Lonely Planet Publications
Melbourne · Oakland · London

Times Sq.
42nd

KU-444-438

Beth Greenfield, Robert Reid &
Ginger Adams Otis

New York City

NYC CITYSCAPES

'THE CITY' IS MORE THAN MANHATTAN, AND MANHATTAN IS MUCH MORE THAN A CITY. BE SEDUCED BY ANY PLACE ON THE NEW YORK CITY MAP. YOU'RE CERTAIN TO BE SURPRISED – AND VERY LIKELY TO BE THRILLED (P108).

New York City cabbies know how to get people to the action

'EVERY DAY THERE'S A NEW EXPERIENCE TO FIND, A NEW PERSON TO MEET OR A NEW CHALLENGE TO CONFRONT.'

Times Square (p156) has its own effervescence

FRANCESCA SMITH
NEW YORK CITY
FIREFIGHTER
WILLIAMSBURG

Best thing about your neighborhood? It's quiet, doesn't quite have the hustle and bustle of Manhattan; not as many cars and highrises, although that's coming. I like the mix of old and new, the shape of the low-lying buildings, and the traditional Polish and Italian shops that are still hanging on. **What's your favorite NYC recreational activity?** Putting out fires. **Have you had any 'only in New York' moments?** I once saw a guy rollerblading down the street with his dog on a leash, while he talked on a cell phone and ate a slice of pizza. Crazy. **Any guilty NYC pleasures?** Pizza. **What are your thoughts on the Ground Zero memorial at the World Trade Center site?** I think the kin of people killed on September 11 should have the majority vote on whatever is built. There is a lot of people involved and they donated a lot of money, so I know their opinions have to be counted too. Maybe the victims' families can't have everything their way, but they should get the final vote on all proposals. **What's the best thing about being a NYC Firefighter?** Every day there's a new experience to find, a new person to meet or a new challenge to confront. I love the discipline and skill firefighting requires. It's one of the best jobs a woman or man could have in the city.

The Lake (p192) in Central Park is hemmed by some very fancy New York addresses

In New York subway stations, anything is possible

3

Grungy or opulent, apartment living is the New York way of life

NEIGHBORHOOD LIFE

AT ITS HEART, NYC IS A COLLECTION OF ECLECTIC, LIVELY LITTLE TOWNS: THE EAST VILLAGE, WHERE OLD-TIMERS BLEND WITH CLUB-GOERS; CHELSEA, RIFE WITH BUFFED GAY MEN; THE UPPER WEST SIDE, WHERE NANNIES PUSH STROLLERS; HARLEM, HOME TO HISTORIC CULTURE SPOTS AND RAPID GENTRIFICATION; BROOKLYN, THE COOLEST OF ALL (P108).

These pampered pooches definitely don't take 'no' for an answer

JANE MADEMBO
SHOP MANAGER/WRITER
HARLEM

Best thing about your neighborhood? I know my neighbors; it's a strong community. There are a lot of friendly faces. It's very diverse and welcoming. **What will your neighborhood look like in five years?** A little more crowded; maybe I won't know all my neighbors anymore. More gentrified, I suppose, with a lot of new people coming in all the time. **Any guilty NYC pleasures?** Going to secondhand and thrift stores. You can get real bargains at flea markets, but the thrift stores also have real steals. When I want a dress or a shirt I'll go to the East Village and just browse the shops. You can find great designer-made clothes and it's a relief to buy something unique that isn't mass-produced. **What's a tourist trap that's worth the trip?** Sylvia's in Harlem for a gospel brunch. **What do you like best about NYC?** I like the sense that all your dreams are possible in this city. Everything is within reach – if you can dream it, you can learn it, and then you can do it. OK, maybe you don't get everything that you want, and you have to work hard, but you have choices. You always have the sense that your dream is just around the corner, waiting for you to catch it. And it's inspiring because you meet people to inspire you, who are doing interesting and different things. Where I came from in Africa, it's beautiful, but you have few choices about your life. Here, you can really feel anything is possible.

Slamdunk success at West 4th Street Basketball Courts (p140)

THE LAWSON FAMILY
JULIAN, CATHERINE AND ANGELINA LAWSON
SOFTWARE ARCHITECT,
EDITOR & MOTHER,
KINDERGARTEN
MIDTOWN EAST

Best thing about your neighborhood? Great family neighborhood with a strong community feel. It hasn't been overrun with high-rises and condos. And scads of great Indian food places. **What's your favorite NYC recreational activity?** Strolling Hudson River Park in summer. **Have you had any 'only in New York' moments?** We were in a dive bar in the East Village and the bathroom was literally a converted broom closet. Some bum had taken up residence there and was charging people a dollar to go in! Nobody kicked him out, so none of us could use the toilet. Oh, and I once saw the Dalai Lama standing outside the Tibetan Kitchen on Third Avenue. **How has NYC changed in past five years?** More expensive, and it's cleaner. **So what will your neighborhood look like in five years?** More expensive, and without brownstones. **Any guilty NYC pleasures?** Eating street kabobs! **Favorite season? What to do then?** The gaps in between the seasons, when it's just the right temperature for a stroll. **What's fun to do with children?** The parks around the boroughs have great kids summer in summer – readings and musical things all geared for those under 12. We go to www.nycgovpark.org and do as much as we can outside all summer. And it's all free!

Lower Manhattan may have its iconic Wall St, but it also has its street graffiti

ARTS & CULTURE

GAZE AT IMPRESSIONIST MASTERPIECES, SEE AN EDGY INSTALLATION, GET A HEADY DOSE OF ORCHESTRA OR MODERN DANCE. THE STATE OF THE ARTS IN NYC HASN'T BEEN BETTER IN DECADES, AND MOST NEW YORKERS SEE THE ARTS AS VITAL. THEY ARE, AFTER ALL, LIVING IN ONE OF THE CULTURAL CAPITALS OF THE WORLD (P52).

George Segal's statues of two gay couples hang out at Christopher Park, Greenwich Village (p140)

ANITA PETRASKE
BOOK EDITOR
GREENWICH VILLAGE

Best thing about your neighborhood? That it is a neighborhood – there's a real community feel to it and it's just like a village most of the time. That, plus the fact that I can get anything I want whenever I want it. **What's your favorite NYC recreational activity?** Jogging, dancing salsa and shopping for books. **Have you had any 'only in New York' moments?** A friend of mine came to visit from Kansas once and as we were walking down the street, one of our neighborhood personalities, a well-known lesbian, came up the street riding a huge tricycle, and she was dressed in something outlandish, playing 'Taps' on a bugle. We stood and watched her go by. Then I turned to my friend and said, 'Well, you're not in Kansas anymore.' **How has NYC changed in past five years?** Unbelievably expensive and it's gotten much more conservative as well, which I think is part of the displacement of artists that occurs whenever more wealth moves in. **So what will your neighborhood look like in five years?** Hopefully it will look exactly the same as it does right now. **What's a tourist trap that's worth the trip?** Manhattan. **Favorite season? What to do then?** Every season – all you have to do is get out and walk. **What's the best NYC book for you, fiction or nonfiction?** Michael Gold's Jews Without Money, about the Lower East Side.

Viewing art in the Museum of Modern Art (MoMA, p154), where the artworks are as big as the artists' egos

Inside the Solomon R Guggenheim Museum (p164), the inspiration for many a shopping mall

MICHEAL DE FEO
ARTIST
CHELSEA

Best thing about your neighborhood? Lots of galleries and the incredibly beautiful High Line. **What's your favorite NYC recreational activity?** When I'm not experiencing the art in galleries and museums, I enjoy installing my own on the streets. **How has NYC changed in past five years?** Ever since 9/11, I've seen the city come together in so many beautiful ways. New Yorkers have always been a caring group and they really showed their stuff in the aftermath of 9/11. **Any guilty NYC pleasures?** Eating the occasional dirty water dog is definitely a guilty pleasure of mine. I'm also a sucker for gyros. **What's a tourist trap that's worth the trip?** La Mela restaurant on Mulberry Street in Little Italy. It's packed with tourists, but the food is top-notch. Also the rotating bar at the top of the Marriott Marquis in Times Square is pretty cool. **Favorite season? What to do then?** My favorite is summer. Walking around barefoot in Sheep Meadow in Central Park, flying a kite, chucking a Frisbee, maybe even napping. I'm a huge fan of the roof-top BBQs on the 4th of July – fireworks! **What's the best NYC book, fiction or nonfiction?** Of course that's my children's book, Alphabet City: Out on the Streets, a traditional alphabet book illustrated with my street art in Manhattan. See it at www.mdefeo.com. **Where's your favorite part of town to work?** As long as it's around 3am or so, it's all good.

FOOD & DRINK

THIS IS A TOWN WITH ROOM FOR EVERY TASTE AND BUDGET, EVERY WHIM AND DIET. ASK FOR 'NEW YORK FOOD' AND YOU COULD GET ANYTHING FROM A HOT DOG TO A SOUTH INDIAN FEAST OR A $29 SIRLOIN-TRUFFLE SHORT-RIB BURGER. CUISINE HERE IS GLOBAL AND CONSTANTLY EVOLVING (P89).

Miss Maude's Spoonbread Too (p252), Harlem

BENNY VRENEZI
PIZZA VENDOR
BROOKLYN
DRITAN SALIHAZ
PIZZA VENDOR
MANHATTAN

Best thing about your neighborhood? You can hear any language anytime and it's impossible to get homesick for Macedonia when I am in Brooklyn. **What's your favorite NYC recreational activity?** Going to the clubs. **Have you had any 'only in New York' moments?** Everyday is like that here for me. I still can't believe my luck, living in a city like this. **How has NYC changed in past five years?** Since I've been here it's gotten busier and more crowded but I think also much more exciting as it grows and expands.

So what will your neighborhood look like in five years? Even more diverse, I think. There are people coming from everywhere to Brooklyn now. **What do you think about the Knicks? Can they be saved?** No, it's really too late for them to be anything but a joke. For me, it's soccer that should be played here in NYC. Time to bring the World Cup here.

Dritan: **What about you? Can the Knicks be fixed?** No, I agree with Benny. Bring us some soccer! **What's your favorite thing about the city?** I can get Albanian food at 3 o'clock in the morning.

Three types of martini

Lombardi's Pizza (p236), Little Italy

Shopping for fresh fruit on Catherine Street in Manhattan's Chinatown (p230)

SIGHTS & ACTIVITIES

STROLL CENTRAL PARK WITHOUT ANY AGENDA. JUMP ONTO A PASSING BUS, EXIT SOMEWHERE AND EXPLORE THE NEIGHBORHOOD YOU'VE LANDED IN. GET LOST AMONG THE ILLOGICAL, DIAGONAL STREETS OF THE WEST VILLAGE. READ THE BULLETIN BOARD AT A LOCAL CAFE, FIND A PERFORMANCE, AND GO (P113).

Catch me if you can, ice-skating at
Rockefeller Center Ice Rink (p313)

Go, Yankees! (p305)

DAVID TAFT
NATIONAL PARKS SERVICE
RANGER FOR THE JAMAICA
BAY WILDLIFE REFUGE
FOREST HILLS, QUEENS

Best thing about your neighborhood? It's wooded; it's got nice trees and parks. **What's your favorite NYC recreational activity?** Fishing **Have you had any 'only in New York' moments?** Bird-watching along Broadway I've seen red-tailed hawks and once I swear I spotted a merlin. **How has NYC changed in past five years?** It just seems more frenetic, although maybe that's me changing. But there are more cars, more SUVs, generally just less patience in the city, I think. **So what will your neighborhood look like in five years?** Well, I hope it will be even greener than it already is. I think people will do more to define their protected spaces and parks, and I hope that physically the city will keep getting greener and greener. **Any guilty NYC pleasures?** Can't resist entering those old wooden pubs that still exist in certain parts of the city. There's a couple around University Place and I love hanging out in those. **What's a tourist trap that's worth the trip?** Times Square at night. It's phenomenal. **Favorite season? What to do then?** I find I'm a spring person lately but I've always loved the fall, too. In spring you can get great striped trout fishing. In the fall, I go for bass. **What's the best NYC book for you, fiction or nonfiction?** Big Oyster by Mark Kurlansky.

Statue of Freedom? Close, but... (p114)

Radio City Music Hall (p155)

STYLE

CHOICE ACCESSORIES ARE DE RIGUEUR: IT'S ABOUT THE RIGHT JEANS (JOE'S, AG'S ANGEL) PAIRED WITH THE RIGHT SNEAKERS (ADIDAS) AND A WHITE OR CANDY-COASTED IPOD IN YOUR POCKET. DON'T EXPECT TO THROW ON WASTE-HIGH LEVIS AND RATTY HIGH-TOPS AND PASS (P31).

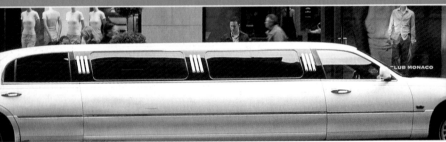

Top Bloomingdale's (p348), the Metropolitan Museum of Art for shoppers **Above** Stretch your budget on Midtown's Fifth Avenue (p341)

DIDEM ATAHAN
PSYCHOTHERAPIST
UPPER EAST SIDE

Best thing about your neighborhood? I love the remains of the Hungarian–German ethnic life. Heidelberg's restaurant and the Schaller & Weber German Market right around my corner and Andrea's patisserie shop. **What's your favorite NYC recreational activity?** Gallery-hopping around the west 20s, and the Egyptian Temple & African Art Halls in Met are my sanctuaries on a freezing or too-hot New York afternoon. **How has NYC changed in past five years?** It's expanded! The city's arts and cultural epicenter used to be Manhattan. Now you can find amazing things going on.

There are art communities and galleries and museums springing up everywhere – even Staten Island has an artist colony. **Any guilty NYC pleasures?** Century 21. **What's a tourist trap that's worth the trip?** Coney Island in summer. Check out the outsider art that pops up on that boardwalk. It's fantastic. **How do you recommend people explore NYC's cultural offerings?** You've got to pace yourself or you'll be wiped out. The big museums, the Met, Guggenheim, MoMA are fabulous, of course, but I usually target a specific exhibit, gallery or era instead of trying to take in everything. One of my favorite places is Museo del Barrio, and I also really like the Noguchi museum in Queens and the galleries in Long Island City. The Lower East Side is a good place to wander for an alternative gallery scene.

NIGHTLIFE

BROADWAY MUSICAL OR ALL-NIGHT CLUBBING? SUPERSTAR ROCK SHOW OR JAZZ JAM IN BROOKLYN? BLOCKBUSTER HOLLYWOOD FLICK WITH STADIUM SEATING, OR FOREIGN INDIE DRAMA? WITH A LITTLE INITIATIVE, YOU CAN EASILY FIND YOURSELF WITH ONE OF THE HOTTEST TICKETS IN TOWN (P278).

Top Trendy bars means queuing. Be chilled, you're on show **Above** Times Square (p281), where everything is in the spotlight

ALEX COLLINS
RUNNER FOR FILM
PRODUCTION COMPANY
**ON THE FORT GREENE/
WILLIAMSBURG BORDER**

Best thing about your neighborhood? I have everything at my fingertips. Fort Greene Park is a two-minute walk. I'm near great restaurants on Dekalb Ave, good clothes shops on Fulton St, and good access to the subway lines that provide a quick ride to Manhattan. **What's your favorite NYC recreational activity?** Riding my bike. I get a great view of the Manhattan skyline every time I cross the Brooklyn Bridge. **What are your favorite clubs or music hang-outs?** Webster Hall always has some good live music but I also like the Bowery Ballroom. I like the Metropolitan, that's a good alternative gay-scene bar, and Barcade on Union St in Williamsburg. Its full of old-school arcade games. **Have you had any 'only in New York' moments?** Ending up in a Polish nightclub deep in Chinatown at 3am on Canal St, listening to Polish rap-music transition into the Beatles. **Is Brooklyn 'over'?** I don't think Brooklyn is over, but I think Williamsburg has reached its zenith of 'hipsterness.' The new areas are Greenpoint and 'East Williamsburg'. It's dirt cheap, filled with twenty somethings in loft spaces. **What's a tourist trap that's worth the trip?** The Empire State Building. Rather than staring up all the time, the view from the top allows you look down at the city, giving you a new perspective. **Favorite season? What to do then?** The fall, seeing the leaves change to red-brown in Central Park.

FREAKS

ONLY IN NEW YORK

PEDIGREE DOG SHOWS, DEEP-FRIED OREOS, WEST INDIAN CARNIVALS, CONEY ISLAND MERMAIDS, GRAND SLAM TENNIS, DOWNTOWN FILM FESTIVALS, FREAKS IN COSTUMES ON PARADE: THERE'S ALWAYS SOME SORT OF CELEBRATION PLANNED IN NEW YORK (P23).

RAVEN SNOOK
WRITER/PERFORMER/DIVA
(AND RECENTLY, MOTHER)
**UPPER EAST SIDE
BORDERING HARLEM**

Best thing about your neighborhood? Central Park. **What's your favorite NYC recreational activity?** Eating out. **Have you had any 'only in New York' moments?** I was waiting for the subway at 110th and Lenox and a guy there asked me if I had a boyfriend. I said yes, and he said, 'Is he white?' and I said, 'No,' and he said, 'I knew it. No white guy could appreciate that ass.' **How has NYC changed in past five years?** For the past decade it's becoming more and more homogenized. 'Hoods blend into each other and are losing their own identities. **So what will your neighborhood look like in five years?** Sadly, probably more of the same. **Any guilty NYC pleasures?** Hitting tourists with my lunch box purse around Times Square. I don't hurt them, I just scare them. **What's a tourist trap that's worth the trip?** Love Saves the Day on Second Ave. and 7th St, if only to gawk at the toys for sale. **Favorite season? What to do then?** Spring so I can walk around. **What's the best NYC book for you, fiction or nonfiction?** The children's book *The Little Red Lighthouse*. It's a little bit of both. **Know any cheap eats in your area?** Flag down those Mexican carts for $1 tamales. I love Nico's for Mediterranean in Morningside Heights and Three Little Guys Diner on 96th and Madison.

Trick or Treat?
Village Halloween Parade (p27)

Naked Cowboy minus the
horse in Times Square

Look! Not in the sky!
It's on herbs? It should be restrained!
It's Superman!

Contents

Published by Lonely Planet Publications Pty Ltd
ABN 36 005 607 983

Australia Head Office, Locked Bag 1, Footscray,
Victoria 3011, ☎ 03 8379 8000, fax 03 8379 8111,
talk2us@lonelyplanet.com.au

USA 150 Linden St, Oakland, CA 94607,
☎ 510 893 8555, toll free 800 275 8555,
fax 510 893 8572, info@lonelyplanet.com

UK 72–82 Rosebery Ave, Clerkenwell, London,
EC1R 4RW, ☎ 020 7841 9000, fax 020 7841 9001,
go@lonelyplanet.co.uk

The Authors

Beth Greenfield

Beth, native to New Jersey, has written about NYC for the 15 years (and counting) that she has lived there including neighborhoods such as Chelsea, Park Slope, the East Village and Boerum Hill. Settled, for now, on the Upper West Side, she is a writer and editor for *Time Out New York*, and writes for the *New York Times* and *Out Traveler*. Her articles have appeared in *Esquire*, the *Village Voice* and *Out*. Beth has written Lonely Planet guides, such as the previous edition of *New York City* as well as *Miami & the Keys*, *Mexico* and *USA*. She lives with her partner, Kiki, and fat cat, Elijah.

Robert Reid

Still a tender Okie, Robert left the panhandle state after graduating from Oklahoma University, and landed in a crappy pad on Manhattan's E 2nd St (now Joey Ramone Pl) where, on occasion, a morning surprise of human excrement awaited outside the entrance door. Robert filled his days with overly crafted memos at *House Beautiful*, unexpected photo sessions at *Glamour*, and co-producing a Manhattan public-access TV show *Unghasted Lake of Splendour* (about a fictional lacrosse league of Saskatchewan, theories linking Roosevelt Island and Delft, and real-live rock music). In 1997, after being in Vietnam, Robert joined Lonely Planet's US office, where he commissioned books, then transferred to the London office. Since 2003 Robert has been back in NYC, where he writes full-time from a Brooklyn apartment overlooking Prospect Park and the Verrazano Narrows Bridge.

Ginger Adams Otis

Ginger is a freelance writer who resides in Manhattan. She writes about the city and local politics for various New York–based publications. She also reports on radio, including AP, the BBC and NPR.

BETH'S TOP NEW YORK CITY DAY

After coffee and an omelet at a fine diner (p92), I'd plan for dinner, at home, by hitting my local Greenmarket (p146) – my favorite communal experience. Then, some shopping and strolling in Nolita (p330) and Soho (p324), where I would find fab new jeans at Atrium (p328) and a cool vintage jacket at Zacharay's Smile (p328). I'll need to refuel at a cozy nook like Café Gitane (p232), before going to the West Village (p140), where I love to stroll the leafy streets in the late afternoon. Sunset calls for a walk around the sparkling Jacqueline Onassis Reservoir (p193) or biking along the Hudson River Park (p143) path. For dinner, I'll save my fresh veggies for another night, and head out for a culinary adventure – the sophisticated Thai cuisine of Kittichai (p230) or upscale vegan of Heirloom (p94), – and then hit a show or concert at PS 122 (p287) in the East Village or Beacon Theater (p279) on the Upper West Side. The perfect ending is 102 stories above street level, with a late-night visit up the Empire State Building (p149).

PHOTOGRAPHER

Dan Herrick has lived in NYC for four years. His favorite photograph opportunity was Coney Island with its characters and history. Recovering on the beach after eating cheese fries, he played booth games with new friends, but Dan didn't leave with stuffed animals. Like most busy locals, he hadn't visited the Statue of Liberty and the Cloisters; these he visited for the first time to photograph.

Introducing New York City

New Yorkers are lucky. But you, dear visitor, are far luckier. This is a city made for explorers; its boroughs are like continents and its neighborhoods are like provinces. NYC streets teem with diverse life; be it a focused crowd of financial traders marching toward the stock exchange or a lone young hipster walking her pit bull in sleepy circles at sunrise. The more you roam, the more you discover, the more you'll want to see – and the more you'll be thrilled by the breadth of prospects.

Take a single topic of interest – theater, let's say. You can start with the obvious, Broadway, with all of its flash and pizzazz. You can choose a musical or a drama, and get butterflies not only as the curtain lifts and the first character steps onto the stage, but before then, as you sit in the darkening theatre and realize 'I am at a Broadway show.' But there are the off- and off-off Broadway gems, the avant-garde and experimental downtown productions, 40-seat houses downtown among them. There are children's theaters, plays in foreign tongues and in sign language, by amateur casts at talent-filled high schools, plus myriad outdoor productions come summertime, like the stellar (and free) Shakespeare in the Park series at the ambient Delacorte Theater.

Add to that the slew of other cultural offerings, such as dance, film, live music, readings, sporting events, art museums and eateries, just for starters. You'll start to get an idea of just how easily, and how often, you'll find yourself wowed.

LOWDOWN

Population Eight million

Time zone Eastern Standard

Three-star room $250

Coffee $1.50

Subway ride $2

Slice of pizza $2

Essential drink Cosmopolitan $6 to $12

No-no Moving slowly

Keep in mind, too, that those are only the structured forms of entertainment. Opportunities for rich experiences lie within every willy-nilly interaction and random setting in this town, from along the energized hubbub on sidewalks and park paths to within the bustling subway trains down below. The situations will reveal themselves with an in-your-face quality that reflects the city's vibrant design, snarling traffic, outstanding culture, spirited politics, and a rich and radical history, infused with a constant surge of renewal that comes through waves of new construction, just-opened businesses and arrivals of foreigners who leave far-flung lands for the challenge of making it here. It's the endlessness of newcomers that keeps the city fresh and bawdy. How else for a place to incorporate such an indefatigable stream of newness than to embrace it full on? New York is an expert in welcoming and accepting newcomers. And that, of course, is one of the best attributes for visitors.

Exploration here can be as simple or complex as you make it. You can plan a thorough itinerary, with highlights that cover the museums, eateries and shows that the city has to offer. Or you can take a more DIY approach, stumbling around in random neighborhoods, getting into the groove of one particular corner or block, park or café, like a New Yorker on holiday. You may wander into a mesmerizing foreign film, or accidentally order the best Mexican *torta* this side of the border. You could listen for foreign tongues on any street corner, order the spanikopita from a Greek diner – at 4am, no less – or wander areas like the surreal Diamond District, where international hawkers will scream, gesture and grab in an amusingly aggressive bid for your business. Or you could happen upon one of endless subcultures: tai chi practitioners posing in parks, pug owners bonding in dog runs, organics adherents pawing through fresh bok choy at a local Greenmarket, ladies who lunch doing high-end shopping sprees along Fifth Ave.

Whomever you encounter, in giddy spring, with its blossoming parklands, or in gilded fall or quiet summer or cozy winter, you can be sure of one thing: it'll be the real deal. Because New Yorkers, for all their routines and survival techniques, truly thrive on spontaneity. And 'real' is the only way they know how to be.

City Life

City Life

NEW YORK CITY TODAY

It's funny to imagine NYC not always being at the top of its game. Despite harsh economic periods and public-safety issues, the city retains its iconic status as a place of unbound energy and opportunity to people who know it well, and to those the world over who imagine it to be that way. But New York City is currently in the midst of a renaissance, which implies, quite correctly, that it's not recently been at such a high. Following a lengthy post-September 11 recession that left many locals scrambling for work and a government wringing its hands, there have been so many booms at once that it feels as if the city is finally finding its place in the exciting 21st century.

With an unemployment rate of 5.8% – the lowest since 2000 – and a steadily decreasing commercial vacancy rate, which implies high demand and increasing rents, financial footing has not seemed better in years. Much of that is thanks to a surge in tourism, which supports more than 329,000 jobs and $12 billion in wages for those it employs. This city welcomed a record 41 million visitors in 2005, with big jumps in both the number of domestic and international tourists that have been on a steady rise since 2001. And new attractions catering to these visitors are not in short supply, with Top of the Rock (p156), the renovated Museum of Modern Art (p154) and the Lower East Side's (LES) hot Hotel on Rivington (p357) among the new spots to be.

Enhancing its healthy economic image has been the recent popularity of all things over-the-top luxurious – expensive, expansive restaurants with lavish, high-style interiors; the building and planning of numerous high-rise residential condos and condo-hotels orchestrated by big-name architects and designers (such as Ian Schrager's swanky 50 Gramercy Park North at the Gramercy Park Hotel, Philip Johnson's Urban Glass House in Soho or the in-process Residence Inn by Marriott, under construction near Bryant Park); and the no-stone-unturned result of gentrification, which has glitzed up formerly scruffy neighborhoods from the Lower East Side to the Meatpacking District. That's meant a reshifting of which areas are 'desirable,' and it has brought about considerable demographic changes, especially in areas like traditionally black Harlem, now on the radar of many a white hipster, and parts of Brooklyn and other outer boroughs, where young artistic types have descended upon low-rent 'hoods, often pushing out long-time black, Latino or other ethnic-minority families in the process.

New and re-development (and how much and what kind is OK, and for whom) is one of the biggest issues facing modern-day NYC. Mayor Michael Bloomberg is pushing a major, five-borough plan to meet housing and commercial demands for the growing population. Chief among the ideas are new residential developments along the East River and in west Chelsea, waterfront parks and completing the east–west No 7 train line so it can connect with Manhattan's far west side. This area was under hot debate as the proposed site of a new stadium, but the plans fell through, coinciding with New York's loss of the 2012 Olympics bid – to the relief of many, who had bitterly opposed Bloomberg's support for it.

HOT CONVERSATION TOPICS

- When are you moving to Brooklyn?
- High-rise development is out of control.
- Johnny Damon? On the Yankees? Now *there's* proof that money talks.
- We're getting ready to buy – but the one-bedrooms are like closets!
- Can you tap into your neighbor's WiFi?
- I saw Matthew Broderick on Perry St last night.
- I *knew* James Frey and JT Leroy were phonies!
- I can't believe they searched my backpack at the subway station entrance.
- Have you seen one of those new electro-powered taxis yet?
- I'll be trapped in my rent-stabilized apartment forever.

NYC EXPERIENCES FOR THE 21ST CENTURY

There are certain stops on the tourist circuit that practically any NYC visitor – young, old, hip or dowdy – can expect to make, and they are of the Statue-of-Liberty, shopping-at-Macy's, Central Park–picnic variety. While the old faithfuls are still well worth making time for, the sightseeing landscape has been changing quite a bit over the years, and there are some fresher experiences you may want to add to your list. You'll probably want to check out at least one or two of the newer museums, including the completely redesigned Museum of Modern Art (p154), with a sleek, updated design and heralded new restaurant, the Modern (p245). Also look into the new Museum of American Finance (p122) and National Sports Museum (p122), both slated to open in 2006 in gorgeous landmark buildings of Lower Manhattan, and the relatively new Skyscraper Museum (p119), an ode to bold city structures. Stroll through some of the neighborhoods that have experienced sweeping changes over the past few years – areas such as the Meatpacking District (p141), home to upscale boutique shopping and hypertrendy clubs and eateries; Nolita (p132), with its tiny quaint streets bursting with cozy cafés and endless retail therapy opportunities; and the borough of Brooklyn (p172), which has a range of culture fixes in areas from Williamsburg (p181) to Fort Greene (p176). Compare and contrast the miniboutiques of downtown with the parade of huge new retail spaces – places like Whole Foods (p341), Adidas (p324) and the mall otherwise known as the Shops at Columbus Circle (p345) – or reserve a table for dinner at one of the many new spacious, design-oriented restaurants. And certainly don't forget to overlook it all from the city's latest lookout point: the historic Top of the Rock (p156), reopened in 2005 and offering bird's-eye views at 70 stories above Midtown.

But no-one is ruffled about the overall crime rate, which has continued its 10-year decline, with NYC remaining a leader in crime reduction out of the 10 biggest US cities, with both murder and other violent crime rates dropping by about 5% in 2005. It's good information for the many out-of-towners who still expect to visit here and find the New York of the '70s. They are shocked – pleasantly so – by the absence of graffiti-covered subway cars, menacing muggers or aggressive hookers plying their trade. The major city cleanup of the former mayor, Rudy Giuliani, has been widely publicized – and continued and flaunted by Bloomberg – but sometimes you just have to see something to believe it. Evidence of the extreme makeover is everywhere: Times Sq and the famous 42nd St thoroughfare continue to evolve into a bright-lights, family-friendly circus, with memories of its seedy porn days becoming more and more difficult to recall.

Even the least savvy, most wide-eyed tourists ride the subways at night – and locals are often spotted riding while working openly on a laptop (an unheard-of image up until just a couple of years ago) – all encouraged by low crime rates, primped signage, increased police presence and immaculate new subway cars. These days, it's nearly impossible to even find a Manhattan neighborhood that's off-limits after dark. Recent proof of how civil New Yorkers have become came during the transit workers' strike of 2005, when thousands were forced to walk home from work in the dark and share cabs with strangers (which is way beyond the comfort level for folks here), and did, for three days, without rioting or acting out on each other. That was the calmer, gentler New York of the 21st century.

CITY CALENDAR

It seems as though there's always some sort of celebration planned in New York. National holidays, religious observances and just plain ol' weekends are perfect times for parades or parties or street fairs. Highlights include the annual Lesbian & Gay Pride March, the Caribbean Day Parade in Brooklyn, and Halloween, which sends mobs of creatively dressed revelers into the West Village streets for an evening parade.

Public holidays may affect business hours and transit schedules. So while they won't affect your ability to eat out, explore or be entertained, they may not be the best days to head to the passport office or local embassy. For additional information of special events in the city, visit www.nycvisit.com. To ensure that your trip does not coincide with a public holiday, see p407.

JANUARY

Each year kicks off with sleeping late after a raucous New Year's Eve. Martin Luther King Jr day is celebrated on the third Monday. It's cold and often snowy as folks trudge back from Christmas holidays, hit the gym with a vengeance and spend lots of time in movie theaters and stores.

THREE KINGS PARADE
☎ 212-831-7272
Every year on January 5, the streets of Spanish Harlem, up Fifth Ave to 116th St, are filled with parading schoolchildren, donkeys and sheep in honor of that one and only holy birth.

WINTER RESTAURANT WEEK
☎ 212-484-1222; www.nycvisit.com
Usually held only for a week in June, the city has added a second Restaurant Week to its calendar, this one beginning near the very end of January. It's a wonderful opportunity to try the expensive, high-profile restaurant of your dreams, as those participating (nearly 200) offer three-course lunches for around $20 and change and three-course dinners for $30.

FEBRUARY

It may be dreary outside – 30°F most days, and often snowy and blustery – but inside, all around town, there's plenty to do. Presidents' Day, which closes down federal and most city businesses, is celebrated on the third Monday.

LUNAR NEW YEAR FESTIVAL
☎ 212-966-0100
One of the biggest Chinese New Year celebrations in the country is this display of fireworks and parades of dancing dragons, drawing mobs of thrillseekers into the streets of Chinatown. The date of Chinese New Year fluctuates from year to year, often falling in late January but sometimes in early February.

OLYMPUS FASHION WEEK
www.olympusfashionweek.com
The second week of February is when the couture world descends upon Manhattan to strut and gawk over new looks. A second fashion week is held in the second week of September.

WESTMINSTER KENNEL CLUB DOG SHOW
www.westminsterkennelclub.org
Catch the much-mocked parade of show dogs at this dead-serious annual showcase for pure breeds.

MARCH

The weather during this month is said to go 'in like a lion and out like a lamb,' steadily getting milder and sunnier, climbing from about 30°F to 50°F or higher as the days pass. The first trickles of spring bring locals to parks in droves, as well as into the streets, where they watch a couple of big parades.

ST PATRICK'S DAY PARADE
☎ 718-793-1600
A massive audience, most with green-painted faces and clutching plastic cups of beer, lines Fifth Ave for this massive, celebratory parade on the 17th, made up of bagpipe blowers, sparkly green floats and clusters of Irish-lovin' politicians. A small but feisty group of gay protesters can be found each year near the beginning of the route, at 42nd St, as the march organizers specifically ban any gay groups from joining in.

APRIL

Flowers bloom, light rains fall and temps finally warm up once and for all, hovering around the 60°F mark most afternoons. It's finally spring, and truly a lovely time to visit the city.

ORCHID SHOW
☎ 212-632-3975; www.rockefellercenter.com
Quickly becoming one of the largest orchid shows in the world, this massive display of the rare flowers, well into its second decade, includes competitions in both orchid-art and fragrance categories. Held around the middle of the month.

MAY

This is perhaps the most perfect month in the city: it's balmy, people have full-on spring fever, and the presummer excitement puts additional electricity in the air, which features average temps of 65°F to 70°F. The official start of the summer is Memorial Day, which generally falls at the end of the month (and sometimes at the beginning of June).

CHERRY BLOSSOM FESTIVAL
☎ 718-623-7200; www.bbg.org
Known in Japanese as Sakura Matsuri, this annual tradition, held the first weekend in May, celebrates the pink, puffy flowering of the Kwanzan cherry trees along the Brooklyn Botanic Garden's famous esplanade. It's complete with entertainment, refreshments and awe-inspiring beauty.

TRIBECA FILM FESTIVAL
☎ 846-941-3378; www.tribecafilmfestival.com
Robert DeNiro co-organizes this annual downtown film fest, held in the first week of May. Quickly rising in prestige and held at various locations around the neighborhood, the week of screenings features several world and US premieres.

BIKE NEW YORK
☎ 212-932-2453; www.bikemonthnyc.org
May is Bike Month here, which brings weekly bike-oriented tours, parties and other events to pedal-pushing New Yorkers. The main event of Bike Month is when thousands of cyclists hit the pavement for Bike New York, a 42-mile ride, much of it on roads closed to traffic or on waterfront paths that takes you through each of the city's five boroughs.

FLEET WEEK
☎ 212-245-0072; www.intrepidmuseum.com
Manhattan resembles a 1940s movie set this week, as clusters of fresh-faced, uniformed sailors traipse around, leaving the docked ships that arrive from around the world for this annual end-of-the-month celebration.

JUNE
The first full summer month brings a slew of parades, street festivals and outdoor concerts – featuring SummerStage shows in Central Park (p293), which bring an amazing lineup of pop, rock and world musicians to the outdoor stage – plus temperatures that head into the 70s.

PUERTO RICAN DAY PARADE
☎ 718-401-0404
The second weekend in June attracts thousands of revelers for the annual Puerto Rican pride parade, around for nearly five decades, up Fifth Ave from 44th to 86th Sts.

RESTAURANT WEEK
☎ 212-484-1222; www.nycvisit.com
The second week of the year (the first is in January) for big-time discounts at topnotch eateries falls in the last week of June, with three-course lunches for around $20 and change and three-course dinners for $30.

LESBIAN, GAY, BISEXUAL & TRANSGENDER PRIDE
☎ 212-807-7433; www.heritageofpride.org
Gay Pride month lasts throughout June, and it culminates in a major march down Fifth Ave (held on the last Sunday of the month) that is a five-hour spectacle of dancers, drag queens, gay police officers, leathermen, parents and representatives of just about every other queer scene under the rainbow. Other weekend events include a Dyke March, which kicks off at 5pm from the New York Public Library (p150) the night before the main event, and a street fair that happens along Christopher Street Pier (p140), as well as countless parties held at various bars and nightclubs. Pride marches are held in **Brooklyn** (☎ 718-670-3337) and **Queens** (☎ 718-429-5648), and many adherents to these marches believe them to be more fun and less corporate than the march in Manhattan. The one in Queens is particularly quirky and multiculti.

MERMAID PARADE
☎ 718-372-5159; www.coneyisland.com
One of the most wonderfully quirky events of the year. This afternoon parade, held on the last Saturday of the month, is a flash of glitter and glamour, as elaborately costumed folks display their mermaid finery along the Coney Island boardwalk. It's not

Jamming in Central Park (left)

JVC JAZZ FESTIVAL

☎ 212-501-1390; www.festivalproductions.net/jvcjazz.htm

More than 40 jazz shows go on in clubs around the city for this mid-June fest, with big names such as Abbey Lincoln, João Gilberto and Ornette Coleman.

RIVER TO RIVER FESTIVAL

www.rivertorivernyc.org

Lasting throughout most of summer but peaking in June, this is the largest free arts event in NYC, with hundreds of creators and performers bringing theatre, music, dance and film to a slew of downtown parks.

JULY

Along with oft-oppressive heat (temperatures can climb into the 90s, but usually hover in the 70s or 80s) comes the explosion of Fourth of July fireworks and weekend treks to nearby beaches, which often leaves the city feeling blissfully deserted to those who remain behind to take advantage of uncrowded bars and restaurants.

JULY FOURTH FIREWORKS

☎ 212-494-4495

The Independence Day fireworks over the East River starts at 9pm. Good viewing spots include the LES waterfront park, waterfront pubs in Williamsburg, Brooklyn, and any high rooftop. The pyrotechnic display, with explosives from the renowned Grucci fireworks company, will rate as the best to see.

NATHAN'S FAMOUS HOT DOG–EATING CONTEST

www.nathansfamous.com

This bizarre celebration of gluttony brings world-champion food inhalers to Coney Island each Fourth of July. The 2005 winner, the slim Takeru Kobayashi of Japan, downed 49 dogs in 12 minutes.

PHILHARMONIC IN THE PARK

☎ 212-875-5656; www.newyorkphilharmonic.org

Free nighttime concerts in the park from the country's premier orchestra are among the most wonderful treats of summer in the city. Grab a blanket and pack a picnic and choose from Central Park, Prospect Park in Brooklyn, or parks in Queens, the Bronx or Staten Island; the symphony visits each one, beginning in early July, bringing a different music program to each.

AUGUST

It's hot – in the 80s – but tourists flock here while locals escape to the beaches and the mountains as frequently as possible. Wear sunblock and enjoy; there are plenty of street fairs and other events to keep you busy.

FRINGE FESTIVAL

☎ 212-279-4488; www.fringenyc.org

This annual mid-August theater festival is the best way to catch the edgiest, wackiest, most creative stage talents in New York.

HOWL! FESTIVAL

☎ 212-505-2225; www.howlfestival.com

A relatively new fest on the scene, this week-long celebration specializes on arts in the East Village, with highlights including the Charlie Parker Jazz Festival in Tompkins Sq Park, the Ave A Processional, Art around the Park, the Allen Ginsberg Poetry Festival and a slew of scheduled readings and performances.

US OPEN TENNIS TOURNAMENT

☎ 914-696-7000; www.usopen.org

One of four Grand Slam tournaments of professional tennis, where top-ranked men and women compete in singles and doubles matches at the USTA National Tennis Center (p316) in Queens.

SEPTEMBER

September is official back-to-school month, as well as the return of cool evenings and bearable warmth. It's an ideal time to visit.

WEST INDIAN AMERICAN DAY CARNIVAL PARADE

☎ 718-467-1797; www.wiadca.com

To most New Yorkers, Labor Day is a wistful day that signals the official end of summer. But to two million Caribbean Americans and other fun-loving onlookers, it's time to head on over to Eastern Pkwy in Brooklyn for the annual Carnival parade – a colorful, day-long march and party featuring over-the-top costumes, delicious Caribbean eats and nonstop music.

OLYMPUS FASHION WEEK
www.olympusfashionweek.com
Round two for designers, fashionistas, jet-setters and assorted others clamoring for advance peeks at the outfits soon to be all the rage come spring.

SAN GENNARO FESTIVAL
www.sangennaro.org
Rowdy, loyal crowds descend on Little Italy for carnival games, sausage-and-pepper sandwiches, deepfried Oreos and more Italian treats than you can stomach in one evening. For more than 75 years, it's been a sight to behold.

OCTOBER
Though the last day of the month, Halloween and its fanfare – bright orange pumpkins at every Korean deli, decorations and masquerade theme parties at bars and clubs – dominate. Cooling temperatures, hovering in the 40s and 50s, usher in the beautiful changing leaves of autumn in New York. If all is well in the baseball universe, October signals playoff season for the Yankees.

D.U.M.B.O. ART UNDER THE BRIDGE FESTIVAL
www.dumboartscenter.org
Celebrating and promoting Dumbo's local artist community, with open studios and galleries, performances and street displays.

OPEN HOUSE NEW YORK
www.ohny.org
The country's largest architecture and design event, at the start of the month, features special architect-led tours plus lectures, design workshops, studio visits and site-specific performances.

HALLOWEEN PARADE
www.halloween-nyc.com
All sorts of freaks and geeks gather in the streets for a wild night of prancing about in costume. The outfits range from very clever to over-the-top raunchy, and the audience lining the streets loves one and all.

NOVEMBER
This month segues from autumn into winter with colder days, bare trees and big Thanksgiving dinners with family at the end of the month. Holiday madness begins the next day, when Black Friday is traditionally the biggest shopping day of the year.

NEW YORK CITY MARATHON
www.nycmarathon.org
Held in the first week of November, this annual 26-mile run through the streets of the city's five boroughs draws thousands of athletes from around the world – and just as many excited viewers, who line the streets to cheer folks on.

THANKSGIVING DAY PARADE
www.macys.com
This famous cold-weather event, for hardy viewers only, parades its famous floats and balloons (watch your head) along Broadway, from 72nd St to Herald Sq. For an even better view, join the throngs who gather at the southwest corner of Central Park to watch the balloons being inflated the night before.

DECEMBER
It's all about Christmas (December 25) for the entire month, when holiday lights appear in the streets and on buildings, and Christmas music seeps into absolutely every store in the city. Temperatures are low, usually in the 30s, and snow is always a possibility.

ROCKEFELLER CENTER CHRISTMAS TREE LIGHTING
☎ 212-632-3975
Join the hundreds who encircle Rockefeller Center in Midtown and watch as the world's tallest Christmas tree is alighted to a chorus of 'ooohs' and 'aaahs.'

NEW YEAR'S EVE
☎ 212-883-2476; www.nycvisit.com
In addition to the world-famous countdown to midnight in Times Sq – which is a raucous, freezing, alcohol-fueled spectacle that you're better off missing – the city has plenty of other celebratory events, namely the Midnight Run in Central Park (☎ 212-860-4455) and midnight fireworks in Central Park, Prospect Park and the South Street Seaport.

CULTURE

IDENTITY

New Yorkers have attitude, and they're not afraid to use it. But it's a lot more complicated than simple rudeness, which has long been how outsiders have mischaracterized the folks of this fair metropolis. Instead, it's a mixture of being tough, brave, on your toes, jaded, overworked and intensely focused. Hang out on a subway, for example, and you'll quickly notice that no-one's making eye contact, but rather studiously avoiding it. The thought is 'who needs to be pulled into a conversation or potential conflict with a crazy person?' Or 'why would I want to be waylaid with small talk when this 15-minute commute is the only time I have to myself all day?' Ask one of those blank-faced people for directions, however, and they'll respond with explicit instructions and a nurturing smile, and perhaps escort you personally – if it's on the way to where they're headed.

Still, they're a street-smart, jaded bunch, and they don't like being played. But the tough outer shell that New Yorkers adopt is simply out of necessity. How else to keep your sanity intact in a city that's rife with homeless people starving before your eyes, the financial pressure of keeping yourself afloat in this expensive town, suspicions that a tragedy – whether it's construction debris raining down from a not-yet-finished high-rise or another terrorist attack – is just around the corner? The locals must balance all that skittish energy with a constant feeling of being stressed out. Sure, some of it's drama; certainly all those people barking into cell phones as they march down the street can't be the VIP they fancy themselves to be. In fact, being swamped with work becomes a point of pride with most New Yorkers, who frequently try to one-up each other with tales of endless responsibilities and deadlines, as if it were all just one big contest on reality TV. But it's true that they are most likely busy, overworked, highly focused and goal-oriented. 'If I can make it there I'll make it anywhere' is more than just a clever line from a song.

All that is enough to make you slightly neurotic, which explains yet another New York obsession: psychotherapy. While Woody Allen and his onscreen characters – usually in therapy for 20 years or more – may be a bit of an exaggeration, the sentiment is right on. There are no official counts of how many locals see a therapist, but anecdotal evidence suggests it's high. New Yorkers want to get everything, including themselves, figured out, and not necessarily in the spiritual, earthy-crunchy way the West Coast is known for (although the spiritual movement is growing here). They want answers and solutions, and they're open about that quest, not thinking twice about explaining to someone that Tuesday night for dinner doesn't work because 'that's therapy night.'

They're also trend-obsessed, tiring of the next big thing before it peaks. Right now it's still all about iPods – what better tool to assist New Yorkers wanting to avoid interaction? – and you'll notice that most subway commuters are hooked up to them. But they'll soon go the way of the former must-haves – Uggs, Seven jeans, North Face jackets, Rollerblades, tribal armband tattoos, pierced septums, hits of ecstasy – probably taking the now-hip Vespas, cell-phones-with-cameras and Joe's jeans right along with them.

But not every one of these wacky characteristics applies to all New Yorkers, of course. This city is, after all, known for its extreme diversity more than anything else. This is a melting pot more than any other place in the country, and while everyone might not always get along perfectly, they're pretty well behaved, considering. In a city of more than eight million people, the economic, racial and religious differences are extreme, so just about any generalization is sweeping. For starters, New York is a city for the young; the median age of residents is 35. Forty-five percent of the population is white, while 26% is black (compared with 12% nationally), 28% is Latino (compared with 14% nationally) and 11% Asian. The median annual household income in all of NYC is $42,000 (slightly higher in Manhattan), and

ONLY IN NEW YORK CITY

Get an only-in-NY opportunity with the following events' unique perspectives:

- Open House New York (p27)
- Howl! Festival (p26)
- Queens Pride March (p25)
- Mermaid Parade (p25)

20% of individuals are living below the poverty line. A whopping 36% of the population is foreign-born (with nearly half in Queens), speaking one of hundreds of languages. An average of 78% of the population over 25 has graduated from high school, while 31% has completed some form of higher education. While 67% of New Yorkers rent their homes, only 33% own.

Religiously, New York is much more Semitic than the rest of the country: about 2% of the national population is Jewish, while about 12% of New Yorkers are Jewish; though that's high, recent studies show that the Jewish population here has dipped below one million (972,000) for the first time in a century, due to Jewish families leaving the city for the suburbs. Around 70% of locals are Christian, many Catholic, with the remainder adhering to Eastern religions, mostly Islam and Hinduism; but about 14% of New Yorkers claim no religious affiliation whatsoever – a figure that is twice what it was about a decade ago. And while outsiders could see that as a signal of defeat, it's more likely a sign of strength. They're looking inward now for answers, and that self-reflection is only adding to the new warmth of today's eclectic but grounded breed of New Yorker.

LIFESTYLE

It doesn't take long to figure out how New Yorkers live while in public – they're harried, hurried and constantly moving – but what about how locals live behind closed doors?

First of all, know that New Yorkers are absolutely obsessed with housing issues, and it's largely due to the simple scarcity of places to live: the housing vacancy rate has never gone above 4%, and rents here are among the highest in the country. The rental market is also governed by a wacky, myriad set of laws. These laws affect the average New Yorker, who lives in a rental apartment, spending about three-quarters of his or her income on those monthly bills. The majority of these folk live in rent-stabilized prewar (before 1940) buildings, meaning the units are covered by city laws that regulate how much rent can go up each year (usually between 3% and 6%). These units can become destabilized, though, when a tenant moves out and a landlord decides to do major upgrade work in the unit. The landlord can then raise the price to what's known as 'fair-market value,' usually an extremely unfair amount that can triple what the price was before. So folks lucky enough to be in stabilized apartments often talk about their home as a 'ball and chain;' if they were to move, they most likely won't land another stabilized home – unless they know someone who needs to transfer a lease, can move into a family member's apartment or has some sort of rare and lucky break. Many other renters live in rent-controlled units – an endangered protection left over from the '30s – or public housing, which offers government-subsidized units to those living below the poverty line. Those who don't rent their home own one – a luxury reserved for the high-income bracket, as an average one-bedroom apartment in Manhattan costs about $680,000 these days.

New Yorkers lucky enough to have jobs (the unemployment rate stands at 5.8%) do any number of things for their income, but most work for one of the city's top-four industries: healthcare, professional services (such as accounting, advertising, finance and public relations), media and entertainment (which includes broadcasting, publishing, film and recording) and tourism (which employs 329,000 people alone). While the average household income is $42,000, figures range wildly, depending on your job. A top editor at a magazine, for example, makes about $100,000, while a government employee in the service sector is more likely to pull in about $35,000 – though working for the city government brings an excellent health-benefit package. People work hard, averaging at least 40 hours a week in many cases; and while the majority still live nine-to-five lives like those in the rest of the country, workers in creative fields are likely to be freelancers who make their own hours and often toil from home – which explains the fact that nightclubs pull in crowds nightly and adults can be found doing anything from laundry to café-lounging smack dab in the middle of what many would define as a 'work day.'

Blame it on advertising or the city's reputation as the center of so many worlds – from fashion to dining out – but New Yorkers are extremely status-conscious. Folks complain about feeling strapped for money no matter how high their income, feeling constantly on edge about whether they have the right clothing, haircuts, apartment decor, laptops, restaurant reservations, summer-home locations, gym memberships, baby strollers, PDAs (Personal Digital Assistant), cell phones, briefcases and even dogs – and you'd better believe that there is a right and wrong dog! Purebreds, of course, are best, especially mini-dachs-hunds and French bulldogs, as are crossbreeds, such as the hyper-popular 'puggle,' which is a beagle-pug mix. This is a city in which most residents do not have access to a car, thanks to a combination of at-capacity street parking, exorbitant parking-garage rates (averaging about $400 monthly) and remarkably good regional mass transit options. But that doesn't stop many from owning vehicles, and from getting caught up in the nation's current SUV obsession; it's amazing how many New Yorkers drive those massive gas- and space-guzzling boats, just so they can keep up with the Joneses. Though some go to the other extreme, choosing cars like the cute and tiny BMW Mini Cooper.

Often, the items they desire are handed to us on a silver platter – for a price, of course. Want fresh, gourmet groceries delivered to your door? Log onto the food-delivery service, Fresh Direct, load the virtual shopping basket, and get actual boxes of groceries within a couple of hours. Caught out on the street in an unexpected rainstorm? Hold tight: vendors hawking $5 umbrellas will appear on practically every corner before you can say, 'I'm wet.' Need to get somewhere quickly? Stick your hand in the air, and a taxi will come to your rescue within minutes.

For New Yorkers with kids, the status thing doesn't end with the stroller (although it's extremely important to have a late-model Maclaren – especially if you're on the Upper West Side). Getting your child into a good private school (even nursery school, as it paves the way for the Ivy Leagues), as well as some trendy outfits and shoes and the care of a top-notch nanny – are also major concerns. In less fortunate 'hoods, though,

WHEN IN NEW YORK CITY, DO AS NEW YORKERS DO

- Only hail a taxi if its roof light is on. This light, though, is actually three; if the middle piece is on, the cab is avail-able; if the lights on the outer edges are on, it's off duty; if no lights are on, there's already a passenger inside. Hailing a taxi with no middle light is the number-one tourist blunder.
- Be aware that most taxis, because of unfathomably ridiculous shift-change hours, are off-duty during rush hour; so avoid needing one between about 4pm and 5pm on weekdays.
- Don't stand on corners waiting for the 'walk' sign. Rather, cross against the light as soon as there's a big enough lull in traffic.
- It's How-sten Street. Not Hew-sten. Got it? Good.
- Be politely aggressive when boarding a crowded subway. Do not stand and wait for your turn to board, or you'll most likely miss your chance.
- While awaiting your subway train's arrival, figure out at which end you'll need to disembark and walk to it, thereby assuring the most efficient use of time.
- Think of yourself on the sidewalk as a car on the street: don't stop short, pay attention to the speed limit, and pull to the side if you need to look at a map or dig through your bag for an umbrella.
- Don't walk down the street saying 'Hello!' to the people you pass. It's sad but true that everyone will think you're crazy.
- Say 'Thank you' to the bus driver as you disembark a bus via the front door (don't yell it from the back). It's one of a just a few pleasantries that New Yorkers really love to honor.

parental concerns are more about having safety – and enough text books – in the local public school.

At the same time that urbanites are stressing over which brand of jeans to buy, however, they're also desperately searching for the best ways to get rid of their stress. New Yorkers are into yoga and fitness in growing numbers, as well as spa services, such as facials and hot-stone massages. But it's often an exercise in irony, as many find themselves feeling competitive in yoga class ('Is my downward dog as good as that skinny, pretty lady's in the corner of the studio?'). But they are also a people who walk everywhere – sometimes around 15 miles daily – so exercise is also built into their lifestyle. There is also rising demand for organic produce and health-food items, judging from the Whole Foods superstores that have popped up around the city.

But being at odds is central to residing in New York – a place where multitudinous types share space, but also clash over lifestyle ideas. Bicycle enthusiasts dislike the motorists in this city, lobbying for more bike lanes and closed-to-traffic park roads and cursing the drivers every time one of them gets doored. Dog owners will go to the ends of the earth for pets' rights in apartments and the creation of more dog runs in parks, while the dogless often hate the massive dog population, pointing to public-health concerns such as the amount of feces that gets generated (and often left on the street). Some people hate the idea of all the chain stores moving into the city, saying it spoils the character of New York; others embrace the change, relieved to finally have as much opportunity for discounts as suburbanites.

FASHION

Contrary to the love-affair-with-fashion image stoked by New York–based films, TV shows and style magazines, it is possible to live an entire life in Manhattan without ever owning a pair of Jimmy Choos. While an improbably high number of women and men in the city do own $400 shoes, there is truth – and comfort – to be found in the fact that most paparazzi shots of local celebs show them wearing simple jeans and boots (albeit pricey ones). Considering that the US taught the rest of the world about blue jeans and that the most famous American designers – Calvin Klein, Ralph Lauren, Michael Kors and Donna Karan – have built their empires on their sportswear, it's not surprising that in New York City, chic equals sleekly casual. The worst fashion sin to commit is to overdress or try too hard.

Though the punk kids hanging out on Ave A or the Broadway hoofers living six to an apartment might opt out of a fashion discussion by rolling their eyes, truth is almost everyone in New York is interested in looking stylish. The definition is different, however, depending on the neighborhood. What works on the classic and conservative Upper East Side (eg Diane Sawyer) doesn't gel with Tribeca's nuanced industrial chic (Robert DeNiro). Fashionable work duds on Wall St won't equate with those from Williamsburg, and vice versa.

While in much of NYC denim and sneakers rule the day, choice accessories are de rigueur; it's definitely a very studied look. It's about the right jeans (Joe's, AG's Angel) paired with the right sneakers (New Balance, Adidas) and a white or candy-coated iPod in your pocket. But not all gadgets and looks are created equal, as Blackberries are viewed as the professional choke-chains preferred by sadomasochistic bosses. And don't expect to throw on high-waisted Levi's and ratty high-tops and pass.

This cult of casual wear might seem strange to someone accustomed to London, where residents are far more experimental and susceptible to fads, or Paris, where haute couture is a more serious affair. But one of the draws of this city life is anonymity, which is why New Yorkers prefer to mix their designer items back in with their regular clothes so that what they're wearing doesn't scream Prada or look like a glorified ad.

What New Yorkers aren't nonchalant about is their grooming. A real metrosexual expresses himself not by the foppishness of his ties but a slavish devotion to scrubs, cuticles, and perfectly coiffed just-rolled-out-of-bed hair. It takes hard work to make that impression of effortlessness. On the other hand, the city will always have plenty of high-maintenance types who have their roots touched up every two weeks or apply leg makeup so they can remain bare-kneed in the dead of winter. Most Manhattan women, though, after a decade of thrice-weekly blowouts and a foray into the $1000 Japanese thermal reconditioning process that leaves hair inalterably limp, have finally learned the value of a good haircut that is 'wash and go.'

Studied casualness aside, there are those – in addition to various thermometer-thin starlets and magazine editors – who you'll find in the front rows of the shows during Fashion Week, held every February and September in tents erected in Bryant Park. With almost all of America's major designers and magazines based in New York, it's no surprise the city is the nexus of the latest inspirations and trends. In recent years, Fashion Week shows have become more diverse, embracing hip-hop's influence and musicians like Sean Combs (aka Diddy) and Beyoncé Knowles as both designers and muses, and with tie-ins to the Bravo reality show *Project Runway,* which searches for the next up-and-coming designer. While some clamor for entrance tickets, most New Yorkers will never attend a runway show during Fashion Week and are content to peruse the highlights on www.style.com.

When they need designer goods, New Yorkers check the sample sales (see p320), which bring out the worst in everyone but are a great way to acquire famous labels for 30% to 90% off. Find out where they're happening at www.nysale.com or www.dailycandy.com. Other delicious bargains are waiting at Century 21 (p321), a designer discount department store which can be crowded with aggressive stylists but is worth a visit. If the end of the season seems too long to wait for a must-have bag, zip down to Canal St where all manner of knockoff bags can be found. Just make sure your Louis Vuitton wannabe isn't plastered with the words Looey Vitawn.

SPORTS

Wall St banks, highbrow arts, global publications, off-the-runway fashion design, punk rock, subway rats – sure, it's all here. But down deep, New York is a sports town for the ages. New Yorkers love their teams, and they love to play.

Urban reality – ie limited green space – has prompted creative liberties of traditional games played in the street, like traditional stickball's take on baseball, or the fresher playground game of pegacide, kind of a cross between dodgeball and handball. All year Central Park is flooded with the active – runners, ice-skaters, cyclists, crosscountry skiers and soccer

Jogging and riding along on their push bikes, honey, on the Hudson River Park path (p143)

players. Little League groups freckle the metropolis – soccer, hockey, softball, flag football, basketball – with other league rosters extending way, way beyond the teens. In summer, crusty old-timer (fully uniformed) softball vets bark calls in Central Park, and dunk-a-thons at outside basketball courts attract pickup-game players and boisterous crowds of onlookers. Sports are so big here that when a historic pier – one built by Grand Central Station architects – faced closure, New York transformed it into a super-sized sports facility called Chelsea Piers (p143).

When New Yorkers don't play, they watch – at stadiums, rinks and courts, or on sports bars' TVs. Seasons overlap, with the famed US Open (played in Queens) coming in August, in the midst of major league baseball and women's basketball, and just before the start of football and men's basketball seasons – so it's a ceaseless passion. And before and after the game, subway commuters pass the stops reading pull-no-punches accounts by sports media (such as the back pages of the *New York Daily News*) – all seemingly bent on throwing coaches into tantrums. It seems that the past couple of years have been even more sports-obsessed than ever, with plans for new stadiums – including a $1.2 billion one for the Yankees (to be built adjacent to the current Bronx site, opening in 2009) and the Mets (with a price tag of $600 million, also with a projected 2009 opening) – recently approved, despite the lost bid for the 2012 Olympics that set the Mets plan in motion. (That bid also included gunning for a Far West Stadium for football's Jets, but the plan was defeated.) Speaking of the Mets, the buzz is that this team, historically in the shadow of the Yankees, may finally be the team to beat thanks to strong new players (Billy Wagner and Carlos Delgado included); though it'll be interesting to see how the Yankees are affected by newcomer Johnny Damon – amazingly snagged from longtime Yankees rivals, the Boston Red Sox. Adding to the baseball drama are recent minor-league baseball stadiums, including those in Coney Island (KeySpan Park of the Brooklyn Cyclones) and Staten Island (Richmond County Bank ballpark of the Staten Island Yankees). Staten Island is also the current site of a battleground between Nascar (National Association for Stock Car Auto Racing), which has proposed a new race track, and its opponents, mainly local residents who fear more traffic congestion.

But nowadays, many would argue, basketball is the king of New York sports (in and out of Madison Square Garden). Unfortunately, the Knicks, in the midst of a many-year losing spell, have a hard time living up to that – and dramas including an early 2006 sexual harassment charge against Knicks president Isaiah Thomas by a former employee certainly don't help matters. But New Yorkers, ever hopeful, have not given up entirely yet.

See the Activities chapter (p304) for information on where to partake.

MEDIA

With all of its magazines, broadcast stations and publishing companies, New York City can stake a claim as the media capital of the world. And the history of this rise is particularly long and strong. It was here, in fact, that the notion of 'freedom of the press' was first truly challenged and upheld. Though the first newspaper here was William Bradford's *New York Gazette,* it was the city's second paper, John Peter Zenger's *New York Weekly Journal,* founded in 1733, that had a profound effect on the future of journalism. Zenger reported some controversial truths about the colony's governor – a bold move during a time when the country's newspapers had been mostly seen as puppets of the government. The governor had Zenger arrested and jailed for seditious libel (his wife continued publishing the paper in his absence), but the journalist's lawyer, one Alexander Hamilton, passionately defended the idea of liberty through the writing of the truth. The jury found Zenger innocent, and it was a major step for the scruples of journalists everywhere.

While journalistic standards – both of quality and integrity – have fluctuated markedly since then, the city has only risen in importance as the home of numerous and influential publications. Today's newspaper offerings are not quite as multitudinous as they were in, say, the late 1800s, when there were no less than 20 dailies published in New York – or even in 1940, when there were eight – but there's certainly no newspaper shortage. The mainstream dailies are the *Daily News* and *New York Post* tabloids, known for screaming headlines and sensationalist takes on grisly crimes or tragic downfalls; and the definitive

New York Times, a hefty, many-sectioned paper that's cited daily by all sorts of professionals and intellectuals. Though the *Times* has long been known by its nickname of 'the gray lady' because of its straightforward, oft-boring approach to news, it's received a major facelift in recent years, as publishers and editors have sought to keep hold of readers who may be more drawn to getting their news in quick, snappy doses delivered either on TV or via the Internet. And though the new reason to poke fun at the paper is its sometimes ridiculous number of modern sections and stilted attempt at hipness, it remains the most widely read news source in the city. Many still say it's the best, although its closest rival is the more financially geared *Wall Street Journal*.

The alternative and ethnic presses are jumping, bringing the latest count of local newspapers to about 280 and leaving little room to complain that there are not enough perspectives available. The *New York Press* and the *Village Voice*, both weeklies, battle it out for liberal, antiestablishment people who like colorful, investigative journalism doled out of newspaper street boxes for free. The salmon-colored weekly *New York Observer* specializes on the political and social escapades of the upper class. And a slew of ethnic papers – the *Haitian Times, Polish Times, Jewish Forward, Korea Times, Pakistan Post, Irish Echo, El Diario* and the *Amsterdam News* among them – offer more comprehensive news reports from a variety of angles. *Metro* and *AM New York* are two new free weeklies – thrust into the paths of zombie-like commuters who are heading on their way to the subway every morning – that now compete for the 'I've-got-no-time-for-news' crowd, offering easy-to-swallow tidbits daily.

In addition to all the publishing houses for trade paperback and hardcover books, New York is home to a slew of magazine publishers. Condé Nast, one of the largest, publishes titles including *Gourmet, Vogue, Vanity Fair* and the *New Yorker* out of its Times Sq headquarters. Other empires include Hearst *(Cosmopolitan, Marie Claire, Esquire)*, which also owns a dozen national newspapers, and Hachette Filipacchi *(Premiere, Elle, Woman's Day)*. Then there are the self-titled empires, such as Martha Stewart Living Omnimedia. Major regional magazines focusing on entertainment and dining include *New York Magazine, Paper* and *Time Out New York* (for details on more newspapers and magazines, see p410).

For all the publications in this town, though, there are really just a few players in the muddled media world – conglomerations that each own way too many news channels and newspapers, making it all too easy to fall into a lull of getting all your news from just one or two powerful sources if you don't seek out alternatives. News Corporation, for example, owns the Fox News network, Fox Sports Net, National Geographic Channel, the Madison Square Garden Network, the *New York Post*, the 20th Century Fox film company and 35 radio stations across the nation – and that's not even all of it. Time Warner, the world's largest media conglomerate, has endless properties, including biggies like CNN, HBO, Warner Books, *Time, In Style, Entertainment Weekly*, Time Warner Cable, the Warner Music Group (with labels including Maverick, Elektra and Rhino), Fine Line Features, and so much more it's scary. It even owns the beloved local TV news station New York 1, which has an unpolished, local style that New Yorkers just love.

The conglomerates provide no real diversity of opinion or analysis, even in this media-saturated city, and news-followers are all the more grateful for publications like the *Village Voice* and the *Jewish Forward*. How grateful New Yorkers are, though, is unclear. Check back in a few years and see which indies have gotten enough support to survive.

TOP FIVE MULTIMEDIA MUSTS

- NY1 (Time Warner cable channel 1; www.ny1 .com) Round-the-clock local headlines, political talk, arts, sports and weather.
- New York Metro (www.nymetro.com) Excellent website of *New York* magazine, with searchable databases for eateries, bars, shops and more.
- Gothamist (www.gothamist.com) Edgy NYC culture website, covering everything from food to sports.
- Curbed (www.curbed.com) Totally hip culture site, featuring juicy 'The Gutter' gossip.
- WNYC (820-AM and 93.9-FM radio; www.wnyc .org) Local WNYC affiliate, featuring great local talk shows like the *Brian Lehrer Show*.

LOCAL PASSWORDS

Knowing the following New Yorkisms can help you make yourself clear – or at least understand what others are talking about:

Bridge-and-Tunnel A disdainful term for folks who come to party in NYC from New Jersey, Long Island or other suburbs that are found across the city's bridges and tunnels; as in 'Yuk, that club's crowd is so bridge-and-tunnel now!'

Hack Old-time nickname for a cabbie, or taxi-cab driver.

Hizzoner A slang term for the mayor, most often used by the *New York Post*.

New York's Finest The New York Police Department.

Regular An old-school way to order coffee, meaning with one sugar and one splash of milk; as in 'Small coffee, regular.'

Schmear A small amount of cream cheese, used when ordering at a bagel counter, as in 'I'll have a sesame bagel with a schmear.'

Slice A serving of pizza, as in 'Let's get a slice.'

Straphangers Subway riders.

The train The subway.

LANGUAGE

To get a sense of the many languages spoken in New York, check out these census figures: of the city's population aged over five and over, a whopping 46% speak a language other than English at home – up 5% from 1990. The foreign-born population here reached a new all-time high as it hit 2.9 million in 2000, and a full 1.7 million residents are not proficient in English. Of those, 52% speak Spanish, 28% speak a different European language (French, German, Swedish etc) and 17% converse in an Asian or Pacific language (mainly Chinese and Korean). Another hint at the range of tongues lies in the city's newsstands: there are hundreds of foreign-language papers published in New York, for those speaking everything from Hebrew, Arabic and German to Russian, Croatian, Italian, Polish, Greek and Hungarian. Or step up to an ATM or Metrocard machine; the first question you'll be asked is what language you'd like to continue in and, depending on the neighborhood, you could find not only Spanish, but Chinese, Russian and French among your options.

Going about your day is an adventure in dialects. Listen on the street or the subway, and you're bound to overhear a five different languages in an hour. You'll hear a blend of English with foreign languages; Jamaican patois peppered with NYC turns of phrase, a fastmoving concoction of Puerto Rican Spanish and New Yorkese known locally as 'Spanglish,' young hip adults of Indian ancestry bringing Hindi words into their 'Desi' American English. Hail a cab and chat to the driver, hearing inflections of Pakistani, Sri Lankan, Russian, Arabic. Take that cab to one of the many ethnic 'hoods around the five boroughs and you'll find closed communities where no English is spoken: Dominican neighborhoods in the south Bronx, Korean pockets of Flushing, Queens, Chinese neighborhoods in Sunnyside, Brooklyn, and the areas of Bukharian (Jews of Central Asian descent) in Rego Park, Queens.

Many American English words have been adapted by the successive waves of immigrants who arrived in New York. From the Germans came words including 'hoodlums,' from Yiddish-speaking Jews terms like 'schmuck' (fool), and from Irish words like 'galore.' And then there are all the long-time locals, speaking with that old-school Noo Yawk dialect that many natives – though they love it – still struggle to understand (see Local Passwords, above).

ECONOMY & COSTS

Since declaring the end of New York's recession in 2004, Mayor Bloomberg's economic news has continued to be strong, steady and generally positive – a big shift from the depressed announcements that characterized the start of NYC's 21st century. In an early 2006 State of the City address, he added these nuggets of good news: Wall St revenues had rebounded to pre–September 11 levels, New York visitors topped 41 million in 2005 (while employment in the tourism sector topped 329,000), and the city's commercial occupancy is the highest in the nation.

So what does all this mean for visitors? The short of it is that, while you will be well-catered to as a tourist, your trip to New York will not be a cheap one. The long of it, though, is that there are many ways to travel in this city, with something for just about every style and budget. Finding deals just takes some forethought and creativity.

Basic costs for a NYC trip start with accommodations, unless you're lucky enough to have a friend or relative who's willing to put you up in their sure-to-be-cramped

HOW MUCH?

- Bottle (8oz) of water: $1.50
- Bagel with cream cheese: $1.50
- Protein shake from a juice bar: $5
- Sunday *Times*: $4.50
- Hot dog: $1.75
- Street-vendor umbrella: $5
- Movie ticket: $10.50
- Pair of AG jeans: $160
- US postcard stamp: 24¢
- Taxi ride from Midtown to the Upper West Side: $12
- Pack of Marlboros: $7.30

apartment. The average night in a city hotel is $250, though beds in hostels can be had for as low as $35, and a room at a budget hotel can go as low as $85. On the high end, those willing and able could easily shell out more like $400 a night or higher, as the sky's the limit when it comes to tricked-out luxury rooms with views and techie bonuses. Bargain rates aplenty can be discovered through various online booking resources, though, and the sheer number of them keeps prices competitive (see p404).

Next comes food. The absolute cheapest way to go is to forgo the foodies' paradise of eateries and stick to making your own meals (if you have access to a kitchen) or subsist on packaged and prepared foods bought at the city's many markets. Basic nongourmet delis, found on practically every corner, make egg-and-cheese sandwiches for breakfast ($2.50 average), and a range of other basic sandwiches throughout the day, whether it's egg salad on rye for $5 or roast beef on a roll for $6. Street food, while not too healthy, is also way-cheap, with everything from hot dogs for $1.75 to gyros for $3. Or you can try to be wholesome by trolling the city's vast array of Greenmarket Farmers Markets (www.cenyc.org) for fresh fruits, breads and cheeses for in-room backpacker meals. Eating at restaurants is gonna cost ya – but the prices range tremendously. Budget options can get you hearty, usually ethnic, meals for under $10. Midrange restaurants with table service can be about $10 to $15 per person for dinner, with the numbers going up from there. Head to a five-star dining establishment, order three courses and throw in a bottle of wine, and you could easily drop $150 per person – even $250 at pricier places. Families should head to diners and other low-key spots with kids menus (see p94), with prices that are less than half that for adults.

If you want to shop while you're here – and who doesn't? – then you'll also find extreme price ranges in just about every category. For clothing, there are bargain spots aplenty, with stores like Daffy's, Century 21, Loehmann's and H&M high on the radar screens of local bargain shoppers for knockoffs and discounted labels (see p322). Also try your luck at sample sales (p320). Entertainment isn't cheap – unless you want it to be. Museums (like expensive MoMA) can charge up to $20 for entrance, but many have 'pay-what-you-wish' days or hours, plus discounts for students and seniors. Broadway tickets, which go for an average of $100, can be bought for half price at one of two TKTS booths (p285) in Manhattan. And plenty of venues all over the city – music, comedy, cabaret, dance and theater – offer frequent cheap ($5 to $10) and free performances; check local arts listings in publications including *Time Out New York* and the *Village Voice* for daily free and cheap activities.

GOVERNMENT & POLITICS

New York City's government is older than that of the USA. Its political history has been spirited, strange and contentious, highlighted by such characters as William 'Boss' Tweed, Fiorello LaGuardia, Nelson Rockefeller and Edward Koch. New Yorkers have had a long record of voting for the Democratic Party, though there are conservative pockets in the blue-collar sections of Queens and Brooklyn, and suburban Staten Island is exclusively

Gateway to the American Dream, Immigration Museum, Ellis Island (p115)

Republican. Despite the Democratic tradition, socially liberal Republican reformers can be elected mayor, as proven by two-term mayor Rudy Giuliani (remembered as a hero based on his post–September 11 performance) and the city's current leader, billionaire Mayor Michael Bloomberg, who switched his party affiliation from Democrat to Republican in order to run against a Democrat mayoral challenger. First elected in 2001 in an atmosphere of turmoil and grief, Bloomberg came under early fire for his severe fiscal policies and draconian moves as head of the beleaguered public school system; later he was criticized for pushing for the 2012 Olympic bid through a controversial West Side development plan, and for effectively halting the move toward legalizing same-sex marriage. Still, 'Bloomie,' as he's been dubbed in the tabloids, predictably won his re-election to a second term (which began in 2006) by nearly 20 percentage points over opponent Fernando Ferrer. His latest proposals include plans to speed up development at Ground Zero and on the No 7 subway line, as well as to improve teacher training and launch new antipoverty programs.

Besides the mayor, the city's political structure includes five borough presidents, who have their own local staff units and smaller budgets for community-level works and patronage. The administration also includes a citywide comptroller (who serves as budget administrator and auditor), a public advocate (who largely is concerned with consumer affairs) and a 51-member city council. These elected officials, who are paid $90,000 a year, are meant to represent individual neighborhoods and serve as a check on mayoral power. As of 2006, the openly lesbian Christine Quinn was elected by her peers as the new City Council Speaker – a powerful position, which wields much control over the city budget. It was monumental news and seen as a major victory for gay and other civil-rights activists, as Quinn has gone head-to-head with Bloomberg in past years over some of his biggest agendas. In addition to being divided into council districts, each city borough is made up of community boards – 59 in total, led by unsalaried members appointed by the borough president, and meant to play an advisory role in zoning and land-use issues, community planning, municipal services and the city's budget process.

ENVIRONMENT

THE LAND

Though it's now a concrete jungle, New York City has a geological history that provides an accurate picture of the entire Earth's evolutionary process. Manhattan's formation dates from over one billion years ago, from a combination of glaciers and the erosion of rocks including quartz, feldspar and mica; the land is marked by a series of faults and underwent its most important topographical changes during the Ice Age. But the movement of the ocean, in a constant cycle of erosion and land shifting, continually alters the miles of shoreline in the city.

It was the waterways of the city that inspired the city's founding, as they have served as a major asset in its growth and development. New York Harbor has 65 sq miles of inland waterways and 772 miles of direct shoreline. The rich marine life provided food to Native Americans and early colonists, and the strategic importance of the New York harbor did not go unnoticed by the British. Through the years, its waters have become ferry routes and host to some of the busiest ports in the world. It's because of all that use – as well as now-prohibited practices such as dumping raw sewage directly into the water and toxic runoff from manufacturing plants – that the waters inevitably became polluted, with most traces of marine life disappearing (the city's drinking water, more than 1.5 billion gallons daily, luckily, comes from upstate reservoirs). Efforts to control the dumping of raw sewage in the 1970s and '80s helped a bit, as did more recent plans, which also targeted the city's air quality.

The air quality in Lower Manhattan has been a topic of much heated debate since September 11, with the Environmental Protection Agency (EPA), City Hall, business interests and community groups all conducting independent tests in an effort to evaluate exactly what is floating around in the air down there. The topic is not one that will die easily, apparently, as a federal judge ruled in early 2006 that Christine Whitman, former administrator of the EPA, misled citizens by declaring the postattack air quality safe; the judge decided not to dismiss a class-action suit against Whitman representing both residents and schoolchildren who say they were put at risk.

GREEN NEW YORK CITY

Today, thanks to environmental reforms, it's actually possible to catch striped bass, blueback herring, yellow perch and blue crab in the Hudson and East Rivers, and health officials say they're safe to eat if you're so inclined. Even more incredible is Brooklyn's Gowanus Canal, a formerly filthy, stinking, lifeless cesspool of rust-colored water that stood stagnant for 30 years following an accident that broke its freshwater propeller. Following its reopening a few years ago and subsequent cleanup project, the waterway is now full of life in the form of blue crabs, minnows, jellyfish and frequent canoeists (see p175). Another fantastic success story has been the return of bald eagles to Inwood Hill Park in far Northern Manhattan.

And, although the environmental awareness here is nowhere near what it is in greener cities, such as those on the West Coast, the tides are definitely changing. When Mayor Bloomberg temporarily suspended the city's comprehensive recycling program as one of his earliest money-saving efforts, there was much outcry, and it was reinstated as of April 2004.

Green spaces tend to unite folks more than any other environmental concern. The city's Community Gardens program

TOP FIVE NATURE BREAKS BEYOND CENTRAL PARK

For a comprehensive list of city parks, both grand and obscure, visit the site of the NYC Department of Parks (www.nycgovparks.org).

- Bird-watching in the marshes of the **Jamaica Bay National Wildlife Refuge** (p49) in Queens.
- Hiking the miles of trails through **Inwood Park** (p171), at Manhattan's northern tip.
- Meditating at the **New York Chinese Scholar's Garden** (p204) in the Staten Island Botanical Garden.
- Strolling the **New York Botanical Garden** (p202) – 40 pristine acres of hemlock, oak and hickory trees, right in the Bronx.
- Wandering along the shoreline in the Bronx' **City Island** (p201).

grew during the Depression, when city-owned land was made available; they were uprooted after WWII and then reappeared in the 1970s, when communities transformed abandoned and garbage-strewn lots, led by activist groups such as the Green Guerrillas. The city's Operation Green Program also made municipal lots available to gardeners for just $1 a year, though various refuges have often found themselves destroyed or at least endangered by sweeping development projects, especially in the rapidly gentrifying East Village. In the past year or so, the concept of 'public spaces' has relaxed quite a bit, with lounge chairs – a longtime no-no based on fears of hijackings by homeless people – have been popping up in many public spaces, including Riverside Park (p160) and the Gantry Plaza State Park in Long Island City.

The desire to eat organically has risen in recent years, as evidenced by the construction of more health markets (most notably, the addition of five new Whole Foods stores in Manhattan and Brooklyn, either open or in planning stages), the growing popularity of the area's Community Supported Agriculture groups (CSAs), and the recent expansion and exploding membership at the Park Slope Food Coop (www.foodcoop.com), a member-owned-and-operated natural-food store in Brooklyn that's been growing since its founding in 1969.

New York is also home to Solaire, the nation's first 'environmentally responsible' high-rise building (located in Battery Park City), which consumes 35% less energy and conserves 50% less water than traditional apartment buildings – as well as a progressive program touting cleaner transportation. The city's Clean Fuel Bus Program made NYC the first public transportation system in the country to switch all diesel buses to those that use ultralow-sulfur fuel as well as clean-air filters. A new test program is also targeting taxi emissions, and introduced six hybrid models into its fleet in 2005.

One group that has a hand in practically all green issues in the city is the Council on the Environment of New York City (www.cenyc.org), a privately funded citizens' organization in the Office of the Mayor. Its programs include Open Space Greening (community gardens), Greenmarket & New Farmer Development Project (supporting 42 greenmarket sites citywide), Environmental Education (for outreach) and Waste Prevention & Recycling, which encourages sustainable practices in schools and other institutions.

URBAN PLANNING & DEVELOPMENT

The topic of urban planning has never been hotter. The reason is a confluence of factors: the city's block-by-block rezoning plan meant to broaden both commercial and residential opportunities, the rise in popular awareness of architecture and development as prompted by the public discussions of what should rise on the World Trade Center Site (p126), and the city's steady economic growth. The most constantly discussed site is still, of course, Ground Zero, especially since Bloomberg's early-2006 promise to the public that he'd speed up development there by offering various 'incentives' to control-freak developer Larry Silverstein. He's also asked the Metropolitan Transit Authority to fast-track extension of the No 7 subway line. The project, hatched during the mayor's unsuccessful campaign to build a sports stadium on the far west side of Manhattan, is seen as a necessary ingredient to the recently approved creation of the Special West Chelsea District, which will bring 24 million sq ft of office space and more than 13,000 residential units to the area within 16th and 30th Sts and Tenth

Cruise the bright lights of Times Sq (p156) in an NYC cab

and Eleventh Aves. The extended train would carry passengers crosstown, well beyond its current western terminus at Times Sq.

Connected to the West Chelsea development – seen generally as a positive outcome of the Jets-stadium–proposal brouhaha – is the much heralded plan to transform the High Line (p141), a 30ft-high abandoned stretch of elevated railroad track, into a long ribbon of parkland. It is a plan which has virtually no opponents (a rarity). Another soon-to-come stretch of green space is the long-awaited Brooklyn Bridge Park (p50), an 85-acre, major recreational park along the Brooklyn waterfront that was granted final approval by the state in early 2006. It's a celebrated plan that will finally put to good use miles of former industrial shoreline – much like the beloved Hudson River Park (p143) has done for the western shore of Manhattan.

Brooklyn & the Outer Boroughs

Brooklyn & the Outer Boroughs

The sign that stretches across the Williamsburg Bridge as you head toward Manhattan says it all: 'You are now leaving Brooklyn. Oy vey!' Placed there by New York City's Department of Transportation in 2005 (at the request of Brooklyn Borough President Marty Markowitz), the sign sums up the prevailing attitude of the day. Manhattan, once the big pot of gold at the end of the rainbow, is just the beginning of the wildly varied New York experience. For a full view of NYC, leave the island behind and expand your travels into the multicultural, multi-colored outer boroughs.

There are five boroughs that make up NYC: Manhattan, Brooklyn, Queens, the Bronx and Staten Island. Manhattan's the best known, but in the past two decades, as skyrocketing rents and constant development turned that sliver of land into an unaffordable dream, waves of working-class families and artists poured into the outer boroughs. Young executives, students and hordes of hip twentysomethings followed, in search of more space and cheaper rents. Each borough has its heritage, and each has developed its own winning personality. While none of them can compete with Manhattan in terms of glistening skyscrapers and bustling corporate headquarters (for now, at least), they hold their own when it comes to cultural diversity, good eats and intoxicating nightlife.

For the traveler, this outer borough bonanza creates a thousand new ways to experience the city. You can still get the best of million-dollar Manhattan, but just a short subway or ferry ride away, you can find an older, purer and, in many ways, more authentic New York that's ready to beguile you with offbeat delights (see p49) and offer up plenty of opportunities to connect to a deeper urban culture.

BROOKLYN RENAISSANCE

Of all the boroughs, none has exploded in popularity like Brooklyn. It's buzzing with the promise of coming development and the ongoing explosion of artistic energy that first awoke this sleeping giant in the early 1990s.

That booming future is visible in the reverse commute that happens nightly in New York. If you're not an urban dweller, the idea of taking a train or a taxi across the East River around 8pm for a bite may sound a bit extreme, but if you're in the city and don't venture across that slender span of steel known as the Brooklyn Bridge, you are missing out. Even if you don't care that many restaurants, bars, and clubs are cheaper once you cross the East River, and that most of NYC's singles and under 35s live on that side of the bridge, remember that you're also ignoring the biggest expression of artistic energy seen in this state since Basquiat lit up the East Village in the 1980s with his spray-painted stick figures.

Where you go usually depends on who you are, or what you're in the mood for. Manhattanites head into Brooklyn in droves every night – usually targeting some foodie event or art gallery opening in Williamsburg, Park Slope or Boerum Hill/Carroll Gardens. If you'd like some kosher meals, try Borough Park (home to a flourishing Bobover religious sect), Flatbush Ave or Williamsburg. For Polish, head to Fort Greene, on the border of Williamsburg. Got a craving for jerk chicken, or anything else Caribbean? Head toward Eastern Parkway or Crowne Heights. Fine dining can be found just about anywhere, but there are some standout restaurants in Brooklyn Heights, Park Slope and Boerum Hill. If you simply want to wander to where your nose takes you, do like the Brooklynites do and stroll Smith St on the border of Carroll Gardens; it's packed with good places.

For an earful or eyeful of creativity, Williamsburg sets the standard, with open-mic nights and movie presentations at Galapagos (p276), and similar events at clubs and venues all along Bedford Ave. But don't forget to check out Dumbo (Down Under the Manhattan Bridge Overpass), the original hipster scene founded after Manhattan rents squeezed out homegrown artists in the 1990s. They migrated to the huge lofts here, and many hold open houses and gallery nights to show off their works (check out the arts section of www.hellobrooklyn.com for some gallery listings). There's also the (in)famous St Ann's Warehouse on Water St, home to some of the most innovative theater being produced in the city. When those twisted geniuses known as the Coen brothers (Joel and Ethan, directors of films such as *Fargo* and *The Big Lebowski*) decided to team up with Charlie Kaufman (*Being John Malkovich* and *Eternal Sunshine of the Spotless Mind*) to produce a radio drama known as *Theatre of the New Ear* (with Meryl Streep, Steve Buscemi and Philip Seymour Hoffman), they turned their backs on the ersatz earthiness of the East Village and instead brought their show to this industrial Brooklyn space, to great critical and popular acclaim.

If you need to break free of the madding crowds, there's always Coney Island, although there's no guarantee you'll actually be alone. On summer nights and weekends, this salty Atlantic beachfront is packed with Brooklynites looking to escape the heat. Regular firework shows lend a sudden and ephemeral beauty to the strange carnival of Coney Island, and of course, the lingua franca is Russian, since the surrounding neighborhood of Brighton Beach, aka Little Odessa, caters to recent émigrés from the former Soviet Union.

To get a taste of old-school Brooklyn, the one that survived due to its port trade and industrial work, head to newly discovered Red Hook, once a Dutch village, now becoming a foodie haven. Some restaurants on Columbia St rival anything on Smith St, or in Manhattan.

QUEENS, THE BRONX & STATEN ISLAND

For some strange reason, most visitors seem to overlook Queens. It's hard to understand why: it's big, vibrant, has two airports and sits just north of popular Brooklyn.

Having always been home to a mix of ethnicities, in recent decades this once quiet and suburban enclave has transformed into a place of mesmerizing cultural diversity. Its furthest reaches, including Sunnyside, retain some of the aura of suburban living that once reigned here, but elsewhere, it's emerging glossy apartment buildings, condominiums and multiple-family houses. The same overflow of exiles from Manhattan that flooded Brooklyn in past decades has reached into Queens, changing the Greek stronghold of Astoria into a neighborhood mixed with Turkish, Korean, Chinese, and more recently, Serbian, Bosnian and Albanian families. From this, a teeming arts scene has been created alongside industrial wharf buildings in Long Island City.

Riding high on the Cyclone roller coaster on Coney Island (p180)

The northern part of Queens leads into the Bronx (via a major thoroughfare over the East River), and the same spillover of gentrification affecting Manhattan's eastern boroughs also affects this one to the north. Leafy, shady Riverdale has always been a beautiful place to live; now the blighted underbelly of the Bronx – the infamous South Bronx of the 1970s – is getting popular too. SoBro, as it's now known, was recently profiled as the next big target for gentrification. What that means in city terms is that artists and other neighborhood pioneers began moving in several years ago – taking dilapidated and depressed loft spaces and turning them into spacious abodes or commercial galleries. As the word spread, developers followed, buying up available buildings and setting off a massive influx that's brought some measure of prosperity to the area, but also displaced many of the area's most vulnerable residents (see The Next Brooklyn? p183).

Just a 25-minute ferry ride from Manhattan's southern tip sits the city's most misunderstood borough: Staten Island. Sure, it consistently votes Republican in an otherwise Democratic city. Sure, it's blue collar. And yeah, it does have a bird's eye view of all the barges trucking trash down to Delaware. But one look at the picturesque enclave of St George that waits at the ferry exit, and all those details will fall by the wayside. Graced with high-ceilinged and turreted brownstones, tons of green trees and big parks, plus plenty of room for biking, roller-blading and running, this borough's been experiencing a slow but steady growth for the last 15 years. And while the island's still short on some amenities (don't expect the plethora of organic or specialty stores found elsewhere) and a car is necessary, the last two Republican mayors (Rudolph Giuliani and Michael Bloomberg) have paid the borough back for its loyalty by keeping the Staten Island Ferry service free.

A BRIEF HISTORY OF THE BOROUGHS

Queens is the largest, but Brooklyn is the most populous. Each of NYC's five boroughs is independently large enough to be considered a major city in its own right.

The story of how these autonomous areas became amalgamated into one fantastic city is long and involved, but the short view can be summed up very quickly: the real estate game, baby! Whatever could be bought was bought, and what couldn't be bought usually got annexed. When emerging technology made it possible to build bridges and subways to even further corners, those municipalities were consumed too.

The only New York borough connected to the mainland, the Bronx was once farmland owned by Jonas Bronck, a Dutch (some say Swedish) sea captain who settled onto a 500-acre farm alongside the Harlem River in 1636. Until WWI, it was sparsely populated, but extensions of the subway system created a housing boom. The arrivals were mostly Irish, but also Polish, Italian and Jewish (the Jewish presence is reflected in the many remaining synagogues, but few are in use today). The Bronx was a haven for bootleggers at the time of prohibition, and became known as a borough of ill repute thanks to its rash of speakeasies.

In the 1930s much of the Polish and German communities moved out as better housing opened up in other parts of the country. The Bronx became predominantly Latino, particularly Puerto Rican, Dominican and Cuban, and African American, with a subset of Italian families, and it remains that way today.

It would be an understatement to say that life in the Bronx took a turn for the worse in the 1960s. Many of the city's renewal programs, such as master planner Robert Moses' Cross Bronx Expwy, destroyed the village-like size of existing nabes and turned them into bleak, high-density housing projects. Simultaneously, many companies moved their industrial projects to the Sunbelt states in the south and left the borough with a bunch of rusty, unusable factories. That double hit hammered the Bronx. Add to that a fiscal crisis in the 1970s and '80s that reduced the city's ability to fund firefighters and cops, and an attitude of near lawlessness took over. Landlords who no longer wanted their buildings would burn them for insurance payouts and the strapped fire department could barely keep up with demand. It led to the signature cry, 'The Bronx is Burning,' used by both the BBC and the *New York Times* in reports on the borough in 1974, but made famous by Howard Cosell, who uttered the line while commenting on a visibly blazing skyline during a World Series game at Yankee Stadium in 1977.

As bad as things were for the Bronx, Brooklyn fared even worse in its first century of annexation. The rural pasture and coastland that had first been occupied by Native American tribes, then the Dutch, and then the British, was its own entity until 1898. With Brighton Beach subway line being established and ferries jumping back and forth between Lower Manhattan and Brooklyn Heights, officially joining New York City seemed a wise thing to do. But it quickly became known as 'The Great Mistake of '98' in most newspapers. Much of Brooklyn's shipping business got shifted to Manhattan's ports, and local shops were encouraged to move into 'the city.' Brooklyn's economic development always got put in second place from that moment on. It became known as 'the bedroom of New York' because just about every resident worked in Manhattan and came home to Brooklyn.

The gentle prosperity enjoyed by many Brooklynites after WWII reduced during the city's later fiscal crisis, and the borough's inner-city neighborhoods were racked with crime. Some parts of Bedford-Stuyvesant, Bushwick and Crowne Heights have still not fully recovered from the poverty that settled on most of Brooklyn nearly 40 years ago, but the present-day borough is an amazing tale of urban reclamation.

Queens, on the other hand, has never looked back since joining the city's fold in 1898. Its larger territory gave local businesses more room to breathe, and companies such as Steinway & Sons (still open today) and other immigrant-run enterprises couldn't be coaxed into Manhattan. The borough had built-in jobs thanks to its proximity to John F Kennedy and LaGuardia Airports in the latter half of the 20th century. It didn't escape the 20th century's economic fluxes unscathed, but its patchwork quilt of immigrant communities seemed better able to absorb some of the financial hits than neighboring Brooklyn.

Staten Island, now often referred to as the forgotten borough (only half in jest), played a crucial role in American history. It was the staging area used by the British (twice) in their battles to regain and then keep control of New York during the American Revolution, and it was there that British leaders first learned of the existence of the Declaration of Independence. The British Army spent so much time on the island during the war that it's largely considered responsible for the deforestation that occurred during the 1700s.

After the Revolutionary War, Staten Island was pretty much overlooked by New York City until the Verrazano Narrows Bridge was built in 1964. That, along with three other smaller Staten Island bridges, connected residents to Brooklyn, Long Island and Manhattan by car, and linked them to New Jersey, which immensely increased the island's profile among commuters. The downside to that, however, was the destruction of many old-style towns and villages that had to be plowed down to make room for roads. The plan was initially drawn up by Robert Moses, who, as the city's lead developer, created some of the best (and worst) public projects that still exist today.

Until recently Staten Island was only known for housing the immense landfill called Fresh Kills. That has been closed off, however, and now it's the fastest growing borough in the county.

QUICK TRIPS TO THE BOROUGHS

Too many people lump the outer boroughs into one monolithic swath of 'everything that's not Manhattan,' and refuse to think about them further. That's too bad, because a tour through New York's boroughs is a tour through the world. There are so many diverse histories, cultures and attractions to be found, that crossing the block is akin to crossing a continent.

Brooklyn

Like any aging Victorian spinster, Brooklyn has her past. An easy initiation to the borough can be had by taking the popular stroll across the Brooklyn Bridge (mind the bike traffic!) and into Brooklyn Heights. That nabe boasts more than 600 historic houses built before 1860 and offers grandiose views of Manhattan's jutting skyline. Important streets to check out their character include Henry, Hicks and Orange Sts. It was while living in this area that Walt Whitman wrote *Leaves of Grass,* his seminal book of poetry, and the abolitionist (anti-slavery) movement arrived in New York via the Plymouth Church of the Pilgrims on Orange St.

If you're feeling experimental, check out the neighborhood around Grand Army Plaza. It's an ornate, mini-rotunda plaza that designers Frederick Law Olmsted and Calvert Vaux (of Central Park fame) wanted to complement the grandiose entry to Prospect Park, a cool slice of green, that often hosts weekend events that far outstrip those hosted by its bigger counterpart in Manhattan. It's filled daily with joggers, bikers and walkers, and in summer, its Great Lawn resounds with laughter as families and friends indulge in easygoing badminton, Frisbee, football and soccer games.

The art deco masterpiece that is the Brooklyn Public Library can be seen from the entrance of Prospect Park, and if you continue past the library and down Eastern Pkwy, the Brooklyn Botanical Garden and the Museum of Art are a 10-minute walk away.

For a jaunt into Williamsburg (known as Billyburg or Billburg), grab the L line to Bedford Ave and start gallery hopping. Don't expect beauty by day – despite its newfound popularity, this gritty, dirty area was never meant to actually house people beyond the Polish immigrants who worked in the factories and ports. Environmentally, Williamsburg has a questionable past, and even though it has now been rezoned to include residential buildings (all the better to absorb the endless influx of hipsters and gallery owners fleeing exorbitant Chelsea), it's still got a toxic waste-management plant right in the middle of town. Outraged residents regularly stage protests, led by the venerable People's Firehouse Organization, calling for more responsible development from city leaders.

Queens

This may be New York's sleeper borough – despite its solidly working- and middle-class demeanor, there is so much going on in Queens! Astoria is probably the most well-known neighborhood, easily reached by train from Midtown, and it's considered the European capital of New York. If you want a night of eating, drinking and dancing to the latest Euro-techno music in a smoky club, head to 'The Mecca,' as Greeks call Astoria. There are some ethnic tensions that occasionally crop up in this area; a shortage of housing has created some unwanted proximity between new Albanian, Bosnian and Serbian immigrants, but generally everybody gets along.

Astoria Blvd is the main drag, but people also gravitate toward Grand Ave (also known as 30th Ave) for its stores and cafés, and Broadway, two blocks south, where the Greek influence diminishes and Bengali and Latin influences take over. Between Astoria Blvd and 28th St, you'll find some of the finest Middle Eastern dining in New York.

If that's not intense enough for you, hold on to your multi-culti hats, because Queens' Jackson Heights has an even more dizzying mix. The neighborhood (most of which is on the National Historic District Register) was laid out after the elevated Flushing train line was erected in the 1920s. It was the first garden community built in the United States: there are more private parks in this area than in any other American city. Most are hidden from view behind apartment buildings, but were designed that way purposefully, so urban dwellers could access their own, semi-private parks. Once populated strictly with Jewish, Polish, Irish and Russian families, it now has an additional Asian population including people from India, Pakistan, Bangladesh, China and Korea, as well as Latino residents from Colombia, Cuba, Ecuador, the Dominican Republic and Mexico. Little India, at Roosevelt Ave and Broadway, is the undisputed king of the city's great Indian food, and, narrowly surpassing Park Slope, this area is considered the most gay friendly outside Manhattan.

Another must-see is Long Island City (LIC), which has turned its fading industrial past into a major hub of the film industry. Remember *Sex and the City*? Almost all of that was shot in rehabbed factories in LIC. Several South American news channels broadcast from this area, as do tons of Korean productions that are set in New York but played back home. It's also teeming with artist lofts and gallery spaces (see Arts & Culture in the Boroughs, opposite).

The Bronx

Offering the best in multifarious living, the Bronx has a seriously split personality. Above 183rd St, Riverdale, Spuyten Duyvil, Woodlawn and other neighborhoods are urbane, sophisticated and densely residential with some commercial development. Throgs Neck, Parkchester and Co-Op City are poor neighborhoods in the East Bronx filling up with working-class families who can no longer afford Manhattan, while the South Bronx – Morrisania, Mott Haven, Morris Heights – once referred to by former US President Jimmy

Carter as The Worst Neighborhood in America, is riding a wave of possible gentrification while still struggling with crime, drug abuse and an unbelievably high poverty rate when compared to rich, neighboring Manhattan.

Except for Yankee Stadium and the Bronx Zoo, which get plenty of visitors, the borough comes off as decidedly anti-tourist, but there are plenty of sights worth checking out. The Bronx holds New York's Botanical Garden, its own Little Italy on Arthur Ave, Fordham University, two of the largest parks in New York City (Pelham Bay and Van Cortlandt), and the Stanford White–designed Hall of Fame for Great Americans, a national landmark overlooking the Harlem and Hudson Rivers.

Don't miss the Edgar Allen Poe Cottage (contact the Brooklyn Historical Society for tour bookings ☎ 718-881-8900), located at Kingsbridge Rd at the Grand Concourse. The tortured poet spent the last years of his life, from 1846 to 1849, in this tiny wooden farmhouse that once had an unobstructed view all the way to Long Island.

Staten Island

On a fine day, a visit to this outlying island is one of the sublime experiences that NYC has to offer. The striking views and breezy fun of Staten Island's free, open-air ferry rides to and from Lower Manhattan are worth the trip in its own right. Some wonderful attractions are available once you arrive at St George, the cheery village perched on the many hills leading down to the dock.

The borough is big, and lacks a subway system, but it does have buses connecting its 20-odd communities. Bay St Landing is the next up-and-coming neighborhood within walking distance of St George. It sits between the ferry terminal and Victory Blvd, and has been revitalized by the 2001 opening of the Richmond County Bank Ballpark, home of a minor-league farm team, the Staten Island Yankees.

The borough's biggest draw is its fabulous, spacious parks – and it has got plenty, including Historic Richmond Town, the 222-acre Blue Heron Park, replete with a

Don't pay the ferryman; the Staten Island Ferry (p116) is free

multi-million dollar nature center, Clay Pit Ponds State Preserve, a rare wetland habitat with great bird-watching, Willowbrook Park, Staten Island Botanical Garden, and many more. Plus, it's got a surprising number of museums, including the Alice Austen House, the Garibaldi-Meucci Museum, and the Staten Island Museum (right across from the ferry landing, and great for kids).

ARTS & CULTURE IN THE BOROUGHS

Queens Arts Scenes

Contemporary art reigns in Queens, starting with PS1 Contemporary Art Center p184, an affiliate of the Museum of Modern Art. It's the oldest and second largest nonprofit arts center in the US. Housed in an old school (hence the name), it nurtures a burgeoning world of artists in nearby Long Island City with grants and fellowships, and its free music festivals in summer play to a packed front yard.

Just a few blocks down the street is 5 Pointz, aka the Institute of Higher Burnin.' It's not exactly a museum or a gallery, although the converted warehouse is full of artist studios and creative types usually eager to talk about their work. The real attraction is the outer facade, covered with brightly colored graffiti easily seen from the elevated 7 subway line that runs behind 5 Pointz.

Sculptures of every type are on display in two places: SculptureCenter, a small, experimental gallery full of contemporary artists; and outside at the Socrates Sculpture Park, which also features community art events in the summer.

Independent curators run the nonprofit Dorsky Gallery Curatorial Program, a 1200-sq-ft exhibition space dedicated to contemporary art.

Of course, the Isamu Noguchi Garden Museum (p183) shouldn't be missed, and the Queens Art Museum (p186) in Flushing Meadows Corona Park is also worth the trek.

Birth of Hip-Hop in The Bronx

Growing directly out of the poverty that took over the Bronx in the late 1960s, hip-hop was created as an antidote to the hopelessness and depression that filled so many young lives.

Jamaican born DJ Kool Herc, considered the pioneer of hip-hop, is credited with bringing the 'toasting' style of chanting over music from Jamaica's dance halls to the Bronx in the late 1960s. He later influenced Kevin Donovan, a young man heavily involved in the Black Spades gang until a trip to Africa in 1973 changed his life, and his name – he became Afrika Bambaataa, a moniker taken from a Zulu chief.

Back in New York, he started the Universal Zulu Nation, which transformed many New York gangs into 'crews' that fought with words. By 1977 he was organizing block parties all over the Bronx and DJing them himself. Combining the toasting he learned from DJ Kool Herc with styles collected from Africa, he realized he needed to extend the songs' duration to get the overlapping rhythms he sought. The birth of the two-record turntable followed, and his musical styling evolved into hip-hop, as break dancing came up alongside it on the dancefloor.

Today, the Bronx' hybrid creation has spread internationally (and become a multimillion dollar industry), but the borough no longer leads the city in churning out hip-hop musicians. That honor goes to Queens, which, thanks to its notorious Queensbridge housing project, the country's largest public housing unit built in LIC in 1933, has turned into a hotbed of hip-hop musicians. Roxanne Shante, The Bravehearts, Mobb Deep, Big Noyd, Nas, Capone, MC Shan and many others all once lived in 'The Bridge,' as it's known. Clubs in Queens showcase hip-hop.

Black Culture in Brooklyn and Queens

The Brooklyn Academy of Music (BAM; p176) fills the mainstream artistic needs of many Queens and Brooklyn residents with top-quality music, dance and theater performances, many of them featuring black artists. But there's plenty more going on in the two boroughs that is deeply connected to the African American experience and there are plenty of ties to subsequent waves of black immigrants from Africa, the Caribbean and parts of South America like Guyana.

Brooklyn pays homage to its history by naming a lot of its attractions after black civil rights and cultural leaders, such as the Simmons African Arts Museum, the Paul Robeson Theater, the Billie Holiday Theater and Medgar Evers College, which has a predominantly black student body. Queens has the African American Museum, waaaay out on the borough's edge, near Long Island, the Museum for African Art (p184) in LIC, the Jamaica Center for Arts & Learning (p187), the Afrikan Poetry Theatre (☎ 718-523-3312; www.afrikapoetrytheatre.com; 176-03 Jamaica Ave, Jamaica), and the Langston Hughes Cultural Center (☎ 718-651-1100; www.queens.lib.ny.us/branches; Northern Blvd, btwn 32nd & 34th Aves, Corona).

Queens also recently designated the redbrick house where Louis Armstrong lived for 30 years of national importance, and made it into a museum, and has always made note of the house in East Elmhurst that Malcolm X resided in with his family for many years. It was actually owned by the Nation of Islam (NOI), and when the Shabazz family resisted an order to vacate from the NOI, the building at 23-11 97th St was firebombed.

Bedford-Stuyvesant, the Brooklyn neighborhood where Spike Lee and Chris Rock grew up, and that features largely in Lee's films and now in Rock's autobiographical TV show, *Everybody Hates Chris*, was the city's first free African American community, founded in 1827, shortly after the abolition of slavery in New York. Some historic African American houses in Hunterfly St are now protected landmark. A museum trip to Brooklyn should also include the multicultural Brooklyn Children's Museum (p178). It's immensely popular for kids of all backgrounds and ages.

OFFBEAT & OFFTRACK OUTER BOROUGHS

If pawing through old car parts is your idea of a great time, you'll be happy to know that in Queens, just beyond Richmond Hill (home to the largest Sikh population outside India), lies Willets Point, an area defined by abandoned junkyards full of decaying vehicles that are often frequented by people looking for a spare set of spark plugs.

Red Hook, a soon-to-be gentrified outer-borough neighborhood, has old Brooklyn docks and maritime museums dedicated to shipping business that energized the local economy. Red Hook can be easily reached by the water taxi, and has several fabulous art events throughout the year. Check out the Brooklyn Artist Waterfront Coalition and Red Hook Waterfront Arts Festival for good times to visit.

If landlocked pursuits are more your thing, Wave Hill in the North Bronx is universally acknowledged as the borough's most entrancing and well-maintained public garden. This former private home (Teddy Roosevelt once stayed here), set on eight acres, has two art galleries, an outdoor summer dance series, and regular jazz and classical music concerts. Canarsie, the Rockaways and Broad Channel offer their own distinct cultures such as a surfing scene that has developed on the rough Atlantic beach off the Rockaways. Bay Ridge, made famous by John Travolta in *Saturday Night Fever*, hasn't changed all that much, nor has neighboring Sheepshead Bay. Still staunchly working class, these neighborhoods have resisted gentrification with all their might – it would take more than a Donald Trump–style developer to shift six generations of Italian Americans. For a more genteel beach experience, City Island in the Bronx is still the place to go – the small hamlet has just the right mix of *haute cuisine* served in elegant B&Bs and beachside shrimp shacks.

To get to New York City's most southern reaches, you need to traverse all of Staten Island to Tottenville, once a wealthy town dedicated to ship building. That industry has long since disappeared, but the stately old mansions remain, including one that was the source of great controversy in 2005. Developers started buying up the houses to build what are known as 'McMansions,' bland townhouses devoid of character. When one particularly beautiful property was snapped up by a developer who wanted to raze it, residents revolted and clamored for it to be declared an historic building. The developer responded by spray painting it with graffiti and promising to fill it with low-income welfare residents from the inner-city. Appalled, Staten Islanders drew on their Republican clout and appealed to Mayor Bloomberg, who made a personal visit to Tottenville in April that year to declare the house a protected landmark.

PARKS, WILDLIFE AND GREEN SPACES

The only US National Park that can be reached by a subway is evenly divided between Queens and Brooklyn. Jamaica Bay National Wildlife Refuge, an important migratory stopover for birds and butterflies, is the least discovered of all New York's marvelous green spaces and perfect for anyone wanting an all-day excursion into nature. It's a tidal area, too, because it stretches down to the water.

For long walks and romantic solitude, you can't beat Van Cortlandt Park or Riverdale Park in the Bronx. Both are huge and treefilled, with lots of private nooks, and Van Cortlandt has horseback riding, boating, golf and tennis.

It's also a favorite among mountain bikers, who find its rolling, wooded surroundings ideal. But if you're craving something really off the beaten path, go to Staten Island's Greenway Park; there are lots of teeth-shattering mountain biking trails off the Ocean Tce path.

For those who like a little city with their park, the best choice is Flushing Meadows Corona Park (p186). Inside the immense park (1½ times the size of Central Park) are several museums, a zoo, Shea Stadium (see p305) and Arthur Ashe Stadium (p316), bicycle rentals, miniature golf and two lakes.

For more information on New York City's best parks, check out: www.nycgovparks.org/or www.nps.gov/gate/.

CHANGES AHEAD

Strange as it sounds, Nascar, which of course makes money from cars that go really fast, has invested $100 million into setting up a racecourse on Staten Island, a borough more likely to have a traffic jam than a speeding problem. That's just one of the many controversial development projects slated for the outer boroughs, as developers fan out in search of affordable real estate.

Brooklyn's Coney Island is expected to get a major facelift soon. The Yankees and the Mets are both working on deals for new stadiums in the Bronx and Queens, respectively. Swedish big-box store IKEA is looking to set up shop in Red Hook and the Brooklyn Bridge Park project is set to completely change the industrialized eastern gateway into the borough. Many say it will change it for the better – with the city and developers promising to turn much of Brooklyn's decrepit waterfront into parklands, similar to what's planned for Manhattan's Lower East Side. But some Brooklynites – perhaps remembering the Great Mistake of '98 – fear the benefit will be greater for Manhattan than their borough.

The most highly debated project pitting residents against developers calls for the installation of a basketball arena in downtown Brooklyn for the New Jersey Nets, and will add 15 new high-rise buildings (one of them reportedly 60 stories tall) into the area around the Metropolitan Transportation Authority's ugly old railyard near Atlantic Ave. The brainchild of developer Bruce Ratner, the project is supposed to contain some affordable housing units and promises at least 15,000 jobs to local residents. But opponents point out that the low-income housing plan is set on regional earning levels, which average out to figures much higher than most Brooklynites in that area can afford. With many condos and units being sold at market rates, and the supposedly low-income units falling to those who make $60,000 or more, residents have furiously labeled the project the Instant Gentrification deal.

Bruce Ratner and his team will probably push approval of the plans through, but hundreds of thousands of residents who face displacement have vowed not to move, leaving the city considering invoking laws of 'imminent domain,' which allow them to move residents who stand in the way of public improvement projects. A court appeal on behalf of the residents has been lodged. That's an approach that surely won't go over well, and for now, developers and elected officials alike are trying to find a solution amenable to all.

Arts

Arts

Though critics can find plenty to complain about when it comes to billionaire Mayor Michael Bloomberg, arts isn't on that list. It wasn't long into the mayor's first term that his role as backer of the arts became clear, as he quietly but quickly took an interest in supporting the cause – reviving arts awards that had been forgotten since the '80s, greatly minimizing budget cuts to the Department of Cultural Affairs, borrowing sculptures and paintings from city museums for prominent display at Gracie Mansion at City Hall, and, most significantly, making 'anonymous donations' to art groups from his personal fortune to make up for where the city's budget has been lacking. Public arts have especially been Bloomberg's big interest, evidenced most prominently in 2005, when Christo's large-scale *The Gates* installation took over Central Park – a direct result of the mayor resurrecting the long-dormant (and controversial) plan.

So how does all this translate into the everyday fabric of arts and cultural life for the casual fan? There's plenty to see, for starters. And though that's nothing new in a city where you could always gaze at impressionist masterpieces in the morning, see an edgy installation made of used tampons in the afternoon and get a heady dose of orchestra or modern dance in the evening, the trend is toward even more to choose from – both now and in the future. One of the biggest developments by far has been the reopening of the Museum of Modern Art (MoMA; p154) following an $850-million expansion project that doubled its space, added sweeping interior design and a high-end destination restaurant. It created a bit of a modern-art frenzy and, to the dismay of many, constant mobs who just can't get enough of the excitement the redesign has generated (despite its sky-high $20 entrance fee). But it's far from the only news. Plenty of institutions have expanded or renovated or are planning on it – the Metropolitan Museum of Art (though its wealthy neighbors are fighting expansion on the grounds of increased crowds), the Guggenheim, Carnegie Hall, the Brooklyn Museum and the Brooklyn Academy of Music (BAM). Even Lincoln Center's planning a $500-million transformation plan (though it's still in the fund-raising phase). And the Seventh Regiment Armory on Park Ave, home to a famous annual art show, has big plans to be transformed into a 55,000-sq-ft visual and performing arts institution.

The latest arts development news has focused on the construction of new museums, namely the New Museum of Contemporary Art (p144) and the Dia Art Foundation (formerly housed in Chelsea and now in Beacon, in upstate New York). The New Museum, formerly located on Broadway in Soho and now temporarily housed in the Chelsea Art Museum on W 22nd St, is slated to move into stunning, 60,000-sq-ft Lower East Side digs in late 2007. Designed by Tokyo architects Sejima and Nashizawa/SANAA, the modern white building that resembles a stack of cubes broke ground in 2005, and will be the first art museum to be constructed in downtown Manhattan in over a century. Dia, meanwhile, is in the very early planning stages of a new home in the Meatpacking District in conjunction with the far-reaching High Line park (p141), whose path, through a concentrated collection of arts institutions, is integral to the park's philosophy. will house its permanent collection in a high-design museum located at the High Line's entrance. Finally, the Museum of Arts & Design (p154) is planning a major and controversial move by 2008 into a Columbus Circle building after preservationists lost their fight to stop the move.

Still, sometimes messages from the government are mixed when it comes to art's place in society – New Yorkers received a not-so-gentle reminder of this during the never-ending redevelopment of Ground Zero. Governor George Pataki and Co effectively ended far-reaching plans for cultural centers by warning art institutions that they could not display art that would offend American patriotism. As a result, places like the esteemed Drawing Center (p128) were forced out.

Also, most artists themselves (except for the very commercially successful) have long been priced out of Manhattan. Still, the city remains fertile ground for young, burgeoning artists of multiple media, who are drawn to New York by its kinetic energy (and all-important patrons of the arts). They're just on unending searches for perfect warehouse spaces, found in the outer boroughs in vibrant arts communities such as Long Island City in Queens, and Williamsburg, Dumbo and Bedford-Stuyvesant in Brooklyn.

Citywide, megaconcerts always sell out, clubs get mobbed and new theater and dance productions lure folks in from all over the tristate area. Because the truth is that most New Yorkers do see the arts as vital, whether that's a conscious philosophy or not. They are, after all, living in one of the cultural capitals of the world.

For information on the city's music scene, see p78. See p66 for architecture.

PAINTING & VISUAL ARTS

Though there may not be much of a place for the so-called starving artist these days – high rents took care of that, thank you very much – artists (and the people who love them) are in grand supply. Some of the major names include Julian Schnabel, Jean-Michel Basquiat, Andy Warhol, Chuk Close and Alice Neel. That's clear in the number of major art museums (25), independent art galleries (about 600), public-art installations and less formal displays of creative talents, from ad-hoc art shows hung in bars and restaurants to all-out graffiti murals scrawled on building facades and walls within the subway's underground labyrinth. The absolute center of the gallery world lies in Chelsea, which has more than 200 art spaces in its neighborhood alone – big names such as Matthew Marks and Barbara Gladstone among them. Parts of the Lower East Side and Williamsburg, Brooklyn, as well as Long Island City, Queens, are also gaining notoriety as more galleries open doors there. But it hasn't always been this way, and it probably won't be for long.

Chelsea Gallery heavyweight, Matthew Marks (p142)

The history of shifting art scenes is a fickle one, with the earliest galleries opening on and around 57th St because it was the vicinity of the immensely popular Museum of Modern Art. Opened in 1929 as a challenge to the conservative policies of traditional museums (such as those of the Met), MoMA spawned a

TEN GREAT NYC ART SPACES

The Met and MoMA are world-class art repositories, and the Guggenheim's got the architectural pedigree. But some of New York City's premier art moments – with blessedly thinner crowds – can be found at these local faves:

- Brooklyn Museum (p178) With its new look, family-friendly theme and moniker (it's dropped 'Art' from the name), this is a joyous place to spend an afternoon – or an evening, at its popular First Saturdays series.
- Cloisters (p170) The Met's charming outdoor cousin resides in northern Manhattan, providing a peaceful, historic retreat.
- Deitch Projects (p54) The installations and quirky special events here keep Soho safely on the gallery map.
- El Museo del Barrio (p169) The best place to catch works by local Latino artists as well as by Latin-American masters.
- Frick Collection (p161) Skip the crowds, not the classics, at this quiet, uptown gem.
- International Center of Photography (p152) Constant stunning exhibits are a must for shutterbug fans.
- Isamu Noguchi Garden Museum (p183) This precious, Zen-like sculpture castle makes Long Island City worth the travel time.
- Neue Galerie (p163) Fans of Klimt and Schiele should not miss this intimate space, housed in a former Rockefeller Mansion.
- Studio Museum in Harlem (p168) Keep up-to-date on up-and-comers on the Harlem arts scene.
- White Columns (p54) A small gallery just south of the Meatpacking District, this is the place to be wowed by odd, contemporary work.

slew of smaller spaces, such as the galleries owned by Julien Levy and Peggy Guggenheim, which showed the progressive work of artists including Mark Rothko and Jackson Pollock. The scene moved uptown for a while during the pop-art movement of the '50s, and then shifted down to the East Village, when showcases for the second generation of abstract expressionism opened along East 10th St. Andy Warhol gained notoriety for his Marilyn Monroe and Campbell's soup can images during this period, displaying much of his work in the early '60s before opening his infamous Factory.

An entrepreneur by the name of Paula Cooper moved all the fun into Soho, though, when she opened the first commercial gallery there, on Wooster St, in 1969. It launched a neighborhood revolution, as artists flocked to Soho lofts that worked as both living and work spaces, and galleries opened here en masse. The year 1980 brought the scene back to the East Village for a while, as the Fun Gallery anchored the district and about 50 other spaces popped up, too, all brandishing a highly ironic set of works that actually helped to bring about the swift gentrification of the 'hood. It ended as suddenly as it began, jumpstarting a brief Soho revival which ended in 1993, when high rents forced the art crowd into West Chelsea, a barren area that was ripe for taking over.

MUSEUMS & GALLERIES

Chelsea is the current heart of the gallery world. It's where the trendy masses roam from opening to opening on Thursday and Friday nights. It's where the hottest artists are bought and sold, where collectors clamor to be and where some of the most innovative yet high-profile pieces are displayed. And it just keeps getting bigger and hotter, as evidenced by the area's most buzzed-about addition, a new gallery group on 27th St between Eleventh and Twelfth Aves. In early 2006, six showcases – Derek Eller Gallery, Foxy Production, Wall-space, Oliver Kamm Gallery, Clementine Gallery and John Connelly Presents – relocated from other Chelsea spots into the old loading dock bays of what used to be the Tunnel nightclub. And the block, with all galleries blessedly located at street level, has become the district's new frontier. (See Walking Tours, p215.)

But all the former hot spots still have plenty to show off. Soho has **Deitch Projects** (☎ 212-343-7300; 18 Wooster St btwn Canal & Grand Sts) and the Drawing Center (p128), both featuring edgy installations. The high 50s and, to a lesser degree, the East Village also have galleries worth trekking to, as do the Lower East Side. There, places such as Rivington Arms (☎ 646-654-3213; 102 Rivington St btwn Essex & Ludlow Sts) and Maccarone Inc (p134) are flexing muscle, similar to Pierogi (☎ 718-599-2144; 177 N 9th St btwn Bedford and Driggs Aves) and similarly edgy spaces out in Williamsburg. Another great spot geared toward fans of more wild, off-kilter creations is **White Columns** (☎ 212-924-4212; 320 W 13th St), a much-admired, unique gallery space in the West Village that's been showing daring works since it opened in 1969. Its openings, held on Fridays, get jam-packed with tuned-in hipsters.

Another couple of areas worth checking out are western Queens, mainly Astoria and Long Island City, and Dumbo in Brooklyn. For years now, Queens has been on the radar of art fans because of places such as PS1 Contemporary Art Center (p184), a massive contemporary-art space which became affiliated with MoMA in 2000; the Socrates Sculpture Park (p184), an outdoor, waterfront patch of land (and former abandoned landfill) with large-scale works by Mark di Suvero and others; and the Isamu Noguchi Garden Museum (p183), with his sculptures presented in a peaceful garden setting.

Dumbo, meanwhile, is where artists flocked in the 1970s and '80s, drawn by the abandoned, industrial feel of the area. But by the end of the '90s, every artistic type – whether they were an artist or not – had discovered the area, falling in love with its couple of eateries, tiny waterfront park and cobblestone streets. Needless to say, it's rapidly gentrified since then, bringing in big restaurants, shops and upscale residences. But the artists remained. The **Dumbo Arts Center** (30 Washington St btwn Plymouth & Water Sts) shows local artists and sponsors an annual Dumbo Art Under the Bridge Festival (p27) in October.

The city's museum classics are still worth visiting – more than ever. The Metropolitan Museum of Art (p162), which houses extensive collections of American, European, Asian, African, Egyptian and Greco-Roman art, plus galleries devoted to fashion, furniture, medieval armor, stained glass, jewelry, written arts and more, is in the process of adding massively to its halls. Others, including the Brooklyn Museum (p178), the Frick Collection (p161), the Solomon R Guggenheim Museum (p164), the American Folk Art Museum (p154) and the Whitney Museum of American Art (p164), are impressive places to spend afternoons, as they are gorgeous structures filled with awe-inspiring works of art that reflect classical, modern or both sensibilities. The Whitney enjoys an explosion of notoriety – from both fans and critics – every two years when it pulls out all the stops for its Biennial, a sprawling showcase of the latest, most cutting-edge rising stars of the art world. It's sometimes derided, often controversial, and occasionally lauded. Other, less prominent museums, such as the brilliant German-Austrian Neue Galerie (p163), near the Met, showcase smaller, more focused collections.

But for art fans more interested in buying than browsing, the most fun and efficient option is to attend art fairs, usually held in the spring and swiftly becoming one of the most high-profile, trendy games in town. Among the hottest is the **Armory Show** (www.thearmoryshow.com), an international modern-art show held every March in pier spaces that jut out over the Hudson. It features fine works from more than 200 galleries, brought together from cities all over the world, from Antwerp to Zurich.

The best way to ensure you've hit all the spaces that might interest you is to pick up the *Gallery Guide,* a small, magazine-like booklet available at any city gallery.

PUBLIC ART

Public art – artwork that graces public spaces, that is – has a rich history in New York that's getting richer with the support of the Bloomberg Administration. It's a tradition that reached its peak in February 2005 with *The Gates* – the long-awaited installation of Christo and Jeanne-Claude that unfurled 7500 bright-orange sheets of heavy fabric from high gates suspended over 23 miles of footpaths in Central Park. The two-week event drew all sorts of opinions, from mind-altering and beautiful to ugly and intrusive. But most importantly, it got people talking about art – and going to check it out, if only out of curiosity – turning it into a public-art event of massive proportion.

But art in public spaces is an ongoing fact in NYC. Two wonderful public-art programs are behind much of the works – the Public Art Fund and the Department of Cultural Affairs' Percent for Art plan. Percent for Art, initiated in 1982 by then-mayor Edward Koch, requires that 1% of the city's budget for construction projects be spent on integrating art into the design or architecture of new facilities. Since its inception there have been nearly 200 such projects at public schools, libraries, parks and police stations – even a **Marine Transfer Station** (59th St & Hudson River) for garbage got the artist's touch when Stephen Antanakos souped it up in 1990 with a neon-light installation that glows pink and green and blue when the sun sets each evening. Other Percent for Art projects include Valerie Jaudon's brick and granite mosaic at Manhattan's police headquarters, Jorge Luis Rodriguez' bright orange steel flower in the **East Harlem Artpark** (Sylvan Place & E 120th St), and Donna Dennis' Dreaming of Faraway Places: The Ships Come to Washington Square Market – a steel fence at **Public School 234** (Greenwich St), and the place where Bloomberg hosted the 20th anniversary celebration of Percent for Art back in 2003.

The Public Art Fund, meanwhile, is a nonprofit organization dedicated to working with both established and emerging artists to present large-scale works to the public. The fund commissions new projects, works with museums to help expand outside of its gallery space (such as when it collaborates with the Whitney to place sculptures in Central Park as part of its Biennial), has open calls for innovative new works every year, and organizes an ongoing lecture series about public art. To find up-to-date locations of commissioned works, visit www.publicartfund.org.

A now-defunct program that has left many beautiful impressions on the city was the 'Creative Stations' project of the Metropolitan Transit Authority (MTA), which runs the subway system. Today you'll find remnants at a slew of stations – including a glass-wall and mural installation at the 28th St stop on the 6 line; colorful tile mosaics at the Bowling Green 4, 5 station; and the sonic, synthesized-music piece hanging overhead at the 34th St N, R platform. Luckily, new art on subway platforms – as well as at bridges and

GRAFFITI & STREET ART

Graffiti art, as we know it, is a movement that began in the 1960s, mostly through 'writers' using public property to make political statements, and for gang members to mark their turf. Early writers were mostly known for their work on subway cars. Tag styles began to quickly evolve, both in style and scale, as a way for writers to distinguish themselves. Early recognition of graffiti as an art form came from scholars and articles, namely in the *New York Times*. NYC's fiscal crisis of the mid '70s gave rise to the height of graffiti, thanks to a poorly maintained transit system; images from that day have been so long-lasting that it's often those tagged-up cars that many tourists expect to still find today.

They won't find it, though, as the Transit Authority made eliminating tag art – known by detractors as vandalism – a priority. Diehards remained throughout the antigraffiti climate of the '80s and '90s and, though many believed that tagging transit spaces was the only real way to go, the hip-hop movement gave rise to writers springing up all over town, adding colorful mural art on the sides of buildings, bridges, rooftops and various hard-to-reach places to the mix. The movement even gave rise to some 'legitimate' pop artists, including Keith Haring and Jean-Michel Basquiat.

Today there's a split between renegade street artists and graffiti that's been co-opted by the art world. A recent, ridiculous example came during plans for a 2005 street fair in Chelsea, during which the hip-hop clothing maker Ecko invited legendary graffiti artists to come and do tagging demos on a display of faux subway cars. Bloomberg would not allow a permit for the event on the grounds that it would incite subway vandalism, but a judge overruled it on Constitutional grounds. The oddly commercial event went off without a hitch.

The best places to glimpse renegade street art today are in the outer boroughs, mainly in the South Bronx and in Queens, from the elevated 7 train before and after the Hunters Point Ave station. There are several options for more organized viewings. **Exhibit 1A Gallery** (147th St at Eighth Ave) is the city's first all-graffiti art gallery, housed in a residential building, and shows 'Graffiti Uptown: You Can't Shut Us Down' every year in November; check www .graffiti.org for upcoming events. Early graffiti supporter Hugo Martinez runs the roving **Martinez Gallery** (www .martinezgallery.com) by showing tagging 'stars' at spaces around the city, including at high schools. Finally, there's the **Graffiti Hall of Fame** (www.graffitihalloffame.org), founded by Ray Rodriguez and consisting of murals on walls of **Junior High School 13** (106th St & Park Ave, Spanish Harlem). Special annual exhibits are held each summer. For more information on tagging artists and history, visit **Streets Are Saying Things** (www.streetsaresayingthings.com) and **@149st** (http://at149st.com).

tunnels, and stations for both the Long Island and Metro-North Rail Roads – keeps on coming, thanks to the ongoing Arts for Transit program of the MTA. Every now and then, New Yorkers will be awakened from their commuting slumber when a new tile mosaic or sculpture appears in their regular subway station, prompting smiles and curiosity. Recent additions include the sparkly glass-mosaic mural *Artemis, Acrobats, Divas and Dancers* by Nancy Spero at the 66th St–Lincoln Center 1 station, and the whimsical cast-bronze sculptures of Tom Otterness, whose untitled installation in the 14th St subway station on the A, C, E, L line features lovable, cartoonish characters that have gotten chuckles out of the most jaded New Yorkers.

For some good public-art viewing above ground, check out *The Sphere,* by Fritz Koenig, moved to Battery Park from the World Trade Center as a memorial piece after it sustained damage during the September 11 attacks (see p118). In other parts of town, be sure to visit Tony Rosenthal's legendary cube sculpture, *Alamo,* on Astor Place (which spins if you turn it with some muscle), Henry Moore's *Reclining Figure* and reflecting pool at Lincoln Center, and Milton Hebald's dramatic *The Tempest* and *Romeo and Juliet* pieces at the Delacorte Theater in Central Park. Search along the ground you walk on for less obvious works, such as Lawrence Weiner's *NYC Manhole Covers,* which say 'In direct line with another & the next' and can be found at 19 locations south of Union Sq; also look for the wonderful *Subway Map Floating on a New York Sidewalk* (by Francoise Schein), an 87-ft-long work of concrete rods embedded in the sidewalk in front of 110 Greene St in Soho. The Socrates Sculpture Park (p184) in Long Island City, Queens, with permanent, massive sculptures by Mark di Suvero and a constant rotation of works by visiting artists, is quite a find for fans of outdoor art. Spend an afternoon climbing on pieces, picnicking in their shadows and gazing out over the East River and the east side of Manhattan just across it.

THEATER

The biggest, splashiest dramas and musicals are probably what's best associated with New York's entertainment world – mainly because of that term known round the world: Broadway. But Broadway shows, while they do make up a significant portion of the local theater scene, refer strictly to productions staged in the 38 official Broadway theaters – lavish, early-20th-century jewels surrounding Times Sq. Public opinion about the state of the Great White Way changes drastically every couple of years, with some folks constantly moaning that, with the constant revivals, there's just no good, original theater anymore. But the very latest wave of innovative musical works – *Avenue Q* and *Wicked* – has changed many minds. And repackaged movie hits such as *Monty Python's Spamalot* and *Grey Gardens* have even taken the town by storm.

New York has a rich history of taking folks by storm when it comes to the development of the theater world. The Theater District as we see it today was begun in 1893 by Charles Frohman, who opened the Empire Theater on 40th St, beginning the shift of the district from the 30s to what would later become Times Sq. That same year, the first-ever industry trade union – the National Alliance of Theatrical Stage Employees, for stagehands – was formed. By 1901, the flood of lights coming from theater facades in the area was so great that designer OJ Gude deemed the Broadway district the Great White Way. Soon after, the Theater Guild began its long and distinguished history of producing big hits, from Eugene O'Neill, George Bernard Shaw and others, and musicals began to soar in quality and popularity. The first Tony Awards took place in 1947, the Theater Development Fund was established 20 years after and, by the late '80s, nearly every Broadway theater was designated as a historic landmark.

Broadway, though, doesn't tell nearly the whole story. Off-Broadway, more adventurous, less costly theater shown in houses that seat 200 to 500 people, or off-off-Broadway, even edgier, more affordable performances housed in theaters for crowds of less than 100, are both big businesses here. They often provide venues for more established actors to let their hair down a bit, and sometimes produce shows that wind up either on Broadway (*Rent*, for example, premiered at the downtown New York Theater Workshop, just as *Angels in America* started at the Public Theater and *The Vagina Monologues* took off at the tiny HERE in Soho). To see a lot of experimental theater in a short amount of time, watch for the Fringe Festival (p26; www.fringenyc.org), held in various downtown venues every August. Also in summer, usually beginning in June, is the acclaimed Shakespeare in the Park festival, produced by the Public Theater and taking place at the Delacorte Theater in Central Park. Tickets are free, but you do need to line up on certain days at specific times to claim yours.

To purchase tickets for any other show in town, you can either head to the box office, or use one of several ticket-service agencies (see p279 for a list).

Bargain-hunters can try to score same-day standing-room tickets for sold-out shows for about $15. You'll get great views and sore feet, but you can always scope out vacant seats at intermission. In Times Sq, the TKTS booth (p285), run by the Theater Development Fund, sells same-day tickets to Broadway and off-Broadway musicals and dramas. The booth's electric marquee lists available shows; availability depends on the popularity of the show you're looking to see, so be prepared to be flexible. On Wednesday and Saturday, matinee tickets go on sale at 10am, and on Sunday the windows open at 11am for afternoon performances. Evening tickets go on sale at 3pm daily, and a line begins to form up to an hour before the booth opens. Note that TKTS accepts cash or travelers checks only.

COMEDY, CABARET & PERFORMANCE ART

If you visit New York City, and especially if you live here, you had better be able to laugh. How else do you expect to make it through life in such a bustling, trying, crazy place? Luckily, there are plenty of funny folks around who are willing to lend a hand. Mayor Bloomberg even joined forces with Carolines on Broadway (p288), Comedy Central and various laugh-centered sponsors to create the annual New York Comedy Festival, which will enter its third year in November 2006 (see www.nycomedyfestival.com for details).

New York has a great history of discovering great comedians – it's the town that brought us Jon Stewart and his *Daily Show,* after all, as well as Jerry Seinfeld, Eddie Murphy and Chris Rock, who began their careers at Carolines on Broadway. Jim Belushi, Dennis Miller, Joe Piscopo, Kevin Nealon, Dana Carvey and Tina Fey (along with many others) all had their careers launched on the hit New York series *Saturday Night Live* (p302).

Similar to many other entertainment forms here, the comedy scene is sharply divided between the big-name, big-ticket clubs and the more experimental and obscure places – which often host the best shows in town, sometimes bending the typical stand-up style to include music, burlesque or comedy sketches. For that kind of anything-goes format, check out the Upright Citizens Brigade Theatre (p289), which specializes in improv and often sees comedy celebs in its audience. Rififi Cinema Classics (☎ 212-677-6309; 332 E 11th St), in the back room of its movie house with Welcome to Our Week and Invite Them Up, as well as the Thursdays at Ten series at Ars Nova Theater (☎ 212-489-9800; 511 W 54th St), also deliver unexpected goods. But to be made fun of, and to hear wisecracks about the state of the country or the city or the $12 drinks you're sipping, stick with the standard stand-up shows. Besides Carolines, perhaps the most well-known such place in the city, there's Stand-Up NY (p289), the Gotham Comedy Club (p288) and many more. See p288 for all venue information.

Cabaret, meanwhile, often has plenty of comedic overtones – but it's much more subtle. Usually consisting of a performer at a piano or a microphone who holds court in an intimate venue, the clever riffs or anecdotes are just highlights to the real purpose: live music. Jazz and standards are the most popular fare, although at Theater District venues – Danny's Skylight Room, Don't Tell Mama (p287) – you'll get a big dose of Broadway show tunes. Styles also differ depending on the pricing and on if the venue is considered 'classic' – such as Feinstein's (p288) or the Carlyle (p287), where cabaret stars including Woody Allen, Betty Buckley and Ann Hampton Callaway grace the stage. Though all cabaret has a gay bent by its very (campy) nature, the queer feel is more evident at the Duplex (Christopher St) where performers will often be in drag; gay bars and lounges often become ad hoc cabaret venues – such as Therapy (p267) and xl (p267), among others.

Some of the gay nightspot shows verge on performance art, although there are plenty of other places to go to find that murky genre as well. One of the hottest styles remains burlesque, which can be seen at various multithemed venues around the city such as Slide/Marquee (p266) and the new Mo Pitkin's House of Satisfaction (p288) in the East Village. Galapagos Art Space (p276) in Williamsburg, La MaMa E.T.C. (p286) and the all-women WOW Café Theater (☎ 212-696-8904; 59 E 4th St btwn Bowery & Second Ave), both in the East Village, are also excellent places to find burlesque, strange music revues, live soap-opera series and all-around cleverness.

CLASSICAL MUSIC & OPERA

If downtown Manhattan is home to all things contemporary – indie rock bands, clever drag shows, cutting-edge art installations and experimental dance theater – then Uptown is the refuge for more classic, timely pursuits. A visit to the Upper West Side, a neighborhood for old-school artists, reveals this quickly enough, as musicians who make their living as cellists, bassists or tuba players for orchestras and ensembles can almost always be spotted lugging their instruments, secured in bulky, odd-shaped cases, home from the 96th St stop on the 1, 2, or 3 trains. For a good number of them, work has probably included gigs at either the Lincoln Center (p280) complex or Carnegie Hall (p279) at one point or another, just as a fair amount have most likely studied – or at least taken a class – at one of the premier schools for classical music and opera in the country: the Juilliard School or the Manhattan School of Music, which are also host to top-notch concerts.

Lincoln Center was built in the 1960s as part of an urban renewal plan under development commissioner Robert Moses, controversially clearing out a slew of slums (the ones used as the basis for *West Side Story,* actually) in the process. And what started as a questionable project for many preservationists and arts fans has largely won over much of New York with its incomparable offerings. Housed in the massive miniworld – complete with fountains and reflecting pools and wide-open spaces – are the main halls of Alice Tully, Avery Fisher, the Metropolitan

Opera House (the most opulent of all the venues here) and the New York State Theater, as well as the Juilliard School, the Fiorello LaGuardia High School for the Performing Arts, and the Vivian Beaumont and Mitzi Newhouse theaters. Resident companies include the Metropolitan Opera and the New York City Opera, the New York Philharmonic, the New York City Ballet and the Chamber Music Society of Lincoln Center, among others. Its programs are far reaching, with some free offerings – such as the popular summer Concerts in the Parks series of the Philharmonic, itself founded in 1842 and America's premier orchestra, currently directed by Lorin Maazel. The Metropolitan Opera – now in an exciting period thanks to its new (and populist) general manager, Peter Gelb – has always been the grand, more classic company, while the New York City Opera is its more unique, imaginative and down-to-earth sibling.

The smaller, more contained and limited Carnegie Hall, meanwhile, is just as beloved a venue – especially since opening Zankel Hall, offering eclectic world-music and jazz sounds, beneath the main Issac Stern Hall, whose stage has been graced by all the big names. This is the place to experience visiting orchestras from all over the world, acclaimed soloists such as violinist Midori and pianist Nelson Freire, and big concerts including the New York Pops series. Fans are watching with anticipation to see what its new general director, Clive Gillinson, will do with the lineup.

Outside of these biggie venues, there's plenty more. But one of the main attractions is the Brooklyn Academy of Music (BAM; p279), the country's oldest academy for the performing arts, where you'll find opera seasons and concerts from its resident Brooklyn Philharmonic, which also plays for free in summer, in nearby Prospect Park. (For other classical performance venues, see p289.) To catch quality classical sounds anytime without paying a penny, tune in to one of the local radio stations that serve as community centers for lovers of the genre: the 75-year-old 96.3-FM WQXR, which is all classical all the time; and 93.9-FM WNYC, the city's local National Public Radio (NPR) affiliate, which goes classical weekdays at 2pm and 7pm and weekend evenings at 8pm.

DANCE

The past couple of years have been banner years for dance in NYC – where five new dance spaces opened and several more are in the works. It wasn't the usual situation, and was one that had dance experts thrilled, but also puzzled as to how such a positive shift had snuck up on their world. New and notable spaces that opened in 2004 or 2005 include the **Baryshnikov Arts Center** (450 W 37th St), a three-story interdisciplinary rehearsal and performance space in Hell's Kitchen. In nearby Chelsea, the Cedar Lake Ensemble (p290) opened a theater and studio, while the Field opened the FAR Space, for artist residencies, also on 26th St. Alvin Ailey American Dance Theater (p290) opened its new $54-million home in Hell's Kitchen in 2004, while still to come are the **Dance New Amsterdam** (280 Broadway) headquarters in Lower Manhattan, as well as a brand new space for the edgy Dixon Place (p286), which offers a healthy dose of dance along with theater, readings and performance art. The new spaces represent a change in tune from the recent past, when all new dance spaces, such as the Mark Morris Dance Group, housed in a relatively new space in Fort Greene, Brooklyn, were sent scrambling for real estate in the outer boroughs.

But good news for dance is nothing new in New York City, where, historically, all dance roads lead. It's a place where the dance world is really comprised of two separate halves – the classical and the modern – and its split personality is what makes it one of the most renowned dance capitals of the globe. You can see this two-spirited self by browsing dance listings, whether you're a fan or not – or you can experience it firsthand, by taking a dance class while you're in town. Almost any dance school in the city, whether it's Steps on the Upper West Side, Dance Space in Soho or anything in between, offers a wild blend of classes – modern or jazz or some blend, or ballet, whose students are known as 'bunheads' by the modern folks. And most amateurs pick one side of the line and stick with it, similar to pros and their fans. The Entertainment chapter has details of dance companies, studios and arts centers (p290).

It all started in the 1930s, when American classic ballet took off here and laid the foundation for what would soon become the world-class American Ballet Theatre (ABT) and New York City Ballet. Lincoln Kirstein envisioned a US ballet for native dancers, and wanted them trained by the ballet masters of the world so they could create a repertory that had a built-in cast. Kirstein met the Russian-trained George Balanchine in 1933 in London, and the two started their now legendary American school, the New York City Ballet, together in New York that year, later performing with Jerome Robbins as assistant artistic director. In 1964 they opened the New York State Theater and have been its resident ballet company ever since. Since then, ballet bigwigs, including Balanchine, Robbins and Peter Martins, have choreographed dances for the troupe, which has boasted stars such as Maria Tallchief, Suzanne Farrell and Jacques D'Amboise.

Meanwhile, the American Ballet Theatre (ABT) was making its own inroads, founded in New York in 1937 by Lucia Chase and Rich Pleasant and made famous through works by Balanchine, Antony Tudor, Jerome Robbins *(Fancy Free)*, Alvin Ailey and Twyla Tharp *(When Push Comes to Shove)*. After defecting from the Soviet Union, Mikhail Baryshnikov found fame with ABT as a principal dancer in the '70s, and remained as its artistic director from 1980 to 1989 before founding his own White Oak Dance Project.

Simultaeously, Martha Graham, Charles Wiedman and Doris Humphrey sowed the seeds of the NYC modern movement, which was continued here after WWII by masters including Merce Cunningham, Paul Taylor, Alvin Ailey and Twyla Tharp. Today both scenes continue to be global forces, with the more experimental, avant-garde dance world constantly growing as well – enabling you to see pretty much anything from muscle-bound women mixing circus-type trapeze acts into their performance to naked troupes rolling around on a bare stage.

Today's up-and-coming dancers continue to move in new directions, bringing their own interpretations to small downtown theaters including the Kitchen, the Joyce Theater and Danspace Project (see p291 for all venue information). And the dancers themselves, often forced to work other jobs to support themselves and their craft in such an expensive city, are remarkably supportive of each other. Dancers can apply for financial grants, studio space and other creative assistance through organizations such as the Field, Movement Research, Pentacle, New York Foundation for the Arts and Dance Theater Workshop – which hosts the Bessies, a prestigious annual awards ceremony for dancers (named after Bessie Schönberg, a highly regarded dance teacher who died in 1997).

The best way to tap into what's going on in dance is to read – especially the words of the dance critics at the *Village Voice, Time Out New York* and the *New York Times*. Or, for a complete list of dance venues, organizations and news updates, visit www.dancenyc.org. Then pick a side in the modern–classical dichotomy – or don't. You can enjoy it all here, the most influential dance capital you'll find.

LITERATURE

New York's lit scene goes way beyond a great selection of bookstores – mainly because so many top-notch writers reside here. Famous writers are practically a dime a dozen, as contemporary scribes including Michael Cunningham, Jonathan Ames, Grace Paley, Tom Wolfe, Frank McCourt, Joan Didion, Jay McInerney and too many others to name all live and write in NYC. Throw in the fact of the still-unknowns – everyone and his mother is writing a book in this town, and can be found on the active public-readings circuit – and the fact that New York is the capital of the book-publishing industry, and you've got yourself quite a bookish city indeed. That should come as no surprise, considering the many sources of inspiration here, coupled with a long and storied literary history.

Greenwich Village has perhaps the most glorified such history in New York, and de-

Architectural books Italiano style at Rizzoli (p345)

NYC IN LITERATURE

- *Bonfire of the Vanities* by Tom Wolfe (1987). The man who recorded the world of 1960s' acid tests and high-class society's love affair with Black Power delved into the status-obsessed '80s with this gripping novel of an uptown investment banker's entanglement with the world of the black South Bronx.
- *Bright Lights, Big City* by Jay McInerney (1984). A Manhattan yuppie with everything on his side has a big downward spiral – featuring sordid scenes in pre-gentrified Soho – when he's forced to deal with his mother's death and the seduction of drugs.
- *Drag King Dreams* by Leslie Feinberg (2006). The new novel from the author of the lesbian classic *Stone Butch Blues* brings readers into the post–September 11, gender-bending world of queer West Village nightlife.
- *Go Tell It on the Mountain* by James Baldwin (1953). This emotional, lyrical, tight novel shares the details of just one day in the life of 14-year-old John Grimes, bringing readers into Harlem during the Depression.
- *Jazz* by Toni Morrison (1992). Pulitzer Prize–winner Morrison explores the Harlem Jazz Age through the tales of three tragic, intersecting lives.
- *The Good Life* by Jay McInerney (2005). Still writing about his city, McInerney's latest deals with affluent New Yorkers and how they were affected by September 11.
- *Motherless Brooklyn* by Jonathan Lethem (1999). This genius novel had a quick rise to cult status among north-Brooklyn residents, as its oddly compelling tale – of grown-up orphan Lionel Essrog, a detective with Tourette's syndrome who is investigating the death of his boss – explores crevices and histories of north Brooklyn 'hoods that newcomers never knew existed.
- *Paradise Alley* by Kevin Baker (2002). Baker's second in a trilogy of historical novels about fires in NYC takes the Draft-Riot fires and weaves stories from them.
- *Push* by Sapphire (1996). Brooklyn writer Sapphire's wrenching modern-age story about an abused young Harlem woman, 16-year-old Precious Jones, is almost too much to bear. But her gorgeous, honest prose pulls you through.
- *Slaves of New York* by Tama Janowitz (1986). This real estate–obsessed collection of deadpan, quirky stories about folks living downtown in the '80s is a nostalgic glance at a time when real-life starving artists could scrape by and find their own little nests, whether in illegal lofts or dilapidated studios.
- *Specimen Days* by Michael Cunningham (2005). In his first novel since *The Hours,* this three-part story explores NYC in past (the '20s), present and future (22nd century), weaving three indescribable tales of disasters and Walt Whitman poetry.
- *The Story of Junk* by Linda Yablonsky (1997). Years after her grim existence as a heroin junkie living in the down-and-out, pre-gentrified artists' Lower East Side, Yablonsky recalls all the shocking, seedy details.

servedly so. Literary figures including Henry James, Herman Melville and Mark Twain lived in the Washington Sq area at the turn of the 19th century. And by 1912, the tightknit, storied clan of John Reed, Mabel Dodge Luhan, Hutchins Hapgood, Max Eastman and other playwrights and poets wrote about bohemian life and gathered at cafés in these parts for literary salons and liquor-fueled tête-à-têtes. But when Prohibition sent too many uptowners searching for hooch downtown and the party broke up, things remained quiet for a time, until Eugene O'Neill and his cohorts came along, followed by such luminaries as novelists Willa Cather, Malcolm Cowley, Ralph Ellison and poets ee cummings, Edna St Vincent Millay, Frank O'Hara and Dylan Thomas, who is said to have died in this 'hood after downing one too many drinks at the local White Horse Tavern in 1953.

The area is still most closely associated with the late 1950s and '60s, when the wild and wonderful Beat movement was led by William Burroughs, Allen Ginsberg, Jack Kerouac and their gang. These poets and novelists rejected traditional writing forms and instead adopted rhythms of basic American speech and jazz music for their literary musings. Ginsberg is best known for *Howl,* which he wrote in 1956 as an attack on American values. Kerouac's prose, as seen in novels including *On the Road, The Subterraneans* and *The Dharma Bums,* similar to that of Burroughs *(Naked Lunch),* reflect a disdain for convention and a thirst for adventure.

In 1966, Ginsberg helped found the Poetry Project at St Mark's Church-in-the-Bowery in the East Village, still an active, poet-staffed literary forum and resource – and sort of all-around community center – for New York writers. Ginsberg gave a historic joint reading here with Robert Lowell, and some of the many other literary legends to read here have included Adrienne Rich, Patti Smith and Frank O'Hara.

That this center took root in the East Village is one of the best proofs that intellectual, writerly activities and inspirations have never been confined to the fabled Greenwich Village. Harlem, for example, has a long literary history. James Baldwin, born in this uptown 'hood, was a black, gay, preacher's son who wrote about conflicts of race, poverty and identity in novels including *Go Tell It on the Mountain* and *Giovanni's Room,* published in the 1950s. Audre Lorde, a Caribbean-American lesbian, activist and writer, was raised in Harlem and attended Columbia University. Her poetry, written mostly in the '70s, and memoir, *Zami: A New Spelling of My Name* (1982), dealt with class, race and gay and lesbian issues. Much earlier, in the 1920s, Dorothy Parker held court at the famous Algonquin Round Table – a private clique of writers who hung out and drank and talked endlessly about American culture, politics and literature. Soon, the regular gatherings – which included *New Yorker* founder Harold Ross, author Robert Benchley, playwrights George S Kaufman, Edna Ferber, Noel Coward, Marc Connelly and various critics – turned into a national amusement, as stories were written about the gatherings and tourists often came to gawk at the intellectual bunch.

In the 1980s, novelists such as Bret Easton Ellis *(American Psycho)* began expounding upon the greedy, coke-fueled era. At the same time, notable poets and writers of the East Village (where Allen Ginsberg actually lived) included Eileen Myles, whose poetry and unconventional novel *Chelsea Girls* took readers into the rebellious downtown art world, as did poets Gregory Masters and Michael Scholnick.

And way before any of this, of course, came Long Island native Walt Whitman, who wrote from his home in the borough of Brooklyn, publishing *Leaves of Grass* in 1855, paving an early way for more contemporary Brooklyn authors, including Betty Smith, who wrote *A Tree Grows In Brooklyn* in 1943, and modern darling Jonathan Lethem, whose *Motherless Brooklyn* (1999) sparked new interest in the area around Cobble Hill and Brooklyn Heights. Other breakout Brooklynites of this century and the late '90s include Rick Moody *(Purple America, The Ice Storm),* who mixes suburban and urban adventure; Paul Auster *(New York Trilogy, Mr Vertigo, Timbuktu),* who writes about current-day New York; and the young Lauren Weisberger *(The Devil Wears Prada, Everyone Worth Knowing),* who has documented the current vapid yet fascinating worlds of magazine publishing and A-list–filled nightclubs.

For information regarding venues where you can catch readings by authors both legendary and up-and-coming, see p291.

FILM & TV

As both a subject and venue, New York has a long and storied life in TV and the movies. At least a dozen films are in production here at any given time, while 20 prime-time TV shows *(Law & Order, The Apprentice, Hope & Faith, American Justice)* are regularly produced here, along with 40 daytime and late-night shows *(All My Children, The Today Show, Saturday Night Live)* and about 30 cable shows *(The Sopranos, Chapelle's Show, Inside the Actors Studio, Queer Eye for the Straight Guy, Project Runway, Court TV).* And while some are set here only in theory and filmed in LA studios *(Seinfeld* and *Friends,* for example, all in reruns), they've definitely added to the city's allure – as has *Sex and the City,* now in reruns. Many of the shows are filmed not only on the city streets, but in Silvercup Studios (42-22 22nd St) in Long Island City, Queens, which is the largest full-service film and TV production facility in the city; it's been here since 1983. And, nestled in with the endless array of TV stations with homes here – NBC, ABC, CNN, the local NY1 news network, and the Food Network and Oxygen Media, both housed in the Chelsea Market – are now a couple of major film companies, including New Line Cinema (a division of Time Warner), New Yorker Films, and Miramax and Tribeca Productions (owned by Robert DeNiro), both housed in the 14-year-old Tribeca Film Center, proving that the entire industry, at least, is not confined to Hollywood. Local cable shows (there are two cable carriers, Time Warner and Cablevision) are popular forms of entertainment, with the public-access Manhattan Neighborhood Network (MNN) channel providing constant cultural programming and just plain weird shows, as the station grants airtime to just about any local resident who wants it (visit www.mnn.org for a schedule). The New York Metro channel (Cablevision 60, Time Warner 70), part of *New York* magazine, features slick NYC-centric program-

NYC ON FILM

- *Angels in America* (2003). Directed by Mike Nichols. Starring Al Pacino, Meryl Streep, Jeffrey Wright. This exquisite, HBO-movie version of Tony Kushner's Broadway play recalls 1985 Manhattan: relationships are on the brink, AIDS is out of control and a closeted Roy Cohn does nothing about it – but fall ill himself – as part of the Reagan administration. Follow characters from Brooklyn to Lower Manhattan to Central Park.
- *Big* (1988). Directed by Penny Marshall. Starring Tom Hanks and Elizabeth Perkins. A seriously heartwarming tale of a little boy who gets his wish to be big, Hanks plays the bogus grown-up who becomes an executive at a toy company, creating wonderful scenes in loft apartments, FAO Schwarz, glitzy restaurants and other hallmarks of 1980s' NYC.
- *Chasing Amy* (1997). Directed by Kevin Smith. Starring Ben Affleck and Joey Lauren Adams. Affleck's breakout film, though far from a cinematic masterpiece, put Meow Mix and other aspects of Manhattan lesbian life on the map.
- *Crossing Delancey* (1988). Directed by Joan Micklin Silver. Starring Amy Irving and Peter Riegert. Isabelle is set up with Sam the pickle man by her grandmother in a romantic comedy showing the Lower East Side before the trendies moved in.
- *Fatal Attraction* (1987). Directed by Adrian Lyne. Starring Michael Douglas, Glenn Close and Anne Archer. This psycho thriller is about a happily married man whose one-night stand turns into a series of run-ins with his trick-turned-stalker. Catch great glimpses of the pregentrification Meatpacking District (and that famous lift scene).
- *Kids* (1995). Directed by Larry Clark. Starring Leo Fitzpatrick, Chloë Sevigny and Rosario Dawson. Shot in documentary style and starring a bunch of then-unknowns, this chilling tale of privileged Manhattan kids growing up with no rules – downtown in the 1990s – tackles sexual promiscuity, drugs and AIDS.
- *Manhattan* (1979). Directed by Woody Allen. Starring Woody Allen, Diane Keaton and Mariel Hemingway. A divorced New Yorker dating a high-school student (the adorable, baby-voiced Hemingway) falls for his best friend's mistress in what is essentially a love letter to NYC. Catch romantic views of the Queensboro Bridge and the Upper East Side.
- *Midnight Cowboy* (1969). Directed by John Schlesinger. Starring Dustin Hoffman and Jon Voight. A Best Picture Oscar-winner despite an X-rating for its provocative (for then) content on the sordid life of big-city hustlers, this thoroughly depressing (and startlingly homophobic) drama now stands as a time capsule for the bygone sleaziness of Times Sq.
- *Party Monster* (2003). Directed by Fenton Bailey. Starring Seth Green and Macauley Culkin. Culkin plays the crazed, famed, murderous club kid Michael Alig in this disturbing look into the drug-fueled club-kid era of the late '80s in downtown NYC. The Limelight club, now Avalon, is featured prominently.
- *Saturday Night Fever* (1977). Directed by John Badham. Starring John Travolta and Karen Lynn Gorney. Travolta is the hottest thing in bell-bottoms in this tale of a streetwise Brooklyn kid who becomes king of the dancefloor. Great glimpses of '70s Bay Ridge.
- *Summer of Sam* (1999). Directed by Spike Lee. Starring John Leguizamo, Mira Sorvino and Jennifer Esposito. One of Spike Lee's best, the sordid tale puts the city's summer of 1977 in historical context by weaving together the Son of Sam murders, the blackout, racial tensions and the misadventures of one disco-dancing Brooklyn couple, including scenes at both CBGB and Studio 54.
- *Taxi Driver* (1976). Directed by Martin Scorsese. Starring Robert DeNiro, Cybill Shepherd and Jodie Foster. DeNiro is a mentally unstable Vietnam-war vet whose urges to lash out are heightened by the high tensions of the city. It's a funny, depressing, brilliant classic that's a potent reminder of how much grittier this place used to be.

ming, including fashion, entertainment, reality and talk shows, as does the new official NYC station, Channel 25.

The Mayor's Office of Film, Theater & Broadcasting (MOFTB) has definitely been a driving force behind the success of the local industry – worth more than $5 billion and 75,000 city jobs. As a result of MOFTB's efforts, through strong incentives which include free permits, free locations, free police assistance and zero sales tax on production consumables, New York City is currently ranked as the second-largest production center in the country, according to a recent study by the US Department of Commerce. Spend just a little time in this city and you will most likely see the evidence of this for yourself, as it's not uncommon to happen upon on-location shoots, which often close down city blocks, blast them with floodlights at night and surround them with massive trucks and bossy assistants who'll stop you in your tracks if you try to walk through the filming area – much to the dismay of the locals, who are often barred from even going home to make dinner after a long day of work until the scene-in-session has ended! See the boxed text, above, for a rundown of movies filmed on-location here.

As a showcase for film, New York is a star as well. There have been quite a few new movie theaters built over the past several years, most with stadium seating, wide screens and other glamorous amenities, such as gourmet snack stands. And the number of annual film festivals held here throughout the year just keeps rising: the number currently stands at around 30, including Dance on Camera (January), Jewish Film Festival (January), New York Film Festival (January), African-American Women in Film Festival (March), Williamsburg Film Festival (March), the fast-rising Tribeca Film Festival (May), Lesbian & Gay Film Festival (June) and the Human Rights Watch Film Festival (June).

New York is home to some of the top film schools in the country – NYU's Tisch Film School, the New York Film Academy, the School of Visual Arts, Columbia University and the New School – and the students get great support from MOFTB, which offers free film permits to students for use of any public property. But you don't have to be a student to learn, as plenty of museums – namely the Museum of the Moving Image (p185) in Astoria, Queens, and the Museum of Television & Radio (p155) – serve as major showcases for screenings and seminars about productions both past and present.

Finally, you can always go and get a glimpse of locations made famous from appearances in TV shows and movies, from the **Dakota building** (Central Park West at 72nd St), the apartment building used in the classic thriller *Rosemary's Baby,* to **Tom's Diner** (Broadway at 112th St), the facade of which was used regularly in *Seinfeld.* The best way to find all the spots you want to see is to take a movie- or TV-location guided tour, such as On Location Tours (p112), which takes you to spots where your favorite TV shows were filmed, including *Sex and the City, Sopranos, Friends* and more.

ARCHITECTURE

Another example of New York City's vertical thrust

ARCHITECTURALLY SPEAKING, THERE'S NEVER BEEN A MORE EXCITING TIME TO BE IN NEW YORK.
Buildings are going up like crazy, many by well-known international architects, such as
Spain's Santiago Calatrava and Tokyo's Sejima and Neshizawa/SANAA. Boring glass-box
office buildings are old news, overpowered by new crystalline towers with experimental
geometric forms and fragmented facades. Stylish apartment buildings designed by American architects Philip Johnson and Michael Graves are sprouting. Museums including the
New Museum of Contemporary Art and the Museum of Arts & Design are getting spanking
new homes. Even old standards including Yankee Stadium and Shea Stadium (of the Mets)
will be getting snazzy new abodes. Much of it has been spurred on by redevelopment plans
for the **World Trade Center site** (p126), which envisions dramatic office towers and retail spaces;
ironically, though, drama and in-fighting keep preventing forward motion here.

New York's neighborhoods are rejuvenating as older, deteriorating areas across the city
such as Harlem, Carroll Gardens in Brooklyn and Mott Haven in the Bronx are sparking
interest, and their historic housing is being restored to earlier glory days. Ever since New
York City enacted the Landmarks Law in 1965, grass-roots preservationists have been
battling big-time developers with some success, as city planners try to keep a balance
between preservation and progress and ordinary New Yorkers keep a watchful eye on
their own turf.

The best local sources for architecture information are the **AIA Center for Architecture** (Map
p448; ☎ 212-683-0023; 536 LaGuardia Pl btwn Bleecker & W 3rd Sts), which is known for
its rather straightforward and academic approach, and the unique **Architectural League** (p292),
whose artists' look at architecture can be seen through its excellent exhibits, publications
and lecture series.

The classy, glassy Time Warner Center (p153)

TOP TEN
NEW ADDITIONS

Adding to the growing lineup of designer-label condos is Gwathmey Siegel's 21-story **Astor Place** (Map p449; Astor Pl at Lafayette St), a luxury tower of curved, reflective green glass – an oddly sparkling addition to the gray-toned, low-rise East Village.

Richard Meier recently added a third to his pair of celeb-filled, minimalist, transparent **Perry Street Towers** (Map p448; Charles & Perry Sts at West Side Hwy) that sit perched at the edge of the West Village.

Frederic Schwartz Architects' new **Staten Island Ferry Terminal** (p116), completed in 2005, is an airy glass-and-steel structure that frames views of the harbor and the Brooklyn Bridge.

The **Time Warner Center** (p153), by David Childs/Skidmore, Owings & Merrill, has two huge crystalline glass towers rising from a six-story curved base, incorporating the world's largest cable-net glass wall.

The Miami firm Arquitectonica adds a dose of shiny color with the **Westin Hotel** (Map p282; 270 W 43rd St), a tower of reflective purple and blue glass.

The Morris-Jumel Mansion, p171, Manhattan's oldest (haunted) house

'MANHATTAN'S LAST SURVIVING FARMHOUSE.'

DUTCH DOMESTICITY

None of the 17th-century stepped-gable buildings from New Amsterdam are left but a few Dutch Colonial farmhouses survive and are open to view. The Pieter Claesen **Wyckoff House** (Map p464; ☎ 718-629-5400; 5816 Clarendon Rd; admission free; ✆ 10am-4pm Tue-Sun), in Brooklyn, is the oldest house in the city. Its first section, constructed in 1652, is easily recognized by the shingled exterior and peaked roof with flaring eaves. Built later, but in a similar style, the **Dyckman House** (p171), 1785, is Manhattan's last surviving farmhouse.

GEORGIAN GENTILITY

British rule brought buildings popular during the reign of the four English Hanoverian kings, Georges I–IV (1714–1830). They were rectangular and symmetrical with hipped roofs, tall end chimneys and, sometimes, topped with a cupola. English originals were created from fine stone;

the transplants built of brick or wood. A model of twhe British City Hall, erected in 1703 but later demolished, is displayed at **Federal Hall National Memorial** (p121). **Fraunces Tavern** (p121), 1907, imitates the original pub where George Washington said goodbye to his officers.

Morris-Jumel Mansion (p171), 1765, the oldest house in Manhattan, is one of the best built in Colonial America. The white-painted, clapboard and shingled mansion boasts a two-story colonnade and exquisite entrance. **St Paul's Chapel** (p119), 1766–94, is a copy of St Martin-in-the-Fields in London, but built of Manhattan fieldstone and brownstone. French architect Pierre L'Enfant designed the high altar, crowned by a golden sunburst, in the sanctuary.

Brownstones also come in churches, St Paul's Chapel (p119)

Take it all the way to City Hall (p124)

FEDERAL FINERY

After the Revolutionary War, heavy solid forms of the Georgian period were replaced by refined Federal architecture of the new republic, based on designs popularized by the Adam brothers, Scottish architects inspired by the delicate details of ancient Roman architecture.

Diminutive **City Hall** (p124), 1812, owes its French form to émigré architect Joseph Francois Mangin and its Federal detailing to American-born John McComb Jr. Originally faced with white marble, the rear was covered in brownstone to cut costs. The interior contains an airy rotunda and curved cantilevered stairway. **Gracie Mansion** (p161), 1799, the official residence of the mayor since 1942, was built as a country villa. The cream-colored frame house features Chinese Chippendale railings, a fan-light doorway with leaded glass sidelights and a porch that runs along the length of its river-view facade. The James Watson House, converted to the **Shrine of the Blessed Elizabeth Seton** (p119), 1792 and 1806, is the sole survivor of a row of elegant redbrick houses. The newer section has a two-story colonnade of slender Ionic columns and Adam touches.

You can recognize Federal row houses by their small size, distinctive Flemish bond (alternating long and short bricks), peaked roofs with dormer windows, and decorative doorways. **Harrison Houses** (p127), 1796–1820, a row of nine modest dwellings, were restored and grouped together. The **Merchant's House** (p139), 1832, has a late Federal exterior with Greek Revival iron-work and interior ornament. It's the city's only home preserved intact from the 19th century and having original furnishings.

GREEK-REVIVAL RELICS

Greek fever spread through the US in the 1820s as Americans linked the populist presidency of Andrew Jackson with ancient Greek democracy. Architects and builders who had never stepped foot in Greece cribbed designs from pattern books. Churches and public buildings dressed up like Greek temples with tall columns supporting a horizontal entablature and a Classical pediment. Two of the best are still standing. The gray granite **St Peter's Church** (246 W 20th St) 1838, replaced the first Roman Catholic church in the city, erected in 1785 and destroyed by fire. The white-marble **Federal Hall National Memorial** (p121), 1842, originally the US Custom House, is now a museum. Narrow redbrick row houses sported takeoffs of ancient Greek architectural elements and ornament. The **Row** (Map p448), 13 Greek Revival houses on the north side of Washington Sq in Greenwich Village, built in 1833 for New York's most fashionable families, is considered the city's finest 19th-century block front.

'AMERICANS LINKED THE POPULIST PRESIDENCY OF ANDREW JACKSON WITH ANCIENT GREEK DEMOCRACY'

Federal Hall (p121), Wall Street, is an iconic classical building where iconic battles on freedoms of speech have taken place

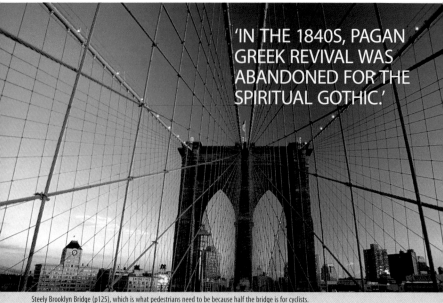

'IN THE 1840S, PAGAN GREEK REVIVAL WAS ABANDONED FOR THE SPIRITUAL GOTHIC.'

Steely Brooklyn Bridge (p125), which is what pedestrians need to be because half the bridge is for cyclists.

GOTHIC GLORIES

In the 1840s, pagan Greek Revival was abandoned for the spiritual Gothic, uplifting toward the heavens, echoing English and French church architecture of the late Middle Ages. Churches were built with advanced vaulting techniques supported by buttresses, filled with colored light shining through stained-glass windows, punctuated by pointed-arch windows and doors, spouting gargoyles and topped by ornamented towers and spires.

Richard Upjohn jumpstarted the Gothic Revival in New York with his **Church of the Ascension** (Map p448, Fifth Ave at 10th St), 1841, a square-towered English country church faced in brownstone. Architect Stanford White gathered a group of artists in 1888 to redecorate the interior with paintings, sculptures and stained-glass windows. Upjohn's next project, **Trinity Church** (p123), 1842, also brownstone, used Gothic forms and ornament but 'modern' building techniques, adding fake buttresses and a plaster ceiling. James Renwick Jr designed two of the city's stunning churches.

Grace Church (p138), 1846, features a pointed French Gothic spire, a splendid stained-glass rose window and lacy stonework. **St Patrick's Cathedral** (p132), 1878, inspired by Cologne Cathedral, has a central gable flanked by identical spires, and plenty of ornament. An enduring icon of the city, the **Brooklyn Bridge** (p125), 1883, with its great stone Gothic towers and webbing of steel cables, was designed by Prussian engineer John Roebling.

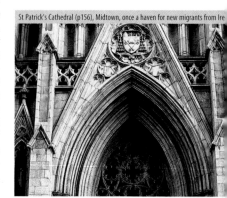

St Patrick's Cathedral (p156), Midtown, once a haven for new migrants from Ire

ITALIANATE IMPERIALISTS

In the mid-19th century, a new style invaded New York, evoking links with great wealth and power, based on imposing palazzi of the Italian Renaissance. McKim Mead & White designed private hangouts fit for the Medici, such as the **Metropolitan Club** (Map pp454–5, 1 E 60th St), 1894, and the **University Club** (Map pp452–3), 1899.

AT Stewart Store (Map pp444–5, 280 Broadway), 1846 with additions to 1884, now a municipal building, was the first department store in America and the first Italianate commercial building in the city. It's faced in white marble with cast-iron columns. New York County Courthouse, known as **Tweed Courthouse** (Map pp444–5, City Hall Park), 1881, was inspired by the US Capitol in Washington DC. A grand staircase leads to a dazzling interior, occupied by the Department of Education and closed to the public.

Villiard Houses (Map pp452–3, Madison Ave at 50th St), 1884, by McKim Mead & White and modeled after Rome's Cancelleria, were six splendid brownstone mansions for the super-rich, surrounding a courtyard, like a unified palazzo. They are now part of the Palace Hotel; some of the exquisite rooms, designed by Stanford White and his artist friends, are intact in Le Cirque 2000 restaurant. Ordinary families moved into rows of Italianate brownstones, forming chocolate-coated streetscapes in neighborhoods such as Chelsea and Murray Hill.

BEAUX-ARTS BEAUTIES

By the start of the 20th century, somber brownstone was out. Gleaming white was the newest fashion, reflecting the impact of the 1893 Chicago World's Fair, a pretend city created by top American architects trained at Paris' École des Beaux-Arts. Public buildings across America were disguised as palaces built with rich materials, lush ornament and sculpture. **Grand Central Terminal** (p150), 1913, engineering by Reed & Stem, facade and interior by Warren and Wetmore, showcases a giant clock and sculptures by Jules Coutan. The breathtaking concourse is topped by a high-vaulted ceiling covered with a zodiac mural by Paul Helleu. Allegorical sculptural figures decorate the facade of the **New York Public Library** (p150), 1911, by Carrere and Hastings. Two marble lions guarding the steps, nicknamed Patience and Fortitude, added in 1920 are by Edward Clark Potter. The monumental US Custom House, 1907, by Cass Gilbert, now the **National Museum of the American Indian** (p122), celebrates trade. Figures on the massive attic portray mercantile nations. Daniel Chester French's culptures on ground level represent the Four Continents. The **Metropolitan Museum of Art** (p162) was built in stages; the Fifth Ave facade in 1902 was by Richard Morris Hunt and the 1926 side wings by McKim Mead and White. Three giant Roman arches alternate with paired Corinthian columns, topped with uncut blocks of stone, originally planned as massive sculptures.

Can Grand Central Terminal's (p150) zodiac ceiling reveal timetable changes?   Sink into the sumptuous reading rooms at New York Public Library (p150)

SKYSCRAPERS

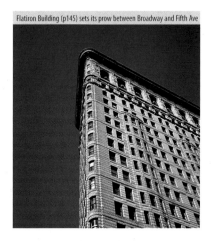

Flatiron Building (p145) sets its prow between Broadway and Fifth Ave

CAST-IRON BUILDINGS

Before steel-frame skyscrapers there were cast-iron buildings pioneering advances in building technology, but with facades chosen from stock books. At first, cast-iron fronts were attached to conventional brick load-bearing outer walls. Later, buildings evolved as primitive cages with interior iron framing and columns. The Venetian-style, cast-iron **Haughwout Building** (p129), 1856, holds the first passenger elevator installed in the US. Soho, once manufacturing, now million-dollar loft apartments and must-have shopping, flaunts the largest concentration of cast-iron buildings in the world.

ECLECTIC OFFICE BUILDINGS

After the elevator was perfected by Elisha Otis in 1853 and steel-frame construction was invented in Chicago in 1885 by William Le Baron Jenney, skyscrapers shot up. The problem for architects was how to cover those steel skeletons; the answer was to suit them up in historic clothing. The 21-story **Flatiron Building** (p145), 1902, by Daniel Burnham, owes its distinctive shape to the triangular site. A wavy midsection is clad in white terra-cotta, decorated with Renaissance ornament. Cass Gilbert, architect of the **Woolworth Building** (Map pp444–5, 233 Broadway), 1913, modeled his designs on the 1830s Houses of Parliament in London and emphasized the upward thrust of his office tower with continuous vertical rows of windows. The building is covered with cream-colored terra-cotta and Gothic ornament. Its ornate lobby is now off-limits to visitors.

King Kong knew how to choose a vantage point, the Empire State Building (p149)

'SILVER RADIATOR HOOD CAPS JUT OUT LIKE GARGOYLES AND CARS RACE IN THE BRICKWORK'

Eccentricities in architecture echo through New York's 20th-century buildings

ART DECO

In the 1930s, architects turned away from history, creating unique buildings, configured with setbacks, required by new zoning laws, and decorated with original ornament. The **Chanin Building** (Map pp452–3, 122 E 42nd St), 1929, by Sloan and Robertson, took the lead with its wedding-cake silhouette, exterior decoration of exotic plant forms and sea life, and singular lobby. The **Chrysler Building** (p148), 1930, by William Van Alen, a corporate headquarters for an automaker, rises with setbacks to a tower with a radiant stainless steel crown of sunbursts. Silver radiator hood caps jut out like gargoyles and cars race in the brickwork. The lobby glows with colorful marble and inlaid wood, its ceiling covered with a mural celebrating technological progress. The **Empire State Building** (p149), 1931, by Shreve, Lamb and Harmon, was conceived as the world's tallest and planned for maximum amount of rental space. The clean lines of the building need little ornament. Soaring from a series of setbacks, the tower pierces the sky with a silver mast.

Sony Building (opposite), reflects a bouillabaise of architectural styles

INTERNATIONAL STYLE

Architects Mies van der Rohe, Walter Gropius and Marcel Breuer, who left Europe in the early 1930s, brought the vision and know-how of the avant-garde German Bauhaus to America. Architecture that rejected the past, it imagined future cities of functional glass towers. United Nations (UN, p151), 1947–52, was the combined effort of many architects: Swiss-born Le Corbusier, Brazil's Oscar Niemeyer, Sweden's Sven Markelius and representatives from 10 other countries, coordinated by America's Wallace K Harrison. The angular slab of the Secretariat, New York's first building with all glass walls, looms over the ski-slope curve of the General Assembly. Lever House (Map pp452–3, 390 Park Ave), 1953, by Gordon Bunshaft/Skidmore, Owings and Merrill, composed of a green glass tower rising from a horizontal slab on freestanding columns above an open courtyard, appears to float over Park Avenue. The Seagram Building (Map pp452–3, 375 Park Ave), 1958, designed by Mies van der Rohe, a stunning amber glass and bronze slab, is set on an open plaza. Van der Rohe, given an unlimited budget, produced a masterpiece of the International Style. Cheaper glass towers that followed didn't measure up.

The flags fly high at the United Nations (p151)

'ARCHITECTURE THAT REJECTED THE PAST, IT IMAGINED FUTURE CITIES OF FUNCTIONAL GLASS TOWERS'

POSTMODERN

Rebelling against glass boxes, architects in the 1980s had a brief fling with vintage styles. Philip Johnson, who designed the pink granite AT&T Headquarters, now **Sony** (Map pp452–3), 1984, borrowed from three eras, producing a giant Romanesque Revival base and Chicago-skyscraper-style midsection, crowned by a neo-Georgian pediment. Most people shrugged off this phase and architecture continued to move forward with hardly a backward glance.

ON THE HORIZON

Real-estate mogul Joel Sitt has proposed a crazy, over-the-top Vegas-type, billion-dollar shopping, entertainment and hotel megacomplex along the **Boardwalk at Coney Island** (p180) – all to be topped with a blimp that would leave for tourist joy rides every 10 minutes. What the…?

Santiago Calatrava's elegant **80 South Street**, an off-set stack of a dozen glass cubes – each intended to house just one or two families – will be a striking condo tower that should rise in Lower Manhattan sometime in 2007.

A 30ft high, abandoned, elevated railroad track on Manhattan's west side has gotten the green light to be transformed into **High Line Park** (p141), a long stretch of parkland, incorporating public art and the new Dia Center for the Arts.

After a long and nasty battle with local preservationists, the **Museum of Arts & Design** (p154) will remake a unique 1964 Columbus Circle building into its sleek, futuristic, white-cube new home.

Ground was broken in 2005 for construction of the 6000 sq ft, all-white, seven-story **New Museum of Contemporary Art** (p144), by Tokyo-based firm Sejima and Neshizawa/SANAA.

THE ARCHITECTURAL SCENE TODAY

Shaking off its notorious reputation for resisting architectural innovation, New York's new buildings are cutting edge and computer generated, catching the beat of the 21st century. Architects are global winners; their latest creations are topnotch, such as Japan's Yoshio Taniguchi's expansion of the **Museum of Modern Art** (p154), and Fumihiko Maki's addition to the **UN** (p151). Coming soon will be the dramatic New York Times Tower by Italy's Renzo Piano and a curvy new tower for Chelsea's Eyebeam museum by Diller + Scofidio (before Renfro joined them). The City Planning Department's proposals for rezoning dying manufacturing districts for mixed use, outside of the city's overbuilt core, will open timeworn neighborhoods for new housing and commercial development. Understandably, some New Yorkers are not happy about losing their old way of life and the struggle continues between holding on to the past and making way for the future.

The Museum of Modern Art (p154) is the new 21st-century kid on the block

Music

Music

You may wonder what that guy's bouncing his head to, listening to his MP3 player on the subway – it could be anything, since much of the music world has built its muscle in New York City. Many people sigh over golden days of past – when Charlie Parker put bebop into jazz, camp hit the Broadway stage, and leather jackets and distortion pedals energized punk rock in the East Village. The jazz clubs of 52nd St have long been replaced by office buildings, while CBGB is looking to shut down for good. But music in New York ain't done. NYC remains *the* destination for musicians of all forms, looking to make it big in the Big Apple and bend the way music is made. Remnants of all music forms are still in New York for the taking: free concerts in Central Park in summer; noise fests in Red Hook, Brooklyn; indie rock galore in Williamsburg; jazz shows in original clubs in Greenwich Village; and Broadway's enduring life, weaving with the changes in Midtown. A look at New York's music is a look at the music of the world.

AGE OF VAUDEVILLE

With the USA urbanizing and industrializing like mad in the decades after the Civil War, vaudeville's musical variety shows grew popular by providing cheap song-and-dance entertainment for increasingly bored Americans. Spurred on by 'minstrel artists' (often comic white actor/singers impersonating African Americans in 'blackface'), much of the art form catered to the lewder interests of drinking and gambling (and womanizing) men, such as on New York's infamously rowdy Bowery. Here flophouses charged pennies for rooms, saloons attracted hordes, and things got a little rough. Most old saloons are selling kitchen appliances these days.

A graduate of the Bowery circuit, Brooklynite Tony Pastor earned his stripes as the 'father of vaudeville' by cleaning up its act in 1881. **Tony Pastor's New 14th Street Theatre** (145-47 14th St), now the ground floor of the Con Ed building, opened that year. Pastor took the beer and cigars out of vaudeville, and sought kid-friendly acts (singers, but also magician Harry Houdini) who would attract a wider audience that crossed class (and gender) lines. Pastor's theater closed in 1908, but vaudeville spread, creating a commercial outlet for the city's diverse ethnic cultures. Singers like Eddie Cantor and actors like Groucho Marx and (at the age of *five*) Mae West cut their teeth on the vaudeville circuit.

After 1913 the **Palace Theatre** (cnr 47th St & Seventh Ave) brought song-and-dance to the present-day turf of Broadway. Alas, movies and television killed (or at least stole) the vaudeville star, typified when the Palace switched gears to celluloid in 1932.

TIN PAN ALLEY

Running strong from 1880 to the dawn of Elvis, New York's 'Tin Pan Alley' changed the music world by churning out sheet music for vaudeville stars to take on the road, theater and film performers to sing onstage and on camera, and vocalist stars to croon via radio waves. (And, of course, for folks back home to play along – like an early, DIY-form of 'ka-

---

THAT NEW YORK SONG

The definitive soundtrack for the Big Apple tends to be Frank Sinatra's take on 'New York, New York.' Actually it exists only because Robert De Niro wasn't pleased with the first-round of theme songs for the 1977 Martin Scorsese flop *New York, New York*. Angry at the rebuff from an *actor*, composers John Kander and Freb Ebb sat down and quickly tore out this classic. Liza Minnelli, who appeared in the film, kept singing it, but it wasn't until Frank Sinatra finally got to it, in 1980, that it achieved its fame.

raoke.') Named in 1900 by a reporter frowning over the competing sounds from publishers' out-of-tune pianos along 28th St (between Sixth Ave and Broadway), Tin Pan Alley was home to tunesmiths of all kinds of music of the times: European-style operettas, ragtime blues, show tunes, jazz, folk.

The machine cranked the songs out and publishers plotted to get songs into set lists of popular singers like Al Jolson, Louis Armstrong or Bing Crosby. An early big-seller, Charles K Harris' 'After the Ball,' sold nearly five million copies in the 1890s. Another early fave was Scott Joplin, an African-American piano player who moved here in the first decade of the 20th century from St Louis to kick off the 'ragtime' craze of rushing, syncopated, polka-inspired piano ditties. After Joplin's ambitious 'black opera' *Treemonisha* flopped in 1911, his success waned.

When sheet-music sales dipped in the 1920s, the focus switched to radio, and by the 1930s to movie soundtracks. The mobile Tin Pan Alley moved its base northward over the years. By 1931 the **Brill Building** (Map p452–3; 1619 Broadway) was its center, home to the sheet-music retailer Colony (p345). Some early rock'n'roll songs were cranked out here by the likes of Jerry Lieber, Carole King and Neil Diamond.

By the mid-1950s Elvis showed that performance beat all, and rock'n'roll (not terribly sheet music–friendly) took over the charts.

BROADWAY & MUSICAL THEATER

Considering Broadway sells 12 million seats annually, the impact it's made on music in New York can't be denied. The sweat of numerous composers has dripped in the effort to create instant hum-along immortal standards, such as 'No Business Like Show Business,' or 'Hello, Dolly!,' or – forget it all – 'California Here I Come.'

The roots of musical theater grew from vaudeville, and the days when theaters clustered around 14th St. Initially shows were light, comic numbers, where audiences were expected to boo and hiss at villains in black hats. Things started to get more interesting as productions moved toward Times Sq.

In its early years, Broadway's ascension in popularity was driven by its songwriters. The statue overlooking the TKTS booth in Times Sq today (p285) is of George M Cohan, a vaudeville graduate who opened a theater near Times Sq in 1911 and, as WWI raged, staged *Over There* – its melody, based on a bugle call, captivated the nation.

In 1914 Irving Berlin, a Russian Jewish immigrant who grew up in the Lower East Side before making it big by moving uptown, added ragtime jazz to the stage with *Watch Your Step*. He'd later pen classics like 'White Christmas' and 'God Bless America.'

Brooklyn-born George Gershwin wrote 'Swanee' for crooner Al Jolson to sing in the Broadway musical *Sinbad* in 1919, then the instrumental 'Rhapsody in Blue' in 1924. Jolson, who kept vomit buckets off stage for his (invisible) nerves, once interrupted a production to ask 'do you want to hear the rest of the story, or do you want me?' (The crowd went for Al.) By 1927 Broadway had 264 shows in 76 theaters – its peak year.

Things got more serious in the late 1920s and '30s, when songs started tackling social issues as the Depression hit full force (including Ira and George Gershwin's satirical songs in jazz-influenced *Of Thee I Sing*). During WWII Richard Rodgers and Oscar Hammerstein II's *Oklahoma!* raised the bar a notch, adding a staged death along with catchy songs that revived a slumbering genre.

Broadway stepped along with the changing moods of the times. Leonard Bernstein and Stephen Sondheim's *West Side Story* (1957) – with vocals by Chita Rivera – put Romeo and Juliet amid New York gang wars, while off-Broadway import *Hair* (1968) added hippies, nudity, profanity and rebel rock to Broadway's checklist.

By the 1980s New York's contribution to musicals faced a crisis (along with the city) as the only successes were imports from the UK (Andrew Lloyd Webber's *Cats* and *The Phantom of the Opera*) or France *(Les Miserables* and *Miss Saigon)*. The unlikely savior came from Jonathan Larson's druggy East Village setting, the rock-fueled *Rent,* which coincided with New York's own renaissance.

For a thorough decade-by-decade history, click 'Broadway 101' at www.talkinbroadway.com.

ALL THAT JAZZ

Survey New York's roster of jazz greats; Louis Armstrong, Duke Ellington, Charlie Parker, Miles Davis, Dizzy Gillespie, Billie Holiday, Ella Fitzgerald, Ornette Coleman, John Coltrane, and you'll see all came here from elsewhere (well, it was easy for Ella – she was born in Yonkers). Jazz's roots lead back to New Orleans and Chicago, but by the late 1920s, jazz was all about New York, and in particular, Harlem. Louis Armstrong moved in, and Chicago's strict Prohibition laws of 1927 caused many jazz musicians to follow. Jazz's subsequent incarnations – from swing to bebop to cool to free jazz to tonal to fusion – all made their first serious steps in Harlem speakeasies, along with downtown basement dives and 52nd St nightclubs.

The late 1920s marked the boom days for Harlem. A DC native, Duke Ellington led his big-band orchestra at the **Cotton Club** (cnr Lenox Ave & 142nd St), a plush Harlem club with African Americans performing for an exclusively all-White crowd. Duke remained at the Cotton – enigmatically decked out like an antebellum plantation (with slave-house murals) – from 1927 to 1931. The Cotton Club moved to Midtown following a Harlem race riot in 1935.

> ## TOP FIVE NYC JAZZ ALBUMS
>
> - *The Complete Savoy & Dial Master Takes* (1944-48) Charlie Parker.
> - *Free Jazz* (1960) Ornette Coleman.
> - *The Black Saint and Sinner Lady* (1963) Charles Mingus.
> - *Love Supreme* (1964) John Coltrane.
> - *Bitches Brew* (1969) Miles Davis.

Another Harlem staple of the era, the **Savoy Ballroom** (596 Lenox Ave btwn 140th & 141st Sts) was a racially integrated club that spurred new dance crazes (like the Lindy Hop, named for Charles Lindbergh). The huge room fit two bands which, like DJs in the '70s, would engage in 'cutting contests' to outdo the other; Chick Webb's house orchestra beat Count Basie and Benny Goodman, while helping to launch the career of local teenager Ella Fitzgerald, who won an amateur contest at nearby Apollo Theater (p168).

In the 1930s jazz began to broaden its appeal to a mainstream audience with swing, typified by the national rise of clarinetist Benny Goodman. He formed a big band in 1934, using many arrangements from Fletcher Henderson, whose band played at the **Roseland Ballroom** (1658 Broadway) from the mid-1920s. While working to 'dignify' jazz by staging shows at Carnegie Hall, Goodman, who was white, helped assemble the first interracial group in popular music.

Bands like Goodman's would rotate singers; one of his was Billie Holiday, a former prostitute. She recorded many songs with Goodman and Lester Young; in 1939 she recorded 'Strange Fruit' – an unsubtle attack on lynchings in the south. Holiday fit in night shows at clubs on 52nd Street (btwn Fifth & Seventh Aves), a two-block, neon-lit jazz haven that was home to Kansas City–import Count Basie's big band and where national jazz players sought their first gigs in the Big Apple. Jazz on 52nd faded after WWII.

New York's first true homegrown jazz came in 1940 and 1941, with an artier, jagged, more nervous version of swing: bebop, or bop. Born from jam sessions by players like Thelonious Monk, Dizzy Gillespie, Miles Davis and – most notably – Charlie Parker (aka Bird), bop thrived at small Harlem clubs like **Minton's Playhouse** (210 W 118th St). (The club closed in 1956, but the sign is still up.) DJs at Columbia University's super WKCR (89.9FM) used to come and record shows to play on the air (tune in, it's still going strong). The heyday of NYC jazz, many claim, was the 1950s and '60s when on any evening jazz greats played on side-by-side venues along 52nd St.

Time passed. Bird died following heroin binges; Billie's reckless life caught up with her too. Many jazz greats, including Armstrong, took their earnings to settle in comfortable homes in Queens (p153). Miles Davis switched gears for 'hard bop' to develop and record, with John Coltrane, the modal-jazz masterpiece *Kind of Blue* in 1959 (the 'blue notes' come when the player hits notes lower, flatter, than expected). That year, saxophonist Ornette Coleman 'played wrong right,' as bassist Charles Mingus would call it, with a confusing, seemingly formless – and certainly influential – free-jazz set at the **Five Spot Cafe** (4 Cooper Sq).

TOP NYC MUSIC MOMENTS

1920 Prohibition in the USA begins, jazz musicians pour to looser Harlem from Chicago.

1940 Duke Ellington explains how to get to Harlem ('Take the A Train').

1961 Minnesotan Bob Dylan arrives and plays Cafe Wha?; John Coltrane starts his own interpretation of jazz a couple blocks away at Village Vanguard.

1962 James Brown records his set at Harlem's Apollo Theater.

1967 Velvet Underground release first album, with collaborator Andy Warhol designing the banana-peel cover.

1969 The Who debut the rock opera *Tommy* at Fillmore East, unfortunate trend of concept albums follow.

1975 Bruce Springsteen shows off new *Born to Run* at Bottom Line, and jumps into stardom.

1978 Sex Pistol Sid Vicious confesses to offing Nancy Spungen at the Chelsea Hotel during a drug-induced blur; he ODs before trial is completed.

1979 Sugar Hill Gang take Bronx rhymes to the studio and record 'Rapper's Delight.'

1980 John Lennon murdered outside his Upper West Side apartment.

1983 Billy Joel gives dorks hope by wooing model Christie Brinkley with 'Uptown Girl.'

1997 Garth Brooks attracts one million fans to Central Park…some call it one of New York's saddest music days.

2001 The Strokes revive New York indie rock, start new East Village haircut.

Know you're at the forefront of jazz experiences at the Village Vanguard (p297)

Beginning in 1961 John Coltrane sanctified his place in jazz by stretching solos and adding instruments like bass clarinets – critics called it 'antijazz' – at a recorded two-week stint at the Village Vanguard (p297), a rare vintage bar that's still kicking. (If you go, note the stage's broken light fixture, knocked out by Mingus long ago.)

Miles continued to base himself in a Manhattan flat. In 1968 he switched gears, playing with musicians like Herbie Hancock and Chick Corea and incorporating rock and funk into jazz, along with wah-wah pedals for his trumpet.

These days most of the classic clubs are long gone. The center for jazz has slowly migrated downtown, with most clubs (often basement dives) in the Greenwich Village. See p295 for a list of some.

TALKIN' NEW YORK BLUES

From the 1930s to the 1970s folk music in New York served as the voice for the politically active. What was long seen as harmless sing-along songs about family and lost loves became purely radicalized, way-left turf in New York. In the 1930s, as the Depression raged, pro-union rallies of the Industrial Workers of the World featured protest folk songs, while the Popular Front, loosely associated with communism, spread political ideals through folk music too.

An unabashed communist with a smile, banjo-picker and Harvard dropout Pete Seeger assembled the Almanac Singers (which included Woody Guthrie) in 1940, penning labor songs like 'The Talking Union Blues.' Seeger formed the Weavers in 1949 – their cover of Louisiana blues singer Leadbelly's 'Goodnight Irene' became a national hit until political pressure of the times resulted in the band being 'blacklisted' from performing. Leadbelly had moved to New York in 1936 – after serving jail time for murder in Texas – where he made many recordings with Library of Congress chronicler Alan Lomax. Author of 'This Land is Your Land,' Okie Woody Guthrie made New York his land in the 1940s, where he lived for many years writing songs and playing. After a fiery 'antifascist' stint as a merchant marine in WWII, Woody toned down the politics for a collection of children's songs (on 1946's *Songs to Grown On*), written for his own kids at his Mermaid Ave home in Coney Island. After his death in 1967, his ashes were spread in the water off the beach at Coney Island.

Bob Dylan came to New York in 1961 hoping to meet Woody. The folk scene at that time in Greenwich Village was akin to the disco or punk scene of the late '70s. His early song 'Talkin' New York' recounts his first show at Cafe Wha? (p213). Dylan's first paid gig was opening for John Lee Hooker at Gerde's Folk City (11 W 4th St) in 1961; Dylan donned a suit allegedly given to him by Woody and debuted his 'Song to Woody.' Dylan – the 'voice of the generation' – created 'protest' classics like 'The Times They Are A-Changin' but always insisted he wasn't a protest or even folk singer. He finally left the scene for good by plugging into rock by 1965. His electrified song 'Positively 4th Street' is often seen as a bitter lashing at the folk scene, who resented him for leaving it.

NEW YORK CITY ROCKS

The man who named 'rock'n'roll,' Cleveland DJ Alan Freed, brought rock to New York in 1954, when he spun records at New York station WINS, staged shows (eg the battling Chuck Berry and Jerry Lee Lewis) at Brooklyn's Paramount Theatre (cnr Dekalb & Flatbush Aves), and went national on CBS radio. As the '60s awoke, doo-wop bands were still slicking back their hair and churning out smooth quartet-style harmonies. Local bands included the Ravens, the Drifters, the Coasters and many Italian groups like Frankie Valli and the Four Seasons.

Artists local and elsewhere sought dreams in New York, often signified by a slot on the Ed Sullivan Show, which was hosted by the stone-faced New Yorker. When Elvis appeared first – in 1956 – he called it his 'greatest honor,' though producers filmed him from the waist up to miss the pelvic mojo. The Beatles' first singles went belly-up in the USA until their 1964 performance on the show was seen by 70 million. Ed expanded with the '60s, hosting the Rolling Stones, Janis Joplin and the Doors. Today David Letterman airs his show from the Ed Sullivan Theatre (Map p282; 1697 Broadway).

By the mid '60s the Tin Pan Alley approach of feeding stars calculated hits was falling by the wayside, courtesy of artists who wrote their own songs. Rock'n'roll became the voice of social consciousness in protest against Vietnam, and in support of the Civil Rights movement and 'loosening the tie a bit.'

TOP FIVE NYC ROCK ALBUMS

That's right: *no* Billy Joel here.

- *Velvet Underground & Nico* by Velvet Underground (1967) Lou Reed's own NYC guide: tells you where to score smack and how to cross-dress
- *New York Dolls*, self-titled, (1973) Trashy and lipsticked (and a little lost), David Johansen's glam-rock brings us 'Lonely Planet Boy'
- *Ramones* (1976) With a 'hey! ho!' Ramones' Joey and company kickstart punk rock in the East Village
- *Some Girls* by the Rolling Stones (1978) Mick and Keith get shadooobied in their new home
- *The Rising* by Bruce Springsteen (2002) The Boss licks wounds after September 11

In 1966 Lou Reed and the Velvet Underground sang about heroin and drag queens as a backdrop to artist Andy Warhol's Exploding Plastic Inevitable shows on St Marks Place (p212).

Jimi Hendrix hung out in the Big Apple, crashing (and recording) at **Electric Lady Sound Studios** (Map p448; 52 W 8th St) before his drug-induced death in 1970. Hendrix and the Stones guitar-shopped at still-strong Manny's Music (p346).

Max's Kansas City (213 Park Ave), now a deli, was a beacon for punk-blooming rock bands (Blondie's Deborah Harry waited tables here). A tape rolled during the Velvet Underground's two-week stint in 1970 – just before Lou Reed left the band – which became the lo-fi classic *Live at Max's Kansas City*.

As the Velvets disbanded, sexually ambiguous glam rock started washing in from the UK. The trashy New York Dolls donned makeup and were thought to be the next thing, but fizzled outside Manhattan. In from Michigan, Iggy Pop was a Max's regular, meeting long-time collaborator David Bowie here. Iggy's band the Stooges – the raunchy descendant of the Underground, led by Iggy's masochistic, often bloody stage presence – helped spur on punk in the years to come. Max's closed in 1980.

No offense to Lou Reed, but New York's favorite son comes from across the Hudson River: Bruce Springsteen. He premiered *Born to Run* in 1975 after marathon recording sessions at the popular 450-seater Bottom Line (Map p448; 15 W 4th St), which sadly shut its doors in 2004 after becoming NYU property.

Tunes needle the audience at Knitting Factory (p234)

Starting in 1974 with a fiery '1-2-3-4!' from Queens' leather-clad Ramones at CBGB (p212), punk rock ignited as a wave of kids angry with their parents hit distortion pedals. Before the Ramones released their first album (in 1976), CBGB was *the* downtown rock scene HQ. Television, Blondie and Talking Heads played shows in 1975, followed by 'no wave' bands like DNA and Teenage Jesus and the Jerks, who incorporated performance rock and atonal sounds and nihilism in the late '70s. Their offshoot (led by enduring New York band Sonic Youth) inspired noise bands and grunge. By the '90s, CBGB breathed solely by its lore, with the stage left for lame metal acts from Long Island. At press time it looked like its 30-year run was ending in late 2006.

During CBGB's heyday, big rock names from abroad started moving to New York – John Lennon, Mick Jagger, Keith Richards, later David Bowie (who says there's no reason to venture north of 14th St). But by the 1980s New York's high costs, coupled with the approach of major record companies, started becoming less conducive for bands, and – curiously – New York's influence started to wane a little (for the mainstream at least). There were exceptions, particularly among the experimental sounds of artists like Glenn Branca and John Zorn; Knitting Factory (p294) and now Tonic (p296) are the most popular playgrounds for experimental music-makers. Sonic Youth made the inspired rock/rap hybrid 'Kool Thing' in 1990, featuring Chuck D of Public Enemy (the song is about LL Cool J). Lou Reed made a comeback in 1988 with his (rather cantankerous) ode to his city, *New York*.

Through it all, the Chelsea Hotel (p142) has been the lodge of choice for bohos and punk rockers. Here, Dylan typed lyrics in room A17, Hendrix was mistaken for a janitor, Madonna filmed for her controversial book *Sex*, and – ick – Jon Bon Jovi shot a video.

Music

NEW YORK CITY ROCKS

BOOGIE NIGHTS

Dance culture took off as the '60s ended in New York, particularly at who-you-know loft parties popularized at the Loft in SoHo, by DJ David Mancusco, from 1971. Diverse crowds ground out the floor together – particularly popular among gay men, and also African Americans and Latin Americans. By 1975 DJs were looking for more bass for the funk and R&B than the wee 45in single could provide, and extended dance versions of songs on better-quality 12in singles started popping out.

1977 was a full-on four-on-the-floor disco breakout, here and worldwide. That year DJ Larry Levon started spinning discs at the **Paradise Garage** (84 King St) in SoHo. More famously, Stephen Rubell and Ian Schrager (of boutique-hotel fame) opened **Studio 54** (254 W 54th St) – the definitive disco in Manhattan, with its mirrored ceilings and decadence for coked-up cool things. *Saturday Night Fever* – with John Travolta strutting under the elevated subway line in Bensonhurst, Brooklyn – came out in '77 too. The famed 2001 Odyssey disco (later renamed as the Spectrum) only closed in February 2005; its light-box dancefloor was sold on eBay.

Rock acts got into the disco action. In 1978 new New Yorker Mick Jagger led the Stones into disco with 'Miss You,' the band's last number-one hit. But New York's 'greatest' contribution to the music followed, when two French songwriters assembled a five-piece band meant to reflect the campy fantasy roles (Native Americans, cops, construction workers etc) seen in gay clubs in the West Village. The Village People quickly churned out a few enduring classics, such as 'YMCA' and 'Macho Man.' Their song 'In the Navy' attracted attention as a potential recruiting theme for US Navy ads, but controversy grew when the band planned to shoot a video – at taxpayers' expense, supposedly – at the naval base in San Diego.

Disco, to some effect, has lingered on as a nod to the past. In the early '90s, downtown band Deee-Lite (with a Russian DJ, a Japanese DJ, an Ohioan lead vocalist and funk-legend Bootsy Collins on bass) had a dance-club hit with 'Groove is in the Heart.'

RAPPER'S DELIGHT

The world comes to Manhattan to make music, but the Bronx made its own. As disco and punk reigned across Manhattan, the Bronx crafted hip-hop, donning iron-on letter shirts and spinning vinyl on Technics turntables. The '70s were a bad time in NYC, when cops dealt smack, gangs claimed territories in the boroughs, President Ford turned his back on the city's rising debt, and Bronx wages were half the city's average. Release was needed – and DJs offered it, playing makeshift 'park jams' by tapping city-light power, or in community centers or high-school gyms (if the janitor unlocked the door).

The 'godfather of hip-hop' and self-proclaimed 'Muhammed Ali of rap,' Kool DJ Herc – who moved to NYC from Jamaica as a kid – introduced the two-turntable system by 1974. He mixed two records together and 'toasted' friends – through heavy reverb – just to get the party started. Inspired, Afrika Bambaataa and Zulu Nation played the Bronx River Center in an often gun-packed environment; Bambaataa expanded the DJ role by incorporating things like Bugs Bunny songs. Grandmaster Flash, who got whupped as a kid for taking apart the family stereo out of curiosity, upped the ante by developing a 'pre-hear' system with headphones so he could extend 'breaks' in songs (the best part!). His partner's brother Grand Wizard Theodore couldn't wait to drop the needle and by 1975 started audibly finding the groove, and 'scratching' was born.

Attention started turning from the dancefloor to the DJs and their MC crew, who made their names with syncopated 'rap' poetry, routines or just call-outs, including Cowboy (who started the 'everybody say ho!' calls), Melle Mel, Rahiem, Grandmaster Caz, Busy Bee, and the first female MC, Sha-Rock. Crews amassed giant sound systems (speakers from 55-gallon steel drums) to 'battle' rival crews, just like jazz bands back at the Harlem Savoy.

Things changed for good in 1979, when producer Sylvia Robinson saw a DJ Love Bug Starski show at Harlem World and hunted out rappers to make a record. Her son Joey spotted part-time bouncer Big Bank Hank in a Jersey pizzeria rapping over a Grandmaster Caz tape and asked him to help form the Sugar Hill Gang, who recorded 'Rapper's Delight' (using many Caz rhymes) and sold two million copies. The real deal in Bronx felt snubbed, but rap boomed.

Robinson's Sugar Hill Records eventually signed on Grandmaster Flash & the Furious 5, whose 1982 song 'The Message' – led by Melle Mel, who described urban life 'like a jungle sometimes' – changed the playing field from 'yo!' Then Sugar Hill signed Funky 4 + 1 – with Sha-Rock ('the best female in this here town'). They become the first rap act on national television (appearing, with Blondie's help, on *Saturday Night Live* in 1981).

Many of the acts recorded little. Movies like *Wild Style* and *Beat Street* showed off the scene of the time. Cold Crush Brothers battled the Fantastic 5 in 1982 at Harlem World, a long-time classic that inspired Run DMC and only made it to CD in 1998.

In 1983 Run DMC – kids from Queens, actually – catapulted rap further with sparse, tougher drum-box and the scratchin' heavy song 'Sucker MCs' – a sound picked up by post-punk rappers Beastie Boys by their first recordings with Def Jam Records, founded by Rick Rubin and Russell Simmons. Run DMC also set the way for politicized rap and eventually the gangsta variety of Boogie Down Productions (locally) and NWA (out in LA). The Def Jam movie *Krush Groove* features both bands.

Another Queens native, James Todd Smith (aka Ladies Love Cool James, aka LL Cool J) has one of hip-hop's most long-lived careers, starting as a teen with 'I Need a Beat' in 1984.

The best Run DMC grads were Long Island imports Public Enemy, with a dense, militarized soundscape of urban life. Chuck D's highly politicized lyrics (eg jabs at John Wayne in 'Fight the Power') were balanced by the cartoony sidekick Flavor Flav, and undermined by controversial, anti-Semitic comments from Professor Griff.

Later rap stars of New York 'hoods depicted violence on the streets. From Bedford-Stuyvesant, Notorious BIG' debut *Ready to Die* (1994) helped spur on the East Coast–West Coats rap feuds. A few months after Tupac Shakur's murder, Biggie fell from bullets in LA. In recent years, 50 Cent (from Jamaica, Queens) and Jay Z (from Brooklyn) have taken over the reins.

21ST-CENTURY ROCK

All that Seattle and Austin and Detroit luster wore off in the early 21st century, when New York – in particular the Lower East Side and Williamsburg – took over at least a chunk of the indie-rock world. It started in downtown clubs like Arlene Grocery (p294) and Mercury Lounge (p295) with the Strokes, whose debut LP *Is This It* (2001) sure came with some pregame hype (leader Julian Casablancas' pop happens to be the head of Elite modeling). The lo-fi nod to new-wave greats like Television and present lo-fi gods Guided by Voices won hearts among hipsters in the USA and UK. (Some swooned more for Julian than the music.)

Since then, less-standard, more experimental fare from bands from or based in Brooklyn are starting to give Williamsburg bragging rights for the city's music scene with a host of new-century darlings: Yeah Yeah Yeahs continued the raunchy White Stripes' bassless nod to past genres; Clap Your Hands Say Yeah went postmod in nomenclature and Talking

Heads in sound; TV on the Radio slapped the Billyburg bridge on their debut; Illinois-imports, brother-and-sister team Fiery Furnaces recorded a piano-based operetta with their grandma; and Animal Collective got weird.

Over in Red Hook, the No Fun Fest (p179) is an annual celebration of noise bands, including No Neck Blues Band who maintain an anonymous lineup.

Throughout this new century out was a shortlived dip to revive the Warhol-style 'events' with 'electroclash' – a campy mix of punked-up lo-fi retro electro dance music. In Williamsburg, Cafe Luxx, now called Trash, staged 'Berliniamsburg' nights from 2001 to 2003. Electroclash is dead, long live electroclash!

Food

Food

Eating out in New York City is an event that rivals going to the opera, theater or symphony in its magnitude. It's a serious situation, an evening in itself and a complete form of entertainment. And while it hasn't always been this way, it's a tradition that began some 180 years ago.

HISTORY

Delmonico's, America's very first restaurant, was a lavish eatery that opened in Lower Manhattan in 1827, starting out as a confectioner's shop and quickly evolving into a gathering spot for high society. It's where a 100-page menu listed items such as Lobster Newburg and baked Alaska (both created here) in French and English, and featured a massive wine cellar that held 16,000 bottles. Before closing in 1923, Delmonico's was the inspiration for other high-class restaurants, where the European foods of the wealthy set, such as boiled salmon, soufflés, mutton chops and charlotte russe, appeared on menus.

Everyday New Yorkers, meanwhile, got their eating-out fixes at either cheap restaurants or pushcarts (25,000 of them by 1900), which, by the turn of the century, proffered foods from all over the world – not surprising for a city that served as a major port for both immigrants and global commodities. Oyster houses, cafeterias, kosher delis, the first hot-dog vendors and pizzerias (the first, Lombardi's, opened in 1905; p236) were everywhere, as were Chinese and German restaurants, all reflecting the ethnic makeup of the time.

While the foreign cuisines served mostly the immigrant communities who were used to such strange foods, this was the beginning of today's thriving global foodie obsession, in which New Yorkers cannot wait to try the latest *huitlacoche* quesadillas (flour tortillas topped with a mushroom-like corn fungus) from Mexico or *arepas* (thick corn cakes topped with melted cheese) from Colombia. And, while the talked-about 'scene' might have revolved around the high-class diners, a simultaneous trend was beginning with the proliferation of affordable dining spots. Today it's the cheap eats of Chinatown and the East Village that draw low-income food aficionados; then it was the Automats, which dropped sandwiches out of vending machines (the last, on 42nd St, closed in 1991), cafeterias, German spots offering 45¢ lunches, Irish pubs in Manhattan and 'penny restaurants' in Brooklyn – especially Coney Island.

Another major influence in the globalization of New York cuisine was the World's Fair of 1939. While it wasn't meant to be a food festival, nearly every country present took it as a chance to show off its national specialties. Many of the foreign-food purveyors at the fair stayed behind to run restaurants, including the French Le Pavillon, which started the ongoing legacy of French food as a standard here. After this period and until the '60s, Greek and Middle Eastern restaurants sprang up all over Greenwich Village, bringing even more tastes to the middle and working classes; French food dominated the upscale scene.

It was during this time that one man, James Beard, revolutionized the idea of cuisine in America – and he did it from his home base, New York City, where he established the James Beard Cooking School. After his death in 1985, the late Julia Child had the idea to preserve his Greenwich Village brownstone as the James Beard Foundation – North America's only his-

Bagels (p91) are NYC's survival secret for life in the fast lane

torical culinary center, offering educational programs, meals from great chefs and annual awards to the biggest players in the industry. Thought it went through a major public scandal in 2005 (after revelations that $1 million had been siphoned off rather than donated to charity), it's still plugging along, prompting chefs and food writers everywhere to covet one of its well-respected honors.

CULTURE

Unlike California or the South or even the Southwest, New York never really gets referred to as having one defining cuisine. Try asking for some 'New York food,' for example, and you could wind up getting anything from a hot dog or a slice of pizza to a South Indian feast or the much-hyped $29 sirloin-truffle-short-rib burger from Times Sq's DB Bistro Moderne. Cuisine here is global by definition, constantly evolving by its very nature. This is a town with room for every taste and budget, every whim and every diet. But, while the healthy, organic and veggie landscape has been expanded and revolutionized a *lot* in recent years (see p94), the serious, deep-pocketed dining-out world is skewed much more toward exotic excess – with the celebrity chefs churning out all manner of duck, pork belly, beef cheek, foie gras, lamb loin, venison and rabbit-sausage concoctions.

Five-star chefs of note – either local, national or both – abound. The most prominent include the orange-clogs-and-shorts-clad Mario Batali (of the Lupa-Babbo p237 etc empire), David Bouley (of the French Danube and Bouley p229), Daniel Boulud (of DB Bistro Moderne, p245, Café Boulud, and Daniel), Wylie Dufresne (of the eclectic 71 Clinton Fresh Food and WD 50, p235, both on the Lower East Side), Tom Valenti (Ouest p248, and Cesca, p273) and Thomas Keller (Per Se, p244, in the Time Warner Center), and you'd better believe food-obsessed New Yorkers know all of their names. In 2005 the James Beard Awards team duly noted their accomplishments, as four out of five nominees in the best-chef category were from New York City (Mario Batali won) and the chosen best new restaurant was Per Se.

The frenzy has made eating out about much more than the grub. It must be presented as a complete experience now – with sweeping designs, tantalizing lighting aesthetics and even physically cool menus – all adding up to a totally transporting ambience for diners. It's a necessity now, in a dining-out climate in which fickle customers will clamor with fever pitch to get into the hottest new place (Spice Market, p239, and The Modern, p245, are good examples), only to grow tired of it and yearn for the next new eatery in a matter of months. It all fuels the constant grand openings and neighborhood shifts; witness, for example, the recent blossoming of the Upper West Side as a dining destination, thanks to restaurateurs such as Tom Valenti, whose 'Cesca (p248) and Ouest (p248) transformed the 'hood into a place foodies could finally be proud of. The easily bored pattern, of course, also leads to monumental closures, which cause nostalgic pangs – but not for long. Recent casualties of changing tastes and rising rents have included: the legendary Second Avenue Deli in the East Village; Jean-Georges Vongerichten's V Steakhouse in the Time Warner Center; the Sugar Hill Bistro, which brought jazz brunches, high-end Southern food and much attention to the northern reaches of Harlem; and, in 2004, Lutece, a renowned French standby that served Manhattan's East Side for 43 years. The local press ran high-profile stories about the monumental closures, and long-time regulars moaned. But in the end, everyone moved on.

ETIQUETTE

Please don't use your cell phone at the table. Also, have some respect for the wait staff; speaking politely, making unusual or last-minute requests with a 'please,' and signaling for a server silently, with a finger in the air (without hisses or whistles or 'hey, you!'), all work wonders. And be sure to leave a fair tip – at least 20% for above-average service. If there is a major slight or mistake on the part of the waiter or chef, a good restaurant will often comp a small part of your meal – a glass of wine, dessert, appetizers. Complaining politely, of course, ups the chances.

MAKING RESERVATIONS

To avoid disappointment, always assume that a reservation is necessary – especially on weekends, when it's almost certainly going to be the case. Cheap-eats places are the exception, as people move in and out quickly (not to mention the fact that there is probably a no-reservations policy). The hottest eateries in town require reservations, and many times you'll be told that there's nothing available for weeks; if you know way ahead of time that you want to be able to experience WD 50 (p235) and La Esquina (p232) before you leave town, for example, reserve your table before you even get to town – or at least the second you arrive. However, as much as New Yorkers like to talk about how you'll *never* get into certain places, there's almost always a way to do it. One trick is to accept a reservation at a less-than-popular dining time – before 7pm or after 10:30pm – which is almost always available. Also, many hot spots have bars, and many of these bars have food service. Sure, it's not the same as getting lavish table service, but it's considered a cool way to experience a place, and getting a seat is rarely a problem.

HOW NEW YORKERS EAT

Table manners of locals here are pretty much the same as in the rest of the country: put the napkin on your lap and do the 'fork-shift' thing, using the fork in your left hand to anchor what you are cutting with the knife in your right, then shift the fork into the right to pick up what you've just cut (or visa versa if you're a leftie). It's cumbersome, it's colonial, it's American. But one way New Yorkers tend to distinguish themselves is by being a bit chopstick-obsessed; in Chinese, Japanese, Thai or any other sort of Asian restaurant – even in an eclectic restaurant in which you are eating an Asian dish – locals ask for chopsticks. It's part respect, part pretension, and pretty much the norm.

But when they don't have time to actually sit down to a meal – whether at home, in the office or in a restaurant – New Yorkers won't think twice about eating on the run, barely stopping their forward movement long enough to swallow. It's common to see locals standing at a pizzeria counter, consuming a slice or two in four long, quick bites before continuing their day. Office workers especially will grab a sandwich or salad-bar concoction from a lightning-fast deli, perch on the nearest bench or stoop, and eat fast, savoring every bit of fresh air while they're at it. Relaxing? No. Normal? Yes.

STAPLES & SPECIALTIES

Cuisines with the longest histories here include a range of tastes. Specialties from Italians and East European Jews, because these groups were among the earliest wave of immigrants, are integral parts of the city's food history; a bagel (Jewish) and slice of pizza (Italian) are just a couple of the uncontested staples of New York eats. The Reuben, a grilled sandwich consisting of corned beef, sauerkraut, Swiss cheese and mustard on rye, was invented in NYC in 1914, by Arnold Reuben at his now-defunct Reuben's sandwich shop; you can find the concoction on most deli menus today. Steakhouses, a tradition that began well before the global influences of the World's Fair, are the best places to go if you want to feel like you're eating in a long-passed era; Peter Luger Steakhouse (p257), in Williamsburg, is among the best, most classic such institution in New York. But while 'New York steak' might mean something in every other part of the country (prime shell steak, rare), the term gets fuzzy here, where steakhouses specialize in forms from aged porterhouse to garlic-rubbed tenderloin. And then there's Chinese. Since the late 1800s, when chop suey is said to have been invented here to suit American tastes by the cooks of Chinese ambassador Li Chung Hang, who was visiting New York at the time, locals – especially Jews, who have a storied love affair

Hot dogs are hot stuff at Nathan's Famous (p285)

with the food because it was available on Sunday, the Christian Sabbath – have embraced the cuisine. Though you can barely find chop suey on any New York menu these days, you can find more evolved versions of the country's food – usually Hunan or Szechuan versions – on practically every corner in Manhattan. 'Chinese,' by the way, has become practically synonymous with 'takeout.'

HOT DOGS

The history of the hot dog is long and storied, with many different versions. A derivative of sausage, one of the oldest forms of processed food, goes back thousands of years, and made its way to New York via various European butchers in the 1800s. German butcher Charles Feltman was apparently the first to sell hot dogs (the origin of that term is a contested history in itself) from pushcarts along the Coney Island seashore. But it was Nathan Handwerker, a German immigrant, who made the food famous. Originally an employee of Feltman's, the shrewd entrepreneur saved up enough money to open his own hot-dog shop across the street. Nathan put up huge signs advertising his dogs, which were half the price of those at Feltman's. His business grew, and when the Stilwell Ave subway station opened right across the street in the 1920s, Nathan's benefited from its location, exploding in popularity and finally putting Feltman's out of business in the '50s. Today the original Nathan's (p256) still stands in Coney Island, at the corner of Stillwell and Surf Aves (while its empire has expanded on a national scale), where it hosts an annual July 4th hot-dog eating contest – a disturbingly amusing display of gluttony. Nathan's also inspired hot-dog sellers all over NYC, and today there is barely a neighborhood in existence that does not have at least a few hot-dog vendors on its street corners. Some locals would never touch one of these 'dirty-water dogs,' preferring the new wave of chi-chi hot-dog shops that have popped up all over town, with strong showing in the East Village. Enjoy yours, wherever it's from, with 'the works': plenty of spicy brown mustard, relish, sauerkraut and onions.

PIZZA

Pizza's not indigenous to the Big Apple. But New York–style pizza is a very particular thing and the first pizzeria in America, Lombardi's (p236), opened in 1905, is here. While Chicago-style is 'deep dish' and Californian tends to be light and doughy, New York prides itself on having pizza with thin crust and an even thinner layer of sauce – and slices that are triangular (unless they're Sicilian-style, in which case they're square). Pizza made its way over to New York in the 1900s through Italian immigrants, and its regional style soon developed, its thin crust allowing for faster cooking time in a city where everyone's always in a hurry. Today there are pizza parlors about every 10 blocks, especially in Manhattan and most of Brooklyn, where you'll find standard slices for $2. The style at each place varies slightly – some places touting cracker-thin crust, others offering slightly thicker and chewier versions, and plenty of nouveau styles throwing everything from shrimp to cherries on top. Some of the most popular local chains include La Famiglia, Grimaldi's (p253) and Ray's (and the various Ray's options, most unrelated, are the source of constant confusion – you'll see Ray's Famous, Famous Ray's, Original Ray's and Famous Original Ray's all over town; don't sweat it, they're all good). No matter where you get your slice, though, you should learn how to eat it properly and walk at the same time: fold in half lengthwise, hold in one hand and chomp away.

BAGELS & BIALYS

Bagels may have been invented in Europe, but they were perfected during the turn of the 19th century in New York City – and once you've had one here, you'll have a hard time enjoying one anywhere else. Basically, it's a ring of plain-yeast dough that's first boiled and then baked, either left plain or topped with various finishing touches, such as sesame seeds or dried onion flakes. 'Bagels' made in other parts of the country are often just baked and not boiled, which makes them nothing more than a roll with a hole. And even if they do

NYC DINERS & COFFEE SHOPS

It's hard to walk five blocks in any direction, in just about any neighborhood, and not come across either a diner or coffee shop (basically an older, crustier version of a diner) – the type of place where George and Jerry spend much of their time on *Seinfeld* (the facade of which was shot at Tom's Restaurant, 2880 Broadway at 112th St, by the way). They're ubiquitous places, traditionally Greek-owned, not so concerned with decor (booths, counter, rotating dessert case, done) and filled with more types of food than you can fathom. The menus – either heavy, bound, booklike objects with side tabs for easy navigating, or long, double-sided, laminated things packed with type – are comforting and predictable, boasting all-day breakfasts, burgers, turkey clubs, grilled fish, steaks, spaghetti and meatballs, pot roast, milkshakes, tuna-salad platters, grilled cheese, eggplant parm, shrimp scampi, pork chops, endless pies and cakes, 'bottomless' cups of so-so coffee and, of course, Greek salads and moussaka. And that's just a very tiny sampling. Plus, they're usually open until very late, if not 24/7, and filled with the most diverse cast of characters you could ever hope for. Those with truly good food (not always the case) include **Brooklyn Diner** (Map p282; 212 W 57th St btwn Seventh Ave & Broadway), **City Diner** (Map pp454–5; 2441 Broadway at 90th St), **Viand Restaurant** (Map pp454–5; 300 E 86th St at Second Ave) and **Village Den Restaurant** (Map p448; 225 W 12th St at Greenwich Ave). **Tiffany Restaurant** (Map p448; 222 W 4th St at Seventh Ave), with a full bar, is gay central and quite an old-school blast.

get boiled elsewhere, bagel-makers here claim that it's New York water that adds an elusive sweetness never to be found anywhere else. You can find 65¢ bagels with cream cheese from street vendors in the morning, though they're not great. Which baker creates the 'best' bagel in New York is a matter of (hotly contested) opinion, but most agree that **H&H Bagels** (main shop on 46th St at the West Side Hwy, Map pp452-3, with locations around Manhattan; www.handhbagel.com) rank pretty high up there. The most traditionally New York way to order one is by asking for a 'bagel and a schmear,' which will yield you said bagel with a small but thick swipe of cream cheese. Or splurge and add some lox – thinly sliced smoked salmon as was originally sold from pushcarts on the Lower East Side by Jewish immigrants back in the early 1900s. Bialys, by the way, are a cousin of the bagel, but more like a crusted roll; they're not nearly as popular as bagels, but just as New York. Find the undisputed best in the Lower East Side at Kossar's (p233).

EGG CREAMS

This frothy, old-fashioned beverage contains no eggs – just milk, seltzer water and plenty of chocolate syrup (preferably the classic Fox's U-Bet brand, made in Brooklyn). But when Louis Auster of Brooklyn, who owned soda fountains on the Lower East Side, invented the treat back in 1890, the syrup he used was made with eggs, and he added cream to thicken the concoction. The name stuck, even though the ingredients were modified, and soon they were a staple of every soda fountain in New York. While Mr Auster sold them for 3¢ a piece, today they'll cost you anywhere from $1.50 to $3, depending on where you find one – which could be anywhere from one of the few remaining old-fashioned soda shops, such as Lexington Candy Shop (p250) on the Upper East Side, or at the new East Village Mo Pitkin's House of Satisfaction (p268), where you can get one spiked with vodka.

NEW YORK–STYLE CHEESECAKE

Sure, cheesecake, in one form or another, has been baked and eaten in Europe since the 1400s. But New Yorkers, as they do with many things, have appropriated its history in the form of the New York–style cheesecake. Immortalized by **Lindy's** (Map pp452-3; Broadway at 50th St) restaurant in Midtown, which was opened by Leo Lindemann in 1921, the particular type of confection served there – made of cream cheese, heavy cream, a dash of vanilla and a cookie crust – became wildly popular in the '40s. Junior's (p253), which opened on Flatbush Ave in Brooklyn in 1929, serves its own famous version of the creamy cake, but with a graham-cracker crust. Today, you'll find this local favorite on more dessert menus than most, whether you're at a Greek diner or haute-cuisine hot spot.

DRINKS

WINE

While wine-making in New York State has a history that stretches back to the 1800s, it wasn't until 1976 that the industry began to explode. That was when the NY State Legislature passed a bill that approved the establishment of small-farm based wineries, allowing entrepreneurs to sprout vineyards wherever the soil and climate would allow. Among the state's biggest producers is the Finger Lakes region, upstate, which is home to more than 60 wineries. Closer to the city are the wineries of eastern Long Island, located mainly on its North Fork but also on the South Fork (otherwise known as the Hamptons; see p380). Vintage New York (p328), with a flagship store in Soho and another on the Upper West Side, sells strictly New York wines, offering free tastings and knowledgeable advice. Perhaps its best quality, however, is that, because it's affiliated with an upstate winery and technically considered such, it's open on Sunday, when all other wine and liquor stores are closed. New Yorkers' appreciation of wine, local or otherwise, seems to only keep getting hotter: just a few years ago there were about a dozen wine bars in the city; now there are more than 50. Among the excellent options are Morrell Wine Bar & Cafe (p272) and Another Room (p263).

BEER

NYC lags far behind most major US cities when it comes to brewing its own suds – but there is one star on the scene. The Brooklyn Brewery (p182), in Williamsburg, is the city's first successful commercial brewery since Schaefer and Rheingold both closed their doors in 1976 (although Rheingold resumed beer-brewing in Brooklyn in 2004). Founded in 1987, it opened its 70,000-sq-ft warehouse and brewery in 1996, and has developed a cultish following. It produces more than a dozen award-winning brews, with its most popular, Brooklyn Lager, widely available at bars and shops around the city. Head over to its factory for tours and occasional weekend happy hours. Two other local breweries, operating on a much smaller scale, are the Heartland Brewery (p262) and Chelsea Brewing Company (p270). And the appreciation of the stuff can be found far and wide, with many bars now offering a slew of on-tap and bottled selections. D.B.A. (p267) and the sprawling new Ginger Man (p271) have a ton of options.

COCKTAILS

Classic martinis are certainly beloved here. But what'll really give you a buzz are all the creative variations of the elixir – cosmopolitans, appletinis, lycheetinis, chocolatinis – even saketinis (with sake replacing the vodka) and Tablatinis (at Tabla, p244), infused with fresh pineapple and lemongrass. Top-shelf liquors are always in fashion, especially vodka and tequila, which can be found at upscale Mexican spots in forms way too precious to poison with margarita mix. A popular up-and-comer is cachaça, a potent Brazilian liquor made with fermented sugarcane and slowly inching its way into the New York market thanks to a few upscale importers. The cachaça cocktail – a *caipirinha,* which adds muddled sugar and lime juice to the mix – is increasingly popular, and steadily gaining on the Cuban *mojito* of rum, mint, sugar and lime. Basically, the more exotic the ingredients – fresh tropical fruits, Asian spices, muddled herbs – the better the cocktail, which is why many restaurants are employing cocktail 'chefs' along with sommeliers these days.

COFFEE & TEA

It wasn't so long ago that nary a good cup of joe could be found in this city – you had to hit the West Coast for that. But something happened several years ago (namely the hijacking of the city by Starbucks), and now gourmet coffee purveyors are a cinch to find. Among the excellent local latte sources are Gorilla Coffee (Map p464; 97 Fifth Ave) in Park Slope, Brooklyn, Joe (Map p448; 141 Waverly Pl) and Porto Rico Importing Co (three downtown locations). But old-school diehards are sticking with the $1 version – served in a to-go cup festooned with a blue-and-gold Roman column design and often ordered 'regular,' which is New York speak for 'with milk and one sugar.' Teahouses have also taken off, with spots

KID-FRIENDLY EATERIES

Where children are and are not welcome is not always so clear at first. But use common sense (no Babbo, Daniel or Per Se), and you'll be just fine. Many places welcome kids with open arms. Diners (see p92), which are bustling, noisy places, are always perfect; one favorite is **EJ's Luncheonette** (Map pp454–5; 1271 Third Ave at 73rd St), which can be found both in the Village (Map p448; 432 Sixth Ave) and the Upper West Side (447Amsterdam Ave). But many eateries go beyond that by offering specific children's menus, activities and other perks, like **Bubby's Pie Company** (p229), in Tribeca and Dumbo, Brooklyn (the latter has a playroom); **Two Boots Restaurant & Pizzeria** (p236; www .twoboots.com), with several Manhattan outposts; ESPN Zone (p156), attached to a massive arcade; and **Peanut Butter & Co** (Map p448; 240 Sullivan St), which has nothing but variations on the PB&J sandwich. **Willy Bee's Family Lounge** in Williamsburg (Map p463; 302 Metropolitan Ave btwn Driggs & Roebling Aves) has a café, playroom and roster of activities; and **Dylan's Candy Bar** (Map pp452–3; 1011 Third Ave) is a two-story sweet shop that rivals Willy Wonka's setup. Meanwhile, the suburban chain **Chuck E. Cheese** – a massive, carnivalesque pizza place with casinos and entertainment (and only passable food, but hey…) – has arrived in Long Island City, Queens (Map p457; 34-19 48th St).

such as Teany (p234) as well as **Wild Lily Tea Room** (Map p448; 511 W 22nd St btwn Tenth & Eleventh Sts) offering book-thick menus of various brews.

CELEBRATING WITH FOOD

New Yorkers, like most people, enjoy a good dinner party. But urbanites' always-busy nature coupled with cramped living quarters makes such occasions rare. It's why dining out has become the solution for any holiday you can think of, even traditionally home-style ones such as Thanksgiving and Christmas dinners, where gathering around someone's dining room table is regarded as the most important aspect of the holiday in the rest of the States. And restaurants in NYC are happy to comply, offering special menus for every conceivable (and usually at-home) holiday from Thanksgiving and Christmas Eve to Easter and Passover; New Year's Eve and Valentine's Day are especially big eating-out nights, with most eateries jacking up prices for four-course meals. Even on July 4th, most New Yorkers are restaurant-bound for their ribs and chicken – unless you live in one of the outer boroughs, where you might just fire up your own BBQ right on your front sidewalk or stoop.

VEGETARIANS & VEGANS

The herbivore scene here has long lagged behind that of California and West Coast areas and it's still mocked by serious foodies. Still, though NYC doesn't have a local version of Alice Waters to call its own, there has been a big shift towards healthfulness and vegetarianism lately, and places catering to those who believe in it have exploded. These new spots realize that 'vegetarian' isn't a synonym for 'boring,' and have been sure to inject healthy doses of cool ambience (and great wine lists) into the mix. Downtown is home to most veggie places, with groovy takes on earthy-crunchy including Pure Food & Wine (p243), Counter (p236), Blossom (p240), Gobo (p238) and the new **Heirloom** (Map p449; 191 Orchard St). But herbivore oases now dot the entire landscape – uptown standouts include Candle Café (p250) and Mana (p248) – and even the most meat-heavy four-star restaurants are figuring out the lure of legume; the market-inspired 'le potager' section on the **Café Boulud** (20 E 76th St) menu is one of the most high-brow and little-known veggie gems in town.

QUICK EATS

For good on-the-go grub, NYC's got it goin' on. From street vendors hawking everything from hot dogs and tacos to homemade soups and falafel sandwiches, to Korean delis offering massive salad bars and sandwich counters, you'll never go hungry. Plus, the entire city, especially in downtown areas such as the East and West Village, is awash with teensy little specialty storefronts and parlors, where you'll find quality crepes, Thai food, curries, gyros, pizza, sushi, pomme frites – anything, really – for under $5 and in under five minutes.

History

History

THE RECENT PAST

DAY OF INFAMY

Good times were already faltering as the electronic-stock bubble burst, but the terrorist attack on the World Trade Center on September 11, 2001, ushered in a period of high unemployment and tightened belts. Downtown Manhattan took months to recover from the ghastly fumes wafting from the ruins of the World Trade Center, as forlorn missing-person posters grew ragged on brick walls. While recovery crews coughed their way through the debris, the city braved constant terrorist alerts and an anthrax scare to mourn the estimated 1749 dead. Shock and grief drew people together, and united the often fractious citizenry in a determined effort not to succumb to despair. Before the year was out, community groups were already gathering together in 'Imagine New York' workshops, to develop ideas for renewal and a memorial at the World Trade Center site.

21ST CENTURY: BIGGER APPLE

In 2002 Mayor Michael Bloomberg began the unenviable task of picking up the pieces of a shattered city that had (finally) thrust all its support behind his predecessor, longtime controversial mayor Rudy Giuliani, who rose in popularity for his selfless reaction to September 2001. Wrestling for his own lore, Bloomberg found his critics during his four-year campaign to build a West Side Stadium atop the West Side Hwy, rescue the Jets back from Jersey, and score a bid for the 2012 Olympic Games. All three failed after Albany said 'no' to a $2.2 billion project (to the cheer of many a New Yorker fearing traffic build-up and cost), but Bloomberg didn't take a dent in the 2005 elections, topping Bronx Democrat Fernando Ferrer by 20 points.

The boom in NYC probably didn't hurt his bid for re-election. For one thing, tourism picked up its pace by 2005, when receipts beat pre-September 11 levels and (taking cue) hotel prices and occupancy rates reached record heights. Sites like the Museum of Modern Art refurbished itself into a bigger, more beautiful being.

Lots of traditionally 'non–New York' things rushed out of the gate in the wake of September 11. One, both exotic and controversial, was the boom in malls and Texas-sized department chains. The Shops at Columbus Circle opened in 2003, with 'upscale' boutiques to take away Central Park strollers. Sixth Ave became, cynics would say, a super-sized ghetto, with Best Buy and Home Depot opening up. Lower East Side hipsters were up-in-arms when Starbucks opened on tangential Delancey St in 2005. Downtown Brooklyn chimed in too, with the 2004 opening of a Target right off Flatbush Ave.

The king of this non–New York movement, perhaps, was its setting in 2004 for the Republican National Convention, where 400,000 protested the president, the war and the clean-cut suits in Madison Sq Garden, but the away-squad Repubs carried the victory banner in the national elections anyway.

Preservation of the past has never been a strong New York trait. In 2005 the landmark downtown-rock shrine CBGB was fighting for life, as its monthly rent doubled to $40,000.

One place where New York said 'yes' to self-preservation, or at least to a bit of its past, is by granting the $100 million go-ahead to the High Line (p141), a 22-block project of greenery and galleries that upon completion in 2008 will stretch atop an abandoned train lane from the West Village through the Meatpacking District and Chelsea to Midtown West. Of

TIMELINE

c. 1500 AD	1625–26
About 15,000 Indians live in 80 different sites around the island	Dutch West India Company imports 11 slaves to New Amsterdam

the 5000-plus new units slated to open, one-quarter will be low-incoming housing, the rest priced to market (meaning about $3 million for a three-bedroom condo).

Gentrification is not new to New York. But its wave is moving at record speed. Over the past 15 years, the East Village has peeled off Alphabet City's avenues (and south into the Lower East Side's tenements), replacing one-time gangs and drug-dealers with young professionals (occasional tokers, surely) able to pay half a million for apartments (and willing to walk the long blocks to the nearest subway). Ave D – with projects still home to nearly 10,000 – is the last possible wall between complete gentrification. Brooklyn's arms have reached wider – and taken more and more hipster and budding families' embraces. See p42.

About the time New York celebrated the centennial of the Staten Island ferry (2005) and the subway (2004), the MTA Authority union grew restless over salaries, pension and health insurance – and engaged a three-day strike in December 2005 that rendered much of the boroughs (in particular) stranded. Mayor Bloomberg walked over from ritzy Brooklyn Heights to show the city was still ready to work. But those further afield struggled more. Commuters took cabs, but a four-person minimum made some ambling for a last-second passenger to get over the bridges to Manhattan. Some savvy homeless found themselves a new profession in charging lunch money to fill the slot. What's New York without a little impromptu entrepreneurship?

FROM THE BEGINNING

NATIVE INHABITANTS

The signature shoreline of New York was sculpted by glaciers between 75,000 and 17,000 years ago. The end of the Ice Age left New York with hills of glacial debris now called Hamilton Heights and Bay Ridge, and the numerous inlets and drowned valleys known as Long Island Sound, the East River and Arthur Kill. Glaciers scoured off soft rock leaving behind Manhattan's stark rock foundations of gneiss and schist. Around 11,000 years before the first Europeans sailed through the Narrows, the Lenape people foraged, hunted and fished the regional bounty. Spear points, arrowheads, bone heaps and shell mounds testify to their presence. Some of their pathways still lie beneath such streets as Broadway, originally part of a trail linking Manhattan with the beaver-trading post, Albany. In Munsee, the Lenape language, the term Manhattan may have translated as hilly island, or more descriptively, 'place of general inebriation.'

The bands of Lenape did not think of themselves as a nation, but rather functioned in small groups whose evocative names still linger as the names of rivers, towns and bays. Hackensacks lived on the Jersey side of the Hudson, Raritans there and on Staten Island, Massepequas, Rockaways and Matinecocks along Long Island Sound. On Manhattan Island dwelled Wiechquaesgecks, Rechgawanches and Siwanoys, whose campsites still sometimes yield archaeological riches when bulldozers dig.

EXPLORERS

In 1524 the Florentine Giovanni da Verrazzano explored the Upper Bay, which he termed a 'very beautiful lake.' Today's seaborne visitors enter that 'lake' under the magnificent Verrazano Bridge (seen from helicopters every fall at the start of the New York Marathon). Only a year later the black Portuguese Estaban Gomez, a former helmsman with Magellan, sailed further up the Hudson. However brief his New World sojourn, he did pause long enough to seize 57 Native American captives to sell as slaves in Lisbon. By the time the Dutch West India Company employee Henry Hudson arrived in 1609, encounters with Native Americans were already beginning to be dichotomized into two crude stories, alternating between 'delightful primitives' and 'brutal savages.'

1664	1788–90
New Amsterdam becomes New York in a bloodless (welcome for most) transition	New York is capital of the USA

COLONIAL ARRIVALS

Like the other foreign outposts of European empires bursting at the seams, the tiny port of New Amsterdam attracted the best and worst of the international flotsam and jetsam of the 17th century. Marked by its sailor-friendly abundance of taverns and endless supply of languages, the trading town was owned by the Dutch West India Company. Common currencies included Indian wampum, Spanish pieces of eight, gold doubloons, silver, furs and tobacco. One early administrator may have sealed the real estate transaction of the millennium by 'purchasing' Manhattan for 60 guilders, or $24. More likely, the Native American side of the deal thought the exchange was about rent, and permission to hunt, fish and trade, rather than a permanent transfer of property – an unfamiliar custom in the New World.

From the beginning New Amsterdam's governors displayed more talent for self-enrichment than for administration. As colonists grumbled about the Dutch West India Company's stingy provisions and primitive wood huts, the walls and ramparts of the 'fort' crumbled under the assault of free-roaming pigs, cattle and sheep. Meanwhile, Governor Willem Kieft stirred up so much trouble with the surrounding Native Americans that they formed an alliance to subdue the aggressive Europeans. By the time Peter Stuyvesant stumped off a ship to clean up the mess in 1647, the population had dwindled to around 700, and Kieft had retreated to count his gains in various corrupt transactions.

PEG LEG PROSPERITY

Peter Stuyvesant busily set about remaking the demoralized colony, establishing markets and a night watch, repairing the fort, digging a canal (under the current Canal St) and authorizing a municipal wharf. His vision of an orderly and prosperous trading port was partially derived from his previous experience as governor of Curaçao. Indeed, the burgeoning sugar economy in the Caribbean helped to inspire an investment in slave trading

TOP HISTORY BOOKS

Check out the ubiquitous street sellers for cheap copies of these books, old and new.

- *Gotham. A History of New York City to 1898* by Edwin G Burrows and Mike Wallace. A hugely entertaining, 1000-page tome that lends itself to chapter-by-chapter sampling. Chock-full of evildoers, absurdity and contention – just what you would expect from an NYC history. Won a Pulitzer Prize.
- *Lowlife* by Luc Sante. Rollicking look at 19th-century criminality, drawing heavily on Herbert Asbury's *Gangs of New York*. Be sure to read about characters such as the fat fence Marm Mandelbaum, who gave dinner parties on chairs her clients stole.
- *Invisible Frontier: Exploring the Tunnels, Ruins and Rooftops of Hidden New York* by LB Deyo and 'Lefty' Leibowitz. Idiosyncratic chronicle of how this team of urban explorers penetrated forbidden spaces in NYC to see the actual bricks, mortar and steel bones of the city's history. After September 11, of course, security concerns have barred entry to many of these places, but their trip diaries are a unique way of experiencing city history.
- *Gay New York* by George Chauncey. The hidden history of dandies, the docks, drag balls and brief encounters, demonstrating how gay urban habits evolved within surprisingly variable sexual cultures and practices.
- *American Ground: The Unbuilding of the World Trade Center* by William Langewiesche. Thought-provoking look at issues surrounding the nine-month recovery efforts at the World Trade Center site, based on long hours with engineers and construction workers underground. Controversial because the firefighters have hotly denied that any looted Gap jeans from the underground Mall were ever found in a fire truck.
- *Rats: Observations on the History and Habitat of the City's Most Unwanted Inhabitants* by Robert Sullivan. In the aftermath of September 11, Sullivan took to the alleyways to watch our four-legged friends seek meals and mates in the after-hours.

1795	1853
Yellow Fever epidemic; wealthy flee to country	The City authorizes the allotment of a massive public park, which later becomes Central Park

that soon boosted New Amsterdam's slave workforce to 20% of the population. After long service some of them were partially freed and given the 'Negroe Lots' areas near today's Greenwich Village, the Lower East Side and City Hall. (You can see the remnants of their African burial ground, p120, recently unearthed on Reade St.) The Dutch West India Company encouraged the fruitful connection to plantation economies on the islands, and issued advertisements and offered privileges to attract merchants to the growing port. Although these 'liberties' did not encompass religious freedom for Jews and Quakers, settlers did come. By the 1650s, warehouses, workshops and gabled houses were spreading back from the dense establishments at the river's edge on Pearl St.

A brisk trade in furs, tobacco and timber supplied residents and Native Americans with liquor, guns, kettles and cloth. The memory of this trade lingers in the city's seal, visible on municipal buildings and documents. Although the city on the tip of the island commanded a strategic position to monitor the fur trade flowing down the Hudson River and over from the Connecticut River, its very success made it vulnerable. The 'wall' along Wall St was meant to keep both English and Indian raiders out of town.

In the long run, prosperity counted for more than nationality, and when the English showed up in 1664 in battleships, Governor Stuyvesant surrendered without a shot. King Charles II promptly renamed the colony after his brother the Duke of York. Nevertheless, Dutch laws and customs coexisted with English ways, which included large land grants to royal favorites in the regions surrounding New York.

TURMOIL

Local forces were prone to squabbling, and one such contretemps called Leisler's Rebellion terminated with its leader being hanged and beheaded in what is now City Hall Park in 1691. Sharp-tongued colonials did not hesitate to publish their complaints in the colonial press. Peter Zenger's *Weekly Journal* flayed king and royal governor so regularly the authorities tried – unsuccessfully – to convict Zenger for libel. His acquittal signaled that juries would no longer help the ruling powers squash criticism. Some 2000 enslaved New Yorkers continued to resist their involuntary servitude. In the Great Negro Plot of 1741, black slaves and white accomplices were accused of plotting arson and rebellion in a tavern not far from today's World Trade Center site. The facts have remained forever unclear, but the city fathers executed as many as 64 people, burning 17 of them at the stake. Remains of two of them may be among the bodies found at the African burial ground.

Trade with the Caribbean accelerated and wharves lined the East River to accommodate the bulging merchant men. By the 18th century the economy was so robust the locals were improvising ways to avoid sharing the wealth with London. Smuggling to dodge various port taxes was commonplace, and the jagged coastline, full of coves and inlets, hid illegal activity well (as 20th-century drug smugglers also discovered). New York, that hotbed of hotheads and tax dodgers, provided a stage for the fatal confrontation with King George III.

REVOLUTION & WAR

From dodging port taxes to formally declaring 'independence' and the right to bear arms, the colonists found themselves well along the road to revolution by the 1760s. The Boston Tea Party was echoed by a similar episode of tea-tax defiance in New York Harbor.

Patriots and the Tories loyal to the king clashed in public spaces – the patriots erected Liberty Poles and the royalists ripped them down. General George Washington's performance in New York consisted mostly of unimpressive battles and a stealthy escape across the East River at night. After winning the Battle of Long Island and chasing Washington's ragtag forces up to Washington Heights in 1776, the British occupied the town for the rest of the American Revolution. Patriots fled, and royal rule was aided by a policy of liberating slaves who fought for the king. When the British fleet sailed out of New York Harbor in

1863	1875
Civil War draft riot erupts in New York	First tattoo parlor opens at Chatham Sq

FIVE TURNING POINTS IN NYC HISTORY

In history as in physics, every action has a reaction:

- The Torching of NYC (Sep 21, 1776) Who burned down NYC during the American Revolution? The triumphant British, who had only captured the port town a fortnight earlier, blamed rebel arsonists. The patriots denied it, saying the vengeful British had torched it. Surveying the smoking ruins of 500 dwellings from his headquarters in Harlem Heights, General George Washington observed: 'Providence or some good honest fellow, has done more for us than we were disposed to do for ourselves.' It was a low point for the patriots in the revolutionary war, but it did send them scurrying to territory where their guerrilla tactics could later defeat the colonial power.

- Commissioners Plan of 1811 (Mar 22, 1811) Orderly but bland, squashing the motley heights and valleys of hilly Manhattan into a flat checkerboard, the plan imposed a grid on a city that had yet to develop above Houston St. It did make city navigation a cinch for strangers. But the plan also forestalled agreeable variety, in the name of creating tidier and more marketable real estate bundles – each rectangle equal to another.

- Triangle Shirt Waist Fire (Mar 25, 1911) A tossed cigarette probably ignited the raging inferno in the top stories of a sweatshop full of young immigrant women. The terrified garment makers collapsed at a locked door to the staircase; the owners had fastened it to prevent employee pilfering. Within minutes, dozens of workers had jumped from the ninth floor. The death toll of 146 spurred public sympathy for workers, and new safety codes to prevent a repetition. But to this day firefighters avoid sleeping on high floors because they know the limits of ladders and hoses.

- Dodgers Leave Brooklyn (1957) The borough's favorite baseball team got its name from fans dodging trolleys that turned around near its playing field. When owner Walter O'Malley moved the team to Los Angeles, cries of pain and rage echoed across the east. Did this mean the end of great cities and their valiant athletic teams? Only two years earlier the Dodgers had finally won the World Series against hated rivals, the Yankees. Since the Dodgers (and Manhattan's Giants) moved to California, many sports-team owners have yanked their teams out to suburban stadiums with big parking lots. And many more threaten to do so, in an intricate game of blackmail to force cities to build new facilities.

- Demolition of Pennsylvania Station (1963) Despite public outcry, the magnificent McKim Mead and White Pennsylvania Station, built in 1910, was demolished. The grand structure modeled on the Roman baths of Caracalla was replaced by the current underground maze. Architectural historian Vincent Scully summed up the difference saying, 'one entered the city like a god...now one scuttles in like a rat.' The infamous preservation defeat led directly to New York City's Landmarks Law in 1965. Jacqueline Kennedy Onassis was a member of the Landmarks Commission when it prevented a repeat demolition of Grand Central Terminal in the 1970s (p150).

1783, it took as many as 3000 ex-slaves along to Canada and the colonies. After a series of celebrations, banquets and fireworks at Bowling Green, General Washington bade farewell to his officers at Fraunces Tavern Museum (p121), and retired as commander-in-chief.

But in 1789, to his surprise, the retired general found himself addressing crowds at Federal Hall (still standing at Wall St, p121) gathered to witness the inauguration of President Washington. Signaling simplicity and patriotism, he wore a suit of American-made broadcloth, and walked to prayers afterwards in a pew still visible in nearby St Paul's Chapel (p119). Characteristically, people distrusted a capitol located adjacent to the financial power of the merchants of Wall St, and New Yorkers lost the seat of the presidency to Philadelphia shortly thereafter.

BIGGER, BETTER, FASTER

After setbacks at the start of the 19th century, the prospering city found mighty resources to build mighty public works. Irish immigrants helped dig a 363-mile 'ditch' from the Hudson to Buffalo, known as the Erie Canal. The canal's chief backer, Governor Clinton, celebrated the waterway by ceremonially pouring a barrel of Erie water into the sea (Clinton's cask is on view at the New-York Historical Society, p159). A great aqueduct system brought Croton Water, relieving thirst and dirt. No longer would cholera sweep the town, as new water meant ordinary folks needn't drink from the brackish river and polluted ground water.

1883	1904
Brooklyn Bridge debuts on May 24 and 150,000 walk across	Luna Park in Coney Island opens, followed by Dreamland amusement park; IRT subway carries first passengers

Another project to boost the health of the people crammed into tiny tenement apartments was a grand park of 843 acres. Begun in 1855 in an area so far uptown some immigrants kept pigs, sheep and goats there, Central Park (p190) was both a vision of green reform and a boon to real-estate speculation. As much as Central Park promised a playground for the masses, the park project also offered work relief for the city when the Panic of 1857 (one of the city's periodic financial debacles) shattered the nation's finance system. Further down, after several winter freezes had underlined the weakness of the ferry system connecting Brooklyn and downtown Manhattan, John Roebling, an inventive German-born engineer, designed a soaring symphony of spun wire and gothic arches to span the East River. The Brooklyn Bridge (p125) accelerated the fusion of the neighboring cities. The proudly independent city of Brooklyn, already nearing a million residents, bowed to the inevitable in 1898 when the five boroughs were consolidated in one big, powerful unit.

POWER & CORRUPTION

Construction fueled great expectations among New York City's political fixers. Boss Tweed, a ward politician from the heavily Irish immigrant neighborhoods, forever known through Thomas Nast's biting caricatures in the 1870s, created a powerful ring of corrupt officials and fee-splitting contractors to build a courthouse that cost nearly $12 million and took 20 years to complete. (See it now elegantly restored in City Hall Park, p124, now home to Mayor Bloomberg's revamped Department of Education.) Running the famous Tammany Hall political machine, the clubhouse bosses passed out patronage jobs, holiday turkeys and free firewood in neighborhoods such as Five Points and Little Germany. The Tweed political style, portrayed in the Martin Scorsese film *Gangs of New York* (2002) included graft, corruption, vote tampering, ballot stealing, cronyism and lots of municipal pork. Then and now, the gargantuan scale of public works has attracted financial geniuses equipped to capture some of the booty – on both sides of the law.

Other big shysters included the private rapid-transit companies that fought for city franchises. By the turn of the 20th century elevated trains carried a million people a day in and out of the city. Rapid transit opened up areas of the Bronx and Upper Manhattan, spurring mini-building booms in areas near the lines. At this point, the city was simply overflowing with the masses of immigrants from southern Italy and Eastern Europe, who had boosted the metropolis to around three million. The journey from immigrant landing stations

New York's own Parthenon, Federal Hall (p121)

at Castle Garden and Ellis Island led straight to the Lower East Side. There, streets reflected these myriad origins with shop signs in Yiddish, Italian, German and Chinese. Ethnic enclaves allowed newcomers to feel comfortable in home languages, buy familiar and New World staples from pushcart peddlers and worship in varied versions of the Christian and Jewish faiths. Experience their extremely tight living quarters today at the Lower East Side Tenement Museum (p134).

1918	1931
Yankees acquire slugger Babe Ruth, to the agony of Red Sox fans everywhere	Empire State Building (1454ft tall) built in 410 days

CIVIL STRIFE

In the 19th century New York also became famous for its radical politics and militant workers, who challenged the system that created both huge fortunes and impoverished workers. Over and over again labor movements went on strike for the eight-hour day and a living wage. In the roller-coaster economies of the time, workers confronted unspeakable hardships when bubbles burst and factories closed. Some winters in the city found 100,000 working men laid off, shivering in soup lines, and shoveling snow for nickels. Children collected rags and bottles, boys hawked newspapers, and girls sold flowers to contribute to family income. In already crowded apartments, a kitchen table or two chairs jammed together could earn rent as beds for boarders. Then, during the day, whole families assembled paper flowers or sewed sleeves in shirts for precious pennies. Family budgets were so meager it was common to pawn the sheets to raise food money before a payday.

Harsh conditions and competition for scarce jobs produced regular outbreaks of violence. New York finally abolished slavery in 1827, and many working-class jobs excluded African Americans. Gangs of young men regularly broke windows in black churches and harassed the worshippers. Writers and community activists responded by publishing appeals for justice and heartening news of progress in *Freedom's Journal,* the first black-owned and operated newspaper in the US, produced on Church St and later Lispenard St. At times mobs expressed their rage on the city's black neighborhoods, or caricatured African Americans in minstrel shows and popular entertainment. The most dramatic clash between the races

WISE GUY NEW YORK

Romanticized by Hollywood and fanned by popular culture, New York's organized crime underground made its greatest marks in the 20th century. Fleeing economic disasters in southern Italy and Sicily, Italian immigrants faced discrimination and dislocation in their new home. But being marginalized can have the unintended side effect of stimulating new underground business. Its economy in New York began before WWI, when the Society of the Black Hand, a band of small-time grafters, tossed Molotov cocktails in storefronts if the owner failed to pay protection money.

The New York Mafia took off during Prohibition, when the Volstead Act banning liquor sales offered a golden opportunity to unofficial business. Running rum down Lake Champlain from Canada, hijacking each other's trucks, hosting backroom gambling, loan-sharking, pimping, the big names – Lucchese, Genovese, Anastasia, Costello, Bonanno, Gambino and Castellano – muscled in on the various branches of entertainment that had long made New York City a mecca for the sporting man. Raw competition unfettered by above-ground rules meant that the families inflicted more damage on each other than law enforcement ever managed.

Lucky Luciano got his nickname after he survived having his throat slashed, ear to ear, in 1929 when he challenged mob leadership with his pals Meyer Lansky and Bugsy Siegel. Crazy Joe Gallo whacked Albert Anastasia as he sat in a barber's chair in 1952, but he himself was shot full of holes less than 20 years later in Umberto's Clam House (still on Mulberry St a few doors up from the original location). Joe Colombo was killed in front of thousands at a 1971 rally, undermining his public statements about the nonexistence of the Mafia. In a successful challenge to the Gambino family control, John Gotti ordered Paul Castellano gunned down in front of Sparks Steakhouse in 1985. Before he finally received a prison term, Vincent Gigante was famous for wandering the village in his bathrobe in the 1970s and '80s to demonstrate his mental incompetence, thus preventing a successful prosecution until 2002.

Sometimes it seems hard to distinguish the movies from the facts. Marlon Brando from *On the Waterfront* to *The Godfather* offers a mythical compendium of society's affection for rule-breakers, outsiders and hoods, which persists through *GoodFellas* and on to Tony Soprano.

Like all big businesses, the Mafia diversified as it grew, moving from petty extortion to large-scale drug trade by the 1960s. By the time of the Pizza Connection, a cocaine and heroin smuggling operation that used pizzerias as fronts to distribute drugs in the 1970s, Mafia entrepreneurship had reached new levels of sophistication. Then in 1986 US Attorney General Rudolph Guiliani successfully prosecuted Gaetano Badalamenti, who was sentenced to 45 years in the pen. The phrase 'Pizza Connection' went on to become the name of a popular video game.

1961	1963
Young folk singer Bob Dylan arrives in NYC, plays Cafe Wha? on his first night in town	Original Pennsylvania Station (from 1910) demolished, prompting the foundation of Landmarks Preservation Commission

occurred in 1863, when President Lincoln instituted a draft to replenish his dwindling Civil War army. Grumbling that wealthy men could buy an exemption from service for $300, the working classes also feared that black men would take their jobs while they were sent to war. Many Irish immigrants resented fighting for the emancipation of people who, as they saw it, stood ready to steal their jobs and drive down wages. So during the first days of the draft, mobs burnt conscription offices, pulled down the houses of abolitionists, attacked police and chased and lynched African Americans in the street. The mob even surged uptown to 42nd St to burn down the Colored Orphan Asylum. Troops had to be yanked from the front to quell the violence in the Union's largest city.

FABULOUS WEALTH

After the Civil War, the old aristocratic elements retreated uptown, far from the sons and daughters of Europe. The newly wealthy began to build increasingly splendid mansions on Fifth Ave. Modeled on European chateaux, palaces such as the Vanderbilt home, on the corner of 52nd St and Fifth Ave, reached for new summits of opulence. Tapestries adorned marble halls, mirrored ballrooms accommodated bejeweled revelers, liveried footmen handed grand ladies from their gilded carriages. Mrs Astor and her friends in old New York tried to resist the onslaught of robber-baron wives eager to break into society. Mrs Astor's idea of the right people encompassed only 400, which, she sniffed, sufficed for all the people one would want to know socially, in any case. Her snobbery could not withstand the tidal wave of fortunes being made by Rockefeller in oil, Gould in railroads, and Carnegie in steel. The latecomers included a substantial group of German Jews such as Jacob Schiff, Otto Kahn, Solomon Guggenheim, and Felix and Paul Warburg, who formed their own elite society known as 'our crowd.'

WOMEN TAKE TO THE STREETS

With the start of the 20th century, piquant accounts of the foibles of the rich competed with rabble-rousing crusades for the masses in the flamboyant press of New York. Joseph Pulitzer and William Randolph Hearst vied for public affection with racy stories, lavish illustrations, and the new fad for comic strips. Even women began to penetrate the Fourth Estate. Nellie Bly, a girl stunt reporter, committed herself to an insane asylum to pen an exposé, before she traveled 'Round the World in 80 Days,' filing telegraphed dispatches all the way.

Woman power was evident on the streets of Manhattan too, as female garment workers 20,000-strong marched on City Hall. Suffragists held street-corner rallies to obtain the vote for women, and Margaret Sanger opened the first birth-control clinic in Brooklyn, where purity police promptly arrested her. Women New Yorkers definitely had a lot to complain about, given their abysmal pay and wretched working conditions in sweatshops and factories.

THE JAZZ AGE

But manufacturing jobs did put change in people's pockets, and they began to spend it on such new entertainment as movies and jolly outings to Coney Island amusement parks (p180). By the 1920s the Great Migration from the South made Harlem the center of African American culture and society, turning out poetry, music, painting and innovative attitude that continues to influence and inspire to this day. The Apollo Theater (p168), still humming on 125th St, began its famous Amateur Night in 1934 – it's a venue that has boosted the careers of unknowns such as Ella Fitzgerald, James Brown and the Jackson Five. Harlem's daring nightlife in the 1920s and '30s attracted the flappers and gin-soaked revelers that marked the complete failure of Prohibition. Indeed, the Jazz Age seems to have taught women to smoke, drink and dance at speakeasies, a foretaste of the liberated nightlife that New Yorkers still enjoy today (although they are forced to smoke their coffin

1973	1976–7
The Knicks win their most recent NBA championship – and the dry spell begins	David Berkowitz says a demon in a dog told him to commit Son of Sam murders

nails outside bars these days.) Broadway seemed to thrive in good times and bad, supplying leggy chorines for Busby Berkeley spectacles such as the cynically titled *Gold Diggers of 1933* and oodles of sporty slang that still permeates American speech today.

THE GREAT DEPRESSION & WWII

New York made it through the Great Depression of the 1930s with a combination of grit, endurance, rent parties, militancy and a slew of public works projects. The once-grand Central Park blossomed with shacks, derisively called Hoovervilles, after the president who refused to help the needy. But Mayor Fiorello LaGuardia found a friend in President Franklin Roosevelt, and worked his Washington connections to great effect to bring relief money home. Riverside Park (p160) and the Triborough Bridge (Map pp458–9) are just two of the still functioning monuments to New Deal projects, brought to New York by the Texas-born, Yiddish-speaking son of an Italian bandmaster.

WWII brought troops galore to the city, ready to party down to their last dollar in Times Sq, before being shipped off to Europe. Converted to war industries, the local factories hummed, staffed by women and African American workers who had rarely before had access to these good union jobs. The explosion of wartime activity led to a huge housing crunch, which brought New York its much-imitated Rent Control Law.

But there were few evident controls on business, as Midtown bulked up with skyscrapers after the war. The financial center marched north, even while the banker David Rockefeller and his brother Governor Nelson Rockefeller dreamed up the twin towers to revitalize downtown.

FROM HEARTBREAKING DODGERS TO POT-SMOKING POETS

A mere decade after Jackie Robinson joined the Brooklyn Dodgers, breaking the color barrier, owner Walter O'Malley moved the team to Los Angeles, breaking Brooklyn hearts. The population of the gutsy borough had peaked at 2.7 million at just about the time that its famous breweries began to close. (The classic Rheingold recommenced beer-brewing in Brooklyn in 2004.) But under the Manhattan approaches to the Brooklyn Bridge, an art movement was brewing that wrested the crown from the previously reigning French. Abstract expressionism, a homegrown, large-scale outbreak of American painters, offended with its incomprehensible squiggles and blotches, but charmed with its color and energy. Artists such as Willem de Kooning, Mark Rothko and Helen Frankenthaler exhibited as much flair in their personal lives as in their canvases. Jackson Pollack, the great dripper, and his friends often quenched their thirst at the Cedar Tavern still there on University Place, then known as the home of alcoholic expressionism.

These cultural high jinks soon broadened into the broader social movements of the 1960s, which parlayed artistic defiance into maverick urban lifestyles. Beat poets such as Allen Ginsberg made the Village the downtown capital of the word, while gay revelers found their political strength in fighting a police raid at the Stonewall Bar (p266). The lesbian and gay community flourished in the tolerant atmosphere of a neighborhood that did not even bother to open its shops till 10am or 11am. And then bearded merchants sold sex toys, drag queen accessories and roach clips.

TAILSPIN/RENEWAL

The fiscal crisis of the mid-1970s demoted the elected Mayor Abraham Beame to a figurehead, turning over the city's real financial power to Governor Carey and his appointees. The president's message to the beleaguered town – Ford to City, Drop Dead! – marked the nadir of relationships between the US and the city it loved to hate. As massive layoffs decimated the city's working class, untended bridges, roads and parks reeked of hard times. Even the bond raters turned thumbs down on New York's mountain of debt.

1977	1980
Studio 54 opens at the height of disco fever; John Travolta struts his stuff in *Saturday Night Fever*	Deranged gunman Mark David Chapman kills John Lennon; Frank Sinatra records 'New York, New York'

But the traumatic '70s actually drove down rents for once, and helped to nourish an exciting alternative culture that staged performances in abandoned schools, opened galleries in unused storefronts and breathed new life into the hair-dye industry. For example, the fees from shooting the movie *Fame* at PS 122 at 10th St and Second Ave, helped pay for the renovation of the still-popular performance space. Blue-haired punks turned former warehouses into pulsing meccas of nightlife, transforming the former industrial precincts of Soho and Tribeca. Immortalized in Nan Goldin's famous performance piece *The Ballad of Sexual Dependency,* this lowlife renaissance bent gender roles into pretzels and turned the East Village into America's center of tattooing and independent filmmaking.

B-BOYS, BREAKING & BASQUIAT

Meanwhile, in the South Bronx, a wave of arson reduced blocks of apartment houses to cinders. But amid the smoke of arson, an influential hip-hop culture was born in the Bronx and Brooklyn, fueled by the percussive rhythms of Puerto Rican salsa. Rock Steady Crew, led by 'Crazy Legs' Richie Colon, pioneered athletic, competitive break-dancing. Kool DJ Herc spun vinyl for break beat all-night dance parties, drawing on his Jamaican apprenticeship in appropriated rhythms. Afrika Bambaataa, another founding DJ of hip-hop, formed Zulu Nation, to bring DJs, break-dancers and graffiti writers together to end violence. Daring examples of the latter dazzled the public with their train-long graphics. Perhaps the best-known 'masterpiece' belied the graf writer's reputation as vandals: Lee 163, with the Fab 5 crew, painted a whole car of trains with the message 'Merry Christmas, New York.' Some of these maestros of the spray can penetrated the art world. Jean-Michel Basquiat, once known by his tag 'Samo,' began to hang with Andy Warhol and sell with the big boys in the go-go art world of the 1980s.

Some of the easy money snagged in the booming stock markets of the 1980s was spent on art, but even more was blown up the noses of young traders. While Manhattan neighborhoods struggled with an epidemic of crack cocaine, the city reeled from the impact of addiction, citywide crime, and an AIDS epidemic that cut a swath through communities. Mayor Ed Koch could barely keep the lid on the city. Homelessness burgeoned as landlords converted the cheap old single-room hotels into luxury apartments. Squatters in the East Village fought back when police tried to clear a big homeless encampment, leading to the Tompkins Sq Park riots of 1988. Hard to imagine that just a few years later, Manhattan would yet again become the shiny apple of prosperity's eye.

THE ROARING NINETIES

A *Time* magazine cover in 1990 sported a feature story on 'New York: The Rotting Apple.' Still convalescing from the real estate crash at the end of the 1980s, the city faced crumbling bridges, tunnels and roads, jobs leaking south, and Fortune 500 companies sniffing the green, green air of suburbia. And then in roared the dot.com market, turning geeks into millionaires and the New York Stock Exchange into a speculator's fun park. Buoyed by tax receipts from IPO (initial public offering) profits, the city launched a frenzy of building, boutiquing and partying unparalleled since the 1920s.

With pro-business, law-and-order Rudy Giuliani at the helm, the dingy and destitute were swept from Manhattan's yuppified streets to the outer boroughs, leaving room for Generation X to score digs and live the high life. Abrasive, aggressive and relentless, Mayor Giuliani grabbed headlines with his campaign to stamp out crime, even kicking the sex shops off 42nd St. The energetic mayor succeeded in making New York America's safest large city, by targeting high crime areas, using statistics to focus police presence, and arresting subway gate-crashers, people committing a minor infringement of city law but who often had other charges pending. So, in the 1990s crime dropped, powering a huge appetite for nightlife in the city that never sleeps. Restaurants boomed in the spruced-up metropolis,

1988	1993
East Village squatters and cops clash in the Tompkins Sq Park riots	Former Van Halen singer David Lee Roth is arrested for buying pot in Washington Sq Park

THE GOOD, THE BAD & THE ABRASIVE MAYOR GUILIANI

In a city ravaged by the crack-cocaine epidemic, tortured with unbalanced budgets, dilapidated from deferred mainte-nance, newly elected Mayor Rudolph Guiliani stepped into a troubled post in a troubled city in 1994. He had stockpiled a glorious list of convictions as a US prosecuting attorney, sending '80s junk-bond traders Ivan Boesky and Michael Milkin to jail, bringing the ruling Mafia families to heel, wreaking the people's justice on old-line corrupt politicians such as Bronx Borough President Stanley Friedman and Congressman Mario Biaggi. But acting as avenging angel was not a possible mayoral policy, so what could the novice politician do with the ungovernable city?

Nephew of four policemen and elected in a law-and-order campaign, the mayor immediately launched a war on crime. He succeeded by targeting high-crime areas, using statistics to focus police presence and mopping up low-level 'quality of life' crimes to create a safer civic atmosphere. Lucky for him, the birth statistics cooperated: since young men 16 to 18 years old commit most violent crime, the drop in the number of teens made crime plummet across the US too.

But aggressive policing can fan fears of police brutality and evaporating civil rights. The NYPD 'spot-checked' cars with minority drivers so often, that the mayor's own African American deputy mayor (Rudy Washington) was issued a special ID to ward off harassment stops of his official NYC car. The citizenry watched in amazement as Guiliani assigned officers to arrest Bowery squeegee men, who washed windshields at stoplights for a quarter.

Had New York really become a place where swaggering bullies in uniform could send cowering citizens running for cover? 'Guiliani Time' incidents began to confirm these anxieties, such as the fatal police shooting of Amadou Diallo, an African immigrant who did not instantly understand a police order. Or the time cops visited a nightclub, and took Haitian immigrant Abner Louima back to the station house for a torture session. These polarizing events reduced Guil-iani's popularity in the African American community, already resentful of its exclusion from city governance. Guiliani did little to counteract bad publicity, when he banned what seemed like permanent demonstrations from the City Hall steps – long a home for protestors exercising the city's late lamented free speech.

But these negative moments faded when Guiliani braved the smoke and chaos to act decisively at the World Trade Center. Much was forgiven on September 11, 2001, when he responded to a reporter's question about the number of victims, saying 'the losses will be more than we can bear.'

Fashion Week gained global fame, and *Sex and the City* beamed a vision of sophisticated singles in Manolos around the world.

Meanwhile, to the delight of unionized plumbers, electricians and carpenters, real estate prices sizzled, setting off a construction spree of new high-rises, converted warehouses and rejuvenated tenements. Throwing off the uncertainty of the era of David Dinkins, a cautious politician who was NYC's first African American mayor, New Yorkers flaunted the new wealth. Areas of the Lower East Side that housed artist storefront galleries in the 1970s and '80s morphed overnight into blocks of gentrified dwellings with double-door security and maintenance charges equal to normal humans' entire take-home pay. Bars switched from pitchers of beer to $9 microbrews and designer vodka cosmopolitans.

Those left behind seldom seemed to bother the mayor. No new housing for ordinary people was built, but plenty of solid apartment stock disappeared from the rent rolls, as landlords converted rentals into pricey cooperative buildings. And yet, the city's population grew and grew, as ambitious young graduates flocked to the financial center. At the new Ellis Island, JFK airport, customs officials greeted wave after wave of South Asians, South Americans and other immigrants willing to double up in cramped quarters in the boroughs. So many Dominicans came to Washington Heights that politicians back in the Dominican Republic launched New York campaigns for their local elections. For refugees from super-slick Manhattan, ethnic enclaves in Brooklyn and Queens beckoned as intriguing places to nosh on exotic foods and sample goods without labels.

All the new New Yorkers didn't exactly bounce back from a troubled economy. Things were faltering in the Big Apple when the new millennium came, and the fateful day in 2001 changed the city's, and world's, perspective.

2002	2005
Mobster boss John Gotti dies of throat cancer while serving a prison sentence for murder and other charges	City loses bid for 2012 Olympics; collective sigh relieves need for air-conditioning for two weeks

Sights

Sights

Sure, New York City is made up of five boroughs. But to most visitors, NYC is synonymous with Manhattan – heck, even outer-borough locals say 'I'm heading into the city' when they venture in, away from homes in Brooklyn, Queens, Staten Island or the Bronx. So what's a poor visitor to believe? Believe this, folks: that 'the city' is more than Manhattan, and Manhattan is much more than a city.

That main borough – home to Times Sq, Central Park, the Empire State Building and just about every other sought-after sight – is truly a collection of eclectic, homey and lively little towns, where you'll find regulars hunkered down at favorite diner tables, or nodding hello to neighbors as they take their dogs for early-morning walks. There's the East Village, where a clutch of old-timers blends in with queer club-goers, shoppers scouring the teensy clothing boutiques, and a diminishing crowd of young street punks. There's Chelsea, rife with buff gay men and souped-up diners that double as lounge clubs; the Upper West Side, where nannies push strollers and musicians lug cellos home on the subway after orchestra gigs; Harlem, home to historic culture spots and a fast-and-furious tide of gentrification; and Soho and Noho, home to high-earning loft dwellers and destination shopping strips.

But cross a bridge or tunnel on any side of the skinny, packed-tight island of Manhattan, and you'll find the city's borders stretch further out than most New Yorkers will let on. In the massive land of Queens, you'll find neighborhoods where English is the second – even third – language, and mother tongues that range from Korean and Cantonese to Colombian Spanish, Gujarati and Guyanese. The Bronx has regions from beautiful parkland and gritty ghettos to purely Italian or Irish 'hoods and stretches of residential housing that mimic nearby suburbia. Staten

CENTRAL PARK

When you're looking for respite from the sights and sounds of the city, Central Park is the perfect place. Our color coverage of this urban oasis begins on p190.

Island, which feels more like its New Jersey neighbor in many spots, is the most ridiculed borough – though with miles of lovely beaches and parkland and pockets of ethnic culinary treasures, it deserves a better rap. The coolest of all, though, is Brooklyn – which now rivals Manhattan with its hip factor, bumped up constantly with its influx of new restaurants, indie shops and residential neighborhoods that woo folks from downtown and uptown, sometimes to visit and oftentimes to live. Feel free to be seduced by any place on the New York City map. You're certain to be surprised – and very likely to be thrilled.

ITINERARIES

Two Days

Plan your attack over a quintessential New York breakfast at a cozy spot near where you're staying – perhaps **Bubby's** (p229) in Tribeca – then pick a neighborhood that most compels you and meander around, ducking into a café or boutique whenever the mood for snacks or shopping strikes. Ride the subway uptown (unless you're already there) and hit the impressively remodeled **Museum of Modern Art** (p154) if it's raining, or the airy green space of **Central Park** (p190). Grab a cab down Broadway, just for the experience, and stop in **Times Sq** (p156), a spectacle that deserves at least a smidgen of attention. Have dinner at a newly opened hot spot such as the **Shoreham** (p370) and have the best nightcap ever with a late-night trip to the top of the **Top of the Rock** (p156), which sends its last elevator up at 11pm. Day two should begin with more food, of course – but something different, like dim sum at **Dim Sum**

NEIGHBORHOODS

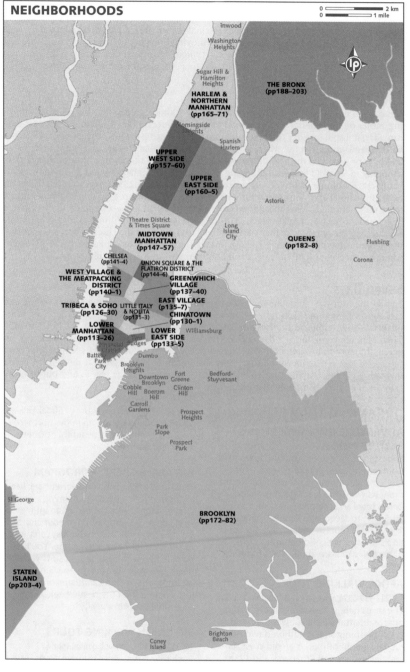

Sights

NEIGHBORHOODS

0 —————————— 2 km
0 —————————— 1 mile

Inwood

Washington
Heights

Sugar Hill &
Hamilton
Heights

**THE BRONX
(pp188–203)**

**HARLEM &
NORTHERN
MANHATTAN
(pp165–71)**

Morningside
Heights

Spanish
Harlem

**UPPER
WEST SIDE
(pp157–60)**

**UPPER
EAST SIDE
(pp160–5)**

Astoria

Theatre District
& Times Square

Long
Island
City

**QUEENS
(pp182–8)**

Flushing

**MIDTOWN
MANHATTAN
(pp147–57)**

Corona

**CHELSEA
(pp141–4)**

**UNION SQUARE & THE
FLATIRON DISTRICT
(pp144–6)**

**WEST VILLAGE &
THE MEATPACKING
DISTRICT
(pp140–1)**

**GREENWICH
VILLAGE
(pp137–40)**

**EAST VILLAGE
(p135–7)**

**TRIBECA & SOHO
(pp126–30)**

**LITTLE ITALY
& NOLITA
(pp131–3)**

**CHINATOWN
(pp130–1)**

**LOWER
MANHATTAN
(pp113–26)**

**LOWER
EAST SIDE
(pp133–5)**

Williamsburg

Battery
Park
City

Dumbo

Brooklyn
Heights

Downtown
Brooklyn

Fort
Greene

Bedford-
Stuyvesant

Cobble
Hill

Boerum
Hill

Clinton
Hill

Carroll
Gardens

Prospect
Heights

Park
Slope

Prospect
Park

St George

**BROOKLYN
(pp172–82)**

**STATEN
ISLAND
(pp203–4)**

Brighton
Beach

Coney
Island

Go Go (5 E Broadway btwn Catherine St & Chatham Sq, Lower East Side) in **Chinatown** (p230) – and then continue with a quirky guided tour (below) of your choice, to get either a lay of the land or a concentrated look at what fascinates you. Take a late-afternoon gallery walk through art-centric **Chelsea** (p141) and, after enjoying some happy-hour cocktails, settle into dinner right in the 'hood or at whatever eatery floats your boat (see Eating, p226). Enjoy a nightcap downtown, where you can rock out to a great local band at **Arlene's Grocery** (p294).

Four Days

Get a small dose of all the major tourist spots by taking a guided tour on your first morning, either on the **Circle Line ferry** (opposite) or a double-decker bus. Then follow the two-days itinerary; it'll spill into day three, so add onto that by hitting the wonderful **Greenmarket Farmers Market** (p146) in Union Sq, where you can sample artisanal cheeses and homemade bread and buy (or just ogle) the beautiful produce. Finish off the afternoon with some heavy-duty shopping in **Soho** and **Noho** (see Shopping Tour, p208) and collapse into a comfy downtown banquette for dinner at a trendy spot like **EN Japanese Brasserie** (p238). Drop your purchases off back at the hotel and venture out for a nearby cocktail nightcap. On your final day venture to an outer borough. Visit the storied **Coney Island** (p179) and take a stroll on the weathered boardwalk to nearby **Brighton Beach** (p181), where you can enjoy beer and pierogi while overlooking the ocean; take the **Staten Island Ferry** (p116) across the Hudson and poke around the neighborhood of St George (p203); or take the 7 train to **Jackson Heights** (p185), Queens, where an excellent blend of Indian and South American food and culture awaits.

Seven Days

Spread the four-day guideline out over five days, spending more time at each venue and tacking on something cultural – an indie flick at the **Film Forum** (p301), perhaps, or some quality theater, either in the **Broadway District** (p281) or at a quirky house like **PS 122** (p287). Then plan an excursion – a day trip via ferry boat to **Sandy Hook** (p391) in summer, or an overnight jaunt to the **Catskills** (p390) no matter what the season. If you have time when you return, choose a neighborhood that really intrigued you and explore it more fully, either through a guided walking tour (p206) or a DIY crawl that takes you in and out of every café, shop and watering hole that moves you.

ORGANIZED TOURS

ADVENTURE ON A SHOESTRING
☎ 212-265-2663; $5
Shoestring founder and tour guide Howard Goldberg believes people deserve to get *more* than their money's worth, not just their money's worth. He leads neighborhood-based tours and themed walks, such as his Salute to Jacqueline Kennedy Onassis. 'We've done tours in driving rain, blackouts and subway strikes,' Goldberg says. What a perfect way to learn about NYC's fortitude.

AFOOT WALKING TOURS
☎ 212-939-0994; www.erickwashington.com; $15
The focus here is a geographically unique one: Manhattanville, a subject that guide Eric K Washington has authored two books on. The neighborhood is an old West Harlem enclave around Broadway and 125th St; get to know it through Eric's lively walks that look at African American history. You

can also choose from tours of Sugar Hill, an architecturally rich region in the northern part of Harlem, or the beautiful northern stretch of Riverside Park.

BIG APPLE GREETER PROGRAM
☎ 212-669-8159; www.bigapplegreeter.org; free
If you find NYC a bit overwhelming – and who wouldn't? – call to set up an intimate stroll, in the neighborhood of your choice, led by a local volunteer who just can't wait to show off his or her city to you. You'll be matched with a guide that suits your needs, whether that means speaking Spanish or American Sign Language, or knowing just where to find the best wheelchair-accessible spots in the city.

BIG ONION WALKING TOURS
☎ 212-439-1090; www.bigonion.com; $15
'Each tour has a very extensive script,' says Big Onion founder Seth Kamil. It's that attention to fine detail in this grand city that

makes the awardwinning Big Onion – whose tours 'explore the many layers of history' – stand apart, and gives it a stellar reputation. Choose from nearly 30 tours, including Brooklyn Bridge and Brooklyn Heights, the 'Official' Gangs of New York Tour, A Gay and Lesbian History Tour – Before Stonewall, and Park Slope.

BIKE THE BIG APPLE
☎ 877-865-0078; www.bikethebigapple.com; $55-69 incl bike & helmet

Biking tours let you cover more breadth than walking tours – and give you a healthy dose of exercise to boot. Bike the Big Apple, recommended by NYC & Company, offers four set tours. Its most popular is the six-hour Back to the Old Country – the Ethnic Apple Tour, 12 miles of riding that covers Williamsburg, Roosevelt Island and the east side of Manhattan. Other tours visit the Bronx's Little Italy, city parks and Manhattan at night.

CIRCLE LINE BOAT TOURS Map pp452-3
☎ 212-563-3200; www.circleline42.com; 42nd St at Twelfth Ave; $18-28

The classic Circle Line – whose local 1970s TV-commercial song is now the stuff of kitschy nostalgia – guides you through all the biggie sights from the safe distance of a boat that circumnavigates the five boroughs. It's got a bar on board and has a bit of a party reputation (especially its two-hour evening cruise); other options include a three-hour day trip and an abbreviated 75-minute journey.

EXPERIENCE CHINATOWN Map pp444-5
☎ 212-619-4785; www.moca-nyc.org; Museum of Chinese in the Americas, 70 Mulberry St at Bayard St; $12

To truly penetrate the layers that make up the bustling, insiders' world of Chinatown, you need a guide. And trusting one from the Chinatown-based Museum of Chinese in the Americas (p131) is definitely a good move. The tours, given weekly from May through December, are led by museum docents with family roots in the community, and give you a sense of Chinatown's past and present.

FOODS OF NEW YORK
☎ 212-239-1124; www.foodsofny.com; $38

The official foodie tour of NYC & Company offers various three-hour tours that help

you eat your way through gourmet shops in either Chelsea or the West Village. Prepare thyself for a moving feast of French bread, fresh Italian pasta, global cheeses, real New York pizza, local fish and fresh-baked pastries.

GRAY LINE
☎ 212-397-2620; www.newyorksightseeing.com; $38-75

The most ubiquitous guided tour in the city, Gray Line is responsible for bombarding New York streets with the red double-decker buses that locals love to hate. Really, though, for a comprehensive tour of the big sights, it's a great way to go. The company offers nearly 30 different options, the best being both the popular hop-on, hop-off loops of Manhattan. Tours are available in various languages, including Japanese, French, German and Italian.

GREENWICH VILLAGE LITERARY PUB CRAWL
☎ 212-613-5796; www.bakerloo.org/pubcrawl; 567 Hudson Ave at 11th St; $15

Every lit-head's heard about Dylan Thomas meeting his alcoholic fate at the White Horse Tavern. But what was the real deal? Join this troupe of Bakerloo actors who take you for drinks at a lineup of neighborhood pubs; actors play the part of different writers and share stories about themselves and the surroundings from back in the day. The group meets Saturdays at 2pm at the White Horse (Map p448).

A HIP-HOP LOOK AT NEW YORK
Map pp452-3
☎ 212-714-3527; www.hushtours.com; 252 Fifth Ave btwn 30th and 31st Sts; $80

Learn about the true roots of local hip-hop with a bus or walking tour led by a 'hip-hop pioneer' (Kool DJ Herc, LA Sunshine and Raheim among them) through Manhattan and the Bronx, complete with a soul-food meal, a dance performance and a freestylin' battle at the end. Kurtis Blow leads a spiritual Harlem Hip-Hop Church Tour, too.

KRAMER'S REALITY TOUR Map p282
☎ 212-268-5525, 800-572-6377; Producers Club Theater, 358 W 44th St; $39

Seinfeld may be ancient TV history by now, but this quirky bus tour given by the real inspiration for the Kramer character still sells out, often weeks in advance. Its focus is, of course, locales made famous by the hit series. For die-hard fans only.

LIBERTY HELICOPTER TOURS

Map pp452-3

☎ 212-967-6464; www.libertyhelicopters.com; Twelfth Ave at W 30th St & East River's Pier 6; per person 2-30min $30-184, 15min Romance Over Manhattan (for up to 4 people) $849

Enjoy a bird's-eye view of the city in a very Donald Trump sort of way, as a helicopter whisks you high above the skyscrapers. Just get ready to shell out for the privilege.

MUNICIPAL ART SOCIETY

☎ 212-935-3960; www.mas.org; $12-15

With an expert focus on architecture, this nonprofit society is dedicated to championing urban design. It takes groups on walking or bus tours of structural gems, including those of Madison Ave, Bedford-Stuyvesant and Jackson Heights. Its most popular is a walk-through of the beaux arts Grand Central Terminal. See the website for schedules.

NEWROTIC NEW YORK CITY TOURS

☎ 718-575-8451; www.newroticnewyorkcitytours .com; adult/child $199/99

Lifelong Queens resident Marc Preven guides you through his largely undiscovered borough, with emphases on the culturally rich neighborhoods of Elmhurst and Jackson Heights. Plus, visit Louis Armstrong's home in Corona, wander through several massive ethnic supermarkets, ride the 'international express' 7 train and check out the Museum of the Moving Image.

NEW YORK GALLERY TOURS

Map pp452-3

☎ 212-946-1548; www.nygallerytours.com; 526 W 26th St at Tenth Ave; $15

You know you're supposed to check out the array of amazing modern-art galleries in Chelsea. But where to begin? This excellent guided tour – with additional gay and lesbian tours that focus on a 'queer aesthetic' – takes you to a slew of galleries and provides helpful commentary along the way.

NY TOUR GODDESS NEW YORK TOURS

☎ 212-535-7798; www.nytourgoddess.com; per hr $150, negotiable with group bookings

Quirky guide Jane Marx, who's made careers of acting, writing and teaching, blends all of her talents for a huge range of tours that focus on providing intimate portraits of her city. 'I'm off the wall,' she admits. 'But I'm so knowledgeable.' Tours, which are not cheap, range from Wall St and Little Italy to Union Sq and Harlem.

ON LOCATION TOURS

☎ 212-209-3370; www.screentours.com; $15-40

Face it: you want to sit on Carrie Bradshaw's apartment stoop and visit the design studio from *Will & Grace*. This company offers four tours – covering *Sex and the City, The Sopranos*, general TV and movie locations, and movie locations in Central Park – that let you live out your entertainment-obsessed fantasies.

PHOTOTREK TOURS

☎ 212-410-2514; www.phototrektours.com; $100-175

If the photo record of your trip is just as – if not more – important than the experience itself (you know who you are), let guide and photographer Marc Samuels (or a member of his capable staff) lead you through some of the most picturesque spots in the city, and take professional photos of you in front of each one. Choose from Central Park, Midtown and downtown; tours are for private groups or couples only.

ROCK JUNKET NEW YORK CITY

☎ 212-209-3370; www.rockjunket.com; $25

Join rockin' guide Bobby Pinn each Saturday at 11am for a two-hour tour that relives the good ol' East Village days of punk and glam rock. Learn cool tidbits about CBGB, the Ramones, the New York Dolls, the Velvet Underground, Fillmore East, Iggy Pop and others through onsite visits and in-the-know discourse.

A SLICE OF BROOKLYN PIZZA TOUR

☎ 212-209-3370; www.bknypizza.com; $45 (incl pizza)

The effusive Brooklyn Borough President Marty Markowitz just loves this focused tour. And who wouldn't want to spend more than four hours downing a gut-busting range of insanely delicious slices, from the brick-oven

DIY NYC

We at Lonely Planet are dedicated to providing comprehensive and in-depth coverage of every country and city we write about. But more than that, we are dedicated to creating a sustainable global traveler culture, which is why we say that the greatest adventure is to fly by the seat of your pants. And so, as antithetical as it may seem, we want you to put the guidebook down for a day – or even a week – and try exploring this big bad city on your own, in ways that you just won't find in the pages of this guide. We'll happily jumpstart your exploration with some ideas: stroll Central Park or Prospect Park without any agenda. Jump onto a passing bus and ride it until you feel like getting off, then explore the neighborhood you've landed in. Get lost among the illogical, diagonal streets of the far West Village. Read the bulletin board at a local café and find an announcement for a performance going on that night – and then go to it. Hail a cab and ask the driver to take you to his favorite lunch spot, where you'll no doubt delight in an obscure and affordable ethnic feast. Afterward, if you've had a great, off-beat travel experience, let us know about it! Tell us your stories at www.lonelyplanet.com/feedback.

Neapolitan style of Grimaldi's to the authentic Sicilian squares of L&B Spumoni Gardens? A guide mouths off about the neighborhoods of Bay Ridge, Red Hook, Bensonhurst and more while you're chewing.

TOURS OF THE CITY WITH JUSTIN FERATE

☎ 212-223-2777; www.justinsnewyork.com; free–$325

A former educator and tour director, Ferate, who also has a background in architecture, now pours all of his knowledge into his extensive tours. He offers a free trip through Grand Central Terminal and Midtown every Friday, as well as intensive walking tours that, as part of the continuing education program of the Cooper Union college, focus on a different neighborhood each week.

WATSON ADVENTURES SCAVENGER HUNTS

☎ 212-726-1529; www.watsonadventures.com; $20-30

Go beyond walking and talking with Watson, which turns each tour into a game by making you hunt for things – be it answers to interesting questions or quirky items – as you go about your journey. Tours vary, but most are great for children, such as hunts in both the Metropolitan Museum of Art and Museum of Natural History, which have you scour the grounds for mummies, knights and bones.

WILDMAN STEVE BRILL

☎ 914-835-2153; www.wildmanstevebrill.com; adult/child $12/6

New York's best-known naturalist – betchya didn't know there were any! – has been leading folks on foraging expeditions through

city parks for more than 20 years. He'll trek with you through Central Park, Prospect Park, Inwood Park and many more, teaching you to identify natural riches including sassafras, chickweed, ginko nuts, garlic and wild mushrooms along the way. It's wild!

LOWER MANHATTAN

Eating p227, Drinking p262, Shopping p321, Sleeping p354

Manhattan comes to a narrow triangle at its southern tip, forming the general swath known as Lower Manhattan. Teeming with iconic images that include Wall St, City Hall, the Statue of Liberty offshore in the distance and, of course, the memory of the Twin Towers and the everlasting scars of September 11, it's a small region that manages to pack quite a diverse wallop. It's come back to life in a big way since the tragedy, and, though developers and government officials and everyday New Yorkers are still bickering over how to best reincarnate the actual World Trade Center (WTC) grounds (see p126 for more on that), there's been quite a stream of positive growth going on all around it. Residents, lured by post–September 11 low rents subsidized by tax-free Liberty Bonds, have entered in droves, creating a young and hip (if quiet-at-night) little neighborhood scene. It's now the fastest growing residential 'hood in New York. New museums – from the International Sports Museum to the newly relocated Museum of American Finance – are moving in and creating a sort of cultural boom. And among the most positive news has been the start of construction on a $2.21 billion project that will create the WTC Transportation Hub – an architecturally slick and joyously practical station that will connect the PATH rapid-transit system of New Jersey to all subway lines and to the

World Financial Center Ferry Terminal via a complex maze of underground passageways. The high-reaching hub is slated for a 2009 completion date.

Meanwhile, life goes on, bustling on weekdays with stock traders, bankers, government employees, housing lawyers and politicians, who rush to and from meetings and power lunches all day long. Among all the action is a steadily increasing rush of visitors 'rediscovering the amazing vitality of the area,' according to Kevin Rampe, president of the Lower Manhattan Development Corporation (LMDC, formed in the wake of September 11). Visitors can choose from more than 25 museums and cultural attractions – browse through the offerings and get updates on the area via the website of a newly formed umbrella group, the Museums of Lower Manhattan (www.lowermanhattan.info/nystarts here), which aims to increase awareness of the area's offerings. And so far, it seems to be working. So go south and discover! While you're there, look for red-vested members of the **Alliance for Downtown New York** (Map pp444–5; ☎ 212-566-6700; www.downtownny.com; Suite 3340, 120 Broadway), who hand out maps and offer neighborhood factoids to intrepid explorers.

Orientation

Lower Manhattan encompasses the area below Canal St (where you'll also find a section of Chinatown) down to Battery Park, including the Financial District and Tribeca, the 'Triangle Below Canal St' (though that 'hood is covered in the next section, along with Soho). Waterfront areas include South Street Seaport and the New York Harbor, home to both Lady Liberty and Ellis Island.

NEW YORK HARBOR

Just like the city's first immigrants, foreigners – whether from as close as New Jersey or as far as Australia – often make a beeline down here to recapture that initial feeling of excitement. And it's a fine way to do it – not only because of the Statue of Liberty and Ellis Island, but because of the gorgeous waterfront lawns and bike paths of Battery Park, festive outdoor concerts at Castle Clinton and overall big-sky feeling you get just from lazing on benches or grassy patches along the shoreline.

STATUE OF LIBERTY Map p442

☎ 212-363-3200; www.nps.gov/stli (or www.circle linedowntown.com for ferry info); admission free, ferry (incl Ellis Island) adult/senior/child $11.50/9.50/4.50; ☻ ferries every 30min 9:30am-3:30pm; ☻ 4, 5 to Bowling Green

The Statue of Liberty is one of the most recognizable icons in the world, right up there with the Eiffel Tower, Mount Rushmore and the Taj Mahal. The image is beloved, and has been coopted by everyone from a local car-rental agency to the city's women's basketball team, New York Liberty. Surprisingly, a great majority of local New Yorkers have never even visited the Lady – though you'd be hard-pressed to find one who didn't greatly admire her from afar as the enduring symbol of freedom that has stood in New York Harbor since 1886.

Following September 11, the statue joined the list of many other city landmarks that became hyper-protected and off-limits to the public. Its interior, crown and museum remained closed for almost two years after that fateful day, until reopening with much fanfare in July 2004 following a multimillion-dollar renovation. Although you still cannot enter the statue itself – a very sad fact for those who have never experienced the thrill

One New York babe you won't forget (above)

of climbing more than 300 steps to the crown for an incredible view – you can now visit its museum and peer into its intricate interior through a glass ceiling at the Lady's base, all under the watchful eye of an official park ranger. Or enjoy the view from the 16-story observation deck, which reopened as well.

Although the ferry ride (run by the Circle Line) lasts only 15 minutes, a trip to both the Statue of Liberty and Ellis Island is an all-day affair. In summer, you may wait up to an hour to embark on an 800-person ferry, and reservations, which yield a 'time pass' (a ticket that specifies a time to enter), are strongly encouraged (although a very limited number of passes are available on a walk-up basis). A less crowded approach to the Statue is via **Liberty State Park** (which can be reached by car, taxi or a combo of the PATH/ light rail; call ☎ 201-435-9499 or visit www .libertystatepark.org for details) in New Jersey.

The Statue of Liberty, modeled after the Colossus of Rhodes, was the brainchild of political activist Edouard René Lefebvre de Laboulaye and sculptor Frédéric-Auguste Bartholdi. In 1865 the pair decided something monumental should be created to promote French republicanism and celebrate friendship between France and the US (this was way before the idea of boycotting French fries was a twinkle in any American's eye). Bartholdi dedicated most of the next 20 years to turning his dream – of creating the monument and mounting it in the New York Harbor – into reality. The American Committee for the Statue solicited donations from the public, and Bartholdi got busy creating his work of art, which included a metal framework designed by railway engineer Gustave Eiffel.

In 1883 poet Emma Lazarus published a poem called *The New Colossus* as part of a fund-raising campaign for a statue pedestal, and her words have long since been associated with the monument, and with its connection to newly arrived immigrants: 'Give me your tired, your poor. Your huddled masses yearning to breathe free. The wretched refuse of your teeming shore. Send these, the homeless, tempest-tost to me. I lift my lamp beside the golden door!' But ironically, these famous words were added to the base only in 1901, 17 years after the poet's death. On October 28, 1886, the 151ft Liberty Enlightening the World was finally unveiled in New York Harbor.

In 1956 the US Congress approved plans for New York to work with the National Park Service to enlarge the base, add a museum and declare it a National Park monument. By the 1980s the statue was in dire need of restoration, and more than $100 million was spent to shore up Lady Liberty for her centennial. The oxidized (and, therefore, green) copper skin required substantial work, and workers installed a new gold-plated torch, the third in the statue's history.

ELLIS ISLAND Map p442

☎ 212-363-3200; www.nps.gov/elis (or www.circle linedowntown.com for ferry info); admission free, ferry (incl Statue of Liberty) adult/senior/child $11.50/9.50/4.50; ⏰ ferries every 30min 9:30am-3:30pm; ◉ 4, 5 to Bowling Green

Ferries to the Statue of Liberty make a second stop at Ellis Island, an icon of mythical proportions for the descendants of the more than 12 million immigrants who passed through here. The process involved getting checked by doctors, being issued new names if their own was too difficult to spell or pronounce, and basically getting the green light to start their new, hopeful and often frighteningly difficult lives here in the teeming city of New York. Now anybody who rides the ferry to the island can get a cleaned-up, modern version of the experience thanks to the impressive **Immigration Museum** that's now housed in the massive redbrick building.

Ellis Island served as New York's main immigration station from 1892 until 1954, and processed a record number of 12,000 individuals daily from countries including Ireland, England, Germany and Austria; in its later years, after WWI and during the paranoia of the 'Red Scare' in this country, the immigration center became more of a de facto holding pen for newcomers believed to be radical threats to the US. After admitting its last arrival (a Norwegian merchant seaman) in 1954, the place closed due to changes in immigration law coupled with rising operating costs.

Fast forward to the 1990s, when a $160-million restoration project turned the abandoned structure into the extensive Immigration Museum, where you can explore the history of the island through a series of interactive galleries. The exhibits emphasize that, contrary to popular myth, most of the ship-borne immigrants were processed within eight hours and that conditions were generally clean and safe (especially for 1st- and 2nd-class passengers, who were processed on board; only immigrants from the steerage class were subjected to whatever conditions prevailed on Ellis Island). The 338ft-long registry room, with its beautiful vaulted tile ceiling, is where the polygamists, paupers, criminals and anarchists were turned around and sent back from where they came. Walking through the roomy, light-filled registry today is probably quite a contrast to the reality faced by thousands of newly arrived foreigners back in its heyday. But you will be joined by a crowd of a different sort, as about two million people now visit Ellis Island annually.

You can take a 50-minute audio tour of the facility for $6. But for an even more affecting take on history, pick up one of the phones in each display area and listen to the recorded memories of real Ellis Island immigrants, taped in the 1980s.

If you want still more, see **Embracing Freedom** (☎ 212-883-1986, ext 742; adult/senior & child over 14 $4/3), a 30-minute play about the Ellis Island experience that shows five times a day. A free 30-minute film on the immigrant experience, *Island of Hope, Island of Tears*, is also worth checking out, as is the exhibition on the influx of immigrants just before WWI; guided tours are available in American Sign Language.

To be sure you get onto a ferry, you should really secure a time pass by making advance reservations. However, if you're not one for planning in advance, you can take your chances by going for one of a limited number of time passes that are available to walkups on a first-come-first-served basis. Also, it should be noted that during the especially crowded summer months, there is a less crowded approach to Ellis Island, via ferry from New Jersey's Liberty State Park (see Statue of Liberty, p114, for more information).

GOVERNOR'S ISLAND Map p442
☎ 212-514-8285; www.nps.gov/gois; admission free; tours twice daily Tue-Sat summer only; ◎ 4, 5 to Bowling Green
For decades, New Yorkers knew this 172-acre swath of land only as an untouchable, mysterious patch of green out in the harbor. As of 2003, the Governor's Island National Monument (encompassing 22 acres) changed all that by beginning to offer

a ferry service to the little gem, along with 1½-hour guided walking tours. Taking them up on their offer is quite a treat, especially on a sunny day, as highlights of the haven, just a five-minute boat ride from Manhattan, include two 19th-century fortifications – Fort Jay and the three-tiered, sandstone Castle Williams – plus open lawns, massive shade trees and unsurpassed city views.

Its historic significance is far-reaching: besides serving as a success story in the Revolutionary War, the central army recruiting station during the Civil War and the take-off point for Wilbur Wright's historic 1909 first-ever flight, it's where the 1998 Reagan-Gorbachev summit signaled the beginning of the end of the Cold War. As far as the future of the island goes, it's yet to be determined, because a general management plan for the entire island – which open-space advocates hope will include plenty of parkland and public activities began in early 2006 and it will most likely require two year to bring this plan to its completion. Until then, services of this new National Monument are limited – tours, for example, take place only in the summertime – but New Yorkers are hopeful that it'll only offer more opportunities for learning and relaxing in the near future.

STATEN ISLAND FERRY Map pp444-5
☎ 311; free; every half hr; ◎ 1 to South Ferry or 4, 5 to Bowling Green
Staten Islanders know the fleet of hulking, dirty-orange ferry boats as commuter vehicles. Manhattanites like to think of the ferries as their secret little romantic, spring-day escape vessels. But the secret is long out, as many a tourist has been clued into the charms of the Staten Island Ferry, which provides one of the most wonderful, free adventures in New York. In service since 1905, the city celebrated its centennial with great fanfare in 2005, using it as a chance to promote the idea of visiting Staten Island – still an oddity to most New Yorkers. Today, the ferry service carries more than 19 million passengers each year across the 5.2-mile stretch of the Hudson River that separates downtown Manhattan from the Staten Island neighborhood of St George. So whether you choose to simply ride it there and back in one run – enjoying grand views of the city skyline, the Verrazano Narrows Bridge (connecting Staten Island to Brooklyn) and the Statue of Liberty – or stay and poke around the shores of St

George before catching a later ferry, it's sure to be a memorable experience. For a great DIY experience, take your bike aboard and head toward one of Staten Island's majestic parklands or sandy beaches.

BATTERY PARK CITY

This corner of the city is made up of beautiful juxtapositions: the gleaming, modern high-rise apartment buildings that look like a real-life Gotham City, and then the soft, tickly green carpet of the lengthy park's North Lawn, which hugs the water's edge. In the background is the fading sadness of September 11, and the empty sockets that used to hold this neighborhood's piece de resistance: the Twin Towers.

But while you're relaxing in the park here, it's easy to forget all that – or even that you're in NYC. Then you can turn around, putting your back to the water, and the glint of sunlight bouncing off the facades of skyscrapers will bring you right back to reality. It's a happy combo, and a wonderful one to experience first-hand.

The 30-acre waterfront swath of parkland stretches along the Hudson River from Chambers St to Pier 1 on the southern tip of the island, encompassing Rockefeller Park, the Battery Park City Esplanade, Robert F Wagner Park and Battery Park. It's a great opportunity for escape, with glorious sunsets and Statue of Liberty views, outdoor concerts and films in summer, playgrounds and soccer games, and smooth paths for cycling, running, strolling or blading.

For added entertainment value, the Park House near Rockefeller Park lets you borrow pogo sticks, basketballs, jump ropes, board games or billiard balls and a cue (for use on the outdoor tables gazing on Lady Liberty), free with identification. Kids will love romping in the playgrounds and climbing on the whimsical bronze sculptures by Tom Otterness. Plus the **Battery Park City Parks Conservancy** (☎ 212-267-9700; www .bpcparks.org) offers a range of free or low-fee walking tours, group swims, children's programs and classes in these parks; for information contact the Conservancy.

WATER, WATER, ALL AROUND

It tends to take a disaster of some level to remind New Yorkers that, living on an island, they are surrounded by water – and that, surrounded by water, boats and ferries are actually viable, if not highly efficient, means of transportation. It was September 11 that really sprang boat operators into action, rescuing survivors from downtown and transporting them to safety in New Jersey or Brooklyn, bringing to life the fleet of fire boats that sat waiting at their docks. With subways out of commission, passenger numbers on water taxis increased – just as they did during the three-day Transit Workers Union strike during the very cold winter of 2005. The waters – comprised of the Hudson River to the west, the East River to the east, and, to the south, the New York Harbor, Upper and Lower New York Bays and Atlantic Ocean – may not be as busy as in the days when New York was a truly bustling port, but they are still plied day in and day out with barges, freighters and tankers en route to Brooklyn's shores; water taxis going back and forth between Manhattan and New Jersey; pleasure voyages on sailboats, kayaks and the famous Circle Line; and gargantuan cruise ships (including the QE2, which has docked here at least twice), which arrive and leave like lying-down skyscrapers along the western shores of Midtown.

For more details on New York's water life of both today and the past, visit the **South Street Seaport Museum** (p123), which is home to a fleet of historic schooners. And then, get yourself out onto the water! Below are various ways for you to do it:

- For a 30-minute rush, take a ride on the **Beast** (☎ 212-630-8855; www.circleline42.com; $17), a tourist fave that will ferry you through the Hudson and around the Statue of Liberty at a brisk 45mph.
- Hop aboard the free and easy **Staten Island Ferry** (see opposite), where you'll join a crowd of commuters and enjoy great glimpses of the skyline.
- Go for a sunset sail aboard one of the South Street Seaport's historic schooners, such as the **Pioneer** (☎ 212-738-8786; $17).
- Take one of various sightseeing cruises with **New York Waterway** (☎ 800-533-3779; www.nywaterway.com) or the **Circle Line** (see p111).
- In the summertime, hop aboard a **SeaStreak** (www.seastreak.com), which will ferry you 30 minutes away to the wonderful beach getaway of Sandy Hook in New Jersey (see p391).
- Sink yourself into a kayak and paddle along the Hudson River with some equipment (and guidance) on a tour with the **Manhattan Kayak Company** (p310), or do some DIY paddling from the **Downtown Boathouse** (p309), where use of kayaks is absolutely free!

CASTLE CLINTON Map pp444-5

☎ 212-344-7220; www.nps.gov/cacl; Battery Park;
☪ 8am-5pm; ⊕ J, M, Z to Broad St, 1 to South Ferry
Built as a fort to defend the New York
Harbor during the War of 1812, the circular wall got its current moniker in 1817
to honor then-mayor DeWitt Clinton.
Later, and before Ellis Island opened to
immigrants, Castle Garden (as it was then
known) served as the major processing
center for new arrivals, welcoming more
than 8 million people between 1855 and
1890. Today it has been restored as a
national monument – after turns as an
opera house, entertainment complex and
aquarium – and now serves as a visitor
center, with historical displays, as well
as a massive performance space, where
musicians from The Stills to Beulah have
recently taken to the roofless stage for
summer shows under the stars.

IRISH HUNGER MEMORIAL

Map pp444-5
290 Vesey St at North End Ave, Battery Park; admission free; ⊕ 1, N, R to Cortlandt St
This compact and poignant labyrinth of
low limestone walls and patches of green
grass is the creation of artist Brian Tolle,
here to increase awareness of the Great
Irish Famine and Migration (1845–52),
which led so many immigrants to leave
the Republic for the opportunity of a
better life in the Big Apple. The winning
proposal in a 2000 design competition
organized by the Battery Park City Authority, Tolle's sculpture is an even more fitting
metaphor than he probably meant it to
be: it's turned out to be a delicate work,
and has already required extensive repairs
due to harsh winters that chipped away at
its structure.

MUSEUM OF JEWISH HERITAGE

Map pp444-5
☎ 646-437-4200; www.mjhnyc.org; 36 Battery Pl;
adult/senior/student $10/7/5, free 4-8pm Wed;
☪ 10am-5:45pm Sun-Tue & Thu, 10am-8pm Wed,
10am-5pm Fri; ⊕ 4, 5 to Bowling Green
This 30,000-sq-ft waterfront memorial museum, with a six-sided shape and three tiers
to symbolize the Star of David and the six
million Jews who perished in the Holocaust,
explores all aspects of what it means to be
Jewish in modern-day New York. Displays
include personal artifacts, photographs,
and documentary films. A centerpiece of
the museum is the *Garden of Stones* – an
outdoor memorial garden, created by artist
Andy Goldsworthy, in which 18 boulders
form a narrow pathway for contemplating
the fragility of life, dedicated to those who
have lost loved ones in the Holocaust. An
onsite kosher café, **Abigael's at the Museum**,
serves light food during museum hours,
and the 375-seat Safra Hall is a great venue
for films, plays, ongoing lecture series and
special holiday performances.

NEW YORK CITY POLICE MUSEUM

Map pp444-5
☎ 212-480-3100; www.nycpolicemuseum.org;
100 Old Slip; adult/senior/child suggested donation
$5/3/1; ☪ 10am-5pm Tue-Sat, 11am-5pm Sun;
⊕ 1 to South Ferry, 2, 3 to Wall St
This small and basic museum is chock-full of
interesting facts and exhibits. Check out the
cool old police vehicles (some which sit right
in the museum, others, like a 1939 beauty,
are simply pictured), photos and weapons
of some of New York's most notorious
criminals (from Willie Sutton to Al Capone),
a collection of police shields and uniforms
from throughout the decades, NYPD leader-

THE SPHERE AND NOW

Partially damaged in the World Trade Center attacks, the **Sphere** (Map pp444–5; Bowling Green entrance, Battery Park;
⊕ 4, 5 to Bowling Green) used to stand atop a granite fountain in a plaza between the WTC towers. Now this 45,000lb,
15ft-wide orb stands as an indestructible reminder of its past home. Creating an overpowering aura of enduring strength
on the edge of this bustling park, the display tends to instantly quiet even the most hyped-up, post–Statue of Liberty
tourists to come upon it. Artist Fritz Koenig's massive steel and bronze sculpture, created in 1971 as a symbol of peace
through world trade, was moved here as a tribute to the dead shortly after September 11, and a hearty gash across
its center is a potent reminder of what it has been through. The piece is now fronted by an eternal flame, and has a
simple plaque at its base: 'In honor of all those who were lost,' it reads, 'the Sphere endures as an icon of hope and the
indestructible spirit of this country.'

ship histories, and a moving September 11 memorial exhibit called the *Hall of Heroes*.

NEW YORK UNEARTHED Map pp444-5
☎ 212-748-8628; www.southstseaport.org /archaeology/nyunearthed.shtm; 17 State St btwn Pearl & Whitehall Sts; admission free; ☽ noon-5pm Mon-Fri; ◉ N, R to Whitehall St, 4, 5 to Bowling Green, 1 to South Ferry

Who knows what you may find here! Shards of dinnerware, pieces of a pipe, old shoes – they help you piece together more than 6000 years of NYC history. This archaeologist-staffed outpost of the South Street Seaport, just across the street from Battery Park, is filled with artifacts mined from city sites, including 850,000 remnants of the 19th-century Five Points neighborhood (depicted in the film *Gangs of New York*) and a three-dimensional cross section of an archaeological site. The exhibits here – and friendly staff – are great for kids.

SHRINE TO ST ELIZABETH ANN SETON Map pp444-5
☎ 212-269-6865; Our Lady of the Rosary, 7 State St; admission free; ☽ 6:30am-5pm Mon-Fri, before & after 12:15pm Mass Sat & 9am & noon Masses Sun; ◉ N, R, W to Whitehall St

This mystical, silent escape from the city is a tiny church and shrine to Mother Seton, housed in the redbrick Federal-style home where America's first saint herself lived in 1801. Born in NYC, Elizabeth Ann married and had five children but was eventually widowed, which inspired her to become a nun and found the Sisters of Charity. Today, devotees can often be found on their knees, praying inside this spiritual space at all hours of the day.

SKYSCRAPER MUSEUM Map pp444-5
☎ 212-968-1961; www.skyscraper.org; 39 Battery Pl; adult/senior & student $5/2.50; ☽ noon-6pm Wed-Sun; ◉ 4, 5 to Bowling Green

Occupying the ground-floor space of the Ritz-Carlton Hotel, this wonderful ode to skyscrapers the world over features two galleries. One focuses on rotating exhibits, with past shows that have looked at the World Trade Center, a new generation of environmentally-sustainable skyscrapers and the top 10 NYC building picks of various experts (the Chrysler Building won by a landslide). The other half of the museum is

dedicated to a permanent study of high-rise history, including a size chart of the world's biggest buildings (Taiwan's Taipei 101 is currently in the lead – in 2004, it's a whopping 1670ft high!), as well as exhibits on building the Empire State Building and an overview of downtown architecture. The museum is also home to the cutting-edge technology known as VIVA: the Visual Index to the Virtual Archive, a visually based interface that uses a 3-D computer model of Manhattan as a click-on map, allowing users to see the city, past and present, and to access the museum's collections through an online database (you can access it via the museum's website).

ST PAUL'S CHAPEL Map pp444-5
☎ 212-602-0800; www.saintpaulschapel.org; Broadway at Fulton St; ◉ 2, 3 to Fulton St

George Washington worshiped here after his inauguration in 1789, and that was the biggest claim to fame for this colonial-era church (part of Trinity Church, which sits further down Broadway) prior to September 11. After that fateful day, when the World Trade Center destruction occurred just a block behind this Classic Revival brownstone, the mighty structure became a spiritual support center for all who needed it. Volunteers worked round the clock, serving meals, setting up beds, doling out massages and counseling rescue workers. Today a moving, interactive exhibit, *Unwavering Spirit: Hope & Healing at Ground Zero*, sits beneath the elegant cut-glass chandeliers, bringing streams of people who are still searching for healing and understanding. The church, which functions more as a spiritual community center, also hosts workshops, special events and the popular Trinity Concerts, a free classical-music series with performances on Monday at 1pm.

WORLD FINANCIAL CENTER Map pp444-5
☎ 212-945-2600; www.worldfinancialcenter.com; 200 Liberty St; ◉ A, C, 4, 5 to Fulton St–Broadway Nassau

This mall-like complex, behind the former WTC site, stands on the landfill created by the excavation for the WTC's foundation. A group of four office towers surrounds the Winter Garden, a palm-and-light-filled glass atrium that hosts free concerts and dance performances throughout the year. This is a good place to head if the weather turns nasty as you can pass an hour or so by shopping at the various chain stores (Ann Taylor, Banana Republic, Gap) or eating at the large food-court area. It's also the best spot to get a bird's-eye view of Ground Zero; head to the second floor of the Winter Garden, where the Lower Manhattan Development Corporation has set up a memorial installation that includes 3-D models and videos to let the public in on (constantly changing) redevelopment plans.

WALL STREET & THE FINANCIAL DISTRICT

Anchored by the mile-long and world-famous Wall St, which was named for a defensive wall the Dutch built in 1653 to mark the northern line of New Amsterdam, this history-steeped area is where the US Congress first convened and where America's first president, George Washington, was inaugurated. The concentrated feel of the area is distinguished by intimate, circuitous and sometimes confusing side streets flanked by stoic Federal homes, Greek Revival temples, Gothic churches, Renaissance palazzos and a fine collection of early-20th-century skyscrapers. Though the New York Stock Exchange has been closed to visitors 'for security purposes' since September 11, tourists still gather on the sidewalk to gawk at harried traders who scurry in and out for cigarettes and hot dogs before getting back to their frenzied business. Nearby is the Federal Reserve Bank, where just glancing at the hushed, guarded exteriors is a good reminder that you have most definitely stumbled into the seat of capitalism.

AMERICAN NUMISMATIC SOCIETY
Map pp444–5

☎ 212-234-3130; www.numismatics.org; 96 Fulton St at William St; admission free; ⏰ 9:30am-4:30pm Tue-Fri, closed noon-1pm; ◉ A, C, J, M, Z, 2, 3, 4, 5 to Fulton St–Broadway Nassau

The society was formerly part of the Audubon Tce collection of museums in Inwood. In 2004 it moved its large permanent collection of coins, medals and paper money downtown, appropriately, to the stately Donald Groves Building in the Financial District.

BOWLING GREEN Map pp444–5

cnr Broadway & State St; ◉ 4, 5 to Bowling Green

New York's oldest – and possibly tiniest – park is believed to have been the spot where Dutch settler Peter Minuit paid Native Americans $24 to purchase Manhattan Island. The verdant triangle was leased by the people of New York from the English crown beginning in 1733, for the token amount of one peppercorn each. But an angry mob, inspired by George Washington's nearby reading of the Declaration of Independence, descended upon the site in 1776 and tore down a large statue of King George III; a fountain now stands in its place. The 7000lb bronze Charging Bull sculpture by Arturo Di Modica, which sits famously at the northern edge of the park, was actually placed here permanently after it appeared mysteriously in front of the New York Stock Exchange in 1989, two years after a market crash. Now it's the unwitting subject of constant tourist photos, and an unintentional Wall St icon.

ASHES TO ASHES: THE AFRICAN BURIAL GROUND

Sitting among the financial movers and shakers and beautiful old official buildings is a quiet piece of very important history: the African Burial Ground (Map pp444–5; ☎ 212-337-2001; www.africanburialground.com; 290 Broadway btwn Duane & Elk Sts; ⏰ 9am-4pm Mon-Fri; ◉ 4, 5 to Wall St). Builders were shocked when, during preliminary construction of a downtown office building in 1991, more than 400 stacked wooden caskets were discovered only 16ft to 28ft below street level. When it became clear that the boxes held the remains of enslaved Africans (the nearby Trinity Church graveyard had banned burial of Africans at the time), construction was halted, an investigation was launched and all hell broke loose – Mayor David Dinkins rallied and citizens held protests and vigils, demanding that no building be erected on such sacred ground. The rally cries worked; today the site is permanently protected as a National Historic Landmark. It's an ongoing project to memorialize those buried here, overseen by both the National Park Service and the Harlem-based Schomburg Center for Research in Black Culture. It's all under the management of the US General Services Administration, which held a ceremonial groundbreaking at the site in late 2005 for a permanent memorial.

FEDERAL HALL Map pp444-5

☎ 212-825-6888; www.nps.gov/feha; 26 Wall St; admission free; ◉ 2, 3, 4, 5 to Wall St, J, M, Z to Broad St

Federal Hall, which contains a museum dedicated to postcolonial New York, was closed to the public for an extensive renovation at the time of research. It is slated to reopen in September 2006.

The building, distinguished by a huge statue of George Washington, stands on the site of New York's original City Hall, where the first US Congress convened and Washington took the oath of office on April 30, 1789, as the first US chief executive. After that structure's demolition in the early 19th century, this Greek Revival building gradually rose in its place between 1834 and 1842. Considered to be one of the country's premier examples of classical architecture, it served as the US customs house until 1862. It's also a place that played a significant role for freedom of the press, as it's where John Peter Zenger was jailed, tried and acquitted of libel for exposing government corruption in his newspaper – a history lesson that cannot be underplayed enough today. Call for details on opening hours.

Wall Street brokers come up for air at Federal Hall (above)

FEDERAL RESERVE BANK Map pp444-5

☎ 212-720-6130; 33 Liberty St at Nassau St; admission free; ◉ tours hourly 9:30am-2:30pm (except 12:30pm) Mon-Fri; ◉ J, Z to Fulton St–Broadway Nassau

The only reason to visit the Federal Reserve Bank is to ogle the facility's high-security vault – more than 10,000 tons of gold reserves reside here, 80ft below ground.

You'll only see a small part of that fortune, but you'll learn a lot about the US Federal Reserve System on the informative tour. You can also browse through an exhibition of coins and counterfeit currency. Reservations – made five days in advance – are required for the comprehensive tour.

FRAUNCES TAVERN MUSEUM

Map pp444-5

☎ 212-425-1778; www.frauncestavernmuseum .org; 54 Pearl St; adult/senior, student & child $4/3; ◉ noon-5pm Tue, Wed, Fri, 10am-7pm Thu, 10am-5pm Sat; ◉ 4, 5 to Bowling Green, 2, 3 to Wall St

This museum-restaurant sits in a block of historic structures that, along with nearby Stone St and the South Street Seaport, comprises the best-preserved examples of early-18th-century New York architecture.

The site was originally built as a tony residence for merchant Stephan Delancey's family; barkeeper Samuel Fraunces purchased it in 1762, turning it into the Queen's Head Tavern in honor of the US victory in the Revolutionary War. It was in the 2nd-floor dining room on December 4, 1783, that George Washington bade farewell to the officers of the Continental Army after the British relinquished control of New York City. In the 19th century, the tavern was closed and the building fell into disuse. It was also damaged during several massive fires that swept through old downtown areas, destroying most colonial buildings and nearly all Dutch-built structures. In 1904, the Sons of the Revolution historical society bought the building and returned it to an approximation of its colonial-era look – an act believed to be the first major attempt at historical preservation in the USA. In 1975 the Fuerzas Armadas de Liberación Nacional, a radical group from Puerto Rico, detonated a bomb here, killing five people.

The museum hosts lunchtime and evening lecture series, historical walking tours and various rotating exhibits, such as the recent *Fighting for Freedom: Black Patriots and Black Loyalists*.

Just across the street from the tavern are the excavated remains of the old Dutch Stadt Huys, which served as New Amsterdam's administrative center, courthouse and jail from 1641 until the British takeover in 1664. This building, destroyed in 1699, was originally on the city's waterfront until landfill added a few more blocks to southern Manhattan. The excavation here between 1979 and

1980 was the city's first large-scale archaeo-logical investigation, and it reaped many artifacts (including the privy and cistern remains displayed under Plexiglas).

MUSEUM OF AMERICAN FINANCE
Map pp444-5
☎ 212-908-4110; www.financialhistory.org; 48 Wall St; ⊖ 2, 3, 4, 5 to Wall St

One of the shining new examples of Lower Manhattan's cultural renaissance is this formerly under-the-radar tribute to finance. Now, with a snappy new name (it used to be called the Museum of American Finan-cial History) and stunning new location (28 Broadway was its former home) that is slated to open in late 2006, this mu-seum is ready for its close-up. Comprising 30,000 sq ft in the old Bank of New York headquarters, it's a grand space featur-ing 30ft ceilings, high arched windows, a majestic staircase to the mezzanine, glass chandeliers, and murals depicting historic scenes of banking and commerce. Exhibits will focus on historic moments in American financial history, and permanent collections include rare 18th-century documents, stock and bond certificates from the Gilded Age, the oldest known photograph of Wall St, and a stock ticker from 1867.

NATIONAL MUSEUM OF THE AMERICAN INDIAN Map pp444-5
☎ 212-514-3700; www.nmai.si.edu; 1 Bowling Green; admission free; ⏱ 10am-5pm Fri-Wed, 10am-8pm Thu; ⊖ 4, 5 to Bowling Green

This museum, an affiliate of the Smithso-nian Institution, is housed in the spectacu-lar former US Customs House on Bowling Green. It's an ironically grand space for the USA's leading museum on Native American art, established by oil heir George Gustav Heye in 1916. The facility's information center is in the former duties collection office, with computer banks located next to old wrought-iron teller booths.

The galleries are on the 2nd floor, be-yond a vast rotunda featuring statues of famous navigators and murals celebrating shipping history. This museum does little to explain the history of Native Americans but instead concentrates on Native American culture, boasting a million-item collection of crafts and everyday objects. Computer touch screens feature insights into Native American life and beliefs, and working

artists often offer explanations of their techniques. The museum also hosts a range of cultural programs, including dance and music performances, readings for children, craft demonstrations, films and workshops.

NATIONAL SPORTS MUSEUM
Map pp444-5
☎ 212-837-7950; www.thesportsmuseum.com; 26 Broadway at Bowling Green; ⊖ 4, 5 to Bowling Green

The newest cultural offering in these parts, set to open in late 2006, is jock heaven: 100,000 sq ft comprising the first-ever all-sports museum in the country. Located in the landmark former Standard Oil Building and funded ($60 million!) by post–September 11 Liberty Bonds and private investors, it's found partnerships in all sorts of athletic organizations, including the Basketball, Hockey, World Golf and College Football Halls of Fame; Nascar; the Negro Leagues Museum; and the Yogi Berra Museum. Expect gallery exhibits on every conceivable sport, from basketball and tennis to swim-ming, hockey, equestrian events and speed racing. Call for details about opening hours.

NEW YORK STOCK EXCHANGE
Map pp444-5
☎ 212-656-5168; www.nyse.com; 8 Broad St; ⊖ 1, 2, 4, 5 to Wall St, J, M, Z to Broad St

Though Wall St is the widely recognized symbol for US capitalism, the world's best-known stock exchange (NYSE) is actually right here on Broad St. Before it closed to the public due to stepped-up security measures, more than 700,000 visitors a year passed behind the portentous Romanesque facade to see where about a billion shares valued at around $44 billion change hands daily.

Feel free to gawk outside the exchange, though, where you'll see dozens of bro-kers dressed in color-coordinated trading jackets popping out for a quick cigarette or lunch from a vendor cart; lucky for you, the street scene outside is often more enter-taining than the money-swapping within.

Truly frantic buying and selling by red-faced traders screaming 'Sell! Sell!' goes on at the **New York Mercantile Exchange** (Map pp444–5; ☎ 212-299-2499; www.nymex .com; 1 North End Ave; ⊖ , C, 4, 5 to Fulton St–Broadway Nassau), near Vesey St. This exchange deals in gold, gas and oil com-modities, but not tourists anymore; like the NYSE, it's closed to visitors, but encourages you to check back periodically to see if the policy has changed.

TRINITY CHURCH Map pp444-5

☎ 212-602-0800; www.trinitywallstreet.org; Broadway at Wall St; ⏰ 8am-6pm Mon-Fri, 8am-4pm Sat, 7am-4pm Sun; ⊚ 2, 3 4, 5 to Wall St, N, R to Rector St

This former Anglican parish church was founded by King William III in 1697 and once presided over several constituent chapels, including St Paul's Chapel on the corner of Fulton St and Broadway. Its huge landholdings in Lower Manhattan made it the country's wealthiest and most influential church throughout the 18th century. The current Trinity Church is the third structure on the site. Designed by English architect Richard Upjohn, this 1846 building helped to launch the picturesque neo-Gothic movement in America. At the time of its construction, its 280ft bell tower made it the tallest building in New York City.

The long, dark interior of the church includes a beautiful stained-glass window over the altar, while the small, fenced-in cemetery out back, filled with ancient headstones smoothed by the centuries, is a fascinating, serene place to wander. Trinity, like other Anglican churches in America, became part of the Episcopal faith following US independence from Britain.

One of the best times to visit Trinity is during weekday lunchtime services or for its excellent Concerts at One midday music series (also held at St Paul's Chapel, see p119) for just a $2 suggested donation. Trinity is also known for its magnificent choir concerts, especially its annual December rendition of Handel's *Messiah*.

SOUTH STREET SEAPORT

Though you'd barely know it now, New York has a long and storied seafaring past, and the best way to get a glimpse of it is down here in the seaport area. Though it's now more of an alfresco mall and food court than an actual seaport, there are plenty of reminders of the salty old days, from the docked wooden schooners to the wonderful South Street Seaport Museum. There's also the strong fish odor – but it's just an olfactory ghost, as the iconic Fulton Fish Market, beloved for its 180 years, closed its doors in late 2005 for an impending move to the Hunts Point section of the Bronx. Plans for the abandoned

waterfront spot are still being hammered out. To get a sense of the gritty history of this waterfront area, check out the writings of the late literary journalist Joseph Mitchell, who wrote about the neighborhood's myriad characters in his now-famous 1952 story 'Up in the Old Hotel,' published in a collection of his writings by the same name.

SOUTH STREET SEAPORT ATTRACTIONS Map pp444-5

☎ 212-732-7678; www.southstseaport.org; ⊚ 2, 3, 4, 5, J, Z to Fulton St–Broadway Nassau

This 11-block enclave of shops, piers and sights combines the best and worst in historic preservation. It's not on the radar for most New Yorkers, but tourists are drawn to the sea air, the nautical feel, the frequent street performers and the mobbed (mostly chain) restaurants. Pier 17, beyond the elevated FDR Dr, is a waterfront development project that is home to a number of shops, one recommended restaurant (**Cabana**, p227) and a rare public bathroom. Clustered around the piers are some genuinely significant 18th- and 19th-century buildings dating from the heyday of this old East River ferry port, which fell into disuse with the building of Brooklyn Bridge and the establishment of deep-water jetties on the Hudson River. The many pedestrian malls, historic tall ships and riverside locale make the seaport a picturesque destination or detour. Schermerhorn Row, a block of old warehouses bordered by Fulton, Front and South Sts, contains novelty shops, upscale boutiques and the **New York Yankees Clubhouse** store at 8 Fulton St (where you can purchase fee-free tickets for the Bronx Bombers and plenty of Yankees souvenirs). Across the street, the **Fulton Market Building**, built in 1983 to reflect the redbrick style of its older neighbors, is a glorified fast-food court and shopping arcade. In the summertime, though, the outdoor courtyard becomes home to an oft-worthy series of performers from local blues, jazz and rock bands.

SOUTH STREET SEAPORT MUSEUM Map pp444-5

☎ 212-748-8600; 207 Front St; adult/senior & student/child $8/6/4; ⏰ 8am-6pm Tue-Sun Apr-Oct, 10am-5pm Fri-Mon Nov-Mar; ⊚ 2, 3, 4, 5, J, Z to Fulton St, A, C to Broadway–Nassau

Opened in 1967, this museum offers a glimpse of the seaport's history and a survey of the world's great ocean liners in its permanent exhibits and interesting sites around the 11-block area. Included here are three galleries, an antique printing shop, a children's center, a maritime crafts center and historic ships. Just south of Pier 17 stands a group of tall-masted sailing vessels, including the *Peking, Wavertree, Pioneer, Ambrose* and *Helen McAllister*, and the admission price to the museum includes access to these ships. You can join sailings aboard the gorgeous, iron-hulled *Pioneer*, built in 1885 to carry mined sand. The two-hour journeys (adult/senior/child $25/20/15) run from Memorial Day through mid-September from Tuesday to Friday evenings and Saturday and Sunday beginning at 1pm; passengers are encouraged to bring snacks and even a bottle of wine for this relaxing, view-rich sail. Reserve a spot by calling ☎ 212-748-8786.

CITY HALL & CIVIC CENTER

Government business is placed in this downtown area, where the infectious buzz of change, progress and pro-action (no matter how delusional it may be) is sure to rub off some of its excited vibes onto you. City council members dash from public hearings to constituent brunches at nearby diners, reporters clamor to City Hall Park for press conferences, and TV satellite vans camp out across from the majestic row of courthouses (where media frenzies have been launched over Martha Stewart, Lil' Kim and Russell Crowe). Resentful locals drag themselves to jury duty each afternoon. Towering over it all is the massive **Municipal Building** (100 Centre St), which houses all from the city's Marriage Bureau to local NPR affiliate radio station WNYC, and the floating span of the Brooklyn Bridge, which has a popular pedestrian entrance just across from City Hall. South of City Hall is Park Row, known as Newspaper Row when it was the center of the newspaper publishing business from the 1840s to the 1920s (now, incidentally, it's the spot of a veritable strip mall, including the excellent computer and electronics purveyor **J&R Music & Computer World**, p324).

CITY HALL Map pp444-5

☎ 212-788-6865; Park Row; admission free, tours by appointment only; ⊕ 4, 5, 6 to Brooklyn Bridge–City Hall, J, M, Z to Chambers St
The hall, in placid City Hall Park facing the entrance to the Brooklyn Bridge, has been home to New York's government since 1812. In keeping with the half-baked civic planning that has often plagued large-scale New York projects, officials neglected to finish the building's northern side in marble, gambling that the city would not expand uptown. The mistake was finally rectified in 1954, completing a structure that architectural critic Ada Louise Huxtable called a 'symbol of taste, excellence and quality not always matched by the policies inside.'

You can explore the interior of City Hall, which is actually rather grand, through **guided tours** offered by the Art Commission of the City of New York, free of charge, on weekdays only (you must call for an appointment, ☎ 311 or ☎ 212-NEW-YORK from outside of the city).

After climbing the formal staircase out front – the site of constant press conferences, as well as demonstrations (only civil ones, with pre-arranged permits) – you'll eventually find yourself under the soaring rotunda, supported by 10 Corinthian columns on the second floor. One highlight inside includes the spot where Abraham Lincoln's coffin sat for a brief time in 1865 (it's at the top of the staircase on the 2nd floor). The Governor's Room, a reception area where the mayor entertains important guests, contains 12 portraits of the founding fathers by John Trumbull, George Washington's old writing table and other examples of Federal furniture, and the remnants of a flag flown at the first president's 1789 inaugural ceremony. If you take a quick peek into the City Council chambers, you might see lawmakers deliberating over controversial legislation, development plans, or, more likely, the renaming of a city street in someone's honor, which is an activity that accounts for approximately 40% of all the bills passed by the 51-member body.

CITY HALL PARK Map pp444-5

Park Row; ⊕ 4, 5, 6 to Brooklyn Bridge–City Hall, J, M, Z to Chambers St
City Hall Park received a multimillion-dollar facelift and its gas lamps, fountains, lovely landscaping, chess tables and benches make it a nice place to kick back for a spell, especially in summer, when a Summerfest concert series brings live R&B and jazz here on weekends. It's often edged by protestors of one issue or another – unless the groups have planned ahead and gotten a protest permit, something required by

BROOKLYN BRIDGE

A New York icon, the **Brooklyn Bridge** (Map pp444–5; ⊕ 4, 5, 6 to City Hall) has seen many protests, joys and tragedies. It was the span that held angry, plunger-wielding marchers who were outraged by the sodomy-based police torture of Haitian immigrant Abner Louima in 1997. In spring 2004 it hosted a crowd of gays and lesbians who marched in support of legalizing same-sex marriage. In December 2005 it was a conduit for masses of commuters – including Mayor Bloomberg himself – who walked to and from their offices due to the three-day Transit Workers Union strike. It's been part of countless marathons and group bike rides, the backdrop for annual Fourth of July fireworks, and the path to refuge for hundreds of traumatized downtown workers, who walked or ran over it, soot-covered, after fleeing their work following the tragic events of September 11, 2001. But its long, long history has many more stories to tell.

When the world's first steel suspension bridge opened in 1883, the 1596ft span between its two support towers was the longest in history. Although its construction was fraught with disaster, the bridge became a magnificent example of urban design, which inspired poets, writers and painters. Today, the Brooklyn Bridge continues to dazzle and many regard it as the most beautiful bridge in the world.

This East River suspension bridge was designed by the Prussian-born engineer John Roebling, who was knocked off a pier in Fulton Landing in June 1869; he died of tetanus poisoning before construction of the bridge even began. His son Washington Roebling supervised construction of the bridge, which lasted 14 years and managed to survive budget overruns and the deaths of 20 workers. The younger Roebling himself suffered from the bends while helping to excavate the riverbed for the bridge's western tower and remained bedridden for much of the project (his wife oversaw construction). There was one final tragedy to come in June 1883, when the bridge opened to pedestrian traffic. Someone in the crowd shouted, perhaps as a joke, that the bridge was collapsing into the river, setting off a mad rush in which 12 people were trampled to death.

The bridge entered its second century as strong and beautiful as ever, following an extensive renovation in the early 1980s. The pedestrian walkway that begins just east of City Hall affords a wonderful view of Lower Manhattan, and you can stop at observation points under the support towers to view brass 'panorama' histories of the waterfront. Just take care to stay on the side of the walkway marked for folks on foot – one half is designated for cyclists, who use it en masse for commuting and pleasure rides, and frustrated pedalers have been known to get nasty with oblivious tourists who wander, camera pressed to an eye, into the bike lane. Barring any such run-ins, you should reach Brooklyn after about a 20-minute trek. Bear left to Empire-Fulton Ferry State Park or Cadman Plaza West, which runs alongside Middagh St in the heart of Brooklyn Heights, taking you to Brooklyn's downtown area, including the ornate Brooklyn Borough Hall and the Brooklyn Heights Promenade (see p221).

Mayor Bloomberg to demonstrate within the actual park, on the steps of City Hall.

WOOLWORTH BUILDING Map pp444-5

233 Broadway; ⊕ 4, 5, 6 to Brooklyn Bridge–City Hall, J, M, Z to Chambers St

Cass Gilbert's magnificent 60-story Woolworth Building was completed in 1913. At 792ft, it was the tallest building in the city – and the world – until it was surpassed by the Chrysler Building in 1929. It's designed in a Gothic style meant to emphasize its height and is constructed of masonry and terra-cotta over a steel frame. It was described at its dedication as a 'cathedral of commerce,' which was meant as an insult, but FW Woolworth, the head of the five-and-dime chain store that was head-quartered here, took the comment as a compliment, and began throwing the term around himself. Today the building houses mainly offices, but, as part of a unique pro-gram offered through the Lower Manhattan Cultural Council, the 33rd floor's raw, open rooms recently housed a dozen artists who were allowed to work in the magnificent space (with 360-degree views of the city) thanks to a grant program.

Woolworth Building (left), skyscraper goes gotharama

WORLD TRADE CENTER SITE

While the physical dust of September 11 may have cleared, the dust of controversy and infighting over what to do with Ground Zero's rebuilding efforts is still being settled. The years of discussion over what kind of redevelopment is appropriately soulful, strong, beautiful and useful has been fraught with drama and politicking, often pitting grieving and angry survivors against the artists and architects who were trying to bring some global meaning to the tragedy.

First, a little recap. Immediately following September 11, the area around Ground Zero was a war zone – covered in thick ash and the smell of death, bustling only with rescue workers, police officers and media folks, and residents trying to grab what was left of their belongings. Ad-hoc September 11 memorials sprang up everywhere – both official, such as the Ground Zero viewing platform that eventually morphed into a Viewing Wall, with display panels showing the history of the buildings' beginning and demise (see also World Financial Center, p119), and unofficial, like the mass of out-of-nowhere vendors who hawked mawkish mementos from framed photos to T-shirts. The true neighborhood spirit was gone for at least a year, until the tax-free Liberty Bond program, created by Congress, started wooing residents and business-owners back here in droves, bringing a feeling of boom to the region that's now at its peak. But always looming was the site of the former towers itself; what to do with it?

At first, all seemed on track. The Lower Manhattan Development Corporation was put in place to oversee plans, and an esteemed architect, Daniel Libeskind, was chosen as the perfect man for the job after winning a design competition that many say was never clear about what was wanted in the first place. Libeskind became the 'master planner,' and drew up plans that were met with approval and included the 1776ft skyscraper that Governor George Pataki promptly dubbed the 'Freedom Tower.' But since then, developer Larry Silverstein has realized that, whatever sort of building goes up, it needs to house businesses that will turn a profit; meanwhile, the New York City Police Department has demanded that a major design be changed to better keep out terrorists. Now several other architects have been brought on board and coerced into what many have dubbed a 'forced marriage' with Libeskind, whose original design has changed significantly and frequently. Meanwhile, developers have still not agreed upon a final version of the official World Trade Center Commercial Design Guidelines – a disconcerting fact that has come to light most recently with the hiring of a prominent new architect, Norman Foster, who has been chosen to design the second largest office tower (at 65 stories) on the sight.

And then there is what many New Yorkers see as the most offensive part of the entire plan: the controversy over art and culture, and how much and what type is appropriate for the memorial. It all came to a head in September 2005, when Pataki scrapped plans for the International Freedom Center, meant to be an extensive art and cultural center that would look at human rights from a global perspective. Relatives of September 11 victims were angry that the culture wouldn't revolve solely around the World Trade Center tragedy, and Pataki, afraid that anything else would be viewed as unpatriotic, evicted the entire museum plan from the plans. Similar arguments ended plans for the relocation of the Drawing Center (see p128), and discussions over the possibility of an on-location performing arts center have stalled. To 'make up for' the Freedom Center loss, Pataki and developers have called for a combination of a retail and office center – a boon to Silverstein but a slap in the face to the artists who had worked on the first plan, and to soulful individuals everywhere.

Visitors are not allowed into the building (though you may be able to sneak a peek at the beautifully preserved lobby), but you can marvel at the facade and height from across the street in City Hall Park.

TRIBECA & SOHO

This pair of neighborhoods, which sit nestled side by side below Houston St, have similar vibes and histories: known today for being the place to find hip bars, fabulous restaurants and quiet side streets that combine industrial starkness and cobblestone coziness, they are also home to wealthy folks who live in massive loft spaces and like to fancy themselves as hipsters. Both have vibrant shopping strips (Soho especially) and the remnants of major art

scenes – perhaps the biggest bond between them.

TRIBECA

Eating p228, Drinking p263, Shopping p328, Sleeping p355

This intimate neighborhood is comprised of landmark 19th-century buildings as well as massive former warehouses that are steadily being converted into condos. Film buffs know it as the indie-movie headquarters for NYC, thanks to Robert De Niro's Tribeca Films production company and his wildly successful **Tribeca Film Festival** (p25), which began as a post–September 11 economic boost but has exploded into a destination fest that gets bigger each year. Local foodies know it as the place to celeb-spot while eating pricey sushi at **Nobu** (105 Hudson St) or fancy French at

Bouley (p229); destination boutique hotels include the Tribeca Grand (p357). The area was so-named by real-estate agents because it sits in a 'Triangle Below Canal St.' First used as farmland for Dutch settlers, years since have seen it become a center for the textile industry, mercantile exchanges for dairy goods, cheap artists' lofts and, by the 1970s, an urban renewal plan that knocked down many of the old buildings and threw up high-rises, parks and educational facilities, including the Borough of Manhattan Community College. Though Tribeca is certainly not known as one of the top spots to see art anymore (most galleries have fled to Chelsea), there's still plenty of it. The best time to see what's cookin' is in late April, during the annual TOAST: Tribeca Open Artist Studio Tour (www.toast artwalk.com), when artists open up their local studios to anyone interested in what they're creating. It's fun, free and a great intro to the neighborhood.

Orientation

Tribeca is bordered by Canal St in the north, West St in the west, Chambers St in the south and Broadway in the east. A good way to get acquainted with the neighborhood is through the Tribeca Organization (www .tribeca.org), though beware that some listings on its website are out of date.

HARRISON STREET HOUSES

Map pp444-5
Harrison St; ⊕ 1, 2 to Franklin St
Built between 1804 and 1828, the eight town houses on the block of Harrison St immediately west of Greenwich St constitute the largest collection of Federal architecture left in the city. But they were not always neighbors: six of them once stood two blocks away, on a stretch of Washington St that no longer exists. In the early 1970s, that area was the site of Washington Market, a wholesale fruit and vegetable shopping area. But development of the waterfront (which resulted in the construction of Manhattan Community College and the Soviet-type concrete apartment complex that now looms over the town houses) meant the market had to move uptown and the historic row of houses had to be relocated. Only the buildings at 31 and 33 Harrison St remain where they were originally constructed.

TRIBECA FILM FESTIVAL

It may have only started in 2002, but the Tribeca Film Festival – founded by Robert De Niro and Jane Rosenthal as a way to boost the post–September 11 downtown economy and provide NYC with a competitive film event – has become a beloved, successful cinematic soiree in its own right, attracting more than 1 million visitors. The part-showcase, part-contest fest is a week-long event in April that features close to 200 films; 2005 screened 24 world premieres. Competitions are held in documentary, feature and shorts categories, and 2005 turned out success stories such *as Rikers High*, a documentary by Victor Buhler that was later broadcast on Showtime, and *Transamerica*, directed by Duncan Tucker, which went on to national release after star Felicity Huffman won the fest's award for Best Actress in a Narrative Feature. In 2006 the festival teamed up with Tropfest, the largest short-film festival in the world, based in Sydney, Australia. Paired with the fastest growing film festival in North America, the two should make quite a team. Visit www.tribecafilmfestival.org for tickets and showtimes.

TRIBECA FILM CENTER Map pp444-5
☎ 212-941-2000; www.tribecafilm.com; 375 Greenwich St btwn N Moore & Franklin Sts; ⊕ 1 to Franklin St
Though this nexus of downtown filmmaking, a labor of love from movie legend Robert De Niro, is mainly an office complex and screening room for film professionals, the public is encouraged to attend the various special screenings here. In 2002, De Niro teamed up with Jane Rosenthal to create the Tribeca Film Festival (see box, above), which includes various screenings and educational panels. Check the website for upcoming events and screening schedules.

WASHINGTON MARKET COMMUNITY PARK Map pp444-5
☎ 212-964-1133; www.washingtonmarketpark.org; Greenwich St & Chambers St; ☽ 6am-dusk; ⊕ 1, 2, 3 to Chambers St
This 3-acre park – which was home to the world's largest food market back in 1858 – is now beloved by local families with kids, mainly because of its popular playground. But it's a great escape for anyone needing a little green space; there's a gazebo, and tennis and basketball courts.

SOHO

Eating p228, Drinking p263, Shopping p324, Sleeping p355

Soho has seen a gentrification process similar to that of Tribeca. It's filled with cast-iron industrial buildings that date from the period just after the Civil War, when this was the city's leading commercial district. These multistory buildings housed linen, ribbon and clothing factories, which often featured showcase galleries at street level. But retail businesses eventually relocated uptown and manufacturing concerns moved out of the city. By the 1950s, the huge lofts and cheap rents attracted artists, misfits and other avant-garde types. Their political lobbying not only saved the neighborhood from destruction but assured that a 26-block area was declared a legally protected historic district in 1973. Unfortunately, as it always goes, the pioneers who were responsible for preserving the attractive district were pushed out by sky-high rents when Soho became gentrified and attained hyperfashionable status. Though there are still some art galleries left here, most of the top spaces have hightailed it to Chelsea, leaving mostly shoe boutiques, like the quirky John Fleuvog (p326), and a growing mass of chain stores – including downtown outposts of both Adidas (p324) and Bloomingdale's (p325) – to carry the torch. Strolling the strip of Prince St on a sunny day is great for shopping, and a good way to get infused with all aspects of Soho. In warm months especially, the wide sidewalks between Broadway and Sixth Ave are lined with local artists hawking quality jewelry, knitwear, paintings, clothing and other sorts of arts and crafts.

Soho's hip cup overfloweth, too, to the northern side of Houston St; this small area, known for excellent shopping and dining, is now known as Noho (see Walking Tour, p208). Add it to Soho and Tribeca for a great DIY experience of strolling, window-shopping and café-hopping, and you'll have quite a lovely afternoon.

Orientation

Houston St marks the northern boundary for Soho, hence 'South of Houston.' Its edges mingle with Little Italy around Lafayette St to the east and Chinatown and Tribeca around the west end of Canal St.

CHILDREN'S MUSEUM OF THE ARTS
Map p450

☎ 212-941-9198; www.cmany.org; 182 Lafayette St; admission $8; ☼ noon-5pm Wed & Fri-Sun, noon-6pm Thu; ◉ B, D, V, F to Broadway–Lafayette St

A place for kids to unleash their inner artist, this small but worthy stop is home to a permanent collection of paintings, drawings and photographs by local schoolkids. For more hands-on activities, check out the museum's vast offering of public programs, which include guided workshops on art forms from sculpture to T-shirt painting, as well as movie nights and other special treats.

DRAWING CENTER Map p450

☎ 212-219-2166; www.drawingcenter.org; 35 Wooster St; ◉ A, C, E, 1 to Canal St

Here since 1977, this is the only nonprofit institute in the country to focus solely on drawings, using work by masters as well as

---

TOP TEN MUST-DOS: DOWNTOWN

- Hop on a ferry, tour boat, historic sailboat or kayak – just get out onto the water (p117), and be sure to look back at the skyline
- Wander aimlessly in the East Village (p135), West Village (p140) or Tribeca (p126), where the residential streets are quirky, intimate and teeming with local life
- Head over the Brooklyn Bridge (p125) for great views and a stroll that rates as a romantic classic
- Chow down in Chinatown (p230) on dim sum, noodles, bubble tea – how could you go wrong?
- Shop till you drop in Soho & Noho (p324) – Lower Broadway and the small streets shooting off it are packed tight with boutiques, bargains and exciting splurges
- Attend the Tribeca Film Festival (p25), the hottest event come springtime
- Be one of the first to visit the New Museum of Contemporary Art (p144) on the Lower East Side
- Party till dawn in Chelsea (p298), home to the biggest, hottest clubs
- Dine out in the Meatpacking District (p238), where new eateries were built to impress
- Visit the Washington Sq Arch (p139), the beautiful icon at the gateway to Washington Sq Park

unknowns to show the juxtaposition of various styles. Historical exhibitions have shown the work of masters including Michelangelo, James Ensor and Marcel Duchamp, while contemporary shows have focused on Richard Serra, Ellsworth Kelly and Richard Tuttle. The Drawing Center was pulled into the controversy over Ground Zero development for a time, as it was one of a handful of cultural centers to be relocated to the new space until infighting over what sort of art was appropriate (see p126) killed the idea, as critics labeled some of the Center's past exhibits as 'anti-American.' So, for now, it remains in Soho.

MUSEUM OF COMIC & CARTOON ART
Map p450

☎ 212-254-3511; www.moccany.org; 594 Broadway; ☾ noon-5pm Fri-Mon, by appt Tue-Thu; adult/child $3/free; ⊚ R, W to Prince St

Recently relocated from its long-time home in Boca Raton, Florida, this new museum has done a good job of capturing the attention of downtown Manhattan. Its mission is to educate the public about comic and cartoon art, and to help everyone appreciate it in all its forms – comic strips, cartoons, animé, animation, gag cartoons, political illustrations, caricature, graphic novels and more. Special exhibits so far have included *Modern Fairy Tales*, showcasing the work of Michael Kaluta and Charles Vess, as well as *Cartoons Against the Axis*, featuring WWII Bonds cartoons from the Terry D'Alessio Collection. Check the website for online exhibits and upcoming lecture series, too.

NEW YORK CITY FIRE MUSEUM
Map p450

☎ 212-219-1222; www.nycfiremuseum.org; 278 Spring St btwn Varick & Hudson Sts; suggested donation adult/senior & student/child under 12 $5/2/1; ☾ 10am-5pm Tue-Sat, 10am-4pm Sun; ⊚ C, E to Spring St

Occupying a grand old firehouse dating from 1904, this museum houses a collection of gold horsedrawn fire-fighting carriages and modern-day red fire engines. Exhibits show the development of the NYC fire-fighting system, which began with the 'bucket brigades.' All the heavy equipment and the museum's particularly friendly staff make this a great place to bring children. The tone was somber here after September 11 – not surprising since the New York Fire Department (FDNY)

lost half of its members in the attacks; memorials and exhibits are now a permanent part of the collection. An excellent gift shop sells official FDNY clothing, patches and books about fire-fighting history.

NEW YORK EARTH ROOM Map p450
www.earthroom.org; 141 Wooster St; admission free; ☾ noon-6pm Wed-Sun (closed 3-3:30pm); ⊚ R to Prince St

Since 1977 this oddity has been wooing the curious with something not easily found in the city: dirt – 250 cu yd, or 280,000lb, to be exact. Walking into the small space is a heady experience, as the scent will make you feel like you've entered a wet forest, and the sight will be pretty darn moving. It's pure earth, after all. Yes, it's been manipulated and stuffed into an urban gallery – but it's fresh and clean. And that's not so common these days.

SOHO ARCHITECTURE Map p450
This area is filled with block upon block of cast-iron industrial buildings (hence its nickname, 'Cast-Iron District') that date from the post–Civil War period. As you walk through fabulous Soho, stop and look up – many of the buildings still have elaborately decorated flourishes on their upper floors. Some of the preserved structures here include the **Singer Building** (561–563 Broadway btwn Prince & Spring Sts), an attractive iron-and-brick structure that used to be the main warehouse for the famous sewing-machine company.

Above a fabric store and gourmet food shop, you can view what little is left of the

You'll light up at the New York City Fire Museum (left)

marble facade of **St Nicholas Hotel** (521–523 Broadway btwn Spring & Broome Sts). This 1000-room luxury hotel was *the* place to stay when it opened in 1854. The hotel, which closed in 1880, also served as the headquarters of Abraham Lincoln's War Department during the Civil War.

Built in 1857, the **Haughwout Building** (488 Broadway at Broome St) was the first building to put to use the exotic steam elevator developed by Elisha Otis. Known as the 'Parthenon of Cast-Iron Architecture,' the Haughwout (pronounced how-out) is considered a rare structure for its two-sided design; look for the iron clock that sits on the Broadway-facing facade.

CHINATOWN

Eating p230, Drinking p264, Shopping p329

Crossing south of Canal St and into the bursting-at-the-seams neighborhood of Chinatown is a feast for all the senses. This is the only spot in the city where you can simultaneously see whole roasted pigs hanging in butcher-shop windows, get whiffs of fresh fish and ripe persimmons, hear the twangs of Cantonese and Vietnamese rise over the calls of knock-off-Prada-bag hawkers along Canal St and be able to buy a brass gong, lacquered chopsticks, rice-paper lanterns, silk Chinese slippers and a jar of Lee Kum Kee sparerib sauce all under one roof (at the fabulous **Pearl River Mart**, see p327). It's also where you can catch one of the best deals anywhere by boarding the **Fung Wah Bus** (see p419), which takes you to Chinatown in Boston for a mere $15.

More than 150,000 Chinese-speaking residents live in cramped tenements and crowded apartments in this neighborhood, in the largest Chinese community that exists outside of Asia. In the 1990s Chinatown also attracted a growing number of Vietnamese immigrants, who set up their own shops and opened inexpensive restaurants here; depending on what street you're on, you'll often notice more of a Vietnamese than Chinese presence. Some of the latest immigrants have been coming from Fuzhou, a Fujian province, as well as Guangdong and Toisan.

The official **Explore Chinatown information kiosk** (Map pp444–5; ☎ 212-484-1216; www.explorechinatown.com; Canal St btwn Baxter and Walker Sts; ☼ 10am-6pm Mon-Fri & Sun, 10am-7pm Sat) is where helpful, multilingual folks can guide you to specific eateries, shops, sights and festivals. But we implore you to explore on your own, too, because this fascinating and many-layered neighborhood is ripe for DIY adventures. Duck into a random produce market and check out the various oddly shaped, sometimes prickly, fruits and vegetables. Buy six cakes of fresh tofu or three luscious turnip cakes for $1 from a street vendor. Try to find the biggest stock of illegal fireworks for sale, wander into one of the musty and mysterious Chinese herb shops, try a red-bean bun or moon cake at one of the various bakeries, or join throngs of hipster teens hanging at one of the popular bubble-tea lounges or video-game halls. Enjoy a Peking-duck feast in honor of the Chinese New Year or stop into a random karaoke bar and belt out a tune from the '80s. Or just stroll up and down the collection of tiny streets – like Pell St, nicknamed 'haircut street' for its preponderance of barber shops.

Orientation

One of Manhattan's most dynamic ethnic enclaves, Chinatown is just north of the Civic Center and the Financial District, sprawling largely south of Canal St and east of Centre St to the Manhattan Bridge; over the years, however, it has steadily crept further east into the Lower East Side and north into Little Italy.

BUDDHIST TEMPLES Map pp444-5

Chinatown is home to Buddhist temples large and small, public and obscure. They are easily stumbled upon during a full-on stroll of the neighborhood; at least two such temples are considered landmarks. The **Eastern States Buddhist Temple** (64 Mott St btwn Bayard & Canal Sts) is filled with hundreds of Buddhas, while the **Mahayana Buddhist Temple** (133 Canal St & Manhattan Bridge Plaza) holds one golden 16ft-high Buddha, sitting on a lotus and edged with offerings of fresh oranges, apples and flowers. Mahayana is the largest Buddhist temple in Chinatown, and its facade features two giant golden lions for protection; its interior is simple, with a wooden floor, red chairs and red paper lanterns, all of which are trumped by the magnificent Buddha, thought to be the largest in the city.

CANAL STREET Map pp444-5

⊕ , M, Z, N, Q, R, W, 6 to Canal St

While the hidden treasures of Chinatown are found on its tiny side streets, this wide avenue is the pulsing artery of China-town, and a walk along it will not only be an exercise in frustration (the crowds are relentless), but also in excitement. You'll pass open, stinky seafood markets hawking bloodied, slippery fish; mysterious little herb shops displaying all manner of roots and potions; storefront bakeries with steamed-up windows and the tastiest 50¢ pork buns you've ever had in your life; restaurants with whole roasted ducks and pigs hanging by their skinny necks in the windows; produce markets piled high with fresh lychee nuts and bok choy and Asian pears; and street vendors selling endless forms of tchotchkes, from knock-off Gucci sunglasses and Rolex watches to whimsical windup toys and three-for-$1 panties. Don't miss it.

COLUMBUS PARK Map pp444-5
Mulberry & Bayard Sts

This is where outdoor mah-jongg and domino games take place at bridge tables while tai chi practitioners move through lyrical, slow-motion poses under shady trees and locals hang out on benches with their caged birds in tow. Judo-sparring and fam-ilies relaxing are also common sights here, in the active, communal space created in the 1890s and now the property of the warm locals. Visitors are welcome, though – or at least ignored. An interesting note is that the Five Points neighborhood, known as home to the first tenements and the inspiration for Martin Scorsese's *Gangs of New York*, was lo-cated at the foot of Columbus Park. The five points were created by the five streets that used to converge here; now you'll find the intersection of Mosco, Worth and Baxter Sts.

MUSEUM OF CHINESE IN THE AMERICAS Map pp444-5

☎ 212-619-4785; www.moca-nyc.org; 70 Mulberry St at Bayard St; suggested donation $3; ☻ noon-5pm Tue-Sun; ⊕ J, M, Z, N, Q, R, W, 6 to Canal St

This tiny, 2nd-floor homage to Chinese Americans is about to get a new home whose size finally matches its breadth of information. Thanks to a city grant, com-bined with private donations, MOCA is slated to move into a new 12,350-sq-ft space designed by architect Maya Lin (who did

the famed Vietnam Memorial in Washington DC). The new museum, which will be on Lafayette St between Grand and Howard Sts, will feature exhibit galleries, a bookstore and visitors lounge, and is set for a 2007 open-ing. Meanwhile, the current space, which grew out of a community-based organiza-tion founded in 1980, will continue to show exhibits about the history of Chinatown and its residents through artifacts, written stories and photographs. Recent special exhibits have included *Archivist of the Yellow Peril: Yoshio Kishi Collecting for a New America*, with a collection of Americana that both demonizes and humanizes the Asian-American community, and *Mapping Our Her-itage Project*, which features an interactive map of New York's Old Chinatown district.

WING FAT SHOPPING Map pp444-5
8-9 The Bowery btwn Pell & Doyers St; ⊕ J, M, Z, N, Q, R, W, 6 to Canal St

One of the most unique malls you'll ever see lies underground, and has businesses offering reflexology, collectible stamps and feng shui services. But the most fascinating aspect is its history, as the tunnel is said to have served as a stop on the Underground Railroad, as well as an escape route in the early 20th century for members of rival Tong gangs who waged battle up on the street and then disappeared down into the darkness before police could even begin to search.

LITTLE ITALY & NOLITA
Eating p231, Drinking p264, Shopping p330, Sleeping p355

In contrast to Chinatown, Little Italy's eth-nic character has been largely diluted in the last 50 years. The area began as a strong Italian neighborhood (film director Martin Scorsese grew up on Elizabeth St), but in the mid-20th century, Little Italy suffered a large exodus as many residents moved to the Cobble Hill section of Brooklyn and the city's suburbs. For that reason, few cultural sites and traditions remain.

One of many newfangled neighborhoods with odd acronyms – Bococa (Boerum Hill/ Cobble Hill/Carroll Gardens in Brooklyn) and Soha (South of Harlem) among them – Nolita (North of Little Italy) is a tiny but much-talked-about region, pulsating with hot shopping and dining spots, and infused with an old-fashioned, local-community feel.

LITTLE ITALY

Once known as a truly authentic pocket of Italian people, culture and eateries, this barely-there remnant is more like a theme-park version of reality – and a constantly shrinking one at that (a growing Chinatown keeps moving in). Still, loyal Italian-Americans, mostly from the suburbs, flock here to gather around red-and-white-checked tablecloths at one of a handful of long-time red-sauce restaurants. That's especially true during the raucous **San Gennaro Festival** (p27), honoring the patron saint of Naples and held for 10 days starting in the second week of September. At this time, Mulberry St from Canal to Houston Sts is closed off to make room for the festival's games of chance, kiddie rides and enough food and wine to sate the Bacchus in all of us.

Locals queue at gourmet-shop counters to purchase fat balls of fresh mozzarella, paper-thin sheets of prosciutto and boxes of sweet cannoli. And walking tours pass through regularly, with in-the-know guides pointing out the various Mulberry St landmarks made infamous by mobsters. There's no harm in bopping through for a look-see, but be aware that more authentic Italian experiences can be had in **Bensonhurst** (p179), Brooklyn, or in the **Belmont** (p201) section of the Bronx (though this, too, is fast becoming more touristy than true).

Orientation

Little Italy takes up most of the small space between Canal St and Houston St to the south and north, and Cleveland Pl to the Bowery to the west and east. The heart lies along the stretch of Mulberry St between Houston and Canal Sts.

MULBERRY STREET Map p450

Ⓒ C, E to Spring St

Although it feels more like a theme park than an authentic Italian strip, Mulberry St is still the heart of the 'hood, as well as being the home of landmarks such as **Umberto's Clam House** (☎ 212-431-7545; 386 Broome St at Mulberry St), where mobster Joey Gallo was shot to death in the '70s, reliable restaurants **Da Nico** (☎ 212-343-1212; 164 Mulberry St btwn Broome & Grand Sts) and **Casa Bella** (☎ 212-431-4080; 127 Mulberry St at Hester St), as well as the old-time bar Mare Chiaro (p265), which was one of the favorite haunts of the late Frank Sinatra. You'll see lots of red,

white and green Italian flags sold in souvenir shops, and you'll also enjoy the lovely aroma of fresh-baked pastries and pizzas wafting out of doorways. Make sure you don't miss the **Ravenite Social Club** (247 Mulberry St). Now, somewhat predictably, it's a gift shop, but it's still a reminder of the not-so-long-ago days when mobsters ran the neighborhood. Originally known as the Alto Knights Social Club, and a place where big hitters such as Lucky Luciano spent some time, the Ravenite was a favorite hangout of John Gotti (and the FBI) before he was arrested and sentenced to life imprisonment in 1992.

ST PATRICK'S OLD CATHEDRAL Map p450

260-264 Prince St at Mott St; Ⓒ R, W to Prince St

Though St Patrick's Cathedral is now famously located in Midtown on Fifth Ave, its first congregation was housed here, in this 1809–1815 Gothic Revival church designed by Joseph-Francois Mangin. Its soaring inner vault stands at 85ft, and the ornate interior features a marble altar and gold-leaf detailing. Back in its heyday, the church was the seat of religious life for the Archdiocese of New York, and an important community center for new immigrants, mainly from Ireland. Today it holds regular liturgies in English, Spanish and Chinese. Its ancient cemetery out back is a beautiful respite in the midst of city chaos; if it's not open when you pass by, sneak a peek through the thick, padlocked gate.

NOLITA

It's hipster heaven in this little corner of the city, home to celebs including Lauren Hutton and David Bowie and Iman, and scores of foodies and fashionistas who are drawn to cool boutiques and trendy eateries that command queues up and down the block. Rice (p232) uses Pan-Asian and **Chibi's Bar** (p264) does it with a range of sake cocktails and a cute canine mascot. Shoppers make daily pilgrimages to **Bond 07** (p328) for designer clothing and vintage bags, and **Rebecca Taylor** (p331) for girly but tailored dresses. (See p208 for shopping tour details.)

At the **Old Police Headquarters Building** (Map p450; 240 Centre St), a landmark structure built in 1908, check out the copper domes, cupolas and skylights; just don't expect to be invited into the luxury condo building, which took over in the '80s, about a decade after the NYPD moved out.

Nolita (which actually lies *within* the borders of Little Italy) can be found on Elizabeth, Mott and Mulberry Sts between Houston and Broome Sts.

LOWER EAST SIDE

Eating p233, Drinking p265, Shopping p331, Sleeping p357

In the early 20th century, half a million Jews from Eastern Europe streamed into the Lower East Side (LES), and today the area remains a magnet – but for a very different crowd. Now the place is either about being cool – by cramming into low-lit lounges and eateries like Suba (p265) – or about being moneyed. You can do the latter either at the low end, by moving into a renovated, walk-up apartment for an average of $2100 a month, or at the super-high end, by buying one of the new luxury condos that are slowly seeping into a 'hood that has been historically downtrodden. At the brand-new Avalon Chrystie Palace, for example, where units go for several million and the building has an onsite Whole Foods market, you can tower above land that used to house tenements and junkie flophouses. Visitors will also find a good selection of clothing boutiques, art galleries, cafés, bars and live-music venues, with places like Tonic (p296) pulling in crowds with eclectic performers – and trying mightily to preserve the edgy, avant-garde nature of the area.

Like Little Italy, the LES has lost much of its historic ethnic flavor, and only a small Jewish community and a handful of traditional businesses remain; see the boxed text on below for a sampling.

But so far, it's still not quite homogenous. Today, the LES is populated by just-arrived youngsters, made-it professionals, and a good many 'lifers' – older artists, musicians and designers – holding for dear life onto their rent-controlled apartments. Also, the Latino community, including many from Puerto Rico and the Dominican Republic, has long spilled over from the lower East Village (known by old-timers as Alphabet City, so-named for its Avenues A, B, C and D), and Chinatown continues to colonize adjacent neighborhoods, making for a flavorful mix that is unique to the LES.

With its array of restaurants and nightlife, the LES still ranks as one of New York City's hottest areas. And in New York, to remain hot means to not remain the same – so don't be surprised if what you saw during a visit here last year is now nowhere to be found.

New additions to the 'hood creating a buzz include the Hotel on Rivington (p357), which offers luxe digs with some serious views, the aforementioned Avalon Chrystie Palace, and the still-in-progress New Museum of Contemporary Art. Formerly located on Broadway in Soho, this house of modern art is now temporarily located in Chelsea (p144), but ground was broken for its new downtown home in late 2005, right on the Bowery between Stanton and Rivington Sts. Already widely heralded for its cutting-edge architecture by the Tokyo-based firm Sejima and Neshizawa/SANAA, the 6000-sq-ft, all-white, seven-story structure is the first art museum to be constructed downtown in over a century.

A visit to the Lower East Side Visitors Center (Map pp446–7; 261 Broome St btwn Allen & Orchard Sts) is a good way to orient yourself once you've arrived in the neighborhood. But don't be afraid to wander around and get lost, either.

www.lonelyplanet.com

Sights

LOWER EAST SIDE

PICKLES, BAGELS & BIALYS

These days, if you're looking to find the Lower East Side Jewish community depicted in the 1988 film *Crossing Delancey* (in which an old-fashioned matchmaker sets up a nice Jewish girl with a pickle vendor), you'd have to head to parts of Brooklyn. But for tastes of that world, you can still score in the LES. Nosh on old-world flavors with a little help from Gus's Pickles (Map pp446–7; 85-87 Orchard St) or the Pickle Guys (Map pp446–7; 49 Essex St), where you can still get new, sour, half-sour or hot pickles – along with pickled tomatoes, peppers and olives – from friendly, apron-clad men. Though you can get amazing bagels and bialys (a cousin of the bagel that's more like a roll) all over the city, it's fun to get a fresh, hot, paper sack of them on the LES, where it just feels like the right thing to do. The best place (and one of the only remaining purveyors here) is Kossar's Bialys (Map pp446–7; 367 Grand St). Find a little bit of everything, including smoked whitefish, herring in cream sauce and chopped liver, at Russ & Daughters Appetizing (Map p449; 179 E Houston St btwn Orchard & Allen Sts).

Orientation

The Lower East Side extends from the Bowery to the East River, bound by Houston St to the north and East Broadway to the south.

EAST RIVER PARK Map p449

Flanked by a looming housing project and the clogged FDR Dr on one side and the less-than-pure East River on the other, you might wonder what the draw is here. But one visit – especially if it's during spring or summer – and you'll understand. In addition to the spanking-new ballparks, running and biking paths, 5000-seat amphitheater for concerts and lovely patches of green thanks to a recent $4 million facelift, it's got cool, natural breezes and stunning views of the Williamsburg, Manhattan and Brooklyn Bridges. A long-time renovation is finally complete, adding four new ball fields, great nighttime lighting and surprisingly clean bathrooms to the mix.

ELDRIDGE STREET SYNAGOGUE

Map pp444–5

☎ 212-219-0888; www.eldridgestreet.org; 12 Eldridge St btwn Canal & Division Sts; ◉ F to East Broadway

The landmark Eldridge St Synagogue, built in 1887, attracted as many as 1000 worshippers on the High Holidays at the turn of the 20th century. Membership dwindled in the 1920s with restricted immigration laws, and by the 1950s the temple closed altogether. It fell into major disrepair due to water damage and neglect, but became the focus of a massive restoration effort – the Eldridge St Project – in the late '80s. While the project is not yet complete, it's getting there, thanks to a $2.9 million boost from the city. The latest phase of work is adding modern cooling, heating and electrical systems to the building (when they say it fell into disrepair they weren't kidding), as well as redesigns that will make the place wheelchair-accessible. Future work will restore stained-glass windows, fix terra-cotta work on the facade, replace the central chandelier and create a multimedia visitors center. For now, you can attend a multitude of cultural programs, including concerts, art exhibitions and educational lectures. Tours (adult/senior & student $5/3; ◷ 11am-4pm Sun & Tue-Thu, or by appointment) of the building are also available.

ESSEX STREET MARKET Map p449

☎ 212-312-3603; www.essexstreetmarket.com; 120 Essex St btwn Delancey & Rivington Sts; ◷ 8am-6pm Mon-Sat; ◉ F, V to Delancey St, J, M, Z to Delancey–Essex St

This 60-year-old historic shopping destination is the local place for produce, seafood, butcher-cut meats, cheeses, Latino grocery items, and even a barber. The Schapiro Wines stall is popular, as its roots in the neighborhood date back to 1899, when the Schapiro family founded its kosher winery (NYC's first winery). It gave tours of its dank cellar and its 50,000-gallon tanks, but moved to upstate New York in the mid-1990s. Taste or purchase the wine and catch the vibe of the place at its new shop – or hit up one of the newer places, like Lower Yeast Side Breads, where you can get fresh treats like baguettes, ciabatta and olive loaves.

LOWER EAST SIDE ART GALLERIES

Map p449

Though Chelsea may be the heavy hitter when it comes to the New York art gallery scene, the LES has its very own collection of quality showplaces, thank you very much. Maccarone Inc (Map pp446–7; ☎ 212-431-4977; 45 Canal St btwn Ludlow & Orchard Sts) and Participant Inc (☎ 212-254-4334; 95 Rivington St btwn Ludlow & Orchard Sts) were both hailed as jump-starting the gallery trend here when they opened several years ago; both exhibit emerging talent, while Participant has the added bonus of varied performances. Gallery Onetwentyeight (☎ 212-674-0244; 128 Rivington St) is also a popular, contemporary space. The best way to get an overview of the area's offerings is to take part in ELS-LES (Every Last Sunday on the Lower East Side) Open Studios (www.lowereastsideny.com/artwalkpartici pant.htm), which typically includes nearly 20 galleries and studios.

LOWER EAST SIDE TENEMENT MUSEUM Map pp446-7

☎ 212-431-0233; www.tenement.org; 90 Orchard St at Broome St; adult/senior & student $15/11; ◷ visitor center 11am-5:30pm; ◉ F, V to Delancey St, J, M, Z to Delancey–Essex St

This museum puts the neighborhood's heartbreaking heritage on full display in several reconstructed tenements. The visitor center shows a video detailing the difficult life endured by the people who once lived in the surrounding buildings, which were more often than not without any running water or electricity. Museum visits are available only as part of scheduled tours (the price of which is included in the admission), which typically operate daily. But call ahead for the schedules, which change frequently.

When you visit, you'll find three recreations of turn-of-the-20th-century tenements, including the late-19th-century home and garment shop of the Levine family from Poland, and two immigrant dwellings from the Great Depressions of 1873 and 1929. On weekends the museum has an interactive tour where kids can dress up in period clothes and touch anything in the restored apartment (from around 1916) of a Sephardic Jewish family. Walking tours of the neighborhood are held from April to December, and usually include stops at the **Streit's Matzo Company** (Map p449; 148-154 Rivington St), which opened in the 1890s, and the **First Shearith Israel Graveyard** (Map pp444–5; 55-57 St James Pl btwn James & Oliver Sts), which was the burial ground of the country's first Jewish community. Gravestones date from the late 1600s and include those who escaped the Spanish Inquisition.

ORCHARD STREET BARGAIN DISTRICT
Map p449
Orchard, Ludlow & Essex Sts btwn Houston & Delancey Sts; 🕙 **Sun-Fri;** 🚇 **F to Delancey St, J, M, Z to Essex St**
When the LES was still a largely Jewish neighborhood, Eastern European merchants set up pushcarts to sell their wares here. While it's no longer as quaint as that, bargain-hunters comb the 300-odd shops in this modern-day bazaar for sporting goods, leather belts, hats and a wide array of 'designer fashions' (which are quite often a little bit cheesy). Rather than searching high and low for label knock-offs – better found at bargain chains elsewhere, such as Century 21 (p321) or Filene's (p341) – know that it's more the type of place for scoring cheap basics like bras, shoes, army-navy bags and leather jackets. While the businesses are not exclusively owned by Orthodox Jews, they still close early on Friday afternoon and remain closed on Saturday in observance of the Sabbath. Serious shoppers should try bargaining to save some cash, although you're up against the world's best here, so don't get your hopes up.

SARAH D ROOSEVELT PARK Map pp446-7
Houston St at Chrystie St
Spiffed up just in time for the arrival of its new tony neighbor, the Avalon Chrystie Palace, this remade little park is a place that most New Yorkers will remember as more of a junkie's spot to score than an actual plot of green space. But it's joined the ranks of former 'needle parks' – such as Bryant Park and Tompkins Sq Park – and is now a three-block respite from urban chaos. Grab an ethnic picnic-to-go at any of the nearby food spots and settle into a shady corner; if you've got kids with you, there's a nice little playground that's perfect for letting off steam.

EAST VILLAGE
Eating p235, Drinking p266, Shopping p333, Sleeping p357
The East Village – home to scruffy stalwarts like **CBGB** (p294), the local chapter of the **Hell's Angels** (look for the parked Harleys on 3rd St between First and Second Aves), and the **Pyramid** (p299), which shot various drag queens to local stardom in the '80s – has an unshakable image as an edgy, radical, be-yourself kind of place. It was the inspiration for *Rent,* the musical-turned-movie about artists trying to get by in the begging days of the AIDS crisis, and Led Zeppelin's album cover for *Physical Graffiti* (the building in the photograph still stands, at 98 St Marks Pl). The **Nuyorican Poets Café** (p292), which played a huge part in the explosion of poetry slams in the '90s, is based here. The **Bowery**, an actual street here that was home to a jumble of flophouses and social freaks throughout most of the 19th and 20th centuries, became known nationally as the epitome of down-and-out. The drug scene was headquartered here in much of the '70s, and the '80s ushered in a major art scene, attracting folks like photographer Nan Goldin, painter Keith Haring and poet Eileen Myles. **Tompkins Square Park** was a tent city for homeless folks – until the famous riots of 1988, when cops struggled for days to kick squatters out. Similar tugs-of-war have come in fits and starts ever since, usually between squatters, community-garden organizers and the constant enemy here: high-end developers.

These days, though, it's pretty clear that the developers are winning. Two controversial, 16-story residences are nearing completion, and the units at these condos – 195 The Bowery and Gwathmey Siegel's glass 'Sculpture for Living' – sell for between $3 and $12 million apiece. The park is totally cleaned

Sights

up, a haven for dog-walkers and stroller-pushing families alike. And the region east of here, historically home to a tight Puerto Rican community and known both as *Loisaida* and Alphabet City, has gone from a scary strip of drug dens (in the '80s) to a series of sleek and fabulous drinking and dining spots. It's the picture of gentrification – which is either awful or wonderful, depending on who you are, of course.

And for visitors in search of good food, interesting crowds, diverse nightlife and indie shopping galore, it's pretty damn good. Ripe exploration grounds in the East Village include First and Second Aves and Aves A and B between 14th and Houston Sts. Among the vintage clothing stores, used-record shops and gay bars, you can find virtually every type of cuisine here, including Italian, Polish, vegetarian, Lebanese, Japanese, Thai and especially Indian – there are about a dozen cheap-ass Indian spots on E 6th St between First and Second Aves. New Yorkers joke that all the spots on this block of **Little India** share the same kitchen and, whether truth or myth, folks looking for a flavorful budget meal can't get enough of the place.

Orientation

The East Village is generally considered the swath of village that's east of Third Ave to the river and north of Houston St to 14th St, with Tompkins Sq Park functioning as its pulsing nexus. Trains don't really go far enough east to carry you to most locations in the nabe, but mostly it's a quick walk (and even quicker cab or bus ride) from the 6 to Astor Pl, F, V to Lower East Side–Second Ave or L to First or Third Aves.

COMMUNITY GARDENS

After a stretch of arboreal celibacy in New York City, the community gardens of Alphabet City are breathtaking. A network of gardens was carved out of abandoned lots to provide low-income neighborhoods with a communal backyard. Trees and flowers were planted, sandboxes were built, found-art sculptures erected, domino games ensued – all within green spaces wedged between buildings or claiming entire blocks. On Saturday and Sunday most gardens are open to the public, for visitors to admire the plantings or chat with gardeners; many gardeners are activists within the community and are a good source of information about local politics.

The **6 & B Garden** (Map p449; www.6bgarden .org; E 6th St at Ave B) is a well-organized space that hosts free music events, workshops and yoga sessions; check the website for details. Three dramatic weeping willows, an odd sight in the city, grace the twin plots of **9th St Garden** and **La Plaza Cultural** (Map p449; E 9th St at Ave C). Also check out the **All People's Garden** (Map p449; E 3rd St btwn Aves B & C) and **Brisas del Caribe** (Map p449; 237 E 3rd St), easily located thanks to its surrounding white picket fence.

Even the community gardens (left) are arty in East Village

RUSSIAN & TURKISH BATHS Map p449

☎ 212-473-8806; www.russianturkishbaths.com; 268 E 10th St btwn First Ave & Ave A; daily/10 visits $25/175; 🕑 11am-10pm Mon, Tue, Thu & Fri, 9am-10pm Wed, 7:30am-10pm Sat & Sun; ◎ L to First Ave, 6 to Astor Pl

The waning of Eastern European traditions on the Lower East Side led to the closure of many old bathhouses in Manhattan, and the AIDS crisis ensured that most of these popular gay romping spots were shut as well. But the historic old Russian and Turkish steam baths still remain. Since 1892, this is the spa for anyone who wants to get naked (or, oddly, stay in their swimsuit) and romp in steam baths, an ice-cold plunge pool, a sauna and on the sundeck. All-day access includes the use of lockers, locks, robes, towels and slippers. Extras such as Dead Sea salt scrubs ($30) and black-mud treatments ($38) are also available, and an onsite Russian café boosts your blissed-out spirit even more with fresh juices, potato-olive salad, blintzes and borscht.

You must wear shorts, unfortunately, when the baths are open to both men and women – which is the case most hours except between 9am and 2pm Wednesday (women only) and between 7:30am and 2pm Saturday (men only). These are widely considered the best times to visit, as the vibe is more open, relaxed and communal.

ST MARK'S-IN-THE-BOWERY Map p449

☎ 212-674-6377; www.stmarkschurch-in-the-bowery.com; 131 E 10th St at Second Ave; ❤ 10am-6pm Mon-Fri; ◎ 6 to Astor Pl, L to Third Ave
Though it's most popular with locals for its cultural-center offerings – poetry readings hosted by the **Poetry Project** (☎ 212-674-0910) or cutting-edge dance performances from **Danspace** (☎ 212-674-8194) – this is also an historic site. This Episcopal church stands on the site of the farm, or *bouwerie*, owned by Dutch Governor Peter Stuyvesant, whose crypt lies under the grounds. The 1799 church, damaged by fire in 1978, has been restored, and you can enjoy an interior view of its abstract stained-glass windows during opening hours.

TOMPKINS SQUARE PARK Map p449

btwn 7th & 10th Sts & Aves A & B; ◎ F, V to Lower East Side–Second Ave, L to First Ave
This park's glory days are long gone, according to long-time residents. But also long gone are the park's upsetting days, when it was a dirty, needle-strewn homeless encampment and unusable for folks wanting a place to stroll or read or picnic. The turning point for the park was sparked by the razing of the band shell and highly publicized eviction of the squatters living in the 'tent city' within the park in 1988. That protest turned violent and the Tompkins Sq Riot, as it came to be known, ushered in the new era of yuppies in the dog run, fashionistas lolling in the grass and undercover narcotics agents trying to pass as hippies or home boys and bust the same.

Today, 16-acre Tompkins Sq Park is still a good spot for a game of hoops, a chess challenge at one of the concrete tables, a picnic with some ethnic takeout or a guitar jam on a sunny day. In warm weather it's often the site of a joyous special event, whether it's the annual May Day art and culture fest, the Howl! Festival (see box, right), summer's yearly jazz marathon or the legendary Wigstock dragfest, which has

HOWL! FESTIVAL OF EAST VILLAGE ARTS

A relatively new and quickly embraced festival in these parts is Howl!, otherwise known as 'eight days of countercultural euphoria' that happen each year at the end of August. It's named, of course, after Allen Ginsberg's famous poem, and it honors the writer's spirit and the spirit of so many other artists, writers and performers who have expressed themselves in and around the East Village over the decades. The fest has events (many free) going on every day and night at a variety of venues, including Tompkins Sq Park. Expect art exhibits, poetry readings, bluegrass concerts, punk shows, queer performance art, new dramas and musicals, film screenings – anything and everything that could ever be considered 'arts.'

returned here to its birthplace after a few years of taking place over on the west side piers. On any day, come here to mingle and play with a good cross section of locals.

UKRAINIAN MUSEUM Map p449

☎ 212-228-0110; www.ukrainianmuseum.org; 222 E 6th St btwn Second & Third Aves; ❤ 11:30am-5pm Wed-Sun; ◎ F, V to Lower East Side–Second Ave, L to First Ave
Ukrainians have a long history and still-strong presence here – thus the existence of several pierogi joints, including the famous Odessa (p268) and Veselka (p241) – and this interesting museum, which just moved into its sleek and expansive newly constructed headquarters. Its collection of folk art includes richly woven textiles, ceramics, metalwork and traditional Ukrainian Easter eggs, as well as the research tools needed for visitors to trace their own Ukrainian roots. Diverse courses in craftwork, from embroidery to bead stringing, are also offered, as are rotating folk-art exhibits and educational lectures.

GREENWICH VILLAGE

Eating p237, Drinking p268, Shopping p335, Sleeping p358
Once a symbol for all things artistic, outlandish and Bohemian, this storied and popular neighborhood will be forever known by visitors as 'Greenwich Village,' although locals don't use the term, and tend to refer to anyplace west of the East Village as, simply, 'the Village.' The

neighborhood's reputation as a creative enclave can be traced back to at least the early 20th century, when artists and writers moved in; by the '40s it had become known as a gathering place for gay folk. In the '50s, the Village's coffeehouses, bars and jazz clubs attracted scores of bohemians, including the Beat poets, who adopted the neighborhood as their east coast headquarters and listened to bebop and poetry throughout the 'hood. And it was here where Norman Mailer helped found the influential *Village Voice* newspaper.

But, like that newspaper – which was recently bought out by an alternative-newspaper chain and had its former editor named in an antigay harassment suit by a laid-off writer – the Village is relatively bland these days. Rents have skyrocketed, tenants have pressured the city to crack down on noisy quality-of-life violations and much of the real estate is being gradually taken over by **New York University** (NYU), which sits smack-dab in the middle of the neighborhood. Still, you'll find plenty to inspire you here, from the eclectic collection of cafés, shops and restaurants that cram the narrow streets to the always abuzz public space of **Washington Square Park**, where pot dealers have been crowded out by students, playground-loving children and dog-owners who flock to the bustling dog run.

The Village is also the birthplace of today's gay rights movement, which began with a legendary, drag-queen-led riot against police harassment at the **Stonewall** (p266), a watering hole that still exists today. Many still think of this area, especially Christopher St, as the center of queer culture in New York – and it is where you'll find the **LGBT Community Center** (p292). But gay life has dissipated, and formed other HQs in both Chelsea and the East Village. Still, crowds of gay men and lesbians continue to make pilgrimages to the Village on the last weekend in June for the annual **Lesbian, Gay, Bisexual & Transgender Pride March** (p25).

Orientation

Roughly bordered by 14th St in the north and Houston St in the south, 'the Village' fills in the space between about Broadway and Sixth Ave, though in some spots it spills as far to the east as Third Ave. West of Sixth Ave begins the West Village (p140).

ASTOR PLACE Map pp446-7
8th St btwn Third & Fourth Aves; Ⓢ **R, W to 8th St–NYU, 6 to Astor Pl**
This square is named after the Astor family, who built an early New York fortune on beaver trading and lived on **Colonnade Row** (429–434 Lafayette St), just south of the square (check out the tile in the wall of the Astor Pl subway platform). Four of the original nine marble-faced Greek Revival residences on Lafayette St still exist, but have seen better days. Astor Place itself is dominated by the large brownstone Cooper Union, the public college founded in 1859 by glue millionaire Peter Cooper. Just after its completion, Abraham Lincoln gave his 'Right Makes Might' speech condemning slavery in the Union's Great Hall. The fringed lectern he used still exists, but the auditorium is only open to the public for special events.

The character of Astor Place has been oddly altered thanks to the addition of the gleaming 'Astor Place: Sculpture for Living' steel-and-glass condo by Gwathmey Siegel architects – which is either an inappropriate horror or a testimony to modernity, depending on whom you ask (though most claim the former). Still, the cube sculpture entitled *Alamo*, in the middle of the square, is a popular spot for skateboarding teens and liquored-up NYU students. Get a group together and give it a whirl; with some powerful backs and legs you can set it spinning. The uptown subway entrance here is an exact replica of one of the first subway kiosks in the early 20th century.

FORBES COLLECTION Map p448
☎ 212-206-5548; www.forbesgalleries.com; 62 Fifth Ave at 12th St; admission free; ✆ 10am-4pm Tue, Wed, Fri & Sat; Ⓢ L, N, Q, R, W, 4, 5, 6 to 14 St–Union Sq
These galleries house curios from the personal collection of the late publishing magnate Malcolm Forbes. The eclectic mix of objects on display includes Fabergé eggs, toy boats, early versions of Monopoly and tin soldiers.

GRACE CHURCH Map p449
800-804 Broadway at 10th St; Ⓢ **R, W to 8th St–NYU, 6 to Astor Pl**
This Gothic Revival Episcopal church, designed by James Renwick Jr, was made of

marble quarried by prisoners at Sing Sing, the state penitentiary in the town of Ossining, 30 miles up the Hudson River (which, legend has it, is the origin of the expression 'being sent upriver'). After years of neglect, Grace Church has been spiffed up in a major way, and its floodlit white marble is an elegant nighttime sight.

MERCHANT'S HOUSE MUSEUM

Map p449

☎ 212-777-1089; www.merchantshouse.com; 29 E 4th St btwn Lafayette & the Bowery; adult/senior & student/child $8/5/free; ☷ noon-5pm Thu-Mon; ◉ 6 to Bleecker St

Located in a difficult-to-pinpoint place that actually straddles the Village, East Village and Noho all at once, this museum is a remarkably well-preserved example of how the business class lived. The house, dating from 1831, once belonged to drug importer Seabury Tredwell. His youngest daughter Gertrude lived here until her death in 1933, so its original furnishings were intact when it began life as a museum three years later. Period clothing and the fully equipped kitchen add to the historical allure.

NEW YORK UNIVERSITY Map p448

☎ 212-998-4636; www.nyu.edu; Information Center at 50 W 4th St

In 1831 Albert Gallatin, secretary of treasury under President Thomas Jefferson, founded an intimate center of higher learning open to all students, regardless of race or class background. He'd scarcely recognize the place today, as it's swelled to a student population of more than 50,000, with more than 16,000 employees, and schools and colleges at six Manhattan locations. It just keeps growing, too – to the dismay of landmark activists and business owners, who have seen buildings (including the legendary Palladium nightclub on 14th St) rapidly bought out by the academic giant and replaced with ugly dormitories or administrative offices. Still, the academic offerings are highly regarded and wide ranging, especially its film studies, writing, medical and law programs. For a unique experience that'll put you on the fast track to meeting locals, sign up for a weekend or one-day class – from American history to photography – offered by the School of Professional Studies and Continuing Education and open to all.

WASHINGTON SQUARE PARK

Map pp446-7

◉ A, C, E, B, D, F, V to W 4th St, R, W to 8th St–NYU, 6 to Astor Pl

This park, like many public spaces in the city, began as a potter's field – a burial ground for the penniless – and the site of public executions, conveniently enough. In recent decades it's had many claims to fame, though its roles as an unofficial campus green for NYU, outdoor stage for street performers and veritable mall for purchasing pot (albeit crappy stuff) have been the most recognized – and not all in a good way. After becoming fed up with the relentless drug dealing, vandalism and rat infestation, a group of neighborhood activists spent years trying to drum up support for a conservancy and a costly renovation. They succeeded in raising $2.7 million for the much-needed renovation of the Stanford White Arch, colloquially known as Washington Sq Arch. Standing over 72ft high and carved of beaming white Dover marble, this landmark dominates the park beautifully, especially since its drawn-out facelift ended in 2004. Originally designed in wood to celebrate the centennial of George Washington's inauguration in 1889, the arch proved so popular that it was replaced in stone six years later and adorned with statues of the general in war and peace (the latter work is by A Stirling Calder, the father of artist Alexander Calder). In 1916 artist Marcel Duchamp famously climbed to the top of the arch by its internal stairway and declared the park the 'Free and Independent Republic of Washington Sq.' These days, the anarchy takes place at ground level, as comedians and buskers use the park's permanently dry fountain as a performance space.

Beyond the arch, though, the rest of the park is still in need of much work – at least according to those who have gotten the city on board to begin an extensive overhaul, with plans that have drawn much debate. Major changes in the $16-million plan include moving the park's fountain to be in line with the arch, relocating the dog run, replacing the plaza with a lawn and, most alarmingly, the addition of a granite and iron fence that would be locked at night. Public-space advocates are up in arms, long-time park fans are upset over the attempt to clean up the ramshackle-charm layout of the place and the whole

Sights

GREENWICH VILLAGE

situation is bound to get uglier before it gets pretty (if you can call it that).

WEST 4TH STREET BASKETBALL COURTS Map pp446-7
Sixth Ave at W 4th St

Otherwise known as 'the Cage,' the small basketball court that stands enclosed within four walls of chain-link fence here is home to some of the best streetball in the country. Though it's more touristy than its counterpart, Rucker Park in Harlem, that's also part of its charm, as games, held right here in the center of the Village, draw massive, excitable crowds, who often stand 10 deep to hoot and holler for the skilled, competitive guys who play here. Prime time is summer, when the W 4th St Summer Pro-Classic League, now in its 26th year, hits the scene. While the height of this court's popularity was back in 2001 – the year Nike capitalized on the raw energy of the place by shooting a commercial here – b'ball-lovin' throngs still storm the place on weekends.

WEST VILLAGE & THE MEATPACKING DISTRICT
Eating p238, Drinking p269, Shopping p337, Sleeping p358

The area of the Village to the extreme west, where meandering streets eventually give way to the landscaped grounds of Hudson River Park and then the wide river itself, is a gem of a 'hood known as the West Village. Just north of it, but still below 14th St, is the Meatpacking District, a corner once known for its lascivious blend of bloody meat factories, S&M clubs and throngs of trannie prostitutes that is now the picture of hyper-gentrification (do we see a trend here in NYC, folks?). Weekends are comically crowded, as folks come from all neighborhoods – especially the suburbs – to search for the latest way to be a part of the in crowd.

WEST VILLAGE

The West Village, made up of leafy, residential blocks sporting an upscale blend of town houses, cafés and boutiques, is more low-key than the Meatpacking District – save for the gay amusement–park stretch of Christopher St that leads to the river, where you'll find a quaintly tacky collection of gay bars and

tchotchke shops selling souvenirs like 'I'm not gay but my girlfriend is' T-shirts, rainbow-flag bandanas and custom-made leather chaps. Find gay solace in tiny Christopher Park (Map p448; Christopher St at Seventh Ave South), where the *Gay Liberation* statues by George Segal are moving testaments to freedom. The rest of the area is a great place for wandering, and even getting yourself happily lost, as it's just about the only place in Manhattan that's not organized in a neat grid due to its past as a collection of navigational horse paths. There's a good chance you'll even run into a celebrity, as the chi-chi neighborhood – which was famously used as the backdrop for shooting *Sex and the City* scenes – is home to quite a collection of A-listers, including Sarah Jessica Parker and Matthew Broderick, Willem Dafoe, Lili Taylor and Nicole Kidman. Perry St is a good place to keep a look out, as its Richard Meier–designed luxury apartment buildings are filled with star residents (who else could afford such places?).

Orientation
Like the Village, its borders are rough, but it's mainly the area west of Sixth Ave, bordered by 14th St in the north (excluding the small, western swath that is the Meatpacking District) and Houston St in the south.

ABINGDON SQUARE Map p448
Hudson St & W 12th St

This historic dot on the landscape (just a quarter-acre small) was recently transformed from an asphalt triangle into a lovely patch of green thanks to a $760,000 capital project fuelled by local representatives. Now home to grassy knolls, beds of perennial flowers and winding bluestone paths – as well as a popular Saturday greenmarket – it's a great place to enjoy a midday picnic or just rest after an afternoon of wandering the winding West Village streets. After getting horizontal, look up at the southern end of the park and you'll see the *Abingdon Doughboy*, a bronze statue of servicemen from the neighborhood who gave their lives in WWI. (A foot soldier then was commonly referred to as a 'doughboy.')

CHRISTOPHER STREET PIER Map p448
Christopher St at Hudson River; ⊙ 1 to Christopher St–Sheridan Sq

Once strictly the domain of young gay hustlers and sassy 'pier queens' (the effeminate

REBIRTH OF THE HIGH LINE

In the pro-development environment of today's New York City, the story of the High Line is more like a fairy tale. The High Line itself is a 30ft-high abandoned stretch of elevated railroad track, which reaches from Gansevoort St in the Meatpacking District up to 34th St. Overgrown with thick weeds and not used since the 1960s, the blissfully empty space has inspired a group of activists to fight with the city for the right to turn it into a long ribbon of parkland – and, miracle of miracles, they've won. The struggle for the site began in 1999, when a group of community activists, Friends of the High Line, lobbied to save the track from being demolished to pave the way for salivating developers. Giuliani opposed the preservation effort, but Mayor Bloomberg supported it – and a heap of financial promises to the tune of $50 million hasn't hurt matters. Construction is slated to begin in 2006, with the first portion of the public green space set to open in 2008. The park, which will create a peaceful continuum that sews together a long swatch of the Lower West Side, will be one of only two elevated parks in the world; the other, created atop an abandoned railroad viaduct, is the Promenade Plantée in Paris.

gay boys and transgender folks who were depicted in the 1990 film *Paris is Burning*), this spiffily renovated concrete finger is now a magnet for downtowners of all stripes (including young gay holdouts). It forms part of the Hudson River Park, which spans the length of Manhattan. The Hudson River Park Project paid special attention to this spot, adding a grass lawn, flowerbed, wooden deck, tented shade shelters, benches and a grand fountain at its entrance. It offers sweeping views of the Hudson and relieving breezes in the thick of summer.

MEATPACKING DISTRICT

Compared to its West Village neighbor, this pocket has more of a hyper, wannabe-star feel to it, and a vibe that is less quaint and more industrial-chic. Try to stroll through on a weekday afternoon, when the streets are quiet and downright pleasant, and you can freely investigate many of this newly-exploded neighborhood's charms, like hot fashion boutiques including **Jeffrey** (p337). You'll have to brave the evening rush, though, to truly get the effect of nightspots like **Cielo** (p298) and **Lotus** (p299), totally hot **Hotel Gansevoort** (p359) and eateries like **Spice Market** (p239).

While you're walking around, it may be distasteful to think about the fact that this 'hood was home to 250 slaughterhouses in 1900. Today there are only about 35, as most have been squeezed out by high rents. The general response to the major development here has been what it always is when a neighborhood begins to rapidly gentrify – a mix of annoyance, disdain and secret excitement. But when developers proposed a 420ft luxury apartment building a few years ago, a group of fed-up citizens, politicians and activists

banded together to make sure the gentrification wouldn't go too far. The group, led by the Greenwich Village Society for Historical Preservation, called itself 'Save Gansevoort Market,' in honor of the neighborhood's old name. It won a major victory in 2004, when it convinced the city to designate a 12-block area of the Meatpacking District as an historic landmark area.

The latest buzz here is over the development of the High Line into parkland (see box, above), and related plans to add some art to the mix by relocating the **DIA: Chelsea Museum** (535 W 22nd St; as part of an incentive to gain High Line park backing) to this 'hood. The new art house, which will sit under the High Line and run along Gansevoort St from Washington to West Sts, is being designed by the renowned Diller Scofidio + Renfro (Eyebeam, Lincoln Center redesign). Another much-anticipated addition is hotelier Andre Balazs' latest outpost of the **Standard**, coming to Midtown in 2006.

The Meatpacking District comprises a small area just south of 14th St, to the west of Ninth Ave and north of W 12th St.

CHELSEA

Walking Tour p215, Eating p240, Drinking p270, Shopping p339, Sleeping p360

During the city's Gilded Age in the late 19th century, this was the dry goods and retail center, drawing well-heeled shoppers to its varied emporia. Closer to the Hudson River, you can still find plenty of old warehouses, and many of the town houses, especially those in the **Chelsea Historic District**, on the low-20s blocks between Eighth and Tenth Aves, are beautifully restored. In the midst of the beautiful region, perfect for wandering and enjoying DIY experiences, is

Sights

CHELSEA

the **General Theological Seminary** (Map pp446–7; ☎ 212-243-5150; 175 Ninth Ave btwn 20th & 21st Sts; ✆ noon-3pm Mon-Fri, 11am-3pm Sat), a campus-cum-garden that is a peaceful haven open to the public.

Today this 'hood is more popular for less-natural attractions, specifically the parade of eye-poppingly gorgeous gay men (who have been known to, ahem, enhance their physiques) who roam the heart of the neighborhood, on the runway of Eighth Ave, making beelines to gyms and trendy happy hours. You'll also be drawn into scads of cafés, shops and restaurants, which have exploded in the past couple of years, especially along Ninth and Tenth Aves.

West of Tenth Ave lies the hub of the city's art gallery scene, which has long since stolen Soho's thunder and grows more expansive by the year. The area is absolutely crawling with jaded reviewers and buyers on Thursday and Friday evenings. But newcomers such as the much anticipated technology-focused museum **Eyebeam** (540 W 21st St), set to open in 2007 with a modern, cantilevered design by Diller + Scofidio, have critics licking their chops in anticipation. Antique-lovers should note that the beloved **Annex Antiques Fair & Flea Market (Chelsea Flea Market)** has moved to Hell's Kitchen (p152), but a smaller, indoor market, the **Antiques Garage** (Map pp452–3; 112 W 25th St btwn Sixth & Seventh Aves; ✆ 6:30am-5pm Sat & Sun) is worth a look-see. Another adventure is to wander through the small but fascinating **Flower District** (around Sixth Ave btwn 26th & 29th Sts) on a weekday morning, when trucks unload massive amounts of fragrant, fresh flowers and plants, and where you can discover great decorative bargains, including cases of votive candles and bamboo reeds.

Orientation

North of the Village and Meatpacking District, Chelsea extends from 14th St north to about 28th St, and west from Broadway to the Hudson River.

CHELSEA ART MUSEUM Map pp446-7
☎ 212-255-0719; www.chelseaartmuseum.org; 556 W 22nd St; adult $6 ($3 after 6pm Thu), student & senior $3; ✆ noon-6pm Tue, Wed, Fri & Sat, noon-8pm Thu; ◉ C, E to 23rd St
One of many new additions to the art scene here, this museum occupies a three-story redbrick building dating from 1850, and stands on land once owned by writer Clement Clarke Moore. Its focus is on post-war abstract expressionism, especially by national and international artists; its permanent collection includes works by Antonio Corpora, Laszlo Lakner and sculptor Bernar Venet. It's also the headquarters of the Miotte Foundation, dedicated to archiving the works of Jean Miotte, a Soho-based artist who has played a big role in the genre of Informel (Informal Art).

CHELSEA GALLERIES
Chelsea is home to the highest concentration of art galleries in the entire city – and the number of them just keeps increasing. Most lie in the 20s, on blocks between Tenth and Eleventh Aves, and wine-and-cheese openings for new shows are typically held on Thursday evenings. For a complete guide and map, pick up a copy of the monthly *Gallery Guide* (www.galleryguide.com), available for free at most art venues. Also, see p215 of this guide for a Chelsea gallery walking tour. Among the showcases that create the most buzz in these parts are: **Andrea Rosen Gallery** (Map pp452–3; 525 W 24th St), which has a gem of holdings by Julia Scher, Rita Ackerman and Felix Gonzalez-Torres; **Mary Boone Gallery** (Map pp452–3; 541 W 24th St), whose owner found fame in the '80s with her eye for Jean-Michel Basquiat and Julian Schnabel in Soho; and the **Matthew Marks Gallery** (Map pp446–7; 522 W 22nd St), a Chelsea pioneer known for exhibiting big names from Nan Goldin to Ellsworth Kelly.

CHELSEA HOTEL Map pp446-7
☎ 212-243-3700; 222 W 23rd St btwn Seventh & Eighth Aves; ◉ 1, 2, C, E to 23rd St
The prime sight on noisy 23rd St is a redbrick hotel with ornate iron balconies and no fewer than seven plaques declaring its literary landmark status. Even before the Sex Pistols' Sid Vicious murdered girlfriend Nancy Spungeon here, the hotel was famous as a hangout for the likes of Mark Twain, Thomas Wolfe, Dylan Thomas and Arthur Miller. Jack Kerouac allegedly crafted *On the Road* during one marathon session here. Musicians have long favored the Chelsea, and it counts many local eccentrics among its permanent residents. Its basement lounge bar, **Serena** (p270), is a sexy, low-lit spot for a martini.

CHELSEA MARKET Map pp446-7

www.chelseamarket.com; 75 Ninth Ave btwn 15th & 16th Sts; ⊖ A, C, E to 14th St, L to Eighth Ave

Gourmet food fans will think they've entered the pearly gates once they've stepped into this 800ft-long shopping concourse, bursting with some of the freshest eats in town. But it's part of a larger, million-sq-ft space that occupies a full city block, home to the Nabisco cookie factory in the 1930s (which created the Oreo cookie), and current home to the Food Network, Oxygen Network and the local NY1 news channel. The prime draw for locals, of course, are the more-than-25 market food shops, including Amy's Bread, Fat Witch Brownies, The Lobster Place, Hale & Hearty Soup, Ronnybrook Farm Dairy and Frank's butcher shop. You can also sit down and indulge at spots including the Green Market organic-food café, and buy non-food items from Chelsea Wholesale Flowers and the expert-staffed Chelsea Wine Vault.

CHELSEA PIERS Map pp446-7

☎ 212-336-6000; www.chelseapiers.com; Hudson River at end of 23rd St; ⊖ C, E to 23rd St

This massive waterfront sports center caters to the athlete in everyone. You can set out to hit a bucket of golf balls at the four-level driving range, ice skate in the complex's indoor rink or rent in-line skates to cruise along the new Hudson Park waterfront bike path down to Battery Park. There's a jazzy bowling alley, Hoop City for basketball, a sailing school for kids, batting cages, a huge gym facility with an indoor pool (day passes for nonmembers are $50), indoor rock-climbing walls – the works. Kayaks are loaned out free at the Downtown Boathouse just north of Pier 64. There's even waterfront dining and drinking at the Chelsea Brewing Company (p270), which serves great pub fare and delicious home brews. Though the Piers are somewhat cut off by the busy West Side Hwy, the wide array of attractions here brings in the crowds; the M23 crosstown bus, which goes right to its main entrance, saves you the long, four-avenue trek from the subway. For more information, see p312.

HUDSON RIVER PARK

Maps pp446-7 & pp444-5

www.hudsonriverpark.org; Manhattan's west side from Battery Park to 59th St

Encompassing way more than Chelsea – though much of its stretch lies along here – is this 5-mile, 550-acre waterfront park, overseen by the Hudson River Park Trust and still in various stages of construction. While for years the west side was known more for snarling highway traffic, unseemly pastimes and smoggy New Jersey vistas, it's recently followed the lead of most other cities that sit on bodies of water – Chicago, Miami, Paris – and turned the shoreline into something spectacular. Among its charms are a bike/run/skate path snaking along its entire length, community gardens, basketball courts, playgrounds, dog runs, and a collection of renovated piers jutting out into the water and serving as riverfront esplanades, miniature golf courses and

Skate, dunk, bowl, sail, bat, rockclimb and kayak your little hearts out at Chelsea Piers (above)

alfresco movie theaters and concert venues come summer. For a detailed map of the entire park, visit the Trust's website.

MUSEUM AT FIT Map pp452-3

☎ 212-217-5800; www.fitnyc.edu; Seventh Ave at 27th St; admission free; ☾ noon-8pm Tue-Fri, 10am-5pm Sat; ◉ 1 to 28th St

The Fashion Institute of Technology is a fashion, design and fine arts school located on the edge of Manhattan's Fashion District (p320). The best way for a visitor to access its unique riches is to visit its museum, which showcases rotating exhibits on fashion and style, including works by students. Its new permanent collection, opened in late 2005, is the country's first gallery of fashion and textile history; it showcases rotating items from its collection of more than 50,000 garments and accessories dating from the 18th century to the present.

NEW MUSEUM OF CONTEMPORARY ART Map pp446-7

☎ 212-219-1222; www.newmuseum.org; 556 W 22nd St; adult/artist, senior & student/child under 18 $6/3/free; ☾ noon-6pm Tue, Wed, Fri & Sat, noon-8pm Thu; ◉ C, E to 23rd St

This museum was recently moved from Soho to here, its temporary location until its fabulous new Lower East Side digs are ready (see p133). Its widespread mission is to give space to works created in the last decade. Some show highlights have included a survey of works by Vancouver-based Brian Jungen, who transforms consumer goods like sneakers and baseball bats into powerful sculptures, and *Andrea Zittel: Critical Space*, in which the artist uses skills of architecture and design to examine life in Western society. Also, check out the museum's Media Z Lounge, with its digital, video and audio installations, and its fine bookstore, featuring an impressive selection of art reference titles and monographs.

RUBIN MUSEUM OF ART Map pp446-7

☎ 212-620-5000; www.rmanyc.org; 150 W 17th St at Seventh Ave; adult/senior & student/child $7/5/free; ☾ 11am-7pm Mon & Sat, 11am-5pm Wed, 11am-9pm Thu & Fri, 11am-6pm Sun; ◉ 1 to 18th St

One of the newest museums in the city is the Rubin, opened in 2004 and the first museum in the Western world to dedicate itself to art of the Himalayas and surround-ing regions. Impressive collections include embroidered textiles from China, metal sculptures from Tibet, Pakistani stone sculptures, intricate Bhutanese paintings and ritual objects and dance masks from various Tibetan regions, spanning from the 2nd to 19th centuries. Rotating exhibitions have included the educational *What is it? Himalayan Art, Female Buddhas: Women of Enlightenment in Himalayan Art*, and *Vanished Kingdoms: The Wulsin Photographs of Tibet, China and Mongolia, 1921-1925*.

UNION SQUARE & THE FLATIRON DISTRICT

Eating p241, Drinking p270, Shopping p340, Sleeping p362

While these two areas are subtly distinct in character – Union Sq more young, bustling and shopping-oriented, Flatiron hip and dining-centric, with more culture in the mix – they tend to easily spill over into each other, and share similar qualities of nonpretension, lovely architecture and a good blend of residences and businesses.

Originally one of NYC's earliest business districts, Union Sq provided a convenient site for many workers' rallies and political protests throughout the mid-19th century. In fact its name has more prosaic origins: this was basically the 'union' of the old Bowery and Bloomingdale (now Broadway) roads. By the 1960s, this area was overrun by junkies and gigolos. But the '90s heralded a massive revival, helped along by the arrival of the Greenmarket Farmers Market (p146). Today, Union Square Park, which underwent restoration work in 2002, hops with activity; it is surrounded by a plethora of bars, restaurants, the enormous Regal Union Square Stadium 14 (850 Broadway) and superstores which include the Virgin Megastore (p341), Filene's (p341), Barnes and Noble and the new Whole Foods (p341). All of these make it a popular place to hang anytime.

For a 10-block radius, the Flatiron District, loaded with loft buildings and boutiques, does a good imitation of Soho without the pretensions, prices or crowds. There are some fine restaurants, some dance clubs and plenty of shopping opportunities. The neighborhood takes its name from the Flatiron Building (opposite), a thin and gorgeous work of architecture that sits just south of Madison Sq Park.

Orientation

Union Sq, the area that juts a few blocks in each direction from the actual Union Sq Park at 14th St and Broadway, runs seamlessly into the newly energized Flatiron District, which is generally the area that juts a few blocks in each direction out of Madison Park, at 23rd St and Broadway.

FLATIRON BUILDING Map pp446-7

Broadway, btwn Fifth Ave & 23rd St; ⊕ R, W, 6 to 23rd St

Built in 1902, the 20-story Flatiron, designed by Daniel Burnham, has a traditional beaux arts–facade and a uniquely narrow triangular footprint that resembles a massive ship. It boasts a limestone facade, built over a steel frame, that gets more complex and beautiful the longer you stare at it. Best viewed from the island on 23rd St between Broadway and Fifth Ave, the unique structure dominated this plaza back in the skyscraper era of the early 1900s. Images of the Flatiron that were published before its official opening – many thanks to the fact that this was also the time of the first mass picture postcards – aroused a buzz of curiosity around the globe. Publishing firm Frank A Munsey was one of the building's first tenants, on the 18th floor, and from there put out *Munsey's Magazine*, which published the writings of O Henry. His musings, along with the paintings of John Sloan and photographs by Stieglitz, best immortalized the Flatiron back in the day – along with a famous comment by actress Katherine Hepburn, who said in a TV interview once that she'd like to be admired as much as the grand old building of the Flatiron. Today it remains one of the most photographed architectural sites in New York.

MADISON SQUARE PARK Map pp452-3

www.madisonsquarepark.org; btwn 23rd & 26th Sts & Fifth & Madison Aves

This park defined the northern reaches of Manhattan until the city's population exploded just after the Civil War. It has enjoyed a rejuvenation within the past few years due to a renovation project and rededication in 2001, and now neighborhood residents head here to unleash their dogs in the popular dog-run area, as workers enjoy lunches – which can now be bought from the hip, on site **Shake Shack** (p243) –

while perched on the shaded benches. These are perfect seats from which to gaze up at the landmarks that surround the park, including the Flatiron (left), art deco Metropolitan Life Tower, and the New York Life Insurance Company Building (topped with a gilded spire). The space also sports 19th-century statues of folks including Senator Rosco Conkling (who froze to death in a brutal 1888 blizzard) and Civil War admiral David Farragut. Between 1876 and 1882 the torch-bearing arm of the Statue of Liberty was on display here, and in 1879 the first Madison Sq Garden was constructed here, at Madison Ave and 26th St.

MUSEUM OF SEX Map pp452-3

☎ 212-689-6337; www.museumofsex.org; 233 Fifth Ave at 27th St; adult/senior & student $14.50/13.50; ⏱ 11am-6:30pm Sun-Fri,11am-8pm Sat; ⊕ N, R, W to 23rd St

Not as racy as you might imagine, this house of culture, which opened in 2002, intellectually traces the interwoven history of NYC and sex, from tittie bars and porn to street hustling and burlesque shows. But don't expect any sex parties or naked go-go dancers here; the collection consists of films, magazines and odd artifacts from vintage blow-up dolls to sex-house coins. Frequently changing exhibitions, which tackle subjects such as how New York has affected sex around the world and ideas of Chinese erotic obsession, are particularly fascinating, as are the varied events including erotica readings, one-person shows and sex-ed seminars.

TIBET HOUSE Map pp446-7

☎ 212-807-0563; www.tibethouse.org; 22 W 15th St btwn Fifth & Sixth Aves; admission free; ⏱ noon-5pm Tue-Fri; ⊕ F to 14th St, L to Sixth Ave

With the Dalai Lama at the head of its board, this non-profit cultural space is dedicated to presenting Tibet's ancient traditions through art exhibits, a research library and publications, and programs which include educational workshops, open meditations, retreat weekends and docent-led tours around the globe. Exhibits here tend to attract a diverse and passionate crowd, and have ranged from *Visions of Tibet*, with color photographs by Brian Kistler and Sonam Zoksang, to *Delicate, Exotic Watercolors Depict 1400 Years of Tibetan Architecture*, featuring works by Michel Peissel.

NYC GREENMARKETS

It's not a feature most visitors expect to find in Gotham, but greenmarkets (www.cenyc.org) are a widespread and beloved part of the culture here. There are 40 greenmarkets scattered throughout the five boroughs and, though the cornucopia at Union Sq (held Monday, Wednesday, Friday & Saturday) remains one of the most popular destination markets, it's the smaller, more infrequent ones in tucked-away neighborhoods that may be even more appreciated. The markets are where regional farmers tote all manner of edibles – such as homemade cheeses and hand milked creams, organic fruits and vegetables, bundled herbs, maple syrup and honey and baked goods – to be sold on stretches of park and pavement including W 97th St (Friday), Isham St in Inwood (Saturday), Poe Park in the Bronx (Tuesday) and Grand Army Plaza in Brooklyn (Saturday). They attract everyone from mothers wanting to feed their families the freshest veggies they can find to celebrity chefs who come to discover just-picked rarities like fiddlehead ferns, fresh curry leaves and purple broccoli. Even if you've no reason to shop, strolling through one of the greenmarkets is a great way to enjoy a true New York experience, as well as a feast for the eyes – and possibly the stomach, if you're lucky enough to happen upon some free samples of cheese or baked goods.

UNION SQUARE Map pp446-7

17th St btwn Broadway & Park Ave S; ⊙ L, N, Q, R, W, 4, 5, 6 to 14th St–Union Sq, W Mon-Fri only

Opened in 1831, this park soon became the central gathering place for surrounding mansions and grand concert halls, and eventually an explosion of high-end shops, giving the area its nickname of Ladies' Mile. Then, from the start of the Civil War until well into the 20th century, this became the site for protests of all kinds – for union workers as well as political activists. By the time of WWI, the area had become neglected and depressed, but eventually was home to all sorts of working-class headquarters, including the American Civil Liberties Union, the Communist and Socialist parties and the Ladies' Garment Workers Union.

The 1960s ushered in an era of lounging hippiedom in the park, spurred on by the fact that Andy Warhol opened his famous Factory on Union Sq West (in a building that, in an amazing sign of the times, now houses Barnes and Noble). Its latest transformation has been an eclectic one, as the park is home to loungers and local workers catching some fresh air, as well as a throng of young skateboarders who like to occupy the southeast corner – along with frequent antiwar or general anti-government protestors. The yearly Christmas holiday bazaar, with all manner of crafts hawked at festive booths, is a wonderful shopping experience – as is the weekly greenmarket (above), which is one of the most popular farmers markets in the city. Fans of the fresh produce worried that it would face too much competition when a massive new Whole Foods (p341) opened on the south side of the park, but so far it doesn't seem to have made a dent.

GRAMERCY PARK & MURRAY HILL

Eating p241, Drinking p270, Sleeping p362

Gramercy Park, loosely comprising the 20s blocks east of Madison Ave, is named after one of New York's loveliest parks – the kind of public garden area found in Paris and other European cities. But while the botanical sentiment did translate across the Atlantic, the socialist sense did not: when developers transformed the surrounding marsh into a city neighborhood in 1830, admission to Gramercy Park was restricted to residents, and still, to this day, you need a key to get in (which, incidentally, you can procure as a guest of the Gramercy Park Hotel, p362). Other attractions in the region include stately brownstones on tranquil streets, including Irving Pl – a short street named after Washington Irving that contains some great little cafés, eateries and the rockin' Irving Plaza (p294) live music venue. One interesting pocket is yet another Little India (others can be found in the East Village and Jackson Heights, Queens), a collection of wonderful Indian restaurants and shops, many featuring South Indian fare, on Lexington Ave between 27th and 30th Sts.

Murray Hill is not only an ubiquitous downtown drag king who can be found hosting campy events on practically a weekly basis, it's a neighboring community just north of Gramercy Park, home to understated inns, more town houses and unique little pockets such as Sniffen Court (Map pp452–3; 150-158 E 36th St), a preserved row of 1860 carriage houses, one of which was used as the backdrop for the cover of the Doors 1967 *Strange Days* LP.

Orientation

The area known as Gramercy Park loosely comprises the 20s east of Madison Ave, while Murray Hill stretches up into the 30s and 40s from here.

NATIONAL ARTS CLUB Map pp446-7
☎ 212-475-3424; 15 Gramercy Park South; ◉ 6 to 23rd St

This exclusive club boasts a beautiful, vaulted, stained-glass ceiling above its wooden bar. Calvert Vaux, who was one of the creators of Central Park, designed the building. The space does hold art exhibitions, ranging from sculpture to photography, that sometimes open to the public from 1pm to 5pm.

PIERPONT MORGAN LIBRARY
Map pp452-3
☎ 212-685-0610; www.morganlibrary.org; 29 E 36th St at Madison Ave; ◉ 6 to 33rd St

This library, recently reopened after beautiful and extensive renovations, is part of the 45-room mansion owned by steel magnate JP Morgan. His collection features a phenomenal array of manuscripts, tapestries and books (with no fewer than three Gutenberg Bibles), a study filled with Italian Renaissance artwork, a marble rotunda and the three-tiered East Room main library. The rotating art exhibitions here are really topnotch.

THEODORE ROOSEVELT'S
BIRTHPLACE Map pp446-7
☎ 212-260-1616; www.nps.gov/thrb; 28 E 20th St btwn Park Ave & Broadway; adult/child $3/free; ⏰ 9am-5pm Tue-Sat; ◉ R, W 6 to 23rd St

This National Historic Site is a bit of a cheat, since the house where the 26th president was born was demolished in his lifetime. This building is simply a re-creation by his relatives, who joined it with another family residence next door. If you're interested in Roosevelt's extraordinary life, which has been somewhat overshadowed by the enduring legacy of his younger cousin Franklin, visit here, especially if you don't have the time to see his summer home in Long Island's Oyster Bay. Included in the admission price are house tours, offered on the hour from 10am to 4pm.

MIDTOWN
Eating p244, Drinking p271, Shopping p341, Sleeping p364

The term Midtown conjures such a range of images that it's sometimes difficult to see it as one fluid place. Is it Donald Trump territory, rife with gleaming high-rises and frenzied suits rushing from subway to office and back again? Is it Christmas windows along Fifth Ave shops, leading to the big ol' tree in Rockefeller Center with a bustling circle of ice underneath? What about the bright white lights of Times Sq and the historic theaters of Broadway, or classic landmarks like the Empire State or Chrysler Buildings? Or the up-and-coming eatery rows of formerly gritty Hell's Kitchen? Midtown is truly all of this, and much, much more. Home to many of the city's most popular attractions, New York's teeming Midtown area is where you'll probably wind up spending plenty of time, which you might find to be a mixed blessing. It can be overwhelming, and extremely crowded on weekdays, but also very exciting, as the energy here is classic New York – the stuff of mainstream Hollywood movies like *Breakfast at Tiffany's, Big* and *Little Manhattan* – and pretty intoxicating, whether it's your first or tenth visit.

Good off-the-beaten tracks ripe for DIY adventures include the ethnic neighborhoods of Little Korea (E 30s blocks), home to karaoke bars and authentic Korean eateries, and Little Brazil (W 46th St btwn Fifth Ave & Broadway), where you'll find Brazilian BBQ and overhear Portuguese conversation and samba music in various shops and restaurants. Hell's Kitchen (W 40s-50s) is also a good spot for mining, especially along stretches of Ninth and Tenth Aves, as is the ritzy Midtown East residential corner of Sutton Place, with homes running parallel to First Ave from 54th to 59th Sts. It's a bit staid over here, but the views of the Queensboro Bridge and the East River, made famous by Woody Allen in *Manhattan,* are amazing.

Orientation

Midtown constitutes such a huge and unwieldy swath that there are many smaller sub-neighborhoods that have been named within it. This book has broken down the region in the following ways: first, by splitting it into Midtown West, which covers the area west of Sixth Ave and north of 34th St to 59th St (where you'll find the start of Central Park as well as Columbus

Sights

MIDTOWN

Circle, now home to the sleek new Time Warner Center), and Midtown East, which also covers 34th to 50th Sts, but moves from Sixth Ave to the East River. Within Midtown West is Hell's Kitchen (also called Clinton), bordered by Eighth Ave on the east and stretching to the Hudson River. The Rockefeller Center and Fifth Ave areas generally refer to regions north of 50th and up to 59th St, while the Theater District and Times Sq comprise a small, overlapping swath within Midtown West in the 40s.

MIDTOWN EAST

Slightly less buzzy than the rest of Midtown is this still-worthy area, which is home to famous spots including Grand Central Station and the Chrysler Building, as well as buttoned-up hotels and cognac and cigar–type lounges. It can be a mellow, interesting place to stroll except at rush hour, when the region is best avoided (unless you like getting jostled).

BRIDGEMARKET Map pp452-3

☎ 212-980-2455; 409 E 59th St at First Ave; ⓔ E, F, 6 to 59th St–Lexington Ave

After decades under restoration, Bridgemarket – a vaulted, Guastavino-tiled space under the 59th St Bridge that served as a farmers market in the early 20th century – was brought back to life in 1999 by design guru Sir Terence Conran. Now it's a thriving retail and dining complex, anchored by the Terence Conran Shop, alive with ingenious modern design accessories, and Guastavino's, a former restaurant (now reserved for private functions) that's worth peeking into.

BRYANT PARK Map pp452-3

☎ 212-768-4242; www.bryantpark.org; W 42nd St btwn Fifth & Sixth Aves; ⓑ B, D, F, V to 42nd St–Bryant Park

Nestled behind the grand public library is this lovely square of green – yet another former patch of squalor, referred to as a 'needle park' throughout the '80s – where local Midtown workers gather for lunchtime picnics on warm afternoons. Among its offerings are impressive skyscraper views, Europe-like coffee kiosks, a Brooklyn-constructed carousel offering rides for $1.50, and frequent special events. This is where the famed Fashion Week tent

goes up every winter, and is the site of a wonderful Monday-night summer outdoor film series, which packs the lawn with post-work crowds lugging cheese-and-wine picnics (for screening details see Bryant Park Film Series, p300, or visit the park's website). Bryant Park Grill (p272), a lovely restaurant and bar situated at the east end of the park, is the site of many a New York wedding come springtime. When it's not closed for a private event, the patio bar is a perfect spot for a twilight cocktail or two.

CHRYSLER BUILDING Map pp452-3

Lexington Ave at 42nd St; ⓢ S, 4, 5, 6, 7 to Grand Central–42nd St

The 1048ft Chrysler Building, just across from Grand Central Terminal, turned 75 years old in the spring of 2005. And since its beginning, it's been widely named as a favorite work of architecture by lay people and building aficionados alike. An art deco masterpiece designed by William Van Alen in 1930, the building briefly reigned as the tallest structure in the world until being superseded by the Empire State Building a few months later. The building was constructed to be the headquarters for Walter P Chrysler and his automobile empire; fittingly, the facade's design celebrates car

The Chrysler Building (above), that's one hell of a syringe

culture, with gargoyles that resemble hood ornaments, amorphous block cars and thatched steel designs, best viewed with binoculars. The 200ft steel spire (known as the 'vertex'), constructed in secret, was raised through the false roof as a surprise crowning touch – which shocked and dismayed a competing architect who was hoping that his new Wall St building would turn out to be New York's tallest skyscraper at the time (it wasn't). Lit up at night, there are few more poignant symbols than the Chrysler Building.

Nestled at the top was the famed Cloud Club, a former speakeasy. For a long time, developers have been planning to convert part of the building into a hotel, but so far that remains only a pipe dream.

The Chrysler Building has no restaurant or observation deck (and is filled with offices for unexciting companies including lawyers and accountants). Still, it's worth wandering inside to admire the elaborately veneered elevators (made from slices of Japanese ash, Oriental walnut and Cuban plum-pudding wood) and the profusion of marble, plus the 1st-floor ceiling mural (purportedly the world's largest at 97ft by 100ft) depicting the promise of industry.

EMPIRE STATE BUILDING Map pp452-3
☎ 212-736-3100; www.esbnyc.com; 350 Fifth Ave at 34th St; adult/senior & student/child $16/15/11; ◷ 9:30am-midnight; ◉ B, D, F, N, Q, R, V, W to 34th St–Herald Sq

Catapulted to Hollywood stardom both as the romantic meeting spot for Meg Ryan and Tom Hanks in *Sleepless in Seattle* and the vertical perch that King Kong was knocked down from, the Empire State Building is one of the most famous members of the New York skyline. It's a limestone classic built in just 410 days, or seven million hours of labor, during the depths of the Depression at a cost of $41 million. Located on the site of the original Waldorf-Astoria Hotel, the 102-story, 1472ft (to the top of the antenna) Empire State Building opened in 1931 after the laying of 10 million bricks, installation of 6400 windows and setting of 328,000 sq ft of marble. The famous antenna was originally meant to be a mooring mast for zeppelins, but the *Hindenberg* disaster slammed the brakes on that plan. One airship accidentally met up with the building: a B25 crashed into

BUYING EMPIRE STATE BUILDING TICKETS

Sure, you can just show up and take your chances. But why stand in line with every other tourist in New York when you can buy your tickets online and get to the summit before others have even entered the elevator? Hit the official website at www.esbnyc.com and go to 'Buy tickets now!' Then you'll be faced with just a couple of decisions – like whether you should purchase straight-up tickets to the observation deck, or whether to spring for optional add-ons, like the official audio tour ($5), available in six languages, or the New York Skyride package (twice the price as the observation-only ticket), which includes a simulated aerial tour of New York that you watch in a big-screen theater. Then just purchase and print out your tickets, which can be used anytime. Buying online does cost an extra $2 service charge per ticket, but once you get a glimpse of the million-dollar view, it'll all seem worth it.

the 79th floor on a foggy day in July 1945, killing 14 people.

Since 1976 the building's top 30 floors have been floodlit in seasonal and holiday colors (eg green for St Patrick's Day in March, black for World AIDS Day on December 1, red and green for Christmas, lavender for Gay Pride weekend in June; visit the website for each day's lighting scheme and meaning). This tradition has been copied by many other skyscrapers, notably the Metropolitan Life Tower at Madison Sq Park and the Con Edison Tower near Union Sq, lending elegance to the night sky.

The view from the Empire State Building is a dandy, but be prepared – the lines to get to the observation decks, on the 86th and 102nd floors, are notorious. And the basement area where you must buy tickets and queue up for the elevator ride is a shabby, poorly ventilated waiting pen, especially in the summer, when big old fans do little but blow hot air in your face. Getting here very early or very late will help you avoid delays – as will buying your tickets ahead of time, online (see box, above).

Sunset is one of the most magical times to be up here because you can see the city don its nighttime cloak in dusk's afterglow. Once up here, you can stay as long as you like. Coin-operated telescopes offer an up-close glimpse of the city, and diagrams map out the major sights. You can even smoke up top, to the great dismay of many non-Europeans.

GRAND CENTRAL TERMINAL

Map pp452-3

www.grandcentralterminal.com; 42nd St at Park Ave; ⊙ S, 4, 5, 6, 7 to Grand Central–42nd St
One of New York's most dramatic public spaces, Grand Central Terminal evokes the romance of train travel at the turn of the 20th century, while enduring the bustle of present-day New York. Thanks to a lovingly tendered 1998 renovation, its interior remains as impressive as ever.

Completed in 1913, Grand Central Terminal (also called Grand Central Station) is another of New York's stunning beaux arts buildings and boasts 75ft-high, glass-encased catwalks, with the constellations of the zodiac streaming across the vaulted ceiling – backwards (the designer must've been dyslexic). The balconies overlooking the main concourse afford an expansive view; perch yourself on one of these at around 6pm on a weekday to get a glimpse of the grace this terminal commands under pressure.

Today, Grand Central's underground electric tracks only serve commuter trains en route to northern suburbs and Connecticut. But whether you're traveling somewhere or not, the station merits a special trip for the architecture alone – not to mention the fine dining, cool bars, funky shops (including a gift shop of the Brooklyn-based Transit Museum, p174), holiday craft fairs, occasional music performances and, particularly worthy, the **StoryCorp Booth** (www.storycorp.net /participate/storybooths). Choose one of the soundproof booths and head inside by yourself or with a loved one to record a personal story. It's an amazing, touching project that began in 2001, and was particularly cathartic in the days and weeks following September 11.

The Municipal Art Society (p112) leads weekly walks (⊙ 12:30pm Wed; $12) through Grand Central, during which you'll get to cross the glass catwalk high above the concourse (usually off-limits). Tours meet at the passenger information booth in the middle of the terminal.

JAPAN SOCIETY Map pp452-3

☎ 212-832-1155; www.japansociety.org; 333 E 47th St; admission free; ⊙ 11am-6pm Tue-Thu, 11am-9pm Fri, 11am-5pm Sat & Sun; ⊙ 4, 5, 6, 7 to Grand Central–42nd St
Founded in 1907 by a group of NYC businesspeople with a deep admiration for Japan, this non-profit society has played a large role in strengthening US–Japan relations. It expanded into a full arts and cultural center with a little help from philanthropist John D Rockefeller, who had a strong interest in Japan. Today its main draw can be found in its galleries, which highlight Japanese art through shows like its recently hailed *Hiroshi Suguimoto: the History of History*, and in its theater, which hosts a range of dance and theater performances. Those who want to dig deeper can browse through the 14,000 volumes of the research library or attend one of myriad lectures.

LITTLE KOREA Map pp452-3

btwn 31st & 36th Sts & Broadway & Fifth Ave; ⊙ B, D, F, N, Q, R, V, W to 34th St–Herald Sq
Herald Sq is a bit on the tasteless side when it comes to finding foodie treats; luckily, you can head for quality refueling at nearby Little Korea, a small enclave of Korean-owned restaurants, shops, salons and spas. Over the past few years this neighborhood has seen an explosion of eateries serving Korean fare, with authentic Korean BBQ available around the clock at many of the all-night spots on 32nd St, some with the added treat of karaoke.

NEW YORK PUBLIC LIBRARY

Map pp452-3

☎ 212-930-0830; www.nypl.org; 42nd St at Fifth Ave; ⊙ 11am-7:30pm Tue & Wed, 10am-6pm Thu-Sat; ⊙ S, 4, 5, 6 to Grand Central–42nd St, 7 to Fifth Ave
This main branch of the public library system is a monument to learning, housed in a grand beaux arts building and reflecting its big-money industrialist roots. When it was dedicated in 1911, New York's flagship library ranked as the largest marble structure ever built in the USA, with a vast 3rd-floor reading room designed to hold 500 patrons. This is not to mention the marble lions at the entrance, profligate use of gold leaf throughout, chandeliers, carved porticos and ceiling murals.

Today this building, now called the Humanities & Social Sciences Library, a research library under the banner of the main library with several other specialist research libraries located elsewhere, is one of the best free attractions in the city. On a rainy day, hide away with a book in the airy Reading Room and admire the original

Carre and Hastings lamps, or stroll through the Exhibition Hall, which contains precious manuscripts by just about every author of note in the English language, including a 'fair copy' of the Declaration of Independence and a Gutenberg Bible. And late 2005 marked the reopening of the incredible Map Division, with a collection that holds some 431,000 maps and 16,000 atlases and books on cartography dating from the 16th century to the present. The free tour is a bonanza of interesting tidbits; it leaves from the information desk in Astor Hall at 11am and 2pm Tuesday to Saturday.

UNITED NATIONS Map pp452-3

☎ 212-963-7539; www.un.org/tours; btwn First Ave & 46th St; adult/senior/student/child $11.50/8.50/7.50/6.50; ⏱ 9:30am-4:45pm Mon-Fri Jan-Feb only, 10am-4:30pm Sat & Sun; ⊕ S, 4, 5, 6, 7 to Grand Central–42nd St

The UN headquarters is technically located on a section of international territory overlooking the East River. Take a guided tour of the facility and you'll get to see the General Assembly, where the annual fall convocation of member nations takes place; the Security Council Chamber, where crisis management continues year-round; and the Economic & Social Council Chamber. There is a park to the south of the complex which is home to Henry Moore's *Reclining Figure* as well as several other sculptures with a peace theme.

English-language tours of the UN complex depart every 30 minutes; limited tours in several other languages are also available. You may sometimes hear this area of Midtown East referred to as Turtle Bay, and even though the turtles are long gone, there is a number of interesting architectural examples around here, in particular among the permanent missions, such as those of **Egypt** (304 E 44th St btwn First & Second Aves) and **India** (245 E 43rd St btwn Second & Third Aves).

If only the walls could talk – United Nations Building (above)

TOP TEN MUST-DOS: MIDTOWN

- Go to the top of the Empire State Building (p149)
- Get a different aerial perspective at the newly reopened Top of the Rock (p156)
- Admire the truly grand interior of Grand Central Terminal (opposite)
- Troll Ninth and Tenth Aves in Hell's Kitchen in search of a fab culinary experience (p230)
- Stroll Fifth Ave and pop into some of the high-end superstar stores (p341)
- Catch a top notch show at Jazz at Lincoln Center (p159)
- Gawk at the lights and action with a night visit to Times Sq (p156)
- Settle in for a Broadway production (p281)
- Stop for late-night BBQ and karaoke in Little Korea (opposite)
- Tour the newly renovated Museum of Modern Art (p154)

MIDTOWN WEST

A general term, Midtown West refers to a collection of neighborhoods that includes the far-west reaches of Hell's Kitchen, and the office-worker crush of food carts and harried suit-wearers along Sixth Ave and Columbus Circle, with its gleaming Time Warner Center. Though at first the area may seem overwhelming, taking the time to pick out the tucked-away riches within the Midtown West sea is fascinating, and a great way to ensure some DIY adventures. Try wandering around Hell's Kitchen, where you may stumble upon tiny community gardens or excellent eateries, or head to one of the specialty districts that make NYC unique: the frenzied **Diamond District** (www.47th-street.com; 47th St btwn Fifth & Sixth Aves) is packed with newly engaged couples shopping for rings and a slew of folks in the biz buying wholesale. It's home to more than 2600 independent businesses, selling all manner of diamonds, gold, pearls, gemstones and watches, and offering engraving and repair services from cramped, hidden-away quarters. Then there's the famed **Garment District** (Seventh Ave btwn 34th St & Times Sq), home to designers' offices and wholesale and retail shops both on and off the avenue, where you'll find a dreamy selection of fabrics, buttons, sequins, lace and more (it's where the kids of *Project Runway* go shopping each week for their challenge on the hit Bravo TV series). Visit the **Fashion Center information kiosk** (Map pp452–3;

www.fashioncenter.com; 249 W 39th St) for maps and details. The tip of this area is **Columbus Circle**, a literal traffic circle that serves as the gateway to both the Upper West Side and Central Park, and is home to the **Time Warner Center** (opposite).

HELL'S KITCHEN Map pp452-3
34th St to 57th St, west of Ninth Ave
For years the far west side of Midtown was a working-class district of tenements and food warehouses known as Hell's Kitchen, a neighborhood that predominantly attracted Italian and Irish immigrants, who drifted into gangs after arriving. Hollywood films have often romanticized the district's gritty, criminal character (*West Side Story* was set here), but by the 1960s, the population of junkies and prostitutes had made it a forbidding place that few cared to enter, including many movie directors.

In 1989 the construction of the **Worldwide Plaza** (Map p282; W 50th St & Eighth Ave) building was supposed to juice the area's revival, as it took over the site of the 1930s-era Madison Sq Garden, which had been a parking lot in the interim. Yet until the mid-1990s, Hell's Kitchen was largely unchanged. Eighth and Ninth Aves between 35th and 50th Sts were still the domain of wholesale food stores, and few buildings rose more than eight stories above the street. But the economic boom of the late '90s seriously changed Hell's Kitchen and developers reverted to using the cleaned-up name Clinton, a moniker originating from the 1950s; locals are split on usage. A perfect link between the Upper West Side and Chelsea, the neighborhood (especially on Ninth Ave) exploded with nightspots and restaurants, as chefs eyed the large quantities of fresh food from nearby wholesalers and the large-ish spaces at cheap(er) rents (which is not the case anymore). Culturally, you can catch unique shows at performance spaces like **Ars Nova** (511 W 54th St) and the Alvin Ailey American Dance Theater (p290), or enjoy the gay nightlife that has crept north from Chelsea at nightspots like Therapy (p267).

HERALD SQUARE Map pp452-3
B, D, F, N, Q, R, V, W to 34th St–Herald Sq
This crowded convergence of Broadway, Sixth Ave and 34th St is best known as the home of Macy's department store, where you can still ride some of the remaining original wooden elevators to floors ranging from home furnishings to lingerie. But the busy square gets its name from a long-defunct newspaper, the *Herald*, and the small, leafy park here bustles during business hours thanks to a recent and much-needed face-lift. Don't bother with the two indoor malls south of Macy's on Sixth Ave, where you'll find a boring and suburban array of chain stores (with the exception of Daffy's, which offers great discounts on big labels).

INTERNATIONAL CENTER OF PHOTOGRAPHY Map p282
212-857-0000; www.icp.org; 1133 Sixth Ave at 43rd St; adult/senior & student $10/7, with 'voluntary contribution Fridays' from 5-8pm; 10am-6pm Tue-Thu, Sat & Sun, 10am-8pm Fri; B, D, F, V to 42nd St–Bryant Park
Consolidated from two locations at this expanded Midtown space, the ICP remains the city's most important showcase for major photographers, especially photojournalists. Its past exhibitions have included work by Henri Cartier-Bresson, Man Ray, Matthew Brady, Weegee and Robert Capa, and have explored a wide range of themes through creative shows such as the recent *Che! Revolution and Commerce* and *The Body at Risk: Photography of Disorder, Illness and Healing*. It's also a photography school, offering coursework for credit as well as a public-lecture series. And its gift shop is an excellent place to stock up on quality photo books or quirky, photo-themed gifts.

INTREPID SEA-AIR-SPACE MUSEUM
Map pp452-3
212-245-0072; www.intrepidmuseum.org; Pier 86 Twelfth Ave at W 46th St; adult/senior & student/child $16.50/12.50/11.50; 10am-5pm Mon-Fri, 10am-6pm Sat & Sun Apr-Sep, 10am-5pm Tue-Sun Oct-Mar; A, C, E to 42nd St
The Intrepid Sea-Air-Space Museum sits on an aircraft carrier at Pier 86 at the western edge of Midtown. The flight deck of the USS *Intrepid*, which served in WWII and Vietnam, features several fighter planes, and the pier area contains the *Growler* guided-missile submarine, an *Apollo* space capsule, Vietnam-era tanks and the 900ft destroyer *Edson*. In 2003 an adjacent barge became home to a 204ft-long, 88-ton Concorde jet. The *Intrepid* is the nexus for the Fleet Week (p25) celebrations each May, when

thousands of the world's sailors descend on Manhattan. Free audio tours in English, French, German, Japanese, Russian and Spanish are available.

JACOB JAVITS CONVENTION CENTER
Map pp452-3

☎ 212-216-2000; www.javitscenter.com; Eleventh Ave btwn 34th & 38th Sts; ❸ A, C, E to 34th St–Penn Station then M11 crosstown bus

NYC's sole convention center is a four-block construction way on the outer reaches of Manhattan's west side. Designed by IM Pei, the behemoth of glass and steel – either totally loved or completely reviled by most New Yorkers – is host to hundreds of events each year, from auto shows and dentist conventions to travel expos and an annual Gay Life Expo (in November).

TIME WARNER CENTER Map pp452-3

☎ 212-869-1890; www.shopsatcolumbuscircle.com; 1 Columbus Circle at 59th St; ⏱ 9am-9pm; A, C, B, D, 1 to 59th St–Columbus Circle

This pair of sleek towers, built for $1.8 billion and completed in early 2004 after much angst and anticipation, created a major buzz with their grand entrance, though much of that has faded. What remains here, in the spot that for years was home to the aging New York Coliseum, is a very tall mall. The seven-floor retail atrium, which affords grand views of Central Park from behind its glass facade and features a wonderful collection of Fernando Botero

sculptures in its common spaces, is rarely crowded anymore. That's probably because its stores – which include Williams-Sonoma, J Crew, Borders Books and Hugo Boss – can be found in so many other places, NYC and otherwise. Same goes for the basement's 59,000-sq-ft Whole Foods, now one of three (and still counting) in the city. Still, it can get crowded with folks who live in the area – including those lucky enough to reside in one of the luxury condominiums at the Time Warner Center, which also houses a Mandarin Oriental Hotel, Equinox Sports Club, Jazz at Lincoln Center (left) and the corporate headquarters of Time Warner, by the way. And then there are the seven high-end eateries above the shopping concourses, which create a continuous buzz - these places include Café Gray, Per Se and Masa (p245).

FIFTH AVENUE

Immortalized in both film and song, Fifth Ave first developed its high-class reputation in the early 20th century, when it was considered desirable for its 'country' air and open spaces. Now it's the battleground for society folks who want to retain their class status without allowing too many others in. 'Fifth Ave is the address against which all others are measured,' writes author Steven Gaines in *The Sky's the Limit: Passion and Property in Manhattan* (Little Brown, 2005). The series of mansions called Millionaire's Row extended right up to 130th St, while Midtown Fifth Ave is the site of airline offices and a number of high-end shops and hotels, especially from 49th St to 57th St.

Most of the heirs to the millionaire mansions on Fifth Ave above 59th St sold them for demolition or converted them to the cultural institutions that now make up Museum Mile. The Villard Houses, on Madison Ave behind St Patrick's Cathedral, are a stunning exception. Financier Henry Villard built the six four-story town houses in 1881, and they flaunt artistic details by the likes of Tiffany, John LaFarge and Auguste St-Gaudens; the mansion and neighboring town houses was later owned by the Catholic church and then sold to a series of hotel magnates.

Today, the avenue's Midtown stretch still boasts upscale shops and hotels, including the famous Trump Tower, where the Big D

Sights

MIDTOWN

JAZZ AT LINCOLN CENTER

Back in 2004 the jazz component of Lincoln Center (www.jazzatlincolncenter.com) left its old home for its grand new digs at the Jazz at Lincoln Center Frederick P Rose Hall in the Time Warner Center, a 100,000-sq-ft, $128-million facility built specifically for jazz. The multiroom space, with a sleek and soaring glass design from Rafael Viñoly Architects, hosts opera, dance, theater and symphony shows, but its main theme is jazz, in the form of education, historical archiving and, of course, performance, with shows curated by its artistic director, none other than Wynton Marsalis. The place is perched high above Central Park – its ring of a glimmering skyline and the magnificent views serves as a backdrop for jazz shows in glass-backed spaces such as the intimate Allen Room and Dizzy's Club Coca-Cola nightclub.

was renowned for firing folks each week on *The Apprentice*, and the endearing anchor of **Plaza Hotel**, which is currently undergoing a major renovation that will convert most of its rooms to high-end condos. This was a change that moved many outraged New Yorkers to form a 'Save the Plaza' campaign and lobby to retain as many rooms and as much of the original interior as possible. They were only partially successful, as demolitions of the most prized rooms went forward as planned.

While a number of the more exclusive boutiques have migrated to Madison Ave, several superstars still reign over Fifth Ave above 50th St, including **Cartier** (p342), **Henri Bendel** (p343) and the movie-famous **Tiffany & Co** (p344).

AMERICAN FOLK ART MUSEUM
Map p282

☎ 212-265-1040; www.folkartmuseum.org; 45 W 53rd St btwn Fifth & Sixth Aves; adult/senior & student/child $9/7/free; ☼ 10:30am-5:30pm Tue-Thu, Sat & Sun, 10:30am-7:30pm Fri; ⊕ E, V to Fifth Ave–53rd St
Housed in a beautiful eight-story building designed by the noted Billie Tsien and Tod Williams, the focus here is on traditional arts tied to moments in history or personal milestones. The expansive collection features objects such as flags, liberty figures, textiles, weather vanes and decorative arts, and recent visiting exhibits have ranged from *Surface Attractions: Painted Furniture from our Collection* to *Obsessive Drawing*, which highlighted five emerging self-taught artists.

MUSEUM OF ARTS & DESIGN
Map pp452-3

☎ 212-956-3535; www.madmuseum.org; 40 W 53rd St btwn Fifth & Sixth Aves; adult/senior/child under 13 $9/6/free; ☼ 10am-6pm Tue, Wed & Fri-Sun, 10am-8pm Thu; ⊕ E, V to Fifth Ave–53rd St
This museum is planning a controversial 2008 move to Columbus Circle, where it will completely redesign an historic building that preservationists lost their fight over. For now, you'll find this fascinating collection directly across the street from Museum of Modern Art. The Museum of Arts & Design, which had its name switched from the American Craft Museum in order to boost its art-world worthiness for those turned off by the term 'craft,' displays innovative and traditional, well, *crafts* in a spectacularly well-designed and airy space. Recent shows have included *Changing Hands: Art Without Reservation*, the second in a series of exhibits that looked at Native American artistry, and especially that which challenged preconceived notions.

MUSEUM OF MODERN ART Map pp452-3
☎ 212-708-9400; www.moma.org; 11 W 53rd St btwn Fifth & Sixth Aves; adult/senior/student/child $20/16/12/free, Fri 4-8pm free; ☼ 10:30am-5:30pm Sat-Mon, Wed-Thu, 10:30am-8pm Fri; ⊕ E, V to Fifth Ave–53rd St
Since its grand reopening in 2004 following the most extensive renovation project in its 75-year history, the Museum of Modern Art has been widely hailed for both its physical design and the soul of its exhibits. The project added a sparkling new design by architect Yoshio Taniguchi and doubled the museum's capacity to 630,000 sq ft on six floors, creating a veritable art universe of more than 100,000 pieces where you could easily hole up for a couple of days and still not properly see it all. Most of the big hitters – Matisse, Picasso, Cezanne, Rothko, Pollock and many others – are housed in the central five-story atrium, where peaceful, airy galleries contain works from the departments of Painting and Sculpture, Architecture and Design, Prints and Drawings, Prints and Illustrated Books, and Film and Media. The museum's sculpture garden – returned to its original, larger vision of the early '50s by Philip Johnson – is a joy to sit in. You can also choose to overlook it from your table at the Modern (p245), a high-end, foodie paradise of French-American cuisine courtesy of celeb restaurateur Danny Meyer (other, more affordable dining options are onsite, too).

The museum's cinema hosts a rich film program, with rotating screenings from its collection of more than 19,000 films, including the works of John Maysles and every Pixar animation film ever produced. Recent special exhibitions inside the high-ceilinged galleries have included *On Site: New Architecture in Spain* and *Dada: Zurich, Berlin, Hannover, Cologne, New York, Paris*, which is the first major US museum show to explore the Dada movement. See p217 for details of a brief walking tour of the museum.

MUSEUM OF TELEVISION & RADIO
Map p282

☎ 212-621-6800; www.mtr.org; 25 W 52nd St btwn Fifth & Sixth Aves; adult/senior & student/child $10/8/5; ⓘ noon-6pm Tue, Wed & Fri-Sun, noon-8pm Thu; ⓘ E, V to Fifth Ave–53rd St

This couch potato's smorgasbord contains a collection of more than 50,000 American TV and radio programs, all of which are available from the museum's computer catalog with the click of a mouse. It's a great place to hang out when it's raining or when you are simply fed up with the real world. Nearly everybody checks out their favorite childhood TV programs and watches them on the museum's 90 consoles, but the radio-listening room is an unexpected pleasure. Your admission fee entitles you to two hours of uninterrupted audiovisual enjoyment. Excellent special screenings are also held here on a regular basis, with recent shows heralding topics from Jim Henson's *Muppets* to women who 'made it' through TV and radio creations.

NBC STUDIOS Map pp452-3

☎ 212-664-3700; www.nbc.com; 49th St at Rockefeller Plaza; tours adult/senior & child 6-16 yrs $18.50/15.50 (child under 6 not admitted); ⓘ tours 8:30am-5:30pm Mon-Sat, 9:30am-4:30pm Sun (extended hrs Nov & Dec); ⓘ B, D, F, V to 47th–50th Sts–Rockefeller Center

The NBC TV network has its headquarters in the 70-story GE Building, which looms over the Rockefeller Center ice-skating rink (the rink doubles as a café in the summer months). The *Today* show broadcasts live 7am to 10am daily from a glass-enclosed street-level studio near the fountain.

Tours of the NBC studios leave from the lobby of the GE Building every 15 minutes; the walkabout lasts for about one hour and 10 minutes, but be advised that there is a strict policy of 'no bathrooms,' so be sure to empty your bladder beforehand!

Tickets to show tapings (eg *Saturday Night Live*, *Late Night with Conan O'Brien* etc) are no longer available by mail, but on a standby basis from 9am to 5pm Monday to Friday. Competition is stiff, so be sure to show up by 7am if you want even a remote chance of getting in. For other shows, visit www.tvticket.com.

RADIO CITY MUSIC HALL Map p282

☎ 212-247-4777; www.radiocity.com; 51st St at Sixth Ave; tours adult/senior/child $17/14/10; ⓘ B, D, F, V to 47th–50th Sts–Rockefeller Center

This 6000-seat art deco movie palace had its interior declared a protected landmark and is looking fine, thanks to extensive renovation work in 1999. In a triumphant restoration, the velvet seats and furnishings were returned to the exact state they were in when the building opened in 1932. (Even the toilets are elegant at the 'Showplace of the Nation.') Concerts here sell out quickly, and tickets to the annual Christmas spectacular featuring the hokey but enjoyable Rockette dancers now cost up to $70. (Samuel 'Roxy' Rothafel, the man responsible for the high-kicking chorus line, declared that 'a visit to Radio City is as good as a month in the country.')

You can see the interior by taking a tour, which leaves every half-hour between 11am and 3pm Monday to Sunday. Tickets are sold on a first-come, first-served basis.

ROCKEFELLER CENTER Map p282

☎ 212-632-3975; www.rockefellercenter.com; btwn Fifth & Sixth Aves & 48th & 51st Sts; ⓘ B, D, F, V to 47th–50th Sts–Rockefeller Center

Built during the height of the Great Depression in the 1930s, the 22-acre Rockefeller gave jobs to 70,000 workers over nine years and was the first project to combine retail, entertainment and office space in what is often referred to as a 'city within a city.' The biggest news here as of late has been the late-2005 reopening of the long-shuttered Top of the Rock (p156) observation deck, which affords stunning views of the city.

Perhaps most impressively, Rockefeller Center features commissioned works around the theme 'Man at the Crossroads Looks Uncertainly But Hopefully at the Future' by 30 great artists of the day. One great artist, however, was looking skeptically at the future. Mexican muralist Diego Rivera, persuaded to paint the lobby of the 70-story RCA Building (now the GE Building), was outraged, along with the rest of the art world, when the Rockefeller family rejected his painting for containing 'Communist imagery' – namely, the face of Lenin. The fresco was destroyed and replaced with a Jose Maria Sert work depicting the more 'acceptable' faces of Abraham Lincoln and Ralph Waldo Emerson.

But even art neophytes will appreciate Prometheus overlooking the ice-skating rink, Atlas doing his thing in front of the **International Building** (630 Fifth Ave), which has a wacky sculpture inset into its lobby walls, and *News* by Isamu Noguchi above the entrance to the **Associated Press Building** (45 Rockefeller Plaza). Anyone interested in artworks within the complex should pick up the *Rockefeller Center Visitors Guide* in the GE lobby, which describes many of them in detail.

Even with the arrival of Top of the Rock, the best-known feature of Rockefeller Center is still its gigantic Christmas tree, which overlooks the skating rink during the holidays. (This tradition dates back to the 1930s, when construction workers set up a small Christmas tree on the site.) The annual lighting of the Rockefeller Center Christmas tree during the week after Thanksgiving attracts thousands of visitors to the area, who cram around the felled spruce, selected each year with fanfare from an unlucky upstate forest. The scene is too crowded to be believed, but skating at the **Rink at Rockefeller Center** (☎ 212-332-7654; www.therinkatrockcenter.com; Fifth Ave btwn 49th & 50th Sts; adult/child $9/7 Mon-Fri, $13/8 Sat & Sun, skate rental $6) under the gaze of Prometheus is unforgettable. Opening hours change weekly, so call for the schedule.

ROCK OUT

Top of the Rock (Map pp452–3; ☎ 212-698-2000; www.topoftherocknyc.com; 30 Rockefeller Plaza; adult/senior/child $17.50/16/11.25; ⏲ 8:30am-midnight) first wowed New Yorkers back in 1933, when John D Rockefeller opened the open-air observation deck. Designed in homage to ocean liners popular in the day, it was an incredible place – 70 stories above Midtown – from which to view the city. But it became off limits for almost two decades starting in 1986, when renovation of the stunning Rainbow Room five floors below cut off access to the roof. The observation deck was reopened with much fanfare (and lines around the block) in November 2005. Now it's an even better bet than the Empire State Building: it's much less crowded and has wider observation decks that span several levels – some indoors, some outside with Plexiglass walls and those at the very top are completely alfresco. Though the Chrysler Building is partially obscured, you do get an excellent view of the Empire State Building itself. The very cool elevator ride to the top is an exciting bonus.

ST PATRICK'S CATHEDRAL Map pp452-3
☎ 212-753-2261; 50th St at Fifth Ave; ⏲ 6am-9pm; ◉ B, D, F, V to 47th–50th Sts–Rockefeller Center

It's worth checking out this cathedral just across from Rockefeller Center, which features an elaborate interpretation of French Gothic styles. The cathedral, built at a cost of nearly $2 million during the Civil War, originally didn't include the two front spires, which were added in 1888. Although it seats a modest 2400 worshippers, most of New York's 2.2 million faithful will have been inside at one time or another. While it may seem like each and every one is there when you show up, muddle through to see some of the exquisite details inside.

After you enter, walk by the eight small shrines along the side of the cathedral, past the shrine to Nuestra Señora de Guadalupe and the main altar to the quiet Lady Chapel, dedicated to the Virgin Mary. From here, you can see the handsome stained-glass Rose Window above the 7000-pipe church organ. A basement crypt behind the altar contains the coffins of every New York cardinal and the remains of Pierre Touissant, a champion of the poor and the first black American up for sainthood (he emigrated from Haiti).

Unfortunately, St Patrick's is not a place for restful contemplation because of the constant buzz from loud, videotaping, generally disrespectful visitors. It's also a regular protest site for gay and lesbian New Yorkers who are systematically excluded and insulted by the Roman Catholic Church. Every March, the banning of Irish gays from the St Patrick's Day Parade triggers protests near the cathedral; it also inspires participants in the spirited Gay Pride March in June to scream 'Shame! Shame! Shame!' as they pass on by.

Frequent masses take place on the weekend, and New York's archbishop presides over the service at 10:15am Sunday. Casual visitors are only allowed in between services.

THEATER DISTRICT & TIMES SQUARE

Now in the midst of a major renaissance – to the dismay of those who gripe about 'Disneyfication' and wax poetic about the prostitute-and-drug-drenched past – Times Sq (◉ N, Q, R, S, W, 1, 2, 3, 7 to Times Sq–42nd St) can once again trumpet its reputation as the 'Crossroads of the World.' Smack in the middle of Midtown

Sights

MIDTOWN

Manhattan, this area around the intersection of Broadway and Seventh Ave has long been synonymous with gaudy billboards and glittery marquees – before the advent of TV, advertisers went after the largest audience possible by beaming their messages into the center of New York. With over 60 mega-billboards and 40 miles of neon, it's startling (and a bit alarming) how it always looks like daytime and how the place has been transformed into a veritable outdoor mall. Massive chains like Sephora, Skechers and Cold Stone Creamery pull in folks who can find this stuff anywhere; multiplex theaters draw crowds with large screens and stadium seating; and gargantuan video-game and sporting compounds like ESPN Zone (Map p282; ☎ 212-921-3776; www.espnzone.com/newyork; 1472 Broadway at 42nd St; ⏱ 11:30am-12:30am Mon-Thu, 11:30am-1am Fri, 11am-1am Sat) and Lazer Park (Map p282; ☎ 212-398-3060; www.lazerpark.com; 1560 Broadway at 46th St; ⏱ noon-11pm Mon-Thu, noon-2am Fri, 11am-2am Sat, 11am-midnight Sun) lure both children and adults with a dizzying array of games, from Area 51 and NBA Showtime Gold to Battlemech and laser tag.

Once called Long Acre Sq, Times Sq took its present name from the famous newspaper, the *New York Times*, which is still located here. Though it has long been the site of bright lights and flashy behavior, Times Sq dimmed quite a bit in the 1960s, as once-proud movie palaces that had previously shown first-run films turned into 'triple X' porn theaters. But in recent years the city has reversed the area's fortunes by extending big tax breaks to businesses that relocated here (most notably Walt Disney) and legislating theaters to the hilt: under Mayor Giuliani an entertainment venue had to be at least 60% 'legitimate' theater to permit the other 40% of the same venue to show or sell porn. Today, the square draws more than 27 million annual visitors, who spend something over $12 billion in Midtown.

Times Sq also continues to serve as New York's official Theater District (see p281), with dozens of Broadway and off-Broadway theaters located in an area that stretches from 41st to 54th Sts, between Sixth and Ninth Aves. Unless it's a very specific show you're after, the best – and most affordable – way to score tickets is at the TKTS Booth (☎ 212-768-1818; www.tdf.org/tkts;

Broadway at 47th St; ⏱ 3-8pm Mon-Sat, 11am-8pm Sun), where you can line up and get same-day half-price tickets for top Broadway and off-Broadway shows. Carnegie Hall (p279) and Town Hall (p281) are classic venues for top notch music shows.

Up to a million people gather in Times Sq every New Year's Eve to see an illuminated Waterford Crystal ball descend from the roof of One Times Sq at midnight. While this event garners international coverage, it lasts just 90 seconds and, frankly, is something of a (very drunk) anticlimax.

TIMES SQUARE INFORMATION CENTER Map p282

☎ 212-869-5667; www.timessquarenyc.org; 1560 Broadway btwn 46th & 47th Sts; ⏱ 8am-8pm; ⊚ N, Q, R, S, W, 1, 2, 3, 7 to Times Sq–42nd St Sitting smack in the middle of this famous crossroads is the official information center, located in the beautifully restored landmark Embassy Theater. More than one million visitors annually stop in to get up-to-date info on the area from both interactive screens and knowledgeable staff guides.

UPPER WEST SIDE

Eating p248, Drinking p272, Shopping p346, Sleeping p372

This lengthy neighborhood stretches up along the western side of Central Park and contains pockets that range from leafy parkland – Riverside Park runs along the Hudson River here – to quaint residential blocks and bustling sections of Broadway that have been hyper-developed recently, with the addition of both chain stores and controversial luxury high-rise condos. It's traditionally home to many creative types, mostly actors and musicians, but you'll also find a high volume of moms pushing strollers, as the parks and the good schools here make it a desirable neighborhood for raising children. Much of the area is an architectural wonderland, with everything from opulent apartment buildings, such as Dorilton (171 W 71st St at Broadway), the Dakota (see p262, 72nd St at Central Park West) and the Ansonia (2109 Broadway btwn 73rd and 74th Sts), to functional public buildings with succulent detail, such as the McBurney School (63rd St) off Central Park West and Frederick Henry Cossitt Dormitory (64th St) near Central Park West.

Orientation

The Upper West Side (UWS) begins as Broadway emerges from Midtown at Columbus Circle and ends at the southern border of Harlem, around 125th St. Many hotels ring Central Park, and many celebrities live in the massive apartment buildings that line Central Park West up to 96th St.

AMERICAN MUSEUM OF NATURAL HISTORY Map pp454–5

☎ 212-769-5000; www.amnh.org; Central Park West at 79th St; suggested donation adult/senior & student/child $14/10.50/8, last hr free; ☽ 10am–5:45pm (Rose Center till 8:45pm Fri); ◉ B, C to 81st St–Museum of Natural History, 1 to 79th St

Founded in 1869, this museum is a classic for kids – school buses deposit loads of excited students day in and day out – and, for most city children, this is a standard introduction to culture. There's nothing standard about the place, though, as its halls are fascinating wonderlands of more than 30 million artifacts, and its interactive exhibits, both in the original museum and the thrilling Rose Center for Earth & Space, added in 2000 for a cost of $210 million, are out of this world. Plan to spend most of a day here so you and your little one can see as much as possible.

The museum is most famous for its three large, recently renovated dinosaur halls, as well as for the enormous (fake) blue whale that hangs from the ceiling of the Hall of Ocean Life. Kids of all ages will find something to be intrigued by, whether it's the stuffed Alaskan brown bear, the Star of India sapphire in the Hall of Minerals & Gems, the IMAX film on jungle life, or the skullcap of a pachycephalasaurus, a plant-eating dinosaur that roamed the earth 65 million years ago. No matter what section of the museum you're in, you'll find enthusiastic volunteer guides who are excited to answer questions.

Visiting exhibitions are also popular, especially the recurring Butterfly Conservancy (November to May), which lets you stroll through a house of glass with more than 600 butterflies from all over the world. It provides an amazing opportunity to truly hang out with – and sometimes serve as a perch for – the creatures.

It's the Rose Center for Earth & Space, though, that has really been the star attraction since its much-heralded opening. Just gazing at its facade – a massive glass box that contains a silver globe, home to space-show theaters and the planetarium – is mesmerizing, especially at night when all of its otherworldly features are aglow. Step inside to trace the origins of the planets, especially Earth, and to grab a cushy seat in the high-tech planetarium, where you can watch either *The Search For Life: Are We Alone?*, narrated by Harrison Ford, or *Passport to the Universe*, with soothing narration by Tom Hanks. Another, smaller theater explores the Big Bang theory with Maya Angelou's voice as your guide.

The live jazz program (called Starry Nights) takes place in the Rose Center from 6pm to 8pm Friday and is highly recommended. Tapas, drinks and top jazz acts are all included with museum admission at these weekly gigs.

CHILDREN'S MUSEUM OF MANHATTAN Map pp454–5

☎ 212-721-1234; www.cmom.org; 212 W 83rd St btwn Amsterdam Ave & Broadway; adult & child over 1/senior $8/5; ☽ 10am–5pm Wed–Sun; ◉ 1 to 86th St, B, C to 81st St–Museum of Natural History

This museum is a favorite for area mommies. It features discovery centers for toddlers, a postmodern media center where technologically savvy kids can work in a TV studio, and the cutting-edge Inventor Center, where all the latest, cool tech stuff like digital imaging and scanners is made available. Expect the kids' stuff to be filtered through a sophisticated city lens, though, as recent exhibi-

Getting a headstart on her media career, this girl presents the weather at the Children's Museum of Manhattan (above)

Sights

UPPER WEST SIDE

tions showed the art of Andy Warhol and shaped interactive art projects around the works of William Wegman, Elizabeth Murray and Fred Wilson. During summer months, little ones can splash around with outdoor waterwheels and boats for lessons on buoyancy and currents. The museum also runs craft workshops on weekends and sponsors special exhibitions. (**Brooklyn Children's Museum**, p178, is an affiliated children's museum.)

LINCOLN CENTER Map pp454-5

☎ 212-546-2656; www.lincolncenter.org; Columbus Ave at Broadway; ⊙ 1 to 66th St–Lincoln Center
The 16-acre Lincoln Center complex includes seven large performance spaces built in the 1960s, which controversially replaced a group of tenements that inspired the musical *West Side Story*. During the day Lincoln Center presents a demure face, but at night the interiors glow and sparkle with crystal chandeliers and the well-heeled. And it will soon be transformed by a $325 million redesign by the famed Diller Scofidio + Renfro, to include a glass-walled restaurant with a grass roof, scrolling electronic billboards, spiffed-up buildings and a 'street of the arts' to span 65th St between Broadway and Amsterdam Ave. Construction is set to begin sometime in 2006.

If you have just a shred of culture vulture in you, Lincoln Center is a must-see, since it contains the **Metropolitan Opera House** (p290), its lobby adorned by two colorful tapestries (viewable from the street below) by Marc Chagall, and the **New York State Theater** (p290), home of both the New York City Ballet and the New York City Opera, which is the low-cost and more-daring alternative to the Met. The New York Philharmonic holds its season in **Avery Fisher Hall** (p280), and you'll find constant high-quality dramas at both the Mitzi E Newhouse and Vivian Beaumont Theaters. To the right of the theaters stands the **New York Public Library for the Performing Arts** (☎ 212-870-1630), which houses the city's largest collection of recorded sound, video and books on film and theater. And then there's the **Walter Reade Theater** (p301), the city's most comfortable film-revival space and the major screening site for the **New York Film Festival** (p301), held each September.

The presence of young drama types keeps the whole area infused with a fresh excitement, as both the Fiorello H LaGuardia High School of Music and Performing

Arts (otherwise known as the *Fame* school) and the Juilliard School are located here; visit the high school's website (www.laguardiahs.org) to check out its diverse performance schedule.

On any given night, there are at least 10 performances happening throughout Lincoln Center – and even more in summer, when Lincoln Center Out of Doors (a series of dance and music concerts) and Midsummer Night Swing (ballroom dancing under the stars) lure those who love parks *and* culture.

Daily **tours** (☎ 212-875-5350; adult/senior & student/child $12.50/9/6) of the complex explore at least three of the theaters (which three you visit depends on production schedules). It's a good idea to call ahead for a space. They leave from the tour desk on the concourse level at 10:30am, 12:30pm, 2:30pm and 4:30pm.

NEW-YORK HISTORICAL SOCIETY
Map pp454-5

☎ 212-873-3400; www.nyhistory.org; 2 W 77th St at Central Park West; suggested donation adult/senior & student $10/5; ⊙ 10am-6pm Tue-Sun; ⊙ B, C to 81st St–Museum of Natural History, 1 to 79th St
As the antiquated, hyphenated name implies, the New-York Historical Society is the city's oldest museum, founded in 1804 to preserve the city's historical and cultural artifacts. It was also New York's only public

---

UPPER WEST SIDE VS UPPER EAST SIDE

These two uptown 'hoods may not seem so very different to the untrained eye. But to New Yorkers, they're as different as the USA and Paris. Upper West Siders would never consider moving to the other side of Central Park (like an ocean to locals on either side); and East Siders feel the same. So what's the big difference? None, really – though perceptions include the UWS having more children, liberals, Jews and artists and the UES having more conservatives, old folks and money. There are some facts backing up the images, though, truth be told: while the West Side's median income is about $65,000, the cross-park average is closer to $75,000; there are also more African Americans living on the West Side, and slightly more registered Republicans in the East. Enter a which-is-better discussion with locals at your own risk.

art museum until the Metropolitan Museum of Art was founded in the late 19th century. Though it's often overlooked by visitors tramping to the nearby American Museum of Natural History, it shouldn't be, as its collection is as quirky and fascinating as NYC itself. Only here can you see 17th-century cowbells and baby rattles and the mounted wooden leg of Gouverneur Morris. The Henry Luce III Center for the Study of American Culture, which opened in 2000, is a 21,000-sq-ft showcase of more than 40,000 objects from the museum's permanent collection, and features items such as fine portraits, Tiffany lamps and model ships. The place always hosts unique special exhibits, too, with recent examples including *Slavery in New York* and *Nature and the American Vision: the Hudson River School at the New-York Historical Society*.

RIVERSIDE PARK Map pp454-5
from 68th to 155th Sts along Hudson River (east of hwy); ◎ 1, 2, 3 to 72nd St or higher
This skinny, lively greenspace is a great place to stroll, bike, run or simply gaze at the sun as it sets over the Hudson River. It's lined with cherry trees that blossom into puffs of pink in the spring, community gardens that are lovingly tended by volunteers, 14 playgrounds that are popular with the local 8-and-under set, basketball courts and baseball fields. There are well-placed

benches and a popular dog run, the seasonal Boat Basin Café, and various works of public art, including an inspiring statue of Eleanor Roosevelt at the 72nd St entrance. It's a gem worth trekking to, especially at sunset, when the Hudson River is bathed in soft gold tones and the city seems like a peaceful place at last.

UPPER EAST SIDE
Eating p249, Drinking p273, Shopping p347, Sleeping p373
The Upper East Side (UES) is home to New York's greatest concentration of cultural centers, including the grand dame that is the **Metropolitan Museum of Art**, and many refer to Fifth Ave above 57th St as Museum Mile. And beyond museums, you'll find intellectual draws that include the **92nd Street Y** (p292), a particular magnet for literature fans, as the theater here is host to an impressive lineup of readings from authors that have included Joan Didion and Margaret Atwood; it's also host to varied theater and dance performances. The neighborhood, whose residents, by the way, are in a never-ending contest with those of the Upper West Side, just across the park (see the boxed text p159), also includes many of the city's most exclusive hotels and residences. The side streets from Fifth Ave east to Third Ave between 57th and 86th Sts feature some stunning town houses and brownstones, and walking through this area at night offers opportunities to see how the other half lives – go ahead, peer inside those grand libraries and living rooms!

Orientation
You're on the UES when you are above 59th St and below 103rd St, between Fifth Ave and the East River. The sole subway line here is the 6, which explains why it's so damned crowded at rush hour – riders often wait for two packed trains to pass them by until they can squeeze into one.

ASIA SOCIETY & MUSEUM Map pp454-5
☎ 212-288-6400; www.asiasociety.org; 725 Park Ave at 70th St; ◎ 6 to 68th St
Founded by John D Rockefeller in 1956 (he was quite a fan of Asia; see also his Japan Society, p150), this cultural center is meant to strengthen understanding of Asia and relations between the continent and the US. Other outposts exist in cities including LA, San Francisco, Hong Kong and Shang-

hai, though New York is the headquarters. You'll find an array of reasons to visit the place, including educational lectures and events, but the biggest draw is its **museum** (www.asiasocietymuseum.org), which features rare treasures from all across Asia, such as Jain sculptures from India, Buddhist paintings from Nepal and jade and lacquer items from China.

CARL SCHURZ PARK Map pp454-5
☎ 212-459-4455; www.carlschurzparknyc.org; East End Ave at 88th St; ◉ 4, 5, 6 to 86th St
The placid Carl Schurz Park is the oldest community-based volunteer park association in the city, and it's long been a favorite spot for a riverside stroll or place to glimpse the blooming garden grounds of Gracie Mansion. That's the 1799 country residence where New York's mayors have always lived – with the exception of the extremely wealthy Mr Bloomberg, who already had plush city digs when he landed the mayoral gig in 2002. To join one of the tours, which take place from March to November at 10am, 11am, 1pm and 2pm Wednesday (adult/senior/student & child $7/4/free), you must first call for a reservation.

COOPER-HEWITT NATIONAL DESIGN MUSEUM Map pp454-5
☎ 212-849-8400; www.si.edu/ndm; 2 E 91st St at Fifth Ave; adult/senior & student/child $12/7/free; ◉ 10am-5pm Tue-Thu, 10am-9pm Fri, 10am-6pm Sat, noon-6pm Sun; ◉ 4, 5, 6 to 86th St
This museum is in the 64-room mansion built by billionaire Andrew Carnegie in 1901 in what was, in those days, *way* uptown. Within 20 years, the bucolic surroundings that Carnegie craved disappeared as other wealthy men followed his lead and built palaces around him. Carnegie was an interesting character; an avid reader and generous philanthropist, he dedicated many libraries around the country and donated some $350 million in his lifetime. To learn more, hop on the 45-minute daily tour at noon or 2pm, included in the admission price.

Part of the Smithsonian Institution in Washington, this house of culture is a must for anyone interested in architecture, engineering, jewelry or textiles. Exhibitions have examined everything from advertising campaigns to Viennese blown glass. Even if none of this grabs you, the museum's

garden and terrace are still worth a visit and the mansion is stunning.

FRICK COLLECTION Map pp454-5
☎ 212-288-0700; www.frick.org; 1 E 70th St at Fifth Ave; adult/senior/student $12/8/5; child under 10 not admitted; ◉ 10am-6pm Tue-Thu & Sat, 10am-9pm Fri, 1-6pm Sun; ◉ 6 to 68th St–Hunter College
This spectacular collection sits in a mansion built by businessman Henry Clay Frick in 1914, one of the many such residences that made up 'Millionaires' Row.' Most of these mansions proved too expensive for succeeding generations and were eventually destroyed, but the wily and very wealthy Frick, a Pittsburgh steel magnate, established a trust to open his private art collection as a museum. It's a shame that the 2nd floor of the residence is not open for viewing, though the 12 rooms on the ground floor are grand enough and the garden beckons visitors – especially on Fridays after 6:30pm, when a cash bar (a counter for buying drinks) opens for business.

The Frick's Oval Room is graced by Jean-Antoine Houdon's stunning figure *Diana the Huntress*; the intimate museum also displays works by Titian and Vermeer, and portraits by Gilbert Stuart, El Greco, Goya and John Constable. An audio tour is included in the price of admission and helps visitors to appreciate the art more fully; you can also dial up information on paintings and sculptures of your choosing on the ArtPhone. Perhaps the best asset here is that it's never crowded), providing a welcoming break from the swarms of gawkers at larger museums, especially on weekends.

JEWISH MUSEUM Map pp454-5
☎ 212-423-3200; www.jewishmuseum.org; 1109 Fifth Ave at 92nd St; adult/senior & student/child $10/7.50/free; ◉ 11am-5:45pm Sun-Wed, 11am-8pm Thu, 11am-3pm Fri; ◉ 6 to 96th St
This homage to Judaism primarily features artwork examining 4000 years of Jewish ceremony and culture; it also has a wide array of children's activities (storytelling hour, arts and crafts workshops etc). The building, a gorgeous 1908 banker's mansion, houses more than 30,000 items of Judaica, as well as works of sculpture, paintings, numismatics, antiquities, prints, decorative arts and photography. Watch for occasional blockbuster exhibitions, such as the recent Modigliani and Max Liebermann

shows, which drew large crowds. The institution also offers frequent lectures and film screenings – especially in January, when it collaborates with Lincoln Center to present the annual New York Jewish Film Festival.

On Thursday between 5pm and 8pm the admission fee is on a pay-what-you-wish basis.

METROPOLITAN MUSEUM OF ART

Map pp454–5

☎ 212-535-7710; www.metmuseum.org; Fifth Ave at 82nd St; suggested donation adult/senior & student/child $15/10/free; ⏰ 9:30am-5:30pm Tue-Thu & Sun, 9:30am-9pm Fri & Sat; ◉ 4, 5, 6 to 86th St

With more than five million visitors a year, the Met is New York's most popular single-site tourist attraction, with one of the richest coffers in the arts world. The Met is a self-contained cultural city-state, with two million individual objects in its collection and an annual budget of over $120 million. And, in 2004, the Met began a $155 million remodeling project that will put every inch of space to use; it will allow loads of works (including an Etruscan chariot) to come out of storage, renovate galleries of 19th-century and modern art, and add a new Roman Court (scheduled to open in 2007) that will increase the number of Hellenistic and Roman artworks from 2500 to 7500.

Once inside the Great Hall, pick up a floor plan and head to the ticket booths, where you will find a list of exhibitions closed for the day, along with a lineup of special museum talks. The Met presents more than 30 special exhibitions and installations each year, and marked floor plans show you how to get to them. It's best to target exactly what you want to see and head there first, before museum fatigue sets in (usually after two hours). Then you can put the floor plan away and get lost trying to get back to the main hall. It's a virtual certainty that you'll stumble across something interesting along the way.

To the right of the Great Hall, an information desk offers guidance in several languages (these change depending on the volunteers) and audio tours of the special exhibitions ($6). The Met also offers free guided walking tours of museum highlights and specific galleries. Check the calendar, given away at the information desk, for the specific schedule. Families will want to see *Inside the Museum: A Children's Guide to the* *Metropolitan Museum of Art* brochure and the kid-specific events calendar (both free at the information booth).

If you can't make it to Cooperstown, home of America's Baseball Hall of Fame, then exit the gallery through the door behind the temple to behold the Met's collection of **baseball cards**, which includes the rarest and most expensive card in the world – a 1909 Honus Wagner worth some $200,000. Continue on to the left and you'll enter the **American Wing** of furniture and architecture, with a quiet, enclosed garden space that is a perennial favorite as a respite from the hordes. Several stained-glass works by Louis Comfort Tiffany frame the garden, as does an entire two-story facade of the Branch Bank of the US, preserved when the downtown building was destroyed in the early 20th century.

Past the popular American Wing, you'll find the pyramid-like addition that houses the **Robert Lehman Collection** of impressionist and modern art, featuring several works by Renoir (including *Young Girl Bathing*), Georges Seurat and Pablo Picasso (including *Portrait of Gertrude Stein*). An unexpected bonus in this gallery is the rear terra-cotta facade of the original 1880 Met building, now completely encased by later additions and standing mutely on view as its own architectural artifact.

The **Rockefeller Collection** contains arts of Africa, Oceania and the Americas, then leads to the Greek and Roman art section. The museum has recently restored much of its Greek and Roman work, including the 2nd-floor Cypriot Gallery, which contains some of the finest pieces outside Cyprus.

Elsewhere on the 2nd floor, you'll see the Met's famous collection of **European paintings**, located in some of the museum's oldest galleries, beyond colonnaded entryways. The exhibition features works by every artist of note, including self-portraits by Rembrandt and Van Gogh and *Portrait of Juan de Pareja* by Velázquez. An entire suite of rooms focuses on impressionist and postimpressionist art. The new collection of modern masters is housed on this level, as well as the photographs recently purchased by the Met, and the museum's exquisite musical instrument holdings. Also of interest up here are the treasures from Japan, China and Southeast Asia.

If you can't stand crowds, avoid a rainy Sunday afternoon in summer. But during horrible winter weather, you might find the

17-acre museum deserted at night – a real NYC experience. The roof garden is also a find, especially in the summer, when it adds a wine bar on weekend evenings.

MUSEUM OF THE CITY OF NEW YORK
Map pp454-5

☎ 212-534-1672; www.mcny.org; 1220 Fifth Ave btwn 103rd & 104th Sts; suggested donation family/adult/senior & student $12/7/5; ☺ 10am-5pm Tue-Sun; ◉ 6 to 103rd St

For a look behind the intriguing facade of NYC, head here, where exhibits focus solely on the city's past, present and future. Housed in a 1932 Georgian-Colonial mansion, the Museum of the City of New York offers plenty of stimulation, both old-school and technology-based. You'll find Internet-based historical resources and a decent scale model of New Amsterdam shortly after the Dutch arrival, and the notable 2nd-floor gallery includes entire rooms from demolished homes of New York grandees, an exhibition dedicated to Broadway musicals and a collection of antique dollhouses, teddy bears and toys. Rotating exhibitions cast a clever eye on the city, with past subjects ranging from Harlem lost and found and the Roaring '20s to moving toward sustainable architecture in the 21st century and Magnum photos of New York.

NATIONAL ACADEMY OF DESIGN
Map pp454-5

☎ 212-369-4880; www.nationalacademy.org; 1083 Fifth Ave at 89th St; adult/senior & student/child under 16 $10/5/free; ☺ noon-5pm Wed & Thu, 11am-6pm Fri-Sun; ◉ 4, 5, 6 to 86th St

Co-founded by painter-inventor Samuel Morse, the National Academy of Design art-school complex includes a permanent collection of paintings and sculptures housed in yet another stunning beaux arts mansion, featuring a marble foyer and spiral staircase. The gem of a space was designed by Ogden Codman, who also designed the Breakers mansion in Newport, Rhode Island.

NEUE GALERIE Map pp454-5

☎ 212-628-6200; www.neuegalerie.org; 1048 Fifth Ave at 86th St; adult/senior $15/10, child under 12 not admitted; ☺ 11am-6pm Sat-Mon & Thu, 11am-9pm Fri; ◉ 4, 5, 6 to 86th St

This showcase for German and Austrian art is a relative newcomer to the museum strip (it opened in 2000), but it stood out as a star right away. The intimate but well-hung collection, housed in a former Rockefeller mansion, features impressive works by Gustav Klimt, Paul Klee and Egon Schiele. And it boasts a lovely street-level eatery, Café Sabarsky, serving Viennese meals, pastries and drinks. And, because of its no-children policy, you'll never encounter noisy stroller blockades.

NEW YORK ACADEMY OF MEDICINE
Map pp454-5

☎ 212-822-7200; www.nyam.org; 1216 Fifth Ave at 103rd St; admission free; ☺ 9am-5pm Mon-Fri; ◉ 6 to 103rd St

With over 700,000 cataloged works, New York Academy of Medicine is the second-largest health library in the world (and in its holdings is the world's biggest cookbook collection). But skip all the books and head straight for the weirdly fascinating medical ephemera like the leper clapper (used by sufferers to warn a town of their arrival), a globule of the world's first penicillin culture, cupping glasses used in phlebotomy procedures, and George Washington's dentures.

ROOSEVELT ISLAND Map pp454-5
◉ F to Roosevelt Island

New York's anomalous, planned neighborhood sits on a tiny island no wider than a football field in the middle of the East River between Manhattan and Queens. It was once known as Blackwell's Island after the farming family who lived here; the city bought the island in 1828 and constructed several public hospitals and a mental hospital. In the 1970s, New York State built housing for 10,000 people along Roosevelt Island's Main St, the island's only one. The planned area along the cobblestone roadway resembles an Olympic village or, as some observe more cynically, cookie-cutter college housing.

Zipping across the river via the four-minute aerial tram is a trip in itself and worth it for the stunning view of the East Side of Manhattan framed by the 59th St Bridge. Instead of heading straight back like most, however, bring a picnic or a bike, as this quiet island is conducive to lounging and cycling.

Trams from the Roosevelt Island tramway station (☎ 212-832-4543; 60th St at Second Ave) leave every 15 minutes on the quarter-hour from 6am to 2am Sunday to Thursday, until 3:30am Friday and Saturday; the one-way fare is $1.50. Roosevelt Island also has a subway station.

SOLOMON R GUGGENHEIM MUSEUM
Map pp454-5

☎ 212-423-3500; www.guggenheim.org; 1071 Fifth Ave at 89th St; adult/senior & student/child $15/10/free; ☼ 10am-5:45pm Sat-Wed, 10am-8pm Fri; ⊕ 4, 5, 6 to 86th St

A sculpture in its own right, Frank Lloyd Wright's sweeping spiral building almost overshadows the collection of 20th-century art housed in this museum. Because of its unusual design, the building sparked controversy during its construction in the 1950s, but today it's a distinctive landmark that architects fiddle with at their peril. An unpopular 1992 renovation added an adjoining 10-story tower that does indeed bear a striking resemblance to a toilet, just as the critics feared, despite being based on Wright's original drawings.

Inside you can view some of the museum's 5000 permanent works (plus changing exhibitions) on a path that coincides with Wright's coiled design – take the elevator to the top and wind your way down. The Guggenheim's collection includes works by Picasso, Chagall, Pollock and Kandinsky. In 1976 Justin Thannhauser's major donation of impressionist and modern works added paintings by Monet, Van Gogh and Degas. In 1992, the Robert Mapplethorpe Foundation gave 200 photographs to the museum, spurring curators to devote the 4th floor to photography exhibitions. Note that you can purchase tickets in advance online via the museum's website, which lets you avoid the sometimes-brutal lines to get in.

TEMPLE EMANU-EL Map pp454-5

☎ 212-744-1400; www.emanuelnyc.org; 1 E 65th St at Fifth Ave; ☼ 10am-5pm; ⊕ N, R, W to Fifth Ave–59th St

Founded in 1845 as the first Reform synagogue in New York, this temple was completed in 1929. It's now the largest Jewish house of worship in the world, and has a membership of some 3000 families. Stop by for a look at its notable Byzantine and Middle Eastern architecture. Its facade features an arch with symbols representing the 12 tribes of Israel, which are also depicted on the grand set of bronze doors. Inside the majestic, buttressed interior are Guastavino

tiles, marble wainscoting and brilliant stained-glass windows.

WHITNEY MUSEUM OF AMERICAN ART Map pp454-5

☎ 212-570-3600, 800-944-8639; www.whitney .org; 945 Madison Ave at 75th St; adult/senior/child $12/9.50/free; ☼ 11am-4:30pm Tue, 11am-6pm Wed, Sat & Sun, 11am-9pm Fri; ⊕ 6 to 77th St

The Whitney makes no secret of its mission to provoke and it starts with the most brutal of structures housing the collection. Designed by Bauhaus architect Marcel Breuer, the rock-like edifice is a fitting setting for the Whitney's style of cutting-edge American art. The collection is highlighted every two years in the much ballyhooed Biennial, an ambitious survey of contemporary art that rarely fails to generate controversy – even if it's over the mediocrity of the works. It last hit town in March 2006.

Established in the 1930s by Gertrude Vanderbilt Whitney, who began a Greenwich Village salon for prominent artists, the stellar collection features works by famous folk including Edward Hopper, Jasper Johns, Georgia O'Keeffe, Jackson Pollock and Mark Rothko. Two upcoming special exhibits worth getting excited about are *Picasso and American Art*, a groundbreaking look at the artist and his countless influences, set for October 2006 through

Whitney Museum (above), remand center of American art

January 2007, and *Kiki Smith: A Gathering, 1980-2005*, which is essentially a retrospective of her diverse contemporary works.

YORKVILLE Map pp454-5
🚇 6 to 77th St
This area, east of Lexington Ave between 70th and 96th Sts, is known today as the one pocket of the Upper East Side with (relatively) affordable rental apartments. It was once the settling point for new Hungarian and German immigrants – the only trace left of that heritage today are places like Schaller & Weber, an old-world German grocery, Heidelberg, a homey restaurant serving sauerbraten and other traditional goodies (both on Second Ave between 85th and 86th Sts) and the **Yorkville Meat Emporium** (Second Ave at 81st St), stocked with fresh meats and prepared Hungarian dishes.

HARLEM & NORTHERN MANHATTAN
Walking Tour p219, Eating p251, Drinking p274, Shopping p349, Sleeping p374

While downtowners used to pride themselves on how they 'get a nosebleed' if they ever travel above 14th St, the growing trend of moving way up instead of down has forced many of these folks to cross over to the other side. They now often travel above 110th St and beyond – either to live or to visit friends who now make their home in Morningside Heights, Washington Heights, Inwood or Harlem. Though it's not as true today as it was just a couple of years ago, the price of real estate and rentals is lower in these parts than in much of the rest of Manhattan, so there has been a mass exodus up here, where it's not quite as trendy (yet) and neighborhoods tend to have a more authentic, community feel to them.

Morningside Heights, located just above the Upper West Side, is anchored by the rambling **Columbia University** (p166); strolling through these parts feels a bit like you've stumbled onto a very hip campus. Part of this area is known by the recently created moniker of Soha (South of Harlem), and has a growing number of hip cafés and eateries. A bit above this area is Washington Heights, known for its large Dominican community and lovely Metropolitan Museum of Art outpost, the **Cloisters** (p170). Inwood comprises

the northernmost tip of Manhattan, and it's filled with peaceful blocks and edged by a mass of lovely waterfront parkland. And then, of course, there's Harlem, eclipsing all other northern 'hoods because of its famous history and buzz of renaissance.

From its origins as a 1920s black enclave, the heart of black culture has always beat in Harlem. This neighborhood north of Central Park has been the setting for extraordinary accomplishments in art, music, dance, education and letters, from the likes of Frederick Douglass, Paul Robeson, Thurgood Marshall, James Baldwin, Alvin Ailey, Billie Holiday, Jessie Jackson and many other African American luminaries.

Despite its past reputation as a crime-ridden no-man's-land, today Harlem – with the exception of some still-abandoned, eerily empty side streets – shouldn't cause you to exercise any more caution than you would anywhere else in New York. It's a great place to add to your touring agenda, for reasons cultural (museums, theaters, jazz, historic architecture and gospel churches), gastronomical (Southern fare at its best) and commercial (shopping opportunities galore). For a great DIY excursion, take a public bus up Broadway or Madison Ave and watch the neighborhoods change; get off at 125th St and see where a stroll takes you.

First-time visitors will probably be surprised to discover that Harlem is just one subway stop away from the Columbus Circle–59th St station. The trip on the express A and D trains takes only five minutes, and both lines stop just one block from the **Apollo Theater** (p168) and two blocks from Malcolm X Blvd (Lenox Ave).

MORNINGSIDE HEIGHTS
This area between the Upper West Side and the way-north Washington Heights is generally the province of Columbia University, as is immediately evident from the scores of students and professors chilling in cafés, filling bookstores and darting to and from classes on the beautiful urban campus. But it's got other draws, too, namely great park areas and some delicious new dining options.

Orientation
Morningside Heights extends north from 110th to 125th Sts, between St Nicholas Ave and the Hudson River.

CATHEDRAL CHURCH OF ST JOHN THE DIVINE Map pp458-9

☎ 212-316-7540; www.stjohndivine.org; Amsterdam Ave at 112th St; ⏰ 7:30am-6pm; ⊕ B, C, 1 to 110th St–Cathedral Pkwy

This is the largest place of worship in the USA – and it's not done yet. When it's finally completed, the 601ft-long Episcopal cathedral will rank as the third-largest church in the world (after St Peter's Basilica in Rome, Italy, and Our Lady of Peace at Yamoussoukro in Côte d'Ivoire). Design highlights include the Great Rose Window, the largest stained-glass window in the country, and the Great Organ, which dates from 1911 and currently awaits cleaning after a devastating church fire in 2001 caused smoke damage that silenced the instrument.

On top of the church construction, the cathedral is involved in some development partnerships so it can generate income from parcels of its unused land: first will be a residential building, and nearby will be a facility for Columbia University.

The cathedral is a flourishing place of worship and community activity. Holiday concerts, lectures and memorial services take place here for famous New Yorkers. Two quirky services worth seeing are the annual Blessing of the Animals, a pilgrimage for pet-owners that's held on the first Sunday of October, and the Blessing of the Bikes, on May 1, which draws helmeted folks with clunkers, sleek 10-speeds and mountain bikes. There's a Poet's Corner to the left of the front entrance but, unlike at Westminster Abbey in London, no-one is actually buried here. Also see the altar designed and built by the late Keith Haring, a popular artist in the 1980s pop-art world.

Other sights are the whimsical Children's Sculpture Garden on the south side, and the Biblical Garden, containing plants that are historically correct for the era, out back. An intriguing Ecology Trail wends its way through the cathedral and the grounds, tracing the creation cycles (birth, life, death and rebirth) from a multicultural perspective. Cathedral tours ($3 per person) are held at 11am Tuesday to Saturday and 1pm Sunday.

COLUMBIA UNIVERSITY Map pp458-9

☎ 212-854-1754; www.columbia.edu; Broadway at 116th St; ⊕ 1 to 116th St–Columbia University

When Columbia University, between 114th and 121st Sts, and the affiliated Barnard College moved to this site in 1897, their founders chose a spot far removed from the downtown bustle. Today, the city has enveloped and moved beyond Columbia's gated campus, but the school's main courtyard, with its statue Alma Mater perched on the steps of the Low Library, is still a quiet place to take some sun and read a book. Hamilton Hall, in the southeast corner of the main square, was the famous site of a student takeover in 1968, and has seen periodic protests and plenty of wild student parties since then. The university also offers endless opportunities for doses of culture through its itinerary of top-notch events; check the school's website or bulletin boards around campus to find out about readings, film screenings, dance and theater performances, art exhibits and sports competitions.

GENERAL US GRANT NATIONAL MEMORIAL Map pp458-9

☎ 212-666-1640; www.nps.gov/gegr; Riverside Dr at W 122nd St; admission free; ⏰ 9am-5pm; ⊕ 1 to 125th St

Popularly known as Grant's Tomb, this landmark holds the remains of Civil War hero and president Ulysses S Grant and those of his wife, Julia. Completed in 1897 – 12 years after his death – the granite structure cost $600,000 and is the largest mausoleum in the country. Though it plagiarizes Mausoleus' tomb at Halicarnassus, this version doesn't qualify as one of the Seven Wonders of the World. The building languished as a graffiti-scarred mess for years until Grant's relatives shamed the National Park Service into cleaning it up by threatening to move his body elsewhere.

MORNINGSIDE PARK Map pp458-9

www.morningsidepark.org; 110th to 123rd Sts btwn Manhattan Ave, Morningside Ave & Morningside Dr

The park that gives this neighborhood its name is a lovely, 13-block finger of green that has much to recommend it. In the region behind the Cathedral Church of St John the Divine you'll find a pond and waterfall, and walking north from here will lead you to several public sculpture memorials, including the Seligman (Bear and Faun) Fountain (1914) by Edgar White and the Carl Schurz Memorial (1913) by Carl Bitter and Henry Bacon. Other draws are playgrounds, shaded pathways and the lush Dr Thomas Kiel Arboretum, near 116th St.

RIVERSIDE CHURCH Map pp458-9

☎ 212-870-6700; www.theriversidechurchny.org;
490 Riverside Dr at W 120th St; ⏰ 7am-10pm;
Ⓜ 1 to 116th St–Columbia University

Built by the Rockefeller family in 1930, this Gothic beauty overlooks the Hudson River. In good weather you can climb 355ft to the observation deck ($2) for expansive river views. The church rings its 74 carillon bells, the largest grouping in the world, with an extraordinary 20-ton bass bell (also the world's largest), at noon and 3pm on Sunday. Interdenominational services are held at 10:45am on Sunday, and there are frequent high-quality events such as concerts and lectures held here, many with an activist, multi-culti, queer-friendly, anti-war bent.

HARLEM

There were two catalysts that spurred Harlem's rebirth: the entire neighborhood being declared an Economic Redevelopment Zone in 1996, and the flocking here of foreign tourists to check out the area's music and spiritual scene. While Harlem's development has attracted buckets of dollars, it has also brought double-decker tour buses and disrespectful crowds clamoring for pews at Sunday services. Cheap rents for amazing spaces have also given rise to a gay (and very white) ghetto, and tensions between the old and new residents are always in the air, as a balance that benefits everyone has yet to be struck. The past couple of years, though, have seen an explosion of black-owned hipsters' shops and cafés; strolling around and popping in and out of places is a good way to spend an exciting afternoon.

City officials have aggressively promoted Harlem to developers, with the alarmingly huge (and extremely popular) Harlem USA (Map pp458–9; 300 W 125th St) entertainment and retail complex acting as the jewel in the crown. It features a dance club, 12-screen cinema, rooftop skating rink and HMV store. The Harlem Visitor Information Kiosk (Map pp458–9; 163 W 125th St at Seventh Ave; ⏰ 9am-6pm Mon-Fri, 10am-6pm Sat & Sun) is a great source for tips, directions and history.

Orientation

In this 'hood – bordered roughly by 125th St to the south and 140th to the north – you'll notice that the major avenues have been renamed in honor of prominent African Americans; however, many locals still call the streets by their original names, which makes finding your way around a little confusing. Eighth Ave (Central Park West) is Frederick Douglass Blvd. Seventh Ave is Adam Clayton Powell Jr Blvd, named for the controversial preacher who served

---

GOING TO THE GOSPEL/HARLEM CHURCH SERVICES

Harlem Sunday services, which are mostly Baptist, pack in the crowds with their deep spirituality and rocking gospel choirs. Unfortunately, the tour buses have been rolling in with their own crowds recently (some of the churches have side deals going with operators), which has resulted in a clash of cultures, with worshippers trying to get in touch with God and sightseers trying to snap the perfect photo.

As the old saying goes, in Harlem 'there's a bar on every corner and a church on every block.' We've listed several churches here, but there are probably twice as many more in the immediate neighborhood, so instead of overwhelming the few we have space to mention, seek out your own – most church marquees proclaim 'all are welcome.' Services usually start at 11am. For a truly unique experience, check out one of the Thursday-night hip-hop services, held at various churches.

The Abyssinian Baptist Church (p168) is quite welcoming to outsiders, as is the Mother African Methodist Episcopal Zion Church (Map pp458–9; ☎ 212-234-1545; 146 W 137th St; Ⓜ 2, 3 to 135th St), around the corner, which usually takes the overflow from the Abyssinian. Canaan Baptist Church (Map pp458–9; ☎ 212-866-5711; 132 W 116th St; ⏰ services 10:45am Sun Oct-Jun, 10am Jul-Sep; Ⓜ 2, 3 to 116th St), near St Nicholas Ave, is an extremely friendly church.

As the churches mentioned above see a lot of traffic, you might try one of the following instead:

- Baptist Temple (Map pp458–9; ☎ 212-996-0334; 20 W 116th St)
- Metropolitan Baptist Church (Map pp458–9; ☎ 212-663-8990; 151 W 128th St)
- St Paul Baptist Church (Map pp458–9; ☎ 212-283-8174; 249 W 132nd St)
- Salem United Methodist Church (Map pp458–9; ☎ 212-722-3969; 211 W 129th St)
- Second Providence Baptist Church (Map pp458–9; ☎ 212-831-6751; 11 W 116th St)

in Congress during the 1960s. Lenox Ave has been renamed for the Nation of Islam leader Malcolm X. The main avenue and site of many businesses, 125th St is also known as Martin Luther King Jr Blvd. Walking in Harlem can be really tiring as the sites are pretty spread out and subway stations are few and far between; up here the crosstown buses can be handier than the train.

ABYSSINIAN BAPTIST CHURCH

Map pp458-9

☎ 212-862-7474; www.abyssinian.org; 132 Odell Pl (W 138th St) btwn Adam Clayton Powell Jr & Malcolm X Blvds; ⊗ services 9am, 11am Sun; ◉ 2, 3 to 135th St

Founded by an Ethiopian businessman, the Abyssinian Baptist Church began as a downtown institution but moved north to Harlem in 1923, mirroring the migration of the city's black population. Its charismatic pastor, Calvin O Butts III, is an important community activist whose support is sought by politicians of all parties. The church has a superb choir and the building is a beauty. If you plan on visiting with a group of 10 or more, the congregation requests that you call in advance to see if space is available.

APOLLO THEATER Map pp458-9

☎ 212-531-5337; 5253 W 125th St at Frederick Douglass Blvd; tours (11am, 1pm, 3pm Mon, Tue, Fri, 11am, 1pm Sat-Sun) pp $12 Mon-Fri, $14 Sat-Sun ◉ A, B, C, D to 125th St

This has been Harlem's leading space for political rallies and concerts since 1914. Virtually every major black artist of note in the 1930s and '40s performed here, including Duke Ellington and Charlie Parker. After a desultory spell as a movie theater and several years of darkness, the Apollo was bought in 1983 and revived as a live venue. After the completion of a two-year renovation (phase one in a long-range plan), the Apollo is more beautiful than ever, as it finally has a restored facade, marquee, glass-and-steel storefront and brand-new box office. Its famous weekly Amateur Night, 'where stars are born and legends are made,' still takes place on Wednesday, with a wild and ruthless crowd that's as fun to watch as the performers. On other nights, the Apollo hosts performances by established artists like Stevie Wonder and the O'Jays.

MALCOLM SHABAZZ HARLEM MARKET Map pp458-9

☎ 212-987-8131; 52 W 116th St btwn Malcolm X Blvd & Fifth Ave; ⊗ 10am-5pm; ◉ 2, 3 to 116th St

Vendors at the semi-enclosed Harlem Market do a brisk business selling tribal masks, oils, drums, traditional clothing and other assorted African bric-a-brac. You can also purchase cheap clothing, leather goods, music cassettes and bootleg videos of films that are still in first-run movie theaters. The market is operated by the Malcolm Shabazz Mosque next door, the former pulpit of slain Muslim orator Malcolm X.

SCHOMBURG CENTER FOR RESEARCH IN BLACK CULTURE Map pp458-9

☎ 212-491-2200; www.nypl.org/research/sc/sc.html; 515 Malcolm X Blvd; admission free; ⊗ noon-8pm Tue & Wed, noon-6pm Thu & Fri, 10am-6pm Sat; ◉ 2, 3 to 135th St

The nation's largest collection of documents, rare books, recordings and photographs relating to the African American experience resides at this center near W 135th St. Arthur Schomburg, who was born in Puerto Rico, started gathering works on black history during the early 20th century while becoming active in the movements for civil rights and Puerto Rican independence. His impressive collection was purchased by the Carnegie Foundation and eventually expanded and stored in this branch of the New York Public Library. Lectures and concerts are regularly held in the theater here.

STUDIO MUSEUM IN HARLEM

Map pp458-9

☎ 212-864-4500; www.studiomuseum.org; 144 W 125th St at Adam Clayton Powell Jr Blvd; suggested donation adult/senior & student $7/3; ⊗ noon-6pm Wed-Fri & Sun, 10am-6pm Sat; ◉ 2, 3 to 125th St

This showcase, a leading benefactor and promoter of African American artists for almost 30 years, provides working spaces for the up and coming. Its photography collection includes works by James VanDerZee, the photographer who chronicled the Harlem renaissance of the 1920s and '30s, and rotating shows feature exhibits from emerging artists in forms from painting and sculpture to video and tattoo work.

EAST HARLEM

Also known colloquially as Spanish Harlem or El Barrio, this is one of the biggest Latino communities – mainly Puerto Rican, Dominican and Cuban, and now more and more Mexican – in the city. And proud of it: Puerto Rican flags fly from vans blaring salsa, men play dominoes in front of ramshackle *casitas* (houses) in the community gardens and people hang out on stoops, shouting to their neighbors in Spanglish.

Interesting stops include **El Museo del Barrio** (right) and **Duke Ellington Circle** (Map pp458–9) – with a statue of the man and his piano – where Fifth Ave and Central Park North (also known as Tito Puente Way) converge. Though **La Marqueta** (Map pp458–9; E 115th St btwn Park and Third Aves), a bustling collection of 200 vendors selling everything from tropical fruits to botanincas and religious items, was the pride of the local Puerto Rican community for decades since WWII, it's recently dwindled into a calm collection of only eight vendors. All that will change in a big way, though, if an exciting, Bloomberg-proposed development project proceeds as planned. Spearheaded by the East Harlem Business Capital Corporation, the far-reaching plans call for a $16 million La Marqueta revival, with new construction that will make way for an 85,000-sq-ft international market with pan-Latin shops, cafés and restaurants. Meanwhile, stopping in and out of the many botanicals and cafés in the vicinity is a great way to find your own market adventures.

Orientation

East Harlem extends from Fifth Ave to the East River, above 96th St.

GRAFFITI HALL OF FAME Map pp454-5
www.graffitihalloffame.org; 106th St btwn Madison & Park Aves; ⊚ 6 to 103rd St

A schoolyard that celebrates all sorts of taggers, this art gallery of the street was founded in 1980 by graffiti artist Ray Rodriguez (aka Sting Ray) and a group of community-minded supporters who saw the lasting value in an art that some politicians and business owners tend to view as vandalism. You can visit the colorful murals at any time, though the actual Graffiti Hall of Fame event, which is when 'writers' come from all over the globe to add their art to the walls, is held in late June. Check the website for updates; another good source of information is Streets are Saying Things (www.streetsaresayingthings.com), a Hall of Fame organizer and constant source of graffiti-related news.

EL MUSEO DEL BARRIO Map pp454-5
☎ 212-831-7272; www.elmuseo.org; 1230 Fifth Ave btwn 104th & 105th Sts; suggested donation adult/senior & student/child $6/4/free; ⊙ 11am-5pm Wed-Sun; ⊚ 6 to 103rd St

The best starting point for exploring Spanish Harlem, this museum began in 1969 as a celebration of Puerto Rican art and culture. It has since expanded into the premiere Latino cultural institution in the city, with a dizzying collection that includes 2000 pre-Columbian ceremonial objects, 900 traditional objects from countries including Brazil and Haiti, more than 3000 Puerto Rican prints and posters, and contemporary paintings and sculptures from artists including Raul Farco, Marcos Dimas and Pepon Osorio. The film and video collection has some rare footage of life in El Barrio from the 1970s to the present, along with educational materials from Puerto Rico. Photographs document life in Puerto Rico during the Depression as well as some of the early years of Latin American migration to the US.

Temporary exhibits are a particular draw, as past showings have focused on the works of big names including Diego Rivera and Frida Kahlo, as well as themed exhibits such as *Retratos: 2000 Years of Latin American Portraits*; *MoMA at El Museo*, which highlighted MoMA's fabulous Latin and Caribbean collection; and, in early 2006, *El Museo's Bienal: The (S) Files/The Selected Files*, which showcased works from an impressive lineup of cutting-edge local artists. Signage and brochures at El Museo, by the way, are in both English and Spanish.

HAMILTON HEIGHTS & SUGAR HILL

This area, which extends north of Harlem from about 138th to 155th Sts west of Edgecombe Ave, is loaded with off-the-beaten path delights, including the delightful **Sugar Hill Bistro** (458 W 145th St) and the **Macombs Dam Bridge** – which stretches east from 155th St and is one of the greatest ways to get to a Yankees game, whether on foot or in a car. In the summer, die-hard basketball fiends will want to check out the legendary competitions at **Rucker Park** (Map pp458–9; W 155th St at Harlem River; ⊙ B, D to 155th St), home to some of the most exciting street-ball games in the city (along with the W 4th St courts in the Village, p137), where players as big as (pre-scandal) Kobe Bryant have even stopped in for some hoops.

HAMILTON GRANGE Map pp458-9

☎ 212-283-5154; www.nps.gov/hagr; 287 Convent Ave at 141st St; admission free; ⊙ 9am-5pm Wed-Fri; ⊙ A, B, C, D to 145th St

Once upon a time this was Alexander Hamilton's original country retreat – Hamilton Heights was named for him, after all, as he owned a farm and estate up here in 1802. When the Federal-style home was moved to this too-small spot from its original location, it had to be turned on its side and squeezed to fit, so now the facade actually faces inward, making it an even more curious sight to behold. Nearby, the Hamilton Heights Historic District stretches along Convent Ave from the City College of New York campus (which has architectural marvels of its own) from 140th to 145th Sts. This gorgeous lineup is one of the last remaining stretches of untouched limestone and brownstone town houses in New York City.

STRIVER'S ROW Map pp458-9

W 138th & 139th Sts btwn Frederick Douglass & Adam Clayton Powell Jr Blvds; ⊙ B, C to 135th St

Also known as the St Nicholas Historic District, Striver's Row has prized row houses and apartments, many designed by Stanford White's firm in the 1890s. When Whites moved out of the area, Harlem's black elite occupied the buildings. It's one of the most visited blocks in Harlem, so lay low, as the locals are a bit sick of gawking tourists. Plaques explain more of the area's history, while excellent alleyway signs advise visitors to 'walk your horses.'

WASHINGTON HEIGHTS & INWOOD

Near the northern tip of Manhattan (above 155th St), Washington Heights takes its name from the first US president, who set up a Continental Army fort here during the Revolutionary War. An isolated rural spot until the end of the 19th century, Washington Heights has attracted lots of new blood as New Yorkers sniffed out its affordable rents over the past several years. Still, this neighborhood manages to retain its Latino – mainly Dominican – flavor, and now what you'll find is an interesting mix of blocks that alternate between hipster expat-downtowners and long-time residents who operate within a tight and warm community.

Most visitors to Washington Heights see the handful of museums, particularly the **Cloisters** (below) in Fort Tryon Park, a beautiful spot in warm weather. Free shuttle buses run among the area's museums between 11am and 5pm. (Call any one of the following museums to find out the schedule.)

Inwood is at Manhattan's northern tip, from about 145th St up, and has drawn folks from downtown with its cheaper real estate, much of which offers great views of the Hudson River. Its most sparkling jewel is the huge waterfront **Inwood Park** (opposite), which offers a great escape between the local neighborhood and the start of the Bronx (p188). There is a modern cultural renaissance thriving in this part of NYC. Not far from the **Morris-Jumel Mansion** (opposite), on the corner of 160th St, is 555 Edgecombe Ave, which, aside from being the address of Jackie Robinson, Thurgood Marshall and Paul Robeson at one time or another, is now the home of **Marjorie Eliot** (Map pp458–9; ☎ 212-781-6595; apt 3F). This lovely lady hosts convivial, free-jazz jams in her home every Sunday at 4pm; they are open to the public and warmly recommended. Two recent in-home attractions include the **Museum of Art & Origins** (Map pp458–9; ☎ 212-740-2001; www.museumofartand-origins.org; 432 W 162nd St; admission $5; ⊙ by appt only), where George Preston has turned three floors of his brownstone into a museum of African masks and figures; two blocks away lives Kurt Thometz, a dealer of rare and out-of-print books who has turned a room of his brownstone into **Jumel Terrace Books** (Map pp458–9; ☎ 646-472-5938; www.jumelterracebooks.com; 426 W 160th St; ⊙ by appt only), a shop specializing in tomes on Africana, Harlem history and African American literature.

CLOISTERS Map pp468-9

☎ 212-923-3700; www.metmuseum.org; 195th St; suggested donation adult/senior & student/child $15/7/free; ⊙ 9:30am-4:45pm Tue-Sun Nov-Feb, to 5.15pm Mar-Oct; ⊙ A to Dyckman St

The Met is a beautiful place to visit on any day, but if it's just too gorgeous to be indoors, you might consider heading to the Met's outside annex instead. Set in Fort Tryon Park overlooking the Hudson River, the Cloisters museum, built in the 1930s, incorporates fragments of old French and Spanish monasteries and houses the Metropolitan Museum of Art's collection of medieval frescoes, tapestries and paintings. Summer is the best time to visit, when concerts take place in the grounds and more than 250 varieties of medieval flowers and herbs are on view.

Works are set in galleries – connected by grand archways and topped with Moorish terra-cotta roofs – that sit around an airy courtyard. Among the many rare treasures you'll get to gaze at are a gold St John the Evangelist plaque from the 9th century, an English ivory Virgin and Child sculpture dating from 1290, ancient stained-glass panels depicting historic religious scenes, and the stunning 12th-century Saint-Guilhem Cloister, made of French limestone and standing 30ft high.

DYCKMAN FARMHOUSE MUSEUM
Map pp468-9

☎ 212-304-9422; www.dyckmanfarmhouse.org; 4881 Broadway at 204th St; admission $1; ☽ 11am-4pm Wed-Sat, noon-4pm Sun; ◉ A to 207th St
Built in 1784 on a 28-acre farm, the Dyckman House is Manhattan's lone surviving Dutch farmhouse – and now, following an extensive two-year renovation, the museum is better than ever. Excavations of the property have turned up valuable clues about colonial life, and the museum includes period rooms and furniture, decorative arts, a half-acre of gardens and an exhibition on the neighborhood's history. To get to the Dyckman House, take the subway to the 207th St station and walk one block south – many people mistakenly get off one stop too soon at Dyckman St.

HISPANIC SOCIETY OF AMERICA
Map pp458-9

☎ 212-926-2234; www.hispanicsociety.org; Broadway at 155th St; admission free; ☽ 10am-4:30pm Tue-Sat, 1-4pm Sun; ◉ 1 to 157th St
Housed in a two-level, ornately carved beaux arts space hung with gold-and-silk tapestries, the Society lives on the serene Audubon Tce, the former home of naturalist John James Audubon. Open since 1908, this is where you'll find the largest collection of Spanish art and manuscripts outside of Spain –

including a substantial collection of works by El Greco, Goya, Diego Velázquez and the formidable Joaquín Sorolla y Bastida, as well as a library with over 25,000 volumes. Head upstairs for a bird's-eye view. All signage and brochures are in English and Spanish.

INWOOD HILL PARK Map pp468-9
Dyckman St at the Hudson River, ◉ A to Inwood–207th St
This gorgeous 197-acre park contains the last natural forest and salt marsh in Manhattan. It's a cool escape in summer and a great place to explore anytime, as you'll find hilly paths for hiking and mellow grassy patches and benches for quiet contemplation. It's so peaceful and un-urban here, in fact, that the treetops serve as frequent nesting sites for bald eagles. You'll also find helpful rangers and a slew of educational programs, many geared toward children at the Inwood Park Nature Center (☎ 212-304-2365; 218th St at Indian Rd; ☽ 11am-4pm Wed-Sun). Let your sporty side rip on basketball courts, horseback riding trails, and soccer and football fields; you can also join locals who BBQ at designated grills on summer weekends. The views of New Jersey and the Bronx from high points in the forest are wonderful.

MORRIS-JUMEL MANSION Map pp458-9
☎ 212-923-8008; www.morrisjumel.org; 65 Jumel Tce at 160th St; adult/senior, student & child $4/3; ☽ 10am-4pm Wed-Sun, other times by appt; ◉ C to 163rd St–Amsterdam Ave
Built in 1765, the columned Morris-Jumel Mansion is the oldest house in Manhattan. It first served as George Washington's Continental Army headquarters. After the war it again became a country house for Stephen Jumel and his wife Eliza, who had a sordid past (not limited to being the second wife of vice president Aaron Burr). Rumor has it that Eliza's ghost still flits about the place. A designated landmark, with grounds that are particularly attractive during spring, the mansion's interior contains many of the original furnishings, including a 2nd-floor bed that reputedly belonged to Napoleon. Guided tours of the house are available on Saturday at noon for $5.

You'll find historic houses nearby on Jumel Tce, including the fine limestone structure at No 16, which was once the home of a noted renaissance man, actor-activist-athlete-singer Paul Robeson.

BROOKLYN

Eating p253, Drinking p274, Shopping p350, Sleeping p375

Booming Brooklyn is the new New York, with a 'who's who' list of stars that rivals Hollywood's Walk of Fame, and new life pouring in courtesy of Manhattanites sick of high rent and too much bustle. Everyone's looking into Brooklyn these days: new parents seeking first-home brownstones in Park Slope, Boerum Hill or Fort Greene; indie-rockers escaping downtown's high rents for Williamsburg or Greenpoint pads; Manhattanites dining at new 'restaurant rows' like Smith St in Boerum Hill, Fifth Ave in Park Slope, and Dekalb Ave in Fort Greene; or real-estate moguls eyeing warehouse industrial areas like Red Hook and Gowanus Canal that can be rezoned, rebuilt and remade into million-dollar lots.

Visitors to New York can hardly afford to miss a day in the world's most well-known borough – even if it's just a walk over the Brooklyn Bridge to Dumbo and Brooklyn Heights (p221), a hot dog at Coney Island (p180), or a wander around New York's second Central Park (p177).

Controversy surrounds all this change. In 2004 Bruce Ratner bought the basketball team the New Jersey Nets and planned to move them to Brooklyn – the would-be first major pro team in Brooklyn since the baseball Dodgers moved to LA in 1957. Locals applaud the idea of having a team again (and the prospective revenue for Brooklyn), but are worried about the price they'll pay for it: the Atlantic Yards commercial complex would include lofts and a convention center for the Nets, all of which would mean relocating many residents in the area. Similar rezoning battles are nothing new – old industrial lofts in Dumbo and Williamsburg have fallen to the might of the potential dollar; and Gowanus Canal and Red Hook are facing a similar fate.

Listen out for the lingo here. Seeping into all boroughs, the glamorized working-class 'New York accent' is sometimes just called 'Brooklynese' – the popular amalgam of Italian, Yiddish, Caribbean, Spanish and even Dutch influences on English: 'da' for the, 'hoid' for heard, 'dowahg' for dog, 'tree' for three, 'fugehdabboudit' for 'forget about it, kind sir.'

The tourist center is downtown (opposite). Another good resource for details on Brooklyn is www.celebratebrooklyn.org.

Orientation

Across the East River from Lower Manhattan, Brooklyn occupies the southeastern tip of Long Island and is connected to Manhattan by the Brooklyn, Manhattan and Williamsburg Bridges (south to north, remember 'BMW'). The prestigious brownstone zone of Brooklyn Heights is nestled between the East River (and Brooklyn–Queens Expressway) to the west, Cadman Plaza West to the east, and Atlantic Ave to the south. Just east are the modern buildings of downtown, bordered by Flatbush Ave to the east.

This section essentially starts at Brooklyn's northwest corner and most common entry point: Brooklyn Heights. From there it makes its way outward west to east, taking in downtown; Dumbo's waterside lofts; residential streets of Cobble Hill, Boerum

---

TOP TEN MUST-DOS: OUTER BOROUGHS

- Drink in front-row views of Lower Manhattan from Brooklyn Heights Promenade (opposite)
- Relive your childhood through the hand painted signs and aged roller coasters of Coney Island (p180), with Little Odessa, a boardwalk stroll away
- Go hip-hop shopping (p187) in Queens' Jamaica (home turf of LL Cool J and 50 Cent), rising in the ranks for its cheap urban wear
- Get square eyes at the Museum of the Moving Image (p185), Queens' fun testament to cinema
- Hunt for the perfect New York slice of pizza – compulsory stops include Totonno's (p256) in Coney Island, and Grimaldi's (p253) under the Brooklyn Bridge
- Join the locals unwinding in Brooklyn's Prospect Park (p177), the sequel to Central Park
- Check out Queens' PS1 (p184), the MoMA outpost giving modern-art edge to an abandoned school
- Take the 7 Train (p185) – Queens' elevated purple line is deemed an historic trail
- Bar-hop in Williamsburg (p223), where the bars are bigger, cheaper and more laid back than Manhattan options
- Cheer at Yankee Stadium (p202) – a tour's fun, but a Bronx Bomber game is a must

TRANSPORTATION

Sixteen subway lines crisscross between Manhattan and Brooklyn, and the G line goes to/from Queens. Here are a few useful stops, broken down by neighborhood:

Bay Ridge R to 77th St, 86th St or Bay Ridge–95th St

Bedford-Stuyvesant C to Kingston–Throop Aves

Bensonhurst D, M to 18th Ave

Boerum Hill F, G to Bergen St, A, C, G to Hoyt–Schermerhorn Sts

Brighton Beach B, Q to Brighton Beach

Brooklyn Heights 2, 3 to Clark St

Carroll Gardens F, G to Bergen St

Cobble Hill F, G to Carroll St

Coney Island D, F, Q to Coney Island–Stillwell Ave

Downtown 2, 3, 4, 5 to Borough Hall, A, C, F to Jay St–Borough Hall, M, R to Court St

Dumbo F to York St, A, C to High St

Fort Greene B, M, Q, R to Dekalb Ave, C to Lafayette Ave

Park Slope F to 7th Ave, B, Q, 2, 3, 4, 5 to Atlantic Ave

Prospect Heights B, Q to Prospect Park

Prospect Park 2, 3 to Grand Army Plaza, B, Q to Prospect Park

Red Hook F to Carroll St, then bus B61

Williamsburg L to Bedford Ave

Hill and Carroll Gardens (aka BoCoCa), then Park Slope and Prospect Heights; industrial Red Hook; far-flung Bay Ridge and Bensonhurst; beachfront neighbors Coney Island and Brighton Beach; historic African American district Bedford-Stuyvesant; and Brooklyn's booming 20-something HQ, Williamsburg and Greenpoint.

BROOKLYN HEIGHTS

New York's oldest unchanged neighborhood, and its first designated historic district, presents the boroughs at their most charming. Some New Yorkers claim this is what 'New York used to look like.' In the Brooklyn Heights Historic District, 19th-century brownstones scale many architectural styles (Victorian Gothic, Romanesque, neo-Greco, Italianate etc) and sit on quiet, treelined streets – some named for fruit or trees in an effort not to canonize particular arriving migrants by name.

These days rents here reach skyscraper heights; long gone are the days when literary folks came for the cheaper housing. Thomas Wolfe wrote *Of Times and the River* at his home at **5 Montague Terrace**. Truman Capote wrote *Breakfast at Tiffany's* at **70 Willow Street**.

In the mid-19th century, Henry Ward Beecher led abolitionist sermons from his pulpit at the **Plymouth Church** (Map p462; Orange St btwn Henry & Hicks Sts), which dates from 1849. Beecher's statue outside was created by Gutzon Borglum of Mount Rushmore fame.

Montague Street is the Heights' main strip, and where downtown and the Heights mingle. During the day its Mexican, Indian, Turkish, Polish, Japanese and American restaurants fill with downtown workers looking for lunch specials.

All east–west lanes head to the neighborhood's number-one attraction: the **Brooklyn Heights Promenade** (Map p462), which hangs over the Brooklyn–Queens Expressway with views of Lower Manhattan and the New York Harbor.

Years ago pedestrians had to watch out for streetcars rattling down the street, inspiring the borough's baseball team name: the Brooklyn Dodgers.

BROOKLYN HISTORICAL SOCIETY

Map p462

☎ 718-222-4111; www.brooklynhistory.org; 128 Pierrepont St; adult/student/child $6/4/free; ⏰ 10am-5pm Wed-Sun; Ⓜ M, R to Court St, 2, 3, 4, 5 to Borough Hall

Built in 1881 and renovated in 2002, this four-story Queen Anne–style landmark building (a gem in itself) houses a library (with some 33,000 grainy digitized photos from decades past), auditorium and museum devoted to the borough. Past exhibits – which tend to stick around for a year or more each – have included Coney Island and the Brooklyn Dodgers' 1955 championship season. The society also leads several Brooklyn walking tours (some free), and an occasional bus tour of the riverside Navy Yard.

DOWNTOWN BROOKLYN

Looming east of Cadman Plaza West and Court St from Brooklyn Heights, and continuing to Flatbush Ave, downtown Brooklyn is a more functional, modern strip of busy streets where weekday workers troll

Sights

BROOKLYN

BROOKLYN WATERFRONT PARK

Looking over the East River from the Brooklyn Heights Promenade, there it is: Manhattan soaring. But below, just past the Brooklyn–Queens Expwy, are ungainly docks poking out into the river. In early 2006 the city and state agreed to front $150 million to create a 1.3-mile-long shoreline patchwork of greenery, basketball courts and fishing piers that will stretch from the Manhattan Bridge (and Empire-Fulton Ferry State Park) to Atlantic Ave. The catch, for many, is that it comes with the condition that the park pays for itself – through hotel rooms and over 1000 new luxury condos. Dumbo residents didn't want a hotel on their waterfront, and the Heights residents worried about extra pedestrians rambling their quiet lanes.

Pending final approval (and it looks to be a done deal), construction will begin in 2007.

sidewalks and Brooklynites come to protest towing fees in the city courts. The Brooklyn Bridge dumps traffic onto busy Adams St; east of here you'll find discount-clothing shops along Fulton St Mall and dated department stores. The many subway connections make this a good jumping-off point to more interesting neighborhoods in the area: Boerum Hill, Brooklyn Heights, Cobble Hill, Dumbo and Fort Greene.

If you're heading to Fort Greene, use the inside ATM at the **Dime Savings Bank** (Map pp460–1; 9 Dekalb Ave btwn Fulton St & Flatbush Ave), now a Washington Mutual, to get a glimpse inside this 1906 Classical Revival marble building.

BROOKLYN TOURISM & VISITORS CENTER Map p462

☎ 718-802-3846; www.brooklyntourism.org; 209 Borough Hall, Joralemon St; ☽ 10am-6pm Mon-Fri; ⊕ 2, 3, 4, 5 to Borough Hall

This information center, on the ground floor of Greek Revival Borough Hall (which dates from 1845), is packed with brochures, walking-tour maps and shopping guides to all things Brooklyn.

NEW YORK TRANSIT MUSEUM Map p462

☎ 718-694-1600; www.mta.info/mta/museum; Boerum Pl at Schermerhorn St; adult/child $5/3; ☽ 10am-4pm Tue-Fri, noon-5pm Sat & Sun; ⊕ 2, 3, 4, 5 to Borough Hall, M, R to Court St

Occupying an old subway station built in 1936 (and out of service since 1946), this museum takes on 100-plus years of getting

around the Big Apple. Many of the exhibits in the station's former waiting area – models of old subway cars, bus drivers' seats to steer, a chronological display of turnstiles from their 'ticket chopper' beginnings in the late 19th century – are geared for kids. Best is the downstairs area, on the platform, where everyone can climb aboard 13 original subway and elevated-train cars dating from the 1904, wicker-seat, army green–and-crimson Brooklyn Union Elevated Car. The museum's gift shop offers popular subway-print gifts.

DUMBO

On the East River north of downtown, Down Under the Manhattan Bridge Overpass (Dumbo) – whatever happened to non-acronym neighborhoods? – is a contained, arty loft-space district with incredible views of Manhattan from between the Brooklyn and Manhattan Bridges. A great way to get here is on foot from the Brooklyn Bridge; see p221 for a walking tour.

WHAT'S IN A NABE?

Brooklyn is a little of everything. Here's who you're likely to find in various 'hoods around the borough:

Bedford-Stuyvesant Historic African American neighborhood

Brooklyn Heights Brooklyn's big money, coming-of-age trust-fund kids

Cobble Hill, Boerum Hill & Carroll Gardens Budding yupsters, Italian long-termers

Coney Island & Brighton Beach Latin Americans, Italians, Ukrainian Jews

Dumbo Smattering of artists, furniture sellers, architects, dot-com millionaires seeking river views

Fort Greene African Americans, 20-something students and young professionals

Park Slope New Brooklynites pushing strollers back to brownstones, 20-something 'downtowners' on Fifth Ave

Prospect Heights Caribbean Americans, Lonely Planet authors

Red Hook Latin Americans, Italians, crusted dock vets, entrepreneurs ahead of the curve

Williamsburg 21st-century East Village hipsters, Polish old-timers, Dominicans, Puerto Ricans, Hasidic Jews

Dumbo was abandoned, rather creepy territory until artists started flowing in as early as the 1970s. That legacy still runs strong, particularly in the blocks east of the blue Manhattan Bridge, where graffiti-dotted buildings remain and you can peek into windows and see artists and sculptors at work. Further east is **Vinegar Hill**, where you can see some historic buildings along Water St between Gold St and Hudson Ave.

Many visitors stay back west, between the bridges – in 'new Dumbo' – where there are more clean-cut million-dollar lofts that attract new wealth and firms eyeing the waterfront view. The most developed is wee Washington St, where one of Dumbo's top galleries is located: **Dumbo Arts Center** (Map p462; ☎ 718-694-0831; www.dumboartscenter.org; 30 Washington St; ◌ noon-6pm Thu-Mon; ◉ A, C to High St, F to York St). The feather in its cap is its annual Dumbo Art Under the Bridge Festival, held each October. It's no small affair – about 200,000 attended in 2005.

On the water, set snug between the bridges and backed by Civil War–warehouses, **Empire-Fulton Ferry State Park** (Map p462; ☎ 718-858-4708; www.nysparks.state.ny.us; 26 New Dock St; ◌ 8am-7pm Thu-Mon, 7am-5pm Tue & Wed; ◉ A, C to High St, F to York St) offers sweeping vistas of the Lower Manhattan skyline that draw many a photographer and filmmaker, amateur and professional. Indeed, it's been featured in a good number of NYC films.

On the other side of Brooklyn Bridge is the **Fulton Landing**, where newlyweds line up for perfectly framed shots of the bridge.

A famous place for a chocolate break is **Jacques Torres Chocolate** (Map p462; ☎ 718-875-

9772; 66 Water St; ◌ 9am-7pm Mon-Sat, 10am-6pm Sun).

COBBLE HILL, BOERUM HILL & CARROLL GARDENS

An easy walk south from Brooklyn Heights, just across Atlantic Ave, this residential trio keeps up the same vibe – with leafy streets and century-old town houses – and ups the ante with a little more life. Not to mention the ever-growing restaurant row of Smith St. The three neighborhoods overlap and share similarities, and in recent years have sometimes gone by the collective name of (don't laugh) 'BoCoCa.'

Cobble Hill runs on and west of Court St (with bookshops, cafés, restaurants and a cinema). Clinton St – where you'll find the quiet **Cobble Hill Park** (Map p465; cnr Congress & Clinton Sts) – is particularly lush. On **Atlantic Avenue**, west of Court St, are a number of Middle Eastern delis and restaurants, including the beloved delicacy shop **Sahadi's** (Map p462; ☎ 718-624-4550; 187 Atlantic Ave; ◌ 9am-7pm Mon-Fri, 8:30am-7pm Sat), where the olive bar boasts two dozen options. East of Smith St (around Hoyt St), Atlantic Ave is lined with furniture and antiques shops, plus a few boutiques – worth a look.

Things feel a little looser over on relentlessly gentrified **Smith Street** in **Boerum Hill**, which expands east to 3rd St. Better food and booze and a slightly younger crowd are found here – along with actors Heath Ledger and Michelle Williams, who moved here in 2005. North, along Atlantic Ave, are a number of furniture shops and boutiques. On the last Sunday of September, the **Atlantic**

GOWANUS CONDO?

A couple of blocks east of Smith St in Carroll Gardens, the factory-lined **Gowanus Canal** (Map p465) won't win awards for beauty, but it carries a special victorious spirit for Brooklynites. In recent times it's become the latest battlefield of gentrification.

As with Red Hook, Gowanus' old warehouses make billionaire city planners salivate over lucrative plans to rezone and build loft-like condos. Many of the 14,000 locals (many of whom are artists) are fighting, but despite a few victories things are starting to change.

For much of the 20th century, the former creek (named for the Gouwane Native Americans who sold the area to the Dutch in 1636) roared with commercial life. Ships from New York Harbor came in to load/unload goods, and tens of millions of pounds of human waste were dumped in each year. Many say it was a favorite body dump for the Mafia too – as they say, nothing floats in black sludge.

A couple of bridges span the thin slice of (now cleaner) water, where (in recent years) canoeists and striped bass come for a look. A good peeking (note the 'k') point is from the retractile bridge on Carroll St.

Antic festival takes up Atlantic Ave. This multicultural festival is one of New York's best, with oodles of food to sample and music to hear (one five-minute walk took in an R&B band in pastel suits, a bluegrass band, a Greek folk band with belly dancers, and Chicago alt-rock band the Ponys).

South of both neighborhoods, beginning around Carroll St, is Carroll Gardens, a long-time Italian neighborhood that continues to where the Brooklyn–Battery Tunnel and Brooklyn–Queens Expwy cut off Red Hook (p179). George Washington watched the disastrous start of the Revolutionary War during the Battle of Long Island from Fort Box (Map p465; cnr Smith St & 2nd Pl); it's now a parking lot.

FORT GREENE & CLINTON HILL

Spreading east and south from the Brooklyn side of the Manhattan Bridge, these residential neighborhoods of late 19th-century brownstones and gospel churches are hot new places to call home for a racially diverse group of working professionals. Spike Lee grew up here, and Erykah Badu and Rosie Perez live here. It's bisected by three main strips – its belly is crossed by Dekalb Avenue, which (between Vanderbilt and Flatbush Aves) offers newer, more stylish restaurants; to the south is Fulton Avenue, with many restaurants and African American businesses; and to the north, gritty Myrtle Avenue is lined with gas stations and discount shops.

It's a good area to wander through, beginning from the Brooklyn Academy of Music behind the art deco clock tower, aka the 1927 Williamsburgh Savings Bank (Map pp460–1; cnr Flatbush Ave & Hanson Pl), Brooklyn's tallest building. Saturday is a good day, when there's a farmers market along Washington Park Ave on the east side of hilly Fort Greene Park. Past the north–south Clinton Ave, Clinton Hill begins – with plenty of remarkable century-old mansions to see along Clinton and Washington Aves. Pratt Institute (Map pp460–1; ☎718-636-3600; www.pratt.edu; 200 Willoughby St) is an art and industrial school with giant sculptures, by some of its 4000-plus students, decorating its courtyard.

Further east and north, toward the Brooklyn–Queens Expwy and East River, things get a little crummier. Now a private industrial yard, the Brooklyn Naval Yard, along Flushing Ave, once cranked out military ships like the USS *Missouri* until business shut down in 1966. It's closed to the public, but the Brooklyn Historical Society (p173) sometimes offers tours.

BROOKLYN ACADEMY OF MUSIC
Map pp460–1

☎ 718-636-4100; www.bam.org; 30 Lafayette Ave; ⊕ 2, 3, 4, 5, B, Q to Atlantic Ave

The oldest concert center in the USA, the Brooklyn Academy of Music has hosted such notable events as Enrico Caruso's final performance. Today it continues to feature first-rate arts programs, including performances by visiting international opera companies and the resident Mark Morris dance troupe. The complex contains BAMCafe (☎ 718-636-4139) with classy dining (and live jazz on weekend nights), a 2109-seat opera house, an 874-seat theater, plus the four-screen Rose Cinemas, the first outer-borough movie house dedicated to independent and foreign films.

PARK SLOPE

Young professionals' brownstone dreams are realized on the gorgeous leafy blocks of Park Slope, between lush Prospect Park West and rougher crosstown thoroughfare Fourth Ave. Cutting through posher North Slope and more working-class South Slope (divided roughly at 1st St) are a couple of key commercial avenues. Along 'Upper West Sidey' Seventh Avenue you'll see some newly arrived émigrés from Manhattan pushing strollers past family-style pizza joints, some chain stores, and secondhand bookshops. Two blocks west, Fifth Avenue is the Slope's own 'downtown' with younger folks mixing in bars, restaurants and clothing boutiques; activity has grown in recent years as Seventh Ave rents grew higher. The area indeed slopes downward, but only a bit, on its way west toward the Gowanus Canal (p175).

The Brooklyn Public Library (Map p464; ☎ 718-230-2100; www.brooklynpubliclibrary.org; Grand Army Plaza) faces the grand entrance to Prospect Park. Its first cornerstone was laid in 1912, but early construction was abandoned – the site became a 'ruin' where kids would play between unfinished walls. With tweaks to its design, it finally opened as a heralded art deco masterpiece in 1941. Presently the library is building an expansive underground auditorium (to be completed in 2007).

GREEN-WOOD CEMETERY

People in big cities die too, and New York is home to many sprawling cemeteries. Of the biggies, however, none beats the gorgeous and historic **Green-Wood Cemetery** (Map p464; ☎ 718-788-7850; www.green-wood.com; 500 25th St; admission free; ☼ 7:45am-6pm Apr, to 7pm May, 7am-7pm Jun-Aug, 7:45am-7pm Sep, to 6pm Oct-Mar; ◉ M, R to 25th St), where 560,000 rest for the ages. (Head to toe, that's 520 miles of folks, minimum.)

Founded in 1838, Green-Wood was the plot where many big names wanted their bones to be. On this massive 478-acre plot (with ponds, rolling lawns and trees), you can take nice strolls past the final resting places of folks like Leonard Bernstein, Horace Greeley, FAO Schwarz, mobster Joey Gallo, Samuel FB Morse and many others.

The park is a hike south of Park Slope; the easiest access is by subway. Walk up from the subway station to the Fifth Ave entrance, and pick up a free map at the entrance.

Big Onion (☎ 212-439-1090; www.bigonion.com; adult/senior & student $12/10) runs terrific walking tours. There are a couple of 60-page booklets detailing walking tours; these are available at the cemetery for $7.

Residents are proud of the Slope. Film director/writer Noah Baumbach, whose 2005 film *The Squid & the Whale* was set in the neighborhood, grew up here. He joked to *Park Slope Reader* (an interesting free quarterly available at cafés; www.psreader.com) that the park and Fourth Ave boundaries 'protected' Park Slope from the rest of Brooklyn. True enough, many Brooklynites feel that Park Slope isn't really the borough – more like a slick enclave of Manhattan in a primo setting.

If you walk the Prospect Park loop, poke around the side-by-side districts **Prospect Park South** and **Ditmas Park**, which look more mid-America than New York City. You'll see two-story stand-alone houses done up in Colonial Revival, neo-Tudor and Queen Anne styles. The best streets are east of dreary Coney Island Ave; try east–west Albemarle Rd (a few blocks south of the park), then south a couple of blocks to streets such as Westminster or Argyle Rd.

PROSPECT PARK

The creators of this 585-acre **park** (Map p464; ☎ 718-965-8951; www.prospectpark .org; subway B, Q, S to Prospect Park, 2, 3 to Grand Army Plaza, F to 15th St–Prospect Park) – Frederick Law Olmsted and Calvert Vaux – considered this an improvement over their other New York project, Central Park. Created in 1866, Prospect Park has many of the same activities in its broad meadows. Many come to lounge, run, boat, bike, skate or BBQ. For information on activities, stop by the **Audobon Center Boathouse** (☎ 718-287-3400; just west of B, Q lines).

Just north of the boathouse is the **Children's Corner**. Here, you'll find a terrific 1912 **carousel** (☎ 718-282-7789; admission $1; ☼ noon-5pm or 6pm Thu-Sun Apr-Oct), which was a former Coney Island resident, and a small **zoo** (☎ 718-399-7339; adult/senior/child $6/1.25/1; ☼ 10am-5pm Apr-Oct, 10am-4:30pm Nov-Mar), with sea lions and 400 other animals. Kids also like the free **Lefferts Homestead Children's Historic House Museum** (☎ 718-789-2822; ☼ noon-5pm Thu-Sun Apr-Nov, by appt Dec-Mar), an 18th-century Dutch farmhouse with toys from the era to play with.

South of the boathouse, on the west edge of Prospect Lake, **Kate Wollman Rink** (☎ 718-287-6431; adult/senior & child $5/3, rental $5; ☼ late Nov-Mar, call for hrs) has enough ice to welcome hundreds of ice-skaters. The nearby lake is open for **pedal boats** (☎ 718-282-7789; per hr $15; ☼ noon-6pm summer, noon-5pm or 6pm Thu-Sun May–mid-Oct).

At the park's northwest entrance, **Grand Army Plaza** (cnr Eastern Pkwy & Flatbush Ave; near Grand Army Plaza station) is home to the 80ft arch, **Soldiers' & Sailors' Monument**, built in 1892 to commemorate the Union army's victory in the Civil War. On occasion its doors are opened and you can walk past stored parade items – giant puppets – to a top viewing deck. The immense art deco **Brooklyn Public Library** (see opposite) faces the arch on its south side.

A free weekend **trolley** connects points of interest around the park (including the Brooklyn Museum) from noon to 6pm.

PROSPECT HEIGHTS

Across Flatbush Ave from Park Slope, Prospect Heights occupies the (flat) blocks north of Prospect Park, centering on Vanderbilt and Washington Aves. It was home to Italian, Irish and Jewish residents in the late 19th century; since WWII the Heights has been a largely working-class barrio of African Americans and West Indies immigrants.

Outside its few attractions, there's not a lot to see by foot. But everyone – locals and tourists – lines up for eggs and breakfasts at one-of-a-kind Tom's Restaurant (p256).

Brooklyn Dodgers fans may want to walk a couple of blocks east of the Brooklyn Botanic Garden (below) to see the site of fabled Ebbetts Field (Map p464; 55 Sullivan Pl). It closed in 1957 when the Dodgers moved west. The site is now home to the towering Jackie Robinson Apartments housing projects.

BROOKLYN BOTANIC GARDEN Map p464

☎ 718-623-7200; www.bbg.org; 1000 Washington Ave; adult/senior & student/child $5/3/free, free to all Tue & 10am-noon Sat; ⏱ 8am-6pm Tue-Fri, 10am-6pm Sat, Sun & holidays Apr-Sep, 8am-4:30pm Tue-Fri, 10am-4:30pm Sat, Sun & holidays Oct-Mar; ◉ 2, 3 to Eastern Pkwy–Brooklyn Museum

The 15-garden museum – most easily accessed from the entrance next to the Brooklyn Museum on Eastern Parkway – features 12,000 plants, a gallery for art exhibits, a Japanese garden and a Celebrity Path (featuring some of the borough's famous past residents, such as Woody Allen, Woody Guthrie, Barbra Streisand and Harry Houdini). It makes for some of Brooklyn's best strolling grounds (and free days can get busy in good weather). The best time to come is at the end of April for the massive Sakuri Matsuri (Cherry Blossom Festival), when trees turn pink and stages host Japanese events (including tako drumming and tearful samurai tales staged to Tokyo pop soundtracks). There's no picnicking in the grounds, but there's a café.

There are guided tours at 1pm on weekends.

BROOKLYN CHILDREN'S MUSEUM

Map p464

☎ 718-735-4400; www.brooklynkids.org; 145 Brooklyn Ave; admission $4; ⏱ 1-6pm Tue-Fri, 11am-6pm Sat & Sun Jul & Aug, 1-6pm Wed-Fri, 11am-6pm Sat & Sun Sep-Jun; ◉ C to Kingston–Throop Ave, 3 to Kingston

This hands-on kids favorite was the world's first museum designed expressly for children, founded in 1899. Emphasizing art, music and ethnic cultures, the museum features a world playground that celebrates different cultures

and a greenhouse designed to teach kids about environmental preservation. The 'Free Friday Family Jam' is held on Friday in July and August, with multicultural dance and music on the rooftop or at nearby Brower Park. By 2007, the museum plans to double its size, adding a Kids Cafe and new galleries.

BROOKLYN MUSEUM Map p464

☎ 718-638-5000; www.brooklynmuseum.org; 200 Eastern Pkwy; adult/senior & student/child $8/4/free; ⏱ 10am-5pm Wed-Fri, 11am-6pm Sat & Sun, to 11pm 1st Sat of month; ◉ 2, 3 to Eastern Pkwy–Brooklyn Museum

The country's biggest art museum after the Met, with 1.5 million pieces and the Americas' biggest Egyptian collection, sees far fewer visitors than its more famous Manhattan friend. The five-floor beaux arts building – built by McKim, Mead and White to be the world's biggest museum in 1897 – certainly sprawls, yet is only a fifth of its planned size. Temporary exhibits often bring weekend hordes here (such as for the Basquiat show in 2005), while at other times it's quiet. One of the best and busiest times to come is the first Saturday of the month, when diverse Brooklyn comes for screenings and concerts (and free entry!) – there's beer and wine on hand.

The museum's still reeling from the 2004 addition of a lovely glass-esplanade and entry; out back is a 1900 replica of the Statue of Liberty (added in 2005). Highlights are many. The African Arts display on the ground floor (near the mint-colored café) features several short video loops that illustrate how traditional masks and costumes are used; note the 'Masquerade' video for the urinating-monkey head puppet from Benin. The 2nd-floor Egyptian collection is the top draw, with 9th-century BC sandstone reliefs of eagle-headed genies covered in script, and 13th-century BC mummy boards decorated like an Assyrian animé. The 4th-floor decorative arts display – with re-creations of art deco apartments and other periods – was being renovated at research time. Definitely leave time for the 5th floor, where 58 Rodin sculptures line the central pavilion, and there's a mix-match of American art and relics (such as fascinating films by Thomas Edison – including footage of the Sioux Ghost Dance in 1894, just four years after the Wounded Knee massacre).

Sights

BROOKLYN

RED HOOK

For over a hundred years the Statue of Liberty has had her gaze on this waterfront district of closed warehouses and projects; it's taken until this new century for anyone else to follow suit. The area is severed from Brooklyn by the Brooklyn–Battery Tunnel and lacks much public transport other than the pokey B61 or B77 bus from the Carroll St subway station in Carroll Gardens. Red Hook – named by the Dutch for its shape and the color of its soil – served as the inspiration for Marlon Brando's brilliant *On the Waterfront* (the film was shot in Hoboken).

Developers are now eyeing it too – the 1132ft *Queen Mary 2* cruise ship began porting at the $45-million Brooklyn Cruise Terminal (at Piers 11 and 12) in April 2006, and IKEA hopes to open its blue-and-gold doors by 2007. Many locals welcome the potential new jobs, while others are worried about yuppified traffic.

Things are pre-boom for now, but there's a trickle of galleries, bakeries, furniture shops and restaurants (p256) on **Van Brunt Street**, a couple of blocks north of the street's terminus. The best place to poke around is the **Beard Street Warehouses** (Map p465; 499 Van Brunt St), two redbrick 1869 warehouses that stored grain, raw sugar, cotton and tobacco. They're now home to the **Brooklyn Waterfront Artists Coalition** (☎ 718-596-2507; www.bwac.org), which hosts some exhibits. Just south you can see the dilapidated loading tracks of a processing plant in ruins.

Held in March since 1997, the three-night **No Fun Festival** (www.nofunfest.com) is a full-on no-wave throwback celebration of noise. It's staged annually at the **Hook** (Map p462; ☎ 718-797-3007; www.thehookmusic.com; 18 Commerce St btwn Richards & Columbia Sts).

The **Waterfront Museum & Showboat Barge** (Map p465; ☎ 718-624-4719; www.waterfrontmuseum.org; Pier 44, 209 Conover St; adult/child purchased in advance $12/6; ☯ check website) stages kid-oriented circus shows on a barge that a former juggler dug up from under the George Washington Bridge.

BENSONHURST & BAY RIDGE

At Brooklyn's southwestern tip is an almost insulated New York that garnered 15 minutes of fame when John Travolta strutted by the elevated subway tracks in Bensonhurst, a little grittier than its westerly cohort Bay Ridge. Coming to either is good DIY turf: a 'real' New York City that sees little fanfare.

After the elevated train line made it to **Bensonhurst** (Map pp460–1; subway D, M to 18th Ave) in 1915, many Italians and Jews poured out of the tight Lower East Side for roomier town houses and apartments. That certain disco film starts famously just outside the 18th Ave subway station. There are plenty of shops and pizzerias to find along 86th St.

Known as Yellow Hook (for its clay color) until the yellow-fever epidemic of the mid-19th century, the more attractive **Bay Ridge** (Map pp460–1; subway R to 77th or 86th Sts, or Bay Ridge–95th St) stretches south along the water to the Verrazano Narrows Bridge. The neighborhood is historically home to many Scandinavians and Italians, and in recent years to many Chinese. The most interesting areas are along **Third Avenue**, roughly from 76th to 95th Sts (lined with many pizzerias, valet-parking trattorias and Irish pubs), as well as the **Shore Parkway Promenade** (unfortunately running alongside the parkway with JFK-bound traffic). The promenade leads south to the **Verrazano Narrows Bridge**, which first connected Staten Island with Brooklyn in 1964.

The *Saturday Night Fever* disco scenes were shot at Bay Ridge's 2001 Odyssey, which only closed – as the Spectrum – in 2005.

CONEY ISLAND & BRIGHTON BEACH

About 50 minutes by subway from Midtown, these two beachside neighborhoods sit on the calm Atlantic tides and are well connected by a beachside boardwalk. It's a fun day trip to visit both – for rides, freak shows, vodka and beach time.

In these ever-changing Brooklyn times, Coney Island's future is up for grabs too. In late 2005 Mayor Bloomberg unleashed an $83-million plan to make Coney Island's amusement park a year-round attraction, with a renovated boardwalk by 2007, plus new entertainment venues and areas for restaurants and shops.

Coney Island is named for wild rabbits (*konijn* in Dutch), which were pretty much all the first Europeans saw on the grassy shoreline in the 17th century. By the end of the 19th century, the island had become a den for gamblers, hard drinkers, boxers and racers – some called it 'Sodom by the Sea.'

MERMAIDS OF HONOR

The official start of the summer season in Coney Island is the wild, wet and wacky annual procession known as the Mermaid Parade, taking place on the last Saturday in June. The lineup of sequined and bejeweled revelers – mostly women (and some flamboyant men) who stuff themselves into teeny bikinis and colorfully freakish aquatic getups – moves chaotically along Surf Ave for an afternoon stroll every year, as wide-eyed observers of all stripes stand and cheer in the sun. Some dress up as pirates.

Founded in 1983 by Coney Island USA (the arts organization that also produces the Coney Island Circus Sideshow), the Mermaid Parade honors Coney Island's forgotten Mardi Gras, which lasted from 1903 to 1954. The event is hosted each year by a different celebrity King Neptune and Queen Mermaid; in 2005, David Johansen (of New York Dolls fame) and Karmen Guy ('voodoo' singer) presided over the madness. It's a truly unique, very New York spectacle-by-the-sea.

The 20th century brought a new era with late-night concerts, settings of Buster Keaton films, and, best yet, amusement parks. The most famous, Luna Park, opened in 1903 and was a dream world of lagoons, live camels and elephants, rides to the moon – all lit by over a million bulbs (fire eventually took it down in 1946). Surviving gems of the time such as the Wonder Wheel (1920) and Cyclone (1927) were mere players in a bigger game.

By the 1960s, Coney Island's pull had slipped (though long-time resident Woody Guthrie still considered it home) and the 'hood became a sad, crime-ridden reminder of past glories. During the 1980s a slow, enduring comeback began, with new rides and 'freak shows' (sword swallowers, bearded women, folks with lizard skin etc) trickling in.

Many visitors start at Coney and return from Brighton Beach. Surf Ave runs parallel to the beach in Coney Island neighborhood, then turns inland as Ocean Pkwy. Brighton Beach's main thoroughfare is Brighton Beach Ave, which connects Ocean Pkwy with Coney Island Ave to the east.

Coney Island's rides run on weekends only from the start of April, then daily from mid-June through Labor Day. Generally rides don't operate from then until April.

CONEY ISLAND Map p466

Ⓞ D, F to Coney Island–Stillwell Ave
Across Surf Ave from the Coney Island–Stillwell Ave subway stop is **Nathan's** (p256), home to Coney's legendary hot dogs – and a belly-stuffing contest on July 4. Beyond (on Surf and Stillwell Aves) are many **games** (batting cages, mini golf, even 'shoot the freak'). Facing the water, to the right is **KeySpan Park**, where the Brooklyn Cyclones play minor-league baseball.

To the left when you exit the subway, toward Brighton Beach, is the bulk of activity. Toward Surf Ave on 12th St (Denos Vourderis Pl) is the nonprofit **Sideshows by the Seashore** (☎ 718-372-5159; www.coneyisland .com; 1208 Surf Ave; adult/child $5/3; ◷ 2-8pm Fri, 1-11pm Sat & Sun Jun-Aug), which hosts a variety of 'nature's mistakes' such as a glass-walking, facial-tattooed bug-eater, a Mormon fire-eater, lots of nails knocked into nostrils etc). It also runs the **Coney Island Museum** (admission $1; ◷ noon-5pm Sat & Sun) upstairs.

Walking east, you'll find **Deno's Wonder Wheel Amusement Park** (☎ 718-372-2592; ◷ 11am-midnight mid-Jun–Aug, noon-9pm weather permitting Apr, May, Sep & Oct), with the long-standing pink-and-mint Ferris wheel (1920; $5) and a collection of kiddie rides (10 rides for $18).

Beyond Deno's is its rival, **Astroland** (☎ 718-265-2100; www.astroland.com; ◷ noon-midnight mid-Jun–Aug, noon-dusk Sat & Sun Apr–mid-Jun & Sep–mid-Oct), under which Woody Allen grew up in *Annie Hall*. A ride on the 1927 **Cyclone** coaster here is $5 ($4 for a 're-ride'). The

Hamburgers, beer and Coney Island (left), a perfect combo

CONEY SIGNS

In 2003, the lore got a boost when Steve Powers and the nonprofit art group Creative Time (www .creativetime.org) brought back the tradition of hand painted signs of freaky characters and such for area games and rides. The artists' shop, **Clubhouse** (Map p466; 1206 Surf Ave; ☺ noon-7pm Thu-Sun mid-Jun–Labor Day; subway D, F, Q to Stillwell Av), sells various sized paintings (from $50).

super clickety-clackety ride winds around a wooden track, down nearly-vertical falls, and slams around bends at nearly 60mph.

For good clean fun for the kids, visit the **New York Aquarium** (☎ 718-265-3400; www .nyaquarium.com; Surf Ave btwn W 8th & 5th Sts; adult/child $12/8; ☺ 10am, call for events & closing times or see website; ◉ F to W 8th St–NY Aquarium), which has a touch pool where kids can handle starfish, plus underwater views of baleen whales and popular feedings of sea lions and walruses.

All along the boardwalk (running to Brighton Beach), of course, is the beach. It's widely used, but still not too dirty. The water is off-limits when lifeguards are off duty during the low season. Plenty of shops sell water-related gear.

BRIGHTON BEACH Map p466
◉ B, Q to Brighton Beach

Named for England's beach resort in 1868, Brighton Beach shows little link with England considering its stream of signs in Cyrillic these days. Now known as 'Little Odessa,' Brighton Beach is home to mostly Ukrainian Jews who emigrated here in the 1970s and 1980s.

A walk along its more residential-feeling boardwalk, and another under the subway line over busy Brighton Beach Ave, is a good finish to a day at Coney Island (it's about a 10-minute walk east, and the B or Q subway link gets you back to Manhattan). Reading most signs requires knowledge of Cyrillic, and if you hold open a door for a babushka, you're likely to get a *spasiba* (thank you). Plenty of shops on Coney Island Ave hawk imported caviar, candies with czar boxes, USSR-themed T-shirts, *matrushka* dolls, and CDs of Russia's (largely unfortunate) pop industry.

See p256 for eating options.

BEDFORD-STUYVESANT

NYC's largest African American neighborhood – where Notorious BIG grew up – gets a bad rap sometimes. Chris Rock's TV show *Everybody Hates Chris* is set here, comically showing 'Bed Sty, Do or Die' graffiti and pimps robbing kids on Halloween. Even Billy Joel slagged it in his 1980 song 'You May Be Right', where he shows off his craziness by walking 'through Bedford-Sty alone.' Some of the neighborhood – which sprawls from Flatbush and Atlantic Aves, somewhat of a cornerstone between Williamsburg and Clinton Hill – earns its rep, with boarded-up town houses and bleak projects. But not all.

Near Bed-Sty's southern reaches, **Stuyvesant Heights**' blocks (Map pp460–1) of leafy late-19th-century brownstones (roughly between Fulton and MacDonough Sts, between Tompkins and Stuyvesant Aves) are on the upswing. Cafés and bookshops are opening on some streets, such as **Lewis Avenue**, and brownstone prices are reaching $1 million. There's even a knockout B&B (p375). The best starting point is from the Kingston–Throop Ave subway stop on the C line. East–west MacDonough St is two short blocks north, with the bulk of the district lying to the east.

WILLIAMSBURG

New York's 'it' neighborhood of the past half-decade or more, Williamsburg has spread along the L line into Brooklyn like a cockroach problem – cockroaches, that is, with tousled hair, uncut beards, just-woke-up expressions, Animal Collective or Deerhoof tunes on the iPod, and an 'East Village? We don't need no stinking East Village' attitude. It's great. Actually 'Billyburg' can be a little ugly by day – warehouses converted into lofts, treeless streets, modern unassuming town houses – but it really lights up, along with cigarettes in some rule-breaking bars, at night, when lights from Manhattan flicker in vain from across the dark East River.

The traditional heart of it is **Bedford Ave** (Map p463; subway L to Bedford Ave), between N 10th St and Metropolitan Ave, where there are side-by-side cafés, indie-rock stores, boutiques, cheap restaurants and bars. Things ebb cooler on side streets – particularly the 'second Bedford', **North 6th St**, toward the river, and parallel thoroughfares Berry and Wythe Aves – and in new scattered eateries

181

and bars that follow each of the next couple of L subway stops, like stepping stones, into **East Williamsburg**, home to many Latin Americans; it begins several blocks east on the other side of the Brooklyn–Queens Expressway. (See p223 for a walking tour.)

South of the eponymous Williamsburg Bridge, on side streets between Broadway and Bedford Ave, you'll find a busy Hasidic Jewish neighborhood. Bedford Ave leads north; based on Manhattan Ave is the traditionally Polish neighborhood of **Greenpoint**.

Time your Billyburg visit right to get a glimpse at the **Brooklyn Brewery** (Map p463; ☎ 718-486-7440; www.brooklynbrewery .com; 79 N 11th St; ☺ 6-11pm Fri, noon-5pm Sat; subway L to Bedford Ave), where those lagers with the cute logo are made. There are eight $3 beers on tap, and free half-hour guided tours – with tastings – at 1pm, 2pm, 3pm and 4pm Saturday. If you can't find a taxi to drive you home, there are late-night car services on Bedford Ave.

Free Williamsburg (www.freewilliamsburg .com) is a community-based site focusing on keeping Billyburg residents cool (album reviews, band features) and has a rolling guide to area bars, restaurants and galleries, with reviews. For the coolest events around, check the precisely clunky website of events staged by one-man show maker **Todd P** (www.toddpnyc.com), who has been staging gigs around Billyburg since 2001.

QUEENS

Eating p258, Shopping p352

While Brooklyn barks its lore and glory to the world, Queens tends to keep quiet about how great *it* is. This is the most ethnically diverse neighborhood or borough in the world – about 150 nations are represented amongst its population of 2.2 million, and close to half its residents were born abroad. Queens is New York's biggest borough, and packs its mighty frame with some seriously rich history – dozens of jazz greats lived here; it's hosted two World's Fairs plus the annual US Open tennis tournament; Run DMC and the Ramones grew up in Queens; Maria from the film *Maria Full of Grace* settled into the Colombian community here; and it's home to New York's two major airports.

At the start of the 21st century there were still clear Greek or Chinese neighborhoods, but things are now getting evocatively mixed up. A walk down 37th Ave

TRANSPORTATION

Here are a few useful subway stops, broken down by neighborhood:

Astoria ⊙ N, W to 30th Ave, Astoria Blvd or Astoria–Ditmars Blvd

Flushing ⊙ 7 to Flushing–Main St, LIRR to Flushing

Jackson Heights 7 to 74th St–Broadway, E, F, G, R, V to Jackson Heights–Roosevelt Ave

Jamaica ⊙ E, J, Z to Suphin Blvd–Archer Ave, LIRR to Jamaica

Long Island City ⊙ E, G, V, 7 to 45th Rd–Court House Sq or Vernon Blvd–Jackson Ave, E, V to 23rd St–Ely Ave, G to Long Island City–Court Sq

Rockaway Beach ⊙ A to Beach 90th St (among other stops)

Shea Stadium & Flushing Meadows Corona Park 7 to Willets Point–Shea Stadium, LIRR to Shea Stadium

in Jackson Heights, for example, passes decades-old Italian restaurants, surrounded by Polish-sausage delis, Afghan kebab shops, Thai noodle shops, and Ecuadorian restaurants in Olde English–style buildings. The attractions, such as **PS1's modern art** (p184) or the **Museum of the Moving Image's** film props (p185), actually outnumber (and beat) Brooklyn's.

Queens was named in the 17th century for Queen Catherine of Braganza, married to Charles II of England. Braganzatown didn't have the same ring to it.

They don't keep a public office, but **Queens Tourism Council** (☎ 718-263-0546; www.discover queens.info) offers information on attractions and tours by phone or on the website. **Queens Council on the Arts** (☎ 718-647-3377; www.queenscouncilarts.org) promotes art in the borough; its website has an 'artMAP' you can download, plus information on many attractions.

Orientation

Many of Manhattan's sunrise-watchers look over Queens. Between the Bronx and Brooklyn, Queens stretches eastward, roughly between Manhattan's 34th and 120th Sts. Queens is bounded by the East River to the north and west (where the Astoria and Long Island City neighborhoods face Manhattan). Queens wraps around its southern neighbor, Brooklyn, to Jamaica Bay (home to JFK International Airport).

Northern Blvd leads east, passing through neighborhoods like Woodside, Jackson Heights, Corona and Flushing. Another

Sights

QUEENS

THE NEXT BROOKLYN?

No-one in the Bronx or Queens is saying this out loud, but the race to be the 'next Brooklyn' is on, and the gloves are off. In the past decades, Manhattan's climbing rent prices (in 2005 nearly $3000 per month, on average) sent artists and downtown budgeteers across the East River to converted warehouses in Brooklyn's Dumbo and Williamsburg (and now Red Hook and Gowanus Canal). But the market, and pretenders, tends to follow the cool kids. In 2005 prices in Brooklyn's up-and-coming Fort Greene were up 35% from a couple of years earlier; a brownstone there often breaks $1 million.

So far Queens is several years ahead of the Bronx. Since 2000 the number of transplants to Queens has skyrocketed, particularly into the riverhugging neighborhoods of artzone Long Island City and already-established Astoria, and at spots scattered along the 7 subway line. Queens' director of economic development Seth Bornstein described the borough to us as the new LES. He said the Brooklyn boom helps Queens and the other outer boroughs, as people start looking for alternatives to Manhattan.

Yet many feel that the Bronx – with its street-cred and hip-hop roots – is more 'legit' than Queens, and rezoned lofts in 'SoBro' (South Bronx, particularly along Buckner Blvd in Mott Haven) have tempted artists and space-seekers to this industrial, formerly rough-edged 'hood. A three-bedroom apartment in 2004 was going for as little as $250,000 – peanuts even in Brooklyn.

main east–west artery is busy Roosevelt Ave, which runs under the 7 subway line from Flushing and splits into Skillman and Greenpoint Aves just east of Long Island City.

LONG ISLAND CITY

Long Island City (Map p457) is Queens' coolest pocket these days (but not its prettiest), and it's definitely on the move. It's home to many Latin Americans and young professionals, and its 'boom' is largely helped by its devotion to art (PS1 is the clear standout, and one of New York's best museums) and its location, just a subway stop across the East River. To look at, it's a bizarre mix of urban life – subway cars rattle along elevated lines over a scene of graffiti-covered warehouses-turned-galleries, 19th-century town houses, and modern condos on the water (attracting a slightly bigger-walleted work-crowd eyeing Midtown across the river). Above it all – and visible for many of the boroughs – is the unlikely modern, 48-story Citicorp Building (Map p457; Jackson Ave), built in 1989 and bringing a lot of life to the area on weekdays.

There's plenty enough reason to linger a bit after checking out PS1 (p184). Across from the Citicorp Building is Court House Square (Map p457; subway 7 to 45th Rd–Court House Sq, E, V to 23rd St–Ely Ave, G to Long Island City–Court House Sq), home to a 1904 beaux arts courthouse. Nearby, standing proud and keeping it real, is 5 Pointz (Map p457; www.5ptz.com), one of the best collections of graffiti left anywhere in New York. Walk under the 7 subway tracks on (unsigned) Davis St, just south of Jackson

Ave, to see the dazzling displays of wall-to-wall art on a cluster of industrial buildings.

A couple of blocks west, Hunters Point Historic District (Map p457; 45th Ave btwn 21st & 23rd Sts) is a stretch of 1880s town houses. A couple of art options reachable by foot include the Dorsky Gallery (Map p457; ☎718-937-6317; 11-03 45th Ave; ☺11am-6pm Thu-Mon) and Sculpture Center (Map p457; ☎718-361-1750; www.sculpture-center .org; 44-19 Purves St; ☺11am-6pm Thu-Mon), a giant brick warehouse with indoor/outdoor space and rotating exhibits.

Some of the eateries around Citicorp stick with weekday hours for the suits. It's better to go for food or beer to the rising scene along Vernon Boulevard between 47th and 51st Aves (see p258). A few more minutes west, by the new condos, is riverside Gantry Plaza State Park (☎718-786-6385) with massive railroad gantries in service until 1967 and nice views of Midtown across the East River. The park will eventually have waterfront access from 46th to 55th Aves; the best access point is via 50th Ave.

ISAMU NOGUCHI GARDEN MUSEUM
Map p457

☎ 718-204-7088; www.noguchi.org; 9-01 33rd Rd at Vernon Blvd; ☺ 10am-5pm Wed-Fri, 11am-6pm Sat & Sun; adult/senior & student/child $10/5/free; ☺ N, W to Broadway

The sculptor and designer was well ahead of everyone, eyeing these lonely Queens streets of warehouses over four decades ago. This former workspace, now proudly strutting a renovation, is an imaginative spot, suitable for Noguchi's works. Outdoor gardens and bare-concrete indoor/outdoor galleries house a few hundred of Noguchi's curling wonders (the man made marble look like cubes of clay) and late pieces like the smooth-sided cobalt well, with a light film of water seemingly stuck to the sides. Some of his home design pieces are available in the café/gift shop. It's a bit of a hike from the subway, but the Socrates Sculpture Park (right) is also nearby. There are free gallery talks at 2pm daily. It's pay-as-you-wish on the first Friday of the month.

MUSEUM FOR AFRICAN ART Map p457
☎ 718-784-7700; www.africanart.org; 36-01 43rd Ave at 36th St; adult/senior & student/child under 6 $6/3/free; ☽ 10am-5pm Mon, Thu & Fri, 11am-5pm Sat & Sun; ⊕ 7 to 33rd St

It's hard to see this amount (and quality) of African tribal crafts, masks, musical instruments and depictions of spirituality outside of that continent. (This is one of only two museums in the USA dedicated to African artists.) The museum is planning to move to a Harlem site at Fifth Ave and 110th St.

PS1 CONTEMPORARY ART CENTER
Map p457

☎ 718-784-2084; www.ps1.org; 22-25 Jackson Ave at 46th Ave; suggested donation adult/student $5/2; ☽ noon-6pm Thu-Mon; ⊕ E, V to 23rd St—Ely Ave, 7 to 45th Rd—Court House Sq, G to Long Island City—Court House Sq

Many visitors to New York miss PS1, but its compelling alternative-space location (a closed 19th-century public school) and excellent exhibits of modern art (lots of video installations; impressionism? no thanks) in five sweeping galleries, make good use of the dramatic, cement-wall garden out front. Rooms are evocative old-student haunts, with wired-in stairways, high ceilings and painted-white wood floorboards that creak. The café has wine – plus sketches of naked people on the walls. PS1 is now run by MoMA, but feels free from the fussy Midtown scene. In summer, the 'Warm Up' series basically consists of hipster parties on Saturdays.

The school had an interesting history. Built controversially after political scandal, it became a landmark for Long Island City, with its stone-tower clock and bell (both destroyed in 1964).

SOCRATES SCULPTURE PARK Map p457
☎ 718-956-1819; Broadway at Vernon Blvd; admission free; ☽ 10am-dusk; ⊕ N, W to Broadway

Transformed from an illegal dumpsite in 1986, this open-air public space (near the Noguchi museum) displays sculptures and installations by local artists in a super location on the East River, with views of uptown and Roosevelt Island's tip. Past exhibits include an outdoor cubicle waiting room (with seats and a potted plant), green balls poking above the river surface, and the top few feet of a brownstone that seems buried in the ground. At 7pm Wednesday in July and August, the garden screens free films – like *Zorba the Greek* – with lots of pre-show food and music. From December to February the park stages light-based installations, illuminating the Queens waterfront shortly after sunset.

ASTORIA

Named for millionaire fur merchant John Jacob Astor, this northwestern edge of Queens is home to the biggest Greek community outside Greece. Greek bakeries, diners and delis line many streets, particularly along Broadway (subway N, W to Broadway); they're slightly more upscale on 31st St and Ditmars Blvd (subway N, W to Astoria–Ditmars Blvd). Before Greeks began moving here in the 1950s, it was primarily a neighborhood of factories (not to mention bridges – arched Hell's Gate and towering Triborough still dominate the views west). These days a lot of folks are brushing shoulders with the Greeks, as there's been an influx of Eastern Europeans (Croatians, Romanians) and Middle Eastern folk, not to mention the hip kids, as Astoria is essentially Queens' answer to Williamsburg.

An easy walk northwest of the Astoria–Ditmars Blvd station, 15-acre Astoria Park (Map p457) is set admirably on the water, with paths looking south toward Manhattan's skyscrapers from under the Triborough Bridge. Near the park is the 1936 art deco beaut Astoria Pool (p316) – the fountains at one end were used as torches when Olympic trials were held here in 1936 and 1964.

In 2003 Astoria became home to the new Queens International Film Festival (www.queens filmfestival.com), held in November.

RIDE ON THE INTERNATIONAL EXPRESS

The elevated, ultra-urban 7 subway line cuts across the guts of Queens on an elevated track, connecting far-off Flushing with Midtown Manhattan. It not only offers views of the borough (and back) to Manhattan, but takes you on a 'national historic trail,' through the longtime immigrant neighborhoods of Woodside (Irish), Jackson Heights (Indian, Filipino), Corona Heights (Italian, Peruvian, Colombian, Ecuadorian, Mexican) and Flushing (Chinese, Korean, Vietnamese). A good day could be spent hopping on and off the burgundy-colored line, taking in some of New York's array of international flavors. Plan on two meals. Ride in the front or back car for the clearest views.

One possible tour would be to take the 7 from Times Sq or Grand Central Terminal to the end of the line (Flushing–Main St), a 35-minute trip. Before you arrive, you'll pass the mammoth Flushing Meadows Corona Park to your right and Shea Stadium to your left.

In Flushing, get some Chinese, Taiwanese or Korean food, and ride back on the subway one stop to Willets Point–Shea Stadium for a walk through the Flushing Meadows park sights. Walk north to Roosevelt Ave, which runs under much of the 7 track. The **Louis Armstrong House** (p187) is a few blocks north.

Meander along Roosevelt Ave for 30 blocks west – past exciting shops and restaurants, all signed in Spanish – to 74th St, where things suddenly become quite Indian. Get a sari here or eat a curry (p258).

Hop on the subway to Woodside–61st St to wander through an old Irish neighborhood, then get onto the subway's front car at the 52nd St–Lincoln Ave or 46th St–Bliss St stations for a full view of Midtown as you inch closer. At Long Island City's 45th Rd–Court House Sq, get out for a look at the **PS1 Contemporary Art Center** (opposite) and a serious show of **graffiti** (p183).

MUSEUM OF THE MOVING IMAGE

Map p457

☎ 718-784-4520; www.movingimage.us; 35th Ave at 36th St; adult/senior & student/child $10/7.50/5, free to all 4-8pm Fri; ☽ noon-5pm Wed & Thu, noon-8pm Fri, 11am-6:30pm Sat & Sun; ⊙ G, R, V to Steinway St

Adults act like kids (kids do too) at this super-fun, three-story museum set in the middle of the sprawling one-time home of Paramount Pictures' east coast HQ. (Kaufman Astoria Studios – where *Sesame Street* is filmed – is next door; it's closed to the public.) It's hard to beat if you like movies. The museum has over 150,000 props and knickknacks from movies and TV in its collection – Robert De Niro's mohawk wig from *Taxi Driver*, the 'dental plumper' for Marlon Brando's heavy jowls in *The Godfather*, Chewbacca's head, Yoda's body, *2001* ape masks, Bill Cosby's sweater from *The Cosby Show*, costumes from *Chicago*, 'top 10' lists from David Letterman. Best are the interactive things: in a sound-edit room you can re-dub the 'we're not in Kansas anymore' scene from *The Wizard of Oz*, or add different soundtracks to scenes from Alfred Hitchcock's *Vertigo*, or act goofy in front of a 19th century–style camera to make a flip-book you can buy for $3. In personal monitors, actors from films such as *Raiders of the Lost Ark* talk about how scenes are made while you watch. There are lots of massive early cameras, plus a Gumby's stop-motion animator from the 1950s show. Temporary exhibits have included a vintage video-game room with tons of arcade gems to play for free. A downstairs area screens films – free with admission – on Friday, Saturday and Sunday. The museum is planning to double its size by 2009 in a $40-million expansion.

JACKSON HEIGHTS

Just below the rattling 7 subway runs **Roosevelt Avenue**, one of the more interesting strolling grounds in the city. This area – home to Indians, Bangladeshi, Vietnamese, Korean, Mexican, Colombian, Ecuadorian and other ethnic groups – is a whirlwind of the international. It's most famous for its 'Little India/Bangladesh' strip of saris, Bollywood DVDs and all-you-can-eat buffet lunches – such as at the **Jackson Diner** (p259) – along **74th Street** between Roosevelt and 37th Aves.

Spread out in a 50-block area to the north of the subway line – out of the smelling shot of fresh tortillas or curries – is one of the nicest New York neighborhoods that next-to-no New Yorkers know about. Following the 1909 opening of the Queensboro Bridge, the **Jackson Heights Historic District** (btwn Roosevelt & 34th Aves, from 70th to 90th Sts) was set up in 1917 as a 'garden city' (popularized in England at the time), with luxe six-story, chateau-style brick apartments sharing long, well-landscaped, (still) private gardens. There are a few good vantage points – try 80th or 81st Sts to 34th Ave. Nearby **37th**

185

Avenue is lined with slightly more polished eateries (Argentine, Ecuadorian, Colombian, American, Japanese) than the cheap taco and chow-mein jobbies on Roosevelt Ave.

Just east of 87th St, and right out of the Amazon, **Horoscopo** (☎ 718-779-9391; 86-26 Roosevelt Ave) is the lively base of the 'Amazon Indian' who tells fortunes amidst colored oils, tarot cards and hanging chicken feet. Pick up a bottle of 'Mr Money' if you're looking to get rich.

FLUSHING & CORONA

Aside from the sites of the widely popular sports events, **Shea Stadium** (p305; the Mets) and the **USTA National Tennis Center** (p308; the US Open), these two otherwise little-known neighborhoods have active streets of locals' shops signed in Chinese, Korean, Spanish and Italian. In between the two areas is the bizarre but interesting Flushing Meadows Corona Park (Map p467), dotted with buildings and monuments built to make statements for the 1939 and 1964 World's Fairs. They still do.

In the 17th century, Quakers met in Flushing to figure out how to avoid religious persecution from Dutch governor Peter Stuyvesant (which they did). Two hundred years later, many escaped slaves found freedom here (via the underground railroad).

By the 20th century, Flushing (in particular) had let itself go. When F Scott Fitzgerald dissed the area as an ash heap in *The Great Gatsby* (1925), he was being kind. The World's Fairs helped turn things around, making the swampy area more attractive for the many jazz greats who lived here.

Flushing – at the end of the 7 subway line – has a flourishing Chinatown that's bigger than Manhattan's. Clusters of shops and eateries center on Roosevelt Ave and Main St.

A couple of subway stops west, Corona's southern reach is a quaint Italian neighborhood that looks like a town square from another era. At **William F Moore Park** (aka Spaghetti Park, 108th St), the clink-clank of bocce balls sounds in summer, while passersby eat lemon ices.

FLUSHING COUNCIL ON CULTURE & THE ARTS   Map p467

☎ 718-463-7700; www.flushingtownhall.org; 137-135 Northern Blvd; gallery admission $5; ☻ 9am-5pm Mon-Fri, gallery noon-5pm; ◉ 7 to Flushing–Main St

Built in 1864, this Romanesque Revival building hosts year-round art shows and jazz and other music concerts. Its claim to fame is the three-hour Queens Jazz Trail trolley tours, held on the first Saturday of the month. The tour goes by old clubs and the homes of a staggering number of greats who lived in the area: Louis Armstrong, Lena Horne, Ella Fitzgerald, John Coltrane, Billie Holiday, Count Basie, Charles Mingus and others. It's $30 for the trolley ride, $40 for the trolley ride and dinner, which includes finishing off with a concert in the jazz hall. The council also has a jazz trail map plus other Queens-related brochures.

FLUSHING MEADOWS CORONA PARK   Map p467

◉ 7 to Willets Point–Shea Stadium

The area's biggest attraction is this 1225-acre park, built for the 1939 World's Fair and dominated by monuments such as Queens' most famous landmark, the stainless steel Unisphere (the world's biggest globe, at 120ft high and 380 tons). Facing it is the former New York City Building, now home to the **Queens Museum of Art** (below) and, on the northern side, which plans to expand, taking over the south side of the building, presently home to the **World's Fair Ice Rink** (☎ 718-271-1996; ◷ Mon, Wed, Fri-Sun Oct-Mar, call for hrs).

Just south are three weather-worn, Cold War–era New York State Pavilion Towers, which were part of the New York State Pavilion for the 1964 fair. More recently, these were used as spaceships in the film *Men in Black*.

Toward the 7 line is the tall **Arthur Ashe Stadium**, and the rest of the **USTA National Tennis Center** (p308), and just beyond, **Shea Stadium** (p305), where the Mets play (and where the Beatles introduced the world to stadium rock).

West, over the Grand Central Pkwy, are a few attractions, including the **New York Hall of Science** (☎ 718-699-0055; www.nyhallsci.org; 47-01 111th St; adult/student & child $11/8, free 2-5pm Fri; ◷ daily, call for hrs) and a small wildlife center.

The park actually has grounds too, on its eastern and southern edges. The top-quality astro-turf soccer fields are legendary for pick-up soccer. And Meadow Lake has boat and bike rentals at the boathouse.

The park is most easily reached from the walkway from the 7 subway stop, Willets Point–Shea Stadium. Check www.nycgov parks.org or call ☎ 718-760-6565 for information.

LOUIS ARMSTRONG HOUSE   Map p467

☎ 718-478-8274; www.louisarmstronghouse .org; 34-56 107th St; adult/senior & student $8/6; ◷ 10am-5pm Tue-Fri, noon-5pm Sat & Sun; ◉ 7 to 103rd St–Corona Plaza

At the peak of his career, with worldwide fame at hand, where did Satchmo choose to live? Queens of course. Louis spent his last 28 years in this quiet Corona Heights home, now a museum and regarded as a national treasure; he died in 1971. Guides offer free 40-minute tours (leaving on the hour; the last goes at 4pm) through the home (past his gold records on the wall). Call for information on visiting the Louis Armstrong Archives.

QUEENS BOTANICAL GARDENS

Map p467

☎ 718-886-3800; www.queensbotanical.org; 43-50 Main St; admission free; ◷ 8am-6pm Tue-Fri, 8am-7pm Sat & Sun Apr-Oct, 8am-4:30pm Tue-Sun Nov-Mar; ◉ 7 to Flushing–Main St

This 39-acre garden – born for the 1939 World's Fair – includes a good variety of non-native flora. The expansive meadows are better picnic grounds than nearby Flushing Meadows Corona Park, and the pathways provide good cycling.

JAMAICA

Where 50 Cent and LL Cool J first penned their rhymes, Jamaica, at the tail end of the E, F, J and Z subway lines, gets missed by most Manhattan residents, but it's getting attention from travelers from afar, specifically from those interested in superb 'hiphop' shopping. Home to many West Indian immigrants (evident in jerk-chicken in the area), Jamaica's name is only coincidentally a nod to many of the new residents' birthplaces. Centuries ago the Algonquin named the area *jameco* (or beaver), a name altered by the first English settlers who moved in – with Dutch permission – during the city's New Amsterdam days in the mid-17th century. After railway links linked Jamaica with the city, the population grew. The area is also home to many Latin Americans.

Although it's not open to the public, **Jamaica Center Business Improvement Association** (☎ 718-526-2422; 90-50 Parson Blvd) hosts occasional walking tours and can send you a few brochures.

The best access for the neighborhood is via the Jamaica Center Parson–Archer subway station on the E, J, Z subway lines, a quick block south of the main strip, Jamaica Ave.

Near the station, amidst 11-acre King Park, is Greco-Roman style **King Manor** (☎ 718-206-0545; www.kingmanor.org; Jamaica Ave at 150th St; adult/student $5/3; ◷ noon-2pm Thu & Fri, 1-5pm Sat & Sun), home to US Constitution signatory Rufus King in the early 1800s. King, an early abolitionist, made a failed run at president in 1817 (the last Federalist to run). The manor's not terribly exciting (most of the interiors are redone), but personalized tours are fun. King is buried a block east in the cemetery outside **Grace Episcopal Church** (155-03 Jamaica Ave).

A couple of blocks east, outside the **Jamaica Center for Arts & Learning** (JCAL; ☎ 718-658-7400; www.jcal.org; 161-04 Jamaica Ave; admission free; ◷ 8:30am-6pm Mon-Sat), is one of only two remaining cast-iron sidewalk clocks (this dates from 1900). Inside the center is a small art gallery showing local artists' works.

Jamaica's main draw, however, is **hip-hop shopping** along the 165th St pedestrian mall, just north of Jamaica Ave, where side-by-side shops hawk Phat Farm, airbrush sweatshirts of Tupac, sports jerseys, Bailey straw hats, Red Monkey, Pepe Jeans, North Face, pastel neo-jazz suits and African dresses. A good catch-all is **Jamaica Coliseum Mall** (☎ 718-657-4400; 165th St at 85th Ave; ☻ 11am-7pm Mon-Fri, 10am-7pm Sat, noon-6pm Sun), with scores of stands.

ROCKAWAY BEACH

The country's largest urban beach – and New York's best – is just a $2 trip on subway line A. Immortalized by the Ramones' 1977 song 'Rockaway Beach,' this terrific four-mile beach is less crowded than Coney Island and – under the jet path to nearby JFK airport – is home to some surprisingly natural, kick-arse scenery including old bungalows from the heyday. Since 2005, surfers have been hitting the waves (legally) around the Beach–90th St subway stop; see p315.

This neighborhood is a close knit Italian and Irish enclave and the further you venture south on Beach Channel Dr and Rockaway Point Blvd, the more evident it will become that you're a day tripper.

Much of the area is part of the 26,000-acre **Gateway National Recreation Area** (for info, check www.nps.gov/gate), which encompasses several parks. One, toward the southern tip of the Rockaways, is **Jacob Riis Park/Ft Tilden** (☎ 718-318-4300; subway A, S to Rockaway Park Beach–116th St), named for an advocate and photographer of immigrants in the late 19th century. The boardwalk, beach and picnic areas are popular in summer.

Extending from near JFK, at the start of the Cross Bay Veterans Memorial Bridge, the 9155-acre **Jamaica Bay Wildlife Refuge** (Map p442; ☎ 718-318-4340; www.nps.gov/gate; Cross Bay Blvd; admission free; ☻ 8:30am-5pm; subway A to Broad Channel) is home to a few hundred bird species. Drop by the visitors center for trail maps (or see the website) for the two trails: the west trail loops 1¼ miles around the West Pond and marshes, just off the bay (plenty of waterfowl to spot). See p309 for information on bird-watching tours in the refuge.

THE BRONX

Eating p259, Shopping p352

North of Manhattan, the Bronx is 'X-treme' New York. Here, the horn-honking is a little louder, the graffiti a little more daring, the swagger a little sharper. (A sign at a

TRANSPORTATION
Subway The B, D, 2, 4, 5 and 6 lines connect Manhattan with the Bronx, with useful stops at Yankee Stadium (B, D, 4 to 161st St–Yankee Stadium), near the Bronx Zoo (2, 5 to Pelham Pkwy) and at the corner of Grand Concourse and Fordham Rd (B, D to Fordham Rd).

Yankees play-off game read: 'Welcome to Da Bronx. Get ready to die!') All this is seemingly bent on proving that the definite article preceding its name – as with the Yucatán or the Hague – helps make the Bronx more than just your ordinary living place. It is. It's given us three of New York's great achievements: the men in pinstripes (the Yankees), hip-hop, and the three-pack of cool – J-Lo, C-Po and, um B-Jo (Jennifer Lopez, Colin Powell and Billy Joel).

Like Queens, the Bronx is home to an ethnically diverse population. Nearly a quarter of the population is Puerto Rican, and there are growing numbers of Jamaicans, Indians, Vietnamese, Cambodians and Eastern Europeans. A quarter of the Bronx is parkland, including Pelham Bay Park.

More of New York is talking about the Bronx these days, and pondering a move to enormous loft spaces at (relatively) cheap rents. 'SoBro', or South Bronx, is still in its infancy stages of gentrification, but is starting to attract its share of artists and folks looking for more elbow room. It's centered on Bruckner Blvd, lined with industrial shops, redbrick loft spaces, and nearly a dozen antique shops between the Third Ave and Willis Ave Bridges. Lincoln Ave leads near the Harlem River, which you can also see by **kayak tours** (p310). Near the 3rd Ave–138th St subway station (on the 6 line) are a number of Caribbean and Spanish restaurants, along 138th St. There's also a pedestrian walkway across the Third Ave Bridge into Harlem.

Bronx Tourism Council (☎ 718-590-2766; www.ilovethebronx.com) offers a visitors guide and regularly updates its website with area events. The council runs a free 'Bronx Tour Trolley' between the zoo and Arthur Ave on weekends. **Bronx County Historical Society** (☎ 718-881-8900; www.bronxhistoricalsociety.org) schedules some walking and bus tours in spring, summer and fall.

(Continued on page 201)

CENTRAL PARK

'THIS IS DEFINITELY A PLACE NOT TO BE MISSED. IT'S AN OASIS FROM THE INSANITY'

Great Lawn (p192), Central Park isn't just a compliment to those who mow it

IF YOU'RE EVER LUCKY ENOUGH TO FLY INTO NEW YORK OVER THE STRETCH OF MANHATTAN, ONE OF THE most stunning views is not the buildings themselves but the lack of them within the 843-acre carpet of green that makes up this stunning park. Located smack-dab in the middle of the borough, this is definitely a place not to be missed. It's an oasis from the insanity: the lush lawns, cool forests, flowering gardens, glassy bodies of water and meandering, wooded paths provide the dose of serene nature that New Yorkers crave. While the park swarms with joggers, in-line skaters, musicians and tourists on warm weekends, you'll find it quieter on weekday afternoons – especially in less well-trodden spots above 72nd St such as the **Harlem Meer** (Map pp454–5; at 110th St) and the **North Meadow Recreation Area** (Map pp454–5; just above 97th St on the west side). Folks flock to the park even in winter, when snowstorms can inspire cross-country skiing and sledding or a simple stroll through the white wonderland, and crowds turn out every New Year's Eve for a popular midnight run. February 2005 had an added bonus – and a major splash of color – with the installation of Christo's *The Gates,* which constituted 7503 massive sheets of orange fabric hung from frames placed along 23 miles of walkways throughout the otherwise stark and frozen park. Some New Yorkers loved it, others despised it, but people visited in droves for the unique and exciting spectacle.

Like the subway, Central Park is the great leveler. Created in the 1860s and '70s by Frederick Law Olmsted and Calvert Vaux on the marshy northern fringe of the city, the immense park was designed as a leisure space for all New Yorkers, regardless of color, class or creed. Olmsted (who also created Prospect Park in Brooklyn) was determined to keep foot and road traffic separate and cleverly designed the crosstown transverses so the two would not meet. That such a large expanse of

GETTING TO CENTRAL PARK

The expanse begins at 59th St at its south border and runs up to 110th St, while the east–west borders are Fifth Ave and Central Park West (the avenue just east of Columbus Ave). For west-side access, take the B or C line, which makes stops at 72 St, 81st St, 86th St, 96th St, 103rd St and 110th St. On the East side, you can take the R, W line to Fifth Ave–59th St or, to get higher, the 6 line, which makes stops along Lexington Ave (three avenues east of the park's border) at 68th St, 77th St, 86th St, 96th St, 103rd St and 110th St. For park visitor information, stop into the **Dairy** (Map p199), which provides maps and tour guides near the E 68th St entrance.

Cross-country skiing should be called cross-city skiing in this instance, and Sheep Meadow (p196) is the place to do it

prime real estate has survived intact for so long again proves that nothing eclipses the heart, soul and pride that forms the foundation of New York City's greatness. Today, this 'people's park' is still one of the city's most popular attractions, beckoning throngs of New Yorkers with free outdoor concerts at the **Great Lawn** (Map p199) the **Central Park Wildlife Center** (Map p199) and the annual Shakespeare in the

'LIKE THE SUBWAY, CENTRAL PARK IS THE GREAT LEVELER.'

Park productions, held each summer at the open-air Delacorte Theater (80th St). Some other recommended stops include the ornate Bethesda Fountain (mid-park at 72nd St), which edges the **Lake** (Map p199) and its **Loeb Boathouse** (Map p199),

where you can rent rowboats ($10 per hour) or enjoy lunch at an outdoor café; the **Shakespeare Garden** (Map pp454–5; west side between 79th and 80th Sts), which has lush plantings and excellent skyline views; and the **Ramble** (Map p199; mid-park from 73rd to 79th Sts), a wooded thicket that's popular with bird-watchers. The Central Park Conservancy offers ever-changing guided tours of the park, including those that focus on public art, wildlife and places of interest to kids. Visit www.centralparknyc.org for tour details, as well as for a great interactive map of the entire park.

Central Park's old reputation as a dark and menacing place, by the way, is generally not justified today, as it now ranks as one of the city's safest parts. If you've any doubts, just stick to the mid-park area around 86th St, where you'll find the headquarters for the official Central Park police precinct.

'THIS MASSIVE EMERALD CARPET WAS CREATED IN 1931 BY FILLING IN A FORMER RESERVOIR'

People enjoy splendour in the grass at Central Park's Great Lawn (below)

GREAT LAWN

Located between 72nd and 86th Sts (Map p199), this massive emerald carpet was created in 1931 by filling in a former reservoir. It is the place for outdoor concerts (this is where Paul Simon played his famous comeback show, and also where you can catch the New York Philharmonic Orchestra each summer), and there are eight softball fields, basketball courts and a canopy of London plane trees. Not far from the actual lawn are several other big sites: the **Delacorte Theater**, which is home to the annual Shakespeare in the Park festival, and its lush Shakespeare Garden; the panoramic **Belvedere Castle**; the leafy **Ramble**, the epicenter of both birding and gay-male cruising; and the **Loeb Boathouse**, where you can rent rowboats for a romantic float in the middle of this urban paradise.

CENTRAL PARK WILDLIFE CENTER

☎ 212-861-6030; www.centralparknyc.org; 64th St at Fifth Ave; ☉ 10am-5pm

The penguins are the main attraction at this modern zoo (Map p199), though you'll find more than two dozen other species to visit, including polar bears and the endangered tamarin monkeys and red pandas. Feeding times are especially rowdy, fun times to stroll through: watch the sea lions chow down at 11:30am, 2pm and 4pm and see the penguins gobble fish at 10:30am and 2:30pm. The **Tisch Children's Zoo**, between 65th and 66th Sts, is perfect for smaller children.

Snow monkeys huddle against the cold in Central Park's zoo (above)

CENTRAL PARK CARRIAGE RIDES

Despite the fact that most New Yorkers wouldn't consider going on a touristy horse-and-carriage ride, Angelina Jolie, Chuck Norris and Hilary Duff are among the celebs who have leapt from their own high horses to go for a jaunt. The rides have appeared in countless feature films, which lends them a romantic air that can't be denied. Pony up the always-rising fee and you can enjoy a ride yourself on the **horse-drawn carriages** (Central Park South; ⊖ 1, A, B, C, D to 59th St-Columbus Circle). They cost $40 for 20 minutes ($10 for every extra 15 minutes) and oh, drivers do expect tips.

Burn off the excess from a meal at Loeb Boathouse with a row around Central Park's Lake (p191)

ARSENAL

Built between 1847 and 1851 as a munitions supply depot for the New York State National Guard, the landmark brick **building** (Map pp454–5, at E 64th St) was designed to look like a medieval castle, and its construction predates the actual park. Today the building houses the City of New York Parks & Recreation and the Central Park Wildlife Center. The reason to visit here is not to see the building, though, but to view Olmsted's original blueprint for the park, treasured here under glass in a 3rd floor conference room.

JACQUELINE KENNEDY ONASSIS RESERVOIR

Don't miss your chance to run or walk around this 1.58 mile track (Map pp454–5, which draws a slew of joggers in the warmer months. The 106-acre body of water no longer distributes drinking water to residents, but serves as a gorgeous reflecting pool for the surrounding skyline and flowering trees. Take a turn around the reservoir's perimeter and you may very well spot the elderly, white-haired Albert Arroyo, the friendly and self-appointed 'Mayor of Central Park,' who used to run laps here and now makes his slow way around and around with the aid of a cane. The most beautiful time to be here is at sunset, when you can watch the sky turn from a brilliant shade of pink and orange to cobalt blue, just as the city's lights slowly flicker on.

Angel of the Waters is more like a snow angel atop Bethesda Fountain (below) in winter

STATUARY **IN THE PARK**

Scattered among the many natural sculptures, otherwise known as trees, are a host of wonderful, freestanding, crafted works of art. Depending on where you enter the park, you might check out the **Maine Monument** (at the Merchant's Gate at Columbus Circle), a tribute to the sailors killed in the mysterious explosion in Havana Harbor in 1898 that sparked the Spanish American War. Further east, toward the Seventh Ave entrance, there are statues of Latin America's greatest liberators, including **José Martí**, 'The Apostle of Cuban Independence' (history buffs will find Martí's proximity to the Maine Monument ironic, to say the least). Further east still at the Scholar's Gate (Fifth Ave at 60th St), there is a small plaza dedicated to **Doris Chanin Freedman**, the founder of the Public Art Fund, where you can see a new sculpture every six months or so.

While almost everyone is familiar with **Angel of the Waters** atop Bethesda Fountain, even those who know Central Park like the back of their hand may have overlooked the **Falconer Statue**, tucked away on a rise overlooking the 72nd St Transverse nearby. This 1875 bronze recreates the remarkable moment of flight, and the connection between master and charge is regal and palpable. Literary Walk, between Bethesda Fountain and the 65th St Transverse is lined with statues, including the requisite **Christopher Columbus** and literati such as **Robert Burns** and **Shakespeare**.

East and north of here is the Conservatory Water, where model sailboats drift lazily by and kids crawl over the giant toadstools of the **Alice in Wonderland** statue. Replete with Alice of flowing hair and dress, a dapper Mad Hatter and mischievous Cheshire Cat, this is a Central Park treasure and a favorite of kids of all ages. Nearby is the **Hans Christian Andersen** statue, where Saturday story hour (11am June to September) is an entertaining draw.

Rose petals strewn across Strawberry Fields, memorial to John Lennon

Sledding with skyscrapers in sight is an only in New York–experience

There is **Cleopatra's Needle** located on the hillock above 82nd St and East Dr. This obelisk was a gift from Egypt to the United States in 1877 for helping build the Suez Canal. Drop down to East Dr and look up to see the crouching cat sculpture, which is poised to pounce on unsuspecting in-line skaters.

At the northeastern extent of the park is the soaring **Duke Ellington** statue, depicting the man and his piano. An oft-overlooked site because of its northern location (at 110th St), this stunning tribute to the jazz master, featuring a 25ft bronze tableau, was unveiled in 1997 and conceived and funded by the late Bobby Short.

STRAWBERRY FIELDS

Standing just across from the famous **Dakota building** (Map p199) – where *Rosemary's Baby* was filmed in 1967, and where John Lennon was fatefully shot in 1980 – is this poignant, tear-shaped garden, a memorial to the slain star. It's the most visited spot in Central Park, and maintained with some help from a $1 million grant from Lennon's widow Yoko Ono (who still resides at the Dakota). The peaceful spot contains a grove of stately elms and a tiled mosaic that's often strewn with rose petals from visitors. It says, simply, 'Imagine.'

WOLLMAN SKATING RINK

☎ 212-439-6900; btwn 62nd & 63rd Sts;
🕑 Nov-Mar

Located on the park's east side, this is a romantic and popular **skating rink** (Map pp454–5) to strap on rented ice skates and glide around, especially at night under the stars. Just try to tune out the blaring pop music, which tends to dampen the peaceful mood.

Enjoy some leaf-peeping right in the heart of the city, with the change of season in Central Park

EXPLORING CENTRAL PARK

THIS GLORIOUS PARK IS IN EVERY WAY A PARK FOR THE PEOPLE. SO TAKE YOUR RIGHTFUL PLACE WITHIN its expansive borders!

A good walk (see walking tour map, p199) begins at the Columbus Circle entrance, at the park's southwest corner. If you're picnicking, fetch supplies at **Whole Foods** (p341) at Columbus Circle before going in (but if you don't want to lug stuff around, there will be a great year-round vendor along the way). Pass through the Merchants' Gate and turn left on West Dr. On your right you'll see the **Umpire Rock** 1, which overlooks the Heckscher Ballfields to the north, the site of fun-to-watch softball league play in summer. Continue north on West Dr to **Sheep Meadow** 2, a wide green expanse where sheep actually grazed in the park's early days at the turn of the 19th century; now you'll find sunbathers and Frisbee players on warm, sunny days. This is a great place for a picnic amid stellar skyline views. A pathway leading to the right takes you along the south side of the meadow. Over the bridge to the right is an enclosed **carousel** (3; 10am-6pm Mon-Fri, to 7pm Sat-Sun Apr-Oct, to dusk Nov-Dec, to dusk Sat-Sun Jan–mid-March; per ride $1.25), which boasts some of the largest hand-carved horses in the country.

From the carousel walk east, through the tunnel, to the **Dairy** 4, opened in the 1870s and designed after an English estate dairy. Its wholesome purpose was to guarantee that children could have a fresh glass of milk after what would've surely been a long family journey to the park. Today the Gothic-style building houses the park's visitor center (212-794-6564; www.centralparknyc.org; 10am-5pm Tue-Sun, 10am-4pm in winter), where you can pick up maps and information about park activities, and survey the gift shop.

From the Dairy, walk along East Dr south about 200m and then left to the **Central Park Wildlife Center** 5 (p192), a small zoo dating from the 1930s but still flaunting its 1980s

Create your own mission impossible; try some rock-climbing (right)

TOP TEN
CENTRAL PARK SURPRISES

- The Central Park Conservancy allows catch-and-release **fishing at Harlem Meer** (Map pp454–5; ☎ 212-310-6600), even supplying you with rods and bait for luring in the bass and bluefish.

- The sight of stately equines clomping along the park's ancient bridal path is to be enjoyed – or do it yourself with a private **horseback riding lesson** (Claremont Riding Academy; ☎ 212-724-5100; per 30min $58).

- You'll find two 15,000 sq ft **bowling lawns** (Map p199; north of Sheep Meadow at 69th St) – one for croquet and one for lawn bowling, where members of the 80-year-old New York Lawn Bowling Club still mix it up with tournaments from May to October.

- On the first Friday of the month, pro-bicycle environmental organization **Time's Up! Moonlight Ride** (☎ 212-802-8222; www.times-up.org) leads packs of riders through the beautiful nighttime version of the park, with only the moon as your guide. Meet at Columbus Circle at 10pm.

- The urban rock-climbing community flocks to **Worthless Boulder** (Map pp454–5; 10ft-tall rock at Park's north end) near Harlem Meer.

- Some scaling skills of your own can be harnessed at the supervised **Climbing Wall** (Map pp454–5; North Meadow Recreation Area just north of 97th St).

- It's news to most New Yorkers, but it's true: the Urban Park Rangers, a division of the NYC Parks Department, lead overnight **camping excursions** (☎ 866 NYC-HAWK; www.nycgovpark.org/sub_about/parks_divisions and then navigate to the schedule of upcoming events in the Urban Park Ranger programs section of the website). These happen in various parks, including this one, throughout the summer.

- For kids, there's **Safari Playground** (Map pp454–5; W 91st St), a jungle-themed play area featuring 13 hippo sculptures, a tree house and a kiddie jogging path.

- A longrunning, weekend gathering spot, **Pug Hill** (Map pp454–5; south of *Alice In Wonderland* statue at E 74th St) is for adorable pugs and their owners.

- Marked by a simple plaque, **Seneca Village** (Map pp454–5; historic area between 81st and 89th Sts on west side) was home to Manhattan's first prominent community of African American property owners (c 1840).

makeover, which was designed to make the animals more comfortable. Zoo residents include lazy polar bears and several sea lions, whose frequent feeding attracts squeals of delight from many a little one. At the entrance, don't miss the **Delacorte Clock 6**, a timepiece festooned with dancing bears, monkeys and other furry friends, who spin and hammer out the time every 30 minutes on the half-hour. Admission to the zoo includes entry to the **Tisch Children's Zoo 7**, a petting center for toddlers; you'll find it across 65th St from the main zoo.

After the Children's Zoo, walk north on the path that parallels East Dr to a group of statues that is known as Literary Walk (including Christopher Columbus and William Shakespeare, p194); this marks the beginning of the **Mall 8**, an elegant promenade lined with benches and a collection of 150 American elms, believed to be the largest surviving stand in the country.

The winter solitude of parts of Central Park is surprising in a city that holds eight million people

At the north end of the Mall, you'll come to the **Naumburg Bandshell** 9. After years of disuse, the bandshell and the area immediately facing it are alive again with occasional performances and a DIY roller disco. (Just behind is the Pergola, a wisteria-festooned walkway, and the Rumsey Playfield, site of the wildly popular Central Park Summer-Stage series, p293.).

Continuing north of the bandshell and across the 72nd St Transverse brings you to **Bethesda Fountain** 10, which brought cinematic closure to the end of the 2003 film *Angels in America*. The fountain, with its *Angel of the Waters* sculpture at the center, has been restored and ranks as one of Central Park's most uplifting sights. In warm weather, you'll find a vendor near here doling out warm, fresh crepes and *empanadas*, providing the perfect opportunity for a snack break.

Continue on the path west of the fountain until you reach **Bow Bridge** 11, an elegant cast-iron suspension bridge that spans 60 feet across the glassy lake. Cross the bridge and enter the **Ramble** 12, a lush wooden expanse that serves as a decent bird-watching pocket. If you manage to emerge from the Ramble without being hopelessly turned around, continue north to the 79th St Transverse until you come to the 19th-century **Belvedere Castle** 13, where you will enjoy excellent views of the **Delacorte Theater** 14 (p286; the site of Joseph Papp Public Theater's free Shakespeare productions, which are held in summer, see p286).

Walk east along the Turtle Pond and north to **Cleopatra's Needle** 15, an Egyptian obelisk dating from 1600 BC; facing it to the east is the massive Metropolitan Museum of Art. Just west is the grand (and appropriately named) **Great Lawn** 16 (p192), where some free concerts take place (including open-air shows by the New York Philharmonic

WALK FACTS

Start 59th St/Columbus Circle
station (Ⓜ A, B, C, D, 1, 2)
End 72nd St station (Ⓜ B, C)
Distance 3.75 miles
Time 2 to 4 hours
Fuel Stops Whole Foods (p341) for
picnic supplies, crepe/empanada
vendor in the park. Or grab a
table at the Loeb Boathouse Cafe
(☎ 212-517-2233 for waterside
diningroom reservations)

Ritzy Manhattan is reflected in Jacqueline Kennedy Onassis Reservoir (p193)

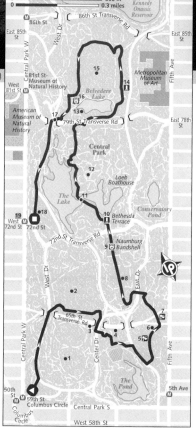

in June and Metropolitan Opera in July,
see p26).

Cut west across the lawn (or around
it when it's closed during winter) and go
south. Past the lawn, nearly to the 79th
St Transverse, is the 19th-century **Swedish Cottage 17**, a sweet little chalet that is
home to the **Marionette Theater** (☎ 212-988-
9093; adult/child $6/5; Ⓨ performances
10:30am & noon Mon-Fri Jul & Aug,
10:30am & noon Tue-Fri & 1pm Sat Sep-
Jun). Reservations are required for these
well-attended shows.

Continuing to the W 72nd St park entrance brings you to legendary **Strawberry
Fields 18** (p195), the three-acre landscape
dedicated to the memory of John Lennon;
it contains plants from more than 100
nations and motley offerings from fans.
The former Beatle had frequently visited
this spot, as he resided across the street in
the **Dakota building 19**, where he was fatally
shot in 1980.

The Metropolitan Museum of Art (p162) has the world's best annex for a museum with its proximity to Central Park

(Continued from page 188)

Orientation

The only borough on the mainland, the Bronx is just north of Manhattan and wedged between the Hudson, Harlem and East Rivers and Long Island Sound. The chief road of the 42-sq-mile Bronx is the north–south Grand Concourse. Its meeting point with Fordham Rd, west of the Bronx Zoo and near the famous Italian neighborhood of Belmont, is the Bronx' main hub of commercial activity.

ARTHUR AVENUE/BELMONT

Map pp468-9

www.arthuravenuebronx.com; ⓖ B, D to Fordham Rd

Some argue that New York's 'real Little Italy' is here, on the blocks south of Fordham University between Bronx Park (to the east) and Third Ave (to the west) – clearly marked with 'Little Italy in the Bronx' banners. Here you'll find pizzerias, trattorias, bakeries (Arthur Ave Baking Co serves many of the city's restaurants), fishmongers, and butchers with bunnies in the window – all prepare their goods for locals and tend to sell them without breaking into English. Do bring an appetite. Many New Yorkers claim that Roberto's (p260) offers the finest Italian eating in the city.

The famous scene in *The Godfather* – where Al Pacino gets the gun from 'behind the toilet with the chain thing' and blasts his way into the family business – supposedly takes place at Mario's (2342 Arthur Ave).

From the Fordham Rd station, walk east 11 blocks downhill along Fordham Rd (a busy commercial strip); turn right at Arthur Ave.

BRONX MUSEUM OF THE ARTS

Map pp468-9

☎ 718-681-6000; www.bxma.org; 1040 Grand Concourse at 165th St; suggested donation adult/senior & student $5/3; ⓨ noon-9pm Wed, noon-6pm Thu-Sun; ⓖ B, D to 167th St–Grand Concourse

Devoted to interesting, largely urban, contemporary art, this museum hosts a wide array of art (graffiti, video installations, paintings) that runs the gamut from Brazilian music from the 1970s to the Yankees–Mets 'subway series.' Often artists featured

are Americans with African, Latin American or Asian ancestry.

BRONX ZOO Map pp468-9

☎ 718-367-1010; www.bronxzoo.com; adult/child $11/8 Apr-Oct, $8/6 Nov-Mar, suggested donation Wed; ⓨ 10am-5pm Mon-Fri, 10am-5:30pm Sat & Sun Apr-Oct, 10am-4:30pm Nov-Mar; ⓖ 2, 5 to Pelham Pkwy

Also known as the Bronx Wildlife Conservation Society, this famous attraction is one of the country's best zoos and receives more than two million visitors a year. Opened in 1899, the 265-acre zoo has been a pioneer in creating naturalistic settings (re-creating African plains and forests, Himalayan mountains and Asian rainforests) for its nearly 5000 animals (gorillas, polar bears, penguins, zebras, giraffes – all sorts). The zoo's bison, acquired in the early 20th century, helped repopulate the animals in the Great Plains in recent years.

Big hits with kids include the hovering bats at the World of Darkness, and penguin feedings (3:30pm). Look out for original structures that date from 1899, including the House of Reptiles. In winter some animals live in sheltered areas and can't be viewed (fewer people visit at this time though) – but the polar bear Blizzard splashes in his icy pool all year.

A few attractions cost extra, including the Congo Gorilla Forest ($3) and the new Bug Carousel ($2), which is a merry-go-round with giant insects.

Liberty Lines Express (☎ 718-652-8400) runs a Bx11 bus ($5) from Madison Ave (pickup locations include 26th, 47th, 54th, 84th and 99th Sts) to the zoo. The trip runs every 20 minutes or so. Exact change or bills are required.

There are five entrances to the zoo. From the Pelham Pkwy subway station, walk south on White Plains Rd, then turn right on Lydig Ave. At Bronx Park East, turn right, then left to the Bronx River Pkwy Gate (where the Bx11 bus drops off passengers). There's a car parking area ($8).

CITY ISLAND Map pp468-9

☎ 718-885-9100; www.cityislandchamber.org; ⓖ 6 to Pelham Bay Park, then ⓠ Bx29

About 15 miles from Midtown, and a world away, City Island is one of New York's most surprising neighborhoods. Founded by the English in 1685, the 1.5mile-long fishing community juts into the Long Island Sound and Eastchester Bay. It's filled with boat slips and half a dozen yacht clubs; Victorian clapboard houses here definitely look more New England than the Bronx. On weekends (even in February), City Island Ave's two-dozen seafood restaurants, including **Tony's Pier** (p259), are mobbed by local families.

If you're serious about diving, sailing or fishing, come here. **Island Current** (☎ 917-417-7557; www.islandcurrent.com) leads fishing tours all year (adult/child $42/25) and sunset tours. **Captain Mike's Dive Shop** (☎ 718-885-1588; www.captainmikesdiving.com; 530 City Island Ave) has two-tank dive trips in the area for $55 ($88 on weekends) including lobster dives.

NEW YORK BOTANICAL GARDEN

Map pp468-9

☎ 718-817-8700; www.nybg.org; adult/senior & student/child $13/11/5, free Wed & 10am-noon Sat; ☯ 10am-6pm Tue-Sun Apr-Oct, 10am-5pm Tue-Sun Nov-Mar; ☺ B, D to Bedford Park Blvd

Spread across 50 acres of primary forest (just north of the Bronx Zoo), the New York Botanical Garden (opened in 1891) is home to several beautiful gardens and the restored Victorian Enid A Haupt Conservatory, a grand iron-and-glass edifice that is a New York landmark. You can also stroll through an outdoor rose garden, just next to the conservatory, and a rock garden with a multi-tiered waterfall.

Metro-North (☎ 212-532-4900; www.mta .info/mnr) trains leave hourly from Grand Central Terminal on the Harlem line and go directly to the garden; the one-way fare is $4.75/6.25/3 at off-peak/peak/weekend. From the Bedford Park Blvd subway stop, walk east down the hill and seven blocks to the gate. A spot in the parking lot costs $7.

WAVE HILL Map pp468-9

☎ 718-549-3200; www.wavehill.org; W 249th St at Independence Ave, Riverdale; adult/senior & student $4/2, free Tue; ☯ closed Mon, see website; Metro-North train to Riverdale

Built by a lawyer in 1843 as a country home, the stone mansion centerpiece of 28-acre, riverside Wave Hill served the needs of the wealthy and connected until it became a city park in 1960. Theodore Roosevelt's family summered here in 1870 and 1871; Mark Twain rented it out from 1901 to 1903.

There are nice views of the Hudson and a café. The easiest way here is by Metro-North train, then walking 15 minutes uphill.

WOODLAWN CEMETERY Map pp468-9

☎ 718-920-0500; www.thewoodlawncemetery .org; Webster Ave at E 233rd St; ☯ 8:30am-5pm; ☺ 4 to Woodlawn

As elegant as Brooklyn's Green-Wood is this 400-acre cemetery, the top resting place in the Bronx. It dates from the Civil War and actually has more big names than Green-Wood (and it is a contest) amongst its 300,000 headstones. Jazz greats resting here include Miles Davis, Coleman Hawkins, Duke Ellington and Lionel Hampton; other famous people include writer Herman Melville and journalist Joseph Pulitzer. Ask at the front for a map, and a photo pass so you can take photos.

YANKEE STADIUM Map pp468-9

☎ 718-293-6000, tour info 718-579-4531; www .yankees.com; E 161st St at River Ave; tours $14-25; ☯ call for hrs; ☺ B, D, 4 to 161st St–Yankee Stadium

The Yankees call their legendary ballpark (built in 1923) the 'most famous stadium since the Roman Coliseum,' and with 26 championships to their name, who's arguing? Of course its days are numbered. The Yanks are building a new 51,000-seat version just north on Macombs Dam Park – it should be ready to play ball by 2009. The Yankees play April to October (see p305 about tickets). Get to games early to take a stroll around Monument Park, presently behind left field, where plaques commemorate such baseball greats as Babe Ruth, Lou Gehrig, Mickey Mantle and Joe DiMaggio. The park closes 45 minutes before the game begins.

Try to resist hollering for the New York Yankees (above)

Sights

THE BRONX

THE HOUSE THAT RUTH BUILT

Pro baseball's biggest team plays in a stadium that brings joy to fans and hatred to rival fans (supporters of the Boston Red Sox come to mind). It's possible, however, it may have had a different size, shape and location, if not for the fateful acquisition of a young pitcher named George Herman 'Babe' Ruth from the Red Sox in 1920.

In the days when pitchers could actually hit, Babe hit better than all of baseball. His home-run blasts brought in huge crowds, and the Yanks soon dwarfed the draws of the New York Giants (now in San Francisco), who served as landlord of the Yanks' field. So the Yanks got pushed out.

Opened in 1923, Yankee Stadium is said to have facilitated Ruth's hitting style (not to mention the numbers of fans clamoring to get a glimpse of Babe in action). He led the Yanks in the stadium's debut season to win the team's first World Series over the New York Giants (bah! to those who say sports can't be poetic).

Renovations have changed the inside – the hard wood seats were replaced by soft plastic ones in the 1970s – but the outer facade is the same one that Ruth fans rushed toward in the '20s.

In 1927 Ruth hit 60 homers, a single-season record until 1961, when North Dakota–born Yankee Roger Maris broke it with 61. Ruth's 714 career homers weren't surpassed until Hank Aaron beat that record in 1974.

On hour-long guided tours (starting from the press gate), you can visit the dugout, press box, field and clubhouse. Individuals can show up at noon without reservations (adult/senior & child $14/7). An expanded tour includes a 20-minute film ($20/14) or looks at the luxury suites and other areas ($25/17). Buy tickets from the website, a Yankee clubhouse shop around town (see website for locations) or Ticketmaster (☎ 212-307-1212).

STATEN ISLAND

Though famed for the ferry, the starting point of the New York Marathon and a (now closed) dump taller than anything south on the East Coast, Staten Island is New York's 'forgotten borough.' Looking at a map, it's practically New Jersey (which is just a short jump across the Kill Van Kull), and in fact the island's first road connection with New York City and State only came in 1964, when the Verrazano Narrows Bridge opened.

Its population – wee, at under half a million – is largely middle-class Republicans, not always jiving with (predominantly) Democratic politics in the city. In 1993 nearly two-thirds of the island voted to secede, but New York State ignored it, and the fantasies have faded.

Many visitors don't leave the ferry (p116), but if you're coming over, there are a few good attractions worth considering leaving the boat for. Taking into consideration ferry time to/from Manhattan, and a couple of hours at Snug Harbor Cultural Center by bus, plan on four hours.

The **Staten Island Chamber of Commerce** (☎ 718-727-1900; www.sichamber.com; 130 Bay St; ☉ 9am-5pm Mon-Fri), three blocks east (left, if facing the water) of the terminal, has a single brochure on the island's attractions.

Orientation

Staten Island is across the New York Harbor, south of Manhattan. The ferry unleashes passengers on downtown St George, on the northern tip of a 58-sq-mile island. Richmond Tce runs along the water to the west.

Twenty-three bus routes converge on four ramps at St George ferry terminal (you can use your MTA Metrocard on any). Buses are timed to coincide with boat arrivals and tend to run every 20 minutes during the day. Routes loosely cover the island, though some destinations require added walks to get there. Staten Island's train service, which departs from the ferry terminal, has less useful routes for attractions.

ST GEORGE

Two blocks from the ferry is the **Staten Island Museum** (☎ 718-727-1135; www.statenislandmuseum.org; 75 Stuyvesant Pl at Wall St; adult/senior & child $3/2; ☉ noon-5pm Tue-Sun), which has a permanent show on the boat you just rode in on. You could take a quick peek, wander around St George's downtown, and hop back on the ferry to Manhattan in less than an hour. The museum is behind the police station.

Sights

STATEN ISLAND

SNUG HARBOR CULTURAL CENTER

☎ 718-448-2500; www.snug-harbor.org; 1000 Richmond Tce; 🚌 S40 to Snug Harbor

Situated in a 19th-century sailors' retirement complex only a few short feet from the water, the Snug Harbor Cultural Center – the island's best attraction – is more like an Ivy League school. In the 83-acre area, some 28 buildings house the center, plus there are a couple of other cultural organizations and a few gardens.

The center opened in 1976 – after famously being saved from the wrecking ball by an impressed Jackie Onassis. In 2005 the (also impressed) Smithsonian granted Snug Harbor 'affiliate' status, which may mean an expanding site in coming years.

Visiting can be a little confusing, with different collections run independently. You can get individual tickets for sites, or a good-value combo ticket for all the following (adult/senior & student $8/7).

From the bus stop, you'll see five side-by-side, seriously columned and seriously Greek-Revival buildings (built between 1833 and 1880) marking the front of the complex. (These are former dorms – and nice ones.) Start at the center one, the Main Hall or Visitors Center (☎ 718-425-3524; adult/senior & child $3/2; 🕐 10am-5pm Tue-Sun); the admission price includes viewing of temporary exhibits in this hall (note the old ceiling mural) and behind in the excellent Newhouse Galleries, home to modern art (one interesting recent show featured giant 1920s banners from Coney Island). These two are frequently called 'Snug Harbor' by other parts of the complex.

To the left (from the bus stop) is the independent Noble Maritime Collection (☎ 718-447-6490; adult/senior & child $3/2; 🕐 1-5pm Thu-Sun), the best place to get in the spirit of Snug Harbor's sailors' days. It features period-piece reconstructions of sailors' dorms, and lithographs of the last days of the wood-mast ships by John A Noble (and his houseboat studio!). Note the collection is closed Monday to Wednesday (other sites are closed Monday only).

Behind the front five buildings, you'll find the glasshouse of the Staten Island Botanical Garden (☎ 718-273-8200; www.sibg .org; admission free), and a maze behind it. Just west, the soothing New York Chinese Scholar's Garden (adult/child $5/4, free 10am-

1pm Tue; 🕐 10am-4pm or 5pm Tue-Sun), built in 1999, offers a walk through ancient-styled pavilions and teahouses (with waterfalls running through). It gets busiest in April and May when many of the plants bloom. You enter from one of five 1880s Victorian cottages, just east of the botanical garden.

There are a couple of old-style cafés serving food.

Get here from the ferry by bus S40. You can make the (rather grim) walk here along Richmond Tce in about 25 minutes.

AROUND THE ISLAND
GREENBELT

☎ 718-667-2165; www.sigreenbelt.org; 200 Nevada Ave

In the heart of Staten Island, the 2800-acre Greenbelt – and its 32 miles of trails for hiking – crosses five ecosystems, including swamps and freshwater wetlands (bring bug spray). There are some easy and tougher hikes here (Staten Island has the highest elevation on the Atlantic seaboard south of Maine). Birders can track 60 species of birds here.

Check the website for many access points. One good place is at High Rock Park, a hardwood forest spot-cut by six trails. Take bus S62 from the ferry terminal to Victory Blvd and Manner Rd (about 15 or 20 minutes), and transfer to the S54.

HISTORIC RICHMOND TOWN

☎ 718-351-1611; www.historicrichmondtown.org; 441 Clarke Ave; adult/child $5/3.50; 🕐 1-5pm Wed-Sun Sep-Jun, 10am-5pm Wed-Sat, 1-5pm Sun Jul-Aug; 🚌 74 to Richmond Rd & St Patrick's Pl

In the center of Staten Island, this 'town' of 27 buildings (some dating back to a 1690s Dutch community) stands in a 100-acre preservation project maintained by the Staten Island Historical Society. The town includes the former county seat of the island; the most famous building, the two-story, 300-year-old redwood Voorlezer's House, is the country's oldest schoolhouse. Every hour, a guide conducts tours, and during July and August folks in period garb roam the grounds.

Hours are sometimes extended in summer; call before you go. It's about 40 minutes from the ferry by bus.

Walking Tours

Walking Tours

You can only know New York from its sidewalks. Make time to walk as much of the busy Midtown avenues, Downtown nooks and riverside trails as you can. You'll see what you can't see from the back of a blazing taxi (or subway car): 19th-century dates marking brownstone facades, storekeepers chatting over a smoke, historical plaques or secondary street names, sometimes even smiles. Manhattan is almost entirely flat, and the boroughs only swell up a little. So no excuses. These eight walks take in a lot – fashion, jazz, rock 'n' roll, architecture, skyscrapers, art, food, nature. Pick your favorite and go.

LOWER MANHATTAN WALKING TOUR

Nieuw Amsterdam was born on the tiny stretch of land that now holds New York's towering skyscrapers and its busy Financial District. The strange scale of things – tiny streets and immense buildings – creates a feeling of concrete canyons waiting to be explored.

For avid walkers, there's no better way to kick off this trip than a subway ride to Brooklyn's High St (A, C line). From there you can march right across Brooklyn Bridge,

WALK FACTS

Start Brooklyn Bridge (Ⓢ 4, 5, 6 Brooklyn Bridge)
Finish Brooklyn Bridge (Ⓢ 4, 5, 6 Brooklyn Bridge)
Distance 2 to 2.5 miles
Duration 1 to 3 hours
Fuel Stop South Street Seaport

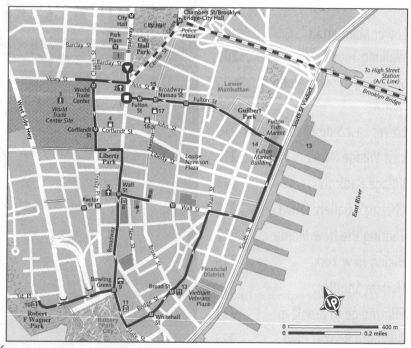

taking in the glorious expanse of Lower Manhattan from between the bridge's graceful Gothic arches.

If you'd rather skip the 30-minute bridge crossing, take a 4, 5 or 6 train downtown and get off at the Brooklyn Bridge stop. City Hall, fronted by a small park, is between Park Row (aka Centre St) and Broadway. Orient yourself by crossing the bottom of City Hall Park and emerging on Broadway and Park Place.

Across the street you'll see the lush facade of the **Woolworth Building 1** (p125), one of the city's most celebrated Gothic structures. It was the tallest building in the world (briefly) when built in 1913. Security is tight, but you usually can poke your head in to inspect the opulent lobby and blue-and-gold tiled ceiling.

Heading south on Broadway, cross Vesey St and you'll see **St Paul's Chapel 2** (p119) on your right – it's the only pre-Revolutionary church left intact in the city. Former US President George Washington worshiped here the day he was inaugurated in 1789, and attended Sunday services throughout his New York residency (he's got a special pew, which you can see inside).

You'll notice many signs that refer to Ground Zero and the September 11 attacks on the World Trade Center Towers; St Paul's served as a refuge for the recovery workers in the months after the disaster, and is now inextricably linked to the site.

If you exit St Paul's and turn left down Vesey St, you'll arrive at **Ground Zero 3** (p126), which now has several commemorative plaques in place and allows visitors to stroll along a platform overlooking the footprint of the former Twin Towers. Wander the perimeter along Church St, Vesey, Liberty and West Side Hwy.

Across Church St you can see **Century 21 4** (p321), New Yorkers' favorite discount clothing store that sells haute couture at bargain prices. At the corner of Liberty and Church Sts, you can follow Liberty St East to the intersection with Broadway, a few blocks south you'll come to **Trinity Church 5** (p123), another one of Old New York's most important houses of worship.

For a quick change of pace, jump across the street and take in the bright yellow-and-red, art-deco lobby of the **Museum of American Finance 6** (p122). It guards the entrance to Wall St, quite a narrow fairway, by New York standards, but stacked with impressively ornate buildings.

The **New York Stock Exchange 7** (p122) is between Wall St and Exchange Pl. Security concerns have closed it to visitors, but you can still take in its 1903 Beaux Arts exterior, looking rather like a Greek temple, except on the days when draped with a company's logo.

Looking diagonally across from the Exchange, you'll see the **Federal Hall 8** (p121) which is where George Washington was sworn in as President after praying for guidance at St Paul's Church. It's also the place where John Peter Zenger in 1735 was acquitted of seditious libel – the first step, historians say, in establishing a democracy committed to a free press. The Federal Hall, which was closed at the time of research and scheduled to be reopened in September 2006, is run by the National Parks Service and offers great tours and many exhibits.

Walk back to Broadway and turn left (south), down the Canyon of Heroes, the stretch of street used by the city every time it wants to fete a New Yorker for some particularly spectacular achievement (like winning the World Series, if you're a Yankee fan). Continue toward the *Charging Bull* sculpture at the end of **Bowling Green 9** (p120) park.

The park is reportedly where Dutch leader Peter Minuit bought Manhattan for $24 from Lenape Indians, although the truth of that tale is often questioned. To find out why, walk into the **National Museum of the American Indian 10** (p122) at the end of the park – it's got another impressive Beaux Arts exterior, built in 1907. Formerly the US Customs House, this museum is now run by the Smithsonian.

If you continue south, you'll enter tranquil and relaxing Battery Park, from where you can see the Statue of Liberty and get a glimpse of Ellis Island. You'll also want to look for the Biosphere, and the Immigrants Statue, two beautiful pieces of art, as you stroll around the edge of Battery Park City, a residential community within the park that abuts the **Museum of Jewish Heritage 11** (p118), which you'll want to check out.

When you're done drifting through the park, get back on Broadway and then follow State St as it curves around the tip of Lower Manhattan. It will bring you to Pearl St, and you want to follow Pearl northeast to **Fraunces Tavern Museum 12** (p121), one of the oldest eating establishments in the city and a good place to break for lunch.

You're now in the heart of the colonial town, and the streets get narrow and confusing, but don't worry too much about getting lost – there's no where really to go! Meander a bit if you like, and then continue up Pearl to Wall St, and turn right (east) on Wall St. You can now saunter down Wall St (the last block is a new pedestrian park) and you'll come to the East River and the beginning of the East Side promenade. You'll also see the tall ships of **South Street Seaport 13** (p123) immediately to your immediate north. If you haven't already eaten, this is also a good place to grab a bite. Across the street is **Schermerhorn Row 14** (p123), reported to be the first city block in New York to get electricity. From there, you can walk up Fulton St until it becomes **Broadway 15**. You can dip in and out of **John St 16** and **Nassau St 17** for a little shopping. When you're done, head north on Broadway, and in a few short blocks you're back at the Brooklyn Bridge.

SHOPPING IN SOHO, NOHO & NOLITA

For consumer-culture vultures, there's really no better place to mine than this small down-town area, its tiny side streets and the main artery of Broadway are studded with gems that'll have your credit-card strip worn clean by day's end. You'll find everything from exclusive boutiques to quality street vendors and some worthy chains, hawking housewares, books, gourmet food stuffs and especially fashion – Levis, couture, handmade jewelry, hip-hop sneakers, silk scarves, you name it.

Begin by exiting the R or W train at Prince St and walking west on Prince St which, though it's become more of a chain-store strip in recent years, still has at least two reasons to visit: the **Apple Store 1** (p325), a massive, circus-like scene where you can test drive anything (and at least check your email), and the interesting mix of jewelry and art vendors, especially when it's warm out. Return to Broadway and head uptown to flashy **Adidas 2** (p324) and on to hyper-trendy **Atrium 3** (p328), which has an excellent range of denim (Seven, Diesel, Joe's, etc) for men and women. From here, go one more block north and turn right on Bond St, home to the adorable **Bond 07 4** (p328), with high-end clothing, hats and eyeglass frames, and **Bond No. 9 5** (p328), a clever perfumery that sells NYC-inspired scents like the sweet Chelsea Flowers and earthy Eau de Noho. Outside, round the corner onto Lafayette St and, if you're peckish, grab a soy hot dog or organic burger at **Sparky's 6** (p230). Then check out **Zachary's Smile 7** (p328), an impressive little vintage shop, before crossing Houston St. Note the beautiful **Puck Building 8**, its shiny gold Puck statue poised over the entrance, and then go to town in this block's boutiques, including multi-label shoe-heaven **Otto Tootsi Plohound 9** (p327) and the local streetwear pusher **Brooklyn Industries 10** (p351).

Turn left onto Prince St and poke into the indie bookstore/café **McNally Robinson 11** (p327) before pawing the wonderfully cartoonish footwear of **John Fleuvog 12** (p326). Then, just past the gorgeous **St Patrick's Old Cathedral 13** (p132), you'll run into a stunning example of Nolita's

Prada princesses (p328)

overwhelming offerings: Mott St, with a dozen overly precious little boutiques like **Bad Dolly 14** 278 Mott St. Check into **Café Gitane 15** (p232) for a Euro-vibe pick-me-up and continue a bit farther on Prince St, where you can paw through the racks of **Ina 16** (p330), a couture consignment shop. Turn right onto Elizabeth St, pausing to admire the fenced-in garden of the curious **Elizabeth Street Gallery 17** (210 Elizabeth St), part of a fireplace, fountain and garden-ornament shop for the wealthy.

At Spring St, turn right. If you're with a child, set them loose in the postage stamp–sized **Desalvio Playground 18** Spring St (between Mulberry and Mott Sts), and then get sugared up in the slick rice-pudding parlor **Rice to Riches 19** (☎ 212-274-0008; 37 Spring St; 🕙 11am-11pm Sun-Wed, 11am-midnight Thu-Sat). Enjoy your stroll along Spring St, which has a nice old-world-meets-new-world feel. At Broadway, you can sneak north half a block for the **Original Levi's Store 20** (p327) or south to the downtown outpost of **Bloomingdale Soho 21** (p325), or just continue west, where you'll come to **Evolution 22** (p326), a strange purveyor of all things creepy, from

WALK FACTS

Start Prince St station (🚇 R, W)
Finish Canal St station (🚇 A, C, E, 1)
Distance 3.75 miles
Duration 3 to 5 hours
Fuel Stops Sparky's (p230), Café Gitane (p232) or Rice to Riches

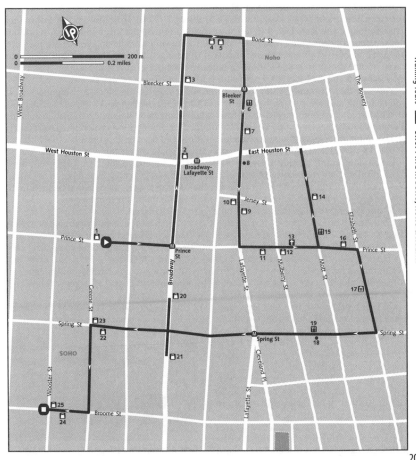

sharks' teeth and scorpions in amber to reproductions of various skulls. Across the street, hit **American Apparel 23** (p324), great for cotton tees and other basics, before going south on the cobblestones of Greene St. Turn right on Broome St and end with two winners: on the left, **Broadway Panhandler 24** (p325), an indie housewares shop where hipster staff can help you choose the perfect cookware or coffeemaker, and, on the right, **Vintage New York 25** (p328), a wine shop selling (and offering tastes of) local reds and whites. For the subway, continue south to Canal St and turn right, or start your evening right in the 'hood.

LOWER EAST SIDE FOOD & DRINK

There are many points of entry into this neighborhood, but let's assume you're headed into the Lower East Side and newly-crowned 'BelDel' district (Below Delancey St) from Lower Manhattan, Chinatown, Little Italy or Soho.

Fortify yourself with a glass of wine and a snack at **Xicala 1** (☎ 212-219-0599; 151-B Elizabeth St, btwn Broome & Kenmare Sts), an atmospheric tapas bar. Wander north on chic Elizabeth St, checking out Lovely Day **2** (196 Elizabeth St) and Public **3** (p232, 210 Elizabeth St), two noteworthy restaurants, the galleries, spray-painters and general scene. At Houston St and Elizabeth St, bookmark **Rialto 4** (on your left) for its fabulous hidden garden dining, and **Colonial Café 5** (on your right for) its laidback service and French/Brazilian fusion food.

But don't stop – continue east on Houston. You'll stroll by Jonah Schimmel Bakery **6**, the city's oldest and cutest knish maker, and **Bereket 7** (p241, 187 Houston St), dishing up Turkish treats, and Katz Deli **8** (205 Houston St), a tourist attraction in its own right, but not a place to linger unless you're looking to fill up on pastrami on rye, . Hang tight for about 10 blocks (you'll pass plenty of bars if thirst starts to overtake you) and then turn right (south) on Clinton St. Go down a block to the intersection with Stanton St and step into **Tapeo 29 9** (☎ 212-979-0002; 29 Clinton St). Time for more snacks and wine.

You can then continue south down Clinton for one looong block to Rivington St. If you're in the mood for sushi, head to **Cube 63 10** (p233), while **Falai 11** (☎ 212-253-1960; 68 Clinton St) has some deep-dish, cheese-laden, homemade Italian. This street also holds a famous foodie haven – **WD50 12** (p235), founded by wunderkind chef Wylie Dufresne. If you're going to try and eat here, make a reservation, and head to the crimson-walled heaven of **Belly 13** (☎ 212-533-1810; 155 Rivington St) for some cheese nibbles while you wait.

If you don't mind making a detour for a really cool joint, go south on Clinton St for a block until you see the **Delancey 14** (☎ 212-254-9920; 168 Delancey St at Clinton St) voted New York's best old-school bar. In summer, the rooftop is open, and the basement's there year-round for rock performances. If you're still in the mood for more, retrace your steps to Rivington and Clinton Sts, and continue west on Rivington.

Continue (west) on Rivington. There's plenty to catch your eye, but your goal is **Schiller's Liquor Bar 15** (p234), where you can cozy up to a chrome-and-gold bar for Belgian beer and fries. When you're finished (if you finish), continue west on Rivington until you reach Essex St. Turn to your left (south) and walk to **Whiskey Ward 16** (☎ 212-477-2998; 121 Essex St). We shouldn't have to tell you what's served here – it comes in jugs, barrels and shot glasses. A friendly saloon's a great place to do some drinking, but don't stay all night – you've still got to check out the scene BelDel. Continue south on Essex St.

Go four blocks south on Essex St to **King Size 17** (☎ 212-995-5464; 21 Essex St), a hoppin' place for a pint, and then continue south to Canal St. Take a right and head west one block, and there, just before the corner of Ludlow and Canal Sts is **Clandestino 18** (☎ 212-475-5505; 35 Canal St), and yes, it is just that – a bar that's very hard to find.

When you're done drinking undercover, head two blocks north on Ludlow St to Grand St and then one block west on Grand St to Orchard St, turning right (north) onto Orchard. You'll soon come to a trio of great snacking and drinking places: **Ronaldo's Pizza 19** (74 Orchard St), **Outlet Bar 20** (76 Orchard

Teeny-weeny pot of tea at Teany (left), Lower East Side

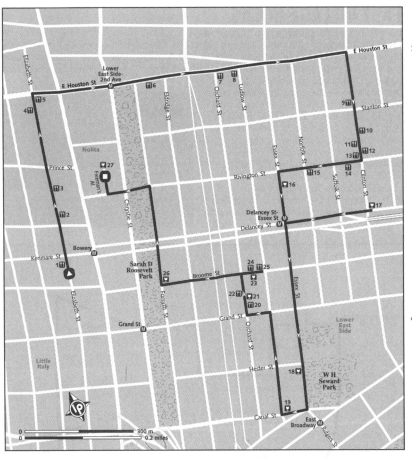

St) and **El Bocadito 21** (☎ 212-343331; 79 Orchard St), which has succulent and affordable Mexican dishes. If you want to continue grazing, go north on Orchard St to Broome St, take a right turn (east) and you'll see **Barrio Chino 22** (p265) with more Mexican, **Broomedoggs 23** (250 Broome St), a stand that sells hot dogs, and **Casanis 24** (☎ 212-777-1589; 81 Ludlow at Broome St), if you're in the mood for fine French fare.

WALK FACTS

Start Elizabeth and Houston Sts (bN, R to Prince St)
Finish Rivington St near Bowery (Ⓜ 6 at Bleecker St–Lafayette St or 6 at Spring St)
Distance 2 miles
Duration Open ended

If you've only been drinking and snacking thus far, you're probably ready for something substantial. Don't give up – you're very close to something special. Retrace your steps west on Broome to Forsyth St, and step into **Happy Ending 25** (☎ 212-334-9676; 302 Broome St) for a little something to keep your blood sugar up. Then head north on Forsyth St, crossing Delancey once again, and turn left (west) at Rivington St. Cross a small park, and continue one more block west on Rivington, and you should see a small road to your right, labeled Freeman's Alley. The pub at the end of the alley, **Freemans 26** (☎ 212-420-0012; off Rivington btwn the Bowery & Chrystie St) is open late, won't take reservations, and welcomes all comers.

EAST VILLAGE ROCKS

It's not as grungy and druggy as it once was, but it's still New York's rock 'n' roll core. From the Bleecker St subway, head east along leafy Bleecker St a few blocks where (for the moment) you can see the fabled site of **CBGB 1** (p294). Opened in 1973, the trashy bar launched punk rock via the Ramones, who yelled out '1-2-3-4' before launching into furious, 1950s-inspired down-strum songs that rarely broke two minutes. Later bands like TV and the Talking Heads played here, but it's been mostly about lame metal for years, and at press time it's lease hung in the balance: CBGB days seem sure to fall. The corner just north marks the block-long **Joey Ramone Place 2**, named after the Ramones' singer who succumbed to cancer in 2001.

Head north on the Bowery to St Marks Place. To the left in Astor Pl is **Cooper Union 3** (p138), where in 1860 president-hopeful Abraham Lincoln punk-rocked a skeptical

WALK FACTS

Start Bleecker St station (🚇 6)

Finish Lower Delancey St–Essex St station (🚇 F, J, M, Z)

Distance 2 miles

Duration 1½ to 2½ hours

Fuel Stop Veselka's (p241) Joey Ramone used to eat farina for breakfast at this Ukranian eatery (he ate with his mouth open, by the way)

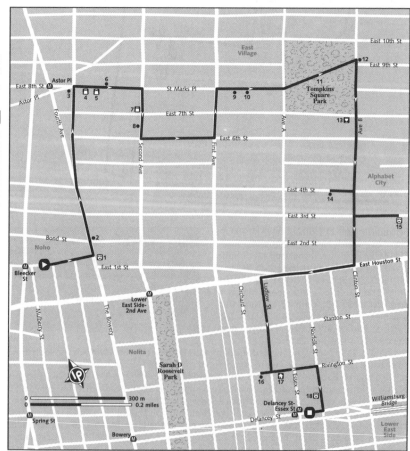

New York crowd with a rousing anti-slavery speech that ensured his candidacy. Turn right on St Marks Place, a block chock-full of tattoo parlors, combat books and 'New York Fuckin City' t-shirt shops that mom will like. Long the center of the East Village, it's a little intentional, but has to be seen. On the right, **Trash & Vaudeville 4** (4 St Marks Pl) is a landmark goth-and-punk shop; in the 1960s, a pre-John Yoko Ono staged happenings at the site. Next door **Mondo Kim's 5** (6 St Mark's Pl) is famed for its diverse CD collection (grab a copy of The Ramones, New York Dolls or Iggy Pop & the Stooges' *Raw Power*). Across the street, the modern mall-strip was the site of the **Dom 6** (23 St Marks Pl), and later Electric Circus, where Andy Warhol staged his Exploding Plastic Inevitable shows in 1966, with the little Velvet Underground providing the live soundtrack.

Ahead, at the corner of Second Ave, turn right, a block down on the right, stop in **Love Saves the Day 7** (p334), a campy shop of Star Wars figurines and clothes; it remains much like in 1985, when Rosanna Arquette came here for Madonna's jacket in *Desperately Seeking Susan*. Another block south is the site of **Fillmore East 8** (105 Second Ave), a seriously big-time 2000-seat live house run by promoter Bill Graham from 1968 to 1971. The Who premiered their rock opera *Tommy* here (Pete Townshend apparently kicked an undercover cop in the testicles during the show), and the Allman Brothers recorded *At Fillmore East* here in 1971.

Cross Second Ave at 6th St and head down the block-long strip of Indian curry shops. At First Ave, turn left – make a scathing comment at McDonald's – and rejoin St Marks Place and turn right. **Fun City Tattoo 9** (94 St Marks Pl) is a 30-year-old monster that's inked up folks from Joan Jett to Boy George. The side-by-side tenements next door are the site of Led Zeppelin's **Physical Graffiti cover 10** (96–98 St Marks Pl), where Mick and Keith sat in 1981 in the Stones' hilarious video for 'Waiting on a Friend.'

The trees looming ahead are the infamous **Tompkins Square Park 11** (p137), where drag queens started the 'Wigfest' summer festival at the bandshell where Jimi Hendrix played in the 1960s, riots broke out in 1988 when police kicked out squatters (immortalized in Lou Reed's *New York* album), and – hey – Ethan Hawke used to play pick-up basketball. A dog walk has replaced much of the junkie activity, but there's lots of life – like live bands, or arguing communists playing chess at the park's southeastern corner. Facing the park is jazz sax great **Charlie Parker's home 12** (151 Ave B), who died at 34 in 1955.

At the park's southeastern corner, **7B 13** (Horseshoe Bar; 108 Ave B) is the eternal East Village dive with fitting jukebox selection; many films have been shot here, including Pentagelli's near death in *Godfather II* and, um, the knife-in-a-mohawk scene in the immortal *Crocodile Dundee*.

Head south on Ave B, perhaps detouring to see **Madonna's first New York home 14** (230 E 4th St) in 1978, or fit in some slam poetry at the enduring **Nuyorican Poets Cafe 15** (236 E 3rd St).

A lot of present-tense rock is starting to filter south in the bar-central Lower East Side. Head there, via Houston and Ludlow Sts. The Beastie Boys chose a local corner for their **Paul's Boutique cover 16** (cnr Ludlow & Rivington Sts) in 1989 – things have changed. A block east, the new **Hotel on Rivington 17** (p357) is where indie rockers bunk these days; the Pixies' Frank Black recorded his speech in a suite here for the Rock 'n' Roll Hall of Fame in 2005. You can ponder your band's demo promise over a beer at the hotel's THOR bar, or see an avant-garde show at **Tonic 18** (p296).

The subway line is half a block southwest.

VILLAGE RADICALS

Manhattan's most unruly maze of streets can be found in Greenwich Village – and that's not only because it's the only corner not laid out in a neat grid. It's historically been a hotbed for upstarts by being home (and protest central) to radicals, bohemians, poets, folk singers, feminists and freedom-seeking gays and lesbians. This walk – which incorporates a corner of the West Village, too, as they haven't always been so clearly defined – is not only gorgeous, but laden with rebellious history.

To begin, disembark the subway at Christopher St and double back east one short block, where you'll find the last remaining LGBT bookstore in the city, the **Oscar Wilde Memorial Bookshop 1** (p336). A simple brick townhouse, it has bucked the mainstream by selling queer books and periodicals since 1967. Now go west to tiny **Christopher Park 2** (p140) where two white, life-size statues of same-sex couples (*Gay Liberation*, 1992) stand guard. On its north side is the legendary **Stonewall 3** (p266), where a clutch of fed-up drag queens rioted for their civil rights in 1969, signaling the start of the gay revolution. Cross Seventh Ave South and continue west along Christopher St, still known as the pulse of gay life here. At Bedford St turn left and enjoy the quietude of the quaint block (if it's a weekday afternoon, that is); stop and peer into **Chumley's 4** (p269), the site of a prohibition-dodging socialist-run speakeasy that is marked by a simple air-conditioning unit over its wooden door. If it's not open yet, return later for drinks and pub grub.

Continue along Bedford St for several blocks, make a left on Downing St and cross Sixth Ave. To the south you'll see a plaque marking '**Little Red Square**' 5, so-named not for communists but for the original site of the experimental Little Red School-house, founded by Elisabeth Irwin in 1921 and still thriving nearby. Continue east on the crooked Minetta St, home to the unremarkable Panchito's Mexican Restaurant. But above its rear red facade is the faded

WALK FACTS

Start Christopher St (Ⓢ 1 to Christopher St–Sheridan Sq)
Finish W 11th St (Ⓢ A, C, E, B, D, F, V at W 4th St)
Distance 2 miles
Duration 1½ hours
Fuel Stops Minetta Lane Tavern, Caffé Reggio

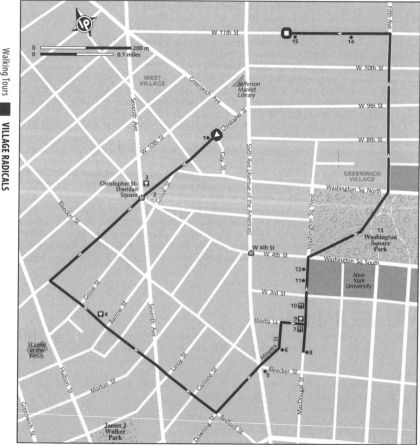

sign for the **Fat Black Pussycat 6** (103 MacDougal St) – called The Commons in 1962 when a young Bob Dylan wrote and first performed 'Blowin' in the Wind' here.

Turn right on Minetta Ln and right on MacDougal St to find the historic **Minetta Tavern 7** (☎ 212-475-3850, 113 MacDougal St, ☉ noon-midnight), a great place for a pit stop. The bar and restaurant, its walls now lined with photos of celebs who have visited, opened as a speakeasy in 1922. It was later frequented by one of the most famous local eccentrics, Joe Gould, who was immortalized through the writings of journalism great Joseph Mitchell (a friendship further depicted in the 2000 flick *Joe Gould's Secret*). Also on this block is the former site of the **Folklore Center 8** (110 MacDougal St), where Izzy Young established a hangout for folk artists including Dylan, who found his first audience at the music venue **Cafe Wha? 9** (☎ 212-254-3706; 115 MacDougal St).

Further along MacDougal is another possible fuel stop, the cozy **Café Reggio 10** (☎ 212-475-9557, 119 MacDougal St), whose original 1927 owners claimed to be the first to bring cappuccino from Italy to the US. Just past here are two former hotspots. The **Provincetown Playhouse 11** (☎ 212-998-5867, 133 MacDougal St), founded on a Provincetown, Massachusetts, wharf in 1915 as an experimental theater, was moved to this converted stable and managed by a young Eugene O'Neill. Next door, the current Research Fellows & Scholars Office of the NYU School of Law is the former site of the **Liberal Club 12** (137 MacDougal St), 'a meeting place for those interested in new ideas' that was founded in 1913 by free thinkers including Jack London and Upton Sinclair.

Beyond here is the southwest entrance to **Washington Square Park 13** (p139), which has a long history of being a magnet for radicals, hosting demonstrations on topics from anti-war to pro-marijuana and dyke pride. Leave the park at the iconic arch and head up Fifth Ave. Make a left on W 11th St, where you'll wrap up the tour with two notable townhouses. First is the infamous **Weathermen House 14** (18 W 11th St), used in 1970 as a hideout and bomb factory for the radical antigovernment group until an accidental explosion killed three members and destroyed the house; it was rebuilt in its current angular form in 1978. Further west, the tour comes full circle with a former, albeit brief, **home of Oscar Wilde 15** (48 W 11th St).

CHELSEA'S GALLERY CRAWL

You know this much: Chelsea = art galleries. But with more than 200 (and counting), where on earth are you supposed to begin? For a complete list of the offerings, you can grab a copy of *Chelsea Art* or the *New York Art World*, available for free at most galleries. But for a more focused taste of everything, follow us. Keep in mind that galleries are open 10am to 6pm Tuesday to Saturday unless otherwise noted.

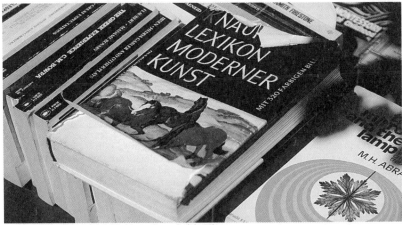

Feed your mind at the markets in Washington Square Park (p139)

A picturesque place to begin is all the way west, at the **Hudson River 1** – which has been painted throughout history by landscape artists including Thomas Cole and Asher Brown Durand. To get there, just take the M23 bus across 23rd St. Gaze out over the water for inspiration before crossing back over the West Side Hwy and entering the gallery district.

Start with one of the more popular gallery strips, 22nd St, home to about a dozen spaces including the temporary home of the **New Museum of Contemporary Art 2** (p144). Note that the bridge running over 22nd St is a closed, weed-covered train line, the old **High Line 3** (p141), which will soon undergo a major renovation to become one of two elevated parks in the world (the other is in Paris).

From here you can peruse whatever moves you on 24th St, at places including **Metro Pictures 4** (☎ 212-206-7100; 519 W 24th St), best known for representing photographer Cindy Sherman, and **Luhring Augustine 5** (☎ 212-206-9100; www.luhringaugustine .com; 531 W 24th St), which often shows large-format photography. Don't miss the seminal **Mary Boone Gallery 6** (p142) – or the very different **Fischbach Gallery** (☎ 212-759-2345; No. 801, 210 Eleventh Ave btwn 24th & 25th Sts) and the **Robert Mann Gallery 7** (☎ 212-989-7600; No. 10, 210 Eleventh Ave btwn 24th & 25th Sts), right around the corner. A block north, on 25th St, stop by **Cheim & Read 8** (☎ 212-242-7727; www.cheimread .com; 547 W 25th St) before hitting 26th St, where you'll find a few smaller, edgier galleries, such as **Lucas Shoormans 9** (☎ 212-243-3159; 508 W 26th St).

Whatever you do, don't miss the area's most buzzed-about addition, a new **gallery group 10** (p54). In early 2006, six showcases – Derek Eller Gallery, Foxy Production, Wallspace, Oliver Kamm Gallery, Clementine Gallery and John Connelly Presents – relocated from other Chelsea spots into the old loading dock bays of what used to be the Tunnel nightclub. And the block, with all galleries blessedly located at street level, has become the district's new frontier.

No doubt you're famished by now, and luckily **Tía Pol 11** (p241), a scrumptious Spanish tapas bar, isn't far, on Tenth Ave between 23rd and 22nd Sts. If you're a photography fan, though, don't miss the **Aperture Gallery 12** (☎ 212-505-5555; 547 W 27th St btwn Tenth & Eleventh Aves) on your way here.

Now stroll south on Tenth Ave and, if your energy isn't sapped, you can check out the fast-rising talents of the **Alexander Bonin 13** (☎ 212-367-7474; 132 Tenth Ave btwn 18th & 19th Sts) and **Bellwether 14** (☎ 212-929-5959; 134 Tenth Ave btwn 18th & 19th Sts) galleries. Then head over to Ninth Ave to check out a work of culinary art: **Chelsea Market 15** (p143), an 800 ft long concourse of gourmet food shops and eateries that's great for snacking, shopping or simply admiring the heady-scented offerings. Just south of here is the trendy Meatpacking District, and you can finish up with a gander at the future home of the **Dia Art Foundation 16** (Gansevoort St at Washington St), where the edgily designed museum will sit nestled beneath the Highline. From here you can begin a night out, as the 'hood is packed with bars, clubs and eateries.

WALK FACTS

Start 23rd St at the Hudson River (M23 bus)
Finish Meatpacking District (⊘ A, C, E to 14th St)
Distance 3 miles
Duration 3 to 6 hours
Fuel Stops Tía Pol (p241), Chelsea Market (p143)

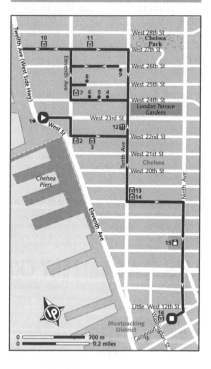

TOURING THE NEW MOMA

Back in Manhattan after a two-year stint in Queens while Japanese Yoshio Taniguchi completed his masterful rehab of the museum's original 1939 building, the MoMA's permanent collection sits in an atmosphere that writer John Updike described as having 'nothing obtrusive, and nothing cheap.'

That includes the hefty $20 entry free, but you can get your money's worth without spending the day in the museum. First, after you've bought your ticket, exit the main lobby on 53rd St and enter the MoMA from the **cantilevered canopied entrance two doors 1** down, heading east. It's the former entrance – it kind of resembles a baby grand piano – and Taniguchi left it intact.

WALK FACTS

Start 11 West 53 Street (btwn Fifth and Sixth Aves; Ⓔ E, V to 5 Avenue–53rd Street, V, B, D, F to 47th–50th Streets–Rockefeller Center)
Finish See above
Distance Open
Duration Open
Fuel Stop

From there, head to the **sixth floor 2**, home to special exhibits, and get used to the white space and bright natural light that pervades the building. Pay attention to the views from the

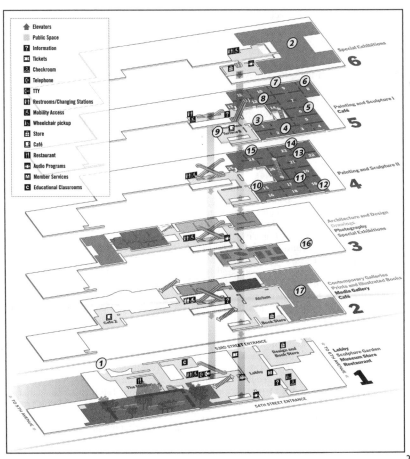

windows – it's here that you can get the best sense of how Taniguchi worked to integrate the new MoMA into older architecture around it.

When you've had your fill, move to the fifth floor. The fifth and fourth floors are basically the MoMA's introduction to modern art – and many of the museums best paintings are displayed here. On the fifth floor, on the back wall of **Gallery 2 3**, you'll find Picasso's Les Demoiselles d'Avignon. Farther down in **Gallery 6 4** is an Henri Matisse, The Moroccans, and of course, no visit to a modern museum is complete without taking in Marcel Duchamp's third version of Bicycle Wheel, in **Gallery 8 5**. The remaining galleries hold a Piet Mondrian, **Broadway Boogie Woogie 6** and Salvador Dali's **The Persistence of Memory 7**. Swing through **Terrace 5 8**, a café with sumptuous desserts and a bird-eye's view of the Sculpture Garden and city. The museum has a few Vincent Van Gogh's sprinkled throughout both floors, including *Starry Nights* in Gallery 1 **9** on the 5th Floor.

On the fourth floor, the standouts include **The Jungle 10** in Gallery 15 by Wifredo Lam, **One: Number 31, 1950 11**, by Jackson Pollock, Willem de Kooning's **Woman 1 12**, Lee Bontecou's **Untitled 13**, Andy Warhol's **Gold Marilyn Monroe 14** and Donald Judd's **Untitled 15**.

If you're looking for an in-and-out tour, head straight to the lobby and spend some time in the **Sculpture Garden 16**. The whole tour can be done in less than two hours, including time for a snack.

For those looking for longer stays, continue down to the third floor, which is dense with the museum's coverage of major movements in architecture and design from the mid-19th century onward, a special collection of drawings from 1880 to the present, and the museum's immense collection of photographs dating from the 1840s to current times. The second floor is given over to **prints and illustrated books 17** – MoMA has more than 50,000 – with installations highlighting individual artists and important movements. The second floor carries exhibits on film and media that often coincide with film series put on by the MoMA – shown in their brand-new theaters, which are below the lobby. If you walk past the atrium on the second floor you'll find **Cafe 2 17**, a full-service caféteria-style deli where food is served at communal tables. There's also an espresso bar, just in case you're energy's flagging. The lobby has a Design & Book Store, but don't leave without stepping into the wondrous and inspiring Sculpture Garden, where the benches and trees are sculptures in and of themselves.

BIKING NEW YORK

There are harder cities than New York to navigate on a bike, but probably few where the traffic moves faster! If you end up on a main street during rush hour – take care. Biking through the Big Apple's fabulous neighborhoods is fun if you know where you are going; nerve-wracking if you don't. For the newbie to the city, you've got two options: go to Central Park and bike your heart out, or combine that with a tour of the not-quite-completed but very good path around the edge of the island, the Greenway Bike Tour.

An easy point of access on the East Side can be found by biking down **14th St 1a** or **Houston St 1b** (both wide, double-lane streets) and following the overpass to the other side of the FDR highway. From there you can head north almost as far as the UN without having to enter traffic again, but a better choice would be to go south, down the **East River Park 2** (p134), past the **Lower East Side 3** (p133), **Chinatown 4** (p111), the **Williamsburg 5a** and **Manhattan Bridges 5b**. You can bike around the tip of southern Manhattan and into **Battery Park City 6** (p117), where there's a walk-only segment to navigate. From there, you're on **Hudson River Park 7** (p143), a 550-acre esplanade stretching up to 59th St. You can get off at **Christopher St** (p140), and enter the **West Village 8** (p140), stop for a lemon ice at **Chelsea Piers 9** (p143), or head up to the **USS Intrepid Museum 10** at 46th St (queue at Pier 86, W46th St & Twelfth Ave). Legend has it that you can follow this route, with forays into traffic on occasion, all the north to Cherry Walk in **Riverside Park 11** (p160), a mile-long stretch from 100th to 125th St that in spring and summer is replete with cherry trees. If you've got legs of steel, and don't mind navigating some walk-only parts with light traffic, you can get all the way up to the **Cloisters 12** (p170), the museum in Fort Tryon Park. If that's too far, you might consider biking up

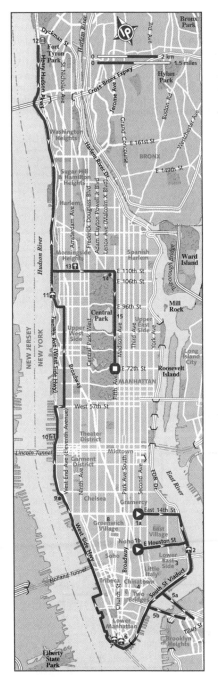

WALK FACTS

Start East River Park (🚇 Union Square if starting at 14th Street, or the F train to Lower East Side–2 Ave/Houston St)

Finish Central Park (🚇 6 at 68 Street–Hunter College–Lexington Ave)

Distance 5 to 10 miles

Duration 2 to 5 hours

Fuel Stop Chelsea Piers

to **Cathedral Church of St John the Divine 13** (p166) and then across the north end of Central Park on 110th St. You can head east along the park, passing Central Park's lake **Harlem Meer 14**,(cnr Fifth Ave & 110th St) and then down the east side of Central Park, along **Museum Mile 15** (p160).

HARLEM SHUFFLE

Harlem, the USA's most famous African American neighborhood, is undergoing a big-time new 'renaissance,' with one-time boarded-up brownstones being restored. Any daytime hours are good to take the walk.

From 145th St station, head a block west to Convent Ave, home to turn-of-the-last-century Queen Anne–style townhouses that make up the Hamilton Heights Historic District. Near the corner of 141st St, stop in the free **Hamilton Grange 1** (p170) to see the home of the $10-bill man.

Head down 141st St around St Nicholas Park to 138th St and turn left two blocks to reach **Striver's Row 2** (p170), filled with 1890s townhouses that got their nickname in the 1920s, when aspiring African Americans first moved here.

West of Adam Clayton Powell Jr Blvd, the unsigned **Abyssinian Baptist Church 3** (p168) has its origins in 1808, when a Lower Manhattan church was formed by African Americans in response to segregated services. Previous pastor Adam Clayton Powell Jr became the first African-American congressional representative in 1944. At Lenox Ave, peek north where two huge jazz clubs roared in the 1920s and '30s (nothing but towering housing projects now): the **Savoy Club 4** (596 Lenox Ave at 140th St) and the **Cotton Club 5** (644 Lenox Ave at 142nd St).

Go south on Lenox Ave to 137th St, where you'll see – on a road which still has many boarded-up buildings – the city's oldest African-American church (originally in Lower Manhattan), the **Mother African Methodist Episcopal Zion Church 6** (p167). The church played an important role in establishing the underground railroad in the mid-1800s.

Walk south on Adam Clayton Powell Jr Blvd to W 135th St. The **Harlem YMCA 7** (181 W 135th St), here since 1919, provided rooms for many newly arrived African Americans who were denied a room in segregated hotels (including James Baldwin, Jackie Robinson and Malcolm X). Note the 'YMCA' in neon atop the tower. Just past the Y there are public b-ball courts that claim 'Harlem plays the best ball in the country.'

Head a block east and see the archives and photos at the **Schomburg Center for Research in Black Culture 8** (p168).

Head south on Lenox Ave. If it's open, stop at the **Liberation Bookstore 9** (p350), then take 130th St east past a row of 1880s brick homes built by William Astor. At Fifth Ave, look north to see Yankee Stadium in the Bronx, where Jackie Robinson and the Brooklyn Dodgers beat the Yanks in the 1955 World Series.

WALK FACTS

Start 145th St station (Ⓜ A, B, C & D)
Finish 125th St station (Ⓜ A, B, C & D)
Distance 2 miles
Duration 1½ to 2½ hours
Fuel Stop Sylvia's (p252)

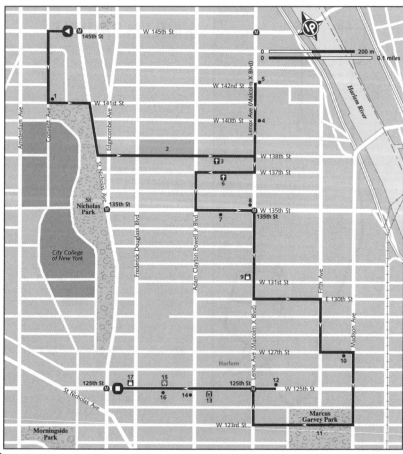

Go south on Fifth Ave and turn east on E 127th St, stopping to see the last **home of poet Langston Hughes 10** (20 E 127th St), who died in 1967. Head south along Madison Ave to 124th St and **Marcus Garvey Park 11**, named for the Jamaica-born founder of the 'Back to Africa' movement who lived in Harlem from 1916 to 1927. There's nice views from the fire watchtower 0n the central hill.

Rejoin Lenox Ave (Malcolm X Blvd) and head north to W 125th St, Harlem's main hub and home to many new residents in the past decade: HMV, Starbucks and **Bill Clinton's office 12** (55 W 125th St).

Walking west on 125th St, under the red, black and green US flag, stop at the **Studio Museum in Harlem 13** (p168), just across from the rather out-of-place State Office Building (1973). On the corner of Adam Clayton Powell Jr Blvd, the giant white-brick **Hotel Theresa 14** (cnr 125th & Adam Clayton Powell Jr Blvd), sometimes known as the 'black Waldorf-Astoria,' hosted Apollo entertainers, and Fidel Castro in 1960. It's now offices only.

West on 125th St is the historic **Apollo Theater 15** (p168), which hosts many performances, including the Wednesday Amateur's Night. Opposite the theater, you will notice the sign for **Blumstein's 16**, a (now closed) store that finally began hiring African-Americans following an eight-week boycott in 1934. (Look back and up to the Theresa from here and see its name still marking the building.)

Around the corner on Frederick Douglas Blvd, finish up at 125th St's first African-American-run shop **Bobby's Happy House 17** (p349) to pick up a gospel or blues CD. Bobby's 'awards' in the front window include a copy of U2's platinum record for their *Rattle & Hum* album.

125th St, Harlem (p165), is one cool 'hood

PILGRIMAGE TO BROOKLYN

New York's favorite bridge (p125) is meant to be walked over. For reward, you get a couple of Brooklyn's coolest areas. From **City Hall Park 1** (p124), cross at the street light to the rising walkway. Keep right (south) – and away from the marked bike lane. The gilded-top building to your left, the **Municipal Building 2** (p124) was originally where the bridge traffic would flow through. Ahead you'll see thick cables leading up the two 'towers' of the bridge. John Roebling's original design included arched tops, but the plans was (thankfully) scrapped to keep on budget.

After the first tower (marked '1875' for its completion), you'll be able to see the Statue of Liberty to the right. Note the squat white building at the foot of Governor's Island (to the right), which serves as ventilation for the Brooklyn Battery Tunnel (originally planned as a potentially view-breaking bridge).

Across, about 150 yards after the wood-plank path ends, follow the fork left – down the steps – to Washington St, under an overpass. Welcome to Brooklyn. Turn left on Washington. To the right you'll see the **Watchtower 3** (p173), the sprawling HQ for the Jehovah's Witnesses. Ahead is Dumbo (aka Down Under Manhattan Bridge Underpass). Not long ago this was an abandoned patch of warehouses taken over by fearless artists – now it's an upscale hot-spot residential area with great views and high-cost loft space. Ahead is a perfectly framed shot of the blue Manhattan Bridge.

To the left on Front St, Jake LaMotta – of *Raging Bull* fame – trained at **Gleason's Gym 4** (☎ 718-797-2872; 2nd fl, 83 Front St). You can look around (for $5) and watch trainers

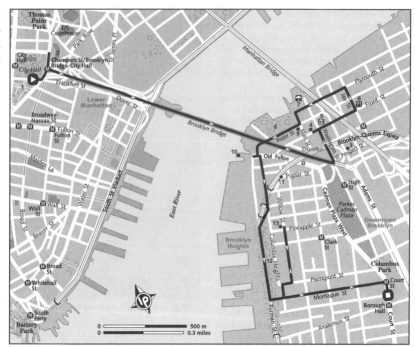

look for the next great thing. Double back on Front St (where the water reached before landfill in the mid-19th-century extended Brooklyn out). Perhaps peek into one of the 10 or so galleries at the orange-entry of **111 Front Street Galleries 5** (111 Front St).

Go under the Manhattan Bridge, to where Dumbo's cobbled streets get bumpier. You can stop for a beer or tamale at the makeshift outdoor seats at long-time Dumbo resident, **Pedro's Bar & Restaurant 6** (p254); beers are $2.50 from 4pm to 7pm. This area has new upscale furniture shops, but much of the rawer past is alive – note the graffiti run rampant, and peek into loft windows to see artists at work.

WALK FACTS

Start City Hall Park, Chambers St/Brooklyn Bridge–City Hall Station (Ⓜ 4, 5, 6)
Finish Court St (Ⓜ 2, 3) or Borough Hall (Ⓜ 2, 3, 4, 5)
Distance 3¼ miles
Duration about 2 hours
Fuel Stop Grimaldi's (p253) Frank Sinatra prints on the wall, fresh pies on the red-checkered tables – it's not New York's front-runner for best pizza for nothing.

Head back on Plymouth St under Manhattan Bridge, then right to two enviably set side-by side parks: **Brooklyn Bridge Park 7** and **Empire Fulton Ferry State Park 8**, near where ferries whisked off to Manhattan for nearly 300 years (stopping in 1924). Head back on Main St a block, then right on Water St; stop in **Jacques Torres Chocolate 9** (☎ 718-875-9772; 66 Water St; ☽ 9am-7pm Mon-Sat, 10am-6pm Sun), an irresistible choco shop with a couple dozen $0.90 fresh chocolates and $2.50 hot chocolate.

Walk along Water St, under the Brooklyn Bridge. To the right is **Fulton Landing 10**, where many newly married couples come to pose – at the far right corner you can see the Statue of Liberty.

Unless you're hungry for Grimaldi's pizza (p253), head up to Columbia Heights St (just past the old Gulf gas station). A couple quick blocks up the hill, past the dog park to the left, you'll get a square-on view of the **split-level Brooklyn–Queens Expwy (BQE) 11** – the Brooklyn Heights neighborhood ahead had to fight to keep it from running through its historic brownstones in the 1950s.

Ahead, follow the sidewalk curving right to the 10-block long **Brooklyn Heights Promenade 12** (p174) A quiet flower-lined strolling ground with straight-on looks at Lower Manhattan (too bad about the BQE noise from the expressway underneath). Afterwards detour on quiet Brooklyn Heights streets. Many literary types escaped Manhattan's high rents here (now Brooklyn Heights is one of New York's most coveted addresses); on lovely Willow St, you can see **Truman Capote's home 13** (70 Willow St btwn Pineapple & Orange Sts), where he penned *Breakfast at Tiffany's*.

Head back to the subway along the Heights' main strip, Montague St. The Court St station is at the end of Montague St, the Borough Hall stop is a block to the right.

BILLYBURG BOOZE CRAWL

The new downtown is over in Williamsburg these days, and the new Williamsburg is east of the Brooklyn–Queens Expressway in 'East Williamsburg.' This tour takes in both. New bars pop up constantly, attracting a mix of 20- and 30-something hipsters and long-term locals (including many Latin Americans and the occasional curious Hassidic Jew). Outside the main strips of N 6th St and Bedford Ave, most bars over here take themselves a little less seriously than Manhattan's; they're generally cheaper, more laid back and bigger too. Some bars mix in live music – often without covers – allowing for 10-minute snoops at a set before moving on.

Life begins well after 11pm, but that doesn't mean you can start sooner.

A good place to start is under the rattling J-M-Z subway tracks at **Moto 1** (p257), a lowlit corner spot that looks straight out of Paris' heyday. Exit the Hewes St subway to the south, and look for hipsters smoking outside the

WALK FACTS

Start Hewes St (Ⓙ J, M)
Finish Bedford Av (Ⓛ L)
Distance 3 miles
Duration 3 hours to ?
Fuel Stop Relish (p257)

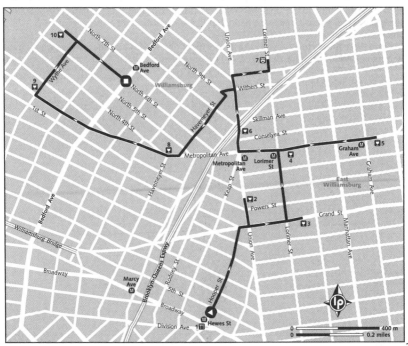

unsigned door. It's more atmosphere than haute cuisine – go for a sandwich and a mug of Australia's Coopers lager.

Head up Hooper St a couple blocks. Stop to play one of the two-dozen vintage arcade games (Asteroids, Berzerk or Star Wars) at **Barcade 2** (☎ 718-302-6464; 388 Union Ave), where's there's a diverse choice of two dozen $5 microbrews and a bottle-cap mosaic in the front smoking area.

Go south on Union St, you'll see a café or two, and turn left on Grand St. Two blocks up is the **Bushwick Country Club 3** (☎ 718-388-2114; 618 Grand St, btwn Powers & Ainslie Sts), a half-hearted but lively take on a 'members only' club with a hokey miniature golf course out back and Spandau Ballet and Billy Joel on the juke. Bartenders are quite nice – maybe it's the flip-off photo of Johnny Cash that urges their good behavior – and drink specials get weird (a can of Pabst comes with a whiskey shot for $5). Munch on the popcorn here, but save space for the *excellent* free pizza (if you're drinking) at **Alligator Lounge 4** (p275), four quick blocks north.

You could head farther east on Metropolitan Ave – **Blue Lady Lounge 5** (☎ 718-218-6997; 769 Metropolitan Ave) includes Metallica and country 'n' western on the jukebox and keeps happy hour going till 9pm.

Back near the expressway, the curving **Union Pool 6** (☎ 718-609-0484; 404 Union St at Conselyea St), once an old pool-supply store, retains a slight '50s feel – the occasional rockabilly DJs and plush booths don't hurt.

Pass under the expressway on Union Ave, then go right to Lorimer St, to reach **Pete's Candy Store 7** (☎ 718-302-3770; www.petescandystore.com; 709 Lorimer St btwn N 10th & 11th Sts), where free music is staged nightly in an slightly seedy ice-cream shop from the 1940s. There's fun planned nightly (eg bingo on Tuesday, quizzes on Wednesday).

Go southwest (via Union Ave, then Havermeyer Ave to Metropolitan Ave to sober up a bit over a plate of cheese and loose tea – or go for the great beer list – at **Spuyten Duyvil 8** (p276).

Head towards the river on Metropolitan – passing a couple bars and eateries. Turn right five blocks up on Wythe Ave, and stop in at no-cover **Zebulon 9** (p276), where there's likely standing-room only in the small bar. Often worldly music and experimental jazz overflows the small stage. There's snacks on hand, but if you're ready to sit a spell, eat at **Relish** (p257) across the street.

Many first-timers to Williamsburg stick with N 6th St. Head up there to see what's happening at **Galapagos Art Space 10** (p276), or one of the bars between Wythe and Bedford Ave.

Eating

Eating

So let's see here. With 18,000 New York City restaurants and only 365 days a year, you'd have to eat at nearly 50 places a day to get to them all. Not an appealing prospect, or even a humanly possible one – unless of course you're one of those professional gorgers who win the annual Nathan's Famous Hot Dog Eating Contest (p26) here in Coney Island every July. Plus, with the rate that things change around here, a good chunk of the restaurants would likely close and be replaced with new spots before you were even close to getting to them! And so, assuming you're not up for a futile and gut-busting game of the Amazing NYC Restaurant Race, here's a better idea: let us help you narrow down the offerings with suggestions for the best (in our humble opinion) eateries in all neighborhoods, in genres from classic diner and Jewish deli fare to helplessly hip upscale celebrity-chef offerings and the authentic, ethnic flavors of Italy, France, Israel, Japan, South India, Brazil, Mexico...shall we go on?

But first here's a quick rundown of the latest NYC dining trends at press time (though we can't guarantee they won't be over by the time you get here). The big phrase these days is 'small plates,' which, in an attempt to be more sophisticated yet still get a taste of practically everything on the menu, has gone over well. Traditional Spanish tapas bars, Turkish meze places and a variety of other ethnic takes – Italian, Middle Eastern and 'eclectic' small-plate spots among them – have been opening all over the city. There's also been strong interest in all things labeled 'organic' – from wine to veggies and beef – as well as pan-Latin cuisine, artisanal cheese courses, desserts in the form of cream puffs and cupcakes, and wines from Argentina and South Africa. Added to the mix is a new feature from the City of New York, meant to address the fear of many New Yorkers that city restaurants can be frighteningly unsanitary places: the new **Restaurant Inspection Website** (www.nyc.gov/health/restaurants). Courtesy of the Department of Health, the site offers a searchable database of restaurant inspection information.

For all of the ambient and not-so-ambient restaurant locations, though, sometimes you just want to stuff your face with lo mein in the privacy of your room, with nothing but the TV to distract you. Other times you may want to create your own stylized atmosphere, be it a picnic in Central Park or a packed lunch on the train to Long Island. That's nothing new in a city where folks can't stay still for long, and it's why virtually every place – from cheap Chinese storefronts to the most high-class dining rooms – offers not only takeout, but door-to-door delivery. Just don't forget to tip the delivery guy, about 15% of your bill.

Opening Hours

Most places are open daily. Those that do have days off usually close on Monday; those that are open Monday are not usually filled with locals, who avoid eating fresh fish and sushi because there are no deliveries on Sunday! Meal times for the varied schedules of New Yorkers are quite fluid, with restaurants complying: many diner-type spots serve breakfast all day or at least start as early as 3am, to accommodate club-goers who rely on stacks of pancakes to sober up. Loosely speaking, though, you can usually find breakfasts served till noon. Lunchtime overlaps a bit, often starting at 11:30am and ending at 4pm, and dinnertime is anywhere from 5pm or 6pm until 10pm during the week and about 11pm on weekends. That said, there are scores of eateries that serve until midnight, 1am or even 2am or 3am; many stay open round-the-clock. Prime time for dinner is between 8pm and 9pm. Brunch, usually limited to Sunday, is generally served from 11am until 3pm or 4pm.

How Much?

If you're on a super-strict budget – or if you have money burning a hole in your pocket – you've come to the right place. You can grab a falafel sandwich, hot dog, fresh fruit, curry, crepe or soup from street vendors (skip those tasty-smelling roasted nuts; they're never as good as they smell) for between $2 and $4, a slice of pizza for $2 or ethnic meals (Chinese, Middle Eastern, Indian, Turkish, Japanese, Korean, Vietnamese) for as cheap as $4 a plate. Midrange restaurants charge about $17 on average per main, while the most upscale spots in town have mains for upwards of $35, or tasting menus for about $75 per person. A treat for foodies who lack expendable incomes is NYC and Company Restaurant Week (see www.nycvisit.com for more) a 10-day stretch in winter and again in summer in which top notch restaurants offer three-course lunch menus for $25 and dinner menus for $35.

Price Guide

The following is a guide to the pricing system in this chapter. Prices are per person and they exclude taxes.

$	under $15
$$	$15-30
$$$	over $30

Booking Tables

Most restaurants take reservations for lunch and/or dinner, although some do not accept them unless you have four or more in your party (such as Tía Pol, p241). For those places that refuse reservations altogether (eg Roberto's, p260), expect rowdy waits that could last a half-hour or more. But hey, it's all part of the experience.

Tipping

Just as in the rest of the USA, you are expected to tip your server an average of 15% of your bill before tax. You can leave slightly less for poor service and slightly more (20% is the standard reward) if it's excellent. Some coffee bars have tip jars next to the register; these are optional, and best fed with a quarter or two.

LOWER MANHATTAN

Food is everywhere during the frenzied lunch rushes down in these parts, with places for three-course power lunches and grab-and-go gyros on what seems like every block. The bigger foraging challenge begins after the workers have gone home – with the notable exception of Tribeca, which has always catered to gourmets. But some stellar options have popped up all around the Lower Manhattan region recently, and they, along with some stalwarts, make it a pretty solid spot for indulging. Fans of the former Windows on the World, the top-floor eatery of the World Trade Center, should note that a group of surviving employees opened a cooperative-owned Greenwich Village restaurant, Colors (p237) in 2006, as a tribute to their 73 coworkers who perished.

BOBBY VAN'S STEAKHOUSE

Map pp444-5   Italian $$$

☎ 212-344-8463, www.bobbyvans.com; 25 Broad St at Exchange Pl; ☼ lunch & dinner; ◉ 2, 3, 4, 5 to Wall St

One of the latest classic, masculine spots to hit the city with classic steakhouse fare of thick porterhouse and sirloin steaks, whole lobsters and lamb chops, Bobby Van's has quickly entered the top 10 lists of many diehard beef fanatics. While the crowd here is pretty staid and upscale – and the prices (averaging $36 for a fine cut of steak) pretty much demand it – the place's history has a bit of artsy intrigue to it. The first Bobby Van's opened in the Hamptons, before it was chi-chi and stuffy, attracting regular Truman Capote and a crowd of other offbeat lit types who loved to chow down and sip whiskey till all hours. The original still remains, along with two others in NYC and an outpost in DC.

CABANA Map pp444-5   Nuevo Latino $$

☎ 212-406-1155; 89 South St Seaport; ☼ lunch & dinner; ◉ J, M, Z, 1, 2, 4, 5 to Fulton St–Broadway Nassau

This branch of the pan-Latin mini-chain (you'll find others on the Upper East Side and in Queens) is a fabulously flavorful addition to the mall-like Seaport staples. The fresh grub includes Cuban *ropa vieja* (dish of shredded beef and tomatoes), fried plantains, seviche, Jamaican jerk chicken, grilled seafood salad marinated in tangy citrus mojo, and thick slabs of *arepa con queso* (thick corn cakes topped with white cheese). The sweeping view of New York Harbor, which can be soaked up through floor-to-ceiling windows as you relax in one of the tropical-fish-patterned banquettes, makes it worth the wait at this bustling haven.

FINANCIER PATISSERIE

Map pp444-5   French Café $

☎ 212-334-5600; 62 Stone St at Mill Lane; ⏲ 7am-8:30pm Mon-Fri, 7am-7pm Sat; ⓜ 2, 3, 4, 5 to Wall St or J, M, Z to Broad St

It's a relief to find French flavors that are both affordable and delicious down in this neighborhood, and this spot manages to pull it off with panache. This graceful café is on the quaint and tiny Stone St. The patisserie's fresh pastries – including almond-crusted fruit tarts and the signature madeleine-type mini-cake – are truly worth raving over. And, as evidenced by the mellow and sophisticated crowd that has clearly sought this spot out, so is the heartier fare. There are homemade soups such as lentil and celery root, sandwiches, including savory chicken with goat cheese on ciabatta or house-cured tuna, and a range of fresh salads.

LES HALLES

Map pp444-5   French Brasserie $$$

☎ 212-285-8585; www.leshalles.net; 15 John St btwn Broadway & Nassau St; ⏲ lunch & dinner; ⓜ A, C to Broadway–Nassau St or J, M, Z, 2, 3, 4, 5 to Fulton St

Celebrity chef Anthony Bourdain still reigns at this packed and serious brasserie where vegetarians need not apply. Among the elegant light-fixture balls, dark wood paneling and stiff white tablecloths you'll find a buttoned-up, meat-lovin' crowd with deep pockets. They've come for rich and decadent favorites including *cote de beouf, choucroute garnis* and steak au poivre, as well as more standard *moules frites,* New York strip steak, salad nicoise and grilled salmon. The lists of wine, single-malt scotches and other liquors are impressive, as are the desserts, from the crème brûlée to the *tarte tatin.*

QUARTINO Map pp444-5   Italian $$

☎ 212-349-4433; 21 Peck Slip at Water St; ⏲ lunch & dinner; ⓜ A, C to Broadway–Nassau St or J, M, Z, 2, 3, 4, 5 to Fulton St

With South St Seaport looming, this is not the place you might expect to find such a sleek and sophisticated wine bar and Italian grazing spot. But join the after-work crowd looking for serenity in this low-lit gem and tuck into some excellent food and drink.

Choose from fresh portions of cured meats and cheeses; pizzas and paninis with luscious options of fontina cheese, anchovies and zucchini; and fresh pastas including vegetable ravioli with walnut sauce and *papardello* with pesto. Pair any choice with a carafe of wine or bottle of Chinotto, a traditional Italian soda, and you'll be good to go – or stay, rather. You'll find another outpost, but with a more organic-vegetarian bent, in the Village, at **Quartino Bottega Organica** (Map p450; ☎ 212-529-5133; 11 Bleecker St).

RUBEN'S EMPANADAS

Map p450   Argentine $

☎ 212-962-5330; 64 Fulton St at Gold St; ⏲ lunch Mon-Fri; ⓜ A, C to Broadway–Nassau St or J, M, Z, 2, 3, 4, 5 to Fulton St

Though there's no decor to speak of at this bustling storefront, which is mainly a quickie takeout shop for office workers tired of hot dogs and deli sandwiches, there are plenty of tasty treats worth talking about. The deal here is, clearly, empanadas, and the non-greasy, stuffed South American pastries are delicious. Find the requisite beef and chicken versions, along with more unique versions including broccoli with mozzarella and ricotta, Argentine sausage; breakfast stuffings include eggs and veggies, while dessert versions are sweetened with gooey guavas or cherries.

TRIBECA & SOHO

Expect a dose of fabulousness in either of these foodie destinations. That means high ceilings, stylish crowds and excited dins rising over the lovely clatter of wine glasses, and of forks happily diving into cuisines that run the gamut from French and Italian to Vietnamese, Japanese, vegan and that ol' fave: haute eclectic.

BALTHAZAR

Map p450   French Bistro $$$

☎ 212-965-1414; 80 Spring St btwn Broadway & Crosby St; ⏲ breakfast, lunch & dinner; ⓜ 6 to Spring St

You'd think folks would be way over this bustling (OK, *loud*) bistro, but it retains its superstar status, attracting A-listers mixed in with eager locals and tourists. Perhaps it's the location, which makes it a convenient shopping-spree rest area. Or it could be the uplifting ambience, with big, mounted mirrors, cozy high-backed booths or the airy high ceilings and wide windows. But it's most likely the something-for-everyone menu, which features a stellar raw bar, steak frites, salad nicoise, roasted beet salad and prawn risotto with sage and butternut squash. The kitchen stays open till 2am Thursday to Saturday. Brunch here is a very crowded (and delicious) production.

BOULEY Map pp444-5 — French $$$

☎ 212-694-2525; www.davidbouley.com; 120 W Broadway at Duane St; 🕑 lunch & dinner; 🚇 A, C, 1, 2, 3 to Chambers St

The home base of celebrity chef David Bouley is the stuff of legend: tender roasted monkfish with a fragrant stew of razor clams and asparagus; lobster with broad beans and haricot verts in a succulent port-wine and blood-orange sauce; Mediterranean rouget with rose olives and saffron. There's even a rare Kobe beef option, a serious splurge at $110 for a decadent 10oz slab. It's all served in one of two elegant rooms – the red room or the white room – to some of the most discriminating eaters in New York. And that's saying something. So book early, or be prepared to accept a dinner seating at 10:30pm or later. Or settle (hardly!) for the **Bouley Bakery, Café & Market** (130 W Broadway at Duane St; $$; 🕑 bakery 7:30am-7:30pm, dinner Tue-Sat) right next door, where you can dine on sushi, wild mushroom salad or grilled halibut, or purchase sinfully rich baked goods to go.

BREAD TRIBECA Map pp444-5 — Italian $$

☎ 212-334-8282; 301 Church St btwn Walker & White Sts; 🕑 lunch & dinner; 🚇 A, C, E to Canal St or 1 to Franklin St

It's all about sandwiches here – get it? – only 'sandwich' is a bit of an understatement when it comes to the delicacies you'll find at this high-ceilinged, hipster-filled spot. Creations flowing out of the open kitchen, courtesy of a former Babbo (p237) chef, include homebaked ciabatta and baguettes slathered with combos like prosciutto with mozzarella, sardines with tomatoes and chicken with avocado. Non-bread–based fare ranges from handmade ravioli served with duck to fresh salads, grilled meats and pizzas. The original **Bread** (Map p450; ☎ 212-334-1015; 20 Spring St btwn Elizabeth & Mott Sts) is in nearby Nolita.

BUBBY'S PIE COMPANY

Map pp444-5 — Comfort Food $$

☎ 212-219-0666; 120 Hudson St at N Moore St; 🕑 breakfast, lunch & dinner daily, brunch Sun; 🚇 1 to Franklin St

Though it started in 1990 as a pie company, 'Bubby's,' as it's fondly called, is now one of the most popular eateries in Tribeca. The old buzz about it being a magnet for local celebs has died down, but the low key standby is a great draw for families with kids – who are welcome and easily sated here with a special kids' menu, brimming with classics from chicken fingers to spaghetti with butter. (Kids under eight even eat free for dinner on Sunday!) Adults find plenty to get excited about, too, from the mellow, high-ceilinged ambience to the excellent takes on homey basics: luscious mac-and-cheese, slow cooked BBQ including Texas-style brisket, grits, matzo-ball soup buttermilk fried chicken and a selection of Mexican plates – all melt-in-your-mouth good. Reviving the buzz lately has been the Dumbo, Brooklyn outpost of **Bubby's** (Map p462; ☎ 718-222-0666; 1 Main St), with a swankier dining room and sweeping views of the city.

FRANKLIN STATION CAFÉ

Map pp444-5 — Malaysian $

☎ 212-274-8525; www.franklinstationcafé.com; 222 W Broadway btwn Franklin & N Moore Sts; 🕑 breakfast, lunch & dinner; 🚇 1 to Franklin St

This small, airy café, with an exposed stone wall and simple wooden tables and chairs, features a unique, refreshing menu that's a thrill to stumble upon any time of day. While breakfast items are an assortment of Eastern and Western cuisine – including brioche French toast, poached eggs with caviar and salmon, and various types of traditional

Think big when it comes to New York breakfasts

congee (rice porridge), including one piled with shredded chicken – lunch and dinner are more focused on Malaysian cuisine. Try the spicy shrimp with noodles and bean sprouts, curried squid or vegetables, or grilled salmon in turmeric ginger sauce.

HONMURA AN Map p450   Japanese $$

☎ 212-334-5253; 170 Mercer St btwn Houston & Prince Sts; ⓨ lunch & dinner Wed-Fri, dinner Tue & Sun; ⓔ R, W to Prince St

Join the fans who flock to this serene and un-hyped space for some of the most wonderful homemade noodles in the city. *Soba* and *udon* noodles are served hot or cold and topped with everything from giant prawn tempura to fish cakes and wild Japanese greens. There's also a small selection of fresh sashimi, and thoroughly unique (if not odd) appetizers grouped in boxes, one of which features '*soba* gnocchi.' If you can't decide what to try, just keep on ordering from the range of small plates; homemade tofu in hot broth, Japanese pickles and sliced smoked duck should all keep you satisfied.

KITTICHAI Map p450   Nouveau Thai $$

☎ 212-219-2000; www.kittichairestaurant.com; ground fl, Sixty Thompson, 60 Thompson St btwn Broome & Spring Sts; ⓨ breakfast, lunch & dinner; ⓔ C, E to Spring St

Ever since this dramatic and soothing space opened in 2004, it's garnered rave reviews – not only for its unique take on Thai food, but for its sleek and highly detailed interior design, which features intricately wood-carved walls, backlit scrims of silk shantung and creatively displayed fresh orchids. The thrills don't stop at the visual, though, as the menu is both traditional and wonderfully creative. Choose from seductive Thai tapas (limestone tartlet with minced chicken, marinated monkfish in pandan leaves, and more) and mains, which include a roasted red curry with vegetables, braised short ribs in green curry or a rich seared aged sirloin with fermented black bean and whiskey sauce. No pad Thai here, sorry.

SPARKY'S Map p450   Organic Fast Food & Snacks $

☎ 212-334-3035; 333 Lafayette St at Bleecker St; ⓨ 8am-midnight Mon-Fri, 10am-midnight Sat, 10am-10pm Sun; ⓔ 6 to Bleecker St

This skinny new snack spot, enclosed on each side by a glass storefront, is only about

8ft wide. But it's filled with cheap, tasty, high-quality fast foods. Its hot dogs, available in beef or soy, are served on fresh challah-like rolls and topped with anything from blue cheese to roasted jalapeños. There are real ice cream or Tofutti sandwiches, grilled cheese, hand cut fries and, for breakfast, locally-made yogurts and granola with milk. Everything is organic and family farmed.

CHINATOWN

In addition to being a long-time haven for authentically Chinese bargain meals – and for the mobs of visitors who seek them – Chinatown has also evolved into a spot for all sorts of pan-Asian fare (still, for the most part, incredibly cheap). The area is now luring foodies from all over the city who hadn't particularly thought of the area as a destination dining spot only five or so years ago. If you're up for a true culinary adventure, leave the guidebook at your hotel room, take a subway to Canal St, and start trolling the crammed and winding streets south of here, stopping in to eat at anyplace that tickles your fancy. For dessert, try to sniff out one of the many bubble-tea lounges or sweet-smelling Chinese bakeries.

BO KY RESTAURANT

Map pp444-5   Pan-Asian $

☎ 212-406-2292; 80 Bayard St btwn Mott & Mulberry Sts; ⓨ breakfast, lunch & dinner; ⓔ J, M, N, Q, R, W, Z, 6 to Canal St

The food here is incredibly cheap and amazingly delicious. This place is home to nearly three dozen types of soup with exotic ingredients and usually featuring some form of noodle, pork or chicken (vegetarians should be wary); the fish-ball flat noodle, curry chicken rice noodle and 'combination soup' are particularly popular. Join the chattering locals who pack into the simple setting for homey meals served by brusque waiters.

CANTON

Map pp444-5   Cantonese $$$

☎ 212-226-4441; 45 Division St btwn the Bowery & Market St; ⓨ lunch & dinner Tue-Sat; ⓔ F to East Broadway

The mild, gracious dishes here rely on quality ingredients – fish, poultry and pork – rather than spicy sauces or deep-fried skins. Tucked away near the Manhattan Bridge, this understated space has turned out authentic favorites for nearly 50 years. With fresh basics like ginger-scallion noodles, breast of duck, sautéed tofu with pork, and the house-special carp (which much be ordered in advance), it's hard to go wrong if it's a real Chinese feast that you're after.

DOYERS VIETNAMESE RESTAURANT

Map pp444-5   Vietnamese $

☎ 212-513-1521; 11 Doyers St btwn the Bowery & Pell St; ☺ lunch & dinner; ◉ J, M, N, Q, R, W, Z, 6 to Canal St

Everything about this place is an adventure: its location, on the curvy little barber–shop-lined street of Doyers; its ambience, in a cave-like, below-street-level hideaway with old-school charm; and the lengthy menu, with curiously yummy dishes including crispy fried tilapia, shrimp-papaya salad, curried eel and a slew of vegetarian offerings, from fried rice stick with vegetables to curried watercress.

18 ARHANS

Map pp444-5   Vegetarian Asian $

☎ 212-941-8986; 227 Centre St btwn Grand & Broome Sts; ☺ 10:30am-7:30pm Mon-Fri, 1-6pm Sun; ◉ 6 to Spring St

Billed as a place serving 'vegetarian comfort food,' the menu here is similar to that of its two pure-veg competitors in the 'hood (Vegetarian Paradise 1 and 2 and Vegetarian Dim Sum House). But the food tastes fresher and lighter here, and the mood inside is a bit more tranquil and friendly. The extensive menu, which offers everything from soba-based noodle dishes to fat dumplings, features unique dishes including its mock-ham omelette served over rice, mock beef with orange, and a vegetarian BBQ with edamame (green soybean), broccoli and tofu in a tangy smoky sauce. Refreshing iced teas and juices, like the ginger honey juice, complement the food deliciously.

JAYA Map pp444-5   Malaysian $$

☎ 212-219-3331; 90 Baxter St btwn Walker & White Sts; ☺ lunch & dinner; ◉ J, M, N, Q, R, W, Z, 6 to Canal St

Though it's not known for its service (not many spots in Chinatown are (it's part of the authentic charm), this place does turn out a mean plate of mai fun (thin, stir-fried rice noodles). The otak-otak (grilled fish

wrapped in a banana leaf) is a tasty and unusual appetizer, and nearly 30 different noodle dishes will keep you occupied through a cocktail or two, and definitely fuel pre-dinner discussions. Egg noodles come swathed in fish paste, tofu and vegetables, while mee siam nyonya adds boiled egg, shrimp and spicy chili sauce to the mix. Wontons are top notch, as are specialties such as pineapple-coconut fried rice and mango chicken in spicy basil sauce. There's an extensive vegetarian selection, too – not always easy to come by in authentic Chinatown spots – with options including eggplant with Thai green curry and mixed vegetables with preserved bean curd.

MEI LAI WAH COFFEE HOUSE

Map pp444-5   Chinese Bakery $

☎ 212-925-5438; 64 Bayard St at Elizabeth St; ☺ breakfast, lunch & dinner; ◉ J, M, N, Q, R, W, Z, 6 to Canal St

You must get here in the morning to witness the true splendor of this teeny, battered old storefront bakery. The city's best steamed pork and sesame buns are doled out warm and fresh to the throngs of Filipinos and Chinese who work in the neighborhood, shoving and yelling to get their morning fix of these heavenly puffs of dough. The coffee is excellent, too – a Chinatown rarity.

ORIGINAL CHINATOWN ICE CREAM

FACTORY Map pp444-5   Ice Cream $

☎ 212-608-4170; www.chinatownicecreamfactory .com; 65 Bayard St; ☺ 11am-10pm; ◉ J, M, N, Q, R, W, Z, 6 to Canal St

Head to this awesome place for scoops of exotic flavors such as avocado, durian, red bean and sesame. It sure beats the nearby Häagen Dazs in terms of ice-cream adventures.

LITTLE ITALY & NOLITA

While Little Italy is barely hanging on, its borders being forever encroached upon by Chinatown and other neighborhoods, shrinking its culinary scene to but a handful of red-sauce spots that attract mostly tourists, Nolita has been picking up where its neighbor leaves off. Though it's just a tiny little geographic pocket, Nolita's draws are many, and its ever-trendy eateries, which range from Asian to Cuban, continue to pack in the hipsters. Still, Little Italy does

Eating

LITTLE ITALY & NOLITA

231

have some tasty charm left; stroll Mulberry St and its surrounding blocks to find old-world bakeries and food shops that'll wow your senses.

CAFÉ GITANE

Map p450   Mediterranean Bistro $$
☎ 212-334-9552; 242 Mott St; ⏲ 5:30-11:30pm; ◉ N, R, W to Prince St

Gitane is the type of place you'd expect to see everywhere in, say, Paris or Barcelona – an ochre-lit space with deep banquettes and warm air, and delicious smells of baking bread and garlic hitting a pan. Outside, slouchy but wealthy artist types are smoking Gauloises, and everyone is drinking coffee. But the food at this perfect shopping-break spot is good, too. The diverse menu features yellowfin tuna seviche, spicy meatballs in tomato turmeric sauce with a boiled egg, Greek salad on focaccia and a heart-of-palm salad.

DA NICO

Map p450   Italian $$-$$$
☎ 212-343-1212; 164 Mulberry St; ⏲ lunch & dinner; ◉ 6 to Spring St

If you're bent on a Little Italy dinner, Da Nico, right in the center of what's left of Little Italy and named for owner Nicholas 'Nico' Luizza, is a classic. Though it hasn't been around all that long, the restaurant is family run and traditional in feel – exposed-brick walls, light-wood tables and chairs centered around a coal-fired pizza oven. The extensive restaurant highlights both northern and southern Italian cuisine that's red-sauce predictable but quite delicious. There's shrimp scampi, chicken cacciatore, aged shell steak and pasta galore – pesto gnocchi, rigatoni with eggplant, tortellini in cream sauce, you name it. Just beware of summer-night tourist mob scenes.

LA ESQUINA

Map p450   Mexican $$
☎ 646-613-1333; 106 Kenmare St; ⏲ 24hr; ◉ 6 to Spring St

This new, unique spot is housed in a long-time greasy spoon that sits within the neat little triangle formed by Cleveland Pl and Lafayette St. It's three places really: a stand-while-you-eat taco window, a casual Mexican café and, downstairs, a cozy, extremely hip cave of a restaurant. You can't even go down the stairs unless you've got a reservation (a woman with a clipboard guards the entryway), but once you're in,

you'll enjoy a feast of melt-in-your mouth chorizo tacos, rubbed pork tacos and mango and jicama salads, among other delicious options.

PEASANT

Map p450   Italian $$$
☎ 212-965-9511; www.peasantnyc.com; 194 Elizabeth St btwn Spring & Prince Sts; ⏲ dinner; ◉ 6 to Spring St

The schtick here is one of old-fashioned simplicity and quality – a warm dining area of bare oak tables structured around a brick hearth and open kitchen, which lovingly turns out hearty, pan-Italian, mostly meat-based fare. And so far it's been working, as Peasant has made it onto various best-restaurant lists in town, and always seems to be filled with a crowd of sophisticates. Chef-owner Frank DiCarlo built an impressive NYC résumé before opening his own place, and here his specialties include solid stunners like gnocchi with wild mushrooms, oven-baked rabbit and *zuppa di pesce*.

PUBLIC

Map p450   Eclectic $$
☎ 212-343-7011, 343-7011; 210 Elizabeth btwn Rivington & Stanton Sts; ⏲ lunch & dinner daily, brunch Sat & Sun; ◉ 6 to Spring St

This place tries, and pretty much succeeds, to be all things to all people – all those who like high-concept gourmet grub with a healthy dose of strange wild game thrown in, that is. The place, designed to honor the concept of public spaces from libraries to schools, features a mix of futuristic and old-fashioned details (such as a card catalogue and gleaming sage tiles in a modern-vibe bathroom). The hip, young clientele seems buoyed by the ambience. The completely eclectic menu includes, among many other delicious oddities, chestnut risotto cake with pickled squash and pine nuts, striped bass with parsnips and edamame, grilled venison with fennel, and a strikingly odd appetizer of grilled kangaroo. Public is a delicious, if newfangled, experience, to be sure.

RICE

Map p450   Asian-Caribbean $$
☎ 212-226-5775; www.riceny.com; 227 Mott St btwn Prince & Spring Sts; ⏲ noon-midnight; ◉ 6 to Spring St

A vegetarian's delight and a delicious cross-continental adventure for just about anyone up for the journey, this reasonably-

KEEPIN' IT REAL: NYC'S MOST AUTHENTIC ETHNIC 'HOODS

Sure, Manhattan's Little Italy and Curry Row are fine – if you like mobs of tourists desperately seeking authenticity. But you can truly find it in the outer boroughs, where the latest waves of immigrants have settled and continue to arrive. Below, a guide to going 'round the world in a few neighborhoods:

- Bukharian: Rego Park (Map p467), Queens, instead of…well…there's nothing quite like this 'hood, which specializes in foods loved by Jews of the former Soviet Republic. Take the R, V or G subway to Rego Park.
- Chinese: Sunset Park (Map pp460–1), Brooklyn, instead of Chinatown. Instead of mobs of New Jersey tourists buying Hello Kitty wallets you get Asian crowds, top notch eateries (including 24-hour dim sum spots) and a feeling that you're far, far away. Take the N train to Eighth Ave.
- Greek: Astoria (Map pp380–1), Queens, or Bay Ridge (Map pp460–1), Brooklyn, instead of Midtown diners. While Astoria is the biggest, most well-known Greek enclave, you can also find the beginnings of feta-cheese shops and grilled-octopus restaurants in the formerly Italian enclave of Bay Ridge. Take the subway N or W to Astoria-Ditmars Blvd for Queens, and the R to 86th St for Brooklyn.
- Indian: Jackson Heights (Map p442), Queens, instead of E 6th St. Go on a cultural adventure filled with sari shops, *thali* plates and *dosas*, and true Bollywood theater. Take subway E, F, G, R or 7 to Roosevelt Ave.
- Irish: Woodlawn (Map pp468–9), the Bronx, instead of Manhattan's Third Ave Irish bars. Say goodbye to drunken frat boys and hello to correctly poured pints of Guinness, authentic bangers 'n' mash, just-arrived youngsters and, of course, about a dozen great pubs. Take the 4 subway to Woodlawn.
- Italian: Belmont (Map pp468–9), the Bronx, or Bensonhurst (Map pp460–1), Brooklyn, instead of Little Italy. Trade in mediocre restaurants for excellent eateries, samples of fresh mozzarella in the Arthur Ave Market (p352), to-die-for-cannoli and serious *Soprano*-character dead ringers. For Belmont, take the B, D or 4 subway to Fordham Rd, then the Bx 12 bus to Hoffman St; for Bensonhurst, take the M or W subway to 79th St.
- Jewish old-world: Borough Park (Map pp460–1), Brooklyn, instead of Manhattan's Lower East Side. Rather than grasping at straws with the handful of remaining bagel and appetizing shops, go for the gusto in this tight knit Hasidic community (just be respectful, of course). Take the subway F to Ditmas Ave.
- Korean: Flushing (Map p467), Queens, instead of Koreatown. Goodbye Macy's shoppers, hello kimchi buyers. Take the 7 train to Flushing–Main St.
- Russian: Brighton Beach (Map p466), Brooklyn, instead of Midtown restaurants. No more vodka-tinis, please – just the rudely staffed food markets, bustling nightclubs and boardwalk that feels like Odessa on the sea. Take subway D to Ocean Pkwy.

priced favorite has expanded to include three other outposts, two of which are in very hip 'hoods in Brooklyn. It's all about rice here, as you may have guessed, and you can choose from one of the 10 types on the menu – from traditional basmati and brown to specialty green (infused with cilantro, parsley and spinach) and Thai black (steamed in coconut milk) – to accompany your main dish. The mains are treats, with highlights that include savory vegetarian meatballs made from a tofu-miso blend, green-lentil stew, jerk chicken wings, and a creamy Thai coconut curry studded with veggies, shrimp or chicken.

LOWER EAST SIDE

It's impossible to keep up with the offerings in these parts, as slinky lounges with elaborate nouveau-fusion menus and instant A-list crowds seem to pop up anew or replace 'old' places on a weekly basis.

Though visitors won't find many remnants of the classic, old-world-Jewish LES dining scene, there are few stellar holdouts: Katz's Deli (p234), Sammy's Roumanian Steakhouse (p234) and Yonah Shimmel Bakery (p235). Otherwise, it's strictly modern, global, hipster fare here, folks.

CUBE 63 Map p449   Sushi $$$
☎ 212-228-6751; 63 Clinton St btwn Rivington & Stanton Sts; ☽ lunch & dinner; ⦿ F to Delancey St or J, M, Z to Delancey–Essex Sts
The fare at this space-age, glowing refuge among the low-lit cubicle dining rooms on this culinary row is outrageously good. You will find standard sushi rolls and sashimi, all fresh and wonderful, plus signature fusions, such as the Mexican roll (jalapeño, spicy sauce and whitefish), volcano (crab meat, toasted shrimp and eel sauce) or the decadent 63 roll (spicy tuna, avocado and lobster salad). The clientele here is as decidedly hip and sassy as the menu.

'INOTECA Map p449 — Italian Snacks $$

☎ 212-614-0473; 98 Rivington at Ludlow St; ⏱ lunch & dinner daily, brunch Sat & Sun; ◉ F, V to Lower East Side–Second Ave

Tuck yourself in at one of the chunky square tables of this airy, dark-wood–paneled corner haven and choose from *tramezzini* (small sandwiches on white or whole-wheat bread), panini (pressed sandwiches) and bruschetta options – or get one of each. The nibbly bits and pressed sandwiches are all delicious and affordable. The truffled egg toast, a square of bread hollowed out in its center and filled with egg, truffles and fontina cheese, is a signature favorite. But you can't go wrong, whether you choose the beet-orange-mint salad, vegetable lasagna built with layers of eggplant rather than pasta, or a plate of garlicky mussels. Best of all is the list of 200 wines, 25 of them available by the glass. There's always a wait here, but it's worth it. The tasty treats are heavenly. And if you find yourself hankering for some truffled toast in the West Village, visit the original pressed-sandwich outpost of 'Ino (Map p448; ☎ 212-989-5769; 21 Bedford St btwn Sixth Ave & Downing St).

KATZ'S DELI Map p449 — Jewish Deli $

☎ 212-254-2246; 205 E Houston St at Ludlow St; ⏱ breakfast, lunch & dinner; ◉ F, V to Lower East Side–Second Ave

This was where Meg Ryan faked her famous orgasm in *When Harry Met Sally*, and, while the classic deli grub may not have the same effect on you, it'll probably come pretty close. The vast, worn-out room is infused with old-world nostalgia – especially the WWII 'Send a salami to your boy in the army' – as are the crusty guys behind the counter who dole out crisp kosher dills, frothy chocolate egg creams and pastrami and corned beef piled high on fresh rye. It's a true New York experience – especially at 2am, when trendy clubbers pile in for sobering sandwiches.

SAMMY'S ROUMANIAN STEAK HOUSE Map p449 — Eastern European $$$

☎ 212-673-0330; 157 Chrystie St btwn Delancey & Rivington St; ⏱ dinner; ◉ F to Delancey St or J, M, Z to Delancey–Essex Sts

A low-ceilinged Jewish old-world holdout that draws mostly nostalgic suburbanites with roots in both Eastern Europe and Brooklyn, Sammy's is a seriously kitschy experience that must been seen to be believed. The food is strictly fat-laden, grandmotherly delicacies – massive skirt steaks bathed in garlic, chopped liver and fat potato pancakes, which many guests flavor with dollops of golden schmaltz, otherwise known as chicken fat, which sits in glass pancake-syrup dispensers on each table. In its 65 years here, Sammy's has seen it all, from junkies strewn in the park across the street to the construction of luxury high-rises all around the neighborhood. A visit here is like a wonderful, innocent time warp.

SCHILLER'S LIQUOR BAR

Map p449 — French bistro/Eclectic $$

☎ 212-673-0330, 260-4555; 131 Rivington St at Norfolk St; ⏱ dinner; ◉ F to Delancey St or J, M, Z to Delancey–Essex Sts

One of the most consistently happening spots in the 'hood, Schiller's brings a glow to this formerly dreary corner – both with its stunning bohemian-antique decor and with its fun and buzzing crowd. The food, which is very reasonably priced, covers all bases, and includes pork chops, steak frites, eggplant parma, cobb salad and spaghetti with pesto sauce. Its cute, sarcastic 'tude is made clear with its wine list – consisting simply of 'Cheap, Decent, Good,' and the pronouncement that 'Cheap is the best.' The bar is also a great place to hang. The huge popularity of Schiller's is easier to understand when you learn it's part of the Keith McNally empire – also responsible for Balthazar (p228) and Pastis (near Paradou, p239), among other faves.

TEANY Map p449 — Vegan Teahouse $

☎ 212-475-9190; 90 Rivington St btwn Ludlow & Orchard Sts; ⏱ breakfast, lunch & dinner till late; ◉ F to Delancey St or J, M Z to Delancey–Essex Sts

This teeny-tiny café, tucked below street level on a quietly hip block, is co-owned by famously vegan pop star Moby – which accounts for the animal-friendly fare served in the mellow, candlelit spot. The book-like menu boasts close to 100 teas, all served in individual teapots and ranging from the typical (spearmint, Irish breakfast) to the sublimely exotic (green sea anemone, white peony). You can also choose from beer and wine, frothy soy-infused coffees and delicious little foods including muffins, tea sandwiches (the cheddar-pickle and peanut butter–chocolate ones rock), excellent salads and scrumptious desserts.

WD 50 Map p449   American Creative $$$

☎ 212-477-2900; 50 Clinton St at Stanton St; ☾ dinner Mon-Sat; ◉ F to Delancey St or J, M, Z to Delancey–Essex Sts

Wylie Dufresne, the genius behind 71 Clinton Fresh Foods (just a few doors down) and one of the leaders in the full-throttle gentrification of this part of the 'hood, added this crowd-pleaser to his growing empire in 2003. It drew in VIPs and wannabes alike in a stream that hasn't slowed. Bamboo floors, a fireplace and exposed beams all highlight the provocative fare in this casual fine-dining hot spot: oysters with apples, olives and pistachios; skate served with preserved-lemon gnocchi and smoked scallions. Get ready to discover all the foods you never knew you loved.

YONAH SHIMMEL BAKERY

Map p450   Knishes $

☎ 212-477-2858; 137 E Houston St btwn Eldridge & Forsyth Sts; ☾ 9:30am-7pm; ◉ F, V to Lower East Side–Second Ave

Shimmel has been selling baked, fist-sized knishes for 92 years and knows how it's done. Choose from a large variety including potato, sweet potato, red cabbage, cheese and kasha – all stellar. You'll also find bagels, blintzes and cookies inside the diminutive old storefront, just a couple of doors away from the wonderful Landmark Sunshine Cinemas (p302) and the perfect pre- or post-movie nosh.

EAST VILLAGE

Here lies the epitome of what's beautiful in New York's dining scene – mind-blowing variety, which can cover several continents as well as the whole gamut of budgets in just a single city block. The neighborhood's roots lie heavily with Ukrainian traditions, and you can still find your fair share of low key pierogi palaces, especially along Avenue A and up and down its lower cross streets. Pizza places are also ubiquitous, along with spots for sushi, vegetarian and Indian fare – especially on the carnivalesque strip of E 6th St between First and Second Aves, otherwise known as Curry Row, where cheap, decent Indian restaurants are a dime a dozen. On a sad note, at the time of writing at least, is the closure due to a major rent hike of the legendary Second Avenue Deli, longtime favorite holdout spot for fat turkey or pastrami sandwiches on wafer-thin rye bread. New Yorkers were keeping their fingers crossed for a possible reopening, but it didn't look hopeful.

B&H DAIRY Map p212   Kosher Dairy $

☎ 212-505-8065; 127 Second Ave btwn St Marks Pl & E 7th St; ☾ breakfast, lunch & dinner; ◉ 6 to Astor Pl

This is a classic lunch counter with some of the most authentic Jewish-dairy comfort food and crusty old 'tude around. Everything is homemade, fresh and vegetarian, including the six types of soups on offer daily (the borscht and mushroom barley rock), which, along with a pillowy slice of fresh-baked challah, will fill you up for hours – and for only about six bucks. Note that just taking a

C'mon, pizza lover, make my day

IN SEARCH OF THE PERFECT SLICE

It's pretty hard to find a *bad* slice of pizza in NYC, where everything from greasy, floppy triangles to thick, whole-wheat squares topped with goat cheese and fennel are fresh, hot and delicious anytime of day or night. But sometimes you're just not satisfied until you can find the best. Here are some Manhattan winners (for Brooklyn, see Organized Tours, p112).

John's Famous Pizzeria (Map p448; ☎ 212-243-1680; 278 Bleecker St) The much-ballyhooed West Village outpost has pies that are thin but chewy, saucy but sweet.

Arturo's Pizzeria (Map p448; ☎ 212-677-3820; 106 W Houston St) Arturo's has matzo-thin, crispy crusts and fresh toppings, with a bustling dining room featuring live piano music.

Stromboli Pizzeria (Map p448; ☎ 212-255-0812; 112 University Pl) For takeout only, this spot makes an impression with spicy, plentiful sauce.

Lombardi's (Map p450; ☎ 212-941-7994; 32 Spring St) A Soho fave, this place offers tangy sauce, fresh mozzarella, sky-high toppings and a thick crust embedded with sesame seeds.

Patsy's Pizzeria (Map p449; ☎ 212-534-9783; 2287 First Ave) The 75-year-old original of five locations, it boasts extra-large, coal-fired triangles.

Two Boots Pizzerias (Map p449; ☎ 212-254-1919; 42 Ave A) Shake things up with slices topped with all sorts of stuff from marinated chicken and plum tomatoes to barbecued shrimp, crawfish andouille and jalapeños, all with cornmeal-dusted crusts.

seat at the lunch counter does not guarantee you'll be waited on – you've got to speak up here, sister! But once you do you'll feel part of a warm, diverse little lunchtime family.

BAO 111 Map p212   Vietnamese $$
☎ 212-254-7773; 111 Ave C at E 7th St; dinner till 2am; M14–Ave C

A new addition to the way-east part of the 'hood, sleek Bao offers an oasis of warm design and upscale versions of Vietnamese classics to a hyper-hip, mussed and gorgeous crowd. Top-shelf sakes, warm sakes infused with fruits and dangerously delicious sake-tinis get you in the right frame of mind to enjoy celebratory dishes like lemongrass curry shrimp, iron-pot chicken with quail eggs, braised vegetable and curry tofu and grilled lemongrass lamb chops. Desserts, like the steamed black rice pudding with roasted mango and coconut sauce, are sublime.

CHIKALICIOUS Map p212   Dessert $$
☎ 212-995-9511; www.chikalicious.com; 203 E 10th St btwn First & Second Aves; 3–11:30pm Wed-Sun; 6 to Astor Pl

First things first: dessert. Chikalicious is New York's first (and only) dessert bar – a place where you get to sit around an open kitchen and settle in as if you were going to have a full-fledged meal, but instead get to live the fantasy of indulging in a three-course dessert feast. 'Meals' include an amusing and assorted petit fours, and

pairing suggestions for dessert wines, ports and champagnes. And the desserts themselves? They're insanely delicious, of course, and include a long list of delicacies such as chocolate pudding with espresso Genoise cake, sweet-potato brûlée with eggnog ice cream, warm chocolate tart with pink peppercorn ice cream and a tableside shaved truffle. Heaven indeed.

COUNTER Map p212   Vegetarian Eclectic $$
☎ 212-982-5870; 105 First Ave btwn E 6th & E 7th Sts; lunch & dinner Tue-Sat; F, V to Lower East Side–Second Ave

Sit at the round counter in the center of the airy space and order one of several organic or biodynamic wines with an elegant plate of cashew-kalamata pâté. Or settle in at one of the tables here, where you'll have more room to linger over fresh and creative fare – much of it enhanced by ingredients grown on the roof garden – like cauliflower 'risotto,' grilled vegetable napoleon or seitan steak au poivre. Daily specials are seasonal and excellent, and the crowd is cool *and* down-to-earth.

IL BAGATTO Map p212   Italian $$
☎ 212-228-3703; 192 E 2nd St btwn Aves A & B; lunch & dinner; F, V to Lower East Side–Second Ave

A bustling yet romantic little nook, this spot has thoroughly delicious Italian creations at exceptionally reasonable prices – plus an excellent wine list and a dedicated sommelier who will pour you tastes before you decide (a wonderful oddity in such an affordable and casual dining room). The frazzled yet warm and quirky owners will greet you like old friends – though be prepared to wait a while even if you've made a reservation; that's just the way it works at this laid-back neighborhood spot. Menu items tend toward the sinful side, with highlights that include cheese and spinach ravioli swimming in butter and sage sauce, homemade gnocchi in gorgonzola sauce, and paper-thin beef slices sautéed in olive oil and white wine. Don't miss the desserts – they're astounding.

PRUNE Map p212   Creative American $$
☎ 212-677-6221; 54 E 1st St btwn First & Second Aves; ⏲ lunch & dinner daily, brunch Sat & Sun; ◉ F, V to Lower East Side–Second Ave
Rich meals are the order of the day here, and you'll find hearty offerings including roast suckling pig, rich sweetbreads and sausage-studded concoctions. The cramped dining room is well lit and wide open, bistro-style, on warm evenings, providing a lovely vantage point onto the quaint stretch of 1st St. It's always crowded – especially for Sunday brunch, when late sleepers rouse themselves for top notch Bloody Marys (in nine varieties), lox and oysters.

GREENWICH VILLAGE

Budget-wise, the Village is home to the highest and the lowest links in the food chain – from through-the-roof Babbo to beautifully cheap Manna Bento and everything in between. This is NYU land, so tasty budget meals like falafel and pizza slices that appeal to penny-pinching students aren't difficult to find; but it's also high-rent territory, so upscale destination dining rooms are also a cinch to come by. Stroll the streets south of Washington Sq Park to find some great cafés, like the wonderful Café Reggio on MacDougal St, where you can kick back with a steaming latte and sweet biscotti and think about how bohemian Greenwich Village got its start.

BABBO Map p448   Italian $$$
☎ 212-777-0303; 110 Waverly Pl at MacDougal St; ⏲ dinner; ◉ A, B, C, D, E, F, V to W 4th St
Redheaded, devilish-grinning celebrity chef Mario Batali – whose empire has expanded to include Lupa in Soho, Esca in the Theater

TOP FIVE EATS DOWNTOWN

- Babbo (left) – Mario Batali's Greenwich Village Italian king
- Chikalicious (opposite) – sweet dessert fests, with the respect of a meal
- 'Inoteca (p234) – perfect wine, panini and ambience
- Kittichai (p230) – stunning Thai like you've never seen it
- WD 50 (p235) – star chef thinks way outside the box

District, Otto Enoteca Pizzeria in the Village, Casa Mono/Bar Jamon in Gramercy, Del Posto in the Meatpacking District and Bistro du Vent in Midtown – is perhaps best known for this, his first and perhaps most popular New York eatery. The split-level dining room in a romantic Village house pulsates with both the excitement of Batali's cult-like fans and the throb of his favorite rock-and-roll dinner soundtracks. Reviews rave consistently about his simple, done-to-perfection fare (not for vegetarians) like lamb's brain with lemon and sage, goose-liver ravioli, grilled guinea hen and osso buco for two. Reserve early or you won't get in.

BLUE HILL Map p448   American $$$
☎ 212-539-1776; 75 Washington Pl btwn Sixth Ave & Washington Sq; ⏲ dinner; ◉ A, B, C, D, E, F, V to W 4th St
A place for Slow Food junkies with deep pockets, Blue Hill is a low-key, high-class dining spot where you can be certain that everything on your plate is fresh and seasonal. Gifted chef Dan Barber, who hails from a farm family in the Berkshires, Massachusetts, uses harvests from that land, as well as from farms in upstate New York, to create his widely praised fare. Expect barely seasoned, perfectly ripe vegetables, which serve to highlight centerpieces of cod in almond broth, Berkshire pork stewed with four types of beans, and grass-fed lamb with white beans and new potatoes. The space itself, slightly below street level and housed in a landmark former speakeasy on a quaint Village block, is sophisticated and serene.

COLORS Map p449   Global Eclectic $$
☎ 212-777-8443; 417 Lafayette St btwn Astor Pl & E 4th St; ◉ 6 to Astor Pl
Just opened in early 2006 by former employees of Window on the World, this is a living

tribute to the owners' former coworkers, who perished atop the towers on September 11. Run as a worker-owned restaurant co-op, the place transfers that loving vibe into its worldly theme, with many of the international eats inspired by family recipes. Varied fare includes smoked seitan with apricot-basil–split pea chutney and a Haitian-style dish of stewed conch with radishes and saffron mayonnaise. A huge map of the world, designed by Maritime Hotel designer Jim Walrod, graces the modern dining room.

EN JAPANESE BRASSERIE

Map p448   Modern Japanese $$

☎ 212-647-9196; 5 Hudson St at Leroy St; ☾ lunch & dinner; ◉ 1 to Houston St

This high-ceilinged space is anchored by a wide sushi bar centered in the room. You'll know you've entered one place special by the amazing earthy yet modern decor and the exuberant welcome you'll get from the chefs in the open kitchen. Menu options are sublime and range from snow crab tempura with avocado, to black cod in miso. Perhaps the biggest excitement, though, is the range of freshly-made tofus.

GOBO

Map p448   Vegetarian $$

☎ 212-255-3242; Sixth Ave btwn Waverly Pl & W 8th St; ☾ lunch & dinner; ◉ A, B, C, D, E, F, V to W 4th St

One of those rare spots that caters to herbivores while also providing the type of low-lit ambience – and fabulous wine selection – that really tells you you're *dining*, Gobo is beloved by vegans and meat lovers alike. Its intricate, creative menu makes clever use of seitan, tofu and fresh veggies, and lets you choose from 'quick bites,' 'small plates' and 'large plates,' which is a perfect setup for ordering a whole lot of food and sharing among friends. Just a few of the many standouts include the pine-nut vegetable medley with lettuce wraps, green tea noodles with vegan Bolognese sauce, and sizzling soy cutlet platter with black-pepper sauce. Desserts make surprisingly mouth-watering uses of tofu and natural sweeteners.

MANNA BENTO

Map p448   Korean $

☎ 212-473-6162; 289 Mercer St btwn Waverly Pl & Eighth St; ☾ lunch & dinner Mon-Sat; ◉ N, R to 8th St–NYU

Blink and you might miss this obscure gem, known almost exclusively by NYU students

who sit solo, hunched over steaming plates and thick textbooks as a sweet lady in a little white bonnet doles out homemade meals. It's the best place around for delicious, bargain, home-style eats such as vegetables, spicy tofu, glass noodles and kimchi served over fluffy white rice for $5 every afternoon.

WEST VILLAGE & THE MEATPACKING DISTRICT

FLORENT

Map p448   French Diner $$

☎ 212-989-5779; 69 Gansevoort St btwn Greenwich & Washington Sts; ☾ breakfast & lunch Mon-Wed, 24hr Fri-Sun; ◉ A, C, E to 14th St or L to Eighth Ave

This all-night cool-person's hang colonized the Meatpacking District many moons ago. There are now endless options on all sides, but it's still a bustling spot that draws local workers and residents, as well as the new wave of tourists and the always-been-there slew of clubbers, who pile in at all hours for hangar steak, burgers, omelets, pork chops and convivial atmosphere. On the weekend closest to July 14, Florent takes over Gansevoort St for an open-air Bastille Day celebration.

MI COCINA

Map p448   Mexican $$

☎ 212-627-8273; 57 Jane at Hudson St; ☾ dinner daily, lunch Sat & Sun; ◉ A, C, E to 14th St or L to Eighth Ave

This festive, romantic spot has a lovely Mexican design – bright tiling, colorful mirrors and terra-cotta floors – and traditional fare. The twist is that it's upscale, slightly fusiony and expertly prepared, with a nod to not only the country's various regions, but to vegetarians as well. Delicious veggie enchiladas are stuffed with Swiss chard and roasted tomato-chipotle sauce, while a roasted zucchini-corn casserole is flavored with roasted tomatoes, cheese and cilantro. Usuals like grilled chicken and

Florent (above right), a Meatpacking District stalwart

roasted shrimp get jazzed up with Mexican oregano, white wine and artistic dabs of guacamole and sour cream. Top-shelf tequilas make for amazing cocktails, and sinful desserts make for dreamy endings.

PARADOU Map p448   French Bistro $$
☎ 212-463-8345; 8 Little W 12th St btwn Ninth Ave & Washington St; ☽ dinner; ☺ A, C, E to 14th St or L to Eighth Ave

Skip the trendy mob scene of Pastis across the street and settle into this minuscule haven instead. The hydrangea-heavy garden out the back is a mini-miracle in springtime, while the romantic little dining room is lovely all year round. Service is well-paced and supportive, not to mention performed by a handsome crew, who dole out tasty buckwheat crepes, panini and grilled fish dishes with a flourish. The wine list is stellar, with plenty of affordable options and by-the-glass pours served in individual mini-carafes.

SOY LUCK CLUB Map p448   Healthy Café $
☎ 212-229-9191; 115 Greenwich Ave at Jane St; ☽ 7am-10pm Mon-Fri, 9am-10pm Sat & Sun; ☺ A, C, E to 14th St or L to Eighth Ave

When it first opened, this storefront café seemed a bit too theme-oriented to last. Soy, after all, isn't the most sexy selling point. But here it stands, several years later – a cool corner filled with hip locals (who love the free WiFi), a flood of sunlight, and a counter bursting with compelling snacks and creative beverages. While many of the menu items are indeed soy-based – the soy chicken and fontina (wheat-free)

crepe, the tofu salad and avocado sandwich, and the mesclun, edamame and soynut salad, just for starters – there's plenty here for the soy-phobic. Panini, salads and brunch items, some even containing meat, abound. Best of all, everything is fresh and tasty, especially the signature drinks, which consist of soymilk, either steamed or iced, mixed with additions from dark chocolate to honey and ginger.

SPICE MARKET Map p448   South Asian $$
☎ 212-675-2322; 403 W 13th St at Ninth Ave; ☽ lunch & dinner; ☺ A, C, E to 14th St, L to Eighth Ave

Part of the Jean-Georges Vongerichten empire (Jean-Georges, Jo Jo, Vong etc), this became an instant fave of the Meatpacking District thanks to its theme-park-like design – 12,000 sq ft of intricately carved walls and traditional pagodas – and for its fun and fancy take on South Asian street foods, with an emphasis on India and Thailand. Shrimp and egg noodles, curried duck and cilantro-lime steak are among the flavorful dishes that get the nightclub-like throngs here all worked up. Beware that its initial days of being 'hot' have passed a bit, and the masses are now more likely to be tourists. Not that there's anything wrong with that.

SPOTTED PIG Map p448   Pub Fare $$
☎ 212-620-0393; 314 W 11th St at Greenwich St; ☽ lunch & dinner till 2am; ☺ A, C, E to 14th St or L to Eighth Ave

Another overnight sensation, this diminutive hideaway on a romantic, residential

Eating

WEST VILLAGE & THE MEATPACKING DISTRICT

LET'S DO BRUNCH

- Amy Ruth's (p251) – chicken 'n' waffles mixed with live gospel music make a Harlem magnet
- Balthazar (p228) – sour cream hazelnut waffles, smoked salmon with crème fraîche and brioche, and hangover drinks such as the potent Ramos Fizz… What's not to love?
- Elmo (p241) – find well-done classics like fat omelets, steak-and-eggs, buttermilk pancakes and diet-diva fruit plates
- Mana (p248) – vegans tired of shunning omelets for dry toast will rejoice in multigrain waffles, excellent tofu scrambles and creamy rice porridge
- Mi Cocina (opposite) – go for something completely different, like upscale *chilaquiles verdes,* of shredded chicken, tortillas and cheese, or *menudo,* the traditional hangover-remedy stew of tripe and hominy
- Park Terrace Bistro (p253) – go to the ends of the earth (or at least Manhattan) for Moroccan surroundings and eclectic options from pulled pork to blueberry pancakes
- Picnic Market and Café (p249) – new UWS gem that draws Sunday crowds with standout French toast and frittatas
- Prune (p237) – it's all about the nine types of over-garnished Bloody Marys – but the oysters, lox, fresh pastries and handsome hipsters don't hurt, either

West Village pocket packs in folks with its hearty, upscale blend of Italian-English-Irish pub fare. But instead of the usual bangers and mash, you get roasted salmon with organic veggies, char-grilled calf's liver with onions, roast pumpkin and pine-nut salad and the requisite (though above average) juicy burger. Pair anything with an icy stout and have yourself a merry little evening.

TAÏM Map p448　　　　　　　　　　Israeli $

☎ 212-691-1287; 222 Waverly St btwn Perry & W 11th Sts; ☽ lunch & dinner; ◉ 1, 2, 3 to 14th St
Not all Middle Eastern fare is alike, and this tiny little falafel joint proves it with its smoothies, salads and sass – and even its falafel, which ranges from the traditional, flavored with parsley and mint, to types spiced up with roasted red pepper or hot harissa. Whichever fried balls you choose, you'll get them stuffed into pita with creamy tahini sauce and a generous dose of Israeli salad – or you can try them all in a platter that gets you three tasty dips. Refreshing salads include carrots spiced with garlic and cumin, and a ruby-red dish of marinated beets. But the coolest part is a tie between the smoothies, which blend exotics from dates to tamarind, and the flow of Israeli regulars, who squeeze into this tiny storefront to chat in Hebrew with the beautiful staff.

CHELSEA

This is one of New York's newest gourmet ghettos, offering a stunning variety of dining options for all budgets. Though you'll find a bit of everything from around the globe here, you'll quickly notice a penchant for all things American – gourmet takes on burgers and diners, mostly. Though Elmo (opposite) is one of the best, there's been an explosion of this sort of diner/swanky lounge hybrid in the last couple of years, from Food Bar, the original, to Diner 24 and Cafeteria and beyond. Stroll up and down Seventh and Eighth Aves and check them all out, and perhaps pop in for a cocktail, as they are all total scenes – and total fun.

AMUSE Map pp446-7　　　　American Creative $$

☎ 212-929-9755; 108 W 18th St btwn Sixth & Seventh Aves; ☽ lunch & dinner; ◉ 1 to 18th St
Housed in a long, soothing dining hall punctuated by lots of backlighting and earth-tone banquettes that wrap around the perimeter, Amuse's main amusement is adding dashes of creativity to American standards. And the local and post-theater crowd that packs in here really loves it. Appetizer-size pulled pork sandwiches get spiced up with cumin, French fries are paired with a side of chipotle-aioli for dipping. Main courses feature handmade ricotta *cavatelli* with *chaterelles* and broccoli rabe (the best bet for vegetarians) and a succulent rack of lamb with a roasted potato gratin.

BETTER BURGER

Map pp446-7　　　　　　　　Organic Burgers $

☎ 212-989-6688; www.betterburger.nyc.com; 178 Eighth Ave at W 19th St; ☽ lunch & dinner; ◉ A, C, E to 14th St or 1 to 18th St
Catering to all the muscled, protein-loving boys in the 'hood is this brilliant take on the tired old burger. It's a sleek, bright, fast-food joint that offers organic, hormone-free burgers made from your choice of beef, ostrich, turkey, chicken, tuna, soy or mashed veggies. All come on homemade whole-wheat buns and are topped with homemade 'tomato zest,' a more sophisticated version of ketchup. To really treat yourself, add an order of the air-baked 'fries,' which are so delicious you'll swear they were dunked in grease, and one of several smoothies or bottled beers. Find other outposts of the fast-growing local chain in Midtown, Murray Hill and the Upper East Side; check the website for locations.

BLOSSOM Map pp446-7　　　　　Vegetarian $$

☎ 212-627-1144; 187 Ninth Ave btwn W 21st & W 22nd Sts; ☽ lunch & dinner; ◉ C, E to 23rd St
Chelsea, brimming with Americana spots that love to get creative with meat, is not known for being particularly vegetarian friendly. Enter Blossom, a fresh new addition to the 'hood that's hoping to turn that beat around. The sweet spot, housed in a Chelsea townhouse and owned by a healthy but creative husband-and-wife team, offers a casual juice-bar vibe by day and ambient, candle-lit, fireplace-warmed dining room by night. That's when its best charms come out, as the dinner-menu items span the globe and enliven the taste buds. Try the delicately sweet pumpkin gnocchi with wild mushrooms or tofu *fra diablo,* which pairs bean curd with spicy tomato sauce and broccoli rabe. Chocolate ganache tortes or pineapple crepes are the perfect way to end.

ALL-NIGHT EATS

In the city that never sleeps, it's not surprising that you'll find plenty of places where urbanites can always eat. Below, a small sampling of 24-hour favorites.

Bereket (Map p449; ☎ 212-475-7700; 187 E Houston St at Orchard St; $; ◉ F, V to Second Ave) Some of the best Turkish food in the city, available 24/7 and wedged between the East Village and the Lower East Side.

Empire Diner (Map pp446–7; ☎ 212-243-2736; 210 Tenth Ave at W 22nd St; $$; ◉ C, E to 23rd St) Dine alfresco, in the fumes, with Chelsea boys and other beauts.

French Roast (Map p448; ☎ 212-533-2233; 458 Sixth Ave at W 11th St; $$; ◉ L to Sixth Ave or F, V to 14th St) Strong coffee, sure, and complete bistro offerings, to boot.

Kang Suh (Map pp452–3; ☎ 212-564-6845; 1250 Broadway at W 32nd St; $$; ◉ B, D, F, N, Q, R, V, W to 34th St–Herald Sq) We're supposed to grill our own meats at 5am? Yep. And sing karaoke, too.

Veselka (Map p449; ☎ 212-228-9682; 144 Second Ave at E 9th St; $$; ◉ F, V to Lower East Side–Second Ave) This East Village classic serves Ukrainian fare – pierogies, stuffed peppers and goulash – all through the night.

ELMO Map pp446-7 — American $$

☎ 212-337-8000; 156 Seventh Ave btwn W 19th & W 20th St; ⏲ 11am-11pm; ◉ 1 to 18th St

One of many epicenters for Chelsea boys who need to refuel after clubbing and before working out (or visa versa), Elmo is on the big bandwagon of diners sporting a nightclub vibe (and it's got an actual clubby lounge, with a rotating performance schedule, in its basement). It's a sexy scene with high ceilings, low lighting, cushy banquettes and a garage door–like facade that gets opened wide to the street come spring and summer. The takes on simple, comfort-food favorites – meatloaf, fried chicken, baked mac 'n' cheese (with added fontina and Gruyère), mussels (steamed in tequila) and big fresh salads – are consistently delicious. And so are the lovely looking wait staff and clientele.

SUEÑOS Map pp446-7 — Mexican $$

☎ 212-243-1333; 311 W 17th St; ⏲ dinner Tue-Sun; ◉ A, C, E to Eighth Ave or 1 to 18th St

Chef-owner Sue Torres, who also runs nearby favorite Rocking Horse Café, touts her bright fuchsia-and-orange space as a proud purveyor of authentic Mexican food. While that claim may be questionable (empanadas stuffed with goat cheese and a 'tortilla lady' who cranks out fresh rounds of cornmeal upon a raised corner stage fit for a DJ?), the upper-crust fusion offerings *are* delicious. Quesadillas topped with *huitlacoche,* an über-trendy corn fungus that's a popular north Mexico delicacy, as well as pan-seared snapper with mango salsa, will thrill your taste buds. Reserve early.

TÍA POL Map pp446-7 — Spanish Tapas $$

☎ 212-675-8805; 205 Tenth Ave btwn W 22nd & W 23rd Sts; ⏲ dinner Tue-Sun; ◉ C, E to 23rd St

This closet-sized, authentic and romantic Spanish tapas bar is the real deal – and the hordes of locals who crowd into the front-bar waiting area to get one of six teeny tables filled with massive doses of deliciousness know it. Come on the early side and you may get seated in under a half-hour. It's a wait well worth its weight in red wine and Spanish tortillas, as both are beyond splendid here. So is just about everything else on the menu, from the fresh salad topped with tuna to the lima-bean-puree bruschetta and sautéed cockles with razor clams. If you find yourself in the 'hood, Tía Pol is a must.

UNION SQUARE, THE FLATIRON DISTRICT, GRAMERCY PARK & MURRAY HILL

A veritable goldmine of eateries, this multi-named area stretches from E 14th St to about the mid-30s. Its most obvious perk is the Union Sq Greenmarket (held Monday, Wednesday, Friday and Saturday; see the boxed text on p146), when discerning chefs both pro and amateur scour the wares of upstate farmers and get inspired for their next meals. Even if you've got no kitchen to go back to, it's fun to roam through the booths and enjoy occasional cheese

SEEK & YOU WILL FIND

Beyond NYC's restaurants is a cornucopia of gourmet food markets, where you can choose your own fresh produce, baked goods and prepared foods without the restaurant price mark ups. The most authentic spots lie in ethnic neighborhoods such as Chinatown, Brooklyn Height's 'fertile crescent' of Middle Eastern shops, the Little India of Jackson Heights or Brighton Beach and Brooklyn's Russian enclave. The cheapest such options are the 24-hour Korean groceries that sport huge salad and hot-food bars that you'll find on every other corner citywide. But the most awe-inspiring are spread around Manhattan.

Chelsea Market (Map pp446–7; www.chelseamarket.com; 75 Ninth Ave btwn 15th & 16th St; A, C, E to 14 St or L to Eighth Ave) Shop for wine, baked goods, cheese and other delicacies. See p143.

Dean & DeLuca (Map p450; 212-226-6800; www.deananddeluca.com; 560 Broadway at Prince St; R, W to Prince St; Map p448; 212-473-1908; 75 University Pl; L, N, Q, R, W, 4, 5, 6 to 14th St–Union Sq) It's got museum-quality produce, chocolates, baked goods, cheeses and prepared items, at exorbitant prices.

Fairway (Map pp454–5; 212-595-1888; www.fairwaymarket.com; 2127 Broadway at 74th St; Map p458–9; 212-234-3883; 2328 Twelfth Ave at 132nd St) Both have stunning arrays of produce and global goods, but the bigger Harlem spot boasts a 10,000-sq-ft 'cold room,' where you can wear a special jacket to pick out meats, flowers, dairy products and other chilly treats.

Gourmet Garage (Map p450; 212-941-5850; www.gourmetgarage.com; 453 Broome St at Mercer St) There are other locations (see Map pp454–5). Each spot varies in size, but the stellar offerings – especially the bulk-olive bar and prepared deli dinners – are equally stand out.

Kalustyan's (Map pp452–3; 212-685-3451; www.kalustyans.com; 123 Lexington Ave at 28th St) An intimate yet extensive shop filled with Indian gourmet items, including endless spices and chutneys, rare produce (like fresh curry leaves), breads, dried beans and oils.

Whole Foods (Map pp452–3; 212-924-5969; www.wholefoodsmarket.com; 250 Seventh Ave at 24th St; Map p282; 212-823-9600; Time Warner Center, Columbus Circle; Map pp446–7; 212-673-5388; 4 Union Sq S) It's taking over, but no one seems to mind. Find miles of aisles blooming with organic products.

Zabar's (Map pp454–5; 212-787-2000; www.zabars.com; 2245 Broadway at W 80th St) A longstanding Upper West Side favorite. The gourmet cheeses, heavenly baked goods, whole-bean coffee and Jewish deli specials inspire pilgrimages from all over the New York area.

or bread samples. But beyond this patch of green is a real range of offerings, both pricey destination dining events and low-key neighborhood gems. Lexington Ave in the high 20s is known as Curry Hill because of its preponderance of spots serving kosher, vegetarian South Indian fare. It's a great place to poke around and pick a place that intrigues you. Bon appetit!

ARTISANAL Map pp452-3 French $$$
212-725-8585; 2 Park Ave S at E 32nd St; lunch & dinner; 6 to 33rd St

You'll find high-end bistro fare in this sumptuous deco dining room, and a serious focus on fine cheese. The menu boasts more than 250 varieties, from the stinky to the sweet, housed in a wonderfully pungent-smelling storage house that greets you upon your entrance. To quote the words of one astute *New York* magazine reviewer, 'If cheese is a religion, this is its bustling, Balthazar-gone-Midtown house

of worship.' Cheese plates and various cheese fondues are the biggest draws here, of course, though a range of well-executed dishes, such as artichoke risotto, olive-crusted cod and the requisite steak au poivre, are also well worth the visit.

CHENNAI GARDEN
Map pp452-3   Kosher Indian $
212-689-1999; 129 E 27th St btwn Park Ave S & Lexington Ave; lunch & dinner; 6 to 28th St

Former owners of the now-defunct Madras Mahal, which was a pioneer of the kosher South Indian trend along this strip, have returned after a spell in Miami to open another winner. Come here for favorite Southern treats like long, paper-thin *dosas* (rice-flour pancakes) stuffed with spicy mixtures of potatoes and peas; spongy *utthappams* (thicker rice pancakes studded with vegetables and herbs); steamed *idli* cakes and *bhel poori*, both ubiquitous Indian street foods that make clever usage of rice and chick peas; and a range of more expected northern favorites, including a range of curries. The interior is bright and bustling – especially for the popular lunchtime buffet, which, for a mere six bucks, lets you reload your plate with menu highlights again and again.

CITY BAKERY Map pp446-7   Café $$
☎ 212-366-1414; 3 W 18th St btwn Fifth & Sixth Aves; ✆ lunch & dinner; ⊕ L, N, Q, R, W, 4, 5, 6 to 14th St–Union Sq

This is the perfect place to take a load off after trolling the Union Sq Greenmarket (p146). The pricey salad-bar offerings here are actually priceless: tofu-skin salad, roasted beets, fresh grilled chicken with sugar-snap peas, soy beans with cabbage. Though hard to snag at lunchtime, plenty of tables line the perimeter of the place. After enjoying the health-bent offerings at the bar, it's likely you won't be able to escape without sampling some of the rich bakery fare, from top notch chocolate-chip cookies to thick, molten hot chocolate, served with or without chubby homemade marshmallow squares.

FLEUR DE SEL Map pp446-7   French $$$
☎ 212-460-9100; 5 E 20th St btwn Broadway & Fifth Ave; ✆ lunch & dinner; ⊕ R, W to 23rd St

A superstar of the dining scene, the Brittany-born chef Cyril Renaud has adorned the brick-walled, white-tableclothed dining room with his very own whimsical watercolor paintings. Once seated, you'll find an extensive, mostly high-end wine list, and a market-fresh, French-infused menu of masterpieces that'll blow your mind. Lobster salad and black truffle mayonnaise, goat cheese and

artichoke ravioli, potato-crusted sea bass and a sugarcane pork chop – just for starters – are not only taste-bud treats, but flawlessly presented works of edible sculpture that are only too fitting for such an artistic chef. Crowds here are well scrubbed, well dressed and well monied, unsurprisingly.

PURE FOOD AND WINE
Map pp446-7   Raw Food/Vegetarian $$
☎ 212-477-1010; 54 Irving Pl btwn E 17th & E 18th Sts; ✆ dinner; ⊕ L, N, Q, R, W, 4, 5, 6 to 14th St–Union Sq

The 'chef' (there's no oven in the kitchen) at this gem achieves the impossible, churning out not only edible, but extremely delicious and artful concoctions, made completely from raw organics that are put through blenders, dehydrators and the capable hands of Pure's staff. Results are creative, fresh and alarmingly delicious, and include the wonderful tomato-zucchini lasagne (sans cheese and pasta); mushroom, avocado and ginger sushi rolls; and the chanterelle, olive and 'ricotta' ravioli with pistachio oil and macadamia cream sauce. In addition, the dining room is sleek and festive; but in warmer months, don't miss a chance to settle into a table in the shady, oasis-like backyard.

SHAKE SHACK Map pp452-3   Fast Food $
☎ 212-889-6600; Madison Sq Park, E 23rd St at Madison Ave; ✆ lunch & dinner Apr-Sep; ⊕ R, W, 6 to 23rd St

The latest addition to spiffed-up Madison Sq Park is this silver cube of a retro burger-and-shake hut. With slick architecture, outdoor café seating and roadside grub that's

Eating

UNION SQUARE, THE FLATIRON DISTRICT, GRAMERCY PARK & MURRAY HILL

Whole Foods (above left) is peppered with fresh food choices

Gourmands make the pilgrimage to Zabar's (p242)

been given the Midas touch of restaurateur Danny Meyer, this is one hip spot to hang come spring and summer. Tuck into juicy burgers topped with cheese or 'shrooms, gourmet dogs from beef to chicken-apple, fries, shakes and heavenly frozen custard in gourmet flavors.

TABLA Map pp452-3   Indian-American Fusion $$-$$$
☎ 212-889-0667; 11 Madison Ave at 25th St; ⏲ lunch Mon-Fri, dinner daily; ◉ R, W, 6 to 23rd St
Ascend the sweeping stairway to this 2nd-floor expanse of light and divine aromas, where some of the best tables in the house overlook placid Madison Sq Park. Everything created by Goa-raised and France-trained chef Floyd Cardoz sparkles with intelligence and love, from lobster and haricot verts in coconut curry to wild mushroom kebab with braised fennel, all served with fruity, flowery flourishes. Desserts, such as Tahitian vanilla-bean *kulfi* (ice cream) and soft cheese with roasted figs and poached quinces, are unsurpassed. For a breezier, hipper experience, head to the more casual and affordable Bread Bar on the ground floor, where food is straight-up Indian (tandoori meats, curries, buttery naan) and just as exquisite.

MIDTOWN
MIDTOWN EAST
AL BUSTAN Map pp452-3   Lebanese $$$
☎ 212-759-5933; 827 Third Ave btwn E 50th & E 51st Sts; ⏲ lunch & dinner; ◉ E, V to Lexington Ave–53rd St, 6 to 51st St
If your only brush with Middle Eastern food has been in a cramped storefront with the hurried gobbling down of a messy falafel sandwich, get thyself to Al Bustan. It's a formal dining room, adorned with a scenic wall mural and filled with well-dressed diners who know a thing or two about hummus – and grilled chicken and lamb kibbeh (tartare) and sautéed quail and soupy, spicy, red-snapper-based *tagine*. Lingering over your meal here, and finishing it off with a triangle of flaky baklava, is the best sort of Middle East peace around.

CHO DANG GOI Map pp452-3   Korean $$
☎ 212-695-8222; 55 W 35th St btwn Fifth & Sixth Aves; ⏲ lunch & dinner; ◉ B, D, F, N, Q, R, V, W to 34th St–Herald Sq
Groups of Korean youngsters flock to this authentic eatery, located in the midst of ever-growing Koreatown, for meals studded with bits of the signature, homemade tofu. Traditional *bibimbops* (dish of rice, veggies and/or meat served with a fried egg on top), sticky-rice dishes and pork stews are all among the best in the 'hood. So, too, are the tiny plates of kimchi surprises (including a pile of teensy dried fish, eyes intact) that you'll get showered with before your meal begins. It's like stepping into another country – one that's just around the corner from very-American Macy's, interestingly enough.

TOP FIVE EATS IN MIDTOWN

- Al Bustan (above) – Lebanese for sophisticates only
- Dawat (opposite) – high-end Indian served with a flourish
- DB Bistro Moderne (opposite) – Daniel Boulud's Times Sq star
- Modern (opposite) – overlook a sculpture garden and eat works of art
- Per Se (opposite) – a Time Warner Center highlight with cultish following

DAWAT Map pp452-3 Indian $$

☎ 212-355-7555; 210 E 58th St btwn Second & Third Aves; ☽ lunch Mon-Sat, dinner daily; ⊙ N, R, W to Lexington Ave—59th St

Famed chef, cookbook author and actress Madhur Jaffrey runs this outpost of Nirvana, which transforms Indian favorites, including spinach *bhajia* (fritter) and fish curries, into exotic masterpieces served with fancy flourishes. Sea bass and lamb chops each get royal treatments with marinades made of various blends of yogurt, mustard seeds, saffron and ginger, and charming, cardamom-flecked desserts cool your palate. The dining room is formal and subdued and the crowd is a bit on the stuffy side (it comes with the territory in this part of town), but none of it'll matter after your first bite of heaven.

MODERN

Map pp452-3 French-American $$-$$$

☎ 212-333-1220; Museum of Modern Art, 9 W 53rd St btwn Fifth & Sixth Aves; ☽ lunch & dinner; ⊙ E, V to Fifth Ave—53rd St

The new high-end restaurant in the sparkling new MoMA is its own work of art, both visually and gastronomically. The glass-walled dining room is sprawling and spare, edged by a sleek backlit bar and overlooking the lovingly restored sculpture garden, which pours in sluices of bright light during the afternoon. It's connected to a formal café space that's younger and hipper in vibe (and more affordable, as there are small-plate options). Crowds are constant and buzzing with excitement at both – as they should be, since the food of Gabriel Kreuther is stellar. You'll find eggplant risotto, licorice poached halibut, duck breast with black truffle marmalade and various tasting menus in the mix. You can't go wrong – especially when you ponder the galleries that you can wander for dessert.

OMS/B Map pp452-3 Japanese $

☎ 212-922-9788; 156 E 45th St btwn Lexington & Third Aves; ☽ 8:30am-7:30pm Mon-Fri, 11am-7pm Sat; ⊙ S, 4, 5, 6, 7 to Grand Central—42nd St

Running from museum to architectural site to a big night out? Skip the usual fast-food options and pop into this oasis, where you'll find a twist on the *omusubi*, a ubiquitous Japanese lunch food consisting of stuffed rice balls. But here the weighty treats are triangular, wrapped in a sheet of nori and stuff with goodies both Japanese – fish

TIME WARNER CENTER: FOOD POWER

The glitzy Time Warner Center (p153) retail, entertainment, office and residential towers that loom over Central Park at Columbus Circle are home not to one, but to seven impressive (extremely) high-end restaurants from celeb chefs. Among the offerings: American creative at the homey Per Se (Map p282; ☎ 212-823-9335); French-Asian fusion at Café Gray (Map p282; ☎ 212-823-6338), where Gray Kunz reigns over an open kitchen; and Japanese-food theater at Masa (Map p282; ☎ 212-823-9800), an insanely expensive (as in $300 per person) lair.

flake, teriyaki chicken, Japanese plum – and otherwise. For the latter, look toward pastrami, fried shrimp and prosciutto. Delicious beverages include a range of soothing teas.

MIDTOWN WEST & THEATER DISTRICT

Pizza joints, Irish pubs and midrange ethnic restaurants fill up the side streets off Times Sq. Finding a truly decent place to tuck into either pre- or post-theater used to be quite a challenge in the not-so-distant past. But in recent years, thankfully, more and more restaurateurs have begun to fill the void – in a big enough way to even lure those for dinner only, sans the Broadway show.

DB BISTRO MODERNE

Map p282 French $$$

☎ 212-391-2400; 55 W 44th St at Broadway; ☽ lunch Mon-Sat, dinner daily; ⊙ N, R, S, W, 1, 2, 3, 7 to Times Sq—42nd St

Peer through the glass façade of this spot, smack in the middle of Times Sq, and you'll see a party that you will definitely want to get in on. That's Daniel Boulud for you, the star chef who infuses all of his projects – Café Boulud and the Daniel Boulud Brasserie among them – with magic. This is a bright and sophisticated spot among the garishness of the neighborhood, with a thoroughly modern interior of beaded curtains, red plaster walls and a fabric-shrouded ceiling, with a stylish crowd to match. It's so cool that the food could be beside the point – except that it isn't. Lobster bisque, grilled tuna, venison stew and the infamous DB

NEW YORK STREET EATS

In addition to the endless wave of cheap pizzerias and falafel storefronts, you'll find plenty of bargain bites being hawked from steaming carts, right on the sidewalk. While some treats, like hot dogs, are universal, others change depending on the neighborhood. Here is a rough guide.

- Doughnuts and coffee – every neighborhood has several come morning, stocked with sticky doughnuts, fresh coffee and even some pre-buttered bagels, with nothing costing more than $1.
- Gyros and falafel – they're ubiquitous – especially around business Midtown and shoppers' Soho (try Broadway between Houston and Lafayette Sts) – but they are delicious.
- Roasted chestnuts – a seasonal treat, proffered all over town right around Christmas time, and the scent is heavenly.
- Soup – thick homemade corn chowder, lobster bisque and cream of potato soup can be found at carts all over the city, but especially in Soho (Prince and Mercer Sts) and Midtown (34th St at Ninth Ave, just for starters).
- Tacos – some of the city's best Mexican tacos, *tortas* (Mexican sandwiches) and *horchatas* (cold rice-water drinks) are doled out of trucks parked on Upper West Side corners – 98th St and Broadway and 104th St and Broadway. Also keep an eye out in the morning (in the same 'hood) for women standing quietly with small coolers, which are filled with homemade tamales and steaming *atole* (hot, flavored rice milk).
- Tarot-root cakes – though you'll find plenty of other delicious and greasy Chinese treats around the streets of Chinatown (including fish balls and spare ribs), these moist, tangy, melt-in-your mouth cubes of mashed tarot are the most delicious.

burger – grilled sirloin stuffed with braised short ribs, foie gras and black truffles for a cool $29 – are really, really good (and really, really rich).

RUSSIAN SAMOVAR Map p282   Russian $$
☎ 212-757-0168; 256 W 52nd St btwn Broadway & Eighth Ave; ⏱ lunch Tue-Sat, dinner daily; ⊕ C, E, 1 to 50th St

Co-owner Mikhail Baryshnikov isn't the only lure at this particular chicken Kiev palace (especially since he is never there). Russians and their fans come in droves for the upscale, authentic dining room, accentuated by hanging fringed lamps and live music on various nights. And it's simple to gorge yourself with dignity here: caviar and blini or smoked salmon appetizers just melt on the tongue, rack of lamb or grilled steak is succulent, and chicken Kiev that is seasoned with dill and mustard seeds is the ultimate way this dish comes. Top off your tank with a cup of traditional cherry tea.

SOUL FIXINS Map pp452-3   Southern American $
☎ 212-736-1345; 371 W 34th St at Ninth Ave; ⏱ breakfast, lunch & dinner; ⊕ A, C, E to 34th St–Penn Station

It's a tiny storefront that's hot and humid inside no matter what the weather, due to the simmering pots of collards, mac 'n' cheese, candied yams and other down-

South specialties that cook all day long. Treat yourself to a $5 breakfast of fish or eggs with grits, and sample all the veggie sides with a lunch combo plate. At dinner, prices and offerings rise with BBQ chicken or ribs, meatloaf and heaped servings of chicken and dumplings. Customers are harried in-and-outers who work in nearby office buildings; you can lounge for as long as you want in the close, steamy quarters.

VIRGIL'S REAL BARBECUE
Map p282   Southern BBQ $$
☎ 212-921-9494; 152 W 44th St btwn Broadway & Eighth Ave; ⏱ lunch & dinner; ⊕ N, R, S, W, 1, 2, 3, 7 to Times Sq–42nd St

Until recently, there were two main cuisines that NYC lacked in a big way: Mexican, which has seen an explosion around town in the past few years, and real Southern BBQ. The latter is finally here, too, and though it's still not exploded, the fact that places like Virgil's exists gives Southern expats – as well as fans of finger lickin' goodness – reason to smile. Rather than specializing in a specific style of BBQ, which varies in both sauce type and meat base in various regions of the US, Virgil's celebrates them all. Menu items cover the entire BBQ map, with Oklahoma State Fair corndogs, pulled Carolina pork and smoked Maryland ham sandwiches, and platters of sliced Texas beef brisket and Georgia chicken-fried steak. Meats are smoked with a combo of hickory, oak and fruitwoods, keepin' it all real.

HELL'S KITCHEN

Long known as being a sort of no-man's land, Hell's Kitchen (also known as Clinton) has finally been able to add some depth to its nickname by developing a truly destination-worthy kitchen culture. You'll find old, cheap standards on these gritty stretches, plus a burgeoning crop of nouveau-American hot spots, thanks to the northern creep of Chelsea and the growing development west of Ninth Ave. Wandering up and down Ninth Ave especially will yield all sorts of ethnic-food market surprises, from Middle Eastern spices sold in bulk to Amish country cheeses proffered by the pound.

CUPCAKE CAFÉ Map p282   Café $

☎ 212-465-1530; 522 Ninth Ave; ⏱ 7am-7pm Mon-Fri, 8am-7pm Sat, 9am-5pm Sun; ⊕ A, C, E to 42nd St–Port Authority

This is *the* place for tasty cupcakes topped with exquisitely decorated buttercream frosting. But it's also a popular, mellow little locals' breakfast and lunch place, where you can find rotating meals from soups and salads to veggie chili and quiche.

A new location has recently opened at 18 W 18th St (btwn 5th and 6th Aves).

EATERY Map p282   Eclectic $$

☎ 212-765-7080; 798 Ninth Ave at W 53rd St; ⏱ lunch Mon-Fri, brunch Sat & Sun, dinner daily; ⊕ C, E, 1 to 50th St

Taking its cue from Chelsea, which is the king of restaurant/lounge hybrids, this slick and happening spot includes a side of DJ-spun techno with its diverse food, wine and specialty cocktail menu. Aim for the fabulous, high-backed horseshoe banquette in the corner (the best spot to see and be seen), but be happy for any seat you get at the always-packed affair. Food choices range from the comfort-leaning salmon club sandwich, chipotle-spiced meatloaf and rum-glazed pork tenderloin to the veggie, Asian-style *udon* noodle salad with tasty citrus tofu, Peking chicken in ginger-plum sauce and bowls of edamame tossed with sea salt. Throw in a fresh watermelon margarita, and you can settle in for a full night out – as long as you move to the cool, adjoining bar once your table is cleared.

44½ Map p282   American $$

☎ 212-399-4450; 626 Tenth Ave btwn W 44th & W 45th Sts; ⏱ lunch & dinner Mon-Sat; ⊕ A, C, E to 42nd St–Port Authority

Owners of the sultry Xth Ave Lounge and the sleek 44 & X, a pioneer dining spot in this stretch of the 'hood, have now added this cute and modern spot to their holdings. The bright speck of a café has meals both great and small – Tuscan chicken orzo soup with a black forest ham panini, for example, or a fat plate of wild mushroom risotto or platter of braised lamb shank – served at either a table or the friendly counter. Better yet, in warm months, you can eat out back in the Zen-like garden.

MARKET CAFÉ

Map p282   American Creative $$

☎ 212-564-7350; 496 Ninth Ave btwn W 37th & W 38th Sts; ⏱ lunch & dinner Mon-Sat; ⊕ A, C, E to 34th St–Penn Station

The Formica tables, white tile walls and bright teal booths will make you think 'old-school diner.' But the charming service, cool steel chandeliers and chic lounge music – not to mention the fresh menu – will show you that this is a special, down-town-hip kinda place. A serving of steak frites is succulent, cod roasted in veal broth is divine and salads are verdant and refreshing. Expect to wait on weekends, but you'll be in good company: the long-running pioneer is still a favorite among local hipsters, despite the fact that there's much more to choose from.

MESKEREM Map p282   Ethiopian $$

☎ 212-664-0520; 468 W 47th St btwn Ninth & Tenth Aves; ⏱ lunch & dinner; ⊕ C, E to 50th St

Located on a placid side street, this place is nothing much to look at – just a sparse, dimly lit dining room that could practically be a diner, save for the little splashes of African decor here and there. But it's about the food here, as a diverse crew of locals know. Sop up huge and fiery, *berbere* sauce–flecked dishes with the spongy, expands-in-your-stomach flatbread called *injera*. Meat eaters will love the garlicky chunks of beef and chicken-meets-egg concoction, while vegetarians will love the spicy lentil or chickpea stews.

UPPER WEST SIDE

This huge swath of neighborhood – from the classic-arts Lincoln Center 60s blocks to the well-heeled, residential 70s and 80s and the more eclectic 90s – has always plenty of good grub to mine. But it wasn't deemed destination-worthy by foodies until the last few years, when chef/restaurateur Tom Valenti made a splash with his creative-American stunner Ouest (right) and other greats followed. Now it's got everything, and keeps getting more.

BEARD PAPA'S Map pp454–5   Café/Bakery $
☎ 212-799-3770; 2167 Broadway at W 75th St; ☽ 10am-8pm; ◉ 1 to 79th St

If you're strolling around Broadway, do yourself a favor and get a cream puff from this place. It's a total phenomenon of a Japanese import, where a small assembly line fills choux pastry shells with fillings from vanilla to green tea, right before your eyes. They're amazing. They're light, delicious and completely addictive. And the bright, butter-yellow store decor puts you right in the mood for happy sweets.

CESCA Map pp454–5   Italian $$$
☎ 212-787-6300; 164 W 75th St btwn Columbus & Amsterdam Aves; ☽ dinner; ◉ 1, 2, 3, to 72nd St

Tom Valenti, who jumpstarted the recent UWS feeding frenzy with Ouest (right), expanded from France to Italy when he brought this place to the 'hood. The handsome, comforting place (stained wood, candelabras and sumptuous leather banquettes) is the setting for mackerel, chicken ragout, wild game and ravioli classics, as well as clever antipasti options such as marinated baby artichokes with fresh ricotta and tiny veal meatballs with pastina. The impressive wine list offers mainly Italian bottles and plenty of by-the-glass choices, which you could opt to sip at the classy up-front bar, while nibbling at more casual (and affordable) fare like a bowl of warm faro salad.

COLUMBUS BAKERY
Map pp454–5   Café/Bakery $
☎ 212-724-6880; 474 Columbus Ave btwn W 82nd & W 83rd Sts; ☽ breakfast & lunch; ◉ B, C to 81st St–Museum of Natural History

An airy bakery-café with a European vibe, this casual spot is a hit with locals, who either rush in and out for a fresh muffin and

cup of coffee or linger for hours over a cup of homemade soup, a sleeping (or screaming) baby in a stroller at their side. It's a great place to take a load off after exploring the streets of the UWS, and also a good source for picnic food, which you can drag one block west to the expanse of Central Park. Either way, the salads (try the hoisin chicken or chickpea with goat cheese), sandwiches (like grilled chicken with poached pears and cheddar) and baked goods (from raisin-pumpernickel bread to chocolate brioche) are to die for.

MANA Map pp454–5   Vegetarian/Macrobiotic $$
☎ 212-787-1110; 646Amsterdam Ave btwn W 91st & W 92nd Sts; ☽ lunch & dinner daily, brunch Sat & Sun; ◉ 1 to 86th St

This place, with its clean and simple atmosphere, is like a second home to many healthful locals, who come for the welcoming service and pure, delicious meals. Greens, grains and beans change daily, as do main specials, which include Asian-influenced stews and noodle dishes and even organic-fish options for those needing a big dose of protein; the main dish of vegetable *gomae* – a rich stew of chunky vegetables, seitan and tofu in a creamy miso-sesame-garlic sauce – is a standout. The vegan chocolate cake, paired with a luscious cup of grain 'coffee' with maple syrup and soy milk, is a perfect way to end.

OUEST Map pp454–5   Modern American/French $$$
☎ 212-580-8700; 2315 Broadway btwn W 83rd & W 84th Sts; ☽ dinner daily, brunch Sun; ◉ 1 to 86th St

Ouest, widely credited with bringing a foodie revolution to the Upper West Side, is the pioneer food-destination that still reigns, along with its delicious followers. They clamor nightly for unique, tantalizing

---

TOP FIVE EATS ON THE UPPER WEST SIDE

- Amy Ruth's Restaurant (p251) – classic Harlem, with an extra dose of waffles
- Cesca (left) – upscale Italian, luscious wines
- Jo Jo (p250) – French destination for uptown foodies
- Ouest (above) – Valenti's original UWS magnet
- Picnic Market & Café (opposite) – surprisingly wonderful French bistro fare

options such as the salmon gravlax with chickpea pancake caviar and mustard oil, a stunning appetizer, and main dishes like seared yellowfin tuna with marinated rice and beans. There's also rich wild-game presentations, like the vegetarians' nightmare called 'rabbit three ways,' offering the little creature's roasted leg, stuffed saddle wrapped in bacon, and in confit form, with preserved lemon and white polenta. A different special reigns daily, like shellfish on Monday and steak on Sunday. Settle in, and enjoy the surprisingly friendly atmosphere.

PASHA Map pp454-5 Turkish $$

☎ 212-579-8751; 70 W 71st St btwn Central Park W & Columbus Ave; ✆ dinner daily, brunch Sat & Sun; Ⓜ B, C to 72nd St

The gourmet grub in this red-walled, festive newcomer goes way beyond simple mezes of roasted eggplant and *cacik* (chilled, homemade yogurt), but those are excellent ways to start. Bump it up a notch by sampling some of the less-standard fare, like the baked zucchini-and-dill pancakes, whipped red caviar, roasted sea bass topped with chopped tomatoes, parsley and lemon, or the vegetarian *sebzeli zuvec*, which is a flavorful blend of green beans, eggplant, zucchini, okra, celery root and tomato baked in an earthenware casserole dish. Dreamy desserts and a healthy selection of wine and cocktails add to the convivial scene.

PICNIC MARKET & CAFÉ

Map pp454-5 French $$

☎ 212-222-8222; 2665 Broadway btwn W 101st & W 102nd Sts; ✆ breakfast, lunch & dinner; Ⓜ 1 to 103rd St

Brought to you by the same couple who created the swoon-inspiring Silver Moon Bakery some years ago, this nearby newcomer has had the same effect on locals here, who clamor at all times of the day for Gallic goodies. Its joyous orange facade and high-ceilinged, sunny interior make it hard not to stop and peer in as you walk by. Once you get a glimpse of the to-go food, neatly arranged behind gleaming glass cases, you'll certainly have to just get a taste. The seasonal menu changes daily, but some examples of the outstanding fare are seared duck breast infused with mint juice, heirloom tomato salad, and pressed goat-cheese and artichoke sandwiches. Take a seat in the spare yet cozy confines or try to score a cov-

eted sidewalk table, or load up on gourmet goodies to go, and celebrate the fact that, with places like this, life really *is* a picnic.

REGIONAL Map pp454-5 Italian $$

☎ 212-666-1915; 2607 Broadway btwn W 98th & W 99th Sts; ✆ dinner daily, brunch Sat & Sun; Ⓜ 1, 2, 3 to 96th St

The hippest addition to this neighborhood in quite some time, Regional, new in 2005, seems to have broken a bad-luck spell at this particular storefront location. It's an industrial-chic spot with a downtown vibe, offering plates both big and small from no less than 20 regions of Italy. Stuffed artichokes, spicy squid and noodles topped with duck *ragu* are all bursting with flavor, and the long list of wines, excellent for pairing, is impressive. It's fun to sit at the bar here, too, or to snag one of just six spots at a freestanding bar table in the window, perfect for watching neighborhood folks go about their business on bustling Broadway.

THALIA CAFÉ Map pp454-5 Café $

☎ 212-864-5400; Symphony Space, 2537 Broadway at W 95th St; ✆ lunch daily, dinner Sat & Sun; Ⓜ 1, 2, 3 to 96th St

A recent addition to the excellent theaters of Symphony Space (p281), this little gem, hidden on the side-street entrance, is rarely crowded – though it deserves to be. The cozy spot has seating options from small, window-front tables to a low, cushy couch. Food and drink are served via counter service and include homemade empanadas, quiche-like tarts, fresh salads, delicious baked goods, great coffee and a huge range of fresh-brewed teas. It's a magnet for local artsy types, retirees wanting a midday slice of pie and moms with little ones, wanting a change of pace from the onslaught of neighborhood Starbucks locations.

UPPER EAST SIDE

High-end diners should prepare for jacket-and-tie wearing movers and shakers, where conversation is hushed and service is extremely formal. But there's plenty more to this traditionally stuffy 'hood, where options take you from Turkey to Belgium to old-school New York and beyond – and let you in wearing jeans and a tank top if that's your pleasure.

BEYOGLU Map pp454-5 — Turkish $$

☎ 212-650-0850; 1431 Lexington Ave at E 81st St; ⊗ lunch & dinner; ⊕ 6 to 77th St

This is one of restaurateur Orhan Yegen's spots – a charismatic, loungey space where yogurt soup, doner kebabs and feta-flecked salads are elegant and excellent. Get in early for your pick of a good table; it's within strolling distance of the subway, making for a tasteful way to end an artistic afternoon. At least the crowds of a sophisticated mix of locals and museum tourists think so. Don't forget to get really festive with a shot or two of the traditional, anisette-flavored raki.

CANDLE CAFE Map pp454-5 — Vegetarian $$

☎ 212-472-0970; 1307 Third Ave btwn 74th & 75th Sts; ⊗ lunch & dinner; ⊕ 6 to 77th St

In a 'hood where quality veggie selections are hard to come by, Candle is a light at the end of a carnivorous cave – it's sandwiched, in fact, by a popular steakhouse and a burger joint. Wealthy New Age types are the norm in this simple storefront, permeated by the constant, clean scent of wheatgrass due to the juice bar stationed up front. Offerings range from the most simplistic, such as 'good food plates,' a custom-made spread of greens, roots, grains and soy-based protein, to the more complex concoctions, such as the beloved 'paradise casserole,' a feast of layered sweet potatoes, black beans and millet topped with mushroom gravy. Vegan cakes are surprisingly moist. The healthful grub is obviously in demand here, as another outpost with a slightly more innovative take on the subject, **Candle 79** (Map pp454-5; ☎ 212-537-7179; 154 E 79th St at Lexington Ave), thrives just a few blocks away.

CENTRAL PARK BOATHOUSE RESTAURANT Map pp454-5 — Seafood $$$

☎ 212-517-2233; Central Park Lake, enter Fifth Ave at 72nd St; ⊗ lunch daily, brunch Sat & Sun year-round, dinner daily Apr-Nov; ⊕ 6 to 68th St

Escape the city and enter this magical lakeside setting, just by taking a 10-minute walk off Fifth Ave. The historic Loeb Boathouse, perched on the shores of the park's lake, is one of the city's most incredible settings for a serene and romantic meal – and the food is top notch, too. Plates are artfully designed – witness the lunch appetizer of yellowfin tuna tartare arranged around mango, jicama relish and lotus-root

chips – and flavorful. Other seasonal treats include homemade gnocchi tossed with slow roasted cauliflower, pine nuts and pesto, and a pan roasted pork tenderloin with grilled sweet onions. Reserve early and aim for an outdoor table – or simply slip up to the bar and enjoy a lakeside cocktail.

JO JO Map pp454-5 — French $$$

☎ 212-223-5656; 160 E 64th St btwn Lexington & Third Aves; ⊗ lunch & dinner; ⊕ 6 to 68th St

It's interesting – and also quite astounding – to note that this intimate townhouse hideaway is brought to you by the same guy behind the trippy and cavernous Meatpacking District hotspot Spice Market (p239). But Jean-Georges is a well-rounded guy. Plus, one taste of the food and you'll recognize the high-class quality. You really can't go wrong here, where French standards get the Midas touch with the addition of a little something special. Foie gras is fashioned into crème brûlée, venison cubes are tossed with pomegranate seeds, roast chicken gets buried under green olives. The warm and gooey chocolate Valrhona cake is widely praised as the best in the city – if not the globe.

LE PAIN QUOTIDIEN

Map pp454-5 — Café/Bakery $

☎ 212-717-4800; 883 Lexington Ave at 64th St; ⊗ breakfast, lunch & dinner; ⊕ 6 to 68th St–Hunter College

A classy Belgian bakery chain, this spot is the perfect place to unwind with a croissant and a mug of thick and addictive hot chocolate. Or go for more substantial fare – an open-faced egg salad sandwich with salty capers, tartins of radish, ricotta and scallions or shrimp and avocado. Settle in for a while, watching the parade of locals who stop in to catch up with each other or to simply while away the hours over a *New York Times*. You won't have trouble finding it, as there are two others right in the 'hood – at 833 Lexington between E 63rd and E 64th Sts and 1131 Madison Ave between E 84th and E 85th Sts.

LEXINGTON CANDY SHOP

Map pp454-5 — Diner $

☎ 212-288-0057; 1226 Lexington Ave at E 83rd St; ⊗ breakfast, lunch & dinner; ⊕ 4, 5, 6 to 86th St

This picture-perfect lunch spot is complete with an old-fashioned soda fountain.

Lexington Candy Shop (opposite) is retro cool

Coming just to look at the mint-condition retro diner is fun enough – it was deemed worthy to be used as the backdrop in both an old Robert Redford film, *Three Days of the Condor,* and a slew of TV commercials. Slip into a booth or grab a seat at the long counter to eavesdrop on local schoolkids or old timers and you'll really have a time. The food is solid, decent fare – burgers, milkshakes, tuna melts – at reasonable prices, right in one of the city's most expensive neighborhoods. It's a great place to bring the kids.

HARLEM & NORTHERN MANHATTAN
MORNINGSIDE HEIGHTS & HARLEM

Columbia and its charges have colonized much of Morningside Heights, but, though you'll stumble across plenty of cheap and late-night diners and bars geared to students, recent years of rising real estate and an influx of yuppie-ish families have brought in more adult options, too. Meanwhile, Harlem, justifiably famous for its traditional soul food, has also undergone some gourmet changes thanks to gentrification. Now you'll find food from soul-fusion to honest-to-goodness upscale Chinese.

AMY RUTH'S RESTAURANT

Map pp458-9   Soul Food $$

☎ 212-280-8779; 114 W 116th St btwn Malcolm X Blvd (Lenox Ave) & Adam Clayton Powell Jr Blvd (Seventh Ave); ⏲ breakfast, lunch & dinner, 24hr Fri & Sat; ⊕ B, C, 2, 3 to 116th St

Though it used to be one of the less frenzied spots on the soul-food-lovin' tourist circuit, notoriety gained by coverage in spots from local magazines to the Food Network have certainly put a dent in that. Still, this place does an exquisite job with all the standards – candied yams, smoked ham, corn pudding, fried okra, you name it – and it has a particularly hard-to-resist specialization in waffles. Choose from chocolate, strawberry, blueberry, smothered in sautéed apples, or paired with fried chicken. Then walk it off – you'll really need to – with a walking tour of the surrounding neighborhood.

CAFFÉ SWISH

Map pp458-9   Pan-Asian $

☎ 212-222-3568; 2953-55 Broadway btwn 115th & 116th Sts; ⏲ 11am-midnight Sun-Thu, 11am-1am Fri & Sat; ⊕ 1 to 116th St–Columbia University

Students especially love this hip hangout, a recent addition to the nabe that sits right across the street from Columbia's entrance. You'll find practically every favorite Asian dish in this bustling and casual spot, from sushi rolls and pad Thai to *udon* soups and the big specialty, *shabu-shabu,* which has patrons cook their own sliced meats and veggies in bubbling pots of broth that are placed right at your table. So skewer that piece of beef and *swish* away.

GINGER Map pp458-9   Chinese $$
☎ 212-423-1111; 1400 Fifth Ave at 116th St; 🕑 lunch & dinner; 🚇 2, 3, 6 to 116th St
It's not where you might expect to find outstanding Chinese fare – it's more the place for greasy fried-rice takeout – but, alas, here it is. The bright and happy room, with red lanterns and bamboo ceiling beams, is the stage for organic, creative treats like ginger beer–braised short ribs with beans and cashews, house-special grilled Angus beef spare ribs, vegetarians' grilled tofu and pineapple-pork fried rice – which is a far cry from the aforementioned version found at battered storefronts all around the 'hood.

MAX SOHA Map pp458-9   Italian $$
☎ 212-531-2221; 1274 Amsterdam Ave at W 123rd St; 🕑 lunch & dinner; 🚇 A, B, C, D, 1 to 125th St
A northern outpost of the beloved Max (Map p449; 51 Ave B btwn 3rd & 4th Sts) in the East Village, this trendy and delicious spot brings a taste of downtown way up. Local gentrifiers can't get enough of the extremely delicious (and budget-minded) creative Italian cuisine, which brings diners wonderful takes on gnocchi in tomato sauce, homemade ravioli of the day, pan-seared cod and sumptuous veggie sides, from rich creamed spinach to zesty eggplant in tomato and basil sauce. Max Soha – whose surname is derived from the 'South of Harlem' nickname for the area – is truly worth getting excited about.

MISS MAUDE'S SPOONBREAD TOO
Map pp458-9   Soul Food $$
☎ 212-690-3100; 547 Malcolm X Blvd (Lenox Ave) btwn W 137th & W 138th Sts; 🕑 lunch & dinner; 🚇 2, 3 to 135th St
Join the tour-bus crowd at nearby Sylvia's if you really must, but if you're really smart you'll sidestep the mob scene for a mellower vibe and more delicious takes on traditional Harlem meals. Melt-in-your mouth short ribs, pecan waffles, heavenly fried chicken and peppery, buttery collard greens are across-the-board good. Friendly service and customers don't hurt, either.

STRICTLY ROOTS
Map pp458-9   Jamaican Vegan $
☎ 212-864-8699; 2058 Adam Clayton Powell Jr Blvd (Seventh Ave) btwn W 122nd & W 123rd Sts; 🕑 lunch & dinner; 🚇 A, B, C, D, 2, 3 to 125th St
This Rastafarian-loved haven is a modest space with a global-sized mission, which is to serve 'nothing that crawls, walks, swims or flies.' And the cafeteria-style spot does quite well with the ingredients that remain, offering a rotating menu of fried plantains, faux-beef curry, stews and stir-fried veggies, along with fresh juices and thick smoothies. The mostly local crowd here is laid-back and healthy looking, happy to find a vegan oasis in a sea of short ribs and fried chicken.

WASHINGTON HEIGHTS & INWOOD

Traditionally known for its preponderance of Dominican joints, Washington Heights has seen hardcore gentrification in recent years, which has given rise to all sorts of cuisines. While still not a foodie scene, there is a tiny burgeoning scene in the 'hood known as Hudson Heights, which overlooks the Hudson River from the cliffs of the high 180s. And Inwood, the last stop before the Bronx and home to suburban-like houses and close knit Jewish communities, has a few good dining spots going for it, too.

BLEU EVOLUTION
Map pp468-9   Eclectic $-$$
☎ 212-928-6006; 808 W 187th St btwn Fort Washington Ave & Pinehurst Ave N; 🕑 lunch & dinner; 🚇 A to 190th St
Sharing space with the velvet-draped Monkey Lounge in this growing crook of the neighborhood is the sultry, funky Evolution, where you can knock back cocktails until 2am and keep your stomach lined with well-done dishes of Middle Eastern salads (hummus, baba ganoush etc) or more substantial roasted monkfish or duck crepes. You'll find a diverse crowd here, especially late at night, as there still aren't too many options in this calm and quiet area.

DR-K Map pp468-9   Dominican $$
☎ 212-304-1717; 114 Dyckman St at Nagle Ave; 🕑 lunch & dinner; 🚇 1 to Dyckman St
Cheap-ass Dominican storefronts abound in these parts, but DR-K is a fancy standout.

It's housed in a slick dining room that feels more South Beach than north Manhattan. You'll be treated to artfully plated options like variously filled empanadas (chicken and seafood among them), spicy seafood stew, coconut shrimp, traditional *pernil* (roasted pork) and a gut-busting platter of grilled steak, pork, chicken, lobster, shrimp and octopus! (Vegetarians, by the way, will have to stick to the usual – rice and beans and plantains – though it's all still delicious.) After your meal, head upstairs with your Dominican *mojito* and bust a move with the pepped-up locals and blaring Latin sounds.

NEW LEAF CAFÉ

Map pp468-9   American Creative $$$

☎ 212-568-5323; Fort Tryon Park, 1 Margaret Corbin Dr; ⏲ lunch & dinner; ⊖ A to 190th St

After feeding your mind with the artistic beauty of the Cloisters, take a peaceful stroll through Fort Tryon Park and feed your belly here, in this beautiful, 1930s stone edifice with nature-lovers' views. The airy dining room features romantic archways, lots of dark wood, sexy night lighting from orange sconces and garden-patio seating for warm afternoons. The tasty food offers something for everyone – handmade *papardelle* with fava beans and ricotta, grilled halibut with risotto, and burgers and salad nicoise for lunch. Thursday nights offer live jazz, but most of all, all profits here are used to maintain the park thanks to an innovative city program.

PARK TERRACE BISTRO

Map pp468-9   French-Moroccan $$

☎ 212-567-2828; 4959 Broadway at 207th St; ⏲ dinner daily, brunch Sat & Sun; ⊖ A to Inwood–207th St

A Moroccan outpost on the tippy top of Manhattan, this place has been widely praised for both its location (beautiful) and its food (luscious). You wouldn't expect such a crowd at these northern reaches, but slammin' it is, both with giddy locals who don't have many options and downtown folks looking for the next big dining adventure. They find it here, through lovely service and rockin' menu items including escargot with fennel confit in a puffed pastry, spicy fish *tagine du jour,* filet mignon in bordelaise sauce, chicken *tagine* with ginger and preserved lemon, and a fresh

vegetable plate, served on request. Brunch is all over the map, pulling in fans with treats from blueberry pancakes to pulled pork, and the wine list is pretty vast, with good picks for every budget.

BROOKLYN
BROOKLYN HEIGHTS, DOWNTOWN BROOKLYN & DUMBO

This broad area – severed by an expressway and two bridge on-ramps – has several eating options. The polite, more upscale crowd will opt for Dumbo's Washington St, or (a bit less formal) on Brooklyn Heights' Montague St. In downtown, cheap slices can be had on Court St or the Fulton Mall. In general, the best stroll-and-see eating options are on Smith St. For excellent chocolate drop by Jacques Torres Chocolate (p351).

GRIMALDI'S Map p462   Pizzeria $

☎ 718-858-4300; 19 Old Fulton St; ⏲ lunch & dinner; ⊖ A, C to High St or 2, 3 to Clark St

Known as Patsy's in a previous life – and still widely recognized as the makers of one of New York's best pizzas – Grimaldi's red-checkered tables bring in a loyal following of local firefighters, guys in leather jackets talking into cell phones, and a tourist or two. Sometimes lines go out the door, but the brick-oven churns out the pizzas fast. This is real-deal New York pizza: Frank (Sinatra – c'mon) is on the walls and jukebox. Four hungry folk can eat two larges (it's thin). You pick the toppings – sun-dried tomato with a little extra basil is tops.

JUNIOR'S Map pp460-1   Cheese Cake $

☎ 718-852-5257; 386 Flatbush Ave; ⏲ breakfast, lunch & dinner till late; ⊖ B, M, Q, R to Dekalb Ave

This 1950 legend is a stylish, well-lit locale that resembles heaven. But really the only other-worldly contribution it makes is the cheesecake. Many locals grab a slice topped with cherry or pineapple to go, or choose to eat in the orange decor inside. Bill Clinton has been known to enjoy a slice, too. It's not a bad place to grab a snack (or a drink – there's a bar too) after a show at nearby BAM (p176) in the evening.

PEDRO'S BAR & RESTAURANT

Map p462   Mexican & Spanish $

☎ 718-625-0031; 73 Jay St at Front St; ☺ breakfast, lunch & dinner; ◉ F to York St

All the fancy eating over on Washington St feels miles apart from Dumbo's oldest resident. Scrappy and loved, Pedro's churns out hearty breakfasts and $2 tamales for the beer-bound. Happy hour runs 4pm to 7pm (beer only, $2.50 a bottle). At the long wood bar inside cocktails are mixed, but the best idea is to settle on the motley crew of outdoor seats on the covered sidewalk.

COBBLE HILL, BOERUM HILL, CARROLL GARDENS & RED HOOK

Smith St, south of Atlantic Ave, is one of Brooklyn's famed hip eating strips (French, Thai, Mexican etc) with many good choices not listed here. A block west, Court St is another strip lined with eating options.

Red Hook's food front is in its crawling stages, but there are a couple choices on Van Brunt St for adventurers.

ALMA Map p465   Mexican $$

☎ 718-643-5400; 187 Columbia St at Degraw St; ☺ dinner Mon-Fri, breakfast, lunch & dinner Sat & Sun; ◉ F, G to Carroll St

Atop a building near the waterfront, split-level Alma packs 'em in less so for the fare (which is tasty) than the list of 20-some tequilas *and* the knock-out views of Lower Manhattan from the rooftop. Most of the food is standard Mexican – steak fajitas are $16. A bit more inventive, corn tortillas stuffed with chicken and cheese and covered in pumpkin sauce is $12.50. Margaritas start at $7. If you don't reserve ahead, you can wait in the downstairs bar for a seat – and it's worth holding out for the rooftop over the 2nd-floor dining area – it's even covered and heated in winter. Weekend brunch begins at 10am.

CUBANA CAFE Map p465   Cuban $

☎ 718-858-3980; 272 Smith St, btwn Sackett & Degraw Sts; ☺ lunch & dinner; ◉ F, G to Carroll St

Juiced on $5 *mojitos* and Cuban beers, the crowd in the miniscule, lively Cubana Cafe linger long over tasty, ridiculously cheap meals. Many of the mains come with rice and beans spilling off the plate – and breakfast is an option all day (as it should be). Most of the dishes are the pulled-pork or pounded-chicken variety, but there's an all-veggie rice with snow peas, tomatoes, corn and bell pepper for $7. The *ropa vieja*, a braised beef with sautéed onions, is lovely. Cheapest snacks in the city: $2 roasted corn with chipotle mayo.

GROCERY Map p465   Modern American $$

☎ 718-596-3335; 288 Smith St; ☺ dinner; ◉ F, G to Carroll St

Minimal and small, the friendly Grocery towers over the Smith St eating options for its well-prepared changing menu of fish and meat dishes. And the success hasn't gone to their heads. Chefs come out to help you pick a wine ($35 to $120 per bottle) from the 50 choices, and put together a few surprise appetizers for starters. The roasted beets atop goat-cheese ravioli and sprinkled with pine nuts ($11) is excellent – you'll want to order another. There are plenty of daily options, the juicy pork chop comes sliced, as does the boneless roasted chicken. An obscure fruit, lemon-lime quinz, is set on the tables, matching the bare walls. In good weather, the back garden doubles the capacity, but you *must* reserve at any time to get in.

PACIFICO Map p462   Mexican $

☎ 718-935-9090; 269 Pacific St; ☺ lunch & dinner; ◉ F, G to Bergen St

This multirooomed Mexican restaurant looks like a Don Quixote hang-out (bell chandeliers, wood-beam ceilings, black-velvet matadors), with three rooms and heat lamps to keep outside decks toasty for the margarita-fueled madhouse. The food is pretty Tex-y and good. The $7.50 taco or enchilada combos aren't overwhelmingly filling; chips and salsa are extra. Margaritas are $6.

360 Map p465   French $$

☎ 718-246-0360; 360 Van Brunt St, btwn Wolcott & Dikeman Sts; ☺ dinner Wed-Sun; ◉ F, G to Carroll St

Facing public basketball courts, this simple but memorable French restaurant brings them in for $25 prixe fixe menu that skips the typical steak-frites menus you find at boilerplate French restaurants city-wide. The menu is seasonal, tapping heavily into local organic farms. Reserve ahead: don't make it all the way here to be turned away for lack of seats. Bus B61 connects Red Hook with the subway stop.

PARK SLOPE & PROSPECT HEIGHTS

It's not hard finding food on Fifth or Seventh Aves in Park Slope. Most fancier options are between the 'named' cross streets – particularly on Fifth Ave – with cheaper options in the 'numbered' cross streets to the south.

Most locals and visitors wander to Park Slope for meals, but Vanderbilt Ave in Prospect Heights is starting to fill its blocks between Eastern Pkwy and Atlantic Ave with cafés and a couple of good restaurants.

The treelined, shockingly Americana-style 'hood of Ditmas Park consists of stand-alone houses on treelined streets. It has relatively few eating options aside from Cinco de Mayo (right).

APPLEWOOD Map p464 American $$
☎ 718-768-2044; www.applewoodny.com; 501 11th St, btwn Seventh & Eighth Aves; ⓥ dinner Tue-Sat, lunch Sun; ⓔ F to 7th Av
Set up in a century-old storefront on a leafy side street, excellent Applewood fills nightly with chatty locals who lounge for hours in a simple Americana space with a lone bookcase, candle-lit tables, a working fireplace, and back bar with cocktails and a long wine list. Unless you really aren't hungry, you'll need an appetizer to yourself (portions are artful but not huge). The creamy lobster broth is a hearty soup for $8. The upstate venison – sliced and grilled – comes with leeks and shallots ($26). There's always a lone veggie option – like the spinach and basil risotto with mascarpone cheese – and several fish dishes. Chef David Shea runs classes once monthly.

BLUE RIBBON SUSHI BROOKLYN
Map p464 Sushi $$
☎ 718-840-0408; 278 Fifth Ave, btwn 1st St & Garfield Pl; ⓥ dinner; ⓔ M, R to Union St
Blue Ribbon's sushi outpost here saves many Brooklynites seeking raw fish a subway ride away in Manhattan. Next to Blue Ribbon's meat- and oyster-filled restaurant, the sushi counterpart features sleek wooden benches and a long list of sashimi, sushi and maki rolls. If you can't pick and choose, the sushi sashimi combo is $27.50.

CINCO DE MAYO Map pp460-1 Mexican $
☎ 718-693-1022; 1202 Cortelyou Rd at Westminster Rd; ⓥ breakfast, lunch & dinner; ⓔ Q to Courtelyou Rd
New York is no San Francisco or LA (or Guadalajara) when it comes to finding a good enchilada, but more and more family-style Mexican eateries are popping up. This one, about 10 minutes' walk south of Prospect Park via Coney Island Ave to Courtelyou Rd, is small but festive, and cranks out *excellente* food. Try the *chilaquiles con huevo* with spicy green or red sauce ($7) – it's egg and cheese covering grilled tortillas. The subway stop is a few blocks east.

TEA LOUNGE
Map p464 Sandwiches & Tea $
☎ 718-789-2762; 350 Union St, btwn Sixth & Seventh Aves; ⓥ 7-1am Mon-Thu, 7-2am Fri, 8-2am Sat, 8-1am Sun; ⓔ 2,3 to Grand Army Plaza or M, R to Union St
Popular and huge, the Tea Lounge smacks of a student hangout on the West Coast. In communal seating nooks, laptop gangs borrow the free WiFi and parents entertain whippersnappers. There's lots of loose teas ($2.75 for personal pot), plus good sandwiches and salads listed on a chalk menu – and a full bar!

TOM'S RESTAURANT
Map p464 Diner $
☎ 718-636-9738; 782 Washington Ave, at Sterling Pl; ⓥ breakfast & lunch Mon-Sat; ⓔ 2, 3 to Eastern Pkwy–Brooklyn Museum
Three blocks from the Brooklyn Museum, this happy greasy spoon woos locals with all-day breakfasts and egg creams. Open since 1936, much of the decor (floral in all possible forms) has been picked up along the way. It's good and cheap: two eggs, toast, coffee, home fries or grits (go for grits) costs $3. *Huevos rancheros* is a recent addition, in addition to a dozen varieties of pancake (the chocolate is like eating syrup-soaked, plate-sized cookies). Saturday mornings mean lines out the door, but staff (the nicest in New York) bring by cups of coffee, 'cold orange slices' and cookies while you wait.

BAY RIDGE

The best strip for food in far-flung Bay Ridge, at the footstep of the Verrazano-Narrows Bridge, is Third Ave between 76th and 95th Sts.

PHO HOAI Map pp460-1   Vietnamese $
☎ 718-745-1640; 8616 Fourth Ave, btwn 86th & 87th Sts; ☽ lunch & dinner; ⓑ R to 86th St
This very friendly restaurant serves fresh Vietnamese dishes – grilled squid, *pho* (beef noodle soup), vermicelli dishes – to a loyal local crowd. It's pretty simple – running the Chinatown template – but keeps its lights softer (and floors cleaner). A good starter is the *goi tom can tay* (shrimp salad; $6 or $8) – ask for rice paper for makeshift summer rolls. This place is half a block from the subway.

CONEY ISLAND & BRIGHTON BEACH

Most of the Coney Island boardwalk eateries are greasy deals catering to the state fair–feel of the neighboring 'shoot the freak' games and kid-oriented rides. More options loom in Brighton Beach.

Along Brighton Beach Ave from Brighton 1st St to Brighton 12th or 13th Sts and along crisscrossing Coney Island Ave you can find several small groceries or restaurants with menus in Cyrillic. Several groceries are stocked with goods from the motherland (including chocolates in Czar boxes).

CAFE GLECHIK Map p466   Russian $
☎ 718-616-0494; 3159 Coney Island Ave; ☽ breakfast, lunch & dinner; ⓑ B, Q to Brighton Beach
Done up in folksy Russian knickknacks, this small cheap restaurant cooks up homey Russian dishes for a loyal local crowd. Prices are cheap, and it offers more lunch life than the bigger banquet-hall restaurants that can feel a little lifeless outside show time at night. The café opens at 10am. When taking your order, staff may ask '*gotovie?*' meaning 'ready?'

M & I INTERNATIONAL
Map p466   Groceries $
☎ 718-615-1011; 249 Brighton Beach Ave btwn Brighton 2nd & 3rd Sts; ☽ 8am-10pm; ⓑ B, Q to Brighton Beach
This is the best of the grocery places, with Russian chocolates in Czar-print fit boxes. It

has a dining area and an outside deck for borscht and Russian fare upstairs.

NATHAN'S FAMOUS Map p466   Hot dogs $
☎ 718-946-2202; 1310 Surf Ave; ☽ breakfast, lunch & dinner till late; ⓑ D, F to Coney Island–Stillwell Ave
If you eat 'em, this is *the* place to stomach the all-beef dog with sauerkraut and mustard. Coneys aren't named as such for nothing, and Nathan's has been serving the local fare since 1916. A frightening time to visit is July 4, when Nathan's holds a hot dog–eating contest (the record stands at Takeru Kobayashi's 50½).

RESTAURANT VOLNA
Map p466   Russian $
☎ 718-332-0501; 3145 Brighton 4th St; ☽ 9am-10pm; ⓑ B, Q to Brighton Beach
This boardwalk place, often filled with crusty locals and teens with carefully blow-dried hair, serves cups of *kvas* ($3; fermented rye bread water). There's a stuffy dining room with lunch specials and sea views too.

TATIANA Map p466   Russian $$$
☎ 718-891-5151; www.tatiana-restaurant.com; 3152 Brighton 6th St; ☽ lunch & dinner; ⓑ B, Q to Brighton Beach
A banquet dinner hall on the Brighton Beach boardwalk, Tatiana is a cheesy mix of glitz and dacha murals on the wall. Meals are huge – with lots of caviar and meats to share, plus vodka. And the place feels like being aboard a Russian cruise – with costumed dancers, magicians and acrobats performing. Banquet meals are from $65 Saturday night, from $85 Saturday lunch and from $55 Sunday.

TOTONNO'S Map p466   Pizza $$
☎ 718-372-8606; 1524 Neptune Ave; ☽ noon-8pm Wed-Sun; ⓑ D, F to Coney Island–Stillwell Ave
Run by the same family since 1924, Totonno's is, many New Yorkers swear, the city's best. Hard to argue, considering the mozzarella is homemade, the tomatoes are imported from Italy and the pizzas are baked in a clay oven. The place is simple (a couple of blocks' walk from the boardwalk), but the sauce itself is enough to justify a trip to Coney Island.

FORT GREENE

A number of neighborhood restaurants line Fort Greene's Dekalb Ave, between Vanderbilt Ave and Fort Greene Park (Cumberland St). Brunch is a big deal here, as are late-night meals at a mix of offerings (Japanese, South African, Italian, Indian, French).

ICI Map pp460-1 — French & American $$
☎ 718-789-2778; www.icirestaurant.com; 246 Dekalb Ave; ☾ breakfast, lunch & dinner Tue-Sun; ◉ G to Clinton–Washington Ave

French by name (and chef), ici fuses different worlds on its menu and wine list. The seasonal menu draws heavily on all-natural ingredients from farmers markets and isn't afraid to pair *pico de gallo* with mackerel. The braised pork shoulder goes South with collard greens and grits. The 40-seat spot, on the ground floor of a brownstone building, has cleanly painted brick walls, a fireplace, wall sconces and a bricked courtyard. Breakfast is a bonus, with croissants made in the back, and excellent takes on the usuals.

WILLIAMSBURG

All the Williamsburg hipsters have to eat *somewhere*. The main crawl, Bedford Ave, has the most options, but they tend to be cheaper, less rewarding, than newbies on side streets such as N 6th St. Many are quite swank jobs built to appeal to splurging locals or uptown folk looking to slum it a night Billyburg-style. For Thai food amid the well-dressed, see SEA (p276).

ENID'S Map p463 — American $
☎ 718-349-3859; 560 Manhattan Ave at Driggs Ave; ☾ dinner daily, brunch Sat & Sun; ◉ G to Nassau Ave

Up in Greenpoint (a 15-minute walk from the heart of Bedford), Enid's is an evocative bar that serves a mean, deeply Southern-style weekend brunch – the 'hungry bear' is a gravy covered biscuit and egg with veggie sausage – that draws long lines. Inside is a bric-a-brac of old Americana – chipped wood floors, tin ceilings and peeling floral wallpaper. The staff say the building is haunted. Every night it's a nice place for dinner, before refocusing as a bar after 10pm.

LODGE Map p463 — American $
☎ 718-486-9400; 318 Grand St; ☾ lunch & dinner; ◉ L to Bedford Ave

On a rare shaded street in Williamsburg, the Lodge is a new, faintly rustic place (fake-antler chandeliers, stone pillars, scuffed-up dark-wood walls, potted plants) serving comfort food to hipster couples. Weekend brunch is $10 including a Bloody Mary. Dinners are pretty gamey, though there's a seitan with polenta ($12). The kitchen has a peep window looking onto the sidewalk, where tables are set in good weather.

MOTO Map p463 — French Bistro $
☎ 718-599-6895; 394 Broadway, cnr Hooper St & Division Ave; ☾ dinner; ◉ J, M, Z to Hewes St

Housed in a former check-cashing spot on a triangular corner almost under the J-M-Z tracks, the remarkably renovated, unsigned Moto – named so because they 'like motorcycles' – is in a dark corner of Williamsburg. There's nightly music (via an accordionist in the corner) and creaky dark-wood floors and chipped painted brick walls, all of which create a rather old-worldly (or at least Quebecois, as in *Delicatessen*) vibe. Appetizers and panini ($8) and macaroni-and-cheese ($11) are probably the best choices. But it's worth it more for the wine, imported beer and scene.

PETER LUGER STEAKHOUSE
Map p463 — Steaks $$$
☎ 718-387-7400; 178 Broadway; ☾ lunch & dinner; ◉ J, M, Z to Marcy Ave

This place has been a Williamsburg meat-eating haven since 1887. Peter Luger serves up some of the city's juiciest, most-famed sirloin cuts (as well as lamb chops, grilled salmon and – for beginners – burgers). It's timeless dining, from its Bavarian design and (rather brusque) waitstaff in aprons. Bring cash: no major credit cards accepted.

RELISH Map p463 — American $$
☎ 718-963-4546; 225 Wythe Ave at N 3rd St; ☾ lunch & dinner; ◉ L to Bedford Ave

Housed in a 1952 Pullman car that's sat here since 1968, Relish has serious atmosphere – with brown leather seats and aluminum blinds and a curving bar with red bulbs and candles that give the dining hipsters (and their parents) a soft glow. The food is good, but standard 'upscale' – with hangar steaks with potatoes ($20) and glazed salmon with mustard and lentils ($17). Vegetarians can opt for falafel with artichoke and eggplant ($13). Locals prefer it, with cheaper prices, for 11am brunch. During good weather, the backyard adds table space.

WILLIAMSBURGH CAFE

Map p463   American $$

☎ 718-387-5855; 170 Wythe Ave; ☻ lunch & dinner Tue-Sun; ◉ L to Bedford Ave

It's kinda ridiculous, and probably the least likely restaurant to hoist the neighborhood's name (though the old-style '-h' gives it separation). However, the Williamsburgh's back room (aka 'garden') is lushly done up in maps, photos and pieces from the 1870s days of the neighborhood. Staff bring hefty plates of beef and fish on the scratched up saloon-plank falls, as a jazz trio plays softly under an indoor garden trellis. Food's good (not super) and it's fun.

QUEENS

Considering its ethnic diversity – Queens is the most diverse 'hood in the world, after all – the thrill of food really can tempt a detour across the East River to this often-missed and underrated borough. Many successful mom 'n' pop eateries in Manhattan only set up shop after testing the waters in areas like Flushing first.

LONG ISLAND CITY & ASTORIA

Vernon Blvd, a couple blocks west of PS1 (p184) and the Citicorp building is up-and-coming, with newish eating options (pizza, Thai, Chinese, Italian).

Astoria teems with Greek, Mexican and Eastern European options – particularly under the elevated subway line on 31st St. Further south, Broadway (between 31st and 35th Sts) is something of a 'Greek row' with diners. Most who make it to Astoria eye the Bohemian Hall & Beer Garden (p276) for fresh pints of Czech beer – it also has food.

CAFE HENRI Map p457   French $

☎ 718-383-9315; 1010 50th Ave at Vernon Blvd; ☻ 8am-midnight; ◉ 7 to Vernon Blvd–Jackson Ave

Good art break potential, this café – a Queens cousin of the Gamin creperies

in Manhattan – is a welcoming place for leisurely snacking, about five minutes' walk from PS1. An open kitchen serves the small space – about 10 tables on wood floors; omelets are $8.50, meat or cheese crepes start at $7. There's live jazz on Thursday and Saturday nights from 8pm.

ELIA'S FISH CORNER

Map p457   Seafood $$

☎ 718-932-1510; 24-02, 31st St; ☻ dinner; ◉ N, W to Astoria Blvd

Take note of the counter of fresh fish as you walk into this corner Greek fish place (right under the elevated subway line) – that's your dinner. The chefs don't get fussy on details – you pick your fish, they grill (whole) your fish, you eat your fish. A host of juicy appetizers are on hand (the grilled octopus is good, but the scallops are particularly tasty). There's Greek beer and wine.

COMMUNITEA

Map p457   Coffee & Sandwiches $

☎ 718-729-7708; 47-02 Vernon Blvd; ☻ breakfast, lunch & dinner; ◉ 7 to Vernon Blvd–Jackson Ave

A casual new café on a Long Island City corner, Communitea has a chalk menu scrawled on the back wall, Eames-style plastic seats and exposed-brick walls. Lite electronica plays for the many locals with laptops, here for sandwiches, coffee and free WiFi.

JACKSON HEIGHTS

A bit further 'in,' Jackson Heights is Queens' most tightly packed smorgasbord of eating options. Cheaper, quicker eats – from tacos to chow mein – can be easily found along Roosevelt Ave, under the rattle of the No 7 subway tracks. More comfortable sit-down places of all stripes are a block north along 37th Ave.

CAVALIER RESTAURANT   International $$

☎ 718-458-7474; 85-19 37th Ave btwn 85th & 86th Sts; ☻ lunch & dinner; ◉ 7 to 82nd St–Jackson Heights

Looking a lot like it did on its opening day in 1950, the long-time family-run Cavalier fills with many aged regulars – some heavy lipsticked and smoking out front. Recently renovated, the graceful dining room, with round booths and well-dressed staff, faces a full bar. The menu runs the gamut from $8 shepherd's pie to $20 veal cavalier or shrimp parmigiana. The $13 brunch on weekends (from noon to 3pm) includes a Bloody Mary. In October the Cavalier goes with '50s prices for a week. From the subway, walk a block northeast to 37th Ave and then turn right. It's a few blocks down on the left.

JACKSON DINER   Map p442   Indian $
☎ 718-672-1232; 37-47 74th St btwn Roosevelt Ave & 37th Ave; ⏱ lunch & dinner; ⓔ 7 to 74th St–Broadway

Most curry-bound diners along Jackson Heights follow their noses to this classic, a converted diner that fills for a daily lunch buffet of changing curries and sweets ($9 weekdays, $10 weekends). The buffet, which runs from 11:30am to 4pm daily, is worth the extra dollar or two over other cheapie buffets in the area. It's tasty and the '90s modern remodeling of an old diner is more comfy. Mixed drinks are $7.50. At least half the buffet options are veggie. The menu kicks in after 4pm. The diner is half a block from the subway stop, on the right-hand side.

LA BOINA ROJA   Map p442   Colombian $$
☎ 718-424-6711; 80-22 37th Ave btwn 80th & 81st Sts; ⏱ lunch & dinner; ⓔ 7 to 82nd St–Jackson Heights

A popular Colombian steakhouse named for the red berets that the staff wear – apparently a tradition from Medellín. A plate of steak or red snapper – there's not much for vegetarians – comes with rice and beans. Start with a *chicharron con arepa* (fried pork belly with corn cake) for $2.50. From the subway, head northwest a block to 37th Ave; it's a block away.

FLUSHING & JAMAICA

Some call Flushing 'Chinatown without the tourists.' And it can feel equally as frantic. Much of the area's inviting Chinese, Vietnamese, Korean and Malaysian restaurants are just on and off the intersection of Main St and Roosevelt Ave.

If you're on the prowl for hip-hop clothing in the neighborhood Jamaica, further along, there are a few takeout conch and jerk-chicken places on 165th St.

PRINCE RESTAURANT
Map p467   Chinese $
☎ 718-888-3138; 37-17 Prince St btwn 37th & 38th Aves; ⏱ 8:30am-11pm; ⓔ 7 to Flushing–Main St

Just west of the main Flushing strip, on quieter Prince St, this buzzing and quite authentic dim sum restaurant draws big lines. Past the front fish tanks, women with burgundy visors and mint-colored skirts wheel around carts with a host of pork-, shrimp- and veggie-filled dim sum dishes you pick-and-point to get. Those not willing to play lottery – English is definitely a distant second language among staff – can order noodles and the like from the menu. Dim sum rolls daily from 9am to 3pm. There's a basement area, but stick with upstairs for the full effect. Expect on paying $12 or so per person.

RINCÓN SALVADOREÑO   El Salvodorean $
☎ 718-526-3220; 92-15 149th St at Jamaica Ave; ⏱ breakfast, lunch & dinner; ⓔ E, J, Z to Jamaica Center–Parsons-Archer

A few blocks west of Jamaica's hip-hop shopping crawl on 165th St, Rincón Salvadoreño is a festive place (with beach murals and fake plants) with families ordering in *Español*. The food is great. *Pupusas* filled with cheese or meats are $1.50. Various combo plates of *pupusas* with mixed beans-and-rice with a huge sausage and a cube of white cheese run from about $8 to $12. There's live music at 8pm on Friday and Saturday night.

THE BRONX

Belmont, the Little Italy of the Bronx where *A Bronx Tale* was filmed, is the borough's most famous culinary enclave with tempting trattorias and pizzerias. It's centered on Arthur Ave, just south of Fordham University.

BRUCKNER BAR & GRILL
Map pp468-9   Sandwiches & Salads $
☎ 718-665-2001; cnr Bruckner Blvd & Third Ave; ⏱ lunch & dinner; ⓔ 6 to 3rd Ave–138th St

Looking like a 100-year-old classic, with chipped-wood floors and historic photos of the area, this place is actually a new version of an elevator factory. It's mostly about beer, wine and some surprisingly good sandwiches (the *cubano* comes with ham, shredded pork and pickles). The grill has a side room with a stage for shows and comedy. It's nearly under the Third Ave Bridge overpass.

ROBERTO'S Map pp468-9   Italian $$

☎ 718-733-2868; 632 E 186th St at Belmont Ave; ⏱ lunch & dinner Tue-Fri, dinner Sat; Ⓑ B, D to Fordham Rd

Just off Arthur Ave (the 'real' Little Italy), Roberto's great reputation is sworn by its fans, with frightening passion, as New York's – not just Belmont's – best Italian restaurant. There's a no reservations policy, so as the night wears on, lines congregate by the bar – for hours. It's well worth it. Ask for the chef's choice, and Roberto – hilariously festive – comes by and lights up your table with dish after dish or Northern Italian specialties. Daily specials are many, including swordfish steaks and veal cutlets, with pasta sides. In nice weather, sidewalk seating is the way to go.

TONY'S PIER Map pp468-9   Fast Food $

☎ 718-885-1424; 1 City Island Ave; ⏱ lunch & dinner

City Island (p201) has plenty of seafood choices, such as this waterside restaurant, a wild fast-food–style place with fried fish and serious drinking at nighttime. There may be more signs to direct people to the cashier than any restaurant in human history. It gets rollicking in the outside seating some nights.

Drinking

Drinking

There are more high brow cultural ventures in this fine city, to be sure. But drinking is a universal pleasure, right? Plus here, along with the usual dose of holes in the wall and gritty dives (fast disappearing), drinking has been elevated to an art form. You'll find dramatic, low lit lounges helmed by DJs with fierce followings. You'll find martini bars where special cocktail experts have been hired to create new elixirs, combining fresh fruit and herbs and muddled sweeteners with the focus of sculptors chipping at marble. Then there are theme bars, with interiors like stage sets and music like film soundtracks, or wine bars, where you'll be transported to Italy or Spain with a pour and a sip.

But, for just a quick dose of reality before you get started, remember that this isn't Italy, because (just one of many reasons) there's no smoking allowed in bars. Unless you're in a specified cigar bar (which, curiously enough, are still allowed, even though the smoke stinks even more...) or at one of the places lucky enough to have outdoor patios or roof decks, you'll be banished to the sidewalk for your tobacco breaks. You also must be 21 years old to get served in a bar, so, though not all places are equal when it comes to being cautious, definitely bring some ID if you don't want to be turned away. But underagers, take note: a handful of clubs are 18-and-over on some if not all nights, including **Spirit** (p299) and **Avalon** (p298).

Some of New York's great bars can be found in hotels, see p371. Most bars stay open until the legal closing time of 4am, though a few stop at 2am; opening times vary, but some start as early as 8am! Nothing like starting a day of touring with a strong Bloody Mary, right?

LOWER MANHATTAN

Let's be honest: This is not exactly the place to head if you're looking for a fun night out of elbow bending. But if you find yourself here after dinner or touring, or if your hotel's in the area and you want a nightcap, you won't go thirsty. Prepare for tie-loosening financial types to be your new drinking buddies.

DAKOTA ROADHOUSE Map pp444-5
☎ 212-962-9800; 43 Park Pl btwn Church St & West Broadway; ⊕ 1 to Park Pl
A crazy urban roadhouse gone wonderfully awry, the kitschy tongue-in-cheek vibe here is highlighted by details like the table hockey game and live lobster machine, which lets you (cover your ears, vegans) pluck your favorite with an automatic claw like you're playing a stuffed-animal game at a carnival. The kitchen will then cook up your prize and serve you a stiff one. Or you can while away the evening at one of the popular pool tables.

JEREMY'S ALE HOUSE Map pp444-5
☎ 212-964-3537; 254 Front St at Dover St; ⊕ J, M, Z to Chambers St, 2, 3 to Fulton St, 4, 5, 6 to Brooklyn Bridge–City Hall
An odd mix of frat house and quirky dive bar, Jeremy's is where you'll find bras hung over the bar, cheap pints served in Styrofoam cups and a lovely view of the Brooklyn Bridge. It's a curious place for a quick stop-in – which can happen at pretty much anytime, thanks to its frighteningly early opening hour (8am on weekdays!).

HEARTLAND BREWERY Map pp444-5
☎ 646-472-2337; South Street Seaport, 93 South St at Fulton St; ⊕ J, M, Z, 2, 3, 4, 5 to Fulton St
The newest and southernmost outpost of this Manhattan mini-chain is housed in a 200-year-old pub space in the Seaport. If it's warm you can drink up at one of the outdoor café areas, or opt for the cozy, antique-clad interior. Pick from delicious brews like oatmeal stout, chocolatey Stumbling Buffalo Ale, Summertime Apricot Ale and the famous Smiling Pumpking Ale. It's like liquid dessert.

RISE Map pp444-5
☎ 212-344-0800; Ritz-Carlton New York, 14th fl, 2 West St at Battery Pl; ⊕ N, R, W to Rector St
Even $14 martinis won't make you think twice about hanging at this Ritz-Carlton (p354) view bar, where the sleek, high-up lounge affords spectacular vistas over sunsets over the Hudson, plus tasty cocktails and amusing people-watching opportunities of the rich and (not) famous. There is a dress code,

of course – 'smart casual' – but you'll want to look slick here, a place striking enough to make you want to make an effort.

ULYSSES Map pp444–5

☎ 212-482-0400; 95 Pearl St (or 58 Stone St); Ⓔ 2, 3 to Wall St

Old-school financial types have been flocking to this Hanover Sq newcomer, which succeeds in blending traditional Irish pub style with the modern lounge vibe. You'll find an impressive list of beers, tequilas, whiskeys and cordials; friendly, fresh-faced staff; and an encouraging stance when it comes to tying one on: Ulysses, which is run by the same folks who own Puck Fair (Map pp452–3; ☎ 212-431-1200; 298 Lafayette St btwn E Houston & Prince Sts) in Soho and Swift (☎ 212-242-9502; 34 E 4th St btwn Bowery & Lafayette St) in the East Village, runs a free shuttle that takes you from one establishment to the other, so you don't have to be responsible for getting yourself around! Oh, there's a menu, too, and it's got oysters on it.

TRIBECA & SOHO

Both 'hoods have always been the place to find a good combo of see-and-be-seen lounges with high ceilings, trendy hotel bars and cozy old-fashioned pubs, to boot. Stroll east along Spring St starting way west, for example, and you'll want to stop every 20 feet to check out one of the many cozy nooks, peopled with beautiful folk who look at ease and mellow in the flickering candlelight.

TRIBECA

ANOTHER ROOM Map pp444–5

☎ 212-226-1418; 249 West Broadway btwn Beach & North Moore Sts; Ⓔ 1, 2 to Franklin St

This is the kind of place that lures you inside, whether you were looking for a drink or not. It's tiny and narrow, with an industrial-chic, cement-floor sort of style, and its walls hold works by local artists. There are no cocktails, but the wine and beer list is great, as is the mellow and diverse crowd that settles in nightly. Additional outposts – in other neighborhoods but with the same lovely vibe – are Other Room (Map p448; 143 Perry St between Greenwich and Washington Sts) and Room (144 Sullivan St between Houston and Prince Sts).

BRANDY LIBRARY Map pp444–5

☎ 212-226-5545; 25 N Moore St at Varick St; Ⓔ 1 to Franklin St

If you see sipping as a serious sort of pastime, the Library will make you feel like you've entered nirvana. With soothing reading lamps, beautiful bottles lining the back-lit, floor-to-ceiling shelves and brown club chairs begging you to sink on in, this place is studiously designed to make you feel smart about your drinking. So choose a top-shelf liquor from the very extensive catalog – Legend XO Extra old reserve French cognac or Orkney Island 18-year-old Highland Park single malt scotch, for example – and focus.

LIQUOR STORE BAR Map pp444–5

☎ 212-226-7121; 235 West Broadway at White St; Ⓔ A, C, E to Canal St

It's located in a Federal-style building that its owners proudly claim has been in commercial use since 1804, and it's got big windows and outdoor tables offering plenty of people-watching opportunities. The bar takes its name from a previous business at the same site, and offers a down-to-earth respite from Tribeca trendies.

SOHO

C TABAC Map p450

☎ 212-941-1781; 32 Watts St btwn Sixth Ave & Thompson St; Ⓔ A, C, E, 1 to Canal St

One of five places left in the city where you can still smoke (and are encouraged to do so) with your drink, Tabac offers more than 150 types of smokes, mainly global cigars. Its specialty drink list ranges from the soothing Cucumber Cocktail (gin, lemon, sugar and cukes) to the pucker inducing Gingersnap (ginger-infused vodka, crystallized ginger and champagne), and the deco-style lounge, with bamboo walls, velvet lounge chairs and circular booths, is as sumptuous as much of its fine-cut tobacco.

EAR INN Map p450

☎ 212-226-9060; 326 Spring St btwn Greenwich & Washington Sts; ⊕ C, E to Spring St

A block from the Hudson River, this great old dive sits in the old James Brown House (the James Brown who was an aide to George Washington, not Soul Brother No 1), which dates back to 1817. Patrons range from sanitation workers and office dweebs to bikers and poets – and all of them love it, as well as the bar's famous shepherd's pie. Its landmarked status ensures that it'll stay around, despite the fact that the just-begun 12-story condo project, Philip Johnson's Urban Glass House, will be towering over it in a couple of years.

MERCBAR Map p450

☎ 212-966-2727; 151 Mercer St btwn Houston & Prince Sts; ⊕ R, W to Prince St

This intimate hideaway, with its mellow, quiet-discussion vibe and ski-lodge sort of look, is a great place to join a true after-work crowd (expect employees in publishing, retail and marketing, among other neighborhood specialties) and get into the sweet elixirs served in those magical martini glasses.

MILANO'S Map p450

☎ 212-226-8844; 51 E Houston St btwn Mulberry & Mott Sts; ⊕ B, D, F, V to Broadway–Lafayette St

For nearly a century, hole-in-the-wall Milano's has withstood the hipster onslaught and stayed true to its divey self – with offerings like $3 Pabst Blue Ribbon beers and a selection of potato chips that hang behind the worn, wooden bar. Crusty regulars and curious young visitors mix it up easily, bonding over pints of Guinness and a great, old-school stacked jukebox with offerings from Tony Bennett to the Chieftains.

PRAVDA MAP p450

☎ 212-226-4944; 281 Lafayette St btwn Prince & Houston Sts; ⊕ B, D, F, V to Broadway–Lafayette St

Pravda tried to remain on the down low, but lines out the door leaked the secret to the entire city. If you dress hip enough and look sufficiently intense, you'll make it past the gatekeepers and enter clouds of cigar smoke in this mock East European speakeasy. The martinis make all the hassle worth it, though; the two-page vodka list includes Canada's Inferno Pepper, a home-grown Rain Organic and a slew of specialty

martinis. Iced racks of global caviar make a perfect match.

CHINATOWN, LITTLE ITALY & NOHO

Once night settles over the city, these three nabes easily blend into one, as drinking in these parts is an equally mixed bag – offering a strange mix of old-man dives and hyper-trendy hideaways. Chinatown is home to various karaoke bars, attracting local youngsters and uptown visitors alike, while Winnie's (opposite) is the classic; strolling around the innards of the neighborhood until you find a more obscure one to pop into is always a fun idea. Little Italy and Noho, meanwhile, are home to varied nooks with old-world, global vibes.

CHIBI'S BAR Map p450

☎ 212-274-0025; 238 Mott St btwn Prince & Spring Sts; ⊕ 6 to Spring St

This tiny, romantic sake bar has a delicately curved wooden bar with ice-blue stools, plus a loungier room to one side. It works its magic through smooth jazz sounds (live on Sundays) and the dangerously delicious flavors of specialty sakes, saketinis and a unique bar menu boasting treats from edamame to salmon caviar. Two other, equally alluring outposts are Chibitini (63 Clinton St between Rivington and Stanton Sts), on the Lower East Side, and the Kitchen Club (30 Prince St), just around the corner from Chibi's and offering up a great menu of homemade dumplings. The best part at each location, though, is the host and namesake, Chibi, a sweet little bulldog.

DOUBLE HAPPINESS Map p450

☎ 212-941-1282; 173 Mott St btwn Broome & Grand Sts; ⊕ J, M, Z to Bowery, 6 to Spring St

This tiled, basement-level bar tunnels through an old apartment with a narrow skylight room and tables tucked into candlelit corners. Pretty girls scan the crowd for a well-dressed Romeo among the wrinkled bards. It's too cool to be signed, but look for the steep stone steps. Or head next door to its newer dive-bar other half, Palais Royale (Map p450; ☎ 212-941-6112; 173 ½ Mott St), where you'll find a lengthy bourbon menu, classic frozen dinners (Hungry Man, anyone?) for noshing, and a pool table for unwinding.

MARE CHIARO Map p450
☎ 212-226-9345; 176½ Mulberry St btwn Broome & Grand Sts; ⓒ B, D to Grand St
Frank Sinatra liked this 100-year-old Little Italy hang, which was also used as a backdrop for scenes in *The Godfather*. And you'll like it for hanging around, even as Little Italy slowly disappears. The gruff, old-school bartenders add to the charm, as does the odd mix of wide-eyed tourists, crusty regulars and the overflow of hipsters from other area watering holes.

WINNIE'S Map pp444–5
☎ 212-732-2384; 104 Bayard St btwn Baxter & Mulberry Sts; ⓒ J, M, Z, N, Q, R, W, 6 to Canal St
Performing drunken, embarrassing karaoke at this Chinatown dive is a rite of passage for New Yorkers. The place is tiny and always packed, the disgusting cocktails (such as the Abortion, a mixture of Sambuca and Baileys) are potent, and the weird karaoke videos, flashed behind you on a movie screen, are shockingly stuck in the '80s.

LOWER EAST SIDE

Change comes and goes in waves in this corner of the city, still populated with a few leftover favorites from decades past, but more likely swelling with the unending addition of new hotspots that seem to sneak in and emerge, trendy crowds in place, overnight. Whatever your style, it's a convenient and overpopulated spot for a full night of drinking and schmoozing, as we prove beyond a shadow of a doubt in our highly focused walking tour, the Lower East Side Food & Drink walking tour (p210). Note that many of the best bars in the area are within great restaurants, so you'll have no problem sating your thirst and hunger in one fell swoop.

BARRAMUNDI Map p449
☎ 212-529-6900; 67 Clinton St btwn Stanton & Rivington Sts; ⓒ F, J, M, Z to Delancey St
This Australian-owned arty place, formerly located on Ludlow St, has taken up residence in this old tenement building after losing its lease at the old spot. Though its garden is gone, it's still home to Barramundi's biggest draws: convivial booths, reason-

ably priced drinks (including some Aussie imports) and some cool tree trunk tables.

BARRIO CHINO Map pp446–7
☎ 212-253 Broome St btwn Ludlow & Orchard Sts; ⓒ F, J, M, Z to Delancey St
Bellying up to the wooden bar here, a small but airy space lit with Chinese lanterns, will yield serious choice. The focus here is on fine sipping tequilas and the menu offers 50 – some of which cost as much as $25 per shot. The $7 options are much more popular, as are the fresh blood-orange margaritas, guacamole and tasty chicken tacos.

EAST SIDE COMPANY BAR Map pp446–7
☎ 212614-7408; 49 Essex St at Grand St; ⓒ F, J, M, Z to Delancey St
Brought to you by the same owner of the now-closed Milk & Honey – a tiny speakeasy sort of joint where you'd have to call ahead to get on the guest list or not be buzzed through the unmarked entrance – this place has a much better door policy. But luckily, it has a similar vibe, which is intimate, hushed and low-lit, with plenty of cozy booths and lots of pressed tin in the décor. DJs spin lounge music on weekends, adding a great soundtrack to your sips of zippy, unique elixirs and on-tap Guinness.

MAGICIAN Map p449
☎ 212-673-7851; 118 Rivington St btwn Essex & Norfolk Sts; ⓒ F to Delancey St, J, M, Z to Delancey–Essex Sts
An unassuming storefront with the requisite low lighting and well-mixed drinks, this neighborhood bar has achieved a magic formula: an unpretentious crowd, wonderfully eclectic jukebox (featuring favorites from Duke Ellington to the Cure) and plenty of space to put your elbows on the bar.

SUBA Map p449
☎ 212-982-5714; 109 Ludlow St btwn Delancey & Rivington Sts; ⓧ 6pm-1am Sun-Wed, 6pm-2am Thu, 6pm-4am Fri & Sat; ⓒ F to Delancey St, J, M, Z to Delancey–Essex Sts
Determined to keep on top of newer, trendier hotspots in the neighborhood, Suba's got an actual water-filled moat around its downstairs dining room, where

BENT BARS

Yes, yes, we know that while bars *used* to be hallowed ground for gay folks – the only place that was free and easy besides the closet – there are much more important ways for queer social butterflies to spend their time nowadays. But still, there *are* endless options – sexy lounges with hunky bartenders, girl bars with pool tables and flowing pints of beer, even a new sports bar for gay men that has Chelsea abuzz. So here's a brief guide (find many more at www.hx.com). You know, just in case. See also Clubs, p298. Also, of the various organizers throwing roving queer events, **Shescape** (www.shescape.com) for lesbians, the **Saint at Large** (www.saintatlarge.com) for circuit boys, and **Motherfucker** (www.motherfuckernyc.com) for rock-'n' art fags, are most worth looking into.

Lower East Side/East Village

Easternbloc (Map p449; ☎ 212-420-8885; 505 E 6th St between Aves A and B; ◉ F, V to Lower East Side–2nd Ave) The newest spot in the 'hood is home to a kitschy iron-curtain theme replete with Bettie Page videos, Communist-era posters and adorable Eastern European–looking bartenders.

Girls Room (Map p449; ☎ 212-254-5043; 210 Rivington St at Pitt St; ◉ F to East Broadway) This place was here to pick up the LES lesbian slack after the sad closing of Meow Mix a couple years back. Downtown divas pile in for nights dedicated to karaoke, open mikes and go-go dancers.

Slide/Marquee (☎ 212-420-8885; 356 Bowery; ◉ F, V to Lower East Side–2nd Ave) This two-level bar (with a drag-queen-heavy stage up top) has a low-key vibe and dedicated local crowds of skinny boys with beards and tattoos, and always some dykes in the mix. Check

out movie nights, live-music shows and more; it's also connected to the fabulous lounge/restaurant Marion's, serving bistro fare at street level.

Starlight Bar & Lounge (☎ 212-475-2172; 167 Ave A; ◉ L to 1st Ave) This is a sultry, loud, straight-friendly lounge with a devoted following of downtown cuties – both boys and girls. But Sunday means Starlette, a long running lesbians soiree for cosmo-sipping kittens. Catch a great comedy show with Keith Price on Wednesday.

Greenwich Village/West Village

Henrietta Hudson (Map p448; ☎ 212-924-3347; 438 Hudson St; ◉ 1 to Houston St) All sorts of cute young dykes storm this place, a former pool-and-pint sort of spot that's now a sleek lounge with varied DJs following a sultry make-over.

Monster (Map p448; ☎ 212-924-3558; 80 Grove St at Sheridan Sq; ◉ 1 to Christopher St–Sheridan Sq) It's old-school gay man–heaven in here, home to a small dancefloor as well as a piano bar and cabaret space. Theme nights range from Latino parties to drag queen–hosted soirees; well-known DJ Warren Gluck spins flashback songs at **Stonewall** (Map p448; ☎ 212-463-0950; 53 Christopher St; ◉ 1 to Christopher St–Sheridan Sq) The site of the Stonewall riots in 1969, when drag queens fought back during a police raid, this historic watering hole still holds its ground. Young ones are even packing the place since its recent redesign.

Chelsea

Eagle (☎ 646-473-1866; www.eaglenyc.com; 554 W 28th St; ◉ C, E to 23rd St) Leather- and Levi-clad men descend on the Eagle for cruisey fun and thematic nights

you can get top notch Spanish food along with your cocktails. The place is a wonder of architecture and design, highlighted by lots of exposed brick, flowing water, mezzanine overlooks and dramatic sweeps of stairs. Sangrias, fruity cocktails and Latin tapas are tasty highlights.

WELCOME TO THE JOHNSONS Map p449

☎ 212-420-9911; 123 Rivington St btwn Essex & Norfolk Sts; ◉ F to Delancey St, J, M, Z to Delancey–Essex Sts

The irony of this Brady Bunch–like theme bar still hasn't worn off, which means it must be pretty cool. It's especially a draw to former suburbanites, who can't get enough of its tacky '70s living-room vibe, cheap-ass drinks (including great margaritas) and its hip crowd of young locals.

EAST VILLAGE

Just like eating options, drinking choices run the complete gamut here, from the dirtiest dive to the loveliest lounge. You can't walk a block without tripping over a bar – or one of its stumbling patrons, especially on weekends – so it's definitely still *the* 'hood for imbibing.

11TH STREET BAR Map p449

☎ 212-982-3929; 510 E 11th St btwn Aves A & B; ◉ F, V to Lower East Side–Second Ave

Grab a spot on one of the soft sofas, call the house cat onto your lap and lean back: This is one of the homiest watering holes in the 'hood, more like a cozy community room than a bar. The pressed-tin ceiling and exposed-brick walls add to the don't-make-me-leave vibe.

that include live S&M action. Come summertime, its open-air roof deck is the place to be.

Gym (Map pp446–7; ☎ 212-337-2439; 167 Eighth Ave at 18th St; ⊙ A, C, E to 14th St, L to Eighth Ave) This new sports bar for men is nothing like the rowdy straight sports bars that pepper Midtown side streets. Here the décor is classy – wide-plank wooden floors, high ceilings and a long, sleek bar – the men are polite, and ice-skating championships are as popular as basketball playoffs (which are beloved only thanks to the hot players' booties).

Splash Bar (Map pp446–7; ☎ 212-691-0073; 50 W 17th St; ⊙ L to 6th Ave, F, V to 14th St) First it was Splash, then SBNY and now Splash Bar. Still, not much has altered (a good thing) at this Chelsea staple, a spot with multilevels that makes it part lounge, part club, and home to some of the hottest, most scantily-clad bartenders around. Sunday's Trannyshack is a popular drag-queen party.

xl (Map pp446–7; ☎ 646-336-5574; 357 W 16th St; ⊙ A, C, E to 14th St, L to Eighth Ave) After-work beautiful boys loom over froofy cocktails at this expansive, high-ceilinged lounge. Flat screen TVs blare music videos, while some nights host quality cabaret or drag-queen shows. A massive fish tank provides a wall in the WC (if those fish could speak...), and workaholics can pair up with their laptops, thanks to the bar's free WiFi.

Midtown

OW Bar (Map pp452–3; ☎ 212-355-3395; 221 E 58th St btwn Lexington & Third Aves) The saving grace for the Upper East Side, this local's favorite (named after Oscar Wilde) has a great jukebox, outdoor garden and expansive lounge, with nightly parties, body (and talent) contests, performances and go-go dancers.

Therapy (Map p282; ☎ 212-397-1700; 348 W 52nd St btwn Eighth & Ninth Aves) Similar in design to xl – multi-leveled, airy and sleekly contemporary – this is the hotspot for 'Chelsea North,' otherwise known as Hell's Kitchen. Theme nights abound, from stand-up comedy to musical shows, and the second-floor lounge has great fare (burgers, hummus, salads) served in front of a roaring fireplace.

Outer Boroughs

Cattyshack (Map p464; ☎ 718-230-5740; 249 Fourth Ave at President St, Park Slope, Brooklyn; ⊙ M, R, W to Union St) After closing her beloved Meow Mix lesbian spot in the East Village, Brooke Webster brought an even bigger, better vibe to the girls of Park Slope (and there are lots of 'em) with this chic, three-level space. Smokers love the rooftop deck, while everyone loves the hot go-go dancers, great DJs and special theme nights. Boys are welcome, too.

Chueca Bar (☎ 718-424-1171; 69-04 Woodside Ave, Woodside, Queens; ⊙ 7 to 69th St) It's a bit of a trip from Manhattan, but beautiful Latina lesbians travel from all over the region – even as far as New Jersey and Connecticut – to hang with their salsa-dancing sisters.

Excelsior (Map p464; ☎ 718-832-1599; 390 Fifth Ave at 6th St; ⊙ M, R, W to Union St) Who says Park Slope is all girls? This long running boy favorite has a cute and friendly crowd, great jukebox and refreshing back patio for summer months (and year-round smokers).

Metropolitan (Map p463; ☎ 718-599-4444; 559 Lorimer St at Metropolitan Ave; ⊙ G to Metropolitan Ave, L to Lorimer St) This friendly and low key Williamsburg spot draws a good blend of arty fags and dykes with its cool staff, cheap drinks, outdoor patio and great DJs.

ANGEL'S SHARE Map p449

☎ 212-777-5415; 2nd fl, 8 Stuyvesant St btwn Third Ave & 9th St; ⊙ 6 to Astor Pl

Sneak through the Japanese restaurant on the same floor to discover this tiny gem of a hideaway, with creative cocktails, well-suited waiters and a civilized policy that states you cannot stay and drink if there's not room enough for you to sit. This often turns out to be the case, so try to stake your claim early.

BEAUTY BAR Map p449

☎ 212-539-1389; 531 E 14th St btwn Second & Third Aves; ⊙ L to Third Ave

A kitschy favorite since the mid-90s, this homage to old-fashioned beauty parlors pulls in a cool local crowd with its gritty soundtrack, nostalgic vibe and free Blue

Rinse margaritas (with a $10 manicure thrown in) from Wednesday to Sunday.

CLUBHOUSE Map p449

☎ 212-260-7970; 700 E 9th St at Ave C; ⊙ F, V to Lower East Side–Second Ave

The folks behind gay-favorite **Starlight** (p289) added this pansexual spot to their repertoire a few years back. It's a grand little space with clever, sweeping design and low light-ing, and rotating DJs that can really pack the small floor with movers and shakers.

D.B.A. Map p449

☎ 212-475-5097; 41 First Ave btwn 2nd & 3rd Sts; ⊙ F, V to Lower East Side–2nd Ave

A dark and bare-bones pub, the draw here is the massive menu, hand-scrawled on a big chalkboard, announcing about 125 beers, 130 single-malt scotches and 50 tequilas. There's also a postage stamp–sized patio out back, but most of the action stays in, near the taps, where a mix of students, business folks and slouchy locals bond over their love of fine liquor.

HOLIDAY COCKTAIL LOUNGE Map p449
☎ 212-777-9637; 75 St Marks Pl btwn First & Second Aves; ⊕ 6 to Astor Pl
You want dive bar? You've got it, right here. This old-school, battered, charming place feels as if it's from another era – and with $3 drinks, it might as well be. Expect crotchety service, the never ending blare of TV shows, and a curious mix of nostalgia seekers, penny-pinching alcoholics and various cheapskates.

MO PITKIN'S HOUSE OF SATISFACTION Map p449
☎ 212-777-5660; 34 Ave A at E 4th St; ⊕ F, V to Lower East Side–Second Ave
Part comfort-food restaurant, part **cabaret/ burlesque lounge** (see p288 for show information) and part retro-style cocktail lounge, Mo Pitkin's is in a league of its own. Drink up at the century-old bar, where you can order various tap beers and unique only-in-New-York drinks like the Absolut egg cream and chat with a variety of East Village characters, both old and new.

ODESSA CAFÉ Map p449
☎ 212-253-1470; 110 Ave A btwn St Marks Pl & E 7th St; ⊕ 6 to Astor Pl
You may not have to be buzzed into the bathrooms for security reasons anymore, but this Polish-diner-turned-bar, right on Tompkins Sq Park, is classic East Village scruff. The decor has never been updated (witness the gaggy red, bumpy ceiling), but liquor was added into the mix a few years ago, and the tattooed, grungy-fun clientele couldn't have been happier. And after your $4 cocktail and plate of rib-sticking pierogi, you'll be right there with them.

GREENWICH VILLAGE

Traditionally quite a gem of a neighborhood when it came to swilling and pontificating, the Village is now generally best avoided for quality bar experiences – unless dodging beer spills from smashed NYU students is your idea of a good time. There are a handful of exceptions, of course, as well as a few worthy gay bars (see boxed text, p266).

BAR NEXT DOOR Map p449
☎ 212-529-5945; 129 MacDougal St btwn 3rd & 4th Sts; ⊕ A, C, E, B, D, F, V to W 4th St
One of the loveliest boites in the neighborhood, this basement of a restored townhouse is all low ceilings, exposed brick and romantic lighting. You'll find mellow, live jazz nightly, as well as the tasty Italian menu of the restaurant next door, La Lanterna di Vittorio.

BOWLMOR LANES Map p448
☎ 212-255-8188; 110 University Pl btwn E 12th & E 13th Sts; ⊕ L, N, Q, R, W, 4, 5, 6 to 14th St–Union Sq
Bowling is just the beginning at this sprawling alley complex, where you can visit just to take a candy-colored, mod-style seat at the lengthy bar – made from the shiny wood of a former bowling lane – and watch glow-in-the-dark games through a massive glass window. The retro atmosphere is popular for large groups, and the groovy DJs might even inspire you to pick up a ball yourself.

MARIE'S CRISIS Map p448
☎ 212-243-9323; 59 Grove St btwn Seventh Ave S & Bleecker St; ⊕ 1 to Christopher St–Sheridan Sq
Aging Broadway queens, wide-eyed out-of-town gay boys, giggly tourist girls and various other fans of musical theater assemble around the piano here and take turns belting out campy numbers, often joined by the entire crowd. It's old-school fun that'll put a spring in your step, no matter how jaded you were when you went in.

STONED CROW Map p448
☎ 212-677-4022; 85 Washington Pl btwn Washington Sq West & Sixth Ave; ⊕ A, C, E, B, D, F, V to W 4th St
One of the divey places worth checking out, this beer-drenched basement space vibrates with blaring classic rock from a killer jukebox, homework-dissing NYU students and a league-favored pool table in its back room.

SULLIVAN ROOM Map p448
☎ 212-252-2151; 218 Sullivan St btwn Bleecker & W 3rd Sts; ⊕ A, C, E, B, D, F, V to W 4th St
This unmarked, basement-level hideaway attracts throngs of good-looking, black-

RACK 'EM UP: BARS WITH POOL TABLES

- Amsterdam Bar & Billiards (p273) Find a dozen pool tables at this UWS perch.
- Dakota Roadhouse (p262) Three pool tables rule here, where Lower Manhattan meets the midwest.
- Gym (p267) Beautiful men shoot pool while cruising at this gay sports bar.
- Stoned Crow (opposite) This Village staple has a league-worthy table.
- West Side Tavern (p270) A popular table entertains the beer-swilling masses here.

clad creatures of the night for DJ'd house parties, stiff cocktails and extensive foreign beer offerings. You'd never know it from the outside – as there's no sign of the place and the other block's offerings are pretty dismal – but this is a very happening affair.

WEST VILLAGE & THE MEATPACKING DISTRICT

Go west of the Village and you'll sidestep much of the frat-boy scenes, finding instead romantic little nooks of both old-fashioned and new-school charms, many housed in historic townhouses. Its winding, hard-to-learn streets are perfect for wandering in search of a watering hole; when something looks inviting, take the cue and head on in. The Meatpacking District is strictly contemporary in vibe, with sprawling, modern spaces boasting long cocktail lists, velvet-roped entrances and dins that'll rattle your brain. Take a drink – it surely helps.

BRASS MONKEY Map p448

☎ 212-675-6686; 55 Little W 12th St at Washington St; ⊕ A, C, E to 14th St, L to Eighth Ave
While most Meatpacking District bars tend toward the chic, the Monkey is down-to-earth, appealing more to folks who put more thought into their favorite beer than which shoes to wear. Entering the small, stripped-wood facade is a comforting way to begin, and the interior just keeps putting you at ease: low, wood-beam ceilings, friendly bartenders and a nice long list of beers and scotches. A small bar menu offers snacks from mussels to bangers and mash.

CHUMLEY'S Map p448

☎ 212-675-4449; 86 Bedford St btwn Grove & Barrow Sts; ⊕ 1 to Christopher St–Sheridan Sq
This is a hard-to-find, one-time speakeasy that serves decent pub grub as well as 11 beers on tap. The best reason to come is to feel the weight of history inside: the worn wood décor and fading photos and book jackets of influential writers lining the walls. Get here on the early side to check it out, though, as late night brings mobs of beer pounding frat types. Look for the unmarked brown door in a white wall to get in.

DOUBLE SEVEN Map p448

☎ 212-981-9099; 418 W 14th St btwn Ninth & Tenth Aves; ⊕ A, C, E to 14th St, L to Eighth Ave
The owner of hipster Lotus (p299) has added a haven for more mature audiences (read: 30s) right across the street. This small cocktail lounge is an intimate den with high, cushiony leather stools, filled with sophisticates who don't mind doling out close to twenty bucks for a single drink – probably because they're uncommonly delicious, and come with a side of designer chocolates.

HUDSON BAR & BOOKS Map p448

☎ 212-229-2642; 636 Hudson St btwn Horatio & Jane Sts; ⊕ A, C, E to 14th St, L to Eighth Ave
A re-creation of a men's club, this is where you'll find a country-library feel, a James Bond drink theme, and plenty of chess games to choose from. It's small, filled with warm wood and as soothing as a big sip of cognac. Bar & Books is so popular, in fact, that it's spawned an uptown Cigar Bar (Map pp454–5; ☎ 212-717-3902; 1020 Lexington Ave at 73rd St) as well as bars in Prague and soon-to-open Bucharest.

PLUNGE Map p448

☎ 212-206-6700; Gansevoort Hotel, 18 Ninth Ave at 13th St; ⊕ A, C, E to 14th St, L to Eighth Ave
Located in the 15th-floor penthouse of the hopelessly trendy Gansevoort Hotel, this Meatpacking District star affords great views of the Hudson River and New Jersey, which are best seen in the glow of sunset. Plus, it helps tremendously to get here early – and on a weeknight, to boot – or else risk being packed like well dressed sardines with hordes of scenester-searching wannabes. And don't even think about plunging into the lounge's pool – it's for guests only, and the security crew will not be fooled.

CHELSEA

Thought mostly the domain of sleek cruising lounges for gorgeous gay men as well as massive, mega-nightclubs for all, there is still some variety to be found here, whether it is for old-school jazz, a sophisticated martini or a plain ol' pint. The pulsating center of the 'hood is gradually moving west, to Ninth Ave, and strolling along here at night will reveal some lovely restaurant-bars and other nooks worth exploring.

CHELSEA BREWING COMPANY
Map pp446-7

☎ 212-336-6440; Chelsea Piers, Pier 59, West Side Highway at 23rd St; ⊖ C, E to 23rd St

Enjoy one of the quality microbrews, waterside, in the expansive outdoor area of this way-west beer haven – a perfect place to re-enter the world after a day of swimming, golfing or rock climbing as a guest at the **Chelsea Piers** (p143) sports center here.

HALF KING Map pp452-3
☎ 212-462-4300; 505 W 23rd St at Tenth Ave; ⊖ C, E to 23rd St

A unique marriage of cozy beer pub and sophisticated writers' lair, you'll often experience top-notch literary readings in this wood-accented, candlelit watering hole. Its myriad seating-area options are bound to provide one that seduces everyone – particularly during warm weather, when a front sidewalk café, main indoor room, cozy back section and mellow backyard patio are all open for business. The food's pretty good too, revving up standard bar fare with nice salad and pasta additions.

SERENA Map pp446-7
☎ 212-255-4646; Chelsea Hotel, 222 W 23rd St btwn Seventh & Eighth Aves; ⊖ C, E, 1 to 23rd St

The lush, underground lounge of the Chelsea Hotel is this dark and sultry space, featuring an array of couches, make-out corners, chill-out DJs and constant theme nights that all go for different crowds. Sunday night is dedicated to classy lesbians, as **Shescape** (p266), which runs roving dance events all over town, has hunkered down here for a weekly stretch-out-the-weekend soiree.

Chill out at this den of indulgence, Serena (left)

WEST SIDE TAVERN Map pp446-7
☎ 212-366-3738; 360 W 23rd St btwn Eighth & Ninth Aves; ⊖ C, E to 23rd St

Talk about normal! This beer-scented tavern has an old-fashioned vibe, loud classic rock and a popular pool table, along with decent pub fare and some roomy tables alongside its lengthy bar. The crowd is filled with groups of regular Joes and the occasional girlfriend, and on alternating Fridays the high straight-boy content (for Chelsea) is especially obvious, as the small basement gets packed with some of the hottest men in the 'hood for Snaxx, a DJ-driven lounge soiree that pulls in a big crowd based on buzz alone.

UNION SQUARE, FLATIRON DISTRICT & GRAMERCY PARK

Look for stylish hotel lounges, fancy-eatery bars and a few down-and-dirty basics thrown in for good measure. You'll be rubbing elbows with a mixture of monied locals, fashion-forward-student spillovers from nearby FIT and a bunch of regular guys who like the preponderance of Irish pubs that start here and get thicker as you move north. Find those perfectly poured pints of Guinness at the clutch of pubs that line Third Ave beginning north of 14th St.

FLATIRON LOUNGE Map pp446-7
☎ 212-727-7741; 37 W 19th St btwn Fifth & Sixth Aves; ⊖ F, N, R, V, W to 23rd St

A simple nook with a classic vibe, this 1927 mahogany bar serves up specialty cocktails

Drinking

CHELSEA

made with fresh, seasonal ingredients – pomegranate, Granny Smith apples, mint, lychee nuts – in a setting that's both historic and retro, decorated with red leather booths and stained-glass lamps. The dramatic entrance, through a low-lit archway, only adds to the elegant excitement.

GALLERY AT THE GERSHWIN
Map pp452-3

☎ 212-447-5700; Gershwin Hotel, 7 E 27th St btwn Fifth & Madison Aves; ◉ F, N, R, V, W to 23rd St

A convenient perk for those bedding down at this hip budget hotel, it's a pretty cool destination for anyone – solo travelers especially, perhaps, as it's a sure bet you'll meet other globetrotters here. Either way, stop in and relax on one of the high-backed red banquettes and enjoy the vibe – artistic (huge paintings grace the walls), mellow (lounge DJs set the vibe) and clever, with cocktails named after luminaries from Pablo Neruda to Jean-Michel Basquiat.

PETE'S TAVERN Map pp446-7

☎ 212-473-7676; 129 E 18th St at Irving Pl; ◉ L, N, Q, R, W, 4, 5, 6 to 14th St–Union Sq

This dark and atmospheric watering hole is a New York classic – all pressed tin and carved wood and an air of literary history. You can get a respectable burger here, plus choose from more than 15 draft beers. The crowd draws in everyone from post-theater couples and Irish expats to no-nonsense NYU students.

SAPA Map pp452-3

☎ 212-929-1800; 43 W 24th St btwn Fifth & Sixth Aves; ◉ N, R, W, 6 to 23rd St

Thanks to an inspired, modern look by award-winning designers, the stylish bar at this French-Vietnamese eatery has become a Flatiron hotspot – drawing not only local professionals and destination diners but the occasional clutch of celebs (who tend to favor the more private booths in the dining area). Take a furtive look around for them, or stare as long as you'd like at the slim walnut bar, whisper-thin scrims and work-of-art lighting schemes. Cocktails tend toward the fresh and fab, making creative use of mint, mulberry syrup, homemade infusions and all things muddled, though you can also get a quality bottle of beer or glass of wine.

MIDTOWN

You'd better believe this massive swath of the city has something for everyone – cheesy tourist, barely-legal suburbanite, high class hipster, buttoned-up businessman – you name it. While bars way west (especially in Hell's Kitchen) are typically less buttoned-up than those way east, the mainstream fare in the middle tends to remain on the non-exciting scale – that is, at least, until very recently, thanks to a handful of smart proprietors who have finally noticed that lack of sophisticated fare near Times Sq. Note that Midtown bars, especially those on the east side, come and go quickly, so be sure to call first before setting out.

MIDTOWN EAST

MANCHESTER PUB Map pp452-3

☎ 212-935-8901; 920 Second Ave St at 49th St; ◉ E, V, 6 to Lexington Ave–53rd St

Thirsting for a taste of England? Head to this popular, cozy pub then, where you'll find solid pub grub, icy pints (Guinness included, natch) and a really cool Internet jukebox that lets you download any song you fancy. Get here early, though, as local fans mob the place by 9pm.

CAMPBELL APARTMENT Map pp452-3

☎ 212-953-0409; 15 Vanderbilt Ave at 43rd St; ◉ S, 4, 5, 6, 7 to Grand Central

Take the lift beside the Oyster Bar or the stairs to the West Balcony and head out the doors to the left to reach this sublime spot for a cocktail. This used to be the apartment of a landed railroad magnate and has the velvet, mahogany and murals to prove it. Cigars are welcome, but sneakers and jeans are not. The Apartment is a great way to enjoy the grandeur of the train station, martini in hand.

GINGER MAN Map pp452-3

☎ 212-532-3740; 11 E 36th St btwn Fifth & Madison Aves; ◉ 6 to 33rd St

The most exciting watering hole to hit Midtown in a while, this high-ceilinged, handsome pub is heaven to those who take their suds seriously. Based in Texas (with three locations in that state and just one in these parts), this is a place that'll thrill beer connoisseurs, as it's got an extensive selection of global bottles and drafts, not to mention a range of scotches, wines and even cigars. The pub fare – Guinness beef stew, cheese and fruit plate or bratwurst sandwiches – is serious, too.

MIDTOWN WEST

AVA LOUNGE Map p282
☎ 212-956-7020; Majestic Hotel, 210 W 55th St btwn Seventh Ave & Broadway; ⊕ N, Q, R, W to 57th St
The modern, palm-studded rooftop lounge of the Majestic Hotel is a high-up gem Midtown, bringing joy to balmy nights with its stellar views of the sparkling skyline around you. Inside, sink into a sumptuous ottoman and enjoy the retro-modern, honey hued décor and stylish crowd. It's oh so South Beach, right in NYC.

BLUE LADY LOUNGE Map p282
☎ 212-245-2422; 104 W 57th St btwn Sixth & Seventh Aves; ⊕ F to 57th St
Tucked above the bustling shopping stretch of W 57th St is this classy hideaway, providing relief from the endless series of quick-lunch delis and serious dining spots that overpopulate the area. Accessible via a flight of stairs that begin beneath a small blue awning next to the main entrance to Shelly's New York (a seafood/steakhouse institution), this is the place for perfect martinis, cozy banquettes and post-theater entertainment, thanks to live jazz bands that play, gratis, in the center of the large deco room each night. You can also order from Shelly's fine raw bar.

BRYANT PARK GRILL & CAFÉ
Map pp452-3
☎ 212-840-6500; 25 W 40th St btwn Fifth & Sixth Aves; ⊕ B, D, F, V to 42nd St–Bryant Park
Nestled toward the east end of Bryant Park's lovely patch of green is this pair of dining and imbibing spots, perfect places to sink into a cocktail and enjoy both the outdoor breezes and the sight of lit-up buildings rising all around the park. The Grill is the more upscale half, and features a sophisticated indoor dining room as well as al fresco bars both on its roof and in a leafy side garden. It's often closed for private events like weddings – but no matter, as the more casual outdoor café, dotted with umbrellas and wicker chairs and a diverse

crew, is also a treat, with strong drinks and a lovely, more affordable-menu to boot.

KEMIA Map p282
☎ 212-333-3410; 630 Ninth Ave at 44th St; ⊕ A, C, E to 42nd St–Port Authority
The perfect pre- or post-theater cocktail spot, Kemia displays plenty of drama of its own: a rose-petal–strewn staircase whisks you down to the underground hideaway, where you'll find low ottomans, billowing tapestries, more roses, excellent DJs, delicious cocktails and Moroccan tapas. It's a hidden treat in a bustling, flashy part of town where it's often difficult to pick winning spots from losers. Kemia is a sure winner.

MORRELL WINE BAR & CAFÉ Map p282
☎ 212-262-7700; 1 Rockefeller Plaza (W 47th St btwn Fifth & Sixth Aves); ⊕ B, D, F, V 49th–50th Sts–Rockefeller Ctr
One of the pioneers of the wine-bar craze in NYC was this mega grape-geeks' haven. The list here is over 2000 long, with a whopping 150 wines available by the glass. And the airy, split-level room, right across from the famous skating rink, is as lovely as the vino.

SINGLE ROOM OCCUPANCY Map p282
☎ 212-765-6299; 360 W 53rd St btwn Eighth & Ninth Aves; ⊕ C, E to 50th St
Just one of a growing number of places that make you do a bit of work to get in – here you have to know to ring the doorbell – SRO is at least one spot that's worth it. It's got a speakeasy vibe in the air and a nice selection of wine and beer on the menu. But it's very small, and kind of cave-like, so claustrophobic tipplers should best not apply. Most others should find it titillating.

UPPER WEST SIDE

A neighborhood for grown-ups, many with children, is not exactly the No 1 destination for hardcore drinkers. But just as this region used to be a wasteland for foodies before the heavy-hitter restaurants came on the scene, better spots for boozing are slowly opening their doors. The northern reaches of the UWS are good for mining more bare-bones, bargain spots thanks to the Columbia students just north of here.

Drinking

UPPER WEST SIDE

AMSTERDAM BILLIARDS & BAR

Map pp454-5

☎ 212-496-8180; 334 Amsterdam Ave btwn 75th & 76th Sts; ◉ 1, 2, 3 to 72nd St

A flight above Amsterdam Ave, this expansive boite featuring exposed brick and a friendly vibe, is way more than a bar – though the drinks are well-mixed and the stools are cozy. The main event, though, is the collection of about a dozen well-maintained pool tables.

'CESCA Map pp454-5

☎ 212-787-6300; 164 W 75th St btwn Amsterdam & Columbus Aves; ◉ 1, 2, 3 to 72nd St

Though it's renowned for its main-dining-room upscale Italian fare, the cozy front lounge and bar area here are also worth a trek. With lots of dark wood, some romantic tables and a large free-floating bar in the center of the room, the front area of Cesca is handsome in a gentlemen's smoking lounge sort of way. But you're likely to find a pretty diverse (for the UWS) crowd bellying up here, happy to have a local spot that offers an impressive list of wines by the glass, as well as expertly mixed cocktails, quality beers and amazing 'bar food,' from Italian cheese plates to a warm faro salad.

BEST BAR JUKEBOXES

- Excelsior (p267) Queerly eclectic in Brooklyn.
- Magician (p265) Plenty of sad-teen faves (the Cure, etc) balanced with jazz.
- Manchester Pub (p271) Internet connection lets you pick anything in the virtual universes.
- Milano's (p264) A dive with picks both classic and Irish.
- OW Bar (p267) Thousands of digital selections at this midtown gay hang.

MARITIME CAFÉ AT PIER 1 Map pp454-5

☎ 917-612-4330; 70th St at the Hudson River; ◉ 1, 2, 3 to 72nd St

Come the warm seasons, this ingenious use of the Riverside Park esplanade – an outdoor café with grilled grub, fruity cocktails and lounge chairs set up on the grass to those who reserve in advance – is totally hopping. It's no wonder, as there are not much better city spots for a front-row view of sunsets, let alone those with such service. Summertime brings frequent live music as well as movies, shown al fresco at the end of the connecting pier.

SHALEL Map pp454-5

☎ 212-799-9030; 65 W 70th St btwn Central Park West & Columbus Ave; ◉ B, C, 1, 2, 3 to 72nd St

Craving some downtown style? Then enter the Greek Metsovo restaurant and head down the candlelit stairway to the cavernous, underground thriller of a Moroccan-themed lounge. You'll find low couches, flickering votives, tossed pillows and even an in-house waterfall. A good selection of spicy wines adds to the mystique, and private little dining rooms can add to the romanticism.

UPPER EAST SIDE

Not exactly the most hoppin' area to party in, this neighborhood relies on its elegant hotel lounges and sprinkling of dives to lure the tippling set. Look for classic dens, along with unique settings, from the Met to Central Park, for the most excitement. But make sure you're dressed the part (not sloppily, in other words).

BEMELMAN'S BAR Map pp454-5

☎ 212-570-7109; Carlyle, 35 E 76th St at Madison Ave; ◉ 6 to 77th St

Waiters wear white jackets, a baby grand piano is always being played and Ludwig Bemelman's Madeleine murals surround you. It's a classic spot for a serious cocktail – the kind of spot that could easily turn up in a Woody Allen film. So get ready for a scene – a completely sophisticated one, of course – that's as fascinating as it is blandly predictable.

BAR EAST Map pp454-5

☎ 212-876-0203; 1733 First Ave btwn 89th & 90th Sts; ◉ 6 to 86th St

Kind of off the beaten path (it's quite a hike from the subway, after all), this friendly neighborhood bar is tricked out with a pool table, good pop-rock DJs, darts and a nice mirror-backed bar. If you want to see locals drinking and yammering without pretense, head east and grab a stool.

SUBWAY INN Map pp454-5

☎ 212-223-8929; 143 E 60th St btwn Lexington & Third Aves; subway 4, 5, 6 to 59th St

This is a classic old-geezer watering hole with cheap drinks and loads of authenticity, right down to the barmen's white shirts and thin black ties. It should truly be landmarked, as the entire scene – from the vintage neon sign outside to the well-worn red booths and old geezers huddled inside – is truly reminiscent of bygone days. The mint dive, which offers plenty of cheapo shots, is an amusing place to recover from a shopping spree at posh Bloomingdale's (p348), just around the corner.

HARLEM & NORTHERN MANHATTAN

A world in itself, the swath of Manhattan above 125th St is ripe for wandering and ducking into, especially if it's a neighborhood vibe or down-home jazz jams you're looking to catch. Particularly good stretches include Broadway between 110th and 125th Sts, where Morningside Heights offers an array of Columbia students' and locals' joints; Lenox Ave around 125th St, the heart of Harlem; and Broadway in the 140s, where you'll find yourself in the middle of Latino/gentrifying Washington Heights.

BLEU EVOLUTION/MONKEY LOUNGE Map pp458-9

☎ 212-928-6006; 808 W 187th btwn Fort Washington Ave & Pinehurst Ave N; Ⓐ A to 190th St

Sharing the velvet-draped space is a sexy spot to knock back cocktails until 2am and keep your stomach lined with well-done dishes of Middle Eastern salads (hummus, baba ganoush, etc) or more substantial roasted monkfish or duck crepes. You'll find a diverse crowd here, especially come late night, as there still aren't too many options in this calm and quiet area, known as Hudson Heights and growing quickly with downtowners in search of affordable real estate.

LA MARINA Map pp458-9

☎ 212-567-8088; 348 Dyckman St at the Hudson River; Ⓐ A to Dyckman St

This top-of-the-borough spot, in the neighborhood of Inwood, is the perfect destination for a warm summer night. You'll find plenty to swallow – including Latin-inspired hits like ceviche and mojitos – and even more to look at, including perfect views of the beautiful George Washington Bridge and an eyeful of talented salsa dancers, who just can't keep still when the DJs or live acts get going on weekends.

LENOX LOUNGE Map pp458-9

☎ 212-427-0253; www.lenoxlounge.com; 288 Malcolm X Blvd btwn 124th & 125th Sts; Ⓞ 2, 3 to 125th St

The classic art-deco Lounge, which hosts frequent big names, is an old favorite of local jazz cats, though it's a beautiful and historic house for anyone who wants a nice place to imbibe. Don't miss the lux Zebra Room in the back.

BROOKLYN

Believe it or not, folk from bottle-shaped Manhattan comes boozing in Brooklyn on occasion, particularly in Williamsburg, just one L stop in. Park Slope's 5th Ave has a mix of bars, including a couple of long-term gay and lesbian bases.

BOERUM HILL, COBBLE HILL, CARROLL GARDENS & RED HOOK

BROOKLYN INN Map p464

☎ 718-625-9741; 138 Bergen St at Hoyt St; Ⓞ F, G to Bergen St

Black on the outside, with dark-oak ornate walls inside, the laid back, neighborhood-y Brooklyn Inn is like an English pub without the smoke – or the English. The back pool room is there for those needing it, but most lingering (and the $5 pints) is up in the front – where the jukebox is (Meat Puppets, Clash, Clap Your Hands). No TV thankfully. Smokers spill onto the street. The bar is featured in the movie *Smoke* (1995).

FLOYD Map p462

☎ 718-858-5810; 131 Atlantic Ave; Ⓞ 2, 3, 4, 5 to Borough Hall

This glass-front bar's claim to fame is a full-size bocce court, but its giant space is equally alluring for comfy seating areas (leather chairs and settees set around coffee tables). It's fun and unique, though the crowd can get a little jock-y at times (we've seen, and this is bad, an exposed single testicle on one occasion – must've been a line at the bocce).

LONG ISLAND BAR & RESTAURANT
Map p462
110 Atlantic Ave, at Henry St; ⏲ 9am-9pm Mon-Sat; Ⓜ 2, 3,4, 5 to Borough Hall
Open since 1951, and looking it, this throwback has flowers in the windows, trophies over the giant bar, and old-timer staff that'll make you a $4 burger to go along with a beer or gin-and-tonic. It closes early, but a good way to kick off a night in 'BoCoCa.' Plenty of seats on the bar, but also red-vinyl booths.

SUNNY'S Map p465
☎ 718-625-8211; 253 Conover St, btwn Beard & Reed Sts; ⏲ 8pm-2am Wed, 8pm-4am Fri & Sat; Ⓜ F, G to Carroll St
This old, out-of-the-way longshoreman bar – sign says 'bar' – in Red Hook, comes right out of *On the Waterfront* – except that Brando didn't go for knitting, as Sunny's does on Wednesday nights. Weekends are about music – when a bring-your-own-banjo policy leads to bluegrass jams on Saturday night. It's a communal environment, as cross-table banter gets going over a couple beers. As soon as you walk in, you're a part. Take Bus B61 from the subway.

PARK SLOPE
GINGER'S Map p464
☎ 718-778-0924; 363 Fifth Ave; Ⓜ F, M, R to 4th Ave–9th St
Let-love-rule lesbian bar with ruby-red walls that sees a lot of gays and straights at its long bar up front and big garden in the back. More laid-back than Manhattan's lesbian bars? Sure, this is Brookburg, baby.

GREAT LAKES Map p464
☎ 718-499-3710; 284 Fifth Ave at 1st St; Ⓜ M, R to Union St
Indie-rock drinkers of the Slope, and beyond, bee-line for the enigmatically named Lakes. The jukebox tributes the littlest bands that could; and a couple photos celebrate caught freshwater fish. Glass front windows make the front sitting area good

if you want to see who's heading to Blue Ribbon next door. Live jazz and rock fill the audiowaves some nights.

O'CONNOR'S Map p464
☎ 718-783-9721; 39 Fifth Ave, btwn Bergen & Dean Sts; ⏲ noon-4am; Ⓜ 2, 3 to Bergen St
All dive-bar infrastructurally – with fluorescent lights, old wall paneling, and Yankees games flickering on the TV – O'Connor's *cheap* drinks (gin-and-tonics are $2.50!), its glorious 1931 roots, and quiet vibe bring in the hipster youth too.

WILLIAMSBURG
Drinking in Manhattan is so '90s. At night Billyburg's industrial warehouses and treeless sidewalks come to life. It's easy to wander from the two L-train stops here, and follow the heel-clicks of 20-somethings seeking alcohol (or other 20-somethings). Bedford Ave is a little cheesy these days, but the peak of action, while North 6th St towards the river is another main hub. See p223 for a walking tour that takes in some more far-flung bars east of the Brooklyn–Queens Expwy.

ALLIGATOR LOUNGE Map p463
☎ 718-599-4440; 600 Metropolitan Ave, Williamsburg; Ⓜ L to Lorimer St)
In Williamsburg's northern reaches, the Alligator draws a mixed crowd of hipsters and working-class locals. The vibe is good and unguarded – with U-shaped leather settees, Japanese tea-house nooks in the back, games on muted TVs, and the Hendrix and Pixies kept low enough to encourage chatter. But the real draw is the *free* freshly

CZECH THIS OUT

Queens' Astoria is New York's other outer-borough back-up to the act of getting drunk, and the **Bohemian Hall & Beer Garden** (Map p457; ☎ 718-274-4925; 29-19 24th Ave btwn 29th & 31st Sts, Astoria; ⏰ 5pm-2am Mon-Thu, 5pm-3am Fri, noon-3am Sat & Sun; subway N, W to Astoria Blvd) is one of New York's greatest happy-drinking grounds. It's a 1919 descendent from the Bohemian Citizen's Benevolent Society (founded for Czech immigrants in 1892) – and one of Astoria's mainstays. It's only worth coming to enjoy, in nice weather, its huge outdoor beer garden – the last of New York's one-time 800 such gardens. The mouthwatering list of cold Czech imports on draft is served with Czech accents. Some warm nights, folk bands set up – occasionally there's a charge of $5 or so – and you're free to linger over a pitcher outside as long as you want (get there early on key nights to ensure a spot). There's plenty of eating options in the area, but the hall serves Czech food, mostly meat-and-potato variety (from $8), but also salads, potato dumplings and burgers. Kids can stay till 9pm.

made brick-oven pizza. And, hey, a pitcher of Yuengling is $14. Karaoke on Thursday, live jazz on Sunday.

BROOKLYN ALE HOUSE Map p463
☎ 718-302-9811; 103 Berry St; ⦿ L to Bedford Ave
Everyone turns their heads (or leaves) for smoking after 10pm on many nights at this wooden floor, hanging-lamp, old-school bar. The jukebox odes the appropriate gods of cool music genres, though the local art that gets the wall space can be sophomoric (political figures with oil-derrick horns). The mix of 20-somethings and crustier pre-boom locals don't pay it mind.

GALAPAGOS ART SPACE Map p463
(☎ 718-384-4586; www.galapagosartspace.com; 70 N 6th St; ⦿ L to Bedford Ave)
They call it an 'art space,' but it's more of an atmospheric hang out of late 20-year-olds in collared shirts and their SOs seeking a diverse line-up of experimental music, disco and campy ukulele bands singing of gay paradise. Some nights Hipsters Feud is held – a spoof on the game-show Family Feud, based

on polls taken of Billyburgians. The entry is a giant dark reflecting pool (the size of some East Village bars), with an elevated stage and long bar (serving $6 cocktails) in back. Some events are free, others are $6 to $8.

SEA Map p463
(☎ 718-384-8850; 114 N 6th St; ⏰ 11:30am-1/2am; ⦿ L to Bedford Ave)
A long-time neighborhood staple, this ultra-glitzy Thai restaurant-bar – with a Buddha statue overlooking a reflecting pool – is about as Williamsburg as the Hard Rock Cafe is East Village. Oh, it's fun (and pretty good food-wise – mains $7-16), but on weekends it's stuffed with non-Williamsburgers looking for a west-side (Manhattan) scene in west-side (Brooklyn). Street-cred points: zero.

SPUYTEN DUYVIL Map p463
(☎ 718-963-4140; spuytenduyvil@verizon.net; 359 Metropolitan Ave, Wiliamsburg; ⏰ 5pm-1/2am Sun-Thu, 5pm-3/4am Fri & Sat; ⦿ L to Bedford Ave)
Low-key bar – named for 'spitting devil' in Flemish – sees ironic youth and grisled 30- and 40-somethings chatter over lightly played jazz while sipping on the impressive beer list, or – and this is cool – a handful of loose teas on hand. Painted-red tin ceilings and vintage maps and ashtray displays look over wood floors, with armchairs set by library racks of old paperbacks no one would want to lift. In good weather, the au-naturale back courtyard is open. There's cheese, pickles and cured meats for snacking.

ZEBULON Map p463
(☎ 718-218-6934; 258 Wythe Ave, ⦿ L to Bedford Ave)
The Zeb is a slightly crusty and improbable space for big events (18-piece bands have spilled off its small stage) of experimental jazz, French poets and Haitian vodou drummers. The vibe is less worldly, sit-in-a-circle than it sounds. Shows start at 10pm nightly. It's always free, so pop in for a drink or two and move on. If the music inspires you, pick up the compilation *This Is It: Live at Zebulon Vol 1*. Beer on draft is $5, bottles of wine start at $20, Moroccan mint tea is $3. There's also soup, toast and tarts.

Entertainment

Entertainment

New Yorkers don't have to try very hard to be entertained. Walking to work, riding the subway, dining out, even food shopping, all have elements of drama, comedy, nightclub sexiness and even musicality (thank you, talented street performers) built right in. But, by picking up a phone or hitting a website, it's possible to find yourself seated, in an actual audience, at one of the hottest tickets in town.

Music, theater, dance, film, opera, readings: everyone has his or her favorite. But it's not hard to become confused by all the sub-genre options: Broadway musical, or downtown drama? Superstar rock show at **Madison Square Garden** (p280), or obscure jazz jam in Brooklyn? Blockbuster Hollywood flick with stadium seating, or foreign indie drama at the **Film Forum** (p301)? Or is it a long night of clubbing that really gets you going? Most New Yorkers tend to pick a preference and stick with it, becoming avid fans of just one genre or another, and maybe, just maybe, sticking a toe or two into something else when they get bored.

If you're a theater fan, think about what style suits you best; it could be the unexpected oddities of downtown avant-garde, the media-hyped star-packed Broadway hits or something in between, like a solid off-Broadway production that's received rave reviews. Though you can probably see a movie anytime back home, consider the expanded options here: is there an obscure documentary that'll never come to your home town? Or perhaps there's a unique **film festival** (p301) going on, providing you a sneak peek at the best indies about to be released. If it's dance that moves you, you probably already know if modern or classical seems more exciting; take your pick here, basing your choice of what to spring for on local listings of who's in town. The same goes for live music, opera and the rest.

But how to get a handle on it all? No single source could possibly list everything going down in the city, but the weekly *Time Out New York, New York Times, New York, The Village Voice, New York Press* and the *New Yorker* all do their damnedest, and include thoroughly subjective reviews, too. You'll be truly informed if you look at them all. Don't spend too much time obsessing over what's best; you'll most likely not be disappointed following your interests. The city tourist agency **NYC & Company** (www.nycvisit.com) lists upcoming events and concerts, while **NYC/On Stage** (www.tdf.org/search) runs an interactive site that publicizes cultural events in every category.

Tchaikovsky is just one of the illustrious range of performers who've played at Carnegie Hall (opposite)

Tickets, Reservations & More

To purchase tickets for shows, you can either head directly to the venue's box office, or use one of several ticket-service agencies (most of which add a surcharge) to order by phone or Internet. Many of them have added perks, from reviews to the latest entertainment news.

The **Broadway Line** (☎ 888-BROADWAY; www.livebroadway.com) provides descriptions and good prices for shows on the Great White Way.

You can skip movie theater lines with **Movie Fone** (☎ 212-777-FILM; movies.aol .com), which lets you buy tickets hours, or even days, ahead of time. For venues not covered by Movie Fone, try **Fandango** (www .fandango.com).

Playbill (www.playbill.com), the publisher of that happy little yellow-and-white program provided by ushers at Broadway plays, also has an online version, offering theater news, listings and a ticket-purchase system.

A less formal site, **Talkin' Broadway** (www .talkingbroadway.com) has dishy reviews as well as a board for posting extra tickets to buy or sell. Alternatively, **Telecharge** (☎ 212-239-6200; www.telecharge.com) sells tickets for Broadway and off-Broadway shows.

A great source for practically anything but Broadway is **SmartTix.com** (☎ 212-868-4444; www.smarttix.com). It has info on comedy, cabaret, performance art, music, dance and downtown theater.

For any form of theater, **Theatermania** (☎ 212-352-3101; www.theatermania.com) provides listings, reviews and ticketing.

Broadening to other genres, try **Ticketcentral** (☎ 212-279-4200; www.ticketcentral .com). It also covers dance, lectures and stand-up comedy.

An old chestnut, **Ticketmaster** (☎ 212-279-4200; www.ticketcentral.com) sells for every conceivable form of big-time entertainment: rock concerts, opera, ballet, Broadway and off-Broadway, museum shows and sporting events. It also operates ticket outlets at Tower Records shops.

Major Halls & Venues

While there are countless little theaters, reading halls, dance stages and holes-in-the-wall scattered throughout every obscure corner in the city, there are just a few (though more than many cities can boast) major venues. Because each one hosts more than one kind of genre – Lincoln Center houses opera, ballet, orchestra, film and theater all at one address – it's helpful to have them altogether in one concise, heavy-hitter list.

BEACON THEATER Map pp454-5
☎ 212-496-7070; 2124 Broadway btwn 74th & 75th Sts; Ⓞ 1, 2, 3 to 72nd St
This Upper West Side venue has a pretty cool atmosphere for such a large, mainstream space. It hosts big acts for folks who want to see shows in a more intimate environment than that of a big concert arena. Phil Lesh, the Allman Brothers, Morrissey and Tina Turner have all played this stage recently, though the theater seating here usually inhibits dancing.

BROOKLYN ACADEMY OF MUSIC (BAM) Map p464
☎ 718-636-4139; www.bam.org; 30 Lafayette Ave at Ashland Pl, Fort Greene, Brooklyn; Ⓞ D, M, N, R to Pacific St, B, Q, 2, 3, 4, 5 to Atlantic Ave
Sort of the Brooklyn version of Lincoln Center – in its all-inclusiveness rather than its vibe, which is much edgier – this spectacular venue also hosts performances from a roster of genres. Its **Howard Gilman Opera House** and **Harvey Lichtenstein Theater** host everything from modern dance (such as the Mark Morris Dance Group, Pina Bausch and Bill T Jones), opera and cutting-edge theater (a recent hit was *Hedda Gabler* starring Cate Blanchett), to music concerts (Laurie Anderson and Patti Smith played recently) and a range of lectures. **BAM Rose Cinemas** is a beautiful setting in which to see the latest (and retro) indie films, with screenings often hosted by their directors; in 2005, Robert Redford moved the office headquarters of the Sundance Film Festival here. Finally, the high-ceilinged but intimate 3rd-floor **Lepercq Space** houses a great café and hosts jazz trios, cabaret singers and more. To catch the most experimental performers, check out the annual Next Wave Festival, held in spring.

CARNEGIE HALL Map p282
☎ 212-247-7800; www.carnegiehall.org; 154 W 57th St at Seventh Ave; Ⓞ N, R, Q, W to 57th St
Since 1891, this mostly classical and world-music historic performance hall has hosted Tchaikovsky, Mahler and Prokofiev, among others. Today it hosts visiting philharmonics from around the world, the New York Pops orchestra, various world-music performers,

including kd lang and Sweet Honey in the Rock, and CarnegieKids family concerts. It's home to three venues: the main (and gorgeous) Isaac Stern Auditorium, and the smaller Joan and Sanford I Weill Recital Hall and Judy and Arthur Zankel Hall.

LINCOLN CENTER Map pp454-5

☎ 212-546-2656; www.lincolncenter.org; Lincoln Center Plaza, Broadway at W 65th St; ◉ 1 to 66th St–Lincoln Center

Every eminent performing-arts genre has a stage at this massive complex, built in the 1960s and about to undergo a major redesign. Avery Fisher Hall is the showplace of the fine New York Philharmonic (www.new yorkphilharmonic.org), the country's oldest symphony orchestra. Alice Tully Hall (☎ 212-875-5050) houses the Chamber Music Society of Lincoln Center, and the New York State Theater (☎ 212-870-5570) is home to both the New York City Ballet (www.nycballet .com) and the New York City Opera (www .nycopera.com). You'll find quality films, as well as the annual New York Film Festival, at the Walter Reade Theater (☎ 212-875-5600; www.filminc.com); wonderful star-studded theater at both the Mitzi E Newhouse and Vivian Beaumont theaters; and frequent concerts at Juilliard School and the Fiorello H LaGuardia High School of Music. But perhaps the biggest draw here – besides the outdoor fountain that was featured in Cher's film *Moonstruck* and in Mel Brooks' *The Producers*, and which hosts the popular summer series Lincoln Center Out of Doors Festival – is the Metropolitan Opera House (☎ 212-362-6000; www.metopera.org). Its spectacular décor includes the two famous Chagall paintings, visible from the street, and the double, winding red staircase that sweeps up from the grand lobby. The house is home to the Metropolitan Opera, which features top

stars and mind-boggling costumes and sets, from September to May, and visiting operas from around the world during the rest of the year – except for spring, when the world-renowned American Ballet Theater takes over the stage. Jazz at Lincoln Center (p153), by the way, has moved to the Time Warner Center.

MADISON SQUARE GARDEN
Map pp452-3

☎ 212-465-6741; www.thegarden.com; Seventh Ave at W 33rd St; ◉ A, C, E, 1, 2, 3, 9 to 34th St–Penn Station

When Madonna, Bruce Springsteen or the Rolling Stones come to town, this is where you'll find them. Perched above Penn Station in Midtown, this 19,000-seat venue is known as 'the world's most famous arena,' and seeing a sold-out show here (as long as you're not up in a nose-bleed seat) is an amazing experience. You'll also find the Harlem Globetrotters, the Ringling Bros and Barnum & Bailey Circus, and the Westminster Kennel Club Dog Show here when they blow into town.

THE MEADOWLANDS Map p442

☎ 201-935-3900; www.meadowlands.com; East Rutherford, NJ; bus service from Port Authority (☎ 800-772-2222)

Located just across the Hudson in New Jersey, this is one of the area's biggest concert and large-event arenas. It contains both the Giants Stadium (home to the Giants football team), which hosts outdoor mega-concerts come summertime, and the Continental Airlines Arena, home to year-round shows from biggies like Coldplay and the Taste of Chaos Tour.

RADIO CITY MUSIC HALL Map pp452-3

☎ 212-247-4777; www.radiocity.com; Sixth Ave at W 51st St; ◉ B, D, F, V to 47th-50th Sts–Rockefeller Center

This grand art deco concert hall, built in 1932 and home to those leggy Rockettes, is where you'll find the Christmas Spectacular every winter. The gorgeous facility, a tour of which is fascinating, is now run by the same folks who book Madison Square Garden. While MSG gets the major superstars, Radio City hosts a mix of A- and B-list performers, with recent visits from Ricky Martin, Il Divo, Martina McBride and David

Roar with pleasure at New Amsterdam Theatre (p284)

Gilmore. Kids' shows breeze through on a regular basis, with recent showings from *Dora the Explorer* and *Peter Pan*.

SYMPHONY SPACE Map pp454-5

☎ 212-864-1414; www.symphonyspace.org; 2537 Broadway at 95th St; ◉ 1, 2, 3 to 96th St

Also a multi-genre space with several facilities in one, this refurbished theater complex is an Upper West Side gem. Consisting of the main Peter Jay Sharpe Theatre and the smaller Leonard Nimoy Thalia, Symphony Space is home to an excellent lineup of series, including Wall to Wall, annual free music marathons focusing on a specific composer; Selected Shorts, which has celebrities reading from famed short stories; and the Just Kidding! children's theater and musical performances. Film classics get good play here, plus you'll find a constant offering of excellent theater, cabaret, comedy, dance and world-music concerts throughout every week. The new onsite café has excellent light fare.

TOMMY HILFIGER JONES BEACH THEATER

☎ 516-221-1000; www.tommyhilfigerjonesbeach .com; Jones Beach, Wantaugh, Long Island; Long Island Rail Road to Freeport, then bus to Jones Beach

It used to be just plain ol' Jones Beach Theater before Tommy took over, but this place does host commercially successful artists, after all. If the mega-concert event is not at the Meadowlands (and sometimes even if it is), it's most likely here, at this huge but lovely concert venue by the sea. Recent visitors have included Tom Petty and Ozzfest.

TOWN HALL Map p282

☎ 212-840-2824; www.the-townhall-nyc.org; 123 W 43rd St btwn Sixth & Seventh Aves; ◉ B, D, F, V to 42nd St–Bryant Park

Classical ensembles regularly play at this landmark venue, as do folk, jazz and blues artists. Even Garrison Keilor plays here, when he brings his live *Prairie Home Companion* radio show to town.

THEATER

From classic song-and-dance Broadway spectacles to naked one-woman shows about breakfast cereals, there's enough drama in this town to please anyone. There are legendary big-hit factories near Times Sq and tiny, ragged downtown theaters as small as a New Yorker's studio apartment. Come summer, there are alfresco performance spaces from Central Park to Washington Sq.

The most celebrated scene is Broadway, the heart of which runs right through Times Sq. Though this area used to proffer plenty of lascivious performances, such as peep shows and porn films, that all came to an end during the Giuliani administration in the 1990s, when Hizzoner got rid of the sleazy scene and replaced it (to the chagrin of many nostalgics) with theaters hawking Disney musicals, from *The Lion King* to *Beauty and the Beast*. Roaming around the brightly lit neighborhood today is as mesmerizing as sitting in the front row of a playhouse; getting inside a playhouse is a bit more comfortable and a lot more entertaining.

Cheesy, bright-lights musicals aside, Broadway offerings have been more diverse than ever lately. The newest wave of innovative, musical works includes *The Color Purple* (the Oprah-produced take on Alice Walker's novel), the cultishly adored *Wicked* (a *Wizard of Oz* prequel starring the witches), Monty Python's *Spamalot* (based on the wacky film) and *Grey Gardens: A New Musical* (based on the disturbingly fascinating documentary by John Maysles). Repackaged movie hits like *The Producers* and *Hairspray* have taken the town by storm, as have several revived musicals, including *Chicago*, *Fiddler on the Roof* and *Sweeney Todd*. Long-running hits that still haven't worn out their welcome include *Rent*, *Phantom of the Opera* and, surprisingly, *Mama Mia!* More adventurous stage buffs should definitely investigate what is happening off-Broadway, downtown and even in the outer boroughs (especially at BAM), as some of the freshest, most accomplished stage work is happening far, far away from the renowned Theater District. The annual Fringe Fest (www .fringenyc.org), held each summer at various downtown theaters, is a great showcase for discovering new, edgy works.

BROADWAY SHOWS

Everyone used to know the name of Broadway's longest running musical: *Cats*. But it's time to learn the new answer because, as of early 2005, that title was won over by yet another Andrew Lloyd Weber hit – *Phantom of the Opera* – which passed its predecessor

TIMES SQUARE & THEATER DISTRICT

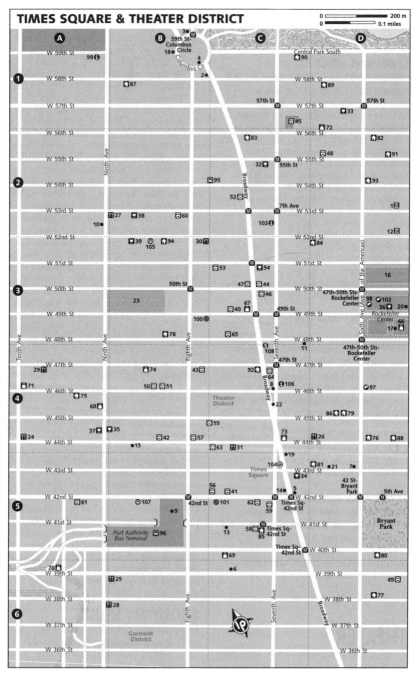

with its 7486th performance at the Majestic Theater. There are plenty of other big-time Broadway shows that just won't stop, as well as newcomers that seem destined for long runs, and they're just the kind of hits that one-time NYC visitors often come looking for. The following listing highlights particular shows, rather than theaters, since it's the specific production that most folks base their Broadway choices on.

'Broadway' productions are staged in the lavish, early-20th-century theaters surrounding Times Sq. They're also pretty costly, with good seats (the only ones worth having) averaging about $80 a pop.

Evening performances begin at 8pm, with Wednesday matinees starting at 2pm. You can reach all of these theaters on the subway by taking N, Q, R, S, W, 1, 2, 3, 7 to Times Sq–42nd St.

AVENUE Q

John Golden Theatre, Map p282; 252 W 45th St btwn Broadway & Eighth Ave; Ⓜ **N, R, 1, 2, 3, 7 to Times Sq–42nd St**
Who knew that puppets could have such popular appeal? Playwright Jeff Whitty, for one, who created this story of pink- and green-faced muppetlike puppets who go about their business in a quirky love

story. Their puppeteers stand on the stage, working their magic, but they soon blend into the background. Songs about *schadenfreude* and scenes of sex will make you blush – and giggle.

CHICAGO

Ambassador Theater, Map p282; 219 W 49th St btwn Broadway & Eighth Ave; Ⓢ N, R, W to 49th St, 1, 9 to 50th St

It's a play! It's a movie! It's a play again! This beloved classic, a musical about Roxy Heart and the fabulously sordid goings-on of the Chicago underworld, has made a great comeback, most likely helped by the recent Hollywood version, which reminded everyone (and taught youngsters) just how fun murder can be.

DOUBT

Walter Kerr Theatre, Map p282; 219 W 48th St btwn Broadway & Eighth Ave; Ⓢ N, R, W to 49th St, 1, 9 to 50th St

One of the darkest hits of late, this new drama tells the mysterious tale of sexual abuse at a Bronx Catholic school in the early '60s. Though you'll no longer get to see lead actress Cherry Jones (played at the time of this writing by Eileen Atkins), who won the 2005 Best Actress Tony for her role as the clever nun, it's still a gripping, disturbing show worth focusing in on.

THE LION KING

New Amsterdam Theatre, Map p282; 214 W 42nd St btwn Seventh & Eighth Aves; Ⓢ N, R, 1, 2, 3, 7 to Times Sq–42nd St

Known by many New Yorkers as the beast that took away Times Sq's bite, this Disney musical is a widely hailed, magically colorful story of kings that kids of all ages love. The marvelous direction and design is by Julie Taymore, with an African-beat score by Tim Rice and Elton John.

MAMMA MIA!

Cadillac Winter Garden Theatre, Map p282; 1634 Broadway at 50th St; Ⓢ N, R, W to 49th St, 1, 9 to 50th St

Taking over grandly in the space still recognized by locals as 'the Cats' theater,' this mother/daughter-story musical, based on the hits of '70s supergroup Abba (and little else), has been a runaway hit since arriving on the scene in 2001.

THE ODD COUPLE

Brooks Atkinson Theatre, Map p282; 265 W 47th St btwn Broadway & Eighth Ave; Ⓢ N, R, W to 49th St, 1, 9 to 50th St

At this writing, it was still a challenge to snag a seat at this instant hit – a revival of the 1965 Neil Simon comedy that stars Matthew Broderick as neat-freak Felix Unger and Nathan Lane as his foil of a messy roommate, Oscar Madison. But it should've eased up by now. Otherwise, you could always rent DVDs of the old favorite TV show that the play inspired.

THE PHANTOM OF THE OPERA

Majestic Theatre, Map p282; 247 W 44th St btwn Broadway & Eighth Ave; Ⓢ N, R, 1, 2, 3, 7 to Times Sq–42nd St

Andrew Lloyd Weber's operetta-like musical, set in 19th-century Paris and serving as the recent inspiration for a Hollywood flick, is now the longest-running Broadway musical. Fans, who often go back several times in a row, just can't get enough of the dark, lush romance.

THE PRODUCERS

St James Theater, Map p282; 246 W 44th St btwn Broadway & Eighth Ave; Ⓢ N, R, 1, 2, 3, 7 to Times Sq–42nd St

Also the inspiration for a recent Hollywood movie is this quirky favorite, which brought a mega-dose of excitement back to the theater world when it first opened in 2001 starring Matthew Broderick and Nathan Lane (now together again, both onstage in *The Odd Couple* and onscreen in a film version of *The Producers*). The musical is based on the 1968 Mel Brooks film, about a tasteless showbiz scheme that winds up creating a runaway Broadway hit.

RENT

Nederlander Theater, Map p282; 208 W 41st St btwn Broadway & Eighth Ave; Ⓢ N, R, 1, 2, 3, 7 to Times Sq–42nd St

With an excellent pop-rock score and storyline based on *La Bohème,* this funky musical from the late Jonathan Larson captures perfectly a long-lost moment in time: early '80s East Village, when artists with AIDS and heroin problems could live in large lofts and thrive on community and love. The stage version, by the way, is much better than the new film.

HALF-PRICE BROADWAY TKTS

An essential NYC experience – a night at the theater – needn't break the bank. Tailormade for the traveler's timetable, and easy to find in Times Sq (look for the queues by the bright red 'TKTS' sign), the TKTS booth (☎ 212-768-1818; Broadway at W 47th St) sells cut-rate, same-day tickets to Broadway and off-Broadway shows. For 8pm shows, line up from 3pm to 8pm Monday to Saturday; for matinees, line up from 10am to 2pm Wednesday to Saturday and from 11am to 3pm Sunday. A downtown TKTS (Map pp444–5; cnr Front and John Sts; 🕙 11am-6pm, closed Sun in winter) can be found at the South Street Seaport, and is often much less crowded; here you must buy Wednesday matinee tickets on Tuesday. Tickets at both outposts sell at 25% or 50% off box-office rates, plus a $3 fee (cash and traveler's checks only!). Check the electric marquee for what's available. There are often plenty of choices, but be flexible. The booth is courtesy of the Theatre Development Fund, an arts advocacy group that sells 2.5 million theater seats annually. If you can't find TKTS in Times Sq, ask the singing naked cowboy, a man whose presence as, well, a singing naked cowboy (he actually wears boots, underwear, a cowboy hat and a sign with his nickname), has stopped many tourists and locals in their tracks.

THE 25TH ANNUAL PUTNAM COUNTY SPELLING BEE

Circle in the Square Theatre, Map p282; 1633 Broadway, entrance on 50th St; Ⓝ N, R, W to 49th St, 1, 9 to 50th St

Small-town America gets its crazy side exposed in this quirky new musical that pits six geeky, eccentric teens (and their respective family baggage) against each other in a spelling bee. It was a surprise hit of 2005, not to mention that same year's Tony Award–winner for Best Book of a Musical and Best Featured Actor (Dan Fogler, as a dad). It's still going strong.

WICKED

Gershwin Theater, Map p282; 221 W 51st St; Ⓑ B, D, F, V to 47th–50th Sts–Rockefeller Center

A whimsical, mythological and extravagantly produced prequel to *The Wizard of Oz*, this pop-rock musical gives the story's witches a turn to tell the tale. Ben Vereen plays the wizard in this play version of Gregory Maguire's 1995 novel. Its followers are a cultish crew, attending frequent performances and launching all sorts of fan clubs, fansites and obsessive blogs.

OFF-BROADWAY & OFF-OFF BROADWAY

Off-Broadway simply refers to theaters where tickets (and production costs) are slightly less, and where houses typically have 200 to 500 seats; you'll find many of these theaters just around the corner from Broadway venues, as well as elsewhere in town. Recent notable off-Broadway productions have included the transsexual tell-all *Christine Jorgensen Reveals,* the trippy long-running *Blue Man Group,* and the Harold Pinter double bill of *Celebration* and *The Room.* Off-off Broadway events include readings, experimental and cutting-edge performances and improvisations held in spaces with fewer than 100 seats. Some of the world's best theater happens in these more intimate venues, providing opportunities for many future stars, John Leguizamo and Whoopi Goldberg among them, to make their mark.

ASTOR PLACE THEATER Map pp454-5

☎ 212-254-4370; 434 Lafayette St btwn W 4th St & Astor Pl; Ⓡ R, W to 8th St–NYU, 6 to Astor Pl

This spot is on the map because of the phenomenally successful Blue Man Group (www.blueman.com), a trio of bald, blue guys who get wild with all manner of props and paint while poking fun at the art-mob mentality. Audience participation is required, like it or not.

CULTURE PROJECT AT 45 BLEECKER ST Map p450

☎ 212-253-7017; 45 Bleecker St at Lafayette St; Ⓖ 6 to Bleecker St, B, D, F, V to Broadway–Lafayette St

This intimate theater, which strives to provide a home to voices of the disenfranchised, was put on the map with the long and successful run of *Exonerated,* about wrongly accused death-row inmates and now the basis for a new TV series. It also hosted *Guantanamo: Honor Bound to Defend Freedom,* and Sarah Jones' *Bridge and Tunnel,* which eventually moved on to Broadway. The Women Center Stage Festival, a spotlight on female playwrights, takes over for two weeks each summer.

DIXON PLACE Map p450

☎ 212-219-0736; www.dixonplace.org; 258 Bowery btwn Houston & Prince Sts; ⓑ B, D, F, V to Broadway–Lafayette St

An intimate showcase for experimental theater that began as a reading space in 1985, Dixon Place is currently campaigning to move to a brand-new spot in the 'hood. For now, though, it's still in apartment-like with mismatched chairs and no actual stage. Still, it doesn't deter the flow of exciting shows – brand-new dramas, comedy and readings, often with a queer bent – or its passionate fans. Its summer HOT! series is a great time to catch the newest works.

JOSEPH PAPP PUBLIC THEATER Map p449

☎ 212-260-2400; www.publictheater.org; 425 Lafayette St btwn E 4th St & Astor Pl; ⓑ 6 to Astor Pl

One of the city's most important cultural centers, the Papp celebrates its 50th anniversary season in 2006. Founded by the late, expansive-minded Joseph Papp, who once returned a massive NEA grant rather than sign its conservative anti-obscenity amendment, the theater is currently run by the visionary George C Wolfe. It's had an almost constant roster of can't-miss productions over the years, such as the world premieres of *Hair, A Chorus Line, For Colored Girls Who Have Considered Suicide/When the Rainbow is Enuf* and *Plenty,* all of which moved to Broadway; the theater also broke ground with Larry Kramer's AIDS play *The Normal Heart,* in 1985. Recent favorites have included *Top Dog/Underground, Take Me Out* and *Caroline, or Change,* all of which have also had successful moves to Broadway. The East Village complex also houses the intimate Joe's Pub (p294) for musical and cabaret shows, and, every summer, it presents its famous and fabulous free productions of Shakespeare in the Park at Delacorte Theater (enter Central Park West at 81st St), which Papp began back in 1954, before the lovely, leafy, open-air theater was even built. Thrilling productions mounted there have included *Macbeth, Hamlet* and a musical take on *Two Gentlemen of Verona,* both in the '60s and in a 2005 revival.

LA MAMA E.T.C. Map p449

☎ 212-475-7710; www.lamama.org; 74A E 4th St btwn Second & Third Aves; ⓑ F, V to Lower East Side–Second Ave

Led by founder Ellen Stewart and begun in a small East Village basement, this home

for onstage experimentation (the 'ETC' stands for 'experimental theater club') has grown into a complex of three theaters, a café, an art gallery and a separate rehearsal studio building. This is the place to find cutting-edge dramas, sketch-comedy acts and readings of all kinds.

MITZI E NEWHOUSE THEATER AT LINCOLN CENTER Map pp454-5

☎ 212-239-6200; www.lct.org; 150 W 65th St at Broadway; ⓑ 1 to 66th St–Lincoln Center

This intimate, 299-seat space is part of the Lincoln Center Theater organization, as is its counterpart, the Vivian Beaumont Theater. Both are home to Broadway-quality dramas (at slightly lower prices). Recent productions have included Wendy Wasserstein's *Third* and, at the Beaumont, the Tony Award–winning musical *The Light in the Piazza.*

NEW YORK THEATER WORKSHOP

Map pp454-5

☎ 212-460-5475; www.nytw.org; 79 E 4th St btwn Second & Third Aves; ⓑ F, V to Lower East Side–Second Ave

This innovative production house originated two big Broadway hits, *Rent* and *Urinetown,* and offers a constant supply of high-quality drama, including recent works from Paul Rudnick and Michael Cunningham and local faves the Five Lesbian Brothers. Early 2005 brought *The Seven,* a hip-hop adaptation of Aeschylus' *Seven Against Thebes,* with choreography by Bill T Jones.

ORPHEUM THEATER Map p449

☎ 212-477-2477; 126 Second Ave at Eighth St; ⓑ 6 to Astor Pl

Located in the East Village, this 349-seat house was a premier Yiddish theater at the beginning of the 20th century. It gained offbeat fame in the '80s with its highly popular musical *Little Shop of Horrors* (which went to Broadway in 2003), and is the current home of the long-running beatfest *Stomp.*

PLAYWRIGHTS HORIZONS Map p282

☎ 212-564-1235; www.playwrightshorizons.org; 416 W 42nd St btwn Ninth & Tenth Aves; ⓑ A, C, E to Port Authority–42nd St

An excellent place to catch a new show that could very possibly be a rising hit, this 34-year-old 'writers' theater' is dedicated to fostering contemporary American theater.

Notable past productions have included *I Am My Own Wife, Sunday in the Park With George, The Heidi Chronicles* and *Driving Miss Daisy*. Early 2005 ushered in *Grey Gardens: The New Musical,* adapted for the stage by Doug Wright (*I Am My Own Wife*) from John Maysles' documentary film.

PS 122 Map p449

☎ 212-477-5288; www.ps122.org; 150 First Ave at E 9th St; Ⓞ R to 8th St–NYU, 6 to Astor Pl
This former schoolhouse has been committed to fostering new artists and their far-out ideas since its inception in 1979. Its two stages have hosted such performers as Meredith Monk, Eric Bogosian, Blue Man Group and the late Spalding Gray, and it's also home to both dance shows and film screenings (especially since the 2006 inception of its 'WYSIWIG Film Festival,' showcasing documentarians and bloggers alike).

ROUNDABOUT THEATRE COMPANY
Map p282

☎ 212-719-1300; www.roundabouttheatre.org; 227 W 42nd St btwn Seventh & Eighth Aves
This main stage for the Roundabout, unfortunately called the American Airlines Theatre, entered its 40th season in 2006. Its attention-grabbing and award-winning productions have included *Twelve Angry Men, The Constant Wife, After the Fall* and *Nine*. The 2006 season kicked off with Harry Connick Jr starring in *The Pajama Game* musical.

SOHO PLAYHOUSE Map p450

☎ 212-691-1555; www.sohoplayhouse.com; 15 Vandam St btwn Sixth Ave & Varick St; Ⓞ C, E to Spring St, 1 to Houston St
Confessions of a Mormon Boy, about a gay Mormon, opened the 2006 season with a blast of energy. The Playhouse was no less head-turning in the past, when it produced the first works of notables including Terrence McNally, Lanford Wilson and Sam Shepard.

CABARET & COMEDY

Oh-so New York, cabaret shows are kind of like mini musical-theater productions, performed in intimate environments and, if done right, no less (even more) thrilling. They have an old-fashioned vibe and

consist usually of a pianist and a vocalist who rely on beloved standards by guys like Cole Porter and Ira Gershwin. Contemporary material will often be thrown in, too, and the distinction between performers can be made based on their style of interpretation as well as where they're onstage. The most acclaimed cabaret clubs include **Café Carlyle** (below where the late Bobby Short reigned for 36 years until his 2005 death), the **Oak Room** (p288) and **Feinstein's at the Regency** (p288), but you can find plenty of less pricey, more casual and much wackier stuff (drag queens and kings, for example) at various little spots around town, like the new **Mo Pitkins House of Satisfaction** (p288) in the East Village.

Laughter, like music, is a good therapy in a city of eight million people. Luckily, there's no shortage of funny folks or fun venues to help crack you up. They range, like theaters, from the big and mainstream (**Carolines on Broadway**, p288) to the small and edgy (**Upright Citizens Brigade Theatre**, p289). One major downtown venue, the Boston Comedy Club in the Village, changed hands in late 2005, and its future is uncertain; check for updates at the informative www.sheckymagazine.com. For an amusing adventure, flip through the local entertainment listings and pick a random open-mic night; you might wind up cringing, but you could also be witness to the making of a star.

CABARET
CAFÉ CARLYLE Map pp454-5

☎ 212-744-1600; 35 E 76th St at Madison Ave; Ⓞ 6 to 77th St
This swanky spot at the Carlyle hotel draws topshelf talent, from Eartha Kitt to Woody Allen, who has been known to play his clarinet here on Mondays. Stars are often spotted in the audience, too.

DANNY'S SKYLIGHT ROOM Map p282

☎ 212-265-8133; 346 W 46th St btwn Eighth & Ninth Aves; Ⓞ A, C, E to 42nd St–Port Authority
This piano lounge for sophisticates, part of Danny's Grand Sea Palace restaurant, features all manner of cabaret pros, from all-original quirky folks to no-frills masters of standards. Annie Ross, Maureen Taylor and John de Guzmán have all done recent stints here.

DON'T TELL MAMA Map p282
☎ 212-757-0788; 343 W 46th St btwn Eighth & Ninth Aves; ⓔ A, C, E to 42nd St–Port Authority
This art deco room, named for a song in *Cabaret*, features some high-quality camp – Tommy Femia doing a jaw-dropping rendition of Judy Garland, for example – as well as the serious stuff, such as green (but talented) performers from nearby music schools.

DUPLEX Map p448
☎ 212-255-5438; 61 Christopher St at Seventh Ave S; ⓔ 1 to Christopher St–Sheridan Sq
It's way gay at this tiny spot, where you'll find a near-constant roster of drag queens as well as piano-bar shows from a range of up-and-comers on the circuit.

FEINSTEIN'S AT THE REGENCY
Map pp454-5
☎ 212-339-4095; 540 Park Ave at 61st St; ⓔ F to Lexington Ave–63rd St, N, R, W to Lexington Ave–59th St (W Sat & Sun only)
You'll be puttin' on the ritz at this high-class joint from cabaret queen Michael Feinstein, where you'll find uniformed waiters, a reservations-only policy and performers ranging from Anne Hampton Callaway and Patti LuPone to Feinstein himself.

HELEN'S Map pp446-7
☎ 212-206-0609; 169 Eighth Ave btwn 18th & 19th Sts; ⓔ A, C, E to 14th St, L to Eighth Ave
A refreshing addition to the circuit that's appropriately located on the main drag of gay Chelsea, Helen's is an eatery that's home to both a piano bar, for mellow tinkling and crooning, and the Hideaway Room, for more powerful cabaret. The 65-seat venue showcases local favorites, from Baby Jane Dexter to leggy drag queen Edie (who recently made her Broadway debut with *The Threepenny Opera*).

MO PITKIN'S HOUSE OF SATISFACTION Map p449
☎ 212-777-5660; 34 Ave A at E 4th St; ⓔ F, V to Lower East Side–Second Ave
Part bar, part comfort-food restaurant, part cabaret/burlesque lounge, Mo Pitkin's is in a league of its own. Conceived as a showcase for the East Village at its best (read: wacky, edgy, delightful), this is where you'll see every hip downtown sensation in town, from über-host (and gaymous drag king)

Murray Hill to acoustic artists like Laura Cantrell and up-and-coming comics and burlesque artists at the weekly variety shows.

OAK ROOM Map p282
☎ 212-840-6800; Algonquin Hotel, 59 W 44th St btwn Fifth & Sixth Aves; ⓔ B, D, F, V to 42nd St–Bryant Park
Order a martini, settle in and get the Dorothy Parker vibe at this famous piano lounge, which is known for launching the careers of Harry Connick Jr and Diana Krall. These days, you're likely to catch A-listers along the lines of Barbara Carroll and Andrea Marcovicci. Its 25th anniversary season began in 2006.

COMEDY CLUBS

CAROLINES ON BROADWAY Map p282
☎ 212-757-4100; 1626 Broadway at 50th St; ⓔ N, R, W to 49th St, 1, 9 to 50th St
This is a big and bright venue in Times Sq. Comedy specials are frequently filmed here, reflecting the caliber of the talent.

COMEDY CELLAR Map p448
☎ 212-254-3480; www.comedycellar.com; 117 MacDougal St btwn 3rd & Bleecker Sts; ⓔ A, C, E, B, D, F, V to W 4th St
This long-established basement club in Greenwich Village features mainstream material and showcases high-profile comics (eg Jon Lovitz and Jon Stewart), a number of whom like to make surprise visits. Drop-ins are of the star-studded variety, like Colin Quinn and Kevin Brennan.

GOTHAM COMEDY CLUB Map pp446-7
☎ 212-367-9000; 34 W 22nd St btwn Fifth Ave & Broadway; ⓔ F, V, R, W to 23rd St
A lovely, intimate venue in the Flatiron District known for its riotous up-and-comers, Gotham now has another theater in its growing empire: the larger new 'flagship' location (Map pp452–3; 208 W 23rd St, btwn Seventh & Eighth Aves), which opened in early 2006. Gotham All-Stars shows feature comics who have already cut their teeth on TV with Letterman, Leno, Comedy Central and HBO. The last Thursday of the month is the popular Homo Comicus, a comedy series dedicated to queer funny folks that has seen the likes of Judy Gold, Poppi Kramer and Michele Balan.

Entertainment

CABARET & COMEDY

NEW YORK IMPROV Map p282

☎ 212-757-2323; 318 W 53rd St btwn Eighth & Ninth Aves; ⓔ C, E to 50th St

It's a Midtown home to rising stars – just like Richard Pryor and George Carlin were when they performed here back in the day. Recent guests, who've already been on TV, have included Mike Yard, Tom Shilue and Jessica Kirson.

STAND-UP NY Map pp454-5

☎ 212-595-0850; 236 W 78th St at Broadway; ⓔ 1 to 79th St

A small club on the Upper West Side, the shows here range from *Hump Day Humor* (Wednesday) to newcomer nights for gay, Latino and other types of specialized humor. It's pretty mainstream, but a bright spot in the mostly humorless (clubwise, at least) UWS.

STARLIGHT BAR & LOUNGE Map p449

☎ 212-475-2172; 167 Ave A btwn 10th & 11th Sts; ⓔ L to First Ave

Funnyman Keith Price hosts queer comics every Wednesday night at this lovely gay bar's low-lit and sofa-strewn rear lounge.

UPRIGHT CITIZENS BRIGADE THEATRE Map pp452-3

☎ 212-366-9176; 307 W 26th St btwn Eighth & Ninth Aves; ⓔ C, E to 23rd St

Pros of comedy sketches and outrageous improvisations reign at this small and popular venue, which offers classes and daily performances, with Sundays a popular time for pros to drop on in.

CLASSICAL MUSIC, OPERA & DANCE

In NYC, the choices for orchestras, chamber music, opera and ballet are abundant, and the lure of cutting edge can often steal center stage. For all things traditional on a grand scale, don't miss Lincoln Center (p280), which has stellar stages for the New York Philharmonic, the Metropolitan Opera, the New York City Opera, the New York City Ballet and the American Ballet Theater; Brooklyn Academy of Music (p176), or BAM, is the outer borough's edgier and more diverse venue. Other venues, varying in size, price and quality, can be found all over town, and include the multistaged Symphony Space

(p281), Carnegie Hall (p279) and Midtown gem Town Hall (p281). Come summer, you'll be lucky if you happen to catch one of a handful of free, outdoor events from the New York Philharmonic at parks, including Central Park, in all five boroughs.

You won't be hardpressed to find good opera here. Although the prestigious Metropolitan Opera is what most people want, it's not what everyone can afford. You can see equally topshelf, although less-luxuriously staged productions at New York State Theater by the New York City Opera and at various budget options downtown. For the Met, you'll be Lincoln Center–bound. Other such productions are staged at BAM (p176).

BAM also hosts fine dance performances. Showcases for styles from ballet to modern, both famous and obscure, are on stages from Brooklyn to the Bronx, and in every part of Manhattan in between. Internationally acclaimed companies including those of Martha Graham, Alvin Ailey and Merce Cunningham are based in New York, and those that are not will surely pass through town at least once or twice a year. Note that there are two major dance seasons here, first in spring, from March to May, then in late fall, from October to December. But there's always someone putting the moves on for you, no matter what the time of year.

CLASSICAL MUSIC

BARGEMUSIC Map p462

☎ 718-624-2083; Fulton Ferry Landing, Brooklyn Heights, Brooklyn; ⓔ A, C to High St, 2, 3 to Clark St

Chamber-music concerts on this 125-seat docked ferry boat are a unique and intimate affair. For almost 30 years it has been a beloved venue, with beautiful waterfront views and performances of Mozart, Brahms, Shostakovich and more throughout the year, from Thursday to Sunday.

MERKIN CONCERT HALL Map pp454-5

☎ 212-501-3330; 129 W 67th St btwn Amsterdam Ave & Broadway; ⓔ 1 to 66th St–Lincoln Center

This 457-seat hall, part of the Kaufman Cultural Center, is one of the city's more intimate venues for classical music. Its unremarkable hall, right in Lincoln Center territory, hosts a remarkable array of performances, from classical and avant-garde to jazz and even a bit of folk and world music thrown in.

METROPOLITAN MUSEUM OF ART

Map pp454-5

☎ 212-535-7710; www.metmuseum.org; Fifth Ave at 82nd St; suggested donation adult/senior & student/child $15/10/free; ✆ 9:30am-5:30pm Tue-Thu & Sun, to 9pm Fri & Sat; ◉ 4, 5, 6 to 86th St

In addition to being a palace of visual art, the Met hosts performances, within the wonderfully acoustic confines of the museum, in its Grace Rainey Rogers Auditorium, by the resident ensemble Metropolitan Museum Artists in Concert. It also offers a roster of performances from noted pianists, viola players and other musicians. Visit www.metmuseum.org/events for details.

TRINITY CHURCH/ST PAUL'S CHAPEL

Map pp444-5

☎ 212-602-0747; www.trinitywallstreet.org; Broadway at Wall St; ◉ 2, 3, 4, 5 to Wall St, N, R to Rector St (St Paul's Chapel Broadway at Fulton St)

This former Anglican parish church offers an excellent series, Concerts at One, on Thursdays (Mondays at St Paul's Chapel) for a mere $2 suggested donation. Call the concert hotline, above, for the weekly schedule.

OPERA

AMATO OPERA THEATER Map p449

☎ 212-228-8200; 319 Bowery at 4th St; ◉ 6 to Astor Pl

To see classics without all the glitz, head to this tiny, alternative opera house, which regularly puts on favorites including *Die Fledermaus*, *The Marriage of Figaro* and *La Bohéme*.

METROPOLITAN OPERA HOUSE

Map pp454-5

☎ 212-362-6000; www.metopera.org; Lincoln Center, W 64th St at Amsterdam Ave; ◉ 1 to 66th St–Lincoln Center

New York's premier opera company, the Metropolitan Opera offers a spectacular mixture of classics and premieres. It's nearly impossible to get into the first few performances of operas that feature such big stars as Jessye Norman and Plácido Domingo, but once the B-team moves in, tickets become available. The season runs from September to April. Though ticket prices start at $65 and can get close to $300, the $12 standing-room tickets are one of NYC's greatest bargains. They go on sale at 10am Saturday for the following week's performances. For a season schedule, visit the website.

NEW YORK STATE THEATER

Map pp454-5

☎ 212-870-5630; www.nycopera.com; Lincoln Center, Broadway at 63rd St; ◉ 1 to 66th St–Lincoln Center

This is the home of the New York City Opera, a more daring and lower-cost company than the Metropolitan Opera. It performs new works, neglected operas and revitalized old standards in the Philip Johnson–designed space. The split season runs for a few weeks in early fall and once again during early to late spring.

DANCE CEDAR LAKE ENSEMBLE CENTER Map pp452-3

☎ 212-868-4444; www.cedarlakedance.com; 547 W 26th St; ◉ C, E to 23rd St

This brand-new 190-seat theater and home base showcases the Cedar Lake Ensemble, a contemporary ballet company with a focus on bringing attention to emerging choreographers.

CITY CENTER Map p282

☎ 212-581-1212; www.citycenter.org; 131 W 55th St btwn Sixth & Seventh Aves; ◉ N, R, Q, W to 57th St

This was formerly the home of three big companies – American Ballet Theatre (ABT), New York City Ballet and the Joffrey Ballet – but that was before Lincoln Center came along. The beautiful Midtown venue still hosts the Alvin Ailey American Dance Theater (which also holds occasional shows in its own Ailey Citigroup Theater at 405 W 55th St, part of its recently built school in Hell's Kitchen) and ABT every December, as well as the Paul Taylor Dance Company in the spring. At other times, there's a steady stream, from the annual New York Flamenco Festival in February to various tapdancer showcases. And the program should only get more expansive, following a 2005 partnership formed with Carnegie Hall (p279).

DANCE THEATER WORKSHOP

Map pp446-7

☎ 212-924-0077; 219 W 19th St btwn Seventh & Eighth Aves; ◉ 1 to 18th St

You'll find experimental, modern works here, a sleek dance center in Chelsea that contains the 190-seat Bessie Schönberg Theater and two dance studios.

DANSPACE PROJECT Map p449
☎ 212-674-8194; St Mark's Church in-the-Bowery, Second Ave at 10th St; ⓒ F, V to Lower East Side–Second Ave
An intimate space with high ceilings, this church-cum-performance-venue presents frequent, edgy showcases of young break-out locals, sometimes backed by live music.

JOYCE THEATER Map pp446-7
☎ 212-242-0800; www.joyce.org; 175 Eighth Ave at W 19th St; ⓒ A, C, E to 14th St, L to Eighth Ave
An offbeat, intimate venue located in Chelsea, the Joyce focuses on traditional modern companies, such as those from Merce Cunningham and Pilobolus, which make annual appearances at this renovated cinema. It seats 470, with great vantage points from every spot.

KITCHEN Map pp446-7
☎ 212-255-5793; 512 W 19th St btwn Tenth & Eleventh Aves; ⓒ A, C, E to 14th St, L to Eighth Ave
A tiny experimental space in west Chelsea that also produces off-beat theater, this is where you'll find new, progressive pieces and works-in-progress on most nights.

METROPOLITAN OPERA HOUSE
Map pp454-5
☎ 212-362-6000; Lincoln Center, W 64th St at Amsterdam Ave; ⓒ 1 to 66th St–Lincoln Center
The American Ballet Theatre (www.abt.org) presents its largely classical season during the late spring and summer at this grand theater of Lincoln Center (p280).

NEW YORK STATE THEATER Map pp454-5
☎ 212-870-5570; Lincoln Center, Broadway at 63rd St; ⓒ 1 to 66th St–Lincoln Center
Established by Lincoln Kirstein and George Balanchine in 1948, New York City Ballet (www .nycballet.com) features a varied season of premieres and revivals, always including a production of *The Nutcracker* during the Christmas holidays, all performed at this 2755-seat Lincoln Center theater. Expect to be dazzled by the works of Balanchine, Jerome Robbins, resident choreographer Christopher Wheeldon and Peter Martins, the company's ballet master.

READINGS & LECTURES
For all the highly stimulating theatrics in town, New Yorkers still can't help being drawn toward a good old-fashioned literary reading. Though the multitudinous Barnes & Nobles around town offer a constant calendar of big-name writers, which often feel like profit-driven highly choreographed commercials, you can find relief at many more literary venues, from intimate indie bookstores and book-minded pubs to well-established theaters, libraries and museums, such as the excellent 92nd St Y (p292). Lectures, a bit stiffer than readings and spoken-word forums but often just as mind-expanding, can be found at virtually every cultural center in town, from universities to museums: not surprising for such an intellectual hub. The following is just a sampling.

READINGS
BLUESTOCKINGS Map p449
☎ 212-777-6028; www.bluestockings.com; 172 Allen St btwn Stanton & Rivington Sts; ⓒ F, V to Lower East Side–Second Ave
A small (but recently expanded), independent radical/feminist bookstore and café, Bluestockings hosts frequent and energizing readings, discussions and spoken-word performances, often with a focus on social or political change. Various readings series highlight new novelists, revolutionary storytellers and, on the last Tuesday of each month, women poets, with a poetry jam and open-mic hosted by 'the hardest-working guinea butch-dyke poet on the Lower East Side.'

BOWERY POETRY CLUB Map p450
☎ 212-614-0505; www.bowerypoetry.com; 308 Bowery btwn Bleecker & Houston Sts; ⓒ 6 to Bleecker St
Just across from CBGB in the East Village, this funky café and performance space has eccentric readings of all genres, from plays to fiction, plus frequent themed poetry slams.

CORNELIA ST CAFÉ Map p448
☎ 212-989-9319; www.corneliastreetcafe.com; 29 Cornelia St btwn Bleecker & W 4th Sts; ⓒ A, C, E, B, D, F, V to W 4th St
This intimate café is known for its various lit series, including monthly storytelling

gatherings, open-mic poetry nights, and readings dedicated to Italian Americans, Greeks, Caribbean Americans, NYC-area grads, members of the Writers Room (a local writers collective), scribes of prose and emerging poets.

HALF KING Map pp452-3

☎ 212-462-4300; 505 W 23rd St btwn Tenth & Eleventh Aves; ⊕ C, E to 23rd St

It looks like a standard-issue Irish pub on the outside, but inside you'll discover flickering votives, high-quality fiction and poetry readings, and a literary crowd along with the pints of Guinness. This atmosphere is thanks to co-owner Sebastian Junger, author of *The Perfect Storm*.

KGB BAR Map p449

☎ 212-505-3360; www.kgbbar.com; 84 E 4th St btwn Second & Third Aves; ⊕ F, V to Lower East Side–Second Ave

This Commie-themed bar, one flight above street level, hosts readings most nights, with occasional appearances from local lit stars such as Rick Moody and Luc Sante, plus popular theme nights that present lineups of journalists, Jewish novelists, poets and fantasy writers.

92ND ST Y Map pp454-5

☎ 212-415-5500; www.92sty.org; 1395 Lexington Ave at 92nd St; ⊕ 6 to 96th St

The Y is a bastion of literary greatness (as well as a venue that caters for music and dance), with its Unterburg Poetry Center hosting frequent readings, plus a Biographers and Brunch lecture series on Sundays, which features topshelf authors. Recent appearances have included Paul Auster, Margaret Atwood, Joan Didion and Michael Chabon. Almost all the big-name readings sell out, so if there's a particular author you're wanting to hear, reserve well in advance.

NUYORICAN POETS CAFÉ Map p449

☎ 212-505-3360; www.nuyorican.org; 236 E 3rd St btwn Aves B & C; ⊕ F, V to Lower East Side–Second Ave

A mover and a shaker back in the earliest days of poetry slams, this funky spot holds plenty of history as well as frequent open mics, hip-hop jams and a whopping 92 poetry slams a year.

SYMPHONY SPACE Map pp454-5

☎ 212-864-1414; 2537 Broadway at 95th St; ⊕ 1, 2, 3 to 96th St

In addition to hosting innovative films, music concerts and dance performances, Symphony Space is home to the beloved Selected Shorts series, hosted by Isaiah Sheffer and broadcast on National Public Radio stations across the country, on frequent Wednesdays in spring. The evening entails high-quality short stories read by celebrities that have included Alec Baldwin, David Sedaris, Jane Fonda and Hope Davis. Additional readings center around various themes, from stories by censored writers or dissidents to those about cats and dogs.

LECTURES

THE ARCHITECTURAL LEAGUE OF NEW YORK Map pp452-3

☎ 212-753-1722; www.archleague.org; The Urban Center, 457 Madison Ave btwn 50th & 51st Sts; ⊕ B, D, F, V to 47th–50th Sts–Rockefeller Center

This unique nonprofit organization, founded in 1881 by a group of young architects who wanted their own venue for creative and artistic development, offers a constant supply of top-notch architecture-based lectures (as well as installations and forums) that focus on development, urbanism, design and planning. The League celebrates its 125th anniversary with a year-long lineup of events throughout 2006.

LGBT COMMUNITY CENTER Map p448

☎ 212-620-7310; www.gaycenter.org; 208 W 13th St btwn Seventh & Eighth Aves; ⊕ 1, 2, 3 to 14th St

One of the largest gay community centers in the world, 'the Center,' as it's lovingly called, is constantly abuzz with performances, support-group meetings, dances, classes and various other events, including an impressive roster of lectures. Topics range from Buddhism and the making of Broadway musicals to safe S&M techniques and coming out. **Out Professionals** (www.outprofessionals.org) hosts frequent seminars about networking, financial planning and other practicalities.

NEW SCHOOL UNIVERSITY Map pp446-7

☎ 212-229-5880; www.newschool.edu; 66 Fifth Ave at 12th St; ⊕ F, V to 14th St

The forward-thinking University, comprised of the Parsons School of Design

FREE FUN, PART I: CENTRAL PARK SUMMERSTAGE

Among New Yorkers, one of summer's most highly anticipated musical pleasures is the return of the **Central Park SummerStage** (Map pp454–5; ☎ 212-360-2756; www.summerstage.org), an annual series of mostly free concerts (with a suggested donation of $25 for those who can afford it) that take place at Rumsey Playfield in the center of the park. A program of the City Park Foundation, SummerStage presents big music concerts of all genres (like Lou Reed, Cassandra Wilson and Dr John), dance performances and readings from a wide variety of artists free of charge, except for the annual blockbuster benefit concerts (which featured a mixed lineup in a Hurricane Katrina fundraising event for 2005). Admission to shows, via the park's Fifth Ave and 69th St entrance, is on a first-come, first-served basis, and though most shows get seriously crowded (especially on weekends), you should always be able to squeeze your way into the back of the throngs. When the summer schedule is released at the end of every May, New Yorkers clamor to see which of their faves will be onstage, as there's always something for everyone.

and various arts, music and urban studies schools, hosts a series of public discourses for anyone interested in listening. And if you can't be there in person, the school's website catalogs lectures and makes webcasts available for downloading. Recent discussions have revolved around the Bush Era and foreign policy, photography and iconic images, curating the Whitney Biennial, affirmative action and sex education.

NEW YORK PUBLIC LIBRARY
Map pp452-3

☎ 212-930-0830; www.nypl.org/events; 42nd St at Fifth Ave; ⏱ 11am-7:30pm Tue & Wed, 10am-6pm Thu-Sat; ◉ S, 4, 5, 6 to Grand Central–42nd St, 7 to Fifth Ave

The public library operates a constant offering of lectures and public seminars at its myriad branch locations, including some of the best at the main **Humanities and Social Sciences Library** (p150) on 42nd St. Just a select sampling of recent evenings includes Tina Brown interviewing Bernard-Hénri Levy on 'America Through Foreign Eyes,' a conversation between Robert Crumb and Robert Hughes, a panel discussion on 'Confronting the Worst: Writing and Catastrophe,' as well as 'The New Literacy: A Conversation with Eric Bogosian & Co.'

92ND ST Y Map pp454-5

☎ 212-415-5500; www.92sty.org; 1395 Lexington Ave at 92nd St; ◉ 6 to 96th St

In addition to its wonderful spectrum of readings, the Y hosts an excellent Lectures and Discussions series, which has recently brought thinkers from Jeff Greenfield and Madeline Albright to Donny Deutsch and

Dan Savage to enthusiastic audiences. **Makor** (☎ 212-601-1000; 35 W 67th St btwn Columbus Ave and Central Park West), the Y's outpost for the 35-and-under crowd, has its very own energized lineup, which is responsible for recent talks including 'Emerging Trends in Creative Thinking,' 'Negotiating the New York Real Estate Market' and 'Punching Back: Jews and Boxing.'

LIVE MUSIC

It's no Austin, but NYC's indie music is nothing to sneeze at, as it's given rise to favorites including the Strokes, We are Scientists, Clap Your Hands Say Yeah, Rufus Wainwright and Babe the Blue Ox in recent years. Dedicated fans make it their business to chart the latest sounds, chatting about them on music blogs and following their favorites to intimate venues around the city, many of which mix up genres and billings. Hip-hop continues to be generated and produced here, too (Queens is in da house!). More traditional sounds are also constants, as a slew of jazz clubs, cabaret houses and classical venues book gigs steadily. Whether you enjoy piano soloists or full symphonies, NYC offers the full range of high culture, performed by renowned house companies and highly regarded touring artists. For updates and news of great indie performers who may be onstage when you're in town, check local listings (and display ads in the *Village Voice*) and notices in downtown music shops. Megastars rarely tour without hitting the New York area: they'll pack Madison Sq Garden, the city's main arena, and, in summer, **Jones Beach** (p385), a fantastic outdoor amphitheater on the Long Island seashore.

ROCK, HIP-HOP & INDIE

ARLENE'S GROCERY Map p449

☎ 212-358-1633; www.arlenesgrocery.com; 95 Stanton St at Orchard St; ⊕ F, V to Lower East Side–Second Ave

This convenience-store-turned-club was just pre-curve enough of the LES' 1990s explosion to entitle it to a snooty vibe. The one-room hothouse incubates local talent, with great live shows for free every night plus cheap beer.

BOWERY BALLROOM Map p450

☎ 212-533-2111; www.boweryballroom.com; 6 Delancey St at Bowery; ⊕ J, M to Bowery

This terrific, medium-sized venue has the perfect sound and feel for acts like We are Scientists, Camper Van Beethoven, Ben Taylor and other bands demanding audience attention.

CBGB Map p450

☎ 212-982-4052; www.cbgb.com; 315 Bowery btwn E 1st & 2nd Sts; ⊕ 6 to Bleecker St

This dark little den is still going strong after nearly three decades thanks to a slew of big-name old punks who came out of the woodwork to save it from its most recent rent-hike-based threat of closure (though it never seems to be totally safe, so don't be surprised if it does disappear someday soon). The name stands for 'Country, Blue-grass and Blues,' but since the mid-'70s the place has heard more rock than any-thing else. Some of the luminaries who've sweated through legendary sets here in-clude Blondie, Talking Heads and the B52s. Today, the bands experiment with rock, Motown, thrash and everything in between. The more mellow downstairs lounge, CB's Lounge, and the addition next door, CB's

313 Gallery, dole out quality jazz, readings and other such diversions.

DELANCEY Map p449

☎ 212-254-9920; www.thedelancey.com; 168 Delancey St at Clinton St; ⊕ F to Delancey St, J, M, Z to Delancey St–Essex St

It's a recent LES hotspot thanks to great indie-band bookings – Clap Your Hands Say Yeah, the Square Johns, the XYZ Affair – and a packed but airy 2nd-floor patio deck.

HAMMERSTEIN BALLROOM Map pp452-3

☎ 212-279-7740; www.mcstudios.com; Manhattan Center, 311 W 34th St btwn Eighth & Ninth Aves; ⊕ A, C, E to 34th St–Penn Station

It's not the most fun place to see a show – mobs being herded through security checks, pricey drinks, oft-rowdy crowds – but the offerings, from Coldplay to Phil Lesh and Friends, can be quite seductive. Plus the interior has a lovely fading grandeur.

IRVING PLAZA Map pp446-7

☎ 212-777-1224; www.irvingplaza.com; 17 Irving Pl at 15th St; ⊕ L, N, Q, R, W, 4, 5, 6 to Union Sq

In the Union Sq area, Irving Plaza is prob-ably the best club of its size hosting inter-esting mainstream indie acts like Lifehouse, the Saw Doctors and Bebel Gilberto. Just be prepared to stand either on the cramped floor in front of the stage or on the balcony up above the entire scene (a better choice if you actually want to see the musicians).

JOE'S PUB Map p449

☎ 212-539-8770; www.joespub.com; Public Theater, 425 Lafayette St btwn Astor Pl & E 4th St; ⊕ R, W to 8th St–NYU, 6 to Astor Pl

Part cabaret theater, part rock and new-indie venue, this intimate supper club has hosted Toshi Reagon, Aimee Mann and Diamanda Galas.

KNITTING FACTORY Map pp444-5

☎ 212-219-3055; www.knittingfactory.com; 74 Leonard St btwn Church St & Broadway; ⊕ 1 to Franklin St

This Tribeca favorite has a long and influ-ential history in the realm of NYC jazz, but today you're more likely to find an eclectic selection of folk, indie and experimental music, from cosmic space jazz to Tokyo

Bowery Ballroom (above), make sure your ballgown is leather

shock rock, plus rock and hip-hop. Listen to bands on the main floor, balcony, lounge or in the bar downstairs.

MERCURY LOUNGE Map p449
☎ 212-260-4700; www.mercuryloungenyc.com; 217 E Houston St btwn Ave A & Ludlow St; ◉ F, V to Lower East Side–Second Ave
Big names may turn up only occasionally, but this beloved club on the LES almost always has something worth hearing. Intimate and comfy, with tables and ample dance space facing the riser stage, the Mercury is a go-to spot for indies from Serena Maneesh to Chad Van Gaalen. It can also boast about its quality sound system – a great combination for local and touring groups, and their audiences.

NORTH SIX Map p463
☎ 718-599-5103; www.northsix.com; 66 North 6th St, Williamsburg, Brooklyn; ◉ L to Bedford Ave
Catch local up-and-comers and occasional name bands at this room just across the river, in Brooklyn. It's one of the favorite music venues in Williamsburg, located in an old warehouse space, and while most fare is of the rock-pop genre, live hip-hop artists will occasionally grace the stage, too.

PIANOS Map p449
☎ 212-505-3733; www.pianosnyc.com; 106 Norfolk St; ◉ F, V to Lower East Side–Second Ave
This is an old piano shop turned hipster's musical haven serving mixed-genre bills (hip-hop, cowpunk, electronica, Asian rock) and pouring plenty of Rheingold for a large and appreciative Lower East Side crowd.

SOUTHPAW Map p464
☎ 718-230-0236; www.spsounds.com; 125 Fifth Ave btwn Sterling & St John's Pls, Park Slope, Brooklyn; ◉ D, M, N, R to Pacific St (M Mon-Fri only), B, Q, 2, 3, 4, 5 to Atlantic Ave
This popular rock venue moved right into the list of favorite spots after opening its doors in 2002. The innovative design gives you a clear view of the stage from wherever you're sitting, whether at the long bar or in one of the comfy banquettes around the perimeter. And the top-notch sound system is perfect for piping the tunes of local rock, funk and world musicians.

JAZZ & IMPROVISATION
The West Village is a veritable jazz ghetto, with many clubs offering long jams, cheap cover charges and a hot buffet of all flavors of jazz. Midtown has plenty of excellent venues, too. But uptown is still the grand-daddy of jazz joints, so old-school enthusiasts might want to hop up to Harlem. The only thing missing nowadays at all these places is that classic cloud of smoke.

55 BAR Map p448
☎ 212-929-9883; www.55bar.com; 55 Christopher St at Seventh Ave; ◉ 1 to Christopher St–Sheridan Sq
This West Village joint hosts jazz, blues and fusion nightly, with regular performances by quality artists-in-residence and stars passing through. Cover ranges from next-to-nothing to about $15 (but that includes two drinks).

BAM CAFÉ Map p464
☎ 718-636-4139; www.bam.org; 30 Lafayette Ave at Ashland Pl, Fort Greene, Brooklyn; ◉ D, M, N, R to Pacific St (M Sat & Sun only), B, Q, 2, 3, 4, 5 to Atlantic Ave
A high-ceilinged restaurant and lounge in the Brooklyn Academy of Music complex, this venue gives you a healthy helping of jazz vocalists, pianists and sax quartets – and sometimes artists dishing up R&B, cabaret or spoken word – along with your supper.

BIRDLAND Map p282
☎ 212-581-3080; www.birdlandjazz.com; 315 W 44th St btwn Eighth & Ninth Aves; ◉ A, C, E to 42nd St–Port Authority
This landmark club was named for Charlie Parker, or 'Bird,' and has been turning out big-name acts since 1949, when Parker often headlined (at the original location, on 52nd St), as did Thelonious Monk, Miles Davis, Stan Getz and everyone else. Today you're likely to catch the Duke Ellington Orchestra (directed by Paul Mercer Ellington), Ann Hampton Calloway with a big band or an Afro-Cuban jazz orchestra.

BLUE NOTE Map p448
☎ 212-475-8592; www.bluenote.net; 131 W 3rd St btwn Sixth Ave & MacDougal St; ◉ A, C, E, F, V, S to W 4th St
This is by far the most famous (and expensive) of the city's jazz clubs. Covers as

high as $75 get you in to hear big stars, from Cecil Taylor to Abbey Lincoln, play short sets to a serious jazz audience (which means no talking – ever!).

CHICAGO B.L.U.E.S. Map p448
☎ 212-924-9755; 73 Eighth Ave at W 14th St; ⑨ A, C, E to 14th St, L to Eighth Ave

This West Village venue hosts visiting blues masters nightly. The up-and-coming also perform at this none-too-flashy club, and if you've got a harmonica in your pocket, you can jump in for Monday night's blues jam.

CLEOPATRA'S NEEDLE Map pp454-5
☎ 212-769-6969; www.cleopatrasneedleny.com; 2485 Broadway btwn W 92nd & 93rd Sts; ⑨ 1, 2, 3 to 96th St

Late-night and open-mic jams are a hallmark at Cleopatra's Needle, where the music goes until 4am. Some of the best band views are from the bar, where you can take a pint on tap and nosh on surprisingly good Mediterranean-influenced fare. There's never a cover, but mind the $10 drink and/or food minimum – as well as the fact that some performers resent being seen as background music to your dinner conversation.

IRIDIUM JAZZ CLUB Map p282
☎ 212-582-2121; www.iridiumjazzclub.com; 1650 Broadway at 51st St; ⑨ 1 to 50th St

The tables are really tight here, but the sound is good and the sight lines fairly clear – plus the food is pretty darn good. High-quality, big-ticket traditional jazz acts play two sets a night from Sunday to Thursday, and three sets on weekends. Monday night is reserved for the talented and hilarious Les Paul trio, as it has been for the past several decades, with the Mingus Big Band following up on Tuesdays. There's also a nice Sunday jazz brunch here.

JAZZ AT LINCOLN CENTER Map pp454-5
☎ 212-258-9595; www.jazzatlincolncenter.org; Time Warner Center, Broadway at 60th St; ⑨ A, B, C, D, 1 to 59th St–Columbus Circle

Of the three venues, which include the fancy Rose Theater and Allen Room, it's Dizzy's Club Coca-Cola that you'll most likely wind up in, as it's got nightly shows. And how lucky for you, since, with the exception of its awful name, the nightclub is flawless, with stunning views overlooking

Central Park and excellent lineups of both local and touring artists.

JAZZ GALLERY Map p448
☎ 212-242-1063; www.jazzgallery.org; 290 Hudson St btwn Dominick & Spring Sts; ⑨ C, E to Spring St

A cultural center rather than your typical jazz club – there's no bar here, folks – the Gallery is for fans who are really serious about their music. The small space with great acoustics hosts several shows per week, with each night offering two sets. Catch astounding pianists, orchestras, quintets and more, from the traditional to the experimental.

LENOX LOUNGE Map pp458-9
☎ 212-427-0253; www.lenoxlounge.com; 288 Malcolm X Blvd btwn 124th & 125th Sts; ⑨ 2, 3 to 125th St

The art deco Lounge, which hosts frequent big names, is an old favorite of local jazz cats and has recently blipped onto the radar of further-flung enthusiasts (especially Harlem-fascinated tourists). Don't miss the lux Zebra Room in the back.

ST NICK'S PUB Map pp458-9
☎ 212-283-9728; 773 St Nicholas Ave at W 149th St; ⑨ A, B, C, D to 145th St

This is an amazing place to hear nightly raw jazz created by musicians for musicians. Monday nights feature an open jam starting at 9:30pm, when axe- and horn-toting tourists take up the creative gauntlet. Later in the evening, big-name jazz cats come from their bigger gigs around town, keeping it real and live here at the Pub.

SMOKE Map pp454-5
☎ 212-864-6662; www.smokejazz.com; 2751 Broadway btwn 105th & 106th Sts; ⑨ 1 to 103rd St

Unobstructed sight lines and plush sofas have hardcore fans of top-notch talent lining up around the block to get in here on weekends. Expect talents like Eddie Henderson, Hilton Ruiz and Lea Delaria, who lives in the 'hood and has been known to stop in and scat. During the week it's not such a mob scene and there's no cover charge.

TONIC Map p449
☎ 212-358-7501; www.tonicnyc.com; 107 Norfolk St btwn Delancey & Rivington Sts; ⑨ F to Delancey St

Expect avant-garde, creative and experimental music at this beloved LES lounge – which

TOP FIVE LIVE MUSIC VENUES

- Jazz at Lincoln Center: Dizzy's Club Coca-Cola (p153) Annoying name, sublime sounds and views.
- Delancey (p294) Trendy hotspot for indie bands and rooftop smoking.
- Central Park SummerStage (p293) Catch top acts of all genres at a shady, alfresco theater.
- Southpaw (p295) Brooklyn's rock spot with killer sight lines and unrivaled sound.
- Tonic (opposite) Venue of choice for NYC's cutting-edge, avant-garde players and their dedicated fans.

would've closed down after a threatened eviction in 2005 if not for the local support and benefactors including Yoko Ono. For jazz, it's known for inspired improvisational jams and percussion trios, but you'll also find great rock, folk and experimental performers onstage here.

VILLAGE VANGUARD Map p448

☎ 212-255-4037; www.villagevanguard.net; 178 Seventh Ave at W 11th St; ⓔ 1, 9 to Christopher St–Sheridan Sq

This basement-level venue in the West Village could possibly be the world's most prestigious jazz club, as it has hosted literally every major star of the past 50 years. There's a two-drink minimum and a serious no-talking policy.

COUNTRY, BLUEGRASS, FOLK & BLUES

BACK FENCE Map p448

☎ 212-475-9221; 155 Bleecker St btwn MacDougal & Sullivan Sts; ⓔ A, C, E, F, V, S to W 4th St

This surprisingly laidback venue is stuck on a depressingly rowdy, college student–mobbed strip of the Village. It offers fine folk, country and blues during the week, classic rock on weekends.

BB KING BLUES CLUB & GRILL Map p282

☎ 212-997-4144; www.bbkingblues.com; 237 W 42nd St; ⓔ N, R, 1, 2, 3, 7 to Times Sq–42nd St

Catch old-school blues performers – along with rock, folk and reggae acts – like Etta James and Merle Haggard at this two-tiered, horseshoe-shaped room in the heart of the new Times Sq, with cool secondary bills at the adjacent Lucille's Grill.

PADDY REILLY'S MUSIC BAR Map pp452-3

☎ 212-686-1210; 510 Second Ave at 29th St; ⓔ 6 to 28th St

It's the place to be for serious pints and even more serious Irish folk bands and jam sessions throughout the week.

PEOPLE'S VOICE CAFÉ Map pp452-3

☎ 212-787-3903; www.peoplesvoicecafe.org; 45 E 33rd St btwn Madison & Park Aves; ⓔ 6 to 33rd St

Members of the group Songs of Freedom and Struggle founded this good old-fashioned peacenik coffeehouse in 1979. Today it's a nonprofit collective of musicians and activists who host shows from political folkies, storytellers and dancers; Pete Seeger graced the stage for a special 25th-anniversary show in 2005.

POSTCRYPT COFFEEHOUSE Map pp458-9

☎ 212-854-1953; www.columbia.edu/cu/postcrypt /coffeehouse; Columbia University, 116th St entrance; ⓔ 1 to 116th St

This small blues, folk, a capella and poetry venue, located in the basement of the University's St Paul's Chapel, has been graced by acoustic talents from Suzanne Vega and Ani DiFranco to Patty Larkin and Martin Sexton. These days you're likely to hear local up-and-comers. Get there early to snag one of only 35 seats and some free popcorn.

RODEO BAR & GRILL Map pp452-3

☎ 212-683-6500; www.rodeobar.com; 375 Third Ave at 27th St; ⓔ 6 to 28th St

A little slice of Texas in NYC, this mellow, roadhouse-style club has quality rockabilly, bluegrass and country, sans a cover fee.

LATIN & WORLD

COPACABANA Map pp452-3

☎ 212-239-2672; 560 W 34th St at Eleventh Ave; ⓔ A, C, E to 34th St–Penn Station

A bit of Miami in NYC, this mega-club has Latin dancing on the main floor and, upstairs, live salsa and merengue complete with dancing showgirls.

EL TALLER LATINO AMERICANO Map pp454-5

☎ 212-665-9460; 2710 Broadway at 104th St; ⓔ 1 to 103rd St

This is a complete Latino cultural institution that hosts everything from Spanish classes and arts exhibits to music and dance lessons. Its livingroom-like performance space also hosts frequent Latin and world-music performances. A recent sampling of performers included a Brazilian jazz singer, live flamenco music and an Argentine jazz series.

GONZALEZ Y GONZALEZ Map p448
☎ 212-473-8787; 625 Broadway btwn Bleecker & Houston Sts; ◉ B, D, F, V to Broadway–Lafayette St, 6 to Bleecker St
The lines getting in here can be fiercely long, and the fiestas inside are a bit raucous, which is great news for those wanting live salsa, strong margaritas and a passionate crowd of dancers.

S.O.B.'S Map p448
☎ 212-243-4940; 204 Varick St btwn King & Houston Sts; ◉ 1 to Houston St
SOB stands for Sounds of Brazil, but it isn't limited to samba: you can shake it to Afro-Cuban music, salsa and reggae, both live and on the turntable. SOB's hosts dinner shows nightly but it doesn't really start jumping until 2am.

DANCE CLUBS & PARTIES

NYC's club scene is constantly changing: partly because New York partiers get bored easily, and partly because club promoters often find themselves in party-ending battles with both the city and their neighbors over noise, drug activity and myriad other quality-of-life issues. In an effort to avoid such drama, most major dance clubs, Cro-bar, Spirit and the new Pacha among them, locate themselves on the less populated outer edges of the city, closer to the West Side Hwy than to bustling residential areas.

Clubs are generally large spaces that revolve around dancefloors and hyped DJs; parties are the special nights that take place in those clubs, and may rove from place to place frequently. For up-to-the-minute listings, check out the 'clubs' section of the weekly *Time Out New York* magazine, the always updated website of the monthly magazine *Paper* (www.papermag.com), and, for gay soirées, either *HX* or *Next* magazine, two monthly bar rags found at most queer clubs. You should also keep an eye out for club and party flyers on walls and billboards while strolling the East Village; sometimes that's the best way to find out about clubs that don't have phones and don't advertise. Oh, and don't even think about going to any of these places before midnight (even on a weeknight) as things don't truly pick up until 1am or later. Peruse the options, and even pay entrance fees, with **Clubfone** (☎ 212-777-2582; www.clubfone.com). For clubs and bars geared toward an exclusively gay or lesbian clientele (in addition to those in the mix below), see p266.

AVALON Map pp446-7
☎ 212-807-7780; 660 Sixth Ave at 20th St; admission $25; ◉ F, V, R, W to 23rd St
The latest incarnation of this labyrinthine church space (formerly known as Lime-light, the troubled clubkid lair of deported scene king Peter Gatien) is most popular on Thursdays, for hip-hop DJs, and Sundays, which are big gay affairs.

CIELO Map p448
☎ 212-645-5700; 18 Little W 12th St btwn Ninth Ave & Washington St; admission $5-20; ◉ A, C, E to Eighth Ave, L to 14th St
Known for its intimate space and free or lowcost parties, this Meatpacking District staple packs in a fashionable, multiculti crowd nightly for its blend of tribal, Latin-spiced house and soulful grooves, especially on Monday with DJ Francois K's 'outerplanetary' sounds at Deep Space.

CLUB SHELTER Map p282
☎ 212-719-4479; 20 W 39th St btwn Fifth & Sixth Aves; admission $10-20; ◉ B, D, F, V to 42nd St–Bryant Park
The night to check out this multilevel behemoth is Saturday, for the beloved, long-

Your fun will go sky high at Cielo (right)

running deep-house party Shelter with DJ legend Timmy Regisford. Meanwhile, Lovergirl packs in lesbian homegirls on a couple of its other floors – on the same night – for a party known more for its cruising than its sounds. Also residing here now on Fridays is Area 10039, the uptown reincarnation of Area 10009 (which took place at the now-closed Opaline); it's the place to find all the ubiquitous freaks on the hosting circuit.

CROBAR Map pp452-3

☎ 212-629-9000; 530 W 28th St btwn Tenth & Eleventh Aves; admission $25; ⊕ C, E to 23rd St
This get-lost-in-another-world mega club, a local sibling of Crobars in Miami, Chicago and Buenos Aires, caters to a largely suburban crowd on weekends, but, come weekdays, it holds plenty of fabulous queer-tinged bashes with super DJs (Victor Calderone, Felix da Housecat and more). There are multiple rooms, which host simultaneous soirées with varying themes, crowds and DJs.

LOTUS Map p448

☎ 212-243-4420; 409 W 14th St btwn Ninth & Tenth Aves; admission $10-20; ⊕ A, C, E to 14th St, L to Eighth Ave
The big night at this slick, VIP-crowd club is Friday, when GBH (not to be confused with GHB) rocks the house with a fresh mix of house, disco and garage for groovy downtown hipsters.

MARQUEE Map pp452-3

☎ 646-473-0202; 289 Tenth Ave btwn 26th & 27th Sts; ⊕ C, E to 23rd St
Glamorous masses, with their fair share of A-listers, try to slip past the velvet rope at this roomy space, where mainstream fare rocks the house and voyeurs gather on the mezzanine to peer through a glass wall at the 1st-floor action.

PACHA Map pp452-3

☎ 212-209-7500; 618 W 46th St btwn Eleventh Ave & West Side Hwy; ⊕ A, C, E to Port Authority–42nd St
The newest club in town is a massive and spectacular place: 30,000 sq ft and four levels of glowing, sleek spaces and cozy seating nooks that rise up to surround the main dancefloor atrium. Resident DJ is Erick Morillo, and big names are on tap for the first full year of 2006.

PYRAMID Map p449

☎ 212-228-4888; 101 Ave A btwn 6th & 7th Sts; ⊕ F, V to Lower East Side–Second Ave
You'll find a happening, themed soirée on just about any night of the week at this mainly gay party cave. But Fridays, offering the long-running '80s party, 1984, draw the biggest mobs.

ROXY Map pp446-7

☎ 212-627-0404; 515 W 18th St btwn Tenth & Eleventh Aves; admission $15-25; ⊕ A, C, E to 14th St, L to Eighth Ave
This legendary megaclub keeps the good times rolling with the freewheeling Wednesday roller disco. John Blair promotes the big, ever-popular Saturday-night bash, a Circuit Party–like massive gathering of shirtless gay men, humping to the sounds of big names from Manny Lehman to Junior Vasquez. The boys are still talking about how Madonna herself made an appearance here to promote Confessions on the Dance Floor in late 2005.

SAPPHIRE Map p449

☎ 212-777-5153; 249 Eldridge St at E Houston St; admission $5; ⊕ F, V to Lower East Side–Second Ave
This tiny, hoppin' venue has survived the crowds of the mid-'90s Ludlow St boom with its hip factor intact. Come here for some steamy dancing on a tightly packed dance floor.

718 SESSIONS Map pp446-7

Deep; ☎ 212-229-2000; 16 W 22nd St btwn Fifth & Sixth Aves; admission $12-25; ⊕ F, V, R, W to 23rd St (W Sat & Sun only)
This monthly party, held at an otherwise unremarkable club space, is a riot of old-school dancing to deep, soulful house from DJ Danny Krivit and occasional live performers, like the recent New Year's Eve show from Joi Cardwell. House parties rage on Friday with DJ Marc Anthony.

SPIRIT Map pp452-3

☎ 212-268-9477; 530 W 27th St btwn Tenth & Eleventh Aves; ⊕ C, E to 23rd St
Taking the place of Twilo hasn't been easy for this massive club, an outpost of a Spirit in Dublin, but weekends have been known to pull in biggies like Danny Tenaglia.

Sundays, promoted by John Blair of Roxy, attract a spirited mob of college-age boys.

TURNTABLES ON THE HUDSON
☎ 212-560-5593; www.turntablesonthehud son.com

An excellent, roving DJ-centric bash with live percussionists and dubs, moves about town throughout the week, attracting a swarm of followers anywhere. It does have a permanent home on Fridays – the **Lightship Frying Pan** (Map pp452–3; Pier 63, Twelfth Ave at 23rd St), a former floating lighthouse that's one of the city's coolest, oddest party spots.

FILM & TV

Cinephiles can sate any film cravings in NYC, from the latest Japanimation import to versions of saucy European films banned elsewhere in the US. And, while it might seem strange to come to NYC and go to the movies, a lot of New Yorkers consider film to be just as evolved an art form as opera or Broadway drama. Besides, nothing beats an air-conditioned movie theater, especially one with a massive screen and comfy stadium seating, in the thick of summer's dog days. Frequent **film festivals** (opposite), the New York, Jewish, Lesbian & Gay and Asian American among them, are special events that give added weight to your movie-watching.

FREE FUN, PART II: BRYANT PARK FILM SERIES

Summers in **Bryant Park** (Map pp452–3; www.bry antpark.org) take a celluloid focus, with the return of the outdoor, Monday-night Film Series. Films, both modern and classic, are projected onto a massive screen that goes up every June on the west side of the tree-lined, European-style patch of green. Folks show up as early as 3:30pm to get a good spot for their blanket, picnics and bottles of wine in tow, with an anxious after-work crowd zipping in by 6pm to enjoy the remaining late-afternoon rays. The movies start at about 9pm, and each summer's series has a different theme, though most are classics or New York–based. Recent screenings have included *The Odd Couple*, *Jaws*, *Whatever Happened to Baby Jane?*, *Sleepless In Seattle* and *Breakfast at Tiffany's*.

Even though movie tickets cost at least $10, long lines on evenings and weekends are the norm. To ensure you'll get in (and not wind up watching with a stiff neck from the front row) it's pretty much imperative that you call and buy your tickets in advance (unless it's midweek, midday or for a film that has been out for months already). Check movie listings for phone numbers and websites for advance sales, but most are handled either through **Movie Fone** (☎ 212-777-3456; www.moviefone.com) or **Fandango** (www.fandango.com). You'll have to pay an extra $1.50 fee per ticket, but it's worth it. Folks who love TV so much they want to be involved with the shows will be in seventh heaven here, as it's where many programs with studio audiences – from *Late Night with David Letterman* to *Good Morning America* – are taped. Read on to see how you can get your 15 minutes.

REVIVAL THEATERS
ANTHOLOGY FILM ARCHIVES Map p449
☎ 212-505-5181; 32 Second Ave at 2nd St; ⊕ F, V to Lower East Side–Second Ave

This East Village theater screens low-budget European and fringe works, plus revives classics, such as *From Here to Eternity*, and puts on festivals that pay homage to films Turkish, Swedish and sports-based, among other themes.

CLEARVIEW'S CHELSEA Map pp446-7
☎ 212-777-3456; 260 W 23rd St btwn Seventh & Eighth Aves; ⊕ C, E to 23rd St

In addition to showing first-run films, this multi-screen complex hosts midnight showings of the *Rocky Horror Picture Show*, as well as a great Thursday-night series, Chelsea Classics, which has local drag star Hedda Lettuce hosting old-school camp Joan Crawford, Bette Davis and Barbara Streisand films.

EAGLE THEATER Map p457
☎ 718-205-2800; 73-07 37th Rd, Jackson Heights, Queens; tickets $5; ⊕ 7 to 74th St–Broadway

King of Bollywood cinema in New York (with hot samosas for sale), the Eagle plays Indian films – with all the bells and whistles – nightly; most action, with locals dressed to impress, is on Friday. English subtitles run on many films, but it's not that important.

FILM FESTIVALS

With so many film festivals in New York – 30 at last count – chances are you'll be able to hit one no matter when you visit. Many credit the highly publicized and quickly growing **Tribeca Film Festival** (p127) for upping the ante on quality of films and screening locations. The topics of New York's film festivals are as varied as the city itself. There's Dance on Camera (January), a celebration of movies about dance, and the Jewish Film Festival (January), which explores Jewish culture and religion onscreen. The old fave New York Film Festival (January) highlights up-and-coming directors every year, and the African-American Women in Film Festival (March) is about, well, you guessed it! The Williamsburg Film Festival (March) has brought the fun to that artsy-trendy Brooklyn neighborhood, and screens local filmmakers, while the Lesbian & Gay Film Festival (June), a highlight of Gay Pride month, has added filmmaker panels in striving to make the queer showcase better than ever. Meanwhile, the Human Rights Watch Film Festival (June) enlightens locals to the evils of global societies, while the New York Hawaiian Film Festival (May), the Asian-American International Film Festival (June) and the Israeli Film Festival (June) focus on those varied cultures.

FILM FORUM Map p448
☎ 212-727-8110; 209 W Houston St btwn Varick St & Sixth Ave; ◉ 1 to Houston St
This is a three-screen cinema in Soho featuring independent films, revivals and career retrospectives. Theaters are small, as are the screens, so get there early for a good viewing spot. There's a great little café in the lobby.

IFC CENTER Map p448
☎ 212-924-7771; 323 Sixth Ave at 3rd St; ◉ A, B, C, D, E, F, V to W 4th St
Formerly the Waverly, which sat in closed decrepitude in recent years, this three-screen art house has a great café and a solid lineup of new indies, cult classics and foreign films.

LEONARD NIMOY THALIA Map pp454-5
☎ 212-864-1414; Symphony Space, 2537 Broadway at 95th St; ◉ 1, 2, 3 to 96th St
This small, just-renovated theater, part of the Symphony Space complex, screens quality double features of a variety of time periods and genres.

MUSEUM OF MODERN ART GRAMERCY THEATRE Map pp454-5
☎ 212-777-4900; 127 E 23rd St btwn Park Ave S & Lexington Ave; ◉ R, W, 6 to 23rd St
This wonderful theater is the site of constant, high-quality retrospectives and some foreign festivals.

WALTER READE THEATER Map pp454-5
☎ 212-875-5600; Lincoln Center, 165 W 65th St; ◉ 1 to 66th St–Lincoln Center
The Walter Reade boasts some good wide, screening-room-style seats. The New York Film Festival takes place here every September, and at other times of the year you can catch independent films, career retrospectives and themed series.

NEW-RELEASE THEATERS

ANGELIKA FILM CENTER Map p450
☎ 212-995-2000; 18 W Houston St at Mercer St; ◉ B, D, F, V to Broadway–Lafayette St
An old favorite, the Angelika specializes in foreign and independent films and is often overcrowded despite the fact that screens can be annoyingly small and you can hear the rumble of the subway during screenings. The roomy café here serves gourmet grub. If you've time to kill before the screening, check out the Stanford White–designed beaux arts building that houses Angelika. Called the Cable Building (the miles of cable here moved the country's first and last cable cars ever installed), it features an oval window and caryatids on its Broadway facade.

BAM ROSE CINEMA Map p464
☎ 718-623-2770; 30 Lafayette Ave at Flatbush Ave, Fort Greene, Brooklyn; ◉ M, N, R, W to Pacific St, Q, 1, 2, 4, 5 to Atlantic Ave
The gorgeous Fort Greene theater at the Brooklyn Academy of Music shows

Angelika Film Center (above). A fave of Angelica Houston?

TV TAPINGS

You can become part of a studio audience for one of the many TV shows taped in town and, though most are booked long in advance, you can always stand in line the day of the taping and keep your fingers crossed for standbys or cancellations.

Saturday Night Live (p155), one of the most popular NYC-based shows, is known for being difficult to get into. That said, you can try your luck by getting your name into the mix in the fall, when seats are assigned by lottery. Simply send an email to snltickets@nbc.com in August, or line up by 8:15am the day of the show at 50th St between Fifth and Sixth Aves (at NBC studios) for standby lottery tickets (16 years and older only). Another late-night show that draws crowds is the *Late Show with David Letterman*. You can try to request tickets for a specific date at www.cbs.com/lateshow, or else secure a standby ticket by calling ☎ 212-247-6497 at 11am on the day of the taping, which begins at 5:30pm Monday to Thursday. Get on the *Daily Show with John Stewart* on Comedy Central by reserving tickets at least three months ahead of time; call ☎ 212-586-2477, or call at 11:30am the Friday before you'd like to attend for a chance at last-minute seats.

Audience members at *Total Request Live* must be at least 16 years old; line up at **MTV studios** (Map pp452–3; 1515 Broadway btwn 43rd & 44th Sts) by noon for weekday tapings, which begin at 3:30pm, or call the **MTV hotline** (☎ 212-398-8549) to try and snag a specific reservation. For *Last Call with Carson Daly*, visit www.1iota.com for reservations, or call ☎ 800-452-8499; you can try your hand at standbys by lining up at the 49th St entrance of 30 Rockefeller Plaza (NBC studios) by 11am. Daytime fans, join the scandal-loving viewers of the *Ricki Lake Show* by filling out a request for tickets at www.sonypictures.com/tv/shows/ricki/index.htm.

For more show ticket details, visit the websites of individual TV stations, or try www.tvtickets.com.

independent and foreign films in spaces that are blessed with excellent seating, huge screens and a lovely, landmark design. You can also catch mini-festivals and revivals here.

LANDMARK SUNSHINE CINEMAS
Map p450

☎ 212-358-7709; 143 E Houston St; ◉ F, V to Lower East Side–Second Ave
A renovated Yiddish theater, the wonderful Landmark shows foreign and mainstream art films on massive screens and is a welcome addition to the LES neighborhood.

LINCOLN PLAZA CINEMAS Map pp454-5

☎ 212-757-2280; 1886 Broadway at 62nd St; ◉ A, B, C, D, 1, 2 to 59th St–Columbus Circle
This underground, six-screen venue is the place to go for artsy independent films on the Upper West Side.

LOEWS 42ND ST E-WALK THEATER
Map p282

☎ 212-505-6397; W 42nd St btwn Seventh & Eighth Aves; ◉ N, Q, R, S, W, 1, 2, 3, 7 to Times Sq
A massive, 13-screen theater in Times Sq, the E-Walk dishes out all the latest Hollywood pabulum in state-of-the-art facilities. It's a good place to catch indies, as they're not as crowded as the mainstream fare, and the digs are plush, with excellent sightlines.

LOEWS LINCOLN SQUARE
Map pp454-5

☎ 212-336-5000; 1992 Broadway at 68th St; ◉ 1, 2, 3 to 72nd St
This Upper West Side behemoth includes a 3-D IMAX theater and 12 large screens that play first-run features. But short folks, beware: there's no stadium seating.

Activities

Activities

Don't say it around the MoMA or the Met, but you could spend a happy, busy lifetime in New York and never see a museum. Those keen for some good ol' fashioned sweat – watching or doing – have a world of options. Actually, subway stations can feel like a sauna and hailing a cab can feel like a game in itself, but there are more traditional ways to enjoy sport and fitness. It's hard to say you've been to New York without sitting and enjoying a hot dog at Yankee Stadium. But you can also chant with stars at downtown yoga centers, swim in pools where the Raging Bull did his laps (or at least hung out), hear trash-talk at a stickball match (the ultimate street sport), get a tennis volley going at he home of the US Open, surf the Atlantic or kayak to Brooklyn.

TOP FIVE SPORTS & ACTIVITIES

- Watch a street-basketball (p306) dunkathon at 'the Cage' or historic Rucker Park in Harlem
- Run (p314), bike (p311), ice-skate (p313) and bird-watch (p309) in Central Park
- Kayak the Hudson River (p309), for free
- Hit the waves (p315) – surf's up in the big Apple; at last the surf ban is lifted
- Help cheer on the Yankees at Yankee Stadium (opposite)

WATCHING SPORTS

New York down deep is as sports-mad as any town with pitch, field, court or alley. If you're not seeing a game in person – and it's really worth trying to catch at least a Yankees game – little sticky-floor neighborhood bars can really light up when a Knicks or Giants or Yankees game is on. Be ready to high-five your neighbor when Eli Manning throws for a Giants' TD or Derek Jeter throws a ninth-inning third out. Look for bars in more residential areas, particularly in the boroughs and away from the trendy districts in Manhattan, that post a New York team logo in neon – ask about game time if you don't know. Those who don't understand the American sports will find more-than-willing (and likely beer-soaked) tutors.

If you need to read up on local sports, skip the overly polite *Times* and head to the holds-no-punches back pages of the tabloids *New York Daily News* or *New York Post*.

Pick me! Pick me! Street basketball (p306) at West 4th Street Courts grips the locals

Tickets

With so many teams and overlapping seasons, a game is rarely a day away. Other than football, tickets are generally available any time. **Ticketmaster** (www.ticketmaster.com) sells individual tickets and the teams handle package deals. There are direct links from 'tickets' links on team websites (see individual entries, later). In some cases, you can buy tickets from team hotlines or ticket box offices directly.

Other buy/sell options include **StubHub** (☎ 866-788-2482; www.stubhub.com) and **BuySell-Tix** (☎ 800-451-8499; www.buyselltix.com).

BASEBALL

New York may be one of the last remaining corners of the USA where baseball runs supreme over football or basketball – and considering tickets start at $5 or $10 it's a real steal. In the years after WWII, New York had three teams, all powerhouses: the New York Yankees, the New York Giants and the Brooklyn Dodgers. Thirteen times, two of them met in the finals for the heralded Subway Series. The unthinkable came in 1957 when both the Dodgers and Giants bolted for Los Angeles and San Francisco, respectively (did it *have* to be California?). The arrival of the Mets in Queens a few years later (strategically with a color combo of the departed teams) was welcomed, but didn't quite dull the sense of betrayal felt by many fans (including ones not yet born in 1957). In 2000 the Yanks beat the Mets in a reprise of the Subway Series, adding more lore for the ages.

Teams play 162 games during the regular season from April to October, when the real action starts – the playoffs.

BROOKLYN CYCLONES

☎ 718-449-8497; www.brooklyncyclones.com; KeySpan Park, cnr Surf Ave & W 17th St, Coney Island; tickets $6-14; ⏰ ticket office 10am-4pm Mon-Fri, 10am-3pm Sat; ⊕ F, D to Coney Island–Stillwell Ave
The Mets' farm team brought baseball back to Brooklyn (finally) in 2001. The minor-league team, part of the New York/Penn League, play at KeySpan Park (Map p466), a few steps from the Coney Island boardwalk. It's a perfect place for getting a hot dog and hearing the ol' bat clank. The team is named for the famed roller coaster (p180), which still runs nearby.

NEW YORK METS

☎ 718-507-8499; www.mets.com; Shea Stadium, 123-01 Roosevelt Ave, Flushing, Queens; tickets $5-70; ⊕ 7 to Willets Point–Shea Stadium
Yankee Stadium had the Babe, but the Shea (Map p467) once hosted the Beatles. New York's 'new' baseball team has represented the National League since 1962. Fans still hold onto the magic of '86, when the Mets last won the World Series in a miraculous comeback. Their blue-and-orange logo shows select buildings from New York's five boroughs, though don't expect many fans to commute from the Bronx on game day. The new favorite Met is one-time Red Sox pitcher Pedro Martinez, who (after famously calling the Yankees 'his daddy') wrought terror over many New Yorkers when he led the Red Sox to victory over the Yanks after being down 0-3 in a best-of-seven AL championship series in 2004. The Mets will need some of this magic, after missing the playoffs in 2005. The trip to Shea is 35 minutes by subway from Midtown.

NEW YORK YANKEES

☎ 718-293-6000, tickets 212-307-1212; www .yankees.com; Yankee Stadium, cnr 161st St & River Ave, the Bronx; tickets $10-115; ⊕ B, D, 4 to 161st St–Yankee Stadium
It would be an Empire State–sized understatement to call the Yanks a baseball dynasty. Playing in the American League, the 'Bronx Bombers' won 26 World Series championships in the last century. These days the Yankees still contend annually for another championship – with Derek Jeter, Alex Rodriguez and (culled from the hated Boston Red Sox) Johnny Damon. The roster is a regular all-star team. Games are held, of course, at fabled Yankee Stadium (p202), 15 minutes from Midtown by subway. Bleacher seats are almost always available. It's not a good idea to wear anything but Yankee blue.

STATEN ISLAND YANKEES

☎ 718-720-9265; www.siyanks.com; Richmond County Bank Ballpark, 75 Richmond Tce, Staten Island; tickets $10; ⏰ ticket office 9am-5pm Mon-Fri, 10am-3pm Sat; 🚢 Staten Island Ferry
Champions of the New York/Penn title three times in the past decade (including

2005), these Yanks play about as well as the guys in the Bronx. If not a fly ball, you can at least catch some fab Manhattan skyline views from Richmond County Bank Ballpark, the stylish waterfront stadium across New York Harbor.

BASKETBALL

Two NBA teams, the Knicks and the Nets, call the New York metropolitan area home. The season lasts from October to May or June. Individual game tickets are available through **Ticketmaster** (www.ticketmaster.com) and **StubHub** (☎ 866-788-2482; www.stubhub .com) or by visiting the team's ticket office.

Last-minute Knicks tickets are tougher to get than Nets tickets. Either way, book way ahead if you're hoping to see either squad play NBA stars like Allen Iverson, Shaq, Kobe Bryant or Lebron James.

BROOKLYN KINGS

☎ 718-775-7524; www.thebrooklynkings.com; Metcalfe Hall, Long Island University (Brooklyn Campus), cnr Dekalb & Flatbush Aves; tickets adult/student $8/5; Ⓜ B, M, Q, R to Dekalb Ave
It's only a matter of time before the minor-league United States Basketball League gets some hipster cred (after all, the 2005 championship was played in Salina, Kansas). Kicking it since 1999 (and finishing second in 2005), the Kings play their 30-game season from late April through June. They're based at Metcalfe Hall (Map pp460–1) in Brooklyn.

NEW JERSEY NETS

☎ 800-765-6387, 201-935-3900, individual tickets 201-507-8900; www.njnets.com; Continental Airlines Arena, Meadowlands Sports Complex, New Jersey; tickets $15-115; ☽ box office 11am-6pm Mon-Sat, though halftime game days
Overshadowed, stuck in the Jersey Meadowlands but – in recent years – plainly better than the Knicks, the Nets play pretty exciting ball, though their closest championship call was being runners-up in the 2001–02 and 2002–03 championship finals. Perhaps what the Nets have needed is a total relocation. In January 2004 Bruce Ratner bought the team and announced controversial plans to move it to Brooklyn by 2007. The final stamp to go is still pending, but it's looking like it will happen. Meanwhile, with players like slick point guard Jason Kidd and Vince 'Vinsanity' Carter, the Nets seem poised to contend for

IS YOUR GAME IN JERSEY?

Home games for the Giants, Jets, Nets, Devils and MetroStars are held at the Meadowlands Sports Complex in East Rutherford, New Jersey. The easiest way to reach the complex is by public bus 351 from the Port Authority Bus Terminal in Midtown. The 20-minute trip is $4.50 each way. (Get a round-trip ticket to avoid hassles on your return.) Buses run continuously from two hours before a game or event until one hour afterward.

By car from Manhattan, take the Lincoln Tunnel from Midtown to Route 3 W and follow signs to Exit 4, Route 120.

Eastern Conference champion each year. See the boxed text on above for directions to the stadium.

NEW YORK KNICKS

☎ 212-465-5867, tickets 212-307-7171; www.ny knicks.com; Madison Sq Garden, btwn Seventh Ave & 33rd St, Manhattan; tickets $10-80; Ⓜ A, C, E, 1, 2, 3 to 34th St–Penn Station
The first rap song of all time gives it up for the beloved Knickerbockers (Sugar Hill Gang sing 'I have a color TV so I can watch the Knicks play basketball'). The blue-and-orange play hoop in front of Spike Lee and 18,999 others at the Madison Sq Garden (Map pp452–3). In recent years, hard times have come to Knicks basketball: a championship has eluded the team since 1973 (when Willis Reed and politician Bill Bradley played); even Patrick Ewing, star center of the '80s and '90s, never claimed the ring (aka 'the Michael Jordan factor'). Some (maniacal) fans believe that, with the additions of Brooklyn native Stephen Marbury and champion coach Larry Brown (snuck in from the Detroit Pistons in 2005), the ever-elusive victory may be within reach. A playoff berth might be a start, as the Knicks have been scraping near the bottom of the Atlantic Division in recent seasons. Generally only tickets from $45 and up are available; book a month in advance.

NEW YORK LIBERTY

☎ 212-465-6293, tickets 212-307-7171; www.ny liberty.com; Madison Sq Garden, btwn Seventh Ave & 33rd St, Manhattan; tickets $10-55; Ⓜ A, C, E, 1, 2, 3 to 34th St–Penn Station
Women's basketball has become another hot ticket since the WNBA league's outset in 1997. Still searching for their first championship, the Liberty, based at the Garden

Activities

WATCHING SPORTS

(Map pp452–3), plays a 34-game season from May to September or October.

FOOTBALL

Both of New York's NFL teams play in New Jersey at Giants Stadium from August to December (and January, if they host play-off games); they play on alternate weekends (16 games per season), but tickets are always sold out. It's possible to get them for $200 and up. Try StubHub (p305) and www.craigslist.com for available tickets. In addition, the Giants have a free ticket-exchange program; see their website or call for details.

See the boxed text on opposite for details on getting to the games.

College football doesn't make much of a blip on the New Yorkers' radar, though Rutgers in New Jersey is the nation's oldest team. Uptown Ivy League team Columbia plays (and usually loses) in Fall to scant crowds.

NEW YORK DRAGONS

☎ 516-501-6700, tickets 631-888-9000; www.new yorkdragons.com; Nassau Veterans Memorial Coliseum, Uniondale, Long Island; tickets $15-55; 🚇 Long Island Railroad to Hempstead
If you're looking to get silly, see New York's arena football team play the mini-version of gridiron in Long Island. The season for the 17-team Arena Football League (AFL) runs from February through May. Team names include, um, Kats and Sabercats. From the

station take bus N70, N71 or N72 to the coliseum.

NEW YORK GIANTS

☎ 201-935-811, tickets 201-935-8222; www.giants .com; Giants Stadium, East Rutherford, New Jersey
One of the NFL's oldest teams, the Giants (part of the NFC conference) are starting to regain control over the NFC's Eastern Division from the Philadelphia Eagles, largely banking on the arm of Eli Manning, legs of team-favorite Tiki Barber, and damn-serious spirit of coach Tom Coughlin (he once fined players for not showing up to a meeting *early*). Seeing ex-coach Bill Parcells in division-rival Dallas Cowboys' gear is hard for many Giants to take. The last Giants Super Bowl appearance (a knock out loss to Baltimore) was in 2000.

NEW YORK JETS

☎ 516-560-8200 ext 1; www.newyorkjets.com; Giants Stadium, East Rutherford, New Jersey
The Jets, generally less popular than the Giants (hell, they play in *Giants Stadium*), have yet to return to the big time since the fabled 1969 Super Bowl when flashy quarterback Joe Namath 'guaranteed' a victory. He was right, and it started an era when AFC teams dominated the once too-tough-to-beat NFC teams. That said, the Jets – despite by the contagious, 'J-E-T-S!' chants – have been finding innovative new ways to lose. In 2004 a missed field goal kept them from the AFC championship; and in 2005 three quarterbacks (including starter Chad

LET THE GAMES BEGIN: NJ VS NYC

Sometimes New York/New Jersey sports can be most interesting behind the scenes. Both 'New York' football teams, which have long played in Jersey, and the other major sports teams here all want new places to play. And both sides of the Hudson River are swinging fists to keep/take/shelter/care for/feed their teams.

In 2004 and 2005 New York City mayor Michael Bloomberg pushed all his political might behind a controversial $1.7-billion plan to move the NFL New York Jets to Manhattan in a new West Side Stadium at Manhattan's traffic-heavy West Side Hwy. The plan finally collapsed in 2005.

Meanwhile, in May 2005, New Jersey officials quietly tightened the reigns on the other NFL team, the New York Giants (who presently share 'Giants Stadium' in the Meadowlands, New Jersey, with the Jets) by signing an $800-million plan for a new 80,000-seat stadium by 2009. For a moment in 2005, it looked like the Jets might split to Queens' Flushing Meadows-Corona Park, but Jersey's offer was too good to pass up.

In the hockey/basketball world, Newark has signed a deal to house the NHL New Jersey Devils in downtown Newark, which Jersey officials hope will keep the NBA New Jersey Nets in Jersey. However, when real-estate mogul Bruce Ratner bought the Nets in 2004, he planned to move them to his proposed $2.5 billion Atlantic Yards project in downtown Brooklyn (set for 2007). Odds look like the Nets are Brooklyn's.

The Yankees seem to be safely the Bronx's, but the Yankees are proposing a new $800-million stadium, which – if approved – would open in 2009.

Pennington) fell to injury and the Jets finished with a dreadful 4-12 season as well as losing their charismatic coach Herm Edwards to Kansas City.

HOCKEY

Of all things, there are more major-league hockey teams in the metropolis than any other sport. Back from a year off after a season-canceling strike in 2004–05, the National Hockey League (NHL) season lasts from September to April; each team plays three or four games a week.

NEW JERSEY DEVILS

☎ 201-935-6050, tickets 212-307-7171; www.new jerseydevils.com; Continental Airlines Arena, East Rutherford, New Jersey; tickets $20-90

The Devils may not be New Yorkers, and they're kind of a team without a city (their victory 'parades' are held in the arena parking lot), but the Devs play some premier hockey. They have won the Stanley Cup three times in the past decade (1995, 2000 and 2003), with present goalie Martin Brodeur playing a key role in protecting the net.

NEW YORK ISLANDERS

☎ 631-888-9000; www.newyorkislanders.com; Nassau Veterans Memorial Coliseum, Uniondale, Long Island; tickets $25-160

New York's other NHL hockey team plays in Long Island. NYC hasn't given much Islander love since their remarkable four-consecutive Stanley Cup streak (1980–83). If you venture out there, give a high-five to Sparky the Dragon (see www.sparky-thedragon.com) for us. Check the contact details on their website for directions.

NEW YORK RANGERS

☎ 212-465-6741, tickets 212-307-7171; www.ny rangers.com; Madison Sq Garden; tickets $27-140; Ⓜ A, C, E, 1, 2, 3 to 34th St–Penn Station

Manhattan's favorite hockey squad ended a 54-year dry spell by hoisting the Stanley Cup in 1994. Though a dip in play has plagued recent seasons (not helped, surely, by Mark Messier's retirement), the Rangers' fans still raise the Madison Sq Garden (Map pp452–3) roof, especially when the Blue-shirts play arch rivals, the New York Islanders. If only right-wing Jaromir Jagr would

grow back his trademark 'hockey hair' (ie business in front, party in back).

HORSE RACING

Horse fans can find a few tracks in the area. Thoroughbreds race Wednesday to Sunday at Aqueduct Race Track (Howard Beach, Queens; Ⓜ A to Aqueduct Racetrack) from October to early May, and at Belmont Race Track (Belmont, Long Island; Ⓡ Long Island Railroad to Belmont Race Track) from May to mid-July, and September and October. Belmont hosts the famous Belmont Stakes in June. For information on either track, contact the New York Racing Association (☎ 718-641-4700; www.nyra.com).

The track at Meadowlands (☎ 201-843-2446; www.thebigm.com; Meadowlands Sports Complex, East Rutherford, New Jersey; admission $1-5) has harness racing December to August and thoroughbreds September to November. Wednesday to Saturday races begin at 7:30pm, and Sunday races at 1:10pm. See the boxed text on p306 for directions to the track.

SOCCER

Yes, the USA *does* play soccer. Unfortunately the women's professional soccer league, which included the New York Power, folded in 2003.

NEW YORK/NEW JERSEY METROSTARS

☎ 201-583-7000, tickets 212-307-7171; www.met rostars.com; Giants Stadium, East Rutherford, New Jersey; tickets $26-38

Awkwardly split betwixt New York and New Jersey by name, the MetroStars' 30-game season (April through October) attracts a diverse crowd of soccer loyalists who can make the games fun. Purists from the Old World may scoff at the level of play, but will recognize players like France's Youri Djorkaeff. See the boxed text on p306 for directions to the stadium.

TENNIS

The pro tennis circuit's final Grand Slam event each year, the US Open (www.usopen .org), takes place over two weeks at the end of August at USTA National Tennis Center (Map p467; ☎ 718-760-6200; www.usta.com;

Flushing Meadows Corona Park, Queens; 7 to Willets Point–Shea Stadium). Tickets usually go on sale at Ticketmaster (www. ticketmaster.com) in April or May, but marquee games (held at Arthur Ashe Stadium) are hard to get. General admission tickets to early rounds aren't though; tickets run about $50 (top bleachers on Court 7 can take in five matches at once). Most who see the games know someone, are playing, or resort to scalpers. Check out the USTA site in January or February for updates.

OUTDOOR ACTIVITIES
New York's activities vary with the season. In summer, parks fill with soccer and basketball players; the river with kayaks and sailboats. In winter, many lace up their ice skates or (after about six inches of snow) cross-country ski the Sheep Meadow in Central Park.

BIRD-WATCHING
One of the country's most important birding areas (no, seriously) is Central Park. Its diverse habitat helps draw some 15% of all migrating birds (some 200 species) to the Big Apple in spring and fall. At those times, the **New York City Audubon Society** (Map pp452–3; ☎ 212-691-7483; www.nycas.org; 71 W 23rd St; F, V to 23rd St) holds four-session Beginner's Birding courses (adult $75), which include two field trips. There's also a Christmas bird count in Central Park, and harbor cruises.

Local birding pro **Starr Saphir** (☎ 212-304-3808) leads three-hour **walking tours** (adult/student $6/3) of Central Park. The bulk of the tours coincide with migration (roughly April to June, September and October), where up to 180 species (eg orioles, sparrows, peregrine falcons) can be spotted. On Monday and Wednesday, she leaves from W 81st St and Central Park West at 7:30am, from W 103rd St and Central Park West on Tuesday 9am, and Saturday at 7:30am. The tours run once monthly in other months (except July). She leads August walks at Jamaica Bay Wildlife Refuge (p49) in Queens during peak of shorebird migration (roughly 200 species, eg egrets, herons, hawks).

The best in-depth guide to city bird life is *The New York City Audubon Society Guide to Finding Birds in the Metropolitan Area*.

Kids enjoy the free Discovery Kit birding backpacks (binoculars, sketchbook etc) available for use at Central Park's **Belvedere Castle** (Map pp454–5; ☎ 212-772-0210; 10am-4:30pm Tue-Sun).

BOATING & KAYAKING
With only one landlocked borough (the Bronx), New York City offers plenty of chances to liaise with water. The free Staten Island Ferry (p116) is New York's ultimate recreational boating trip – and it's free. Central Park and Brooklyn's Prospect Park have rowboats to rent, and City Island, a fully fledged fishing community in the Bronx, has charter opportunities. Manhattan's Circle Line (p111) offers classic round-the-island boat cruises, while the new-fangled yellow-and-black New York Water Taxis (p418) provide hop-on, hop off Manhattan and Brooklyn access. For a true adventure, try Manhattan Kayak Company (p310), and paddle over to Jersey for a sushi lunch.

DOWNTOWN BOATHOUSE Map p448
☎ 646-613-0740; www.downtownboathouse.org; Pier 40, near Houston St; admission free; 9am-6pm Sat & Sun May 15-October 15; 1 to Houston St
This terrific public boathouse offers free 20-minute kayaking (including equipment) in the protected embayment in the Hudson River. You don't need to book tours, just walk up. It's also open some weekday evenings. The boathouse has two other locations: at Clinton Cove (Map pp452–3; Pier 96, west of 56th St; 9am-6pm Sat & Sun, 5-7pm mid-Jun–Aug); and at Riverside Park (Map pp454–5; W 72nd St; 10am-5pm Sat & Sun). Tips are given to first-timers. After a few times, you can go on the

Kayaking the Hudson from Downtown Boathouse (above)

TEN-PIN MANIA

Among retro-crazed New Yorkers (and Americans in general, for that matter), a night of bowling qualifies as quite a hoot. Maybe it's the shoes, or all the pitchers of beer. Go with a group to get goofy (and drunk).

AMF Chelsea Pier Lanes (Map pp446–7; ☎ 212-835-2695; Chelsea Pier, btwn Piers 59 & 60; ☑ 9am-midnight Sun-Thu, 9-2am Fri & Sat; ◉ C, E to 23rd St) Forty lanes for $5.50 per game ($3 shoe rental) before 5pm weekdays. The price jumps to $7.50 per game ($4.50 shoe rental) at other times.

Bowlmor Lanes (Map pp446–7; ☎ 212-255-8188; 110 University Pl; ☑ 11-4am Mon, Fri & Sat, 11-1am Tue & Wed, noon-2am Thu, 11am-midnight Sun; ◉ L, N, Q, R, W, 4, 5, 6 to 14th St–Union Sq) Open since 1938, Bowlmor is New York's bowling alley of choice. Games cost $7.50/8.50 before/after 5pm Monday to Thursday, $8.50/9 Friday, $9 on Saturday and $8.50 on Sunday. Shoe rental is $5. After 10pm Monday, it's all glow-in-the-dark bowling, with live DJs ($20 for all-you-can-bowl including shoe rental); for 21 and older only.

Leisure Time Bowling Center (Map p282; ☎ 212-268-6909; 2nd fl, Port Authority Bus Terminal, 625 8th Ave; individual games before/after 5pm Mon-Fri $6/8, Sat & Sun $8; ☑ 10am-midnight Sun-Thu, 10-2am Fri & Sat; ◉ A, C, E to 42nd St) Thirty lanes smack dab amidst Port Authority's bus frenzy. David Letterman once rushed here from the Ed Sullivan show for a quick bowl during a broadcast of his TV show. Renting a lane for an hour is $30/45 before/after 5pm weekdays, $45 per hour Saturday and Sunday.

five-mile harbor kayak trip from the Clinton Cove location (show up for sign-in before 8am on weekends and holidays).

FRIENDS OF BROOK PARK Map pp468-9

☎ 646-206-5288; www.friendsofbrookpark.org; 111 Lincoln St at Bruckner Blvd; kayak tours $50-150; ◉ 6 to 3rd Av–138th St

This Bronx community organization can arrange kayak tours (with equipment) including a picnic on an island in the Harlem River. The group also holds tango and yoga classes, all to help fund efforts to maintain a nearby community garden. It's also rallying the borough to build a (sorely needed) park on the river waterfront.

LOEB BOATHOUSE Map pp454-5

☎ 212-517-2233; Central Park, btwn 74th & 75th Sts; per hr $10; ☑ 10am-5:30pm Mar-Oct; ◉ B, C to 72nd St or 6 to 77th St

Central Park's boathouse rents row boats from April to October (weather permitting). There are Vienna-style gondolas in summer ($30 per 30 minutes). The water here really is not as dirty as Woody Allen suggests in the boat scene in *Manhattan*.

MANHATTAN KAYAK COMPANY

Map pp452-3

☎ 212-924-1788; www.manhattankayak.com; Pier 63, btwn W 23rd St & West Side Hwy; rates $25-250; ◉ C, E to 23rd St

With over 30 tours spanning more than 150 nautical miles of New York Harbor,

Manhattan Kayak Company offers a huge swathe of waterborne options from April to November. The five-hour 'sushi' trip leads across the Hudson to a Japanese-Jersey community, where lunch is included ($100). It also offers full-moon tours at night, five-hour trips to Red Hook in Brooklyn ($150), or tough full-day trips to Riker's Island near La Guardia ($250). All levels of paddlers are accommodated. Orientation classes are $30.

SCHOONER ADIRONDACK Map pp446-7

☎ 646-336-5270; www.sail-nyc.com; Chelsea Piers, Pier 62, btwn W 23rd St & West Side Hwy; daytime weekday/weekend $35/40, sunset & night tours $50; ☑ daytime 1pm & 3:30pm, sunset 5:30pm, night 8:30pm; ◉ C, E to 23rd St

The two-masted '*Dack* hits the Hudson and New York Harbor with four two-hour sails daily from May to October – be sure to book ahead. The 1920s *Manhattan* yacht makes three-hour circumnavigations around Manhattan Wednesday to Sunday from March to December for $55 to $75, or $155 with dinner; call for times.

BIKING

Unless you're an experienced city cyclist, you may prefer limiting your New York rides to designated bike areas. The few bike lanes on city streets (Lafayette St, Broadway, Second Ave) are frequently blocked by double-parked cars or cars weaving around slower ones to make a turn. Much

Activities

OUTDOOR ACTIVITIES

ado has been made by the proposed 300-mile Manhattan Greenway plan, a citywide 350-mile network of pedestrian and bike lanes – some 17% of which already exists in patches across the city. Mayor Michael Bloomberg has made it one of his administration goals to accomplish.

On streets, wear a helmet and signal your turns. Don't ride on sidewalks. It's possible to take a bike on the last door of subways, but avoid rush hours and stand with your bike (for details about tickets for taking bikes on the subway, see p418). Most city bridges have bike lanes (Brooklyn Bridge is the most fun). See **Bike Network Development** (www.ci.nyc.ny.us/html/dcp/html/bike/home.html) for cycling map downloads and more information on New York biking.

Where to Ride

Central Park is a natural choice for New York biking. Wide, well-paved roads run north–south and in between, making excellent 1.7-, 5.2- and 6.1-mile loops (see Map pp454–5). Roads have a bike lane and are always open to cyclists; roads are closed to traffic from 10am to 3pm and 7pm to 10pm Monday to Friday, and all day Saturday and Sunday.

Rides along the rivers are possible (and popular) along much of Manhattan's 32-mile perimeter. The best stretches are along Hudson River pathways from Battery Park in Lower Manhattan up the west side to Riverside Park in the Upper West Side. Alternatively, take the bumpier east side route, south from E 37th St towards Battery Park.

Brooklyn's gorgeous Prospect Park (p177) has 3.35-mile Park Dr to ride anytime. Note the road is open to traffic from 7am to 9am and 5pm to 7pm Monday to Friday.

The more ambitious can ride the 15-mile Shore Parkway Bike Path from Coney Island to Queens. Ask at a bike shop for details.

Not to be forgotten, Staten Island's **Greenbelt** (☎ 718-667-2165; www.sigreenbelt.org) has miles of developed bike paths (and some hills), and you can take a bike over on the ferry.

Some clubs sponsor various rides. The **Five Borough Bicycle Club** (Map pp454–5; ☎ 212-932-2300 ext 115; www.5bbc.org; 891 Amsterdam Ave; ◎ 1, 2, 3 to 96th St)

leads free trips for its members ($20 annual fee); the club office is at Hostelling International–New York (p372). Another useful club, the **New York Cycle Club** (☎ 212-828-5711; www.nycc.org) lists weekly rides on its website for member access (membership is $19).

Fast & Fabulous (☎ 212-567-7160; www.fastnfab.org) is the city's only bicycling club for gays and lesbians; it hosts frequent rides both in and around the city.

Several hundred cyclists (and in-line skaters) promote safer streets and bike lanes in Critical Mass, a traffic-halting ride leaving from Union Sq at 7pm the last Friday of the month. See **Time's Up** (www.times-up.com) for more information, including regularly scheduled fix-your-bike workshops.

Bike Rental

CENTRAL PARK BICYCLE TOURS & RENTALS Map p282
☎ 212-541-8759; www.centralparkbiketour.com; 2 Columbus Circle; bike hire per day $35, tours adult/child $35/20; ◎ A, B, C, D, 1 to 59 St–Columbus Circle

This place rents mountain bikes and leads various tours of the park – one tour takes in movie sights. Closed in winter. Tour prices include bike rental.

LOEB BOATHOUSE Map pp454-5
☎ 212-517-2233; Central Park, btwn 74th & 75th Sts; bike hire per hr $9-21; ◎ B, C to 72nd St or 6 to 77th St

Various types of bikes are available, 10am to 6pm April to October. You'll need ID and a credit card to rent one. Helmets provided.

MANHATTAN BICYCLE Map p282
☎ 212-262-0111; 791 Ninth Ave btwn 52nd & 53rd Sts; bike hire per hr/day $5/25; ◎ 9:30am-7pm Mon-Fri, 11am-6pm Sat, 11am-5pm Sun; ◎ C, E to 50 Street

Helmets included.

RECYCLE-A-BICYCLE Map p462
☎ 718-858-2972; 55 Washington St; bike hire per 24hr $35; ◎ noon-7pm Mon-Sat, noon-5pm Sun; ◎ F to York St

Near the river in Dumbo, Brooklyn, this small shop has good prices on used bikes, and rents 'em all year.

CHELSEA PIERS

New York's biggest sporting center is at the historic **Chelsea Piers** (Map pp446–7; ☎ 212-336-6666; www.chelsea piers.com; West Side Hwy, btwn W 16th & 22nd Sts; ✪ C, E to 23rd St), a 30-acre sporting village where you can golf, work out, play soccer and basketball, get a massage, swim, box and bowl – and more.

Opened in 1995, the red-white-and-blue Chelsea Piers served as New York's chief port during the heyday of transatlantic ocean voyages. Constructed in 1910 by the makers of Grand Central Terminal, Chelsea Piers was where the *Titanic* was hoping to land in 1912 and the disembarkation point for many Europe-bound WWII soldiers. Its pier days ended in 1967.

Following is a selection of activities that you can do.

Batting cages (☎ 212-336-6500; Field House, Pier 59; 10 pitches $2; ⏰ 11am-10pm Mon-Fri, 9am-9pm Sat & Sun) Four modern cages offer fast, medium and slow-pitch baseball and softball. Call for hourly rentals.

Golf (☎ 212-336-6400; Golf Club, Pier 59; ball cards from $20, golf simulator games per hr $45; ⏰ 6am-midnight Apr-Sep, 6:30am-11pm Oct-Mar) Manhattan's only driving range has four levels of weather-protected tees in nets – you can aim for New Jersey! Golf clubs are available ($4 for one, $6 for three).

Ice skating & hockey (☎ 212-336-6100; Sky Rink, Pier 61; adult/child general skating $11/8.50, skate rental $6, helmets $3) There are two year-round rinks. Schedules vary, usually beginning at 1pm. Open hockey hours are limited, usually weekday lunches and Saturday nights ($27, goaltenders are free). Phone ahead for opening hours.

In-line Skating (☎ 212-336-6200; the Roller Rinks, Pier 62; adult/child skating $7/6, rental $18/13, pad rental $7; ⏰ outdoor rinks May-Aug) For more excitement (ramps, obstacles), 'extreme' skating is $20 for three- or four-hour sessions. There are also roller-hockey leagues here. Phone for opening hours.

Soccer (☎ 212-336-6500; Field House, Pier 62) Mostly for indoor soccer and basketball leagues and gym classes. Call ahead to check schedules for pick-up indoor soccer ('open soccer'), usually an hour or so midday weekdays only ($8).

Spa (☎ 212-336-6780; Pier 60; massages $25-145, facials from $90, body scrubs $65; ⏰ 10am-9pm Mon-Fri, 10am-7pm Sat & Sun) Massage comes in plenty of forms and there's also other treatments available. A 75-minute seaweed body wrap is $125. Package deals include full-day treatment for $500, and a 90-minute sampler is $130.

Sports center (☎ 212-336-6000; Pier 60; per day $50; ⏰ 6am-11pm Mon-Fri, 8am-9pm Sat & Sun) Indoor running track, swimming pool, workout equipment, basketball, boxing, kickboxing, volleyball, yoga classes, rock climbing, great views from inside and sundecks.

SIXTH AVENUE BICYCLES Map pp446-7
☎ 212-255-5100; 545 Sixth Ave; bike hire per day/24hr $35/45; 545 Sixth Ave; ⏰ 9:30-6pm; ✪ F, V to 14th St or L to 6th Ave
Bike shop with parts. Rates include helmets.

TOGA BIKE SHOP Map pp454-5
☎ 212-799-9625; www.togabikes.com; 110 West End Ave, btwn 64th & 65th Sts; bike rental per 24hr $30-100; ⏰ 11am-7pm Mon-Fri, 10am-6pm Sat, 11am-6pm Sun; ✪ 1 to 66th St–Lincoln Center
This friendly and long-standing bike shop rents bikes all year – though it sells off most of its cruisers in winter. Located midway between Central Park's looping paths and the paths along the Hudson River, it's a good base to pick up the bike. You'll need to leave a deposit on a credit card. Rental price includes a helmet. Its Lower Manhattan location rents bikes from April to October only: **Gotham Bikes Downtown** (Map pp444–5; ☎ 212-732-2453; 112 W Broadway btwn Duane & Reade Sts; bike rental per 24hr $30;

⏰ 10am-6:30pm Mon-Sat, 10:30am-5pm Sun; ✪ A, C, 1, 2, 3, 9 to Chambers St).

GOLF

It's not just yuppies raising the five iron, and three wood, and pitching wedge. There's plenty of golfing going on in New York City, but – other than a driving range – the courses are all outside Manhattan. They all have slightly higher fees at weekends and you'll need to reserve a tee-off time.

If you feel like belting a few balls without the walking, head to the driving range at Chelsea Piers (see above).

Also see www.nycteetimes.com for several courses' listings.

BETHPAGE ST PARK
☎ 516-249-0707; Farmingdale, Long Island; green fees $29-39, Black Course $78-98, state residents $39-49, club rental $30
Five great public courses, including the Black Course, which was the first public

course to host the US Open (2002). There's a LIRR rail station at Farmingdale, where you can get a taxi.

DYKER BEACH GOLF COURSE
Map pp460-1

☎ 718-836-9722; cnr 86th St & 7th Ave, Dyker Beach; green fees Mon-Fri $25, Sat & Sun $37; ⓞ R to 86th St

This is a scenic public course in Brooklyn and is the easiest to reach by subway. There's a lone set of old right-handed clubs for loan sometimes. It's between 7th and 10th Aves, to the right, when approaching from the subway station.

FLUSHING MEADOWS PITCH & PUTT
Map p467

☎ 718-271-8182; Flushing Meadows Corona Park; green fees Mon-Fri $11.50, Sat & Sun $12.50, club rental per club $1; ⓞ 7 to Willets Point–Shea Stadium

If your woods are hurting you, you only need a couple of clubs to pace this mini three-par 18-hole course. The shortest hole is 40 yards, longest is 80 yards. Not on the US Open circuit, but fun for beginners.

LA TOURETTE

☎ 718-351-1889; 1001 Richmond Hill Rd, Staten Island; green fees Mon-Fri $29, Sat & Sun $35, club rental $20

This public course is on Staten Island. Take a taxi from the ferry docks. It's an extra $6 or $8 for out-of-state residents.

VAN CORTLANDT PARK GOLF COURSE
Map pp468-9

☎ 718-543-4595; Bailey Ave; green fees Mon-Fri $29, Sat & Sun $35; ⓞ 1 to Van Cortlandt Park

This is the USA's oldest 18-hole public golf course. Out-of-state residents pay an extra $6 or $8. You can ride horseback through the Bronx's mammoth Van Cortlandt Park (☎ 718-548-0912) call for more information. There are also tennis courts at the park (☎ 718-430-1838); call for permit information.

ICE SKATING

Outdoor rinks are open during the winter months, though the rink at Chelsea Piers (opposite) is open all year. See also p186 for Queens' Flushing Meadows Corona Park.

KATE WOLLMAN RINK Map p464

☎ 718-287-6431; Prospect Park, near Ocean Ave; adult/senior or child $5/3, skate rental $5; ⓨ late Nov-Mar; ⓞ B, Q, S to Prospect Park

On the west edge of Prospect Lake in the mid to southeastern part of Brooklyn's park, this rink is cheaper and generally less crowded than Manhattan rinks. Call ahead for hours. There are free lockers and lessons are available (call ☎ 718-282-1226 for information).

ROCKEFELLER CENTER ICE RINK
Map pp452-3

☎ 212-332-7654; Rockefeller Center, cnr 49th St & Fifth Ave; adult $9-17, child $7-12, skate rental $8; ⓨ 8am-midnight Mon-Thu, 8:30am-midnight Fri & Sat, 8:30am-10pm Sun; ⓞ B, D, F, V to 47th–50th Sts–Rockefeller Center

New York's most famous rink, under the gaze of the gold statue of Prometheus in the art deco plaza, is an incomparable location for a twirl on ice, but it gets sardine-busy. Try to show up for the first skating period (from 8am or 8:30am). Waits reach two hours after noon, and it's particularly crammed at weekends. Prices range per times.

WOLLMAN SKATING RINK Map pp454-5

☎ 212-439-6900; Central Park, near 59th St & 6th Ave entrance; adult/child incl skate rental Mon-Fri $14.50/9.50; ⓨ 10am-2:30pm Mon & Tue, 10am-10pm Wed & Thu, 10am-11pm Fri & Sat, 10am-9pm Sun; ⓞ F to 57 St or N, R, W to 5th Ave–59th St

Larger than Rockefeller's, and allowing all-day skating (as if…), this rink is at the southern edge of Central Park. Your slides, stops and slips will be in full view of the buildings peeking over Central Park; skating here is best at night. The rink is open October through April.

IN-LINE SKATING

Freestyle skaters have flaunted their footwork in a disco skate circle near the Naumberg Bandshell in Central Park for decades. Of course in-line skating is a somewhat popular mode of recreation (and transport) around the city: notably, the counterclockwise six-mile loop at Central Park (with no cars on weekends, or from 10am to 3pm, and 7pm to 7am on weekdays), and along

NYC STREET SPORTS

Who needs lawns? With all that concrete around, New York has embraced a number of sports and events played on it.

Handball

Irish immigrant Phil Casey built New York's first four-wall handball court in 1882, and following his rise in the sport (he challenged, and whipped, the Irish world champ in 1887), it quickly became big in New York. In the early 20th century, South Brooklyn started putting up one-wall handball courts around Coney Island, reviving an Irish tradition that had died out long before. It led to one-wall paddleball, still widely played around town. These days, you'll find one-wall courts in outdoor parks all over the city (there are 260 courts in Manhattan alone). See www.nycgovparks .org for a list of handball courts.

Pick-up Basketball

People with hoop dreams, small and large, hit the city's courts throughout the year. The most famous is **'the Cage'** (Map pp446–7; cnr W 3rd St & Sixth Ave), which draw summer audiences on the weekends, and games sometimes fade into elongated dunk-a-thons. Up in Harlem, **Rucker Park** (Map pp458–9; cnr Frederick Douglass Blvd & 155th St) is where NBA stars like Dr J, Kareem Abdul Jabaar, Kobe Bryant, Allen Iverson and Kevin Garnett have shown up to play; it's more for watching, and the organized games are a thing to behold – starting at 6pm Monday to Thursday in summer. Eye goggles, knee pads and tight 80s-era uniforms will probably not win you many potential teammates.

You can also find pick-up games at Tompkins Sq Park (p137) in the East Village and at Riverside Park (p160) in the Upper West Side.

Stickball

Nothing is more street than stickball, New York's decades-old offshoot of English games like 'old cat' and 'town ball.' It's essentially a crude form of baseball – but the pitcher usually throws a pink Spalding ball off the bounce, batters hit with a broom handle, the bases are manhole covers, and parked cars and fire escapes serve as obstacles.

Stickball has stormed its way back in the past 20 years. Of the most successful league is the eight-team, Bronx-based **Emperors Stickball League** (☎ 212-591-0165; www.nyesl.org), which plays 10am to 2pm or 3pm Sunday at Stickball Blvd (Map pp468–9), between Seward and Randall Aves; call for directions. Compared with baseball, one player said, 'It's louder, more in your face; we taunt…but with respect.'

Hudson River Park from Battery Park to Chelsea Piers (using bike lanes and promenades) and to the north of Manhattan via multitiered Riverside Park in the Upper West Side.

Some good Brooklyn options include the 3.5-mile looping Park Dr around Brooklyn's Prospect Park, and the Shore Parkway, just north of the Verrazano Bridge (a smooth waterside promenade; access is from overpasses at 80th or 92nd Sts, or near Bay 19th Ave – all in Bay Ridge).

Rental

The trend towards renting, even buying, in-line skates is on the wane in recent years, but you can rent skates all year at **Blades West** (Map pp454–5; ☎ 212-787-3911; 120 W 72 St; per 24hr incl pads $20; ◉ 1, 2, 3 to 72nd St). You can buy only at **Blades Downtown** (Map p449; ☎ 212-477-7350; 659 Broadway; ◉ 6 to Bleecker St).

JOGGING

You'll find several goods spots for a run in Manhattan. Central Park's loop roads are best during traffic-free hours (see p311), though you'll be in the company of many cyclists and in-line skaters. The 1.6-mile path surrounding the Jacqueline Kennedy Onassis Reservoir (Map pp454–5; where Jackie O used to run) is for runners and walkers only; access it between 86th and 96th Sts. Running along the Hudson River is a popular path, best from W 23rd St to Battery Park in Lower Manhattan. The Upper East Side has a path that runs along FDR Dr and the East River (from E 63rd St to E 115th St). Brooklyn's Prospect Park has plenty of paths.

The **New York Road Runners Club** (Map pp454–5; ☎ 212-860-4455; www.nyrrc.org; 9 E 89th St; ☷ 10am-8pm Mon-Fri, 10am-5pm Sat, 10am-3pm Sun; ◉ 6 to 96th St) organizes weekend runs citywide, including the New York City Marathon.

New York City Marathon

Equally as awe-inspiring as the runners chugging through New York's streets is how the world's most famous marathon grew from a $1000 budget race with 55 finishers in 1970, to a premier running event that spans New York's five boroughs. However, you need a little luck, not just conditioning and strength, to run the race. The final list of 30,000 runners is completed by lottery; applications are accepted until April or May of each year (see www.nycmarathon.org for more information). Held on the first Sunday of November, it's easy to watch the spectacle of over a million people lining the streets. the marathon starts from Staten Island, and crosses the Verrazano-Narrows Bridge. The best vantage may be its end point – Tavern on the Green (Map pp454–5) in Central Park.

ROCK CLIMBING

Central Park contains a couple of rocks that attract boulderers' attention, including Chess Rock, just north of Wollman Rink, and the more challenging Rat Rock, north of Heckscher Playground (around 61st St) – however, the best is City Boy, a 20-footer around 107th St, west of the Harlem Meer.

CITY CLIMBERS CLUB Map pp452-3

☎ 212-974-2250; Parks & Recreation Center, 533 W 59th St; ☾ 5-10pm Mon-Fri, noon-5pm Sat; day pass $15, annual membership $150; ⊕ A, B, C, D, 1 to 59th St–Columbus Circle
New York's first climbing wall still serves as a key HQ for climbers, with 11 belay stations and 30 routes, plus a climbing cave. The first Tuesday and last Thursday of the month are for members only.

SOCCER

Soccer leagues generally don't allow drop-in, single-game players. You can find pick-up soccer games in Central Park's East Meadow around E 97th St and the North Meadow at weekends during the season (April to October). Games at Flushing Meadows Corona Park (p186) are legendary and are in action whenever the weather allows (even February); Chelsea Piers (p312) has games of the indoor variety. Riverside Park (p160) in the Upper West Side has weekly pick-up soccer times in its outdoor field; call for the weekly schedule.

SURFING

In early 2005 the ban on surfing at Queens' Rockaway Beach (p188) was finally lifted, prompting a new crew of surfers to hit the waves, especially August to October when hurricanes down south prompt the biggest action. The open area is between Beach 88th and 90th Sts, near the Beach 89th St subway stop on the A line.

For more information, check out www .surfrider.org/nyc.

TENNIS

Playing on New York's nearly 100 public tennis courts requires a permit (annual fee adults/seniors/children $100/20/10) from April to November; it's free at other times. You can pick up single-play tickets for $7 at the Central Park permit center at Arsenal (Map pp454–5; E 65th St & Fifth Ave, enter park from E 65th St & Fifth Ave; ☾ 9am-4pm Mon-Fri & 9am-noon Sat Apr-Jun). Paragon Athletic Goods (p341) also sells permits. Those with an annual permit can make reservations at the Central Park Tennis Center and Prospect Park Tennis Center (see entries below). Otherwise, take a single-play ticket to a public court, where it's first-come, first-serve; an attendant on hand will collect the ticket. For more information on permits call ☎ 212-360-8133 or check www.nyc.gov/parks.

Riverbank State Park (Map pp454–5) in the Upper West Side also has courts.

CENTRAL PARK TENNIS CENTER

Map pp454-5

☎ 212-280-0205; Central Park West; ☾ 6:30am-dusk Apr-Oct or Nov; ⊕ B, C to 96th St
The daylight-hours-only facility has 26 clay courts for public use (and four hard courts for lessons). You can buy single-play tickets ($7) here. Those with permits can reserve a court for $7. The least-busy times are roughly noon to 4pm on weekdays.

PROSPECT PARK TENNIS CENTER

Map p464

☎ 718-436-2500; www.prospectpark.org; cnr Parkside & Coney Island Aves; ☾ 7am-11pm; ⊕ F to Fort Hamilton Pkwy or Q to Parkside Ave
Open all year, this 11-court facility takes permits or sells single-use tickets on location from mid-May to mid-November. Off-season,

Activities

OUTDOOR ACTIVITIES

it covers the courts to create an indoor facility; hourly rates range from $20 to $60 (there are seasonal passes available, from $560).

USTA NATIONAL TENNIS CENTER
Map p467

☎ 718-760-6200; www.usta.com; Flushing Meadows Corona Park; per hr outdoor court $16-24, indoor court $17-51; ⏱ 6am-midnight Mon-Fri, 8am-midnight Sat, 8am-11pm Sun Oct-Jul; Ⓜ 7 to Willets Point–Shea Stadium

Be like Serena, Venus or Andre on the courts where the US Open is staged every year – no-one minds if you wear a headband. USTA takes reservations up to two days in advance for the 22 outside courts and nine indoor ones. Walk-ins can play indoors for $16 per hour from 6am to 8am weekdays (when available). After-dark lights for outside courts are $8 extra.

TRAPEZE
NEW YORK TRAPEZE SCHOOL
Map pp444-5

☎ 917-797-1872; www.newyork.trapezeschool.com; West Side Hwy btwn Piers 26 & 34; classes $47-65; Ⓜ 1 to Canal St

Fulfill your circus dreams, like Carrie did on *Sex and the City*, flying trapeze to trapeze in this open-air tent by the river (it's covered and heated in winter – NO time is the WRONG time when it comes to trapezing). Call or check the website for the daily schedule.

HEALTH & FITNESS
GYMS & SWIMMING POOLS
If you're just looking to ride an exercise bike for half an hour or so, all but the cheapie hotels have small fitness centers. Elsewhere, Manhattan alone has 17 public recreation centers (such as the Tony Dapolito, opposite). Most of these centers have gym facilities and an indoor or outdoor swimming pool. See www.nycgovparks.org for more information on other outdoor pools (there are 52 parks with pools, free to use from late June through Labor Day). Check out the *Village Voice* for other gym listings.

Chelsea Piers (p312) sports center is a massive riverside center with pretty much every activity you can imagine.

ASPHALT GREEN Map pp454-5
☎ 212-369-8890; www.asphaltgreen.org; 555 E 90 St; gym & pool pass $25; ⏱ 5:30am-10pm Mon-Fri, 8am-8pm Sat & Sun; Ⓜ 4, 5, 6 to 86th St

This super nonprofit fitness center in the Upper East Side is known for its excellent 50m Olympic-sized pool (with an observation window for coaches to check technique). There's also a smaller pool for classes. Some hours are for members only; call ahead or check the website. Many programs cater to kids.

ASTORIA POOL Map p457
☎ 718-626-8620; Astoria Park, cnr 19th St & 23rd Dr; ⏱ 11am-7pm Jun-Aug; Ⓜ N, W to Astoria Blvd

This Works Progress Administration Olympic-size outdoor pool, built in 1936, is an art deco wonder, with views of Manhattan and the Triborough Bridge. Nice spot – that is if you can handle the crowds, which reach 1000 a day during summer.

CRUNCH Map pp452-3
☎ 212-594-8050; www.crunch.com; 555 W 42nd St; day pass $24; ⏱ 6am-10pm Mon-Fri, 9am-7pm Sat & Sun; Ⓜ A, C, E to 42nd St–Port Authority Bus Terminal

This popular fitness center has several locations throughout town, and is equipped with a full fitness center, sauna and spa. Classes include trampolining and yoga. This is New York City's only Crunch location with a pool.

METROPOLITAN POOL Map p463
☎ 718-599-5707; 261 Bedford Ave at Metropolitan Ave; annual membership $50-75; ⏱ 7am-9:30pm Mon-Fri, 7am-5:30pm Sat; Ⓜ L to Bedford Ave

This 1922 gem, fully renovated in 1997, is one of New York's nicest public pools. All the Williamsburg hipsters (who swim) are happy to have it here. There's a fitness room as well.

NEW YORK SPORTS CLUB Map p282
☎ 646-366-9400; www.mysportsclubs.com; 230 W 41st St; day pass $25; ⏱ 6am-10pm Mon-Thu, 6am-9pm Fri & Sat, 8am-6pm Sun; Ⓜ N, Q, R, S, 1, 2, 3, 7 to Times Sq–42nd St

A day pass to this popular fitness chain includes group classes on exercise bikes ('spinning') and entry to the fitness center. Visit the website for information on Manhattan's 37 locations (some with pools).

RIVERBANK STATE PARK Map pp458-9

☎ 212-694-3600; 679 Riverside Dr at W 145th St; pool adult/child $2/1, fitness room $8; ☽ park 6am-11pm; ☉ 1 to 145th St

This modern five-building facility, perched atop a waste refinery (not as crazy as it sounds) and covering 28 acres, has an indoor Olympic-size pool, an outdoor lap pool, a fitness room, basketball and handball courts, a running track around a soccer field, a carousel for the whippersnappers, an 800-seat cultural theater, and a softball field. Ice-skating is $5/3 for adults/children, skate rental is $4; during summer there's roller-skating. Admission to the general park area is free. It's a friendly place, with a mind-numbing array of schedules. Call for activity hours and more information.

TONY DAPOLITO RECREATION CENTER Map p448

☎ 212-242-5228; 1 Clarkson St; annual membership $75; ☽ 7am-10pm Mon-Fri, 9am-5pm Sat & Sun; ☉ 1 to Houston St

This Greenwich Village center (formerly the Carmine) has one of the city's best public pools, but it's only available by annual membership. There's an indoor and outdoor swimming pool (the latter was used for the pool scene in *Raging Bull*) and a gym that's open to the public.

WEST SIDE YMCA Map pp454-5

☎ 212-875-4100; www.ymcanyc.org; 5 W 63rd St; day pass $25; ☽ 6am-11pm Mon-Fri, 8am-8pm Sat & Sun; ☉ A, B, C, D, 1 to 59th St–Columbus Circle

Near Central Park, the West Side Y – one of 20 Ys in the Big Apple – boasts two swimming pools, an indoor running track, a basketball court, five racquetball/squash courts and a big weight room. Membership is $76 monthly (with a $125 initiation fee). See the website for the other locations.

MASSAGE & DAY SPAS

Make an appointment at the following places in advance.

BLISS49 Map pp452-3

☎ 212-219-8970; www.blissworld.com; 4th fl, W New York, 541 Lexington Ave; ☽ 8am-10pm; ☉ 5 to 51 St

This new hotel spa – in the ever-mod W New York – keeps things 21st-century

with personal headsets. A 90-minute body smoother with carrot mulch and oil rub down is $165; massages start at $55. All the Bliss lotions and products are on hand for sale.

BODY CENTRAL Map p448

☎ 212-677-5633; www.bodycentralnyc.com; 5th fl, 99 University Pl; ☽ 12:30-9pm Mon & Wed, 8:30am-9pm Tue & Thu, 8:30am-5pm Fri, 11am-4pm Sat; ☉ L, N, Q, R, W, 4, 5, 6 to 14th St–Union Sq

Relieve pavement-pounded feet with the relaxing 30-minute 'Standing Ovation' foot massage ($50) or treat the rest of the body with a choice of nine other clarity-inducing massages. Body Central also offers chiropractic and nutritional services.

CORNELIA DAY RESORT Map pp452-3

☎ 212-871-3050; www.cornelia.com; 663 Fifth Ave; ☽ 9am-9pm Mon-Fri, 9am-7pm Sat, 11am-6pm Sun; ☉ F to 57 St, E, V, to Fifth Ave–53rd St

Above the chic Salvatore Ferragamo department store, the new Cornelia offers serious pampering on Fifth Ave, like the 'Royal Romanian' mud treatment (90 minutes, $245) or the 'Watsu Flow' massage while you relax in the rooftop saltwater pool (one hour, $200). There's also a salon.

GRACEFUL SERVICES Map pp452-3

☎ 212-593-9904; 1097 Second Ave; ☽ 10am-10pm; ☉ 4, 5, 6 to 59th St or N, R, W to Lexington Ave–59th St

Heaps of New Yorkers looking for relief, not frills, go to barebones Grace for a hot-stone massage or facial. Or to get bruised by a kept-real imported-from-China, dizzying Guasha technique (involving a bull's horn scraped on your oiled self; $80 with massage). An hour massage or acupuncture session is $60.

PAUL LABRECQUE EAST Map pp454-5

☎ 212-988-7816; www.paullabrecque.com; 171 E 65th St; ☽ 8am-9pm Mon-Fri, 9am-8pm Sat, 10am-9pm Sun; ☉ 6 to 68th St–Hunter College

Sit back with the stars at this swank uptown spa (with a salon just for the guys). Reese Witherspoon was enticed to add a translucent sheen to her locks with a color varnish (from $50), and 'I don't take coffee, I take tea' Sting indulged in an hour-long indulgent shave ($80). Paul also offers facials from $120, a host of massages and body treatments (including a $125 body wrap). A haircut from Senor Paul is $250.

SPA AT MANDARIN ORIENTAL
Map pp452-3

☎ 212-805-8880; www.mandarinoriental.com; 80 Columbus Circle at 60th St; ☾ 9am-9pm; ◉ A, B, C, D, 1 to 59th St–Columbus Circle

You might not be able to afford the $15,000 suites, but a splurge at the split-level spa/ fitness center might be worth the plastic. Rooms are ultra exotic – one has a modern 'Chinese wedding bed' plus mid-room fireplace and most tower 35 floors over the Hudson. There's a wide array of pricey treatments you can customize: 80-minute massages run $285, a 'life dance massage' $410, half-day programs start at $485. There's a lap pool on hand, plus yoga courses.

YOGA & PILATES

BIKRAM YOGA NYC Map pp446-7
☎ 212-206-9400; www.bikramyoganyc.com; 3rd fl, 182 Fifth Ave; per class $23; ☾ 7am-8:15pm Mon-Fri, 10am-5pm Sat & Sun; ◉ N, R, W to 23rd St

So very Hollywood (but taking off in Manhattan), Bikram is hot stuff: striking the 26-pose *asana* in a heated room (in the Flatiron Building, no less) means you're going to sweat

All roads for sports nuts lead to Chelsea Piers sporting complex (p312)

into shape. There are showers. Bikram has two other locations. Call for the schedule.

JIVAMUKTI Map p449
☎ 212-353-0214; www.jivamuktiyoga.com; Suite 3, 404 Lafayette St; per class $17; ☾ classes 7:15am-8:15pm Mon-Thu, 7:15am-6:45pm Fri, 10am-5pm Sat & Sun; ◉ 6 to Bleecker St

Quite posh, hip and large for a yoga house – there's a wall waterfall – Jivamukti sees many hipster locals and celebs striking *halasana* poses in the *vinyasa* and hatha classes (and chanting for 10 or 15 minutes too). Russell Simmons and Helen Hunt are regulars. But this is challenging stuff. Not all classes are open to drop-ins. There are showers and a shop.

LAUGHING LOTUS Map pp446-7
☎ 212-414-2903; www.laughinglotus.com; 59 W 19th St; per class $15, 1st-week pass $20; ☾ classes 6:45am-8:30pm Mon-Thu, 6:45am-10pm Fri, 9am-7pm Sat & Sun; ◉ F, V to 23rd St

Happy, popular and pink, the Laughing Lotus has drop-in 1½-hour classes, ranging from devotional sun celebrations, basic stretching/breathing classes, more advanced *vinyasa* and family hour.

OM YOGA CENTER Map p449
☎ 212-254-9642; www.omyoga.com; 6th fl, 826 Broadway; per class $16; ◉ L, N, Q, R, W, 4, 5, 6 to 14th St–Union Sq

This inviting space – with redwood floors, high ceilings and showers – has popular *vinyasa* classes run by former dancer (and choreographer of videos like *Girls Just Want to Have Fun!*) Cyndi Lee, a practitioner of hatha yoga and Tibetan Buddhism. There are several class types, including ones geared for specific parts of the body, plus pre-natal and an hour-long 'yoga express' for $10. Call or see website for class times.

YOGA WORKS Map pp452-3
☎ 212-935-9642; www.yogaworks.com; 160 E 56th St; classes $5-20; ◉ N, R, W, 4, 5, 6 to 59th St

One of four Manhattan locations, Yoga Works is a 'chain' from Santa Monica devoted to different types of yoga and pilates, with classes for athletes, kids and seniors. Check online for class schedules and other Manhattan locations.

Activities
HEALTH & FITNESS

Shopping

Shopping

You want it? New York's got it. Kate Spade bag (real or knockoff), Levis super-low 518 boot-cut jeans, cashmere socks, Tibetan decorative masks, Turkish carpets, bulk organic catnip, out-of-print books, custom-made leather chaps or the newest iPod: you'll find it all here. The city's thousands of shops satisfy all desires, quirks and interests, while megastores shine their 21st-century sheen, and decades-old mom-and-pop shops hold their ground. You can spend a few dollars on a beaded bracelet from a street vendor, spend hundreds of thousands on a diamond-encrusted watch at Tiffany & Co, pick up a stack of 'I ♥ New York' T-shirts for your friends and then break for lunch. That's just the beginning, and there really is no end.

As far as where to go for your spree, the quick answer is 'anywhere.' The more complex one depends on what sort of items and experiences you're seeking. Midtown's Fifth Ave and the Upper East Side's Madison Ave have the famous high-end fashion and clothing by international designers, sold to monied masses (if it's winter, get ready to see lots of fur coats) at places like Bergdorf Goodman, Tourneau, Barneys New York and the like. The coolest offerings – local-designer creations, hipster jeans and indie-made jewelry – are found downtown, with high-end versions in Soho, Noho and Nolita boutiques. Other 'hoods down here – the Lower East Side, East Village and West Village – provide a bridge between the high-end and affordably funky ones, with expensive fashion, design and antiques shops interspersed with those selling music, gifts and clothing for a younger (read: budget) crowd. Greenwich Village has an eclectic mix of antiques, high-end fashion and tourist-geared shops catering to gays and lesbians with lots of rainbow jewelry and tees. Parts of Brooklyn – generally Park Slope, Boerum Hill, Fort Greene and Williamsburg – are chock-full of indie boutiques, and great places to find gifts, houseware items and funky accessories.

Midtown is the place for super-size department stores like Macy's, multi-storied Gaps and other chain stores. It's also where you'll find endless rows of ticky-tacky tourist shops selling fun souvenirs from mini–Statue of Liberties to Big Apple snow globes. Hell's Kitchen's flea markets are a popular weekend draw for locals, while Chelsea has an ever-growing collection of clubwear and home-item boutiques – as does the Meatpacking District, which is home to designer havens like Jeffrey and Stella McCartney.

SAMPLE SALE SURVIVAL GUIDE

While clothing sales happen year-round, usually when the seasons change and the old stock must be moved out, sample sales are held frequently, mostly in the huge warehouses in the Fashion District of Midtown or in Soho. While the original sample sale was a way for designers to get rid of one-of-a-kind prototypes that weren't quite up to snuff, most sample sales these days are for high-end labels to get rid of overstock at wonderfully deep discounts. The semi-annual **Barneys Warehouse Sale**, held at the Chelsea Barneys Co-op location, is one such frenzied event, bringing pushy crowds that resemble bread lines in their zeal for finding half-price Manolo Blahniks or Diane Von Furstenburg dresses.

To truly do well at such an event, there are two golden rules: first, wear uncomplicated clothing with nice undergarments to the sale. That's because sample sales, set up in temporary, slap-dash ways, have no dressing rooms, so you'll have to drop trousers and model your possible spoils in front of shared (and often way too small) mirrors placed in the middle of the room. Second, remember to hold fast to your own fashion reality. That's because, when you find yourself suddenly able to afford an item with an honest-to-goodness 'Louis Vuitton' or 'Marc Jacobs' tag in the collar, you may wind up throwing your taste out the window and purchasing something so ugly that it'll never make it out of your closet once you get it home.

To find sales that are happening when you're in town, check **NY Sale** (www.nysale.com), the Sample Sale Seconds page of **Daily Candy** (www.dailycandy.com), **Lazar Shopping** (www.lazarshopping.com) or the Check Out section of *Time Out New York* magazine.

Most museums – the Met, MoMA etc – have super shops if you're looking for NYC gifts. For junky souvenirs (T-shirts, cheap Yankees hats), Chinatown and Times Sq are the best bets.

As of September 2005, the city permanently did away with its 4% sales tax on clothing and shoe purchases under $110. You'll still pay the state's 4.375% sales tax, but note that, during several occasions throughout the year, the governor will announce completely sales-tax-free weeks – exciting times that make shopping even more of an adventure. Check www.nyc.gov for schedules.

Opening Hours

With the exception of Lower Manhattan and shops run by Orthodox Jews (which are closed Saturdays), nearly all stores, boutiques and megastores are open daily. Few stores open before 10am, though many stay open until 7pm or 8pm. Things open a little later (at 11am or noon) in more residential pockets (such as the East Village, Lower East Side and Brooklyn). Many stores, particularly on Madison Ave, stay open later on Thursdays.

LOWER MANHATTAN

While Manhattan's financial zone may not be the place for a day-long shopping excursion, there are a few big blockbuster options, mainly for clothing and electronics. **South Street Seaport** (p123), a big, 100-store mall with outdoor plazas, is home to chains including J Crew, Coach and Ann Taylor; a similar set up can be found cross town at the **World Financial Center** (p119), an indoor mall that's home to the usual chains: Gap, Banana Republic, Sunglass Hut and more. Unless you're a mall junkie (or have never seen one before), the big reason to come to each is its location: South Street Seaport is on the breezy East River, while the Financial Center affords bird's-eye views of the former World Trade Center site.

CENTURY 21 Map pp444-5   Discount Dept Store
☎ 212-227-9092; 22 Cortland St at Church St;
◷ 7:45am-8pm Mon-Wed & Fri, to 8:30pm Thu, 10am-8pm Sat, 11am-7pm Sun; ◉ A, C, J, M, Z, 2, 3, 4, 5 to Fulton St–Broadway-Nassau
This four-level, marble-floor department store is a favorite New Yorker 'secret.' Problem is, everyone and his mother knows about it. To beat the almost constant mobs, come early in the morning (it opens before most stores on weekdays) and then go out to breakfast. Its popularity is due to its deep discounts on men's and women's designer clothes, accessories, shoes, perfumes and linens (sometimes at less than half the original price). Big design names – Donna Karen, Marc Jacobs, Armani, you name it – can be found here. Just be prepared for long dressing-room queues – and for the impulse to purchase just about everything you see. It's hard to leave without finding something.

CITYSTORE
Map pp444-5   Official NYC Gifts & Books
☎ 212-669-7452; Municipal Bldg, 1 Centre St, North Plaza; ◷ 9am-4:30pm Mon-Fri; ◉ 4, 5, 6, J, M to Brooklyn Bridge
This small, little-known city-run shop is the perfect place to score only-in-New-York memorabilia, including authentic taxi medallions, manhole coasters, silk ties and newborn baby items bearing the official 'City of New York' seal, Brooklyn Bridge posters, NYPD baseball caps, actual streets signs ('No Parking,' 'Don't Feed the Pigeons' and more) and baseballs signed by famous Mets and Yanks. There's also a great collection of

At work on shopfront creative solutions

SHOPPING CATEGORY INDEX

- Bouley Bakery & Market (p329)
- Chelsea Market (p143)
- Chinatown Ice Cream Factory (p329)
- Chocolate Bar (p337)
- Economy Candy (p332)
- Essex St Market (p332)
- Fairway (p346)
- Jacques Torres Chocolate (p351)
- McNulty's Tea & Coffee (p338)
- Murray's Cheese (p336)
- Patel Brothers (p352)
- Sherry-Lehman (p349)
- Sunrise Mart (p334)
- Vintage New York (p328)
- Whole Foods (p341)
- Zabar's (p347)

Gifts, Crafts & Collectibles

- 360 Toy Group (p333)
- Alphabets (p333)
- Citystore (p321)
- Evolution (p326)
- Forbidden Planet (p335)
- Harlem Market (p350)
- Kate's Paperie (p327)
- Mud, Sweat and Tears (p346)
- New York Transit Museum Shop (p343)
- Pearl Paint Company (p330)
- Village Chess Shop (p337)

Health & Beauty Aids

- Aedes de Venustas (p335)
- Bond No 9 (p328)
- CO Bigelow Chemists (p335)
- Kiehl's (p334)
- Shun An Tong Health Herbal Co (p352)

Housewares & Furniture

- ABC Carpet & Home (p340)
- Authentiques Past and Present (p339)
- Bed, Bath & Beyond (p339)
- Broadway Panhandler (p325)
- Delphinium Home (p345)
- Gracious Home (p347)
- Kam Man (p330)
- Las Venus (p333)
- Moss (p327)
- Mxyplyzyk (p338)
- Susan Parrish Antiques (p338)
- Tiffany & Co (p344)

Lingerie

- AW Kaufman (p331)
- Mixona (p331)
- Town Shop (p347)

Music

- Bobby's Happy House (p349)
- Breakbeat Science (p332)
- Colony (p345)
- Footlight Records (p334)
- J&R Music & Computer World (p324)
- Manny's Music (p346)
- Matt Umanov Guitars (p336)
- Other Music (p334)
- Rebel Rebel (p336)
- Today's Music (p352)
- Tower Records (p337)
- Virgin Megastore (p341)

Pets

- Whiskers Holistic Petcare (p335)

Sex Toys/Clothing

- Babeland (p325)
- Leatherman (p338)
- Purple Passion (p340)

Shoes

- Giraudon New York (p340)
- Harry's Shoes (p347)
- Jimmy Choo (p343)
- John Fleuvog (p326)
- Otto Tootsi Plohound (p327)

Sports & Active Wear

- Adidas (p324)
- Capezio Dance Theater Shop (p348)
- NBA Store (p343)
- Niketown New York (p343)
- Paragon Athletic Goods (p341)
- Tent & Trails (p324)

Travel

- Complete Traveller (p342)
- Flight 001 (p337)
- Hagstrom Map & Travel Center (p344)

Vintage & Consignment Apparel

- Beacon's Closet (p351)
- Chelsea Girl (p326)
- Everything Goes (p352)
- Foley + Corinna (p332)
- Housing Works Thrift Shop (p340)
- Ina (p330)
- Love Saves the Day (p334)
- Rags A-Go-Go (p340)
- Screaming Mimi's (p334)
- Tatiana's (p256)
- Tokio 7 (p334)
- Zachary's Smile (p328)

Shopping

SHOPPING CATEGORY INDEX

city-themed books – including the famous *Green Book*, an official directory to city agencies, published annually and not available anywhere else.

J&R MUSIC & COMPUTER WORLD

Map pp444-5   Music & Electronics
☎ 212-238-9000; 15-23 Park Row; ☾ 9am-7:30pm Mon-Sat, 10:30am-6:30pm Sun; ◉ A, C to Broadway-Nassau, J, M, 2, 3 to Fulton St
Located on what used to be known as Newspaper Row – the center of New York's newspaper publishi ng biz from the 1840s to the 1920s – this is now a communications hub of a more modern sort. Occupying a full block with J&R shops and their separate entrances, this is considered by many to be the best place in the city to buy a computer of any sort. You can buy any other electronics item here, including cameras, recorders and stereos, as well as DVDs and CDs of every kind. You'll find good deals and knowledgeable staff.

SHAKESPEARE & CO Map pp444-5 Bookstore
☎ 212-742-7025; 1 Whitehall St; ☾ 8am-7pm Mon-Fri; ◉ R, W to Whitehall St, 4, 5 to Bowling Green
This popular New York bookstore chain – with other store locations in Greenwich Village (p336), Gramercy (Map pp446-7), Midtown (pp452–3) and the Upper East Side (p349) – is a great indie option, featuring a wide array of contemporary fiction and nonfiction, art books and tomes about NYC. A small but unique collection of periodicals is another great feature.

STRAND BOOK STORE Map pp444-5 Used Books
☎ 212-732-6070; 95 Fulton St; ☾ 9:30am-9pm Mon-Fri, 11am-8pm Sat & Sun; ◉ A, C, J, M, Z, 2, 3, 4, 5 to Fulton St–Broadway-Nassau
See the famous Downtown (p336) flagship.

TENT & TRAILS

Map pp444-5   Outdoor Sporting Goods
☎ 212-227-1760; 21 Park Pl; ☾ 9:30am-6pm Mon-Wed & Sat, to 7pm Thu & Fri, noon-6pm Sun; ◉ 2, 3 to Park Pl
This fantastic outdoor outfitter – an NYC rarity – sells top-of-the-line gear like tents, backpacks and footwear, from favorite brands including North Face, Kelty and Eureka, with a small selection available to rent. The staff is knowledgeable, too.

SOHO, NOHO & TRIBECA

SOHO

It's a virtual shopping party along just about every little street in Soho – a neighborhood so packed with retailers of every kind, you could easily spend a day or two and not see it all (though you might run out of funds). Broadway and West Broadway, the main corridors, are home to several chains and more affordable, mainstream outfitters, such as the Original Levi's Store, Adidas, Banana Republic, Miss Sixty and Urban Outfitters. Prince St, which runs in between the two, also has its share of chain stores, but they're well mixed with a diverse array of street vendors, hawking jewelry, art, hats and other crafts, especially during warmer months. The jumble of other streets are packed with boutiques selling clothing, shoes, furniture and housewares; over on Lafayette St, you'll find a collection of shops catering to the DJ and skate crowd.

ADIDAS Map p450   Sports Footwear & Active wear
☎ 212-529-0081; 610 Broadway at Houston St; ☾ 10am-8pm Mon-Sat, 11am-7pm Sun; ◉ B, D, F, V to Broadway–Lafayette St
When this 29,5000-sq-ft sneaker emporium came along a few years ago, the character of the neighborhood shifted once and for all from low-key and rough hewn to large-scale and glossy. Inside, you'll find sneakers for just about every sport, plus a vast array of workout gear. For more classic, fashion-driven looks, head around the corner to Adidas Originals (☎ 212-673-0398; 136 Wooster St; ☾ 11am-7pm Mon-Sat, noon-6pm Sun), which brought mobs of patient folks who queued up for hours when it first opened, just to have a look.

AMERICAN APPAREL

Map p450   Basic Clothing
☎ 212-226-4880; 121 Spring St btwn Broadway & Mercer St; ◉ R, W to Prince St
It's all blissfully simple inside these shops (visit www.americanapparel.net for more city locations) from a Los Angeles–based company that eschews sweat shops for its conscientious inhouse production. The racks are filled with the kind of basic T-shirts and sweatshirts you might buy with

slogans or band photos printed across the chests, but here they're all free of graphics. You'll also find tanks, hoodies, underwear, bras, socks and scarves, with styles geared toward men, women, children, babies – even dogs – in a huge range of colors from the primaries to pink and olive green.

ANNA SUI Map p450 Women's clothing
☎ 212-941-8406; www.annasui.com; 113 Greene St; ⏰ 11:30am-7pm Mon-Sat, noon-6pm Sun; Ⓜ R, W to Prince St
This purple-walled wonderland is a whimsical, high-end showcase for the New York–based Sui, whose deliciously filmy dresses and blouses marry a hippie flow with a hipster vibe. They're sexy-girly, in an old-school Courtney Love sort of way.

APPLE STORE SOHO
Map p450 Computers & Electronics
☎ 212-226-3126; 103 Prince St; ⏰ 10am-8pm Mon-Sat, 11am-7pm Sun; Ⓜ N, R, W to Prince St
Apple's uplifting, airy flagship location – with translucent stairway and upstairs walkway and fully fledged theater, used for how-to presentations – bustles with Soho shoppers picking up iPods, iBooks and other items from the iUniverse. The young, hip-geeky staffers are friendly and helpful, either answering questions or leaving you alone as you test-drive any and all of the gadgets, from computers to digital video cameras, that are displayed for sampling.

BABELAND Map p450 Sex Toys & Books
☎ 212-966-2120; 43 Mercer St; ⏰ noon-9pm Mon-Sat, to 7pm Sun; Ⓜ A, C, E to Canal St
The women-owned sex shop formerly known as Toys in Babeland has shortened its name. It's still the queen bee of sex toys, aflutter with open and supportive staffers who will gladly talk you through the chore of picking out the very best silicone dildo or butt plug, matching it with an appropriate leather harness and inspiring you to toss in a quality vibrator (such as the ever-popular High Joy Bunny) while you're at it. But it's also much more: purveyor of sex-related books, magazines, adult DVDs, flavored lube and Babeland tees, and educator, with a constant roster of how-to lectures, for all genders, from the knowledgeable staff. The original, but smaller shop, is on the Lower East Side (p449).

New items that are the Apple (left) of their owners' eyes

BLOOMINGDALE SOHO
Map p450 Dept Store
☎ 212-729-5900; 504 Broadway; ⏰ 10am-9pm Mon-Fri, 10am-8pm Sat, 11am-7pm Sun; Ⓜ R, W to Prince St
The smaller, younger outpost of the Upper East Side (p348) legend, this Bloomie's sheds housewares and other department-store items for a clear focus on fashion. Find clothing, shoes and outerwear for both men and women, plus a substantial collection of cosmetics and perfume at street level. Labels run the gamut from Marc Jacobs to the totally hip clubwear of Heatherette.

BROADWAY PANHANDLER
Map p450 Kitchenware
☎ 212-966-3434; 477 Broome St; ⏰ 10:30am-7pm Mon-Fri, to 7pm Sat, 11am-6pm Sun; Ⓜ A, C, E to Canal St
As well stocked – if not more so – as any of the big-name housewares chains, this awesome indie is an homage to home chefs, stocking cookware from Le Crueset, All Clad and Calphalon; knives by Wusthof; and a range of food processors, coffee makers and other gadgets from Cuisinart, Waring, Bodum and Braun. Also find cool whisks, aprons, glassware and storage containers, and a hip, young, well-informed staff ready to chat you up about it all.

Shopping

SOHO, NOHO & TRIBECA

325

BROOKLYN INDUSTRIES Map p450 Streetwear

☎ 212-219-0862; 286 Lafayette St; ☽ 11am-8pm Mon-Sat, noon-7:30pm Sun; ◉ B, D, F, V to Broadway–Lafayette St

The Manhattan outpost of a growing Williamsburg-based den of urban wear is one of the most light and airy. Behind the massive glass storefront are smart, basic and affordable styles, including 'Made in Brooklyn' tees and sweatshirts, plus plenty of sweaters, hoodies, jackets, denim, coats, hats, bags and even laptop sleeves in earthy colors. All boast the catchy Brooklyn Industries label – an industrial skyline that prominently features a water tower. Find other locations in Williamsburg (☎ 718-486-6464; 162 Bedford Ave) and Park Slope (Map p464; ☎ 718-789-2764; 206 Fifth Ave at Union St), plus a factory store in South Williamsburg (☎ 718-218-9166; 184 Broadway at Driggs St). See www.brooklyn industries.com for more locations.

CHELSEA GIRL Map p450 Vintage Clothing

☎ 212-343-1658; www.chelsea-girl.com; 63 Thompson St btwn Spring & Broome Sts; ☽ noon-7pm; ◉ C, E to Spring St

You won't be able to walk by this burst of whimsy and color without stopping in for at least a quick peek. A small boutique packed with vintage gems from all decades, this treasure chest, owned by eagle-eyed Elisa Casas, has made all the big fashion mags and pulled in its share of celebrity fans. Racks are filled with mint-condition dresses, gowns, sweaters, shoes and suits; don't be surprised if you find a Pucci silk dress from the '70s sharing space with an Adrian wool gabardine jacket from the 1940s.

DAFFY'S

Map p450 Discount Designer Clothing & Accessories

☎ 212-334-7444; 462 Broadway at Grand St; ☽ 10am-8pm Mon-Sat, noon-7pm Sun; ◉ A, C, E to Canal St

Although one of many locations around the city (see www.daffys.com for details), this has one of the best selections, probably due to its cool downtown location. It's got two floors of designer duds and accessories (and a random handful of housewares) for men, women and children, with prices that can be shockingly low. And the tags – like those at most discount shops – show you the item's suggested retail price on top of Daffy's price, which, at an average of 50 percent off, just gives you more incentive to buy.

EVOLUTION Map p450 Weird Science

☎ 212-343-1114; 120 Spring St btwn Broadway & Mercer St; ☽ 11am-7pm; ◉ R, W to Prince St

Partial to insects, skulls, teeth and other usual gross-outs? Then you'll be in heaven here, home to all of that and more. Filled with natural history collectibles of the sort usually seen in museums, this is the place to buy – or just gawk at – framed beetles and butterflies, bugs frozen in amber-resin cubes, anatomical models (ear, larynx and hand skeleton, to name a few), shark teeth and animals' penis bones.

HOTEL VENUS Map p450 Clubwear

☎ 212-966-4066; 382 W Broadway; ☽ 11am-8pm; ◉ C, E to Spring St

A long-time but now-defunct W 8th St staple, Patricia Field's bright, bizarre fashion collection is just as wild and wacky here in Soho. Find implausibly colored frizzy wigs, all sorts of spandex and lingerie, clubwear and tees by Hysterical Glamour and Heatherette, and fur-trimmed jackets and cropped hoodies from 'Tricia. There's a hair salon out the back.

HOUSING WORKS USED BOOK CAFÉ

Map p450 Used Books

☎ 212-334-3324; 126 Crosby St; ☽ 10am-9pm Mon-Fri, noon-9pm Sat, to 7pm Sun; ◉ B, D, F, V to Broadway–Lafayette St

With the look of a real library, complete with mezzanine, this café positively crawls with locals on weekends. Browse through over 45,000 used books and CDs. Prices are good, and all proceeds benefit Housing Works, a charity serving New York City's HIV-positive and AIDS homeless communities. See also Housing Works Thrift Shop (p340).

JOHN FLEUVOG Map p450 Shoes

☎ 212-431-4484; 250 Mulberry St; ☽ noon-8pm Mon-Sat, to 6pm Sun; ◉ R, W to Prince St

Remember those heavy, clunky, almost-clown-like shoes that every art student worth their salt wore back in the mid '80s and early '90s? No, not Doc Martens – the other ones, with swirlier designs and more eye-catching hues. Well you'll find them here, with the trademark signed, thick latex 'Angel' soles and candy-colored uppers, for both men and women. Boots and ironic pumps join the more familiar clunky shoes in this small, light-filled corner shop.

Shopping

SOHO, NOHO & TRIBECA

KATE SPADE Map p450   Handbags

☎ 212-274-1991; 454 Broome St; ⏰ 11am-7pm Mon-Sat, noon-6pm Sun; Ⓜ R, W to Prince St, 6 to Spring St

Here's where you'll find the inspiration for endless Chinatown knockoffs: Kate's latest collection of famed, '50s-inspired nylon and leather bags as well as accessories, plus shoes and sunnies. Men's sacks – laptop sleeves, soft briefcases, day bags and the like – by Kate's hubby, Andy, are at nearby **Jack Spade** (☎ 212-625-1820; 56 Greene St; same hours).

KATE'S PAPERIE Map p450   Stationery

☎ 212-941-9816; 561 Broadway; ⏰ 10am-8pm Mon-Sat, 11am-7pm Sun; Ⓜ R, W to Prince St

The go-to place for engraved bridal invitations, this New York classic also has a huge and inspired selection of journals, photo albums, greeting cards, wrapping paper, fine pens and, of course, bulk paper, from handmade flaxen sheets with pressed flowers in the weave to stacks of white recycled card stock.

MCNALLY ROBINSON

Map p450   Books

☎ 212-274-1160; 52 Prince St at Crosby St; 10am-10pm Mon-Sat, to 8pm Sun; Ⓜ R, W to Prince St

A new indie bookstore – what a promising sign! Right in the heart of Soho, this cozy spot is a gem. Find a great selection of magazines, plus sections devoted to subjects that include food writing, architecture and design, teen novels and LGBT (lesbian-gay-bi-transgender) literature. There's a great café, too, which is the perfect place to settle in with some reading material or just watch the shoppers of Prince St go by.

Shimmy and shake in chemises from Pearl River Mart (right)

MOSS Map p450   Designer Housewares

☎ 212-204-7100; 146 Greene St; ⏰ 11am-7pm Mon-Sat, noon-6pm Sun; Ⓜ N, R, W to Prince St

Converted from a gallery space, Moss' two showrooms prop slick, modern and fun industrial designs behind glass, exhibitlike, but they're definitely for sale. It's easy to find something – a Yoshitomo Nara flip clock with 84 original drawings, say, or a sleek black La Cupola espresso maker – that you'll just have to own, and that you probably won't find many other places.

ORIGINAL LEVI'S STORE

Map p450   Jeans & Clothing

☎ 646-613-1847; 536 Broadway at Spring St; ⏰ 10am-8pm Mon-Sat, 11am-7pm Sun; Ⓜ R, W to Prince St

Stock up on all your favorite Levi's jeans here – 501 button-fly, super-low boot-cut, zip-fly straight-leg cords – plus check out the great selection of Western shirts, tees, sweaters, jackets and always-evolving new styles for both men and women.

OTTO TOOTSI PLOHOUND

Map p450   Shoes

☎ 212-431-7299; 273 Lafayette St; ⏰ 11:30am-7:30pm Mon-Fri, 11am-8pm Sat, noon-7pm Sun; Ⓜ B, D, V, F to Broadway–Lafayette St

New York hipsters looking for designer-label deals frequent one of Tootsi's four shops (including Union Square and Midtown), which arrange their exciting collections like small museums. Take a slow walk around the perimeter and check out all the fab styles and labels – Miu Miu, Cynthia Rowley, Helmut Lang, Paul Smith and Prada Sport among them – before settling in and trying them on your own tootsies.

PEARL RIVER MART

Map p450   Chinese Dept Store

☎ 212-431-4770; 477 Broadway; ⏰ 10am-7pm; Ⓜ J, M, N, Q, R, W, Z, 6 to Canal St

This one-stop Canal St classic, now in its fancier Broadway location, is still Chinatown's best shop. Find everything Asian here – cheap Chinese and Japanese teapots, dragon-print dresses, paper lanterns, Chinese slippers in all colors, jars of Chinese spices and sauces, imported teas, pecking chicken wind-up clocks that look like throwbacks to the Mao era, and various (loud) Asian instruments. Eastward ho!

PRADA Map p450 — Designer Clothing

☎ 212-334-8888; 575 Broadway; ⊗ 11am-7pm Mon-Sat, noon-6pm Sun; ⊚ N, R, W to Prince St

The Italian designer's ever-chic outfits and shoes are one thing, but the space! Transformed from the old Guggenheim Soho location by Dutch architect Rem Koolhaas, and recently restored following extensive damage in an early 2006 fire, this shop, with sweeping wooden floors and tucked-away downstairs rooms, is a marvel to see. For a thrill, try something on, as the clear glass walls of the fitting rooms fog when the door closes.

VINTAGE NEW YORK

Map p450 — New York Winery Shop

☎ 212-226-9463; 482 Broome St at Wooster St; ⊗ 10am-9pm; ⊚ A C, E to Canal St

This excellent wine shop and wine bar features vintages from boutique wineries all over New York State, including Long Island, the Hudson Valley and the Finger Lakes region. Popular local varieties include sparklers, chardonnay, riesling, pinot noir, merlot and cabernet sauvignon, and all are available for tasting. The best part about the place, though, is that, because it's technically a winery, it's allowed to stay open on Sunday – something no other wine shop in the city can claim. That is, of course, except for its **Uptown branch** (☎ 212-721-9999; 2492 Broadway at 93rd St; ⊗ 10am-10pm).

NOHO

It's just a tiny spit of a 'hood, with one of those newfangled acronym monikers, but if it has a strong point, it's retail opportunities. It's all trendy and pricey here, with just a couple of streets, Bond and Lafayette, acting as the main players. Stroll up and down them, and the other small ones, too, and you'll find some good art supplies, furniture and dancewear.

ATRIUM Map p450 — Clothing & Denim

☎ 212-473-9200; cnr 644 Broadway & Bleeker St; ⊗ 10am-8pm; ⊚ B, D, F, V to Broadway–Lafayette St

A real standout along a particularly ho-hum stretch of retailers, Atrium has an excellent selection of funky designer wear, including shoes and accessories, for both men and women from Diesel, G-Star, Miss Sixty and other popular labels. Best, though, is the

grand range of high-end denim, from folks including Joe's, Seven, Blue Cult and True Religion.

BOND 07 Map p450 — Women's Clothing & Eyewear

☎ 212-677-8487; www.selimaoptique.com; 7 Bond St; ⊗ 11am-7pm Mon-Sat, noon-7pm Sun; ⊚ R, W to Prince St

Selima Salaun reigns here with her stylish, celeb-favored glasses frames, which dominate one section of this sweet boutique in gleaming glass cases. But up front you'll find a couple of eclectic racks of truly special clothing, mainly filmy blouses and supple frocks from edgy young designers like Alice Roi.

BOND NO 9 Map p450 — Perfume

☎ 212-228-1940; 9 Bond St; ⊗ 11am-7pm Mon-Sat, noon-6pm Sun; ⊚ R, W to Prince St

'Making scents of New York' is this thoroughly unique perfume boutique, where the gimmick is NYC. Each bottle of home-brewed potion (which begin at about $100) not only comes labeled with a trademark round label inspired by an old New York subway token, it gets filled with one of 20 fragrances that are named after and inspired by local nabes. There's Riverside Drive, Chelsea Flowers, Central Park, Eau de Noho and Chinatown, none of which smells like wet pavement, exhaust fumes *or* hot pretzels. There's also a great selection of vintage bottles with squeeze balls, which can be filled with the scent of your choice.

ZACHARY'S SMILE

Map p450 — Vintage Clothing & Shoes

☎ 212-965-8248; 317 Lafayette St btwn Bleecker & Houston Sts; ⊚ B, D, F, V to Broadway–Lafayette St

This second, smaller version of the new vintage darling of downtown, which is based in the **West Village** (☎ 212-924-0604; 9 Greenwich Ave btwn Christopher and W 10th Sts), has a wonderful array of mint-condition finds from several decades past. Find chic dresses, sequined sweaters, T-strap heels, well-worn cowboy boots, faux fur coats, clutch purses and more. The salespeople are friendly, to boot.

TRIBECA

Though it doesn't hold a candle to its Soho neighbor in terms of sheer breadth, this small neighborhood does have its fair share of high-end havens that are favorites with local residents. But they're not bad places for a wayward visitor to rack up debt, either. Try strolling the lower reaches of Hudson St and its surrounding lanes for quirky home furnishings and various antiques.

BOULEY BAKERY & MARKET

Map pp444-5   Gourmet Food

☎ 212-608-5829; 130 W Broadway; ⏰ 7:30am-7:30pm; Ⓜ 1 to Franklin St

Want to be able to recreate the exquisite culinary art of celeb chef David Bouley when you get home? Then you'd better get yourself enrolled in chef school. In the meantime, you can at least use some of the same high-quality ingredients as the man himself, now available at the small bakery-market next door to his famed **Bouley** (p229) restaurant. Though the fresh seafood, including halibut, skate, yellowtail and other seasonal delicacies, probably won't do too well in your hotel room, a high-end cheese, such as Jean de Brie, could be paired with organic fig cake and some picholine olives to make for a gourmet picnic. Raspberry vinegar and fancy sea salt could even return home on the plane.

BU AND THE DUCK

Map pp444-5   Children's Clothing

☎ 212-219-7788; 106 Franklin St at Church St; ⏰ 10am-6pm Mon-Sat, 11am-5pm Sun; Ⓜ 1 to Franklin St

Geared toward stylish mothers who are not at all concerned about their toddlers spitting up on their $46 Italian-cotton jerseys (which they'll outgrow in another month anyway), this precious little boutique has classically fashionable clothing, shoes, toys (such as $50 crocheted giraffes), belts, bags and socks, for babies and little ones up to about eight years old.

ISSEY MIYAKE

Map pp444-5   Designer Clothing

☎ 212-226-0100; 119 Hudson St at N Moore St; ⏰ 10am-6pm Mon-Fri, 11am-6pm Sat, noon-5pm Sun; Ⓜ 1 to Franklin St

Find the designer's runway designs, by Naoki Takizawa, and several of the other collections – Pleats Please, APOC, Me and more – at this downtown showcase for the high-end silky, modern, sugary confections for both men and women.

CHINATOWN

Chinatown sprawls for many blocks, and though you'll find almost everything you'd ever want here along Canal and Mott Sts, the real adventure is going off the beaten path, heading into one of the mall-like spots that are definitely not geared to tourists. You'll find bridal shops, video arcades, herbal shops and endless bakeries that fit that description; go ahead and wander inside. But also don't miss the sidewalk-spilling stores that line mobbed Canal St between the Bowery and 7th Ave, offering tees, jewelry (it's not all tacky – poke around), quick watch repair and some electronics (it's best for extension cords and plugs). For big electronics, such as stereo equipment or cameras, it's best to avoid buying anything that requires a warranty. For fun imports, such as bulk teas, silk dresses, exotic produce, woks and fancy chopsticks, try the stores along Mott St. Need a shave and a haircut? On tiny Pell St you'll find a large preponderance of barbers.

Note that Chinatown's best shop, **Pearl River Mart** (p327), is no longer in the 'hood, but is now a few blocks north on Broadway.

AJI ICHIBAN   Map pp444-5   Candy

☎ 212-233-7650; 37 Mott St; ⏰ 10am-8:30pm; Ⓜ J, M, N, Q, R, W, Z, 6 to Canal St

This Hong Kong–based chain, the name of which means 'awesome' in Japanese, is a ubiquitous sight in Chinatown, as this is just one of five locations here, with another in Queens (see www.ajiichiban-usa.com for more). And though it is a candy shop, get ready for something a bit more exciting than malted balls and peppermint sticks. Here's where you'll find sesame-flavored marshmallows, Thai durian milk candy, preserved plums, mandarin peel, dried currant gummies and dried guava, as well as savory snacks like crispy spicy cod fish, crab chips, wasabi peas and dried anchovies with peanut.

CHINATOWN ICE CREAM FACTORY

Map pp444-5   Ice Cream & T-shirts

☎ 212-608-4170; 65 Bayard St; ⏰ 11am-10pm; Ⓜ J, M, N, Q, R, W, Z, 6 to Canal St

Totally overshadowing the nearby Häagen Dazs is this busy ice-cream shop, where you can savor scoops of green tea, ginger, red bean and black sesame. The Factory also sells ridiculously cute, trademark yellow

Shopping

CHINATOWN

T-shirts ($15) with an ice cream–slurping happy dragon on them.

KAM MAN Map pp444-5   Kitchenware
☎ 212-571-0330; 200 Canal St; ☾ 9am-9pm;
Ⓜ J, M, N, Q, R, W, Z, 6 to Canal St
Head past hanging ducks to the basement of the classic Canal St food store for cheap Chinese and Japanese tea sets, plus kitchen products like chopsticks, stir-frying utensils and rice cookers.

PEARL PAINT COMPANY
Map p450   Art & Craft Supplies
☎ 212-431-7932; 308 Canal St; ☾ 10am-7pm Mon-Fri, 10am-6:30pm Sat, to 6pm Sun; Ⓜ J, M, N, Q, R, W, Z, 6 to Canal St
Artists looking for supplies come to this sprawling, multilevel, red-and-white warehouse for anything from simple gesso and tubes of Winsor & Newton oil paint to pre-stretched canvases, potter ribs, vellum pads and graphite sketching sets. Amateur creative types will find plenty of equipment for experimenting, such as Italian gold leaf, Fimo modeling clay, glue guns and big tubs of glitter. There's a whole section devoted to children's art supplies, too.

LITTLE ITALY & NOLITA

Let's face it: the real shopping in this area takes place strictly in Nolita, where a mind-boggling number of cute boutiques line the tiny lanes, and an equal amount of credit-card wielding trend spotters eagerly snap up the offerings. Mott St is particularly packed with shops, though Prince, Mulberry and Elizabeth Sts factor into the mix nicely, too. As far as Little Italy shopping goes, don't go there looking for hip clothes and accessories. But if it's a gallon of extra-virgin olive oil, a bakery box of Napoleons or a 'Little Italy' tee you're after, go for it. You'll find all that and more along Mulberry St and the small blocks poking off it in both directions, just above Canal St.

CALYPSO Map p450   Women's Clothing
☎ 212-965-0990; 280 Mott St; ☾ 11:30am-7:30pm Mon-Sat, noon-6:30pm Sun; Ⓜ B, D, F, V to Broadway–Lafayette St
It's summer forever at this St Bart's–born shop, which stocks tropical clothing, such as light dresses, Dr Boudoir swimwear, flip-flops and slinky blouses, year-round. Calypso has several boutiques (the jewelry shop is a few doors down on Mott St), including one at 74th St and Madison Ave in the Upper East Side. Call for details, or visit www.calypso-celle.com.

HIGHWAY Map p450   Bags
☎ 212-966-4388; 238 Mott St btwn Prince & Spring Sts; ☾ 11am-7pm; Ⓜ B, D, F, V to Broadway–Lafayette St
You'll find a very simple offering at this small Nolita storefront: bags, homespun by Jem Filippi and available in about 20 styles, all laid out on counters like delicious free samples at a cheese shop. Made of materials including nylon, PVC and tooled leather, the playfully functional bags hover around the $125 mark, with a design for every need – be it pocketbook, change purse, wallet or laptop carrier.

HOLLYWOULD
Map p450   Women's Clothing & Shoes
☎ 212-243-8344; 198 Elizabeth St btwn Prince & Spring Sts; ☾ 11:30-7pm Mon-Sat, noon-5pm Sun; Ⓜ 6 to Spring St
Holly Dunlap, former designer at Lilly Pulitzer, has created her own empire with a cultish following and far edgier version of the screaming flower prints that Pulitzer's known for. She's mainly known for her shoe designs: complicated wedge-heeled strappy sandals, simple flats with pointy toes, metallic thong sandals encrusted with gems, gilded mules and pink-and-white candy-striped pumps (all in the $700 range, mind you). But her sealife-print gowns, mother-of-pearl embellished polo dresses, and Mexican-inspired yellow flouncy sundresses deserve props, too.

INA Map
p450   Designer Consignment Clothing
☎ 212-334-9048; 21 Prince St; ☾ noon-7pm Sun-Thu, to 8pm Fri & Sat; Ⓜ N, R, W to Prince St, B, D, F, V to Broadway–Lafayette St
Locals love this super consignment shop that stocks choice designer clothes for women (the men's shop is around the corner at 262 Mott St). Recent finds included a Louis Vuitton dress for $775, Seven jeans for $65 and a cropped Chanel jacket for $1300. Bargain bins go even lower, filled with belts and scarves.

CLOTHING SIZES

Measurements approximate only, try before you buy

Women's Clothing

Aus/UK	8	10	12	14	16	18
Europe	36	38	40	42	44	46
Japan	5	7	9	11	13	15
USA	6	8	10	12	14	16

Women's Shoes

Aus/USA	5	6	7	8	9	10
Europe	35	36	37	38	39	40
France only	35	36	38	39	40	42
Japan	22	23	24	25	26	27
UK	3½	4½	5½	6½	7½	8½

Men's Clothing

Aus	92	96	100	104	108	112
Europe	46	48	50	52	54	56
Japan	S		M	M		L
UK/USA	35	36	37	38	39	40

Men's Shirts (Collar Sizes)

Aus/Japan	38	39	40	41	42	43
Europe	38	39	40	41	42	43
UK/USA	15	15½	16	16½	17	17½

Men's Shoes

Aus/UK	7	8	9	10	11	12
Europe	41	42	43	44½	46	47
Japan	26	27	27½	28	29	30
USA	7½	8½	9½	10½	11½	12½

MIXONA Map p450   Lingerie

☎ 646-613-0100; www.mixona.com; 262 Mott St btwn Houston & Prince Sts; ☼ 11am-8:30pm Mon-Sat, to 7:30pm Sun; ◉ B, D, F, V to Broadway–Lafayette Sts

An oft-cited favorite lingerie shop for New Yorkers, the spacious, industrial-chic space is bursting with sexy scores that'll make you and your loved one go bump in the night. Lacy, pretty, sexy, slutty, stretchy or cute ol' cotton – you'll find it all here, from the best brands in underthings, including Cosabella, Andres Sarda, Dolce & Gabbana, Kenzo, La Perla, Moschino and more.

REBECCA TAYLOR

Map p450   Women's Designer Clothing

☎ 212-966-0406; 260 Mott St btwn Houston & Prince Sts; ☼ 11am-7pm Mon-Sat, noon-7pm Sun

Flirty, feminine and romantic, Taylor's sheer, drapey dresses and blouses are favored by celebs including Cameron Diaz and Uma Thurman. Though the flagship store is in Japan, this Nolita boutique has a grand selection of the designer's goodies, including

racks of frilly frocks, swinging A-line skirts and low-slung trousers.

LOWER EAST SIDE

Similar to the dense concentration of tiny hipster boutiques in Nolita is the vast collection on the LES, although offerings here tend to skew toward the edgier, slouchier, more experimental young customer, whether it's books, vintage dresses or modern home design they're after. You'll find the most shops on Orchard and Ludlow Sts, between Houston and Delancey Sts, but it's worth wandering to other strips, too. Oh, and before the neighborhood's recent hipster makeover, shopping here was generally limited to Orchard St's leather-jacket, old-school lingerie and Judaica shops on Essex St, between Grand and Canal Sts. They're still there today, and can be fun to browse in, as can the few lingering pickle, bagel and Jewish delis sprinkled around the area.

AW KAUFMAN

Map pp446-7   Bras & Undergarments

☎ 212-226-1629; 73 Orchard St at Grand St; ☼ 10:30am-5pm Sun-Thu, to 2pm Fri; ◉ B, D, F to Grand St

Though there's plenty of high-quality underwear of all sorts here, for both men and women, this family-run shop (open since 1924) has a particular obsession: bras. More specifically, bras that fit absolutely perfectly. The salespeople can tell which style and size is right for you with just a quick eyeballing of your goods, and then they'll pull out a couple from drawers and make sure they feel just right. It's old-fashioned customer service, a dying breed in this town.

BABELAND Map p449   Sex Toys

☎ 212-375-1701; www.babeland.com; 94 Rivington St; ☼ noon-10pm Mon-Sat, to 7pm Sun; ◉ F, J, M, Z to Delancey St–Essex St

See Babeland of Soho (p325) for details.

BLUESTOCKINGS

Map p449   Radical Bookstore & Café

☎ 212-777-6028; 172 Allen St; www.bluestockings .com; ☼ 1-10pm; ◉ F, V to Lower East Side–Second Ave

This independent bookstore, first opened with a lesbian bent, has now expanded its turf to radicalism of all kinds. It's still

Shopping

LOWER EAST SIDE

women-owned, though, and its shelves have a strong selection of dyke and feminist lit and crit – along with tomes on gender studies, global capitalism, democracy studies, black liberation and police and prison systems. It's also the site of a vegan, organic, fair-trade café, as well as myriad readings and speaking events, including women's poetry readings, workshops on radical protests and even a monthly Dyke Knitting Circle (see Readings & Lectures, p291, for more details on events here).

BREAKBEAT SCIENCE Map p449   DJ Music
☎ 212-995-2592; 181 Orchard St; ⏱ 1-8pm Sun-Wed, to 9pm Thu-Sat; Ⓞ F, V to Lower East Side–Second Ave
The namesake music label's shop stocks drums-and-bass and jungle vinyl as well as CDs, with turntable stations to preview. It's also stocked with DJ-style tees, hoodies and jewelry, plus equipment like record-cleaner kits, DJ sling bags, DJ cartridges and Breakbeat Science toy figurines.

ECONOMY CANDY Map p449   Candy
☎ 212-254-1531; 108 Rivington St at Essex St; ⏱ 9am-6pm Mon-Fri, 10am-5pm Sat; Ⓞ F, J, M, Z to Delancey St–Essex St
Bringing sweetness to the 'hood since 1937, this sweet shop is stocked with floor-to-ceiling goods in package and bulk, and is home to some beautiful antique gum machines. You'll find everything from the kid-worthy jellybeans, lollipops, gumballs, Cadbury imports, gummy worms and rock candy to more adult delicacies like halvah, green tea bonbons, hand-dipped chocolates, dried ginger and papaya, Brazil nuts and pistachios, and sesame-honey bars.

ESSEX ST MARKET Map p449   Food Market
☎ 212-312-3603; 120 Essex St btwn Delancey & Rivington Sts; ⏱ 8am-6pm Mon-Sat; Ⓞ F, V to Delancey St, J, M, Z to Delancey St–Essex St
This 60-year-old historic shopping destination is the local place for produce, seafood, butcher-cut meats, cheeses, Latino grocery items, even a barber. The Schapiro Wines stall is popular, as its roots in the neighborhood date back to 1899, when the Schapiro family founded its kosher winery. NYC's first winery, it gave tours of its dank cellar and its 50,000-gallon tanks, but moved to upstate New York in the mid-1990s.

FOLEY + CORINNA
Map p449   Girly Clothing & Vintage Shoes
☎ 212-529-5042; 143 Ludlow St at Stanton St; Ⓞ F, V to Lower East Side–Second Ave
A whimsical, girly space with dark wood flooring and pretty, antique murals, this place is a favorite among romantic-era vintage fans, including a large handful of celebs. It's part new designs, courtesy of the Dana Foley collection blouses, dresses and tanks, and part high-end vintage, thanks to Corinna's one-of-a-kind shoes and accessories. Also head around the corner to visit the men's store (114 Stanton St at Ludlow St).

48 HESTER
Map pp446-7   Men's & Women's Fashions
☎ 212-473-3496; 48 Hester St at Ludlow St; ⏱ noon-7pm Tue-Fri, 11am-6pm Sat & Sun; Ⓞ F, V to Lower East Side–Second Ave
High-profile publicist and fashion-showroom manager Denise Williamson has opened this well-stocked boutique, filled with threads from some of her most beloved clients: Ulla Johnson, Kristen Lee, Sass & Bide and Rag & Bone. Soon joining the racks of flapper dresses, blouses, blazers and trousers will be Williamson's own cotton separates, under the new label Franck.

FUCK YOGA Map p449   Sarcastic T-shirts
☎ 212-995-9171; 132A Ludlow St at Rivington St; Ⓞ F, V to Lower East Side–Second Ave
What started out as a joke has become a T-shirt phenomenon with a cult following (which has even included wardrobe designers on *Sex and the City*). Find men's and women's tees with snarky, perfectly New York phrases, which include, along with its namesake, 'Fuck Frank Gehry' and 'Prayer ain't cutting it.'

JUTTA NEUMANN
Map p449   Leather Accessories
☎ 212-982-7048; www.juttaneumann.com; 158 Allen St at Rivington St; ⏱ 11am-7pm; Ⓞ F, V to Lower East Side–Second Ave
German-born Neumann spent several years assisting an old-school New York leathersmith before striking out on her own. Now her own accessory designs – thick leather cuffs with buckles, expertly crafted, simple sandals, handbags with or without straps, a range of wallets and supple belts – enjoy

a huge following by stylish urbanites and fashion-mag stylists alike.

LAS VENUS Map p449   Vintage Furniture
☎ 212-982-0608; 163 Ludlow St; ☼ noon-9pm Mon-Thu, noon-midnight Fri& Sun, to 8pm Sun; ◉ F, J, M, Z to Delancey St–Essex St

Down a couple of steps from the street, this colorful shop packs in cool Danish modern furniture (from the 1950s, '60s and '70s) and other vintage furnishings. Much of it edges toward the pricey line, but some deals await the prodder (as well as old *Playboys*, if that's your thing). Las Venus stocks its chrome furnishings on the 2nd floor of **ABC Carpet & Home** (p340).

MARY ADAMS THE DRESS
Map p449   Women's Clothing
☎ 212-473-0237; www.maryadamsthedress.com; 138 Ludlow St; ☼ 1-6pm Wed-Sat, to 5pm Sun or by appt; ◉ F, J, M, Z to Delancey St–Essex St

Drop by to see what lacy, romantic, boldly colored dresses and gowns Mary has done lately, or you can collaborate with the designer to get one made from scratch. She's known as the go-to girl for over-the-top romantic, unique and eye-catching wedding dresses that can incorporate anything from a lace-up cotton corset to layered, bias-cut silk organza. Custom dresses start at $1500.

360 TOY GROUP
Map p449   Japanese Collectibles
☎ 646-602-0138; 239 Eldridge St btwn Houston & Stanton Sts; ☼ 11am-7pm Sun, noon-6pm Mon; ◉ F, J, M, Z to Delancey St–Essex St

Owner and curator Jakuan is dedicated to showcasing (and selling) the finest, quirkiest toy art from the US, Japan and Hong Kong. Not for kids, these serious (but smile inducing) figures include the street-wise characters of Eric So, the whacked-out children series of Michael Lau, rain-hat-wearing Bathing Apes, robotic Bounty Hunters, and abstract characters from Jakuan's Rock Hard clothing line.

EAST VILLAGE

Still straddling the line of fresh and new alongside crusty and old, the East Village offers a combination of precious clothing boutiques from hot young designers and a more '80s version of itself, through dirty-word T-shirt shops, street vendors selling jewelry and socks and a slew of dusty vintage clothing and furniture boutiques. Find the old-school stuff on St Marks Pl between Third and First Aves, and much of the new stuff along its parallel strips, from E 13th to E Houston, and as far east as Ave D. On weekends, vendors line St Marks Pl and Ave A, and a Greenmarket hits Tompkins Sq Park. The blocks of E 2nd through E 7th Sts, between Second Ave and Ave B especially, are good for finding vintage wear, tattoo shops and record stores. Oh, and you'll find the odd (and massive) Kmart on Astor Pl.

A CHENG Map p449   Women's Clothing
☎ 212-979-7324; www.achengshop.com; 443 E 9th St; ☼ 11:30am-8pm Mon-Fri, noon-7pm Sat & Sun; ◉ L to First Ave, 6 to Astor Pl

A hit with East Village girls in recent years, local designer A Cheng stocks her latest collection of tailored yet funky women's wear, such as trench coats with fun piping and big buttons, bright herringbone halter tops, polka-dotted cardigans and flowery sundresses.

ALPHABETS Map p449   Gifts, T-Shirts
☎ 212-475-7250; 115 Ave A btwn 7th St & St Marks Pl; ◉ F, V to Lower East Side–Second Ave

A cool gift shop mainstay, the shop is actually divided into two distinct halves: one is for the massive variety of kitschy tees, greeting cards and nostalgic toys (along the lines of Silly Putty and Slinky), while the other side stocks higher-end goodies that still have a playful side, such as Michael Graves tea kettles, Precidio nesting bowls, one rack of men's button-downs and dart-board patterned cufflinks. Its shop on the **Upper West Side** (☎ 212-579-5702; 2284 Broadway btwn 83rd and 84th Sts) adds life to that more staid 'hood.

DINOSAUR HILL
Map p449   Toys & Baby Clothes
☎ 212-473-5850; 306 E 9th St; ☼ 11am-7pm; ◉ 6 to Astor Pl

A small, old-fashioned toy store that's inspired more by imagination than Disney movies, this shop sports an amazing puppet selection including Czech marionettes and international finger puppets, along with unique jack-in-the-boxes, art and science kits, quality wooden blocks and glass marbles, plus natural-fiber clothing for infants.

FOOTLIGHT RECORDS Map p449   Music

☎ 212-533-1572; 113 E 12th St; ☽ 11am-7pm Mon-Fri, 10am-6pm Sat, noon-5pm Sun; Ⓜ R, W to 8th St–NYU, 6 to Astor Pl

Home to a well-chosen collection of out-of-print Broadway and foreign-movie soundtracks, Footlight is also big on jazz, vocalists and (brace yourself) documentaries, all on the good ol' LP format. It's a must-visit for vinyl hounds.

KIEHL'S Map p449   Beauty Products

☎ 212-677-3171, 800-543-4571; 109 Third Ave; ☽ 10am-7pm Mon-Sat, noon-6pm Sun; Ⓜ L to Third Ave

Making and selling skincare products since it opened in NYC as an apothecary in 1851, this Kiehl's flagship store has doubled its shop size and expanded into an international chain, but its personal touch remains – as do the coveted, generous sample sizes. Pick up some of the legendary moisturizers, masks and emollients, including Creme with Silk Groom for the hair, Creme de Corps for the body or Abyssine Serum for the face.

LOVE SAVES THE DAY

Map p449   Vintage Apparel and Kitsch

☎ 212-228-3802; 119 2nd Ave; ☽ noon-8pm Mon-Fri, to 9pm Sat & Sun; Ⓜ 6 to Astor Pl

As the waves of change engulf the East Village, Loves Saves the Day stays true to its original form. Its campy collection of old polyester clothes, fake fur coats, glam-rock spiked boots, GI Joes, *Star Wars* '77 figurines and other dolls and vintage toys is not much changed since the days when Rosanna Arquette bought Madonna's pyramid jacket here in the viva-los-'80s film *Desperately Seeking Susan*.

OTHER MUSIC Map p449   Indie Music

☎ 212-477-8150; 15 E 4th St; ☽ noon-9pm Mon-Fri, to 8pm Sat, to 7pm Sun; Ⓜ 6 to Bleecker St

Facing Tower Records (tsk, that mecca for mainstream conformistas!), this indie-run CD store has won over a loyal fan base with its informed selection of, well, other types of music: offbeat lounge, psychedelic, electronica, indie-rock etc, available new and used. Friendly staffers like what they do, and may be able to help translate your inner musical whims and dreams to actual CD reality.

ST MARKS BOOKSHOP

Map p449   Bookstore

☎ 212-260-7853; 31 Third Ave; ☽ 10am-midnight Mon-Sat, 11am-midnight Sun; Ⓜ 6 to Astor Pl

Actually located around the corner from St Marks (it moved a long while back), this indie bookshop specializes in political literature, poetry, new nonfiction and novels and academic journals. There's also a superior collection of cookbooks, travel guides and magazines, both glossy and otherwise. Staffers are a bit on the unsociable side, but hey, they're bookish and they really know their stuff.

SCREAMING MIMI'S

Map p449   Vintage Clothing

☎ 212-677-6464; 382 Lafayette St; ☽ noon-8pm Mon-Sat, 1-7pm Sun; Ⓜ 6 to Bleecker St

A warm and colorful storefront that just begs to be entered, you'll find accessories and jewelry up front, and an excellent selection of clothing – organized, ingeniously, by decade, from the '40s to the '70s – in the back. It's all in great condition, from the prim, beaded wool cardigans to the suede mini dresses and well-matched white leather go-go boots.

SUNRISE MART

Map p449   Japanese Groceries

☎ 212-598-3040; 29 Third Ave at Stuyvesant St; ☽ 10am-11pm Sun-Thu, 10am-midnight Fri & Sat; Ⓜ 6 to Astor Pl

A bright, 2nd-floor supermarket dedicated to all foods Japanese, this is where you'll find clutches of homesick, well-dressed NYU kids stocking up on wasabi, plus plenty of locals who have discovered a new craving for Poki sweets. Paw through aisles of pre-sliced fish, rice noodles, ponzu sauces, sushi rice, white soy sauce, fresh yuzu, miso, tofu, and endless amounts of colorful candies.

TOKIO 7 Map p449   Consignment Store

☎ 212-353-8443; 64 E 7th St; ☽ noon-8:30pm Mon-Sat, to 8pm Sun; Ⓜ 6 to Astor Pl

This revered and hip consignment shop, down a few steps on a shady stretch of E 7th St, has good-condition designer labels for men and women at some 'come again?' prices. Best is the selection of men's suits – there's nearly always something tip-top worth trying on in the $100 to $150 range. You could try to sell off your own labels that you might be tired of, but be prepared to have them sniffed at and promptly rejected.

UNDERDOG EAST

Map p449   Men's Clothing

☎ 212-388-0560; 117 E 7th St btwn First Ave & Ave A; ◉ 6 to Astor Pl

Why should women get all the good boutiques? This 2005 addition to the neighborhood is all about men – very well dressed ones, that is. Its low-key, exposed-brick space features high-end denim, sweaters, shirts and accessories (including some delicious cashmere hats) from designers including Earnest Sewn, Steven Alan, Filippa K and La Coppola Storta.

WHISKERS HOLISTIC PETCARE

Map p449   Natural Pet Products

☎ 212-979-2532; 235 E 9th St btwn First & Second Aves; ◉ 6 to Astor Pl

Newly renovated but a long-time neighborhood favorite, this thoroughly unique pet shop is definitely worth a visit. No, you're probably not vacationing with your pooch or puss, but you may very well want to bring them home a treat of the holistic variety. Like a health-food emporium for furry friends, the natural-activist staff will guide you to the best in organic catnip, shampoos, flea powders, flower remedies, fish-based treats and safe, all-natural toys.

GREENWICH VILLAGE

While not as rich with shopping treasures as the next-door West Village, the streets of the Village make for fun and eclectic retail-based strolls. Places to acquire gifts are in large supply, especially the various candle, housewares and souvenir shops along Sixth Ave. You'll find a collection of CD and guitar shops on Bleecker St, between Broadway and Seventh Ave, and great food shops on practically every corner. The famous 'shoe street' is on 8th between Fifth and Sixth Aves and, despite having fewer shoe stores than there were say five or 10 years ago, there are still quite a few, mainly places filled with affordable knockoffs and staffed by particularly aggressive salespeople. You'll need to be firm when you say you're 'just looking.'

AEDES DE VENUSTAS

Map p448   Bath & Beauty

☎ 212-206-8674; 9 Christopher St; ◷ noon-8pm Mon-Sat, 1-7pm Sun; ◉ A, B, C, D, E, F, V to W 4th St, 1, 9 to Christopher St–Sheridan Sq

Plush and inviting, Aedes de Venustas ('Temple of Beauty' in Latin, if you're tempted to impress the staff) provides more than 30 brands of luxury European perfumes, including Chergui, Mark Birley for Men, Costes, Nirmala and Shalini. They have also got skincare products created by folks such as Patyka and Jurlique, and everyone's favorite $60 scented candles from Diptyque.

CO BIGELOW CHEMISTS

Map p448   Health & Beauty Products

☎ 212-473-7324; 414 Sixth Ave btwn 8th & 9th Sts; ◉ A, C, E, B, D, F, V to W 4th St

The 'oldest apothecary in America' is now a slightly upscale fantasyland for the beauty-product obsessed (though there's still an actual pharmacy and drugstore items on the premises, too). In addition to its own CO Bigelow label products, including lip balms, hand and foot salves, shaving creams and rosewater, browse through lotions, shampoos, cosmetics and fragrances from makers including Acqua di Parma, Dr Hauschka, Weleda, Frédéric Fekkai, Propoline and many more.

EAST-WEST BOOKS

Map p448   Spiritual Bookstore

☎ 212-243-5994; 78 Fifth Ave; ◷ 10am-7:30pm Mon-Sat, 11am-6:30pm Sun; ◉ L, N, Q, R, W, 4, 5, 6 to 14th St–Union Sq

With a calming effect that takes place upon entering, this groovy bookstore stocks a wide array of books on Buddhism and Asian philosophies, plus chill-out music, yoga mats and earthy-crunchy jewelry.

FORBIDDEN PLANET

Map p449   Books & Games

☎ 212-473-1576; 840 Broadway; ◷ 10am-10pm Mon-Sat, 11am-8pm Sun; ◉ L, N, Q, R, W, 4, 5, 6 to 14th St–Union Sq

Indulge your inner sci-fi nerd. Find heaps of comics, books, video games and figurines (ranging from *Star Trek* to Shaq). Fellow Magic and Yu-Gi-Oh! card-game lovers play upstairs in the public sitting area.

MATT UMANOV GUITARS

Map p448   Musical Instruments

☎ 212-675-2157; 273 Bleecker St; ☺ 11am-7pm Mon-Sat, noon-6pm Sun; Ⓜ A, B, C, D, E, F, V to W 4th St, 1, 9 to Christopher St–Sheridan Sq

A friendly guitar house that goes easy on the blaring distortion (though they do sell the pedals), this shop stocks and services an excellent collection of our fretted friends (including some mouth-watering Gibson, Fender and Gretsch guitars, plus steel guitars and banjos).

MURRAY'S CHEESE Map p448   Gourmet Cheese

☎ 212-243-3289; www.murrayscheese.com; 254 Bleecker St btwn Sixth & Seventh Aves

Founded in 1914, this is hailed repeatedly as the best cheese shop in the city. Owner Rob Kaufelt is known for his talent of sniffing out devastatingly delicious varieties from around the world. You'll find (and be able to taste) all manner of *fromage,* be it stinky, sweet or nutty, from both European nations and small farms in Vermont and upstate New York.

OSCAR WILDE MEMORIAL BOOKSHOP

Map p448   Gay & Lesbian Bookstore

☎ 212-255-8097; 15 Christopher St; ☺ 11am-7pm; Ⓜ 1 to Christopher St–Sheridan Sq

The world's oldest bookshop geared to gay and lesbian literature (open since 1967) lives in a lovely red-brick town house and stocks both new and used books, a fine range of magazines, rainbow flags, bumper stickers and other gifts. It nearly closed in 2003, but was rescued from the brink of collapse by Washington DC–based LGBT bookstore.

REBEL REBEL Map p448   Music

☎ 212-989-0770; 319 Bleecker St; ☺ noon-8pm Sun-Wed, noon-9pm Thu-Sat; Ⓜ 1 to Christopher St–Sheridan Sq

This is a tight-fit, tiny music store with CDs and rare vinyl defying limits of space. Ask for what you don't see, as there is loads more in the back, out of view.

RICKY'S Map p448   Health & Beauty & More

☎ 212-924-3401; 466 Sixth Ave at 11th St; ☺ 9am-11pm Mon-Sat, to 10pm Sun; Ⓜ A, C, E to 14th St, L to Eighth Ave

Ricky's may technically be a drug store, but it's not like one you've ever seen before. Here, behind the glittery hot-pink toothpaste tube that serves as the Ricky's symbol, you'll find a bright space with blaring club music. There are endless shelves of goodies, including bright wigs, a wall of hair brushes, cosmetics, imported candies and gums, aisles of both foreign and 'only in salons' hair-care products, hosiery, kitschy tees and toys and, in the back, a selection of sex props. Just browsing is pure fun – and, luckily, there are 15 other locations throughout the city (visit www .rickys-nyc.com for details).

SHAKESPEARE & CO Map p449   Bookstore

☎ 212-529-1330; 716 Broadway; ☺ 10am-11pm Sun-Thu, to 11:30pm Fri & Sat; Ⓜ N, R, W to 8th St, 6 to Astor Pl

See p324. This branch, near NYU's Tisch film school, stocks many theater and film books and scripts. Other shops are in **Lower Manhattan** (p324), **Midtown** (Map pp452–3) and the **Upper East Side** (p349).

STRAND BOOK STORE

Map p449   Used Books

☎ 212-473-1452; 828 Broadway at 12th St; ☺ 9:30am-10:30pm Mon-Sat, 11am-10:30pm Sun; Ⓜ L, N, Q, R, W, 4, 5, 6 to 14th St–Union Sq

Book fiends (or even those who have just casually skimmed one or two) shouldn't miss New York's most-loved used bookstore. Operating since 1927, the Strand presents its towering aisles display (a bit confusingly) 'eight miles', or well over two million, books. Check out the staggering number of reviewers' copies in the basement, or sell off your own tomes before you get back on the plane, as the Strand buys or trades books at a side counter on weekdays. See also its **Lower Manhattan** (p324) location.

TOWER RECORDS Map p449   Music

☎ 212-505-1500; 692 Broadway; ☺ 9am-midnight; Ⓜ 6 to Bleecker St

Before Virgin, there was Tower – three expansive floors of CDs with collections of almost every music type you can think of, including world sounds, musicals, film soundtracks and, most notably, rock on the ground floor and jazz and blues on the 2nd; singles are in the basement. Keith Richards used to live above the place. As they say, coolness seeps downward.

VILLAGE CHESS SHOP LTD

Map p448   Games

☎ 212-475-9580; 230 Thompson St; ⏰ 11am-midnight; ⊕ A, B, C, D, E, F, V to W 4th St

A crusty crew of chess-perts frequent this hole-in-the-wall chess shop for $1 games in a no-frills sitting area. Come to play, buy a book to study up, or buy one of the chess sets (the best ones are thematic: Aztec, Crusades, Vegas etc). There's coffee on, too.

WEST VILLAGE & THE MEATPACKING DISTRICT

The winding, picturesque streets of the West Village are chock full of quaint boutiques with a more worn-in, comforting feel than those in some of the newest retail areas. Expect a mix of quirky gift and food shops, homespun clothing boutiques and, along Bleecker St, an impressive clutch of antiques dealers that quickly gives way to upscale designer-specific shops, including Marc Jacobs and Cynthia Rowley. The Meatpacking District, meanwhile, is all about that new, sleek, high-ceilinged industrial-chic vibe, with edgy designers reigning at expansive boutiques that are among the hippest style haunts in town. The two areas melt into each other at around W 12th St, all the way west.

CHOCOLATE BAR Map p448   Chocolate

☎ 212-367-7181; 48 Eighth Ave at 13th St; ⊕ A, C, E to 14th St, L to Eighth Ave

It's all chocolate all the time at this tiny storefront, where you can create custom gift boxes of fancy artistic chocolates (in flavors from chocolate mint tea to pistachio marzipan) by Brooklyn Willy Wonka Jacques Torres (p351), stock up on rich bricks of the stuff or simply hover over a steaming cup of some of the best hot cocoa ever.

DESTINATION Map p448   Jewelry & Accessories

☎ 212-727-2031; www.destinationny.net; 32-36 Little W 12th St at Washington St; ⊕ A, C, E to 14th St, L to Eighth Ave

The eclectic merchandise provides the spots of color in this vast, all-white space. You'll find hard-to-get jewelry from European designers including Les Bijoux de Sophie, Serge Thoraval and Corpus Christie. Then there are the military chic fashion pieces – funky leather boots with buckle by Gianni Barbato, sailor-inspired pants by John Rocha, cargo bags by Orca – all mixed in with whimsical vests and jackets, bags from Mik and Comptoirs de Trikitrixia shoes (with scented soles, no less!).

FLIGHT 001 Map p448   Travel Gear

☎ 212-691-1001; www.flight001.com; 96 Greenwich Ave; ⏰ 11am-8:30pm Mon-Fri, 11am-8pm Sat, noon-6pm Sun; ⊕ A, C, E to 14th St, L to Eighth Ave

Travel's fun, sure, but it's really only about getting fun travel gear. Flight 001 is definitely one of the most exciting places to get it. Check out the range of luggage and smaller bags by makers from Samsonite to Orla Kiely, brightly colored passport holders and leather luggage tags, wallets sized to hold international bills, travel guidebooks (Lonely Planet included), toiletry cases and a range of mini toothpastes, eye masks, jetlag pills and the like.

INTERMIX

Map p448   Women's Clothing & Handbags

☎ 212-929-7180; 365 Bleecker St at Charles St; ⏰ 11:30am-8:30pm Mon-Fri, to 7:30pm Sat; to 6pm Sun

This pleasant little pop-pink storefront is packed with stylish tops, frocks and jeans from favorite designers like Chloe, Givenchy, True Religion, Stella and Splendid. It's cool, cute and sexy all at once.

JAMES PERSE

Map p448   Men's & Women's Clothing

☎ 212-620-9991; 411 Bleecker St at W 11th St; ⊕ A, C, E to 14th St, L to Eighth Ave

The beloved Los Angeles designer, known for sexy, free-form, layering tees in soft, pliable cottons, opened an East Coast store here in 2005, much to the delight of his fans who love the combo of comfort and coolness.

JEFFREY NEW YORK

Map p448   Designer Clothing

☎ 212-206-1272; 449 W 14th St; ⏰ 10am-8pm; ⊕ A, C, E to 14th St, L to Eighth Ave

One of the pioneers in the recent Meatpacking District makeover, Jeffrey sells several high-end designer clothing lines – Versace, Pucci, Prada, Michael Kors and company – as well as accessories, shoes and a small selection of cosmetics. DJs spinning pop and indie add to the very hip vibe.

LEATHERMAN

Map p448 Leather Kink Apparel

☎ 212-243-5339; 111 Christopher St; noon-10pm, noon-8pm; 1 to Christopher St–Sheridan Sq

Famous for its racy window displays, this long-time sex shop stocks a lot of leather, clothes, toys, jockstraps and videos in its little frame. It's geared toward leather men, but friendly staff help anyone. Why not treat yourself with a custom-made pair of leather trousers? Or at least take a peek at the rowdier stuff downstairs.

MARC JACOBS Map p448 Designer Clothing

☎ 212-924-0026; www.marcjacobs.com; 405 Bleecker St, 403 Bleecker St & 385 Bleecker St; noon-8pm Mon-Sat, to 7pm Sun; A, C, E to 14th St, L to Eighth Ave

With three small shops located on just over a block, each with massive windows for easy peeking, Marc has made a Bleecker St hopscotch pattern of himself: his famous leather bags and other accessories are located at No 385, men's clothing is at No 403, and his Marc by Marc Jacobs women's line at No 405.

MCNULTY'S TEA & COFFEE CO, INC

Map p448 Coffee & Tea

☎ 212-242-5351; 109 Christopher St; 10am-9pm Mon-Sat, 1-7pm Sun; 1 to Christopher St–Sheridan Sq

Next to the LeatherMan's sex toys, sweet McNulty's, with worn wooden floorboards and fragrant sacks of coffee beans, flaunts a different era of Greenwich Village. It's been selling gourmet teas and coffees here since 1895.

MXYPLYZYK Map p448 Gifts & Housewares

☎ 800-243-9810; www.mxyplyzyk.com; 125 Greenwich Ave at W 13th St; 11am-7pm Mon-Sat, noon-5pm Sun; A, C, E to 14th St, L to Eighth Ave

There's nothing usual about this totally fun home shop – including its odd name. Even the cloth napkins, in vibrant, psychedelic patterns, are worth getting excited about – as are the calculators (huge, flat and in neon colors), games (like Doggie Dominoes), bath mats (topped with photos of real grass), and outdoor grill knives (with lights at the tip, for checking whether the meat is cooked to perfection at night-time).

NY ARTIFICIAL

Map p448 Non-Leather Handbags

☎ 212-255-0825; 233 W 10th St btwn Bleecker & Hudson Sts; 11am-7pm; 1 to Christopher St

Tucked down below street level is this thoroughly unique bag shop, filled with quirky, sexy and functional sacks from a variety of designers, all with one thing in common: no leather. It's a vegan shop for folks with a conscience *and* a sense of style.

SUSAN PARRISH ANTIQUES

Map pp446-7 Antiques

☎ 212-645-5020; 390 Bleecker St; noon-7pm Mon-Sat, or by appt; 1, 9 to Christopher St–Sheridan Sq

On a block of antiques dealers, Susan Parrish's impressive selection of Americana (a rarity in NYC) includes quilts and various one-of-a-kind peeling-paint furnishings.

ZACHARY'S SMILE

Map p448 Vintage Clothing & Shoes

☎ 212-924-0604; 9 Greenwich Ave btwn Christopher & W 10th Sts; 1 to Christopher St

See its **Noho** (p328) shop for details.

TOP TEN LOCAL DESIGNERS

- Urban streetwear brand Brooklyn Industries (p326) lives up to its name.
- The darling of the runway, Heatherette (p326) does clubwear by, for and about clubkids.
- Frocks by Anna Sui (p325) are filmy, sexy, and high-end hippie.
- Kudos goes to the eyewear design by Selima (at Bond 07, p328), who knows how to have fun with glasses frames.
- Bags by Jem Filippi (at Highway, p330) are for every reason and season, with seductive sophistication.
- The sexy wear by Holly Dunlap (at Hollywould, p330) is a looser take on Lily Pulitzer.
- Leather tooled with attitude, Jutta Neumann (p332) is the place for cuffs, bags and sandals.
- NYC's 'it' boy Marc Jacobs (left) is still going strong.
- At Mary Adams (p333), it's all about 'the Dress' – any one you can imagine.
- Fresh East Village style is the forte of A Cheng (p333), which the gals can't get enough of.

CHELSEA

Though it's known more for its nightlife and foodie scenes, Chelsea does have its fair share of retail outlets, from antiques dealers to great gift shops and some cool clubwear boutiques. And what are art galleries, really, but glitzed-up art stores? The stretch of Eighth Ave is where you'll find the most eclectic offerings, with some chain stores, including a Banana Republic, thrown in. And Ninth Ave is home to the beloved **Chelsea Market** (p143), a huge concourse with 25 minimarkets offering top-notch baked goods, produce, wines and other gourmet goods. Note that the **Chelsea Flea Market** has moved to **Hell's Kitchen** (see p141).

192 BOOKS Map pp446-7 — Books
☎ 212-255-4022; 192 Tenth Ave btwn 21st & 22nd Sts; ◷ 11am-7pm Tue-Sat, noon-6pm Sun & Mon; ◉ C, E to 23rd St
Located right in the gallery district is this small indie bookstore, with sections on literature, history, travel, art and criticism. A special treat is its offerings of rotating art exhibits, during which the owners organize special displays of books which relate, thematically, to the featured show or artist.

AUTHENTIQUES PAST & PRESENT
Map pp446-7 — Vintage Housewares
☎ 212-675-2179; 255 W 18th St btwn Seventh & Eighth Aves; ◷ noon-6pm Wed-Sat, 1-6pm Sun; ◉ 1 to 18th St
Tucked on a quiet side street is this thoroughly dramatic and kitsch-filled vintage shop. Find groovy and colorful lamps from the '50s and '60s, pastel vases and cache pots, quirky barware, nostalgic cartoon figurines and glasses and flashy costume jewelry.

BALDUCCI'S Map p448 — Gourmet Food
☎ 212-741-3700; 81 Eighth Ave at 14th St; ◷ 9am-10pm; ◉ A, C, E to 14th St, L to Eighth Ave
Housed in a landmark, turn-of-the-century bank building, this new Balducci's shop (which had reigned for years just south of here in the Village) came to Chelsea recently, bringing with it its highest quality gourmet produce, international cheeses, olives, bakery goods, fresh roasted coffee and packaged items from around the globe. Just walking through is a treat in itself, especially under the high ceiling of this majestic location.

BALENCIAGA Map pp446-7 — Designer Clothing
☎ 212-206-0872; 522 W 22nd St at Eleventh Ave; ◷ to 7pm Mon-Sat, noon-5pm Sun; ◉ C, E to 23rd St
Come and graze at this cool, grey, Zen-like space, the gallery-district's showcase, appropriately enough, for the artistic, post-apocalypse avant-garde styles of this French fashion house. Expect strange lines, goth patterns and pants for very skinny (and deep pocketed) gals.

BARNES & NOBLE Map pp446-7 Books & Music
☎ 212-727-1227; 675 Sixth Ave at 22nd St; ◷ 9am-10pm Mon-Sat, 10am-10pm Sun; ◉ 1 to 18th St
With more than 20 locations in NYC (visit www.bn.com for more), this heavy-hitter superstore is not well loved among the city's indie bookstores. But still, *somebody's* keeping them in business. Check out the massive space, with books displayed by endless topics including travel, cooking, classic literature, memoir, biography, children, art, dance, theater, health, gay and lesbian, and new fiction. One half is dedicated to CDs of all genres, and there's a Starbucks in the back. Frequent readings from new-book authors also happen onsite.

BARNEYS CO-OP
Map pp446-7 — Designer Clothing
☎ 212-593-7800; 236 W 18th St; ◷ 11am-8pm Mon-Fri, to 7pm Sat, noon-6pm Sun; ◉ 1 to 18th St
The edgier, younger, more affordable version of **Barneys** (p348) has (relatively) affordable deals at this expansive, loft-like space, which has a spare, very selective inventory of clothing for men and women, plus shoes and cosmetics. Its biannual warehouse sale (February and August) packs the place, both with endless merchandise and mobs of customers.

BED, BATH & BEYOND
Map p448 — Housewares
☎ 212-255-3550; 620 Sixth Ave at 18th St; ◷ 8am-9pm; ◉ F, V to 14th St
Though it's part of a national chain, this massive home-product emporium must be seen to be believed (if you've never entered one before). It's got every kitchen, bath, bed, office and outdoor home product you can imagine. There are fun shower curtains, high-threadcount sheets, plush towels, and pots and pans spread before you like a consumer

ocean, and rising high on floor-to-ceiling displays. Beware of the mobs on weekends.

BOOKS OF WONDER

Map pp446-7   Children's Bookstore

☎ 212-989-3270; 16 W 18th St; ⏰ 11am-7pm Mon-Sat, 11:45am-6pm Sun; ◉ F, V to 14th St

Chelsea-ites love this small, indie, funloving bookstore devoted to children's and young-adult titles. It's a great place to take the kids on a rainy day, especially when a kids' author is giving a reading, or a storyteller is on hand.

GIRAUDON NEW YORK
Map pp446-7   Shoes

☎ 212-633-0999; 152 Eighth Ave btwn 17th & 18th Sts; ⏰ 11:30am-7:30pm Mon-Wed & Fri-Sun, to 11pm Thu; ◉ A, C, E to 14th St, L to Eighth Ave

This small shoe boutique has been selling finely made leather foot sculptures since way before the 'hood was hip. The designs are classic with a touch of edginess, with both casual and glamorous options. It's a tiny space, but rarely crowded. The staffers are friendly and encouraging.

HOUSING WORKS THRIFT SHOP

Map pp446-7   Thrift Store

☎ 212-366-0820; 143 W 17th St; ⏰ 10am-6pm Mon-Sat, noon-5pm Sun; ◉ 1 to 18th St

This thrift shop, with its swank window displays, looks more boutique than thrift, and its selections of clothes, accessories, furniture and books are great value. All proceeds benefit the charity serving the city's HIV-positive and AIDS homeless communities.

LOEHMANN'S
Map pp446-7   Discount Dept Store

☎ 212-352-0856; 101 Seventh Ave at 16th St; ⏰ 9am-9pm Mon-Sat, 11am-7pm Sun; ◉ 1 to 18th St

A starting point for local hipsters looking for designer labels on the cheap (though some may not admit it), Loehmann's is a five-story department store that, it is said, inspired a wee-young Calvin Klein to make clothes good. The original store of the successful chain is in the Bronx; see www.loehmanns.com for other locations.

PURPLE PASSION
Map pp446-7   Kinky Wear

☎ 212-807-0486; www.purplepassion.com; 211 W 20th St btwn Sixth & Seventh Aves; ◉ 1 to 18th S

Behind this quiet, unassuming storefront lurks a kinky, sexy, intriguing selection of items for folks with (or seeking) adventurous sex lives. Paw through fetish fashions in leather, latex, PVC, chain mail and patent leather, plus corsets, vibrators, chastity belts, hoods, floggers and motorcycle boots, and a large selection of books, DVDs and magazines.

RAGS A-GO-GO
Map p448   Vintage Clothing

☎ 646-486-4011; 218 W 14th St btwn Seventh & Eighth Aves; ⏰ 11am-7pm Mon-Sat, noon-6pm Sun; ◉ A, C, E to 14th St, L to Eighth Ave

With a vibe that's more Austin, Texas, than Gotham, this fun vintage shop has racks of '50s dresses, worn-in denim, plenty of country and western shirts and skirts, and a great collection of cowboy boots.

UNION SQUARE & THE FLATIRON DISTRICT

Besides the wondrous **Union Square Greenmarket** (p146), which hits the park several times a week all year round, huge chain stores, most of which are clustered around Union Sq to the north or south, are the mainstay of this area. Fourteenth St, more to the west than to the east, is a shopping adventure all its own, with store upon store hawking discount electronics, cheap linens and a great range of shoes and hit-or-miss clothing, from both bargain indies and chains like Urban Outfitters and Diesel. The fascinating **Flower District** (p141) runs along Sixth Ave between 26th and 30th Sts, and the best time to stroll through is early in the morning, when the wholesale deliveries of exotic blooms are arriving.

ABC CARPET & HOME

Map p448   Home Furnishings

☎ 212-473-3000; 888 Broadway; ⏰ 10am-8pm Mon-Thu, to 6:30pm Fri & Sat, noon-6pm Sun; ◉ L, N, Q, R, W, 4, 5, 6 to 14th St–Union Sq

Home designers and decorators stroll here to brainstorm ideas. Set up like a museum on six floors, ABC is filled with all sorts of furnishings, small and large, including easy-to-pack knick-knacks, designer jewelry, global gifts and more bulky antique furnishings and carpets. Come Christmas season, the shop is a joy to behold, as the decorators here go all out with lights and other wondrous touches.

FILENE'S BASEMENT

Map p448   Discount Dept Store

☎ 212-348-0169; 4 Union Sq S; ☺ 9am-10pm Mon-Sat, 11am-8pm Sun; ⊕ L, N, Q, R, W, 4, 5, 6 to 14th St–Union Sq

This outpost of the Boston-based chain is not actually in a basement, but three flights up, with a tremendous view of Union Sq. The best stuff to see is inside, though, where you will find labels for up to 70 percent less than the price at regular retail outlets. Like similar discount department stores, it's got clothing, shoes, jewelry, accessories, cosmetics and some housewares (like bedding). Fashionistas willing to go on painstaking searches could unearth many treasures, including apparel from Dolce & Gabbana, Michael Kors, Versace and more.

OTTO TOOTSI PLOHOUND

Map pp446-7   Shoes

☎ 212-460-8650; 137 Fifth Ave; ☺ 11:30am-7:30pm Mon-Fri, 11am-8pm Sat, noon-7pm Sun; ⊕ R, W to 23rd St

See branch in **Soho** (p327).

PARAGON ATHLETIC GOODS

Map pp446-7   Sporting Goods

☎ 212-255-8036; 867 Broadway; ☺ 10am-8pm Mon-Sat, 11:30am-7pm Sun; ⊕ L, N, Q, R, W, 4, 5, 6 to 14th St–Union Sq

A maze-like, windowless behemoth, Paragon offers a comprehensive collection of sports merchandise featuring basketballs, tennis rackets, hiking gear, swim goggles, ski poles, baseball bats, all sorts of sneakers and apparel, you name it. It has better prices than the chains and an excellent selection of in-line skates. Watch for end-of-season sales, which can get devastatingly mobbed.

REVOLUTION BOOKS

Map pp446-7   Radical Bookstore

☎ 212-691-3345; 9 W 19th St; ☺ 10am-7pm Mon-Sat, noon-5pm Sun; ⊕ 1 to 18th St

The Rev has New York's biggest and most outstanding radical collection of books, leaflets and journals. You will find bookshelves devoted to Lenin, Mao and Marx, many books in *español*, as well as cute red-star earrings. The shop also hosts radical discussions.

VIRGIN MEGASTORE

Map p449   Music & Videos

☎ 212-598-4666; 52 E 14th St; ☺ 9-1am Mon-Sat, 10am-midnight Sun; ⊕ L, N, Q, R, W, 4, 5, 6 to 14th St–Union Sq

This always bustling Union Sq branch of the massive music store has serious collections of CDs and DVDs. There's another Virgin at **Times Square** (p346).

WHOLE FOODS

Map p448   Gourmet Supermarket

☎ 212-673-5388; 4 Union Sq S; ☺ 8am-10pm; ⊕ L, N, Q, R, W, 4, 5, 6 to 14th St–Union Sq

One of several locations of the healthy food chain that is sweeping the city (there's also one in the Shops at Columbus Circle, p345), this is an overwhelming spot to shop for a picnic. Find endless rows of gorgeous produce, both organic and conventional, plus a butcher, bakery, health and beauty section, and aisles packed with natural packaged goods.

MIDTOWN

Midtown sprawls, and so do its shopping options. The movie-famed Fifth Ave, from 42nd St to Central Park South, is bursting with flagship stores of international designers, along with high-style department stores like Bergdorf Goodman and Henri Bendel, and jewelers like Tiffany & Co and Cartier. Fans swarm here more feverishly than ever, as designers go all out to create display windows more spectacular each year. Herald Sq, meanwhile, where Broadway meets Sixth Ave and 34th St, is home to the world famous Macy's and many huge outposts of some of the most popular chain stores, including Gap (the city's largest), H&M, Daffy's and more. Though Hell's Kitchen, way west, isn't much known for its shopping opportunities, it's slowly becoming home to several enchanting little boutiques, offering both home products and apparel. Fine jewelry seekers should not miss the wonderful **Diamond District** (p151), a wild and wacky only-in-NYC experience, while true fashion mavens should hit the Fashion District, around Seventh Ave in the 30s and home to massive, wonderfully stocked fabric shops, with others dedicated to buttons, thread, zippers, sequins and other notions.

MIDTOWN EAST
BANANA REPUBLIC

Map pp452-3   Clothing
☎ 212-974-2350; www.bananarepublic.com; 626
Fifth Ave; ◯ 10am-8pm Mon-Sat, 11am-7pm Sun;
◉ B, D, F, V to 47th-50th Sts–Rockefeller Center
Good ol' Banana Republic sells its slick,
stylish staid wear in no less than a dozen
Manhattan stores; check the website for locations. This branch, at Rockefeller Center,
has one of the bigger selections.

BERGDORF GOODMAN

Map pp452-3   Dept Store
☎ 212-753-7300; 754 Fifth Ave; ◯ 10am-7pm
Mon-Wed & Fri, to 8pm Thu, noon-8pm Sun; ◉ N,
R, W to Fifth Ave, F to 57th St
This classy, legendary, high-end department
store is all about labels and fabulousness –
the serious, not pretentious kind. Women's
collections include Eli Tahari, Dolce & Gabbana, Yves Saint Laurent, Emilio Pucci, Stella
McCartney, Alice + Olivia and Moschino,
to name just a few. And then there are the
departments selling jewelry, fragrance,
shoes, handbags, housewares and mens-
wear – with apparel from Gucci, Etro and
Paul Smith – and the terrific organic Susan
Ciminelli Spa on the 9th floor.

CARTIER Map pp452-3   Jewelry
☎ 212-753-0111; www.cartier.com; 653 Fifth Ave;
◯ 10am-5:30pm Mon-Sat, noon-5pm Sun; ◉ E, V
to Fifth Ave–53rd St
Cartier's first-rate jewelry and watches are
as good (and as pricey) as it gets. Here, or
in the Upper East Side (Map pp452–3; ☎ 212-
472-6400; 828 Madison Ave btwn 69th and
70th Sts) boutique, you'll find the French
company's rings, diamond-encrusted
watches, glasses, cufflinks and leather
bags spread out (and locked up) in plush,
hushed almost religious retail spaces.

COMPLETE TRAVELLER

Map pp452-3   Used Travel Books
☎ 212-685-9007; 199 Madison Ave at E 35th St;
◯ 10am-6:30pm Mon-Fri, 10am-6pm Sat, noon-
5pm Sun; ◉ 6 to 33rd St
Stocking two rooms full with travel guides
and maps from the travelways of days
past, the Complete Traveller arranges its
stock by destination. It's the perfect browsing ground for travel bugs: old Baedeker

guides, the complete WPA series of US state
guides, maps and some newer titles, too.

THE CONRAN SHOP

Map pp452-3   Home Designs
☎ 212-755-9079; 407 E 59th St at First Ave;
◯ 11am-8pm Mon-Fri, 10am-7pm Sat, noon-6pm
Sun; ◉ 4, 5, 6 to 59th St
Find slick kitchenware and tableware, linens, furniture and home accessories at this
sleek emporium, nestled in a marvelous
space under the Queensboro Bridge, from
British design king Terence Conran. Browse
through streamlined sofas, Missoni china,
Ducati pens, retro Jacob Jensen alarm
clocks, Rob Brandt tumblers, Mandarina
Duck luggage, Lucite photo frames and
much more.

FAO SCHWARTZ Map pp452-3   Toys
☎ 212-644-9400; 767 Fifth Ave; ◯ noon-7pm
Mon-Wed, to 8pm Thu-Sat, 11am-6pm Sun; ◉ 4, 5,
6 to 59th St, N, R, W to Fifth Ave–59th St
The toystore giant, where Tom Hanks
played footsy piano in the movie *Big*, is

Hands up for FAO Schwartz toy store (above)

number one on the NYC wish list of most visiting kids. Why not indulge them? The magical (over-the-top consumerist) wonderland, with dolls up for 'adoption,' life-size stuffed animals, gas-powered kiddie convertibles, air hockey sets and much more, might even thrill you, too.

HENRI BENDEL Map pp452-3 Dept Store
☎ 212-247-1100; 712 Fifth Ave; ☼ 10am-7pm Fri-Wed, to 8pm Thu; ⊕ E, V to Fifth Ave–53rd St, N, R, W to Fifth Ave–59th St

As boutique-cozy as a big-name, high-class department store can be, Bendel's makes for an easy pop-in-and-out. Its European collections include curious, stylish clothing of established and up-and-coming designers, as well as cosmetics and accessories. Look out for the original Lalique windows.

JIMMY CHOO Map pp452-3 Shoes
☎ 212-593-0800; 645 51st St; ☼ 10am-6pm Mon-Sat, noon-5pm Sun; ⊕ E, V to Fifth Ave–53rd St, 6 to 51st St

This is where you'll find the elegant shoes for the stars. Or anybody who's willing to plunk down $700 for a pair of sexy sling-back sandals (and there are many such folks in fashion-obsessed NYC). Styles are classic, with clean lines and dainty heels. Oh, and just FYI: Madonna picked her bridal digs here.

LORD & TAYLOR Map pp452-3 Dept Store
☎ 212-391-3344; www.lordandtaylor.com; 424 Fifth Ave; ☼ 10am-8:30pm Mon-Fri, to 7pm Sat, 11am-7pm Sun; ⊕ 6 to 33rd St, 7 to Fifth Ave, S, 4, 5, 6, 7 to Grand Central–42nd St

Staying true to its traditional roots (Ralph Lauren, Donna Karen, Calvin Klein etc), this 10-floor classic tends to let shoppers browse pressure-free (even in the cosmetics department), and has a great selection of swimwear.

NBA STORE Map pp452-3 Sporting Goods
☎ 212-644-9400; 767 Fifth Ave; ☼ 10am-7pm Mon-Sat, 11am-6pm Sun; ⊕ E, V to Fifth Ave–53rd St

Amid posh department stores and designer outlets, why not hoops? Pick up team jerseys, basketballs and other (rather marked-up) memorabilia, or shoot some free baskets inside before slam-dunking your way to Takashimaya or Saks.

NEW YORK TRANSIT MUSEUM SHOP
Map pp452-3 Gifts
☎ 212-878-0106; Shuttle Passage at Grand Central Station; ☼ 8am-8pm Mon-Fri, 10am-6pm Sat & Sun; ⊕ S, 4, 5, 6, 7 to Grand Central–42nd St

This annex of the Brooklyn Museum (p178) sells some of the best NYC-centric gifts you can find. They all revolve around a ⊕ theme, of course, and include shirts, umbrellas printed with the transit map, watches with the letters of subway lines on their faces, Christmas ornaments, tote bags designed like big Metrocards, historic subway maps and jewelry made of now-defunct tokens.

NIKETOWN NEW YORK
Map pp452-3 Athletic Wear
☎ 212-891-6453; 6 E 57th St at Fifth Ave; ☼ 10am-8pm Mon-Sat, 11am-7pm Sun; ⊕ E, V to Fifth Ave–53rd St

Leave Gotham and enter Niketown, an athletic wonderland where you'll find the full line of Nike products, including sneakers, clothing and gizmos for every sport. You can even test-drive your footwear on the in-store treadmills, making shopping even more fun than it already is.

SAKS FIFTH AVE Map pp452-3 Dept Store
☎ 212-753-4000; 611 Fifth Ave at 50th St; ☼ 10am-7pm Mon-Wed, Fri & Sat, 10am-8pm Thu, noon-6pm Sun; ⊕ B, D, F, V to 47th-50th Sts–Rockefeller Center

Anyone heard of Saks? Here's where it started. This lovely flagship offers its updated collection of high-end women's and men's clothing, plus other lines including Gucci, Prada, Juicy Couture, Theory, Eli Tahari and Burberry. Its January sale is legendary. (Also note the good view of Rockefeller Center from its upper floors.)

SALVATORE FERRAGAMO
Map pp452-3 Clothing
☎ 212-759-3822; 655 Fifth Ave at 52nd St; ☼ 10am-7pm Mon-Sat, noon-6pm Sun; ⊕ E, V to Fifth Ave–53rd St

Opened in 2003, Salvatore's flagship store fills its two floors with the Italian designer's glamorous men's and women's collections, including gold-soled shoes, ostentatious women's outerwear and boho-chic men's turtlenecks.

TAKASHIMAYA
Map pp452-3   Dept Store

☎ 212-350-0100; 693 Fifth Ave; ☺ 10am-7pm Mon-Sat, noon-5pm Sun; ⊚ E, V to Fifth Ave–53rd St

The Japanese owners upped the ante on Fifth Ave's elegant, minimalist style with this stunning store, which sells high-end furniture, clothing and (less costly) homewares from all over the world; the top floor's beauty emporium has classy cosmetics and a serene day spa. Purchases come gorgeously packaged. Even if you're not buying, don't miss the ground-floor floral arrangements and the chance to sip some green tea at the relaxing **Tea Box café** in the basement.

TIFFANY & CO
Map pp452-3   Jewelry & Home

☎ 212-755-8000; 727 Fifth Ave; ☺ 10am-7pm Mon-Fri, 10am-6pm Sat, noon-5pm Sun; ⊚ F to 57th St

This famous jeweler, with the trademark clock-hoisting Atlas over the door, has won countless hearts with its fine diamond rings, watches, silver Elsa Peretti heart necklaces, and fine crystal vases and glassware. It's the high-end bridal registry spot of choice, and the store's little blue boxes have been known to provoke squealing from any teenage girl lucky enough to get a gift from here. The classy elevators are operated by old-school humans – and whatever you do, don't harass them with tired 'Where's the breakfast?' jokes. Okay?

URBAN CENTER BOOKS
Map pp452-3   Architecture Bookstore

☎ 212-935-3592; 457 Madison Ave; ☺ 10am-7pm Mon-Thu, 10am-6pm Fri, to 5:30pm Sat; ⊚ 6 to 51st St

This impressive shop of the **Municipal Arts Society** (p112), in the courtyard of the historic Villard Houses at Madison Ave, carries 7000 new (and some out-of-print) books on architecture, urban planning, design, landscape, history and all aspects of NYC.

Breakfast, lunch & dinner at Tiffany & Co (above)

MIDTOWN WEST
B&H PHOTO-VIDEO
Map pp452-3   Cameras & Electronics

☎ 212-502-6200 (photo), 212-502-6300 (video); www.bhphotovideo.com; 420 Ninth Ave; ☺ 9am-7pm Mon-Thu, to 1pm Fri, 10am-5pm Sun; ⊚ A, C, E to 34th St–Penn Station

Visiting B&H, the city's most popular camera shop, can be an experience in itself. Its shop is massive and crowded, and bustling with black-clad (and quite knowledgeable) Hasidic Jewish men who get bussed in from communities in distant Brooklyn neighborhoods. When you select an item, it gets whisked away from you and dropped into a bucket, which then moves up and across the ceiling to the purchase area (which requires a second queue). It's all very orderly and fascinating, and the selection of cameras, film, computers and many other electronics is outstanding.

GOTHAM BOOK MART
Map pp452-3   Bookstore

☎ 212-719-4448; 16 E 46th St btwn Fifth & Madison Aves; ☺ 9:30am-6:30pm Mon-Fri, 9:30am-6pm Sat; ⊚ B, D, F, V to 47th-50th Sts–Rockefeller Center

Overflowing with choice lit since 1920, the Gotham Book Mart is what bookstores are meant to be. It's historic too (despite having recently moved a block from its original location). Frances Stelof (who died in 1989) founded the James Joyce Society here in 1947, and snuck some of his books and other naughty ones like Henry Miller's *Tropic of Cancer* past US obscenity laws.

HAGSTROM MAP & TRAVEL CENTER
Map pp452-3   Travel

☎ 212-785-5343; 51 W 43rd St; ☺ 8:30am-6pm Mon-Fri; ⊚ B, D, F, V to 42nd St–Bryant Park

Hagstrom is a wonderful, Queens-based maker of maps and atlases, and this travel store, previously stationed in Lower Manhattan, packs a wide assortment of its products, plus various travel guides and accessories.

H&M
Map pp452-3   Budget Fashions

☎ 646-473-1164; www.hm.com; 1328 Broadway at 34th St; ☺ 10am-10pm Mon-Sat, 11am-8pm Sun; ⊚ B, D, F, N, Q, R, V, W to 34th St–Herald Sq

The flagship H&M, at Herald Sq, is one of six (and counting) of the Swedish knockoff discount clothing stores. Check the website for locations. This store and the branch at 51st St and Fifth Ave have large selections.

J LEVINE JEWISH BOOKS & JUDAICA

Map pp452-3 — Jewish Bookstore

☎ 212-695-6888; 5 W 30th St; ☯ 9am-6pm Mon-Wed, to 7pm Thu, 10am-5pm Sun; ⊕ B, D, F, N, Q, R, V, W to 34th St–Herald Sq

The Levine family has been peddling bibles, Jewish-themed books, menorahs, yarmulkes, kiddush cups and ritual wedding items, from huppahs to ketubahs, for five generations.

MACY'S Map pp452-3 — Dept Store

☎ 212-695-4400; 151 W 34th St at Broadway; ☯ 10am-8:30pm Mon-Sat, 11am-7pm Sun; ⊕ B, D, F, N, Q, R, V, W to 34th St–Herald Sq

The world's largest department store has a bit of everything – clothing, furnishings, kitchenware, sheets, cafés, hair salons. It's less high-end than many Midtown department stores but it's useful if you're looking for simpler things, like a good pair of jeans or a work shirt, not necessarily an only-from-Manhattan 21st-century outfit. Plus, riding the creaky old wooden elevators on the Broadway side is a must-do NYC experience.

RIZZOLI Map pp452-3 — Bookstore

☎ 212-759-2424; 31 W 57th St; ☯ 10am-7:30pm Mon-Fri, 10:30am-7pm Sat, 11am-7pm Sun; ⊕ F to 57th St

This handsome store of the Italian bookstore/publisher sells great art, architecture and design books (as well as general-interest titles). There's also a good collection of foreign newspapers and magazines onsite.

SHOPS AT COLUMBUS CIRCLE

Map pp452-3 — Mall

☎ 212-823-6300; 10 Columbus Circle; ⊕ A, B, C, D, 1, 9 to 59th St–Columbus Circle

If you want to hit a big handful of good chain stores all in one spot, head to the four retail floors of the Time Warner Center. You'll find 50 largely upscale shops (and several restaurants) including Coach, Williams-Sonoma, Hugo Boss, Thomas Pink, Sephora, J Crew, Borders Books & Music, Armani Exchange, Esprit and Benetton. If you're bent on a Central Park picnic, visit the absolutely enormous Whole Foods (p341; ☯ 8am-10pm) in the basement for ready-to-go salads and sandwiches.

TIMES SQUARE, THE THEATER DISTRICT & HELL'S KITCHEN

The former 'porn, pimp and drug zone' looks more like Disney World these days, and the bright, flashing, gigantic retail sprawls are only adding to that image. Take a walk up and down Broadway, just above 42nd St, and you'll find one huge store after another, including Sephora (for cosmetics), Toys 'R' Us (which will make your kids slobber), Skechers (for footwear) and the Hershey store (for chocolate and candy bar–themed gifts).

On W 48th St, you'll find several musical-instrument shops (such as Manny's and Sam Ash), where rock stars come to pick up a pedal or a new beast-slaying ax. Way west, in Hell's Kitchen, really lights up on weekends, when flea marketeers hit the area around the Annex/Hell's Kitchen Flea Market (Map p282; ☎ 212-243-5343; 39th St btwn Ninth and Tenth Aves; ☯ 7am-4pm Sat & Sun), formerly in Chelsea, to comb bins and tables packed with furnishings, accessories, CDs, clothing and plain weird stuff from past eras, courtesy of 170 wonderfully choosy vendors.

COLONY Map p282 — Music

☎ 212-265-2050; 1619 Broadway; ☯ 9:30am-midnight Mon-Sat, 10am-midnight Sun; ⊕ R, W to 49th St

Located in the Brill Building (the onetime home of Tin Pan Alley song crafters), the historic Colony once sold sheet music to the likes of Charlie Parker and Miles Davis. Its collection remains the city's largest. Plus there's a giant collection of karaoke CDs (show tunes, mariachi, AC/DC etc) and cases of memorabilia (Beatles gear, original Broadway posters, unused Frank and Sammy tickets etc), all for sale.

DELPHINIUM HOME

Map p282 — Gifts & Housewares

☎ 212-333-3213; 652 Ninth Ave btwn 45th & 46th Sts; ☯ 11am-8pm Mon-Sat, noon-7pm Sun; ⊕ C, E to 50th St

A breath of fresh air on a strip mostly clogged with (quite good) eating options, this blessed retail spot sings with color and quirkiness. It's well stocked with a range of unique gifts and home items, including kids' terry bath mitts with either five chicks or piggies for your fingers, fanciful shower curtains, retro ceramic cookie jars and a great range of well-designed desk and alarm clocks. The staff is friendly, too.

DRAMA BOOKSHOP

Map p282   Theater Bookstore

☎ 212-944-0595; www.dramabookshop.com; 250 W 40th St; ⏰ 10am-8pm Mon-Sat, noon-6pm Sun; ◉ A, C, E to 42nd St–Port Authority Bus Terminal

Treasures in print for Broadway fans are shelved at this expansive bookshop, which has taken its theater (plays and musicals) seriously since 1917. Staffers are good at recommending worthy selections. Check out the website for regular events, such as talks with playwrights.

MANNY'S MUSIC

Map p282   Musical Instruments

☎ 212-819-0576; 156 W 48th St; ⏰ 10am-7pm Mon-Sat, noon-6pm Sun; ◉ R, W to 49th St

Guitar junkies and gear-heads should pay tribute to W 48th St's most famous music shop, Manny's. It's where Jimi Hendrix bought new guitars, the Stones bought the distortion pedal they used on 'Satisfaction,' and, before all that, where jazz greats like Benny Goodman picked up a reed or two. Wall photos tell the tale, and Manny's still stocks all the goods (guitars, basses, drums, keyboards) for you to make your band. **Sam Ash** (☎ 212-719-2299; 160 W 48th St; ⏰ 10am-8pm Mon-Fri, to 7pm Sat, noon-6pm Sun) is another top-notch music outfitter on the block.

MUD, SWEAT & TEARS

Map p282   Pottery & Ceramics

☎ 212-974-9121; 654 Tenth Ave at 46th St; ◉ C, E to 50th St

Also a popular pottery school, this small storefront sells the top work of students and local pros, with a great selection of both functional and display-worthy items from both glazed red clay and fine white ceramic. It's a down-to-earth, pleasantly intimate spot to pick up a gift (just get it wrapped well for the trip).

TOYS 'R' US Map p282   Toys

☎ 800-869-7787; 1514 Broadway; ⏰ 10am-10pm Mon-Sat, 11am-8pm Sun; ◉ N, Q, R, S, W, 1, 2, 3, 7, 9 to Times Sq–42nd St

Sure you have one of these at home, but this super-size Toys 'R' Us is its greatest bastion, with three thematic floors including a huge

video-game area downstairs, an alley of stuffed animals and an indoor Ferris wheel. Just avoid it like the plague before Christmas, when all hell tends to break loose here.

VIRGIN MEGASTORE

Map p282   Music & Video

☎ 212-921-1020; 1540 Broadway; ⏰ 9-1am Sun-Thu, to 2am Fri & Sat; ◉ N, Q, R, S, W, 1, 2, 3, 7, 9 to Times Sq–42nd St

This claims to be the world's largest music store, and also hosts frequent big-name signings. See the location at **Union Square** (p341).

WEAR ME OUT Map p282   Gay Clubwear

☎ 212-333-3047; 358 W 47th St btwn Eighth & Ninth Aves; ⏰ 11:30am-8pm; ◉ C, E to 50th St

A fun little boutique for 'Hellsea boys' who need the perfect outfit to wear to **Roxy** (p299) this weekend, this is a friendly place to pick up a pec-promoting tight tee, a pair of sexy Energie jeans, provocative undies and various types of jewelry. The flirtatious staff is full of encouragement, too.

UPPER WEST SIDE

Not a record-breaking shopping area, the residential Upper West Side has, nevertheless, stacks of shops catering to its well-to-do, sporty (OK, yuppie) residents along its three main avenues (Broadway, Amsterdam and Columbus). Best for the shop-and-walk is by far Columbus Ave, particularly between about W 66th St and W 82nd St, where you can find high-end boutiques and shops. You'll find endless chain stores including Barnes & Noble, Banana Republic, Club Monaco and Gap on the stretch of Broadway between about 80th and 90th Sts. It's worth noting that staffers on the UWS tend to be a bit less pushy than on the other side of Central Park.

FAIRWAY Map pp454-5   Gourmet Food

☎ 212-595-1888; 2127 Broadway at 75th St; ⏰ 6-1am; ◉ 1, 2, 3 to 72nd St

Like a museum of good eats, this landmark grocery spills its lovely mounds of produce into its sidewalk bins, seducing you inside to its aisles of international goodies, fine cooking oils, nuts, cheeses, prepared foods and, upstairs, an organic market and chi-chi café. Even more impressive, though, is the bigger, more gimmicky **Harlem** (p349) branch.

GRACIOUS HOME

Map pp454-5 — Housewares

☎ 212-231-7800; 1992 Broadway at W 67th St; ⌚ 9am-9pm Mon-Sat, 10am-7pm Sun; ⊕ 1 to 66th St–Lincoln Ctr

What started as a Cuban-owned hardware shop has grown exponentially into a multi-storied home department store, with quality pickings for every room in your house. There's an especially extensive selection of cookware and glassware, plus high-quality linens, kitchen utensils, lamps and lighting, and fun accessories like classy scented candles. There are also three locations on the Upper East Side; see www.gracious home.com.

HARRY'S SHOES Map pp454-5 — Shoes

☎ 212-874-2035; 2299 Broadway at 83rd St; ⌚ 10am-6:45pm Tue. Wed, Fri & Sat, to 7:45pm Mon & Thu, 11am-6pm Sun; ⊕ 1 to 86th St

Harry's is a classic, staffed by classy older men who actually measure your foot in one of those old-school metal contraptions and then wait on you patiently, making sure your toe's not pressing into the top of the shoe you're trying on. You'll find mostly sturdy, quality, comfort-trumps-style labels here, such as Merrel, Dansko, Birkenstock, Ecco, New Balance and Mephisto. But fashionable types will find fun stuff, too, mainly from Ugg, Moon Boots and the like. The children's section is extensive.

MURDER INK/IVY'S BOOKS

Map pp454-5 — Mystery Bookstore

☎ 212-362-8905; 2486 Broadway at 93rd St; ⌚ 10am-7:30pm Mon-Sat, 11am-6pm Sun; ⊕ 1, 2, 3 to 96th St

The city's first shop devoted to crime and mystery fiction has been stocking everything of the genre, plus stacks of out-of-print titles, since 1972. Its space-partner, Ivy's Books, carries a broad selection of new and used books, with tasteful journals, greeting cards and kids' books in the mix. Gus the dog works here.

PENNY WHISTLE TOYS

Map pp454-5 — Toys

☎ 212-873-9090; 448 Columbus Ave btwn 81st & 82nd Sts; ⌚ 9am-6pm Mon-Fri, 10am-6pm Sat, 11am-5pm Sun; ⊕ B, C to 81st St

A small, indie, old-fashioned toy store, this bright shop is full of quality fun stuff,

including display-worthy kites, Brio train sets, Czech marionettes, puzzles, costumes and collectible dolls.

PLAZA TOO Map pp454-5 — Shoes

☎ 212-362-6871; 2231 Broadway at 79th St; ⊕ 1 to 79th St

If Harry's Shoes (left) is a bit too practical, find your high-fashion footwear at this brand-new outpost of the suburban favorite – the first and only NYC location. It's got fancy footwork from the likes of Marc Jacobs, Chloe, Adrienne, Cynthia Rowley, Sigerson Morrison and many more. The prices are frequently reduced by nearly half at fabulous sales events.

TOWN SHOP Map pp454-5 — Bras & Lingerie

☎ 212-724-8160; 2273 Broadway at 82nd St; ⊕ 1 to 79th St

Your bra doesn't fit! No, really – statistics say that 80% of women are wearing an ill-fitting bra, and here at the more-than-century-old Town Shop, the attentive saleswomen want to help you. They'll hustle you into a private fitting room and bring you a selection of pretty, quality bras, and not let you leave until they find you one that fits properly. You'll also find great lingerie and sleepwear from Cosabella, Wolford and Hanro.

ZABAR'S Map pp454-5 — Gourmet Food & Kitchenware

☎ 212-787-2000; 2245 Broadway; ⌚ 8:30am-7:30pm Mon-Fri, 8am-8pm Sat, 9am-6pm Sun; ⊕ 1 to 79th St

A New York classic gourmet emporium, Zabar's is famous not only for its food – especially the amazing array of cheeses, olives, jams, coffee, caviar and smoked fish – but also its large 2nd-floor kitchenware department. A $1 Zabar's mug, with its distinctive orange lettering that reflects a kind of uptown Dodge City font, is a great insiders-type gift from New York.

UPPER EAST SIDE

The glamor of Midtown's designer shops and department stores slides its way along Madison Ave into the Upper East Side, a posh neighborhood filled with residents who shop at Gucci, Prada and Cartier as regularly as most folks hit the Gap. The main shopping is on, and just off, Madison Ave, from Midtown up to about E 75th St.

You'll also find little nuggets of trendsetting boutiques, mainly on Lexington and Third Aves in the 70s and 80s, as well as frequent gourmet food shops. For truly unique gifts, hit the museum shops, including those at the **Met** (p162), the **Whitney** (p164), the **Jewish Museum** (p161) and the **Neue Galerie** (p163).

ARGOSY Map pp452-3   Used Books

☎ 212-753-4455; www.argosybooks.com; 116 E 59th St; ⊙ 10am-6pm Mon-Fri, to 5pm Sat; ⊕ 4, 5, 6 to 59th St, N, R, W to Lexington Ave–59th St

Since 1925, this landmark used-book store has stocked fine antiquarian items such as leatherbound books, old maps, art monographs and other classics picked up from high-class estate sales and closed antique shops. Books range from a Matisse-illustrated 1935 copy of James Joyce's *Ulysses*, signed by the artist, for $4000, to less expensive clearance items.

BARNEYS Map pp454-5   Dept Store

☎ 212-826-8900; 660 Madison Ave; ⊙ 10am-8pm Mon-Fri, to 7pm Sat, 11am-6pm Sun; ⊕ N, R, W to Fifth Ave–59th St

Perhaps offering Manhattan's best designer clothing selection, Barneys justifies its occasionally nose-raised staff with its spot-on choice collections of the '00s' best designer duds (Marc Jacobs, Prada, Helmut Lang, Paul Smith and Miu Miu shoes). For less expensive deals (geared to a younger market), check out Barneys Co-op on the 7th and 8th

Barneys (above), the holy of holies for hipsters

floors, or on the Upper West Side, in Soho or in **Chelsea** (p339).

BLOOMINGDALE'S

Map pp454-5   Dept Store

☎ 212-705-2000; 1000 Third Ave at 59th St; ⊙ 10am-8:30pm Mon-Thu, 9am-10pm Fri & Sat, 11am-7pm Sun; ⊕ 4, 5, 6 to 59th St, N, R, W to Lexington Ave–59th St

Massive 'Bloomies' is something like the Metropolitan Museum of Art to the shopping world: historic, sprawling, overwhelming and packed with bodies, but you'd be sorry to miss it. Navigate the mass (and dodge the dozens of automaton types trying to spray you with the latest scent) to browse and buy clothing and shoes from a who's who of designers, including an increasing number of 'new-blood' collections.

CANTALOUP

Map pp454-5   Designer Clothing

☎ 212-288-3569; 1359 Second Ave at 72nd St; ⊙ 10am-9pm Mon-Thu, to 7pm Fri, 11am-7pm Sun; ⊕ 6 to 68th St–Hunter College

Jeans from True Religion and Paper Denim Cloth here, on the uptight Upper East Side? Sure, why not? There are plenty of hipsters here, really, and most of them find their way into this brightly colored, pop-vibe emporium at one time or another, which also stocks sexy dresses, filmy blouses and fab accessories. Nearby is **Cantaloup 2** (☎ 212-249-3566; 1036 Lexington Ave at 74th St).

CAPEZIO DANCE THEATER SHOP

Map pp454-5   Dancewear

☎ 212-348-7210; 1651 Third Ave at 93rd St; ⊕ 6 to 96th St

One of many locations around the city (visit www.capeziodance.com for more), this large favorite of the dance and theater community is chock full of beautifully designed leotards, unitards, dresses, skirts, tights, legwarmers and the like, plus dance shoes for ballet, jazz and musical theater.

NELLIE M BOUTIQUE

Map pp454-5   Women's Clothing

☎ 212-996-4410; 1309 Lexington Ave; ⊙ 10am-8pm Mon-Fri, 11am-8pm Sat, to 7pm Sun; ⊕ 4, 5, 6 to 86th St

Located off Madison, this inviting boutique carries upscale-but-hip clothing from smaller designer labels (such as Rebecca Taylor) than are found at most Upper East Side (UES) giants. There's also plenty of evening wear and accessories, as well as more sporty finds.

RALPH LAUREN

Map pp454–5   Designer Clothing

☎ 212-606-2100; 867 Madison Ave; ⏰ 10am-6pm Mon-Wed & Fri, to 7pm Thu, noon-5pm Sun; ◉ 6 to 68th St–Hunter College

Housed in a beautiful 1890s mansion (one of Manhattan's few remaining residences of that era), Ralph's flagship store rewards the long stroll up Madison Ave, even if you've already stocked up on Polo gear elsewhere. There's a big selection here, with an emphasis on more formal wear (particularly for men).

SHAKESPEARE & CO

Map pp454–5   Bookstore

☎ 212-570-0201; 939 Lexington Ave; ⏰ 9am-8:30pm Mon-Fri, 10am-7pm Sat, 10am-5pm Sun; ◉ 6 to 68th St–Hunter College

See **Lower Manhattan** (p324), **Greenwich Village** (p336) and **Midtown** (Map pp452–3).

SHERRY-LEHMAN Map pp454–5   Wine

☎ 212-838-7500; 679 Madison Ave; ⏰ 9am-7pm Mon-Sat; ◉ 4, 5, 6 to 59th St

Reigning on Madison Ave since 1934, this family-run spot's founder made a name for himself during the Prohibition. Over the years the place has introduced such high-end spirits as Dom Perignon and Chivas Regal to the US market, and it now offers more than 7000 items from its sprawling 65,000-sq-ft space. Expect helpful and knowledgeable staffers, and more selection than you can fathom.

TATIANA'S

Map pp454–5   Consignment Clothing

☎ 212-755-7744; 767 Lexington Ave; ⏰ 11am-7pm Mon-Fri, to 6pm Sat; ◉ N, R, W to Lexington Ave–59th St, 4, 5, 6 to 59th St

No church-basement tag sale, this consignment shop, just a couple of steps from Bloomingdale's, is one of the best places to find gently used duds like women's designer-label evening wear, suits, skirts, tops and shoes. Often you can find last year's luxury pieces, practically new, at much lower prices. Thank the wealthy neighbors.

HARLEM

Harlem's main shopping strip has always been 125th St; it's just the shopkeepers who have changed. The recent and ongoing 'Harlem renaissance' is evident in new malls and big-time chains popping up (such as Nine West and H&M). NBA great Magic Johnson has opened an eponymous cinema and a Starbucks. But, while small, old-time businesses are often forced to fight for their lives, there has been a new wave of indie boutiques, where hip young owners focus on the legend of Harlem and their own talent for fashion. At the other end of that spectrum is the Harlem USA! mall (where you'll find HMV, Magic Theatres and Old Navy), at 125th St and Frederick Douglass Blvd.

BOBBY'S HAPPY HOUSE

Map pp458–9   Gospel & Blues Music

☎ 212-663-5240; 2335 Frederick Douglass Blvd; ⏰ 11am-8pm; ◉ A, B, C, D to 125th St

This fantastic shop has a small but cherished collection of gospel ('oooollllddd-time gospel'), R&B and blues videos, CDs and cassettes. When it opened (on 125th St) in 1946 it was the first African American business on the street. Original owner Bobby Robinson, who has produced blues artists like Elmore James, still runs the place (he's usually there Sunday afternoons, and is happy to have a chat). These days, you're likely to hear the shop before you see it, as the Happy House sets up blaring gospel videos in its can't-miss window showcase to attract passersby.

FAIRWAY Map pp458–9   Gourmet Food

☎ 212-234-3883; 2328 Twelfth Ave at 132nd St; ⏰ 8am-11pm; ◉ 1 to 137th St–City College

Folks like to drive to this outpost of the one on the **Upper West Side** (p346), not only because it's one of the rare retail spots in Manhattan that has a parking lot (though it's small), but because it's next to impossible to leave here with a load small enough to carry onto the subway. This Fairway has all of what the UWS shop has and more, including a very popular Cold Room – a 10,000-sq-ft space where you can wander around (in provided thermal jackets) to choose among the crème de la crème of meats, cheeses, butter, eggs, juices, fresh pastas, sauces and more.

HARLEMADE

Map pp458-9 Wearable Harlem Art

☎ 212-987-2500; 174 Lenox Ave btwn 118th & 119th Sts; ⏱ 11:30am-7pm Mon-Fri, 11am-7pm Sat, noon-6pm Sun; ◉ 2, 3 to 116th St

Decked out with beautiful vintage tables and sporting a mellow vibe, this boutique is filled with designer-made clothing and memorabilia that celebrates the 'hood. Check out the tees and tote bags silk-screened with the profile of a woman with a 'fro, plus earth-tone messenger bags, caps, mugs and aprons that say 'Harlem'.

JUMEL TERRACE BOOKS

Map pp458-9 Rare Books

☎ 646-472-5938; www.jumelterracebooks.com; 426 W 160th St; ⏱ by appt only; ◉ 163rd St-Amsterdam Ave

Housed in an historic private home is this new shop specializing in tomes on Africana, Harlem history and African American literature. You've got to call to set up an appointment, but if you're fascinated by rare books, and rare opportunities to shop at a beautiful home, then it's worth it.

LIBERATION BOOKSTORE

Map pp458-9 Bookstore

☎ 212-281-4615; 421 Lenox Ave at 131st St; ⏱ 3-7pm Tue-Fri, noon-4pm Sat; ◉ 2, 3 to 125th St

This small bookstore has the city's best selection of African and African American

Stick to taxis when wearing your Jimmy Choo (p343)

history, literature and art books. Support it, as it has been threatened with closure due to financial difficulties in recent years, often causing long-time fans to rally around the place. You'll get a nice sense of community spirit here, mixed in with the treats on the shelves.

MALCOLM SHABAZZ HARLEM

MARKET Map pp458-9 Arts & Crafts

☎ 212-987-8131; 52 W 116th St; ⏱ 10am-5pm; ◉ 2, 3 to 116th St

Enjoy some alfresco shopping at this popular marketplace, where you'll find items including African crafts, essential oils, incense, traditional clothing, CDs and bootleg videos. See also p168.

PIECES OF HARLEM

Map pp458-9 Designer Clothing

☎ 212-234-1725; 228 W 135th St; ⏱ noon-6pm Sun & Mon, 11am-7pm Tue-Thu, to 8pm Fri & Sat; ◉ 2, 3 to 135th St

Owned by the husband-and-wife duo who opened the first Pieces in Brooklyn, this new outpost has the same eclectic, hand-picked collection of clothing and accessories from local and national designers. Find funky and sexy halter dresses, flouncy blouses and Pucci-like tunics, plus a range of hip accessories and unique outerwear.

SCARF LADY Map pp458-9 Scarves & Hats

☎ 212-862-7369; 408 Lenox Ave; ⏱ 11:30am-7pm Tue-Sat; ◉ 2, 3 to 125th St

Mystery revealed: Paulette Gay *is* the Scarf Lady. Her small boutique is crammed with hundreds of her handmade, colorful scarves, hats and other accessories.

BROOKLYN

Across the East River, Brooklyn has a well-established shopping scene, notably in three neighborhoods. Williamsburg's youthful hipster district centers along Bedford Ave, with side-by-side shops and cafés. Several vintage shops are here, including a thrift store, as well as more upscale boutiques.

Atlantic Ave, running east–west near Brooklyn Heights, has long been heralded as a hub for antique and furnishings shops, and heading south from Atlantic, both Court and (especially) Smith Sts are lined with local designers' boutiques. Pick up shopping guides to Atlantic and Bococa for neighborhood shops. Residential Park Slope, just west of Prospect Park, has a good selection of laidback clothing shops and bookstores along Fifth Ave (Lower East Side–hip) and Seventh Ave (slightly more Upper West Side).

BEACON'S CLOSET Map p463 Vintage Clothing
☎ 718-486-0816; 88 N 11th St, Williamsburg; ☻ noon-9pm Mon-Fri, 11am-8pm Sat & Sun; ⊙ L to Bedford Ave

Twenty-something groovers find this giant Williamsburg warehouse of vintage clothing part goldmine, part grit. Lots of coats, polyester tops and '70s-era tees are handily displayed by color, but the sheer mass can take time to conquer. From the subway station, walk along Bedford Ave from 7th St to 11th St, turn left (toward Manhattan), and go two blocks; it's between Berry and White Sts. The smaller, more manageable branch on Fifth Ave (Map p464; ☎ 718-230-1630; 220 Fifth Ave, Brooklyn) stocks the cream of the crop only.

BREUKELEN/BARK
Map p462   Gifts & Accessories
☎ 718-246-0024, 718-625-8997; 369 Atlantic Ave, Boerum Hill; ☻ noon-7pm Tue-Sat, to 6pm Sun; ⊙ A, C, G to Hoyt Schermerhorn St

These two modern accessories shops – selling swank products for the home and body, many not found elsewhere in town – share a space on Atlantic Ave. Check out Bark's cameras that (willfully) distort images with color lenses and softened corners.

BROOKLYN INDUSTRIES
Map p463   Streetwear
☎ 212-486-6464; www.brooklynindustries .com; 162 Bedford Ave at N 8th St, Williamsburg; ☻ 11am-9pm Mon-Sat, noon-8:30pm Sun; ⊙ L to Bedford Ave

See the location in Soho (p326) for a full description of the mini-empire that keeps on growing. There's also a factory store in South Williamsburg (Map p463; ☎ 718-218-9166; 184 Broadway at Driggs Ave) and other branches in Park Slope (Map p464; ☎ 718-789-2764; 206 Fifth Ave at Union St) and Boerum Hill (Map p465; ☎ 718-596-3986; 100 Smith St at Atlantic Ave).

FLIRT Map p465   Women's Clothing
☎ 718-858-7931; 252 Smith St, Cobble Hill; ⊙ F, G to Bergen St

The name says it all at this girlishly sexy boutique, where a trio of stylish owners (two of whom are sisters) comes up with funky but feminine creations such as adjustable-snap wrap skirts, custom-made skirts (pick your cut and fabric) and tiny tops in soft knits. It has been stationed here in Cobble Hill for several years, with a newer outpost in Park Slope (Map p464; ☎ 718-783-0364; 93 Fifth Ave).

JACQUES TORRES CHOCOLATE
Map p462   Gourmet Chocolate
☎ 718-875-9772; www.mrchocolate.com; 66 Water St, Dumbo; ☻ 9am-7pm Mon-Sat; ⊙ A, C to High St, F to York St

Serious chocolatier JT runs this small European-style store with three-table café, filled with the most velvety and innovative chocolates ever crafted. Take a few to the nearby Empire Fulton Ferry State Park for a snack and a view between the Brooklyn and Manhattan Bridges. The shop also does a brisk Internet business, and makes its delicacies available at Chocolate Bar (p337) in the West Village.

SODAFINE Map pp460-1   Vintage Clothing
☎ 718-230-3060; 246 Dekalb Ave, Fort Greene; ⊙ M, N, Q, R, W to Dekalb Ave

With a quirky collection of one-of-a-kind pieces from about 30 area designers (plus a selection of vintage wear), Sodafine has the vibe of an artists' collective. Its airy, 2nd-floor space does have a gallery feel, with a constantly rotating, always unexpected selection, from grandma-chic crocheted sweaters to billowy slip dresses and a range of bags you'll want to carry.

UMKARNA
Map p464   Asian Clothing & Local Jewelry
☎ 718-398-5888; 69 Fifth Ave, Park Slope; ⊙ 2, 3 to Bergen St

Like a mini-Eastern bazaar right in Brooklyn, Umkarna is stocked with the owner's handmade dresses, tees, children's outfits and luxurious bedding, all created from materials she's purchased in places including India, Turkey and Uzbekistan. Her husband, who hails from Kashmir, has been a big inspiration, as has his grandmother, who is the store's namesake. Local jewelry, such as the 24-karat-gold creations from Nora Kogan, really makes the place sparkle.

OUTER BOROUGHS

Once you leave the comfort zones of Manhattan and Brooklyn, the best way to approach shopping is by area, looking at, say, a stretch of several blocks on one street as a mini bazaar, with a collection of various shops that you can wander into aimlessly, either laying down cash or simply taking in the other-worldly vibes. In **Jackson Heights, Queens**, the stretch of 74th St that begins at the Roosevelt Ave subway station is a good example. The Little India strip is chock full of shops selling saris, like **India Sari Palace** (☎ 718-426-2700; 37-07 74th St at 37th Ave); 24-karat-gold jewelry, at spots like **Mita Jewelers** (☎ 718-507-1555; 37-30 74th St at 37th Rd); Bollywood DVDs and CDs at **Today's Music** (☎ 718-429-7179; 73-09 37th Rd at 73rd St); and all manner of Indian groceries, from fresh curry leaves to jars of mango pickle. Roaming the food aisles of **Patel Brothers** (☎ 718-898-3445; 37-27 74th St at 37th Ave) is a feast for all the senses. Plus, the neighborhood's beauty salons will thread your eyebrows rather than wax them; hanging out in one of these spots is a great way to spend some time around the relaxed locals.

On and around Main St in **Flushing, Queens** (p186), you'll find a wonderfully hectic array of items both Chinese and Korean. The **Flushing Mall** (Map p467; ☎ 718-762-9000; 133-31 39th Ave at Prince St) is an indoor collection of East Asian items, including electronics, clothing, Chinese pop

star music and memorabilia, and a huge wedding photography studio (a joy to behold). Browse the area outside, stopping into spots like **Magic Castle** (Map p467; 136-82 39th Ave), packed with Korean pop culture from stickers and CDs to hair clips and jewelry, and **Shun An Tong Health Herbal Co** (Map p467; 135-24 Roosevelt Ave, off Main St), one of the oldest Chinese herbalists in the 'hood.

Arthur Ave in **Belmont, the Bronx** (p201), is the place to stock up on Italian delicacies, many of which – from olive oils to spices – could easily be packed for the trip back home. Find a series of vendors right inside the **Arthur Avenue Market** (☎ 718-295-5033; 2344 Arthur Ave), including purveyors of fresh-roasted coffee, olives, bakery items, imported canned goods, fruit, fresh pasta and cheeses.

In **Staten Island** (p203), Ganas – a rare NYC commune of about 90 people – runs one of NYC's best-kept shopping secrets: a collection of four vintage shops called Everything Goes. Run as cooperatives, each location specializes in a different sort of item: there's **Everything Goes Clothing** (☎ 718-273-7139; 140 Bay St; 🕒 10:30am-6:30pm Tue-Sat); **Everything Goes Book Café** (☎ 718-447-8256; 208 Bay St; 🕒 11am-7pm Tue-Sat, noon-5pm Sun); **Everything Goes Furniture** (☎ 718-273-0568; 17 Brook St; 🕒 10:30am-6:30pm Tue-Sat); and **Everything Goes Gallery** (☎ 718-273-0568; 123 Victory Blvd; 🕒 10:30am-6:30pm Tue-Sat), which features eclectic artwork, antiques and collectibles. For directions to each store, which are all within walking distance from the Staten Island Ferry terminal, visit www.well.com/user/ganas/etgstores/.

Sleeping

Sleeping

This will cost you. At $292 per night on average in 2005, New York City hotel rates are about $200 more expensive than the national average. (Even private rooms in hostels generally break $100.) And that's not keeping anyone away, of course.

Meanwhile, the New York–hotel turf wars are heating up, as various hoods try to set themselves apart as the Big Apple base of choice (with new boutiques and groovy hotels in the Meatpacking District and the Lower East Side). Long the number-one base for first-time tourists and theaterbound (and business) travelers, Midtown continues its probe into the chic boutique ground that celeb hotelier Ian Schrager fostered with the still-fresh Morgans (p369) in 1985. The old stalwart Plaza Hotel closed, but a nearby fussy Best Western has been turned into the shockingly modern Dream (p366), and the budget boutique QT Hotel (p367) – with entry pool and cube-like rooms – opened within a few footsteps of Times Sq's 'Naked Cowboy.'

LOWER MANHATTAN

Set up to serve the gods of Wall Street and the Financial District, hotels in Lower Manhattan see streams of weekday business travelers and relatively few travelers – and things can get quiet on weekends. Yet, there are tempting weekend deals at some of the hotels, and big-time tourist attractions are close at hand, such as the Statue of Liberty, the somewhat tacky South Street Seaport, the World Trade Center site, and the canyons of art-deco skyscrapers built atop crooked lanes dating from the days of New Amsterdam.

BATTERY PARK CITY RITZ-CARLTON

Map pp444-5   Deluxe International $$
☎ 212-344-0800; www.ritz-carlton.com; 2 West St at Battery Pl; d/ste from $260/$800; ⊕ 4, 5 to Bowling Green; ⊠ ⊑
Lower Manhattan's nicest hotel – c'mon, it's the Ritz – overlooks the southern tip of Manhattan, many of its 298 luxurious rooms come with telescopes carefully pointed toward Lady Liberty. The bottom 14 floors of the modern 38-floor tower are home to the hotel. All rooms come with marble baths –

and unique 'bath butler' services, including one for kids with milk and cookies – and Bulgari soaps and lotions. Rooms are roomy and not too posh for comfort. The balcony bar Rise (p262) serves light meals and has stunning views of the harbor. Suites sprawl – the Liberty (from $995) is an L-shaped suite with two rooms and a kitchen. There's also a spa and gym.

BEST WESTERN SEAPORT INN

Map pp444-5   Chain Hotel $$
☎ 212-766-6600, 800-468-3569; www.seaportinn .com; 33 Peck Slip btwn Front & Water Sts; d from $209; ⊕ A, C to Broadway–Nassau St, J, M, Z, 2, 3, 4, 5 to Fulton St; ⊠ ⊑
It's chainy and dull, sure, but that can be forgotten if you get a terrace room, with brick decks overlooking the East River and Brooklyn Bridge – not to mention cheaper rates than most hotels within walking distance of Wall Street. The 72 rooms are a lot like Best Western in Kansas City – with 27-inch TVs with VHS players and Internet access – but this one's in historic South Street Seaport, with brick lanes filled with sports bars and Body Shop chains. At least the Brooklyn Bridge pedestrian lane is a few blocks west. There's free breakfast in the TV room downstairs and a small gym.

MILLENIUM HILTON

Map pp444-5   Business Hotel $$$
☎ 212-693-2001, 800-445-8667; www.hilton.com; 55 Church St; d $219-459, ste from $319; ⊕ N, R to Cortland St; ⊑ ⊠ ⊠
Designed to match the ape-confusing obelisk in *2001: A Space Odyssey* – and facing the

TYPES OF ROOMS

Check the neighborhood intros throughout this chapter to gauge the eternal 'midtown versus downtown' sort of question. As far as the type of room to hang your hat, there's essentially five types:

B&Bs or family-style guesthouses, with mix-match furnishings and some serious savings (if you don't mind some Victorian styles or eating brekky with strangers); Brooklyn's (p375) are particularly good; these options cost about the same as the travelers' hotels

Boutique hotels, usually small spaces with minimalist design, staff in all-black uniforms and donning headsets, and lite electronica greeting you in the lobby and room; expect a stylish bar on a rooftop or in the basement that locals will line up behind a velvet rope to get into (but could someone please yank the chain on the trend for all boutiques putting an old-fashioned phone in the lobby); starting rates begin from $200 to $300

'Classic' hotels, typified by the chintzy rooms at the Waldorf-Astoria (p371), stick with a modernized, but loyal European style; these usually cost the same as boutiques and aren't always any larger

European-style 'travelers' hotels' have some creaky floors and small rooms in cheap, but clean, floral patterns, and often a shared bath; good choices are the Hotel 17 (p363) or Hotel 31 (p367); these run about $100 to $150

Hostels have some functional (often lifeless and tight) dorms, but often oozing in life, with backyard gardens, kitchens and TV rooms; Chelsea has many, but the Upper West Side's Jazz on the Park (p373) or Hostelling International (p372) may be the best (if you don't mind late-night subway rides); dorms run about $30 to $35

chilling World Trade Centre site – the narrow 55-floor Hilton has more character than your average chain rep. Rooms have earthy tones – still looking new from a full post-September 11 renovation – with nice extras like in-room WiFi, 42-inch plasma-screen TVs, and a full gym with a swimming pool. For a little extra room, go for a corner junior suite, which has a living room with sleeper sofa.

WALL STREET INN
Map pp444–5   Business Boutique $$
☎ 212-747-1500, 800-695-8284; www.thewall streetinn.com; 9 South William St at Broad St; d incl breakfast Mon-Thu/Fri-Sun from $259/159; ⊙ 2, 3 to Broad St, 4, 5 to Bowling Green; 🕸 🖵
Off cobbled Stone Street in the shadows of old and new skyscrapers, the Wall Street's rooms are pretty homey, if a little predictable. Geared mostly to business folk, the country-style floral bedspreads and curtains hoke-ify the room. Marble

The industrial-chic lobby Soho Grand Hotel (p357)

tubs in the bathrooms are nice, and the TVs have VHS players if renting flicks is your thing. The building is a piece of history too – the 'LB' tile in the entry dates from the previous tenants, the Lehman Brother's banking company. There's a small fitness center.

TRIBECA, SOHO & NOLITA

Downtown's poshest neighborhoods offer plenty of cool inns and big-deal boutiques for those wanting a swank place to set down your Prada shopping bags (or meet up with your film's producers). But it'll cost you to stay in these brick-lane neighborhoods, roughly spread out between Chinatown and the Hudson River. Most double rooms start at $300 or $400 per night. They justify the upped ante with their own sceney bars and brunch spots.

COSMOPOLITAN HOTEL
Map pp444-5   Budget Hotel $
☎ 212-566-1900, 888-895-9400; www.cosmohotel .com; 95 West Broadway at Chambers St; d from $145; ⊙ 1, 2, 3 to Chambers St; 🕸
The most un-Tribeca choice, the cheap Cosmo is a hero for those wanting to save their bills for the area's chic eateries and boutiques. On a busy street corner, the 122-room hotel isn't much to brag about – clean carpeted rooms with private bath-

rooms, a double bed or two, and IKEA knock-off furnishings. Corner rooms – Nos 422, 522 and 622 – are best, offering views of the far-off Empire State Building. All renovated inside, the Cosmo is proud of its age. A hotel has been operating here since 1852 – making it the city's oldest.

MERCER Map p450   Boutique Hotel $$$

☎ 212-966-6060; 147 Mercer St at Prince St; d/ste from $440/680; ◉ N, R, W to Prince St; 🔀 🖳
Right in the heart of Soho's brick lanes, the grand Mercer is where stars sleep. Up from the leisurely lobby with fat, plush sofas, and Jean George's excellent basement restaurant, the 75 rooms offer a slice of chic loft life in a century-old warehouse. Flat-screen TVs, dark-wood floors and white-marble, mosaic-tile bathrooms (some with square tubs under a skylight) add a modern touch to rooms that sport the building's industrial roots – with giant oval windows, steel pillars and exposed-brick walls.

OFF-SOHO SUITES

Map p450   Budget Hotel $

☎ 212-979-9815; www.offsoho.com; 11 Rivington St btwn Chrystie St & The Bowery; r/ste from $129/209; ◉ J, M, Z to Bowery; 🔀 🖳
More Lower East Side than ritzy Nolita, most guests staying at Off-Soho's 40

rooms eye bars to the east. Suites – which sleep four – are like cheapie starters' apartments for downtown life: functional kitchenettes (including microwave, stove, oven, fully-stocked shelves), pull-out sofas across from the satellite-access TV, and a private bedroom with closet. Lots of indie rockers have stayed here, as seen on framed promo pics in vinyl-floored hallways. There's WiFi access in the lobby sitting area.

SIXTY THOMPSON

Map p450   Boutique Hotel $$$

☎ 212-431-0400, 877-431-0400; www.60thompson .com; 60 Thompson St btwn Broome & Spring Sts; s/d/ste from $360/425/715; ◉ C, E to Spring St; 🔀 🖳
Built from scratch in 2000, the snazzy 98-room Sixty Thompson is definitely a place to be seen, and many locals can be overheard greeting the all-blue staff with headsets. They come to dine in the futurist Thai restaurant Kittichai, or swirl cocktails on the rooftop Thom Bar. Minimal rooms are more comfortable than some such boutiques – beds have goose-down duvets and leather headboards, and you can watch DVDs on the flat-screen TVs from a wing-backed seat or creamy tweed sofa. WiFi and high-speed Internet is free hotel-wide.

PRIVATE APARTMENTS

The tight hotel market – not to mention the massive expense of renting an apartment here – has given birth to a cottage industry of sorts, with enterprising New Yorkers turning into part-time innkeepers. After getting approved by one of several rental agencies, a residence – usually that of a part-time New Yorker or someone who travels frequently – becomes available for long or short stays. It's often excellent value, plus a way to fly below the radar as a tourist, coming and going as you please without being forced to make any strained conversation around a B&B's breakfast table. Some rooms are in 'hosted' households, with owners present, which will save you from the 13.625% hotel city tax at least. The following companies offer a range of apartments in neighborhoods all over the five boroughs:

A Hospitality Company (☎ 212-965-1102, 800-987-1235; www.hospitalityco.com; studio/apt per night $225/309) Rents a few fully furnished apartments with features such as data ports, cable TVs and fully equipped kitchens. Its website, which is available in five languages, posts some discounts.

CitySonnet (☎ 212-614-3034; www.westvillagebb.com; hosted s/d from $80/110, private apt $135-185) Rents private apartments or (hosted) guest rooms in an occupied apartment, many in the hippest downtown locations plus locations in Williamsburg and Brooklyn.

Gamut Realty Group (☎ 212-879-4229, 800-437-8353; www.gamutnyc.com; studios from $115, 1-bedroom apt from $150, 1-bedroom apt per month from $1350) Handles a number of short- and long-term apartment rentals, in spaces such as high-rises with doormen, and townhouses. Few options south of 14th St.

Manhattan Lodgings (☎ 212-677-7616; www.manhattanlodgings.com; apt per night/month from $150/2250, hosted stays per night/month from $140/1550) A selection of studio, one-bedroom and two-bedroom apartments across Manhattan.

SOHO GRAND HOTEL

Map p450   Deluxe International $$

☎ 212-965-3000, 800-965-3000; www.sohogrand .com; 310 West Broadway; d $250-350; ◉ A, C, E to Canal St; 🐾 💻

Since it opened in 1997, the industrial-gone-chic Soho Grand has kept its slot as a high-status cool-folks HQ for downtown. A nondescript 17-story tower outside, the Grand is striking inside, where a glass and cast-iron stairway leads to a towering lobby (and swank Grand Lounge) topped with warehouse-like beams and 'chicken wire' ceiling. Light pours into the 363 rooms from over Chinatown or Soho rooftop water towers, through wide-open windows. Rooms are decorated in more somber tones, punctuated with studded leather headboards, free-standing wardrobes and plasma flat-screen tellies. There's a courtyard restaurant in summer, and the lobby's Grand Lounge bristles with action all year.

TRIBECA GRAND HOTEL

Map p450   Deluxe International $$$

☎ 212-519-6600, 877-519-6600; www.tribecagrand .com; 2 Sixth Ave at Church St; d from $399; ◉ 1 to Franklin St, A, C, E to Canal St; 🐾 💻

Located a few blocks south of its sister the Soho Grand (above), the eight-floor Tribeca Grand is more hyped – hosting the Tribeca Film Festival in its private 90-seat theater helps. Opened in 2000, the rooms aren't spacious, but plush with primo details – BOSE CD players, Herman Millar chairs tucked under compact desks, or-ange-felt armchairs looking out huge windows. Situated on its own triangular block, rooms look inward over an interior Church Lounge, where DJs and some binge-drinking or brunching celebrities hang out. If you don't gawk, everyone will probably assume you have your own Sundance film in editing stage.

LOWER EAST SIDE

Having a friend with an extra bed used to be the closest you'd get to trendy digs amid the Side's boutiques and clubs. But the hotel craze is starting to hit these hipster streets long hallowed with lore from Beastie Boys' album covers and Jewish and Latino immigrants.

HOTEL ON RIVINGTON

Map p449   Boutique Hotel $$

☎ 212-475-2600, 800-915-1537; www.hotelonriving ton.com; 107 Rivington St btwn Essex & Ludlow Sts; r/ste from $295/490; ◉ F to Delancey St, J, M, Z to Delancey–Essex Sts; 🐾 💻

If your iPod has all the right songs, opt for where the indie rockers with cash go (Moby shot the album cover of his album *Hotel* in the penthouse, Frank Black and the Killers crashed here). Opened in 2005, the 20-floor THOR – that's the hotel acronym, not the viking – looks like a shimmering new-Shanghai building towering over 19th-century tenements. Best of all, it's all-glass rooms with enviable views over the East River and downtown's sprawl. Best of the barebone-minimal rooms are 'unique suites,' some with corner positions and hanging flat-screen TVs. Some have balconies. Bathrooms are a grab-bag – some are window-side and outsiders can see in too (until the windows fog); others are all-lime tiled or with three-head showers for 'multi-tasking' cleaning. Plenty of hang-out space, like the second-floor lounge and ground-floor restaurant.

HOWARD JOHNSON EXPRESS INN

Map p449   Chain Hotel $$

☎ 212-358-8844; www.hojo.com; 135 E Houston St at Forsyth St; r incl breakfast from $249; ◉ F, V to Lower East Side–Second Ave; 🐾 💻

Sure, it's bland and not so hip but it's only a few years old, and the location is prime. Beds are comfy, there's TV and small desks, photos from local artists adorn the walls of the teeny lobby and you get free muffins, cereal and juice in the morning. It's a better deal in late winter when prices drop about $100.

EAST VILLAGE

Not much going on, bed-wise, in this part of town. A couple homes turned into cheap guesthouse-deals sweeten the scene – but the lack of options means things get filled up quick.

EAST VILLAGE B&B   Map p449   B&B $

☎ 212-260-1865; evband@juno.com; apt 5-6, 244 E 7th St btwn Aves C & D; s incl breakfast $75, d incl breakfast $100 & $120; ◉ F, V to Second Ave–Lower East Side; 🐾 💻

This lesbian-owned find is a popular oasis for Sapphic couples who want peace and quiet in the midst of the noisy East Village scene. Housed in a residential apartment building on a lovely block, the three rooms (one single and two double) are way stylish – bold linens, modern art, gorgeous wooden floors – and the huge (by NYC standards) shared living-room space is filled with light, beautiful paintings from around the globe, exposed brickwork and a big-screen TV. Beyond Ave E, though, it's a particularly long walk to the subway station.

JAZZ ON THE TOWN Map p449   Hostel $

☎ 212-228-2780; www.jazzhostel.com; 307 E 14th St, btwn First & Second Aves; dm from $28; Ⓛ L to 1st Ave; 🔀 🖳

A newby downtown hostel – affiliated with the superior Jazz on the Park (p373) this crammed, four-floor walk-up is, despite the smiles, a by-the-numbers hostel with functional, slightly depressing dorm rooms of four or six beds. There's a rooftop deck with artificial turf and seats overlooking loud 14th St (it's OK to bring in beer, but note the 'no jumping' sign). There are a few computers to check email, a storage room and laundry facilities. There are some all-you-can-drink deals in the basement bar ($12 on Tuesday and Thursday), but it's hard to skip out on area bars.

SECOND HOME ON SECOND AVE
Map p449   Guesthouse $

☎ 212-677-3161; www.secondhomesecondavenue .com; 221 Second Ave, btwn E 13th & E 14th Sts; r from $100; Ⓛ L to 3rd Ave; 🔀

A great option for the downtown-bound on a budget, the Second Home has only seven artful rooms – each with wooden floors, TVs with cable, and worldly themes based on hand-made furnishings or random finds at New York antiques markets. The roomiest, perhaps best, is the Modern Suite ($195), which features French doors separating a sitting area and two double beds on frames put together with assorted pipes. Five rooms have clean shared bath.

ST MARKS HOTEL Map p449   Budget Hotel $

☎ 212-674-0100; www.stmarkshotel.qpg.com; 2 St Marks Pl at Third Ave; s/d $100/110; Ⓑ 6 to Astor Pl; 🔀

A long-time East Village institution, and still a bit rough at the edges despite recent renovations, the 70-room St Marks is in the heart of the combat-boot, tattoo-parlor, ob-scene t-shirt zone of St Marks Place. Rooms are tiny – just enough room to scoot past a full- or queen-size bed. All have a TV bolted to the wall, and a small tiled bathroom attached. A few second-floor rooms pick up some pizza smells from the pizzeria downstairs – anything facing the street will get a lot of traffic noise. Staff store bags for night flights, or you can rent a room for the day for $50 (nothing hourly).

UNION SQUARE INN Map p449   Budget Hotel $

☎ 212-614-0500; www.unionsquareinn.com; 209 E 14th St, btwn Second & Third Aves; d incl breakfast Sun-Thu/Fri & Sat $119/$129; Ⓛ L, N, Q, R, W, 4, 5, 6 to 14th St–Union Sq; 🔀

It ain't on Union Sq, but this 47-room chea-pie cuts its corners on decor (just cheesy floral bedspread and untouched-up nicks on walls) to offer the downtown-bound what they need: a bed and roof for under $150. Rooms lack much natural light, but have a small hanging racks for coats, satel-lite TV, a small refrigerator and tiny private bathrooms. No doubt, 14th St picks up noise – if you're used to locusts singing you to sleep, ask for a back room.

WEST (GREENWICH) VILLAGE

Old-school charm, intimate quarters, reasonable prices and lots of gay-friendliness are what you'll find here – not to mention a couple of slick, impressive newcomers. Those who prefer the East-side grit, and can tolerate the 15- or 20-minute walk, will find more options here (some nicely priced).

ABINGDON GUEST HOUSE Map p448   B&B $

☎ 212-243-5384; www.abingdonguesthouse.com; 13 Eighth Ave, btwn W 12th & Jane Sts; s/d incl breakfast from $149/164; Ⓐ A, C, E to 14th St, L to Eighth Ave; 🔀 🖳

Four-poster beds, elegant antique pieces and scads of exposed brick make Abingdon guests feel like they've landed in a New England country inn. Too bad there's only nine rooms! Occupying two three-floor, 1850 townhouses, rooms mix up the themes (the Ambassador goes safari, with a kitchenette; the Garden has private access to its small namesake out back). There's Internet access and private bathrooms in all rooms. The only catch is the four-night minimum stay over weekends, two-night for weekdays.

HOTEL GANSEVOORT

Map p448   Boutique Hotel $$$

☎ 212-206-6700, 877-426-7386; www.hotelganse voort.com; 18 Ninth Ave at W 13th St; r/ste incl breakfast from $395/625; ⊖ A, C, E to 14th St, L to Eighth Ave; 🖭 🛂 🖳
Coated in zinc-colored panels, and booming up top where rooftop bar Plunge attracts block-long lines (and guests swim in the skinny pool overlooking the Hudson River), the 14-floor Gansevoort has been a swank swashbuckler of the Meatpacking District since it opened in 2004. Light pours in all of the 187 rooms' windows – full-wall deals. Rooms are luscious and airy, with fudge-colored suede headboards, plasma-screen TVs and illuminated bathroom doors. Some have balconies. Breakfast is served in the lovely Ono restaurant, a hot-spot for sushi and evening drinks.

INCENTRA VILLAGE HOUSE

Map p448   B&B $$

☎ 212-206-0007; 32 Eighth Ave, btwn W 12th & Jane Sts; r $169 & $199; ⊖ A, C, E to 14th St, L to Eighth Ave; 🛂 🖳
An easy walk to Chelsea clubs, these two red-brick, landmark townhouses were built in 1841 and later became the city's first gay inn. Today, the 12 rooms get booked way in advance by many queer travelers; call

TOP FIVE BUDGET SLEEPS

- 414 Hotel (p365) Super-friendly, simple guest-house puts 'heck' in Hell's Kitchen.
- Chelsea Lodge (p361) Americana lives in this historic townhouse.
- Gershwin Hotel (p363) Retro rooms outfitted with pop art.
- Hotel 17 (p363) Old-style travelers' hotel, where Woody Allen filmed.
- Second Home on Second Avenue (opposite) East Village guesthouse with home-made furnishings.

early to get in on its gorgeous Victorian parlor (featuring a baby grand piano that's often the site of a show-tune sing-along) and antique-filled, serious-Americana rooms (one is fully red-white-and-blue, with a possibly stunned George Washington watching over the brass bed). The 'Garden Suite' has access to a small garden in back and there's WiFi access in the parlor.

LARCHMONT HOTEL Map p448   Indie Inn $

☎ 212-989-9333; www.larchmonthotel.com; 27 W 11th St, btwn Fifth & Sixth Aves; $; s/d from $75/99; ⊖ F, V to 14th St; 🛂 🖳
This European-style inn has 60 popular rooms on a leafy residential block, mid-distance from the West and East Villages. It's great cheap sleeping if you don't mind tip-toeing in the provided robe and slippers for a tinkle or shower down the hall. Rooms are small, but fine – with wicker furnishings,

Hotel Gansevoort (above) has a rooftop bar, plasma screens and every trendy lure to win over the punters

Sleeping

WEST (GREENWICH) VILLAGE

359

cable TV, wall air-con units, and high-speed Internet connections. For an extra $20, rooms with queen-size beds come with flat-screen TVs and get some townhouse views on the street. Rates are $10 to $15 higher on weekends.

SOHO HOUSE Map p448   Boutique Hotel $$$

☎ 212-627-9800; www.sohohouseny.com; 29-35 Ninth Ave at W 13th St; d/ste $395/550; ◉ A, C, E to 14th St, L to Eighth Ave; 🚇 ❌ 🖳
A new sibling of London's Soho House, this private social club for the high-fashion VIP crowd has 24 guest rooms for nonmembers – but don't expect to snag one easily. (Even Carrie on *Sex and the City* had to sneak her way in to the rooftop pool.) If you get a room, opt for the 'playroom' suites with loft-like space, showers that double as steam rooms, a drawer full of 'naughty' oils, and stand-alone Boffi baths on wood floors. To be a member, sharpen your schmoozing skills, and hang out in the rooftop bar, private screen room, or sixth-floor lounge/reading room – the waiting list is already at 2000.

WASHINGTON SQUARE HOTEL

Map p448   Budget Hotel $$
☎ 212-777-9515, 800-222-0418; www.washingtonsquarehotel.com; 103 Waverly Pl btwn MacDougal St & Sixth Ave; d $166; ◉ A, C, E, B, D, F, V to W 4th St; ❌ 🖳
This nine-floor jazzy hotel keeps art deco going, with vintage-Hollywood pics and cheesy rose petals on the walls of its 160 arty rooms, half recently renovated. Across from Washington Sq Park – surrounded by New York University – there's a lot of life here, and free WiFi connections. The deluxe rooms ($34 extra) are slightly nicer, with all-new furnishings (granite-top vanities) and lush crimson-fuchsia walls. The basement North Square Restaurant & Lounge

Delve into deco land in Washington Square Hotel (above)

is good for a jazz brunch on Sunday; the lobby Deco Room has a slick afternoon tea on other days.

CHELSEA

This historic area – filled with nightclubs, galleries and Chelsea boys – is something of an indie-hotel ghetto, with many options, from backpacker hostels to B&Bs and big-buck boutique hotels. Considering its location between Midtown's theaters and sites, and downtown restaurants, bars and shops, it's a pretty good place to be. And the choices here seem *particularly* fond of the area, with seven here that squeeze 'Chelsea' into their name in the most creative of ways.

CHELSEA CENTER HOSTEL

Map pp452-3   Hostel $
☎ 212-643-0214; www.chelseacenterhostel.com; 313 W 29th St btwn Eighth & Ninth Aves; dm incl breakfast $33; ◉ A, C, E to 34th St–Penn Station; ❌
A little more personal than most hostels, this 18-bedder is a quiet, affordable favorite for backpackers and European budget travelers. There's a kitchen to use, a sitting area, and a small garden in back. Women-only dorms are available. Unfortunately their East Village location closed in early 2006.

CHELSEA HOTEL Map pp446-7   Indie Inn $$

☎ 212-243-3700; www.hotelchelsea.com; 222 W 23rd St, btwn Seventh & Eight Aves; r/ste from $225/585; ◉ C, E, 1 to 23rd St; ❌ 🖳
Immortalized by poems, by overdoses (Sid Vicious did the deed here, after allegedly killing Nancy Spungen), by Ethan Hawke in the house – urgh! – the one-of-a-kind Chelsea still keeps its artsy, bohemian vibe. Bohemian with a credit card. It's New York's most timeless hotel: squint and you can imagine Bob Dylan penning lyrics in a lost scene from *Don't Look Back*. Priced largely for its lore, the mix-match of rooms lovingly show off their decades – most are huge, with ruby red carpets or drip-drop designs on drugs over wooden floors. Some have kitchenettes and separate living rooms. Staying here can feel like life in a film/photo shoot – probably because one's going on next door. Originally a co-op apartment built in 1884, it

became a hotel in 1905. It's known as the 'Chelsea Hotel,' but the real name is 'Hotel Chelsea.' Crazy what rock'n'roll can do to nomenclature. There's Internet access for $7 per hour.

CHELSEA INN Map pp446-7 B&B $

☎ 212-645-8989, 800-640-6469; www.chelseainn .com; 46 W 17th St btwn Fifth & Sixth Aves; s/d/ste incl breakfast from $89/140/160; ◉ Sixth Ave–14th St; ☒

Made up of two adjoining 19th-century townhouses, this funky-charming hideaway (a four-storey walk-up) has small but comfortable rooms that look like they were furnished entirely from flea markets or grandma's attic. It's character on a budget, just a bit east of the most desirable part of this happening 'hood. Rates drop in winter.

CHELSEA INTERNATIONAL HOSTEL

Map pp446-7 Hostel $

☎ 212-647-0010; www.chelseahostel.com; 251 W 20th St btwn Seventh & Eighth Aves; dm/r $28/70; ◉ C, E, 1 to 23rd St; ☒

A festive, international scene defines this hostel, where the back patio serves as party central (until midnight closing time) for up to 350 guests. Bunk rooms sleep four to six and amenities include communal kitchens and laundry facilities. It's kind of run like an urban camp – with some staff loving their jobs less than others. Everyone – even Americans – must show their passport to check in. There's a two-week maximum stay.

CHELSEA LODGE Map pp446-7 B&B $

☎ 212-243-4499; www.chelsealodge.com; 318 W 20th St btwn Eighth & Ninth Aves; r/ste from $114/150; ◉ C, E to 23rd St; ☒

Housed in a landmark brownstone of Chelsea's lovely historic district, the European-style, 20-room Chelsea Lodge is a super deal, with homey well-kept rooms. Decor flies the Americana flag, with color prints of train scenes in rooms, Native American busts and hunting duck decoys propped up over doorways. Rooms are small – just a bed, with TVs (with cable) plopped on an old wooden cabinet. There are showers and sinks in room, but toilets are down the hall. Six suite rooms have private bathrooms, two come with private garden access.

CHELSEA PINES INN Map p448 B&B $

☎ 212-929-1023, 888-546-2700; www.chelseapines inn.com; 317 W 14th St btwn Eighth & Ninth Aves; r incl breakfast from $139; ◉ A, C, E to 14th St, L to Eighth Ave; ☒ ▯

With its five walk-up floors coded to the rainbow flag, the 26-room Chelsea Pines is serious gay-and-lesbian central, but guests of all stripes are welcome. It helps to be up on your Hitchcock beauties, as vintage movie posters not only plaster the walls but rooms are named for starlets like Kim Novak, Doris Day and Ann Margaret. There's a sink in the walk-in closet of standard rooms, with clean bathrooms down the hall. The small café downstairs has free WiFi access, and opens to a tiny courtyard out back. Plenty of advice on cruising, partying and eating by the lively staff.

CHELSEA STAR HOTEL

Map pp452-3 Hostel $

☎ 212-244-7827; www.starhotelny.com; 300 W 30th St at Eighth Ave; dm/r from $29/109; ◉ A, C, E to 34th St–Penn Station; ☒

This three-floor hotel sports a serious hostel vibe with blue-and-gold hallways, a great back deck, and wacky thematic rooms (such as *Star Trek,* Coney Island and *Absolutely Fabulous*). Private rooms are quite small, but spotlessly clean – with shiny dark-wood floors, a small closet and cable TV. There are a couple shared bathrooms for every half-dozen rooms. Dorms have attached bathroom. More sedate, carpeted 'superior rooms' (from $199) are a bit overpriced, but have private bathrooms. Nearby Eighth Ave can produce some serious traffic noise. At research time, the Star was planning to expand next door. Madonna lived here briefly in 1981.

COLONIAL HOUSE INN

Map pp446-7 B&B $

☎ 212-243-9669, 800-689-3779; www.colonialhouse inn.com; 318 W 22nd St btwn Eighth & Ninth Aves; r incl breakfast with shared bath/bathroom from $85/135; ◉ C, E to 23rd St; ☒

Friendly and simple, this 20-room gay inn is tidy but a bit worn and small. Most rooms have small walk-in closets (with a small TV and refrigerator) and sinks. The owner, Mel Cheren, ran the legendary hip-hop club Paradise Garage. He lives on the ground

BLUELIST: BEST WAY TO LOOK LIKE A LOCAL IN NYC

Headphones: the Ultimate Prop. Doesn't matter if they're connected to your iPod, cell phone or cigarette lighter. Gives you an instant out when approached by panhandlers, lost tourists, or would-be muggers. Simply point to the headphones and keep moving.

Tell-Tale Reading Material. Review travel literature BEFORE you leave your hotel. Rip out pages you need (like maps) and stick them in a paperback novel befitting a true New Yorker, i.e. Catcher in the Rye. Nose in a novel = another great way to avoid unwanted interaction.

And They're Off! Native New Yorkers walk at an accelerated pace. It is important to move through the crowds with urgency (as if you're late for an audition or you're about to lose your reservation at Club 21). Burns more calories, too.

Diss Matt & Katie. Of course we all love the *Today Show*, but you never see a local frothing at the mouth in a crowd shot from Rockefeller Plaza.

Release the Chains that Bind. NYC is home to some of the best restaurants in the world. Avoid the chain restaurant experience you can get at home. There are lots of online resources to help you find restaurants without super-size options.

Back in Black. If you want to blend in with the locals, leave your home town sports attire at home. Keep it simple. Black is always good. And ladies, bring at least one pair of impractical shoes. Better yet, buy some while you're in the city.

Check out more Bluelists at http://www.lonelyplanet.com/bluelist/

---

floor and lines the walls with his colorful paintings. Breakfast in the small café leads to chat sessions. When weather is chummy, the rooftop deck up top sees some nude sunbathing.

INN ON 23RD ST

Map pp452-3   B&B $$

☎ 212-463-0330; www.innon23rd.com; 131 W 23rd St btwn Sixth & Seventh Aves; s & d incl breakfast from $229; ⊖ C, E, 1 to 23rd St; ✂ ▭
Housed in a lone 19th-century, five-storey townhouse on busy 23rd St, this 14-room B&B is a Chelsea gem. The hotel's kitchen shares its counters with the New School Culinary of Arts, meaning lots of free cakes and breads from promising students appear on the second-floor, all-Victorian library/dining room. Rooms are big and welcoming, with fanciful fabrics on big brass or poster beds and TVs held in huge armoires. There's an honor-system bar (beer is $3!) and an ol' piano to play boogie woogie.

MARITIME HOTEL

Map pp446-7   Boutique Hotel $$$

☎ 212-242-4300; www.themaritimehotel.com; 363 W 16th St btwn Eighth & Ninth Aves; r from $325; ⊖ A, C, E to 14th St, L to Eighth Ave; ✂ ▭
Originally the site of the National Maritime Union headquarters (and more recently a shelter for homeless teens), this white

tower dotted with portholes has been transformed into a marine-themed luxury inn by a hip team of architects. It feels like a luxury *Love Boat* inside, as its 135 rooms, each with their own round window, are compact and teak-paneled, with gravy in the form of 20-inch flat-screen TVs and DVD players. The most expensive quarters feature outdoor showers, a private garden and sweeping Hudson views. Big names show up at the chic Hiro club in the basement, while La Bottega is a popular trattoria and bar with 6000 sq ft of patio space out front.

UNION SQUARE & FLATIRON DISTRICT

Though often overlooked, this area is prime lodging ground for two main reasons: it's quiet, and it's in a great location. You'll find inns that feel like you have discovered them, and leafy, residential streets, in close proximity (walking distance) to both Midtown and East Village attractions. It's long on character and short on space, so book early.

The **Gramercy Park Hotel** (Map pp446–7; ☎ 212-475-4320; www.gramercyparkhotel .com; 2 Lexington Ave at 21st St) was undergoing a major renovation at research time, but is likely to re-emerge as a major player in the neighborhood.

CARLTON HOTEL

Map pp452-3   Boutique Hotel $$$

☎ 212-532-4100, 800-601-8500; www.carltonhotel ny.com; 88 Madison Ave btwn 28th & 29th Sts; r from $399; ⊕ N, R, W to 28th St, 6 to 28th St; 🔀 🖳 Opened in 2005, this jazzy luxury hotel feels like walking into a sepia-toned portrait of the art-deco age. In the lobby, big-band and jazz standards play as, along a wall, water gently falls over a fuzzy Madison Ave street scene. Overlooking is the hot-spot eatery Country Restaurant, and a classy lobby bar-café popular for drinks or brunch. The rooms are traditional and homey, with brown floral carpets, creamy walls and drapes hanging over bed headboards. In addition to TVs and work desks, in most rooms there are iHouse alarm clocks for your iPod. There's free Internet access and meeting rooms that appeal to business folk.

CARLTON ARMS HOTEL

Map pp452-3   Budget Hotel $

☎ 212-679-0680; www.carltonarms.com; 160 E 25th St btwn Third & Lexington Aves; d with shared/ private bathroom $87/101; ⊕ 6 to 23rd St; 🔀 Like a stray adrift from the East Village, the 54-room Carlton Arms can feel like sleeping in a rehearsal space. The four-floor walk-up has themed floors and rooms (one floor is done up like Little Egypt). Adding to the vibe, there are occasional room-to-room 'plays.' One room has a ruby bedspread, blue shag carpet and Venetian murals. It's a little gritty but fine – and only a 15-block walk to the East Village. All rooms have ash trays ready for rock'n'rollers with cigs.

GERSHWIN HOTEL

Map pp452-3   Indie Inn $

☎ 212-545-8000; www.gershwinhotel.com; 7 E 27th St at Fifth Ave; dm $33, r $43/119; ⊕ 6 to 28th St; 🔀 🖳 Next to the Museum of Sex, and four blocks north of the Flatiron Building, the 13-floor Gershwin is one of the Manhattan greats: a mostly hotel, part-hostel Chelsea Hotel for many younger folk (not exclusively) not wanting to spend several hundred dollars a night. Its facade is lined with tear-shaped drop-drop bulbs, and inside there's framed pop art in the lobby and rooms. Of the 159 rooms, a handful are carpeted dorms with four, six or 10 bunks (most co-ed, one is women only); all have private bathroom.

Rock 'n' roll Gershwin Hotel (left) next to the Museum of Sex

Appealing private rooms have wooden floors, with yellow walls, clean bathrooms, vintage furnishings, cable TV and a dresser. The rooftop deck was closed for renovation at research time, but should once again provide a great hang-out spot.

HOTEL 17 Map pp446-7   Budget Hotel $

☎ 212-475-2845; www.hotel17ny.com; 225 E 17th St btwn Second & Third Aves; d $120-150; ⊕ N, Q, R, 4, 5, 6 to 14th St–Union Sq, L to Third Ave; 🔀 Right off Stuyvesant Sq on a leafy residential block, this popular eight-floor townhouse has old–New York charm with cheap prices. Plus Woody Allen shot a frightening dead-body scene here for his film *Manhattan Murder Mystery* (1993). Only four of the 120 rooms have private bathrooms (all are free of the film's dead bodies). Rooms are small, with traditional, basic furnishings (gray carpet, striped wallpaper, chintzy bedspreads, burgundy blinds) and lack much natural light.

HOTEL GIRAFFE

Map pp452-3   Boutique Hotel $$$

☎ 212-685-7700, 877-296-0009; www.hotelgiraffe .com; 365 Park Ave South at 26th St; r/ste incl breakfast from $325/425; ⊕ 6 to 23rd St, N, R, W to 23rd St; 🔀 🖳 Up a notch in posh for most of the boutiques this far south, the new 12-floor

Giraffe earns its stripes, or dots, with sleek, modern rooms in a stretch of art-deco office buildings and a sunny rooftop area for drinks or tapas. Most of the 72 rooms have small balconies. All come with flat-screen TVs (and DVD players), granite work desks, and automatic black-out shades to open/shut (the big) windows from your bed. Corner suites add a living room with pull-out sofa.

INN AT IRVING PLACE

Map pp446-7   B&B $$$

☎ 212-533-4600, 800-685-1447; www.innatirving .com; 56 Irving Pl btwn 17th & 18th Sts; r incl breakfast from $325; ⊕ L, N, R, 4, 5, 6 to 14th St–Union Sq; ✖ ▢

Richly Victorian, this intimate 11-room red-brick townhouse dates from 1834 and bursts with period pieces and rosy patterns of softer days past. Rooms are named for area writers and figures, such as the Edith Wharton, which has smooth dark-wood floors and a sitting area in front of the original (and now just decorative) fireplace. Breakfast is served in the atmospheric parlor Lady Mendl, which stages a five-course tea service Wednesday to Sunday ($35).

MARCEL Map pp452-3   Boutique Hotel $$

☎ 212-696-3800, 888-664-6835; www.nychotels .com; 201 E 24th St at Third Ave; d from $227; ⊕ 6 to 23rd St; ✖ ▢

Billing itself as boutique for less, the eight-floor, minimalist Marcel doesn't equal the comfort you find in boutiques that cost $100 more – but if modern and the Flatiron District are your thing, it's hard to look past it. Most of the 98 rooms are small, done up in earth tones. Atop cube-designed carpets, beds are surrounded by wall-hugging shelving consoles. All rooms have WiFi

Internet access. There's a coffee area downstairs, but little public space.

W NEW YORK – UNION SQUARE

Map pp446-7   Classy Chain Hotel $$$

☎ 212-253-9119, 888-625-5144; www.whotels .com; 201 Park Ave South at 17th St; r from $400; ⊕ L, N, Q, R, 4, 5, 6 to 14th St–Union Sq; ✖ ▢

The ultra hip W demands a black wardrobe and credit card. Of the five W's in Manhattan, it's the only downtown option – and the UnderBar gets busy in evenings. Everything is top of the line. Lots of somber tones in rooms, like framed leather headboards and lavender duvets for the feather beds. There's DVD players for the TVs and high-speed Internet connections. Rooms aren't big, but – set in a 1911, one-time insurance building – all rooms benefit from high ceilings.

MIDTOWN

Options are endless in Midtown, the accommodations capital of New York City. Prices and conditions range from $75 cheapies with shared toilets down the hall, to thousand-dollar suites with private terraces overlooking the skyline's blinking lights. Basically Midtown comes in four parts: the Times Sq frenzy, including nearby Hell's Kitchen – best for theater-goers and first-time visitors; the ritzier blocks between Sixth and Fifth Avenues with boutique hotels and stalwarts like the Iroquois (p368) catering to those more keen on art museums and Fifth Ave shopping; the somewhat grimier and busier blocks south of 42nd St and west of Broadway are filled with more budget hotels; and the more residential and classy boutiques east of Park Ave from the underrated Murray Hill in the '30s to the outskirts of business in the '50s.

TOP FIVE THEMES

- Casablanca Hotel (p366) Moroccan. Let the tiled mosaics, sculptures and carved details take you away.
- Chelsea Pines Inn (p361) Vintage Hollywood. OK, so it's only got loads of framed film posters. But we'll bet any of the boys bunking here can belt out some lines from the big hits as well.
- Harlem Flophouse (p374) Jazz. The renaissance for real, kinda. Budget guesthouse aims for '20s glory.
- Library Hotel (p369) Dewey Decimal System. Third floor? Social Sciences. Eighth floor? Literature. Pick your favorite type of read, then snag the room with all the books that suit you.
- Maritime Hotel (p362) Nautical adventure. Snuggle into your cabin and peer out your porthole – no seasickness here, but maybe stars shagging next door.

414 HOTEL Map p282 | Budget Hotel $$

☎ 212-399-0006; www.414hotel.com; 414 W 46th St btwn Ninth & Tenth Aves; r incl breakfast $139-239; ⊕ B, D, F, V to 42nd St; ✦ ▣

Set up like a guesthouse, this great budget deal offers 22 tidy rooms a couple blocks west of Times Sq. Staff hand out maps and brim with tips. All rooms are simple deals – with desks, dressers, closets with mini safe, cable TV and sinks outside tiled bathrooms. There's a small courtyard between the townhouse's two buildings; breakfast is served up front, where there's a computer and a small kitchen to use.

ALGONQUIN Map p282 | Luxury Hotel $$

☎ 212-840-6800, 888-304-2047; www.algonquin hotel.com; 59 W 44th St btwn Fifth & Sixth Aves; d from $300; ⊕ B, D, F, V to 42nd St, 4, 5, 6, 7 to Grand Central; ✦ ▣

A storied classic a couple blocks from Times Sq, the 174-room Algonquin was where Dorothy Parker staged a lit-lunch round table in the 1920s. These days, the vibe still roars in the superb public places (Oak Room for cabernet and jazz brunches, lobby lounge for drinks, the dark Blue Bar for $13 martinis). Rooms still smart from a recent renovation, accented by red-and-gold carpet, flat-screen TVs, WiFi access, and framed black-and-whites of hotel details. Rates are high, but – in Dorothy's honor – writers get a break on their first night!

AMERICANA INN Map p282 | Budget Hotel $

☎ 212-840-6800; 69 W 38th St btwn Fifth & Sixth Aves; r from $95; ⊕ B, D, F, N, Q, R, V, W to 34th St–Herald Sq; ✦

Clean as in clinical, central as in a few blocks from Times Sq, and cheap as in (often) two-digit rates – the 52-room Americana isn't the home-away-from-home you dream of. Fluorescent lights bounces from bare white walls, there's local channels (only) on the TV, and the bathroom is down the hall. But it's clean and safe.

AVALON Map pp452-3 | International Hotel $$

☎ 212-299-7000, 888-442-8256; www.avalonhotel nyc.com; 16 E 32nd St btwn Madison & Fifth Aves; r from $275; ⊕ B, D, F, N, Q, R, V, W to 34th St, 6 to 33rd St; ✦ ▣

This Spanish-run 100-room hotel aims for the Old World, with a frenzy of pillars and marble in its lobby, and chintzy rooms, adorned with English-landscape art on striped walls, green floral carpets, and fussy items like a TV-packing armoire and mini bar. Suites, for an extra $50, grant you wood-floor entries and a sofa-bed in the TV room by the window. Guests can use a nearby Bally's Sports Club.

BELVEDERE HOTEL

Map p282 | International Hotel $$

☎ 212-245-7000, 888-468-3558; 319 W 48th St btwn Eighth & Ninth Aves; d incl breakfast $250-400; ⊕ C, E to 50th St; ✦ ▣

Open since 1928, the 400-room Belvedere's roots (and facade) are art-deco originals, even if the make-over is a modern version of the era's glory. Rooms have the usual amenities (including Internet access). There's a fitness centre, business centre and a café in the intentionally '20s-style lobby.

BENJAMIN

Map pp452-3 | Business Hotel $$$

☎ 212-320-8002, 888-423-6526; www.thebenjamin .com; 125 E 50th St at Lexington Ave; d/ste from $400/500; ⊕ 6 to 51st St; ✦ ▣

Just east of the bulk of Midtown business, the Benjamin's 209 rooms aim to please those wishing to settle in for a bit. Most rooms are suites, and all come with fully stocked kitchens (microwave and refrigerator – but no stove or oven) and a giant work desk that pulls out for more space. Four people will do better with a suite than paying $40 for a roll-away bed. Rooms have BOSE stereos. There's a 24-hour fitness centre too.

BIG APPLE HOSTEL Map p282 | Hostel $

☎ 212-302-2603; 119 W 45th St btwn Sixth Ave & Broadway; dm/r from $35/92; ⊕ B, D, F, V to 42nd St–Bryant Park; ✦

Half a block from Times Sq, the characterless, no-frills Big Apple has clean and safe rooms and surprisingly friendly staff. Added treats are the courtyard and kitchen, plus laundry facilities in the basement. Private rooms are like the dorms – with access to shared bath – but add a cable TV and a couple chairs.

BRYANT PARK

Map p282 | Boutique Hotel $$$

☎ 212-869-0100; www.bryantparkhotel.com; 40 W 40th St btwn Fifth & Sixth Aves; d/ste from $365/465; ⊕ B, D, F, V to 42nd St, 7 to Fifth Ave; ✦ ▣

All eyes from nearby Bryant Park naturally fixate on this gem, a black-and-gold-brick tower looming to the south. Originally the American Standard Building (1934), this 130-room hotel is chic central, with bare-bone minimalist rooms and huge views from most rooms. The lift up is padded in red leather; rooms come with flat-screen TVs, cashmere robes, full-size soaking tubs and Pipino lotions. If you're loaded, opt up for a suite that faces the park (higher priced ones have terraces). The adjoining KOI is a classy sushi restaurant.

CASABLANCA HOTEL

Map p282   Boutique Hotel $$
☎ 212-869-1212, 888-922-7225; www.casablanca hotel.com; 147 W 43rd St btwn Sixth Ave & Broadway; d incl breakfast from $269; ⊙ N, Q, R, S, W, 1, 2, 3, 7 to Times Sq; ⊠ ▣
Low-key and tourist-oriented, the popular 48-room Casablanca flexes the North African motif throughout (eg tiger statues, Moroccan murals, framed tapestries, and a second-floor lounge named Rick's Cafe after the movie). Rooms are pleasant and comfortable, with sisal-like carpets and a window-side seating area. There's free Internet, all-day espresso, wine at 5pm, and roll-away beds.

CHAMBERS

Map p282   Boutique Hotel $$$
☎ 212-974-5656, 866-204-5656; www.chambersnyc .com; 15 W 56th St btwn Fifth & Sixth Aves; d from $350; ⊙ F to 57th St, N, R, W to Fifth Ave—59th St; ⊠ ▣
This 77-room – near Fifth Avenue's ritziest department stores – aims for a bit of high-style class. The towering lobby has a great mezzanine lounge with anime-like art on walls and a mix of area rugs, sofas and armchairs. Upstairs rooms give illusions of more space with a small hallway. Plush cushions are plopped on the duvets of wood-frame beds; bathrooms have concrete floors and giant shower heads in clear-glass showers. Business visitors will enjoy the tear-away tracing paper on the glass-top work desks. Room service is handled by the swank neighbor Town restaurant.

DREAM Map p282   Boutique Hotel $$$
☎ 212-247-2000, 866-437-3266; www.dreamny .com; 210 W 55th St btwn Broadway & Seventh Ave; d from $365; ⊙ N, R, Q, W to 57th St; ⊠ ▣
A new transformation of a blah chain, the 220-room Dream is certainly surreal. The

bizarre lobby features a two-story aquarium filled with Caribbean fish and a giant three-figure statue culled from a Connecticut Russian restaurant. Minimal all-white rooms have blue lights shining from under beds and inside glass-top desks. There's Internet and flat-screen TVs on the wall. Best is the penthouse bar with open-air areas overlooking Broadway. At research time, a basement spa was in the works.

DYLAN Map pp452-3   Boutique Hotel $$
☎ 212-338-0500, 866-553-9526; www.dylanhotel .com; 52 E 41st St btwn Madison & Park Aves; r/ste from $259/69; ⊙ S, 4, 5, 6 to 42nd St—Grand Central; ⊠ ▣
Now a house of style, this 108-room luxury boutique hotel was once home to the Chemists Club (seems that science nerds used to go for ornate beaux-arts, evident in the original swirling marble staircase and 1903 facade). Somber lighting in cushy rooms may be too dark for some, but it's hard to not be moved by full-marble bathrooms, cube-like armchairs and color schemes of sky blue, green and lavender. Best is the Alchemy Suite (about $899), created in the 1930s as a mock medieval lab. (Those are the nerds we love most.) The ground-floor Chemist Club is a classy clubhouse restaurant serving breakfast and a $75 tower of oysters and other seafood.

FLATOTEL Map p282   Business Hotel $$
☎ 212-887-9400, 800-352-6863; www.flatotel.com; 135 W 52nd St btwn Sixth & Seventh Aves; r from $225; ⊙ B, D, F, V to 47th-50th Sts—Rockefeller Center; ⊠ ▣
Set up for business chiefly, this reborn condo offers 288 luxurious, if a little unexciting, rooms – and one of the best fitness-centre views in the world. Rooms feature comfy

TOP FIVE BOUTIQUE HOTELS

- Hudson (p368) Ian Schrager's trompe l'oeil entry is the epitome of boutique.
- W Hotel – Times Sq (p364) Corner suites seem a mile off Broadway.
- Hotel Gansevoort (p359) Sceney rooftop pool and bar evokes Miami.
- Mercer (p356) It's so, Soho cool.
- Morgans (p369) Schrager's pioneer from 1985 is still strong.

king-size platform beds with built-in wooden headboards. There are Aenon work chairs tucked under small work desks, and the usual DVD players for the TV, plus microwaves, and a lobby Moda restaurant-bar worthy of a martini or two. Most exciting is the 46th-floor fitness center for that exercise-bike-in-the-sky sensation.

FOUR SEASONS

Map pp452-3   International Chain Hotel $$$
☎ 212-758-5700, 800-819-5053; www.fourseasons .com/newyorkfs; 57 E 57th St btwn Madison & Park Aves; r/ste from $725/1600; Ⓜ N, R, W to Fifth Ave–59th St; 🅿 🖳
Rising like a pyramid – up 52 floors – the Four Seasons' massive lobby (designed by IM Pei) hits you like a Gothic cathedral gone mod, with limestone arches leading to the glass-tile skylight – plus there's an adjoining bar and restaurant. Even the smallest of the 368 ('superior') rooms are giant things, with latte-colored carpets, and 10-inch plasma TVs in the full-marble bathrooms. The views north, over Central Park, are practically unfair. There's a 24-hour fitness centre and top-hatted doormen will set you up for the free car service (limit: two-mile radius) from 8am to 11pm.

HOTEL 31
Map pp452-3   Budget Hotel $
☎ 212-685-3060; 120 E 31st St btwn Park Ave South & Lexington Ave; s/d/tr $60/75/100; Ⓜ N, R, W to 28th St, 6 to 28th St; 🅿
A cast of kooky characters and long-term guests make the fun Midtown-version of Hotel 17 something like a Coen Brothers film set. Half of the 70 available rooms have small, clean private bathrooms. It's good budget-hotel fodder. All are small, decorated in blue-checkered carpets, floral bedspreads and burgundy blinds, with cable TV in all. Ziggie, an elderly staffer, has worked in the building for 20 years and is fond of telling one-liners (eg 'only the old lady's allowed on the rooftop… mother nature'). Remember the rules.

HOTEL 41
Map p282   Boutique Hotel $$
☎ 212-703-8600, 877-847-4444; www.hotel41.com; 206 W 41st St btwn Seventh & Eighth Aves; r from $189; Ⓜ N, Q, R, W, 1, 2, 3, 7 to Times Sq–42nd St; 🅿 🖳
Right off Times Sq, the 41's 47 carpeted rooms are tiny to the point of a capsule:

standards are just 100 square feet, enough room for a wall-mounted TV with DVD player, small writing desk, full-size double bed and a clean bathroom. Nothing fancy, but it's nicer than some budget deals – and it's a few steps from your Broadway show (*Rent* is next door). There's free Internet access. The ground-floor lounge has a little style – and a plethora of games on mute.

HOTEL METRO
Map pp452-3   International Hotel $$
☎ 212-947-2500; www.hotelmetronyc.com; 45 W 35th St btwn Fifth & Sixth Aves; d incl breakfast from $199; Ⓜ B, D, F, N, Q, R, V, W to 34th St–Herald Sq; 🅿 🖳
A slightly tacky, half-hearted take on 1930s art deco, the 179-room, 13-floor Metro has a rooftop deck with full-frontal looks at the nearby Empire State Building. Up from the black-and-gold lobby, rooms are rather plain but certainly comfortable, with caramel color schemes and more thinking space than most hotels at this price range. There's a library area with flat-screen TVs, next to where breakfast is served. In peak season, rates often start at $295 – a bit beyond its worth.

HOTEL QT
Map p282   Boutique Hotel $$
☎ 212-354-2323; www.hotelqt.com; 125 W 45th St btwn Sixth & Seventh Aves; d incl breakfast from $170; Ⓜ N, Q, R, W, 1, 2, 3 to Times Sq–42 St, B, D, F, V to 47th-50th Streets–Rockefeller Center; 🚣 🅿 🖳
Oh how modern! Opened in 2005, this 139-room Times Sq newby brings boutique for cheap to the area. The reception area – a bodega-style counter – is backed by a bar looking onto the small swimming pool, with a mezzanine lounge and spa above. Tight rooms – named by size-based grades (A to F) – barely fit the beds on wall-to-wall padded platforms. Some tiled bathrooms lack shower doors, so there's no escaping your travel companion's bum while showering. But it's clean and cool and right in the action.

HOTEL STANFORD
Map pp452-3   Budget Hotel $$
☎ 212-563-1500, 800-365-1115; www.hotelstanford .com; 43 W 32nd St btwn Fifth Ave & Broadway; d incl breakfast from $199; Ⓜ B, D, F, N, Q, R, V, W to 34th St–Herald Sq; 🅿 🖳
Calling all karaoke fans, the 122-room Stanford is your base. On a busy stretch of

Koreatown noodle shops and karaoke bars, the Stanford has fairly chintzy rooms, with floral bedspreads and curtains, and framed Monet prints. You can borrow videos (primarily in Japanese and Korean) for the VHS player, or take the mike at the second-floor Maxim Lounge.

HOTEL WOLCOTT

Map pp452-3   Budget Hotel $$

☎ 212-268-2900; www.wolcott.com; 4 W 31st St btwn Fifth Ave & Broadway; d from $180; ◉ B, D, F, N, Q, R, V, W to 34th St–Herald Sq; ⌘ ▣

Buddy Holly stayed in this 1904, beaux-arts fossil when recording in the '50s, and things do sport that '80s-doing-the-'20s feel, with green carpets, striped wallpapers and out-of-date furnishings. Original moldings of the building – which was designed by the maker of Grant's Tomb (p166) – add some flair, as do the chandeliers and cherubs of the gilded lobby. Plus, it's only two blocks from the Empire State Building. A full (much-needed) renovation could work wonders.

HUDSON   Map p282   Boutique Hotel $$

☎ 212-554-6000, 800-697-1791; www.hudsonhotel.com; 356 W 58th St btwn Eighth & Ninth Aves; r $285-450; ◉ A, C, B, D, 1 to 59th St–Columbus Circle; ⌘ ▣

One of boutique-hotel king Ian Schrager's jewels, the all-too-hip Hudson is as much a nightclub as a hotel. Entering it is a trick: fluorescent lemon-lime doors lead to an escalator tub leading to a surprising lobby done up in fake vine and red brick. Adjoining is the chic, floor-lit Chambers Bar. Rooms are cruise-ship small, but cushy in the bare details. Translucent curtains separate the wood-floor entry and bedroom, with a tiny TV tucked in a desk-side cabinet. Bathrooms have glass walls for the peek-oriented. The 15th-floor sky terrace has drinks and views looking toward the namesake river. The location – a block from Central Park, and a few from Broadway theaters – is a bonus.

IROQUOIS   Map p282   International Hotel $$$

☎ 212-840-3080, 800-332-7220; www.iroquoisny.com; 49 W 44th St btwn Fifth & Sixth Aves; r/ste from $385/600; ◉ B, D, F, V to 42nd St, 4, 5, 6, 7 to Grand Central; ⌘ ▣

James Dean's old haunt – he lived in No 803 from 1951 to 1953 – the 114-room

Iroquois boasts history, along with mod cons from a recent renovation. Most who check in are of affluent, mid-aged ilk. The mid-century French look to the rooms is certainly classy – with greens and cream colors, ceiling-reaching Italian marble in the bathrooms, Frette bathrobes and WiFi access. Ask for 'zero line' rooms for nicely framed Chrysler Building views. The lobby restaurant, La Petite Triomphe, buzzes at pre-theater hours. Wear your leather pumps – there's a free shoeshine upon arrival.

IVY TERRACE   Map pp452-3   B&B $$

☎ 516-662-6862; www.ivyterrace.com; E 58th St btwn Lexington & Third Aves; r Mon-Fri/Sat & Sun from $180/200; ◉ 4, 5, 6 to 59th St, N, R, W to Lexington Ave–59th St; ⌘

This lesbian-owned urban B&B is popular with couples who don't want to stay in the fray of the downtown scene. But with gay bars – Townhouse and OW Bar – right on the block, there's still plenty of nearby entertainment, not to mention Bloomingdale's and the rest of the shopping district for all guests, straight or gay. The four rooms have Victorian charm – lace curtains, sleigh beds and hardwood floors, kitchens with breakfast supplies – and fill up fast, so call ahead.

KIMBERLY HOTEL

Map pp452-3   Business Hotel $$

☎ 212-755-0400, 800-683-0400; www.kimberlyhotel.com; 145 E 50th St btwn Third & Lexington Aves; d from $225; ◉ 6 to 51st St, E, V to Lexington Av–53rd St; ⌘ ▣

Generally geared for business travelers and long stays, Kimberly's 186 stately rooms – all with kitchenettes – come with a little fun too: all guests can take a free ride on the hotel yacht on Wednesday, Saturday or Sunday nights. Traditional, European-style rooms come with big desks and fax machines. Guests get entry at the New York Health & Racquet Club. A downstairs bar, the Nikki Beach Bar, is surprisingly hip.

KITANO   Map pp452-3   Deluxe Indie Inn $$$

☎ 212-885-7000, 800-548-2666; www.kitano.com; 66 Park Ave at 38th St; d/ste from $350/750; ◉ S, 4, 5, 6, 7 to Grand Central–42nd St; ⌘ ▣

The long-time hotel location of the Rockefellers' Murray Hill Hotel, the cool,

Japanese-run Kitano was completely rebuilt in 1995, predominantly because the owners were so unhappy with Manhattan hotels. This sleek 18-floor business hotel indeed has a hushed Eastern vibe. At research time, rooms were scheduled for a (slightly overdue) renovation – carpeted rooms are simple, with fluffy duvets, WiFi access, flatscreen TVs and larger work desks are included in the plan. If you wish to have the whole deal, the *ryokan*-style Japanese suite (from $890) is decorated like a traditional Japanese inn, with tatami mats, tea areas and wood floors. Mayor Michael Bloomberg is a big fan of the basement sushi bar.

LE PARKER MERIDIEN

Map p282   International Hotel $$$
☎ 212-245-5000; www.parkermeridien.com; 118 W 57th St btwn Sixth & Seventh Aves; d from $395; ⊕ Q, W to 57th St, F to 57th St; 🚻 🍴 🖥
Luxury all the way but geared for leisure, this 730-room tower has a rooftop pool with a vertigo-defying jogging track, basement racquetball, cartoons in the elevator and 'fuhgettaboudit' privacy door signs. Rooms have extraordinary views and are lined in cherry-wood paneling, and come with useful rotating entertainment centers, with 32-inch TVs and DVD players. Breakfast is not included, but don't skip the famous ones at Norma's in the lobby. Located nearby, a neon hamburger points to an unlikely real-deal burger joint that is a smashing recreation of mid-America.

LIBRARY HOTEL

Map pp452-3   Boutique Hotel $$
☎ 212-983-4500, 877-793-7323; www.libraryhotel .com; 299 Madison Ave at 41st St; d incl breakfast $300; ⊕ S, 4, 5, 6 to Grand Central–42nd St; 🍴 🖥
Each of the 10 floors in this cleverly themed space is dedicated to one of the 10 major categories of the Dewey Decimal System: Social Sciences, Literature, Philosophy, and so on, with a total of 6000 volumes split up between quarters. The handsome style here is bookish, too: mahogany paneling, hushed reading rooms and a gentlemen's-club atmosphere, thanks largely to its stately 1912 brick-mansion home. A bonus is the rooftop deck bar, where you can peek down 41st St to the real library.

MANDARIN ORIENTAL NEW YORK

Map p282   International Chain Hotel $$$
☎ 212-885-8800, 866-801-8880; www.mandarin oriental.com; 80 Columbus Circle at 60th St; r from $850; ⊕ A, B, C, D, 1 to 59th St–Columbus Circle; 🚻 🍴 🖥
Occupying the 35th to 54th floors of a modern 84-floor tower at the southwestern edge of Central Park, the Mandarin is the hotel all New York hotels look up to. With some suites breaking $13,000 a night, it's tip-top, Eastern-influence opulence, with superb views over the park and Midtown skyline. Even standard rooms get many of the higher-priced suite touches – with Japanese writing-box desks, TVs in the all-marble bathrooms and chaise lounges by the full-wall windows. Those without the bucks can splurge for a $17 martini or $38 tea service at the towering lobby lounge. The hotel has a seriously pampering spa and a narrow lap pool in the split-level fitness centre.

MORGANS HOTEL

Map pp452-3   Boutique Hotel $$
☎ 212-686-0300, 800-334-3408; www.morgans hotelgroup.com; 237 Madison Ave btwn 37th & 38th Sts; d incl breakfast from $300; ⊕ 6 to 33rd St, B, D, F, N, Q, R, V, W to 34th St; 🍴 🖥
This Ian Schrager classic, the pioneer for New York's boutique hotels, looks as cutting-edge as it did when it opened in 1985. The 113-room, sleek hotel has some surprises. Curtains hide doorways from the lobby into the swank Morgans Bar and split-level Asia de Cuba restaurant; in the rooms, Robert Mapplethorpe prints (done specifically for the hotel) provide lone wall decoration in small, but well laid-out spaces. Bathrooms are lined in black-and-white tile with the same stainless-steel sinks used in Concord jets. The living room has a computer for guests and sunken sitting areas overlooking Madison Avenue.

MURRAY HILL INN

Map pp452-3   Budget Hotel $
☎ 212-683-6900, 888-996-6376; www.murray hillinn.com; 143 E 30th St btwn Lexington & Third Aves; d from $129; ⊕ 6 to 33rd St; 🍴 🖥
Named for its pleasant, leafy residential nook of Midtown, this friendly 47-room

budget option is better than most in the price range. A recent renovation added wood floors and flat-screen TVs to the rooms, which also have small refrigerators and a small closet. All but two rooms have private bathrooms.

RITZ-CARLTON – NEW YORK, CENTRAL PARK

Map p282   International Chain Hotel $$$
☎ 212-308-9100, 800-241-3333; www.ritzcarlton .com; 50 Central Park South btwn Sixth & Seventh Aves; r from $995; ⊙ N, R, Q, W to 57th St, F to 57th St; ✳ 🖳

It's about as lux as Manhattan goes: a landmark building with views of Central Park so giant you almost can't see New York. Inside the opulent lobby bar, a harp player plucks on strings while the ritzy set sip on cocktails. All 261 rooms are faintly French colonial, with tasseled arm chairs, lovely inlaid-tile bathrooms and loads of space. If you're splurging, do go for a park view, where a *Birds of New York* field guide is set by a telescope. Three-course dinners at high-class Atelier run to about $85. There's also a great spa and business center.

ROGER WILLIAMS

Map pp452-3   Boutique Hotel $$
☎ 212-448-7000, 888-448-7788; www.hotelroger williams.com; 131 Madison Ave at 31st St; d from $250; ⊙ 6 to 33rd St; ✳ 🖳

Here's a boutique not afraid of a little color. A geometric splash of orange, blue and green greets guests of this hotel named for the founder of Rhode Island (and the church next door). Rooms are small, but homey – with quilts folded at the end of comfy beds, and flat-screen TVs over small work desks. Garden Terrace rooms (from $295) have balconies. The second-floor lounge has a great breakfast ($13) featuring the best of bakeries from all over New York.

ROYALTON

Map pp452-3   Boutique Hotel $$
☎ 212-869-4400, 800-635-9013; www.royalton.com; 44 W 44th St btwn Fifth & Sixth Aves; d from $225; ⊙ B, D, F, V to 42nd St; ✳ 🖳

A funky mix of modern and classic (glam cruise liner theme inside, Greek columns outside), this Ian Schrager and Philippe

Starck creation is a mainstay chic choice in this primetime spot Midtown. Deep blue carpet rushes by curving hallways with 'porthole' numbers on doors. Short bed frames are topped with down duvets. For an extra $50, superior rooms have more space. The sunken lobby lounge is a cool hang-out spot, with Chinese checker boards and cocktail gurglers.

SHOREHAM

Map p282   Boutique Hotel $$
☎ 212-247-6700, 800-553-3347; www.shoreham hotel.com; 33 W 55th St btwn Fifth & Sixth Aves; d from $300; ⊙ F to 57th St; ✳ 🖳

Boosted by an ongoing renovation at research time, the artful and chic Shoreham is a rising scenester hotel in the heart of Midtown. In the lobby, there are video loops of hummingbirds, while the 175 rooms are said to be inspired by lilies – abstract black-and-white photos of flowers make up feather-bed headboards. Extras include clear-door iceboxes stocked with your requested treats, flat-screen TVs, all-white tile bathrooms, and work desks with Internet access. The lobby bar sports a futuristic look and attracts an artful professional crowd.

THIRTYTHIRTY

Map pp452-3   Boutique Hotel $$
☎ 212-689-1900, 800-497-6078; www.thirtythirty -nyc.com; 30 E 30th St btwn Park & Madison Aves; $$; d from $159; ⊙ 6 to 33rd St; ✳ 🖳

This 252-room hotel aims to be a boutique stay for cheap, but gets sidetracked by a

W New York Times Square (p371) the kingpin of the Ws

few tacky touches – such as handmade ads in the elevators, or playing an '80s pop radio station (and their ads) in the lobby. Still, many visitors toting Macy's bags check into simple rooms with fudge-colored rugs, TVs bolted to the walls, a small closet with safe, and teddy bears between pillows. Worth considering at under $200 only.

W NEW YORK – TIMES SQUARE

Map p282   Boutique Hotel $$

☎ 212-930-7400, 877-946-8357; www.whotelsthe world.com; 1567 Broadway at 47th St; d/ste from $300/450; ⊕ C, E to 50th St, N, R, W to 49th St; ✂ ▣

The best of Manhattan's five Ws, this ultra-swank 507-room hotel affords a knock-out look at the crazy scene of neon. 'Wonderful' rooms are below the 31st floor, identical 'spectacular' above – all have loads of light, white-tile entries leading to rooms where beds burst with pillows. Glass desks face a full wall of glass. The corner 'urban suite' includes two flat-screen TVs and a cool living room with pull-out sofa. All guests can bypass the $20 entry (and lines) to the Whiskey bar downstairs – if the velvet-rope scene is your scene. Other good W hotels in Midtown include side-by-side **W New York – The Court & The Tuscany** (Map pp452–3; ☎ 212-685-1100; 130 E 39th St; d from $399), with stylish Icon restaurant with red-velvet seats and a lovely garden; and **W New York** (Map pp452–3; ☎ 212-755-1200; 541 Lexington Ave; d from $409), the original W amid stodgy old-timer hotels. Also see **W New York – Union Square** (p364).

WALDORF-ASTORIA

Map pp452-3   Legendary Chain $$

☎ 212-355-3000, 800-925-3673; www.waldorf astoria.com; 301 Park Ave btwn 49th & 50th Sts; s & d $200-500; ⊕ 6 to 51st St, E, F to Lexington Ave; ✂ ▣

An attraction in itself, the 416-room, 42-floor legendary hotel – now part of the Hilton chain – is an art-deco landmark. It's massive, occupying a full city block – with 13 conference rooms and shops and eateries keeping the ground floor buzzing with life. Elegant rooms conjure some old-world fussiness, with rose-petal rugs and embossed floral wallpaper. Staff tell us three-quarters of daily visitors come just to look. Plenty to gawk at:

the *Wheel of Life* mosaic tile entry (at the Park Ave entrance) features nearly 150,000 tiles.

WARWICK

Map p282   International Chain Hotel $$

☎ 212-247-2700, 800-223-4099; www.warwick hotels.com; 65 W 54th St at Sixth Ave; r from $225; ⊕ B, D, F, V to 47th-50th Sts–Rockefeller Center; ✂ ▣

Lots of business folk and gray-haired travelers on package trips check into this stuffy classic, which William Randolph Hearst purportedly built in 1927 for his infamous mistress Marion Davies who 'performed' at Ziegfeld's a block away. The 33-floor hotel has traditional rooms, recently redone. The lobby Murals on 54 restaurant features some slightly naughty murals (ie bare bums, a bloke urinating) painted by a feisty artist upset at Hearst balking on his bill. There's a fitness centre and business centre.

WJ HOTEL

Map p282   Bargain Hotel $$

☎ 212-246-7550, 888-567-7550; www.wjhotel.com; 318 W 51st St btwn Eighth & Ninth Aves; d from $159; ⊕ C, E to 50th St; ✂ ▣

Still proud of a 2003 scrub-up, the Washington Jefferson (gone hip now as 'WJ') offers modern, comfortable rooms with platform beds, goose-down comforters and big padded headboards to lean your head back on and watch cable TV. The downstairs sushi restaurant Shimizu attracts Hell's Kitchen locals looking for low-priced lunch specials (from $14).

Sleeping

MIDTOWN

UPPER WEST SIDE

You'll find a broad selection of midrange and budget hotels in this part of town, but none of the fanfare you would discover in the fashionable inns to the south. It's strictly old-school New York – character, bargain and no-nonsense grandeur – and Central Park is no more than a couple blocks' walk.

COUNTRY INN THE CITY

Map pp454-5   B&B $$

☎ 212-580-4183; www.countryinnthecity.com; 270 W 77th St btwn Amsterdam & Columbus Aves; apt from $185; ⊕ 1 to 79th St; ✷ ▢

Just like staying with your big-city friend: this 1891 limestone townhouse sits on a stellar, tree-lined street, and the four often-filled, self-contained apartments are cool and sophisticated, with four-poster beds, glossed wooden floors, warm color schemes and lots of light. Most furnishings – sofa, lamps, rugs – have been picked up in area antique shops, spurring on the 19th-century feel. There's some welcome food supplies for the kitchenettes in each room (including stove and micro-waves). Rooms are for two people only and have Internet access; there's a three-night minimum. No credit cards.

HOSTELLING INTERNATIONAL – NEW YORK Map pp454-5   Hostel $

☎ 212-932-2300; www.hinewyork.org; 891 Amsterdam Ave at 103rd St; dm $29-40, d $135; ⊕ 1 to 103rd St; ✷ ▢

Occupying an impressive red-brick 1883 mansion that once served the HQ for the 'Relief of Respectable, Aged, Indigent Females,' these days 624 well-scrubbed bunks welcome all. There's little of the history inside the rather clinical hallways and rooms, but heaps of public spaces (like a back lawn and brick courtyard, plus a giant communal kitchen) and a friendly help desk offering walking tours (a few are free). Because many groups stay (including girl scouts!), the hostel is alcohol-free. Three private rooms come with private bathroom. Dorm rooms have a lot of space, and have new carpet, plus lockers and air-con. We heard a rumor of a ghost here (away from the sleeping quarters, thankfully). There's WiFi access and computers handy to check email.

HOTEL BELLECLAIRE

Map pp454-5   Budget Hotel $$

☎ 212-362-7700; www.hotelbelleclaire.com; 250 W 77th St at Broadway; d from $199; ⊕ 1 to 79th St; ✷

Nothing fancy, the nine-storey Belleclaire is a budget option that rises above the usual stuffy, ruffly international hotels at this price range. Rooms are small and have varying lay-outs and attempt a modern (read: no floral patterns) look. All come with tiled bathrooms, TVs mounted on the wall, and fluffy duvets over the comfy beds. There's a claustrophobic fitness centre, but Central Park is just three blocks east!

HOTEL NEWTON Map pp454-5   Budget Hotel $$

☎ 212-678-6500; www.newyorkhotel.com/newton; 2528 Broadway btwn 94th & 95th Sts; s & d from $150; ⊕ 1, 2, 3 to 96th St; ✷ ▢

Fairly by-the-numbers, this clean and cheap, pretty uninspiring, 109-room hotel has all-new furnishings and caters to a mix of international visitors and academic folk wanting a base for Columbia University 30 blocks north. Framed still lifes certainly don't make a case for 'swank,' and higher-priced suites only add an enigmatic sitting area with a sofa facing a wall. But all rooms have refrigerators, microwaves, Internet access and double-paned windows. In January and February, rates drop to $80 – can't beat that.

INN NEW YORK CITY

Map pp454-5   B&B $$

☎ 212-580-1900, 800-660-7051; www.inn newyorkcity.com; 266 W 71st St at West End Ave; ste from $300; ⊕ 1, 2, 3 to 72nd St; ✷

Four massive, quirky suites occupy a whole floor in this 1900 townhouse, which allows you to feel as if you're living in a mansion. It's far west, and close to both Riverside Park and Central Park, and its rooms feature antique chestnut furnish-ings, feather beds topped in down com-forters, Jacuzzis and stained-glass panels, if just a bit too much flowered carpeting. The Opera Suite has a private terrace. Three suites are $575 during peak season, $475 other times; the smaller Vermont Suite starts at $300. All rooms have cable TV with DVD and VCR. It's stately, massive and heavy with history.

BIDDING FOR TRAVEL

Finding bargains is really not such a skill any more – as long as you know how to use the Internet and decide on a price that's right for you, you're in. It's thanks to the slew of websites that help you find discounted quarters and even name your own prices, just like the mega-popular sites that do the same for discounted airline tickets.

Priceline.com is a straightforward site that lets you choose the area of Manhattan you'd like to stay in, the grade of hotel room (one to five stars) and then bid on the price you'd like to pay. A different version of this is **Hotwire.com**, which allows you to pick a neighborhood and tells you a price, but not the hotel. The catch, on all such sites, is that you must enter your credit card information before you know where you'll be staying; if the type of hotel you requested agrees to match your price, you'll automatically be charged for the room and notified that you indeed have a reservation.

Travelers who want to know where they'll be up front are better off browsing the offerings at one of the following discount sites: **Orbitz.com**, which lets you choose your hotel's star rating and amenities and then gives you several options, as do **Hotels.com**, **Hoteldiscounts.com** and **Travelzoo.com**, all claiming prices that are up to 70% less than the rack rates. **Justnewyorkhotels.com**, **Newyork.dealsonhotels.com**, **Newyorkcityhotelstoday.com** and **NYC-hotels.net** work the same way, but are focused strictly on NYC. Checking individual hotel websites is also worth a shot, especially during slow seasons suc has mid-January through March, when inns offer discounts themselves.

JAZZ ON THE PARK HOSTEL

Map pp454-5   Hostel $

☎ 212-932-1600; www.jazzhostel.com; 36 W 106th St btwn Central Park West & Manhattan Ave; $; dm incl breakfast $27-32, d incl breakfast $85; ⊕ B, C to 103rd St; 🚲 🖳

This former flophouse on a street named for Duke Ellington is deservedly popular. In addition to simple but small rooms, there's lots of hang-out options: two terrace sitting areas and a basement lounge (for jazz and comedy) under renovation at research time. Also, the common snack bar serves espresso and $3.50 lasagna. Dorms are co-ed and single-sex, ranging from four to 12 bunks per room. They're all small but have lockers. Shared bathrooms are clean but have no changing space outside the showers. There's Internet and locked luggage areas on the main folder. Private rooms are little but walls and a bed; all but one are at a nearby annex (54 W 105th St). Also see Jazz on the Town (p358). They were planning to open a Harlem location at research time.

ON THE AVE

Map pp454-5   Boutique Hotel $$

☎ 212-362-1100, 800-497-6028; www.ontheave.com; 2178 Broadway at W 77th St; r/ste from $225/625; ⊕ 1, 2, 3 to 79th St; 🚲 🖳

An excellent uptown hotel, the stylish and cool 16-floor On the Ave boasts 266 rooms done up in warm earthy tones and brimming with extras from a recent renovation (eg fudge-colored suede headboards backing new featherbeds, flat-screen TVs and bedside CD players). Sunlight pours into the huge windows. All rooms have a data port with WiFi access. There's a super glassed-in top-floor balcony with seats facing the north.

PHILLIPS CLUB

Map pp454-5   Business Hotel $$$

☎ 212-835-8800; www.phillipsclub.com; 155 W 66th St btwn Broadway & Amsterdam Ave; ste from $390, per month from $6600; ⊕ 1 to 66th St–Lincoln Center; 🚲 🖳

Most often used for long stays – one month or more – but the suites are also available nightly. They're classy and spacious, with high-end linens and original framed photographs, and they offer business amenities including data ports, multiphone lines with voicemail and conference spaces. All guests get access to the exclusive Reebok Sports Club gym.

UPPER EAST SIDE

Some of New York's poshest, most elegant hotels are up here, allowing you to stay near some of the city's wealthiest residents and greatest cultural institutions, such as the Met and Central Park. Rooms run upwards of $300 on average, and nightlife is pretty much a non-happening event, so be prepared to crawl downtown (or cross-town) for any action.

BENTLEY Map pp454-5   Boutique Hotel $$
☎ 212-644-6000, 888-664-6835; www.nychotels.com; 500 E 62nd St at York Ave; r/ste from $268/359; ⊕ F to Lexington Ave–63rd St; 🚲 🖳
A little enigmatic and way east – it's practically under the tram to Roosevelt Island

and spitting distance from the riverside FDR expressway – this 197-room transformation of an old office building packs some boutique, modern style into tight spaces. Dark gray carpet and all-leather chaise lounges by the window add a somber effect. Suites grant two rooms, and some straddle corners, but the mini kitchenettes are dated after-thoughts. Best is the top-floor lounge with food from 5pm and an excellent spot for after-dinner drinks under a gaze of city lights.

CARLYLE Map pp454-5   Deluxe Indie Inn $$$
☎ 212-744-1600; www.thecarlyle.com; 35 E 76th St btwn Madison & Park Aves; d/ste from $650/1075; ⊕ 6 to 77th St; ✂ ▭
A classic since its 1930 opening, the 179-room Carlyle is where Woody Allen plays clarinet on Monday night, JFK and Jackie O stayed, and where Louis XIV might feel at home. You're in good company – if you can afford it. Opulence is at notch 11 here. The lobby's black-marble floors look like a pool of oil, the Bemelmans Bar is a slick art-deco bar, rooms are as big as suites elsewhere, with old-fashioned luxury (eg 430-thread-count linens, Jacuzzi bathtubs).

FRANKLIN Map pp454-5   Boutique Hotel $$
☎ 212-369-1000, 800-607-4009; www.franklin hotel.com; 164 E 87th St btwn Lexington & Third Aves; d incl breakfast from $290; ⊕ 4, 5, 6 to 86th St; ✂ ▭
A good choice for an Upper East Side bed for under $300 (usually), the 49-room Franklin has seriously small rooms, but they fit a lot in. Quilts hang off the end of hefty beds and there are fresh flowers. There's a computer to use in the lobby, where French accordion music is piped in and staff set out wine and cheese from 5pm to 7pm.

Carlyle (above) where black marble and good cotton abound

MARK NEW YORK
Map pp454-5   Luxury Indie Inn $$$
☎ 212-744-4300, 800-526-6566; www.mandarin oriental.com; 25 E 77th St at Madison Ave; d/ste from $310/735; ⊕ 6 to 77th St; ✂ ▭
Little bro to the super-glam Mandarin Oriental (p369), the regal Mark isn't exactly a cheap travelers' version – but the 176-room building, a transformation of a 1920s art-deco residence, retains a more homey base for the heart of the Upper East Side. Standard rooms have a chintzy, airy feel, plus writing desks looking out the windows, but the deluxe rooms (for an extra $30 or $50) are worth the splurge for a fully stocked Euro-style kitchen and more space. There's a small fitness centre.

WANDERERS INN Map pp454-5   Hostel $
☎ 212-289-8083; www.wanderersinn.com; 179 E 94th St; dm incl breakfast $30-36, r with shared/ private bathroom $75/85; ⊕ 6 to 96th St; ✂ ▭
This four-floor walk-up townhouse is a surprising hostel on a respectable residential block on the ever-respectable Upper East Side. There are free pizza nights and a backyard to light up or get out the beer-bong. Opened in 2002, the Wanderers' carpeted dorms feature four-to-ten army-style bunks (and army-style lockers) – some have private bathrooms. Dorms on the basement floor are a little stuffy. **Wanderers** (☎ 212-222-8935; 257 W 113th St) runs a similar hostel in the Upper West Side too.

HARLEM
With gentrification comes waves of visitors, and the smartest entrepreneurs have capitalized on that fact – but in a classy, quirky way. Just be aware that some side streets may feel slightly menacing after dark.

HARLEM FLOPHOUSE
Map pp458-9   Guesthouse $
☎ 212-662-0678; www.harlemflophouse.com; 242 W 123rd St btwn Adam Clayton Powell & Frederick Douglass Blvds; s/d $100/125th; ⊕ A, B, C, D to 125th St
A superb alternative Manhattan base, this gorgeous four-room, 1890s townhouse conjures up the jazz era, with period-piece antiques, glossed-wood floors and vintage radios tuned to a local jazz station. There's shared bathrooms – one with a sink hauled back from the historic Blumstein's shop

(see p221) – but no air-con or TVs. It's a kept-real trip to the past. The owner can point out the real-deal gospel church services that the tour buses miss and good soul food eateries nearby.

BROOKLYN

It used to take a funeral to get many Manhattanites to cross the East River, but the jump – as the tired Brooklynite cliché goes – is just a quick subway ride. And it really is. Though Brooklyn is still an infant in the lodging scene, it's an underrated base for New York. Nearly all its worthy options are well-priced B&Bs in appealing residential hoods of its northwest – and you get extras like 'hellos' on the sidewalks.

AKWAABA MANSION INN

Map pp460-1   B&B $$
☎ 718-455-5958, 866-466-3855; www.akwaaba
.com; 347 MacDonough St btwn Lewis & Stuyvesant Aves, Bedford Stuyvesant; r incl breakfast from $150; ◉ A, C to Utica Ave; ⊠

A New Yorker's dream – an 1860 mansion fenced-off on a block of century-old townhouses – the four-room Awkwaaba's only drawback is its remote location in the misunderstood neighborhood Bedford Stuyvesant. Presently the setting of Chris Rock's 'Everybody Hates Chris' TV show, beautiful Bed-Sty (at least this part) has a hard time escaping its 'do or die' reputation from its gritty past. The Awkaaba, along with a couple eateries and shops nearby, are doing their part in getting Bed-Sty back on the map. Its original parquet floors and ceiling moldings are accented with new African-themed touches (eg imported statuettes in bathroom nooks, safari paper-border above original wood paneling). Rooms are themed – the 'regal retreat' is the most traditional, with claw-foot tub in the bathroom. Giant southern-style breakfasts are served family-style in the parlor. The inn caters to many local weddings.

AWESOME B&B Map p462   B&B $$
☎ 718-858-4859; 136 Lawrence St btwn Willoughby & Fulton Sts; r incl breakfast from $140; ◉ M, R to Lawrence St, 2, 3 to Hoyt St; ⊠ ▯
In busy downtown Brooklyn, this basic B&B has six small rooms overflowing with detail (lots of small lamps, entry tables,

textured hand-painted walls showing their smears) and a hostel-like vibe. It's fun too: 'Gothic Nights' gets medieval on your arse, while the 'Dragon Palace' room has a mural of an Asian-style dragon wrapping around three walls. Staff will print out maps based on your NYC plan. There are two shared bathrooms. Downtown isn't Brooklyn's most atmospheric hood, but Smith Street's restaurants and Brooklyn Heights' brownstones are a few blocks away by foot.

BAISLEY HOUSE Map p465   B&B $$
☎ 718-935-1959; 294 Hoyt St btwn Union & Sackett Sts; r incl breakfast $162 & $192; ◉ F, G to Carroll St; ⊠
The childhood home of Hollywood starlet Susan Hayworth, the three-room Baisley House is a five-minute walk from the subway on a side-street of 18th-century townhouses – and a step back 150 years. It's lushly decorated with a Victoria-rama of 17th- to 19th-century pieces (busts and clocks on mantels, wing-back chairs, period-piece landscapes). All rooms access a shared bathroom. Breakfast – a big, daily changing one – is served on nice days in the back garden. The owner is an encyclopedia of area knowledge.

BED & BREAKFAST ON THE PARK
Map p464   B&B $$
☎ 718-499-6115; www.bbnyc.com; 113 Prospect Park West btwn 6th & 7th Sts; d incl breakfast from $155; ◉ F to Seventh Ave–Park Slope; ⊠
Across from Brooklyn's Prospect Park in yuppified Park Slope, this homey Victorian B&B has seven rooms splashed out in oriental rugs, potted plants, poster beds covered in pillows, gas-operated fireplaces and original wood floors and wall moldings. Family-style breakfasts of soufflés and kielbasa get chatty and can last hours. All rooms have private bathroom. The WiFi signal reaches some rooms and the garden out back.

MARRIOTT AT THE BROOKLYN
BRIDGE Map p462   International Chain Hotel $$
☎ 718-246-7000, 888-436-3759; 333 Adams St; d from $199; ◉ 2, 3, 4, 5 to Borough Hall, A, C, F to Jay St; ▨ ⊠ ▯
Though a blah chain, the 374-room (and expanding) Marriott is – for the time

being – the only big-time hotel on this side of the East River. Rates drops on weekends, when the business travelers head home. Rooms are predictable, but comfy – with new king-size mattresses, chintzy bedspreads, word desks and Internet access. There's a giant fitness center with a lap pool.

UNION STREET B&B Map p465   B&B $
☎ 718-852-8406; www.unionstbrooklyn bandb.com; 405 Union St, btwn Smith & Hoyt Sts; s/d incl breakfast $100/150; ◉ F, G to Carroll St; ✂
On a fine strip of townhouses in Carroll Gardens, this slightly peeling 1898 brownstone is a little scrappy, decorated in half Victorian and half assorted pieces from later years. But it's cheap and friendly, and the neighborhood is great. All six rooms

have shared bath (there are two, one with an old claw-foot tub).

QUEENS

Sprawling Queens has a few unexciting chains scattered about, which cater to visiting relatives.

HOWARD JOHNSON

Map p467   Chain Hotel $
☎ 718-461-3888; info@howardjohnsonny.com; 135-33 38th Ave; s or d $119; ◉ 7 to Flushing–Main St; ✂ ▢
This basic chain won't surprise you inside, and it's at the end of the 7 line, but it's in the heart of Flushing – a safe, cheap backup with tons of great Chinese, Vietnamese and Korean restaurants.

Excursions

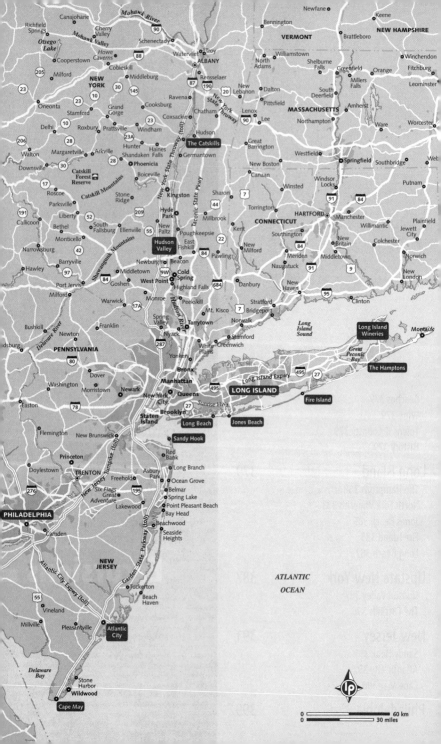

Excursions

Some New Yorkers tend to get stuck in ruts, often not leaving the city for months at a time. 'There's nowhere tranquil nearby,' they moan. 'There's too much traffic – and it's too inconvenient without a car.' But don't believe it for a minute – because, come summer, locals disappear in spades. The surrounding environs – New York's Hudson Valley and the mountainous Catskills, New Jersey's refreshing beaches and glitzy casinos, Long Island's ritzy Hamptons and plentiful wineries, and Philadelphia's rich history – offer a slew of wonderful year-round options, from beaches and country towns to wine trails and nature preserves. You can get to just about any excursion in this chapter via public transportation (which, if combined with cycling, gives you even more options), but if you want or need a car, be aware that rental rates here are high (upwards of $60 a day), and simply plan your escape during a weekday, when most of the city is stuck at work. Beating traffic is one of the advantages of being on vacation, after all.

BEACHES

It may seem surprising, but New York City is surrounded by beaches – sandy stretches of parkland that abut the frothy Atlantic Ocean. While the closest lie within the city limits (Coney Island, the Rockaways, City Island), urban beaches can be crowded, noisy and dirty, and heading out of town will definitely provide a more tranquil experience. Long Island has several options: **Jones Beach**, the sprawling city of sand; **Fire Island**, a peaceful, car-free gem; hip **Long Beach**, a quick train ride from Manhattan; and the **Hamptons**, with miles of white beaches edging the area's tiny towns. In New Jersey you'll find the entire Jersey Shore, with highlights including **Sandy Hook** and **Cape May**.

WINE

While New York's Finger Lakes region, way upstate, is the state's most renowned wine producer, Long Island is quickly catching up. You'll find more than 30 vineyards on Long Island's eastern end, with most on the **North Fork** and more and more uncorking on the **South Fork** (the **Hamptons**) as well.

TOWNS & COUNTRY

Leisurely paced villages surrounded by nature are closer than you may think. New York State's **Hudson Valley** has endless little hubs great for exploring, and the area is laced with historic mansions and small museums. Further north are the mountainous **Catskills**, dotted with artsy hamlets, scenic hiking and camping spots and antique shops galore. On Long Island, the **Hamptons** truly offer a bit of everything, in a series of quaint towns known for picture-perfect main streets, high-end boutiques and a five-star restaurant scene (with plenty of celeb sightings). Connected to the Hamptons by a ferry is the **North Fork** of Long Island, which is a more low-key version of its Hamptons counterpart known more for its mellow B&Bs and myriad wineries.

HISTORY

A quick bus ride takes you to the historic heart of the nation. **Philadelphia** – a smaller, mellower city than NYC – has plenty of its own offerings, such as the Liberty Bell, Independence Hall, the US Mint and tasty cheese steaks, to name but a few.

LONG ISLAND

The largest island in the US (120 miles long), Long Island begins with Brooklyn (Kings County) and Queens (Queens County) on its western shore. New York City then gives way to the suburban housing, strip malls and working-class heroes in neighboring Nassau County. You might hear reference to the north and south shores here; the north is the ritzy part. The terrain becomes flatter, less crowded and more exclusive in rural Suffolk

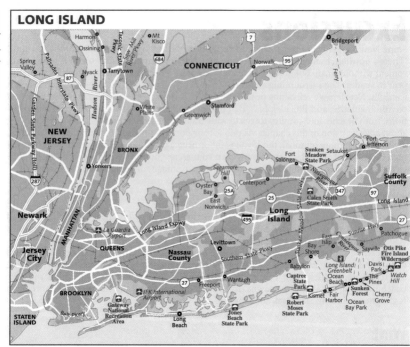

LONG ISLAND

County, which comprises the eastern end of the island. Suffolk County itself contains two peninsulas – commonly called the North and South Forks – divided by Peconic Bay. It's the South Fork that lures the most visitors, as it's what is also known as the East End – or, commonly, the Hamptons.

THE HAMPTONS

What began as a tranquil hideaway for city artists, musicians and writers has developed into a frenetic summer getaway mobbed with jet-setters, celebrities and throngs of curious wannabes. That said, there is still plenty of the original peace and beauty to discover. The beaches and farmlands (what's left of them) are indeed stunning and there's plenty of opportunity for outdoor activity, from kayaking to mountain biking. You can easily combine your peace-seeking with some boutique shopping and serious dining, as both the shops and restaurants are top notch. You're also quite likely to spot celebs if you're here in summer. But bargain travelers be warned: absolutely everything costs a pretty penny out here, with most inns charging well over $300 a night (you could also get up early and do a long day trip). Summer is high season; prices do drop a wee bit and traffic jams disappear about a month after Labor Day. This lessening of crowds, combined with the balmy weather of the fall harvest season, make autumn the most beautiful time for a visit.

The Hamptons is actually a series of villages, most with 'Hampton' in the name. Those at the western end – or 'west of the canal,' as locals call the places that are on the other side of the Shinnecock Canal – include Hampton Bays, Quogue and Westhampton, and are less frenzied than those to the east, which start with the village of **Southampton**. This is an old-moneyed and rather conservative spot compared to some of its neighbors, home to sprawling old mansions, a main street with no 'beachwear' allowed, but some lovely beaches. Pick up maps and brochures about the town at the **Southampton Chamber of Commerce office**, squeezed among a group of high-priced artsy-crafty shops and decent restaurants. Within the town is a small Native American reservation, home to the Shinnecocks, who run a tiny **Shinnecock Museum** with unpredictable hours. The **Parrish Art Museum** has quality exhibitions (and be sure

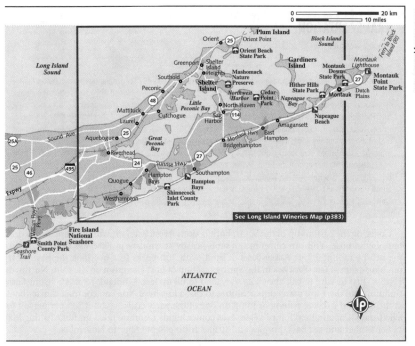

See Long Island Wineries Map (p383)

to pick up a copy of the *East Hampton Star* or *Southampton Press* for listings of myriad local art galleries). Dining at the new **James on Main**, on orange-glazed sea bass and the like, is an unforgettable experience.

To the east, **Bridgehampton** has the shortest of all the main drags, but it's packed with trendy boutiques and restaurants. The **Bridgehampton Inn** is a plush and classic inn with WiFi service.

Seven miles north of Bridgehampton on Peconic Bay is the old whaling town of **Sag Harbor**. There are bunches of historic homes and points of interests here and you can pick up a historic walking tour map at the **Windmill Information Center** on Long Wharf at the end of Main St. **Sag Harbor Whaling Museum** is fascinating, and the village's tiny Cape Cod–style streets are a joy to stroll; there are several excellent restaurants to discover. The **Bike Hampton** shop rents bicycles and sells maps of cycling trails. Get gourmet sustenance without going broke at the delicious new **Fat Ralph's Deli**. **American Hotel**, right on Main St, has eight luxurious rooms and a highly regarded restaurant catering to scotch-and-cigar types from the city.

A quick ferry ride on the South Ferry (see p382) from the edge of North Haven, which borders Sag Harbor, will take you to sleepy Shelter Island, nearly a third of which is dedicated to the **Mashomack Nature Preserve**, dotted with biking and hiking trails.

Long Island's trendiest town is **East Hampton**, where you can catch readings and art exhibitions at **Guild Hall**. **Babette's** is an outstanding organic and mostly vegetarian eatery. Restaurants where you'll most likely spot celebrities include **Della Femina** and **Nick & Toni's**, where the Italian-influenced meals are flawless. **Mill House Inn**, a renovated property, offers eight lovely rooms.

More honky-tonk than the rest of the Hamptons, **Montauk** has relatively reasonable restaurants and a louder bar scene, largely because all the service personnel – mainly students and new Mexican immigrants – live here in communal housing. For a kitschy 'bargain,' try staying at the **Memory Motel**, a scruffy but comfortable spot where Mick Jagger often stayed in the 1970s and was inspired to write the Rolling Stones song of the same name. To get pampered, book a room at the beachfront, spa-equipped **Gurney's Inn Resort**. For some real beachy eatin', head to the **Lobster Roll** ('Lunch') for what else but a lobster roll – rich lobster-meat salad stuffed into a fresh hot-dog roll.

TRANSPORTATION

Distance from New York City 100 miles (East Hampton)
Direction East
Travel time 2¼ hours

Car Take the Midtown Tunnel out of Manhattan, which will take you onto I-495/Long Island Expressway. Follow this for about 1½ hours to exit TK, which will take you onto TK East. Take it for about 5 miles and then merge onto the Montauk Hwy/Rte 27, which will take you directly into Southampton. Follow Rte 27 to get to all towns east.
Bus The **Hampton Jitney** (☎ 800-936-0440; www.hamptonjitney.com; one way $29, round-trip $51) is a luxury express bus. It departs from Manhattan's East Side – 86th St; 40th St between Lexington and Third Aves; 69th St; and 59th St at Lexington Ave – and makes stops at villages along Rte 27 in the Hamptons.
Train The **Long Island Rail Road** (LIRR; ☎ 718-217-5477; www.mta.nyc.ny.us/lirr; one way $14.50) leaves from Penn Station in Manhattan and the Flatbush Ave station in Brooklyn, making stops in West Hampton, Southampton, Bridgehampton, East Hampton and Montauk.
South Ferry (☎ 631-749-1200; Rte 114, North Haven; ☯ 5:45am-1:45am Jun 1-Labor Day, 9am-5pm Mon-Fri, 9am-1pm Sat, closed Sun Labor Day-May 30) Trips occur every 10 to 15 minutes between Sag Harbor and Shelter Island.

Covering the eastern tip of the South Fork is **Montauk Point State Park**, with its impressive Montauk Lighthouse. You can camp in the sand nearby at windswept **Hither Hills State Park** or hike the nearby mountainous **Walking Dunes** of sand, with 80ft peaks that overlook the bay. Or try pitching a tent at **Cedar Point Park** in the Springs section of East Hampton on the calm Northwest Harbor. Just be sure to call ahead, as sites tend to fill up fast. Montauk retains a strong fishing tradition and there are many opportunities to cast a line here. You can contract charter boats at the dock for a day of fishing or jump on one of the party cruises (about $35 per person for a half-day). Captain Fred E Bird's **Flying Cloud** comes highly recommended for fluke fishing May to September and sea bass, porgies and striper fishing September to November.

Sights & Information

Bike Hampton (☎ 631-725-7329; 36 Main St, Sag Harbor; rental per day $25-40)

Cedar Point Park (☎ 631-852-7620)

Flying Cloud (☎ 631-668-2026; 67 Mulford Ave, Montauk)

Guild Hall (☎ 631-324-0806; www.guildhall.org; 158 Main St, East Hampton)

Hither Hills State Park (☎ 631-668-2554)

Mashomack Nature Preserve (☎ 631-749-1001)

Montauk Point State Park (☎ 631-668-3781)

Parrish Art Museum (☎ 631-283-2111; 25 Jobs Lane, Southampton; adult/senior & student $5/3; ☯ 11am-5pm Mon-Sat, 1-5pm Sun Memorial Day–Sept 14, closed Tue-Wed rest of year)

Sag Harbor Whaling Museum (☎ 631-725-0770; www .sagharborwhalingmuseum.org; Main St at Garden St, Sag Harbor; adult/senior & student $5/3; ☯ 10am-5pm Mon-Sat, 1-5pm Sun May 17–Oct 1; closed Oct-May)

Shinnecock Museum (☎ 631-287-4923; Montauk Hwy, Southampton; admission $5; ☯ 11am-4pm Fri-Sun)

Southampton Chamber of Commerce (☎ 631-283-0402; 76 Main St, Southampton; ☯ 9am-5pm Mon-Fri)

Windmill Information Center (☎ 631-692-4664; Long Wharf at Main St, Sag Harbor; ☯ 9am-4pm Sat & Sun)

Eating

Babette's (☎ 631-537-5377; 66 Newtown Lane, East Hampton; mains $12-18)

Della Femina (☎ 631-329-6666; N Main St, East Hampton; mains $18-30)

Fat Ralph's Deli (☎ 631-725-6688; 138 Division St, Sag Harbor; sandwiches $7-10)

James on Main (☎ 631-283-7575; 75 Main St, Southampton; mains $19-28)

Lobster Roll ('Lunch') (☎ 631-267-3740; 1980 Montauk Hwy, Montauk; mains $12-20)

Nick & Toni's (☎ 631-324-3550; 136 N Main St, East Hampton; mains $18-30)

Sleeping

American Hotel (☎ 631-725-3535; Main St, Sag Harbor; r low season $155-250, high season $210-335)

Bridgehampton Inn (☎ 631-537-3660; 2266 Main St; r low season $165-350, high season $310-450)

Gurney's Inn Resort (☎ 631-668-2345; 290 Old Montauk Hwy, Montauk; r $190-500)

Memory Motel (☎ 631-668-2702; 692 Montauk Hwy, Montauk; r $95-120)

Mill House Inn (☎ 631-324-9766; 31 N Main St, East Hampton; r low season $200-600, high season $350-800)

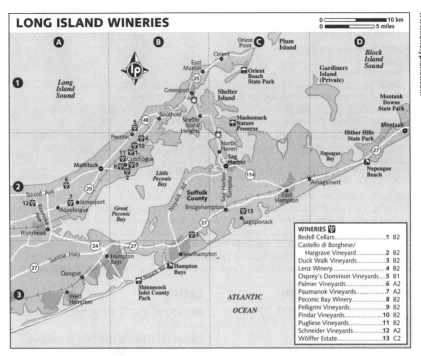

LONG ISLAND WINERIES

0 — 10 km
0 — 5 miles

WINERIES
Bedell Cellars............................1 B2
Castello di Borghese/
Hargrave Vineyard.............2 B2
Duck Walk Vineyards.................3 B2
Lenz Winery..............................4 B2
Osprey's Dominion Vineyards....5 B1
Palmer Vineyards......................6 A2
Paumanok Vineyards.................7 A2
Peconic Bay Winery...................8 B2
Pelligrini Vineyards...................9 B2
Pindar Vineyards.....................10 B2
Pugliese Vineyards..................11 B2
Schneider Vineyards................12 A2
Wölffer Estate.........................13 C2

NORTH FORK WINERIES

In just over 25 years, Long Island's wine scene has grown from one small winery to a thriving industry that takes up more than 3000 acres of land. A vast majority of the 50-plus vineyards are at the East End's North Fork, where distinctive green 'wine trail' road signs mark the way along Rte 25 once you pass the town of Riverhead, where the two forks split. If you want to include the few South Fork stops in your travels (**Duck Walk Vineyards** and **Wölffer Estate**), you can explore the Hamptons and then continue on to the North Fork via the North Ferry service (see p384). But staying out of the paparazzi-filled fray and just settling into the easy pace of the North Fork is a worthy trip in itself. Harvest time is in fall, which, coupled with foliage and pumpkin-picking opportunities, makes it an ideal time to visit, however most places remain open year-round. Several wineries offer full-scale tours of their facilities. The following (all on the map above) are just some of the wineries that offer tastings: **Bedell Cellars, Castello di Borghese/Hargrave Vineyard, Lenz Winery, Osprey's Dominion Vineyards, Palmer Vineyards, Paumanok Vineyards, Peconic Bay Winery, Pelligrini Vineyards, Pindar Vineyards, Pugliese Vineyards, Schneider Vineyards** and **Wölffer Estate**. For individual winery information, as well as maps for touring the wine trail, contact the **Long Island Wine Council**.

However, there's plenty to do beyond sipping and spitting. **Greenport** is friendly and more affordable than South Fork villages, and you'll find plenty of open-air restaurants clustered around the marina. **Claudio's** is a landmark that gets noisy at the long wooden bar as tourists clamor for lobster dinners. **Aldo's** is a more refined option – it serves sublime food and is known for its home-baked biscotti. Reservations are essential. Stop at **Greenport–Southold Chamber of Commerce** for maps and other information, and take a spin on the restored waterfront **carousel**.

Also worth a visit is the tiny hamlet of **Orient**, about 3 miles from the Orient Point ferry terminal. There's not much of a business district in this 17th-century hamlet, just an old wooden post office and a general store, but Orient features a well-preserved collection of white clapboard houses and former inns. Further out of town, you can bike past the Oyster Ponds just east of Main St and see the beach at **Orient Beach State Park**.

A drive along the back roads of the North Fork affords some beautiful, unspoiled vistas of farms and rural residential areas. But if you're too bushed to make the trip out and back in

www.lonelyplanet.com

Excursions

LONG ISLAND

383

TRANSPORTATION

Distance from New York City 100 miles
Direction East
Travel Time 2¼ hours
Car Take the Midtown Tunnel out of Manhattan, which will take you onto I-495/Long Island Expressway. Take this until it ends, at Riverhead, and follow signs onto Rte 25. Stay on Rte 25 for all points east.
Hampton Jitney (☎ 212-362-8400; www.hamptonjitney.com; one way $18, round-trip $35) picks up passengers at 44th St at Third Ave in Manhattan and makes stops in 10 North Fork villages.
Train The Long Island Rail Road (LIRR; ☎ 718-217-5477; www.mta.nyc.us/lirr; round-trip $13-19) has a North Fork line, with trips leaving from Penn Station and Brooklyn. Tickets can be bought at the station from agents or automatic machines.

one day (a doable, but tiring, prospect), you'll find plenty of classic inns to rest your head for the night. Two good options are the **Red Barn B&B**, a cozy, antique-filled inn in Jamesport, and the **Quintessentials B&B Spa**, an 1840s Victorian place in East Marion outfitted with a full-service spa, plush quarters and peaceful, flowering grounds. If you do wind up driving out, a stop in **Riverhead** is worthwhile – both for the **Tanger Outlet Center**, a massive tangle of factory outlet stores such as Banana Republic and Nautica, and for its **Polish Town**, a tiny, insular community of Polish immigrants with various ethnic bakeries and restaurants such as **Polonez Polish Russian Restaurant**.

Sights & Information

All wineries are generally open from 11am to 5pm, with closing time extended by an hour in summer.

Bedell Cellars (☎ 631-734-7537; Cutchogue)

Carousel (Front St, Greenport; admission $1; ☺ 10am-10pm summer, weather permitting rest of year)

Castello di Borghese/Hargrave Vineyard (☎ 631-734-5158; Cutchogue)

Duck Walk Vineyards (☎ 631-726-7555; Southampton)

Greenport–Southold Chamber of Commerce (☎ 631-765-3161; www.greenportsoutholdchamber.org; Rte 25, Southold; ☺ 9am-4pm Mon-Fri)

Lenz Winery (☎ 631-734-6010; Peconic)

Long Island Wine Council (☎ 631-369-5887; www.liwines.com; 104 Edwards Ave, Calverton)

Orient Beach State Park (☎ 631-323-3400)

Osprey's Dominion Vineyards (☎ 631-765-6188; Peconic)

Palmer Vineyards (☎ 631-722-9463; Riverhead)

Paumanok Vineyards (☎ 631-722-8800; Aquebogue)

Peconic Bay Winery (☎ 631-734-7361; Cutchogue)

Pelligrini Vineyards (☎ 631-734-4111; Cutchogue)

Pindar Vineyards (☎ 631-734-6200; Peconic)

Pugliese Vineyards (☎ 631-734-4057; Cutchogue)

Schneider Vineyards (☎ 631-727-3334; Riverhead)

Tanger Outlet Center (☎ 631-369-2732; 1770 W Main St, Riverhead)

Wölffer Estate (☎ 631-537-5106; Sagaponack)

Eating

Aldo's (☎ 631-477-1699; 103-105 Front St, Greenport; mains $15-25)

Claudio's (☎ 631-477-0715; 111 Main St, Greenport; mains $18-30; ☺ mid-Apr–Jan 1)

Polonez Polish Russian Restaurant (☎ 631-369-8878; 123 W Main St, Riverhead; mains $12-20)

Sleeping

Quintessentials B&B Spa (☎ 631-477-9400; 8585 Main Rd, East Marion; r $175-275)

Red Barn B&B (☎ 631-722-3695; 733 Herricks Lane, Jamesport; r $150-275)

Mashomack Nature Preserve (p381) on Shelter Island

JONES BEACH

The offerings of Jones Beach State Park are simple: 6½ miles of clean sand covered with bodies. The type of character differs depending on which 'field' you choose – for example, 2 is for the surfers and 6 is for families, and there is a gay beach followed by a nude beach way east – but it's a definite scene no matter where you choose to spread your blanket. The ocean gets quite warm by midsummer, up to about 70°F, and there are plenty of lifeguards. In between sunning and riding waves, though, you might also hop into one of the two massive on-site pools for a swim, play shuffleboard or basketball on beachside courts, stroll the 2-mile boardwalk, visit the still waters of the bay beach or, at the Castles in the Sand museum, learn how master builder Robert Moses transformed Long Island with the creation of Jones Beach in the 1940s. Burgers, nachos, ice cream and other beach foods are available at snack bars, located at each beach field, and there's a sit-down eatery, the Boardwalk Restaurant, with ocean views and serious fare, from seared tuna to buckets of steamers. When the sun goes down, you can grill at one of the many barbecues in the sand, or head to the Tommy Hilfiger Jones Beach Theater (recently renamed to serve as a constant advertisement, unfortunately), where alfresco concerts under the stars feature headliners along the lines of Judas Priest, Kid Rock and Britney Spears.

TRANSPORTATION

Distance from New York City 33 miles
Direction East
Travel Time 45 minutes
Car Take the Midtown Tunnel from Manhattan onto I-495/Long Island Expressway. Take this to exit TK and get on the Northern State Parkway or Southern State Parkway until the Wantagh Parkway, which will take you directly to Jones Beach State Park.
Train The Long Island Rail Road (LIRR; ☎ 718-217-5477; www.mta.nyc.ny.us/lirr; round-trip $14) offers round-trips from Penn Station and Brooklyn's Flatbush Ave station to the Freeport station on Long Island; the trip takes less than 40 minutes and, between Memorial Day and Labor Day, includes a shuttle bus to Jones Beach.

Sights & Information

Castles in the Sand (☎ 516-785-1600; admission $1; ⏰ 10am-4pm Sat & Sun Memorial Day–Labor Day)

Jones Beach State Park (☎ 516-785-1600)

Tommy Hilfiger Jones Beach Theater (☎ 516-221-1000; www.tommyhilfigerjonesbeach.com) Phone for opening hours and admission.

Eating

Boardwalk Restaurant (☎ 516-785-2420; mains $10-15)

FIRE ISLAND

This skinny barrier island of sand runs parallel to Long Island, and contains much wonder, beauty and flaming adventure along its scant 32 miles. Federally protected as the Fire Island National Seashore, the land offers sand dunes, forests, white beaches, camping, hiking trails, inns, restaurants, 15 hamlets and two villages. Its scenes range from car-free residential villages of summer mansions and packed nightclubs to stretches of sand where you'll find nothing but pitched tents and deer (overpopulation is a big problem here). Robert Moses State Park, the only part of the island that's accessible by car, lies at the westernmost end and features wide, soft-sand beaches with mellower crowds than those at Jones Beach. It's also home to the Fire Island Lighthouse, which houses a history museum. Walk way east along the shore here and you'll stumble upon a lively nude beach.

The gemlike parts of Fire Island, though, are found further east, in the tranquil, car-free villages. Davis Park, Fair Harbor, Kismet, Ocean Bay Park and Ocean Beach combine small summer homes with tiny towns that have groceries, bars, nightclubs and restaurants – just keep in mind that almost everything in every town shuts down a couple of weeks after Labor Day. Each village has slightly different crowds – some more geared toward singles, others family-friendly; you can rely on the South Bay Water Taxi service to shuttle you between villages. To find out more, check out the town guide at www.fireisland.com.

Perhaps the most infamous villages are those that have evolved into gay resorts: Cherry Grove and The Pines. These, too, attract different crowds – Cherry Grove a more down-to-earth, rainbow-flag–touting person who likes burgers, beers and nude sunbathing. Cherry Grove attracts lesbians, too, while The Pines is exclusively men – affluent men, with sculpted bodies, Manhattan apartments and a taste for drug-fueled soirees, either at each others' large houses or at the recently remodeled **Pavilion** nightclub. The boys from either side often meet in the middle, of course, namely for an anonymous encounter at the tangle of forest that separates the two villages (nicknamed 'the meat rack'). While day trips are easy to Fire Island, staying on this oasis, where boardwalks serve as pathways between the dunes and homes, is wonderful. If you can't stay in someone's summer share-house, there are few options: **Belvedere** (for men only), **Holly House**, and **Grove Hotel**, all in the Grove; Grove Hotel offers the main source of entertainment with its nightclub. In The Pines, there's a (barely) renovated inn, **Hotel Ciel**.

None of the eateries are worth writing home about, but **Rachel's** has great ocean views, while **Cherry's** sits on the bay. Both are popular Grove gathering places.

If you want to skip the scene altogether and just get back to nature, enjoy a hike through the **Sunken Forest**, a 300-year-old forest, with its own ferry stop (called Sailor's Haven). At the eastern end of the island, the 1300-acre preserve of **Otis Pike Fire Island Wilderness** includes a beach campground at **Watch Hill** (reservations are a must, as sites fill up a year in advance); just beware of the fierce mosquitoes.

Sights & Information

Cherry Grove (☎ 914-844-7490; www.cherrygrove.com)

Fire Island Information (www.fireisland.com)

Fire Island Lighthouse (☎ 631-681-4876)

Fire Island National Seashore (☎ 631-289-4810; www.nps.gov/fiis)

Otis Pike Fire Island Wilderness/Watch Hill (☎ 631-289-9336; campsite $25)

Pavilion (☎ 631-597-6677; admission $5-20)

The Pines (www.thepinesfireisland.com)

Robert Moses State Park (☎ 631-669-0449; www.nys parks.state.ny.us)

South Bay Water Taxi (☎ 631-665-8885; www.southbay watertaxi.com; fares $10-20)

Sunken Forest (☎ 631-289-4810)

Eating

Cherry's (☎ 631-597-9736; Cherry Grove; mains $10-15)

Rachel's (☎ 631-597-4174; Cherry Grove; mains $10-12)

Sleeping

Belvedere (☎ 631-597-6448; Cherry Grove; r from $250)

Grove Hotel (☎ 631-597-6600; Cherry Grove; r $80-500, ste $90-500)

Holly House (☎ 631-597-6991; Cherry Grove; r from $250)

Hotel Ciel (☎ 631-597-6500; The Pines; r $225)

TRANSPORTATION

Distance from New York City 60 miles
Direction East
Travel Time 2 hours (including ferry ride)
Car Take the Midtown Tunnel out of Manhattan onto I-495/Long Island Expressway. For Sayville ferries (to The Pines, Cherry Grove and Sunken Forest), get off at exit 57 onto the Vets Memorial Hwy. Make a right on Lakeland Ave and take it to the end, following signs for the ferry. For Davis Park Ferry from Patchogue (to Watch Hill) take the Long Island Expressway to exit TK. For Bay Shore ferries (all other Fire Island destinations), take the Long Island Expressway to exit 30E, then get onto the Sagtikos Parkway to exit 42 south, to Fifth Ave terminal in Bay Shore. You can also take Tommy's Taxi Service (☎ 631-665-4800), with pick-up points in Manhattan and it takes you directly to the Bay Shore ferry for $16. To get to Robert Moses State Park by car, take exit 53 off the Long Island Expressway and travel south across the Moses Causeway.
Train The Long Island Rail Road (LIRR; ☎ 718-217-5477; www.mta.nyc.ny.us/lirr) makes stops in both Sayville and Bay Shore, and has a connecting summer-only shuttle service to the Fire Island Ferry Service (☎ 631-665-3600; Bay Shore), Sayville Ferry Service (☎ 631-589-0810; Sayville) and Davis Park Ferry (☎ 631-475-1665, Davis Park). Visit www.fireislandferries.com. One-way tickets from Manhattan and Brooklyn are about $13; round-trip ferry tickets average $14.

LONG BEACH

Beautiful Long Beach, closer to the city than either Jones Beach or Fire Island, is one of the best stretches of sand within an hour of the city. It's easily accessible by train, has clean beaches, a hoppin' main town strip with shops and eateries within walking distance of the ocean, a thriving surfing scene and many city hipsters. Pick up information at the **Long Beach Chamber of Commerce** and the official **City of Long Beach** office to help navigate the area.

You'll probably do just fine on your own, though, as Long Beach is compact and easily negotiated. **Lincoln Beach**, at the end of Lincoln Blvd, is the main spot for surfing; you can rent boards or even sign up for a surfing lesson at **Unsound Surf**. The skinny sand strip sits in front of this wave-churned spot in the Atlantic, with plenty of other sunning and swimming areas along either side. Behind the beach scene is a sweet residential 'hood, made up of cute beach houses and larger year-round homes, seemingly all equipped with porches and wind chimes. Strolling or biking through is a nice break from the surf and sun; you can also bike along the boardwalk that fronts the beach, which has lanes reserved for cyclists. You can rent bikes at **Buddy's**.

There's plenty of good eats in the town around the beach. Stroll around and find whatever takes your fancy, or make a beeline for one of the following: **Baja California Grille**, serving up tasty Mexican fare, or **Kitchen Off Pine Street**, a great place for an eclectic dinner before heading back to the city – just be sure to dust all the sand out of your hair and put your shoes back on first. Long Beach doesn't have much in the way of hotels, but getting back to NYC is so easy, it doesn't really matter anyway.

TRANSPORTATION

Distance from New York City 30 miles
Direction East
Travel Time 45 minutes
Car Follow the Grand Central Parkway east to the Van Wyck Expressway, toward JFK Airport. Take exit 1E to the Nassau Expressway, which heads right into Long Beach.
Train The **Long Island Rail Road** (LIRR; ☎ 718-217-5477; www.mta.nyc.ny.us/lirr; round-trip $12) goes directly to Long Beach from both Penn Station and Flatbush Ave in Brooklyn.

Sights & Information

Buddy's (☎ 516-431-0804; 907 W Beech St; 3-hr bike hire $16)

City of Long Beach (☎ 516-431-1000; www.longbeachny.org; 1 W Chester St; ☺ 9am-4pm Mon-Fri)

Lincoln Beach (☎ 516-431-1810)

Long Beach Chamber of Commerce (☎ 516-432-6000; 350 National Blvd; ☺ 9am-4pm Mon-Fri)

Unsound Surf (☎ 516-889-1112; surf-report line ☎ 516-892-7972; 359 E Park Ave; lessons per hr $55)

Eating

Baja California Grille (☎ 516-889-5992; 1032 W Beech St; mains $6-10)

Kitchen Off Pine Street (☎ 516-431-0033; 670 Long Beach Blvd; mains $13-22)

UPSTATE NEW YORK

Heading north from New York City the landscape quickly mellows into a long lush stretch of historic riverfront towns and thickly treed hills, the dynamic colors of which set New Yorkers scrambling each fall to locate their driver's licenses so they can rent a car and peep at the foliage.

HUDSON VALLEY

Winding roads along the Hudson River take you by picturesque farms, Victorian cottages, apple orchards and old-money mansions built by New York's elite. **Hudson Valley Tourism** has regional information about sites and events. Painters of the Hudson River school romanticized these landscapes – you can see their work at art museums in the area as well as in the city. Autumn is a particularly beautiful time for a trip up this way, either by car or train (though having a car makes site-hopping much easier); cyclists also love the beauty and challenge of riding through the area (for further information, read *25 Mountain Bike Tours in the Hudson Valley* by Peter Kick, Backcountry Books). The season's changing foliage and opportunities for pumpkin- and apple-picking make this excursion a classic Americana experience.

On the west side of the river, 40 miles north of NYC, **Harriman State Park** spans across 72 sq miles and provides swimming, hiking, camping and a visitors center. Adjacent **Bear Mountain State Park** offers great views from its 1305ft peak. The Manhattan skyline looms beyond the river and surrounding greenery. You can enjoy hiking in summer, wildflowers in spring, gold foliage in fall and crosscountry skiing in winter. The **Storm King Art Center**, in Mountainville, is definitely worth a visit. It showcases stunning avant-garde sculpture

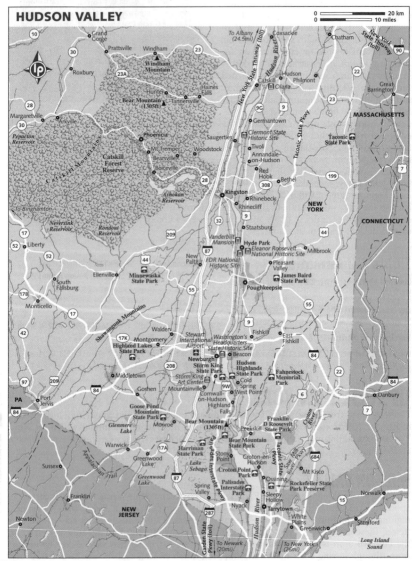

HUDSON VALLEY

TRANSPORTATION

Distance from New York City 95 miles (to Hyde Park)
Direction North
Travel Time 1¾ hours
Car To leave Manhattan, take the Henry Hudson Parkway to I-95 to the Palisades Parkway. Follow this to the New York State Thruway to Rte 9W or Rte 9, the principal scenic river routes. Most towns can also be reached by taking the faster Taconic State Parkway, which runs north from Ossining and is considered one of the state's prettiest roads when the leaves turn in autumn.
Bus Short Line Buses (☎ 212-736-4700; www.shortlinebus.com; round-trip $28) runs regular trips to Hyde Park and Rhinebeck.
Train While **Amtrak** (☎ 212-582-6875, 800-872-7245; www.amtrak.com) trains run the length of the river and connect with several communities on the eastern shore, your best and cheapest bet from New York City is the **Metro-North commuter train** (☎ 212-532-4900, 800-638-7646; www.mnr.org; one-way off-peak $5.50-9.50), which departs from Grand Central Terminal (take the 'Hudson Line'). On weekends, Metro-North runs special summer and autumn tourist packages that include train fare and transportation to and from specific sites such as Hyde Park and the Vanderbilt Mansion.
Boat One of the most relaxing and pleasant ways to take in several sites is by the **NY Waterway** (☎ 800-533-3779; www.nywaterway.com; tours from $40), which offers ferry trips up the Hudson River. Full-day tours on offer include many of the area's mansions and historic sites.

by Calder, Moore and Noguchi, among others. Tucked among rolling hills, this outdoor park occupies 400 acres, successfully combining art in a natural setting. The nearby **Storm King Lodge** is a stately 1800s home with tasteful rooms featuring private bathrooms and fireplaces.

The largest town on the Hudson's east bank, **Poughkeepsie** (puh-*kip*-see) is famous for **Vassar**, a private liberal-arts college that admitted only women until 1969. Its modern **Francis Lehman Loeb Art Center** features Hudson River–school paintings and contemporary work. The office **Dutchess County Tourism** has regional information. Another attraction on the east side is the town of Beacon – basically a scruffy waterfront village with one very worth stop: **Dia Beacon**, an outpost of NYC's soon-to-be-reopened **Dia Center for the Arts** with a renowned contemporary collection.

Cheap motel chains in Poughkeepsie are clustered along Rte 9, south of the Mid-Hudson Bridge. But for a stay with some character, try the **Copper Penny Inn**, a tasteful B&B in a converted 1860s farmhouse.

Hyde Park has long been associated with the Roosevelts, a prominent family since the 19th century. The **Franklin D Roosevelt Library & Museum** features exhibits on the man who created the New Deal and led the USA into WWII. Eleanor Roosevelt's cottage, **Val-Kill**, was her retreat from Hyde Park, her mother-in-law and FDR himself. The **Vanderbilt Mansion**, a national historic site 2 miles north on Rte 9, is a spectacle of lavish beaux arts and eclectic architecture. A **combination ticket** (☎ 800-967-2283; adult $18) is available for the three sites; reservations are recommended. There are plenty of other grand mansions to explore –

THE OTHER CIA

Also in Hyde Park, the renowned **Culinary Institute of America** (☎ 800-285-4627; www.ciachef.edu) trains future chefs and can satisfy anyone's gastronomic cravings. Most of its five student-staffed restaurants are formal, but **St Andrew's Cafe** (☎ 845-471-6608; dinner around $30) is more casual and the least expensive – reservations are required. A nearby inn, the **Willows Bed & Breakfast** (☎ 845-471-6115; 53 Travis Rd; r $135-165) has quirky, contemporary rooms.

Kykuit, a Rockefeller home with antique carriages and gardens sits in Tarrytown along with the Gothic Revival mansion Lyndhurst Castle; **Olana**, built with Moorish touches by Hudson River–school artist Frederic Church, is in Hudson; and **Springwood**, in Hyde Park, was FDR's boyhood country home.

Sights & Information

Bear Mountain State Park (☎ 845-786-2701)

Dia Beacon (☎ 845-440-0100; www.diaart.org; Beacon; ☺ 11am-6pm Thu-Mon Apr 14-Oct 17, otherwise 11am-4pm Fri-Mon)

Dutchess County Tourism (☎ 800-445-3131; www .dutchessny.gov; 3 Neptune Rd, Poughkeepsie)

Franklin D Roosevelt Library & Museum (☎ 845-229-8114; www.fdrlibrary.marist.edu; 511 Albany Post Rd/Rte 9, Hyde Park; admission $10; ☺ 9am-5pm)

Harriman State Park (☎ 845-786-5003)

Hudson Valley Network (www.hvnet.com)

Hudson Valley Tourism (☎ 800-232-4782; www.hud sonvalley.org)

Kykuit (☎ 914-631-9491; Pocantico Hills, Tarrytown; adult/senior/child $22/20/18; ☺ tours 9:45am, 1:45pm, 3pm)

Lyndhurst Castle (☎ 914-631-4481; www.lyndhurst .org; Rte 9, Tarrytown; guided tours ☺ Tue-Sun 10:30am-4:15pm; castle/grounds $10/4)

Olana (☎ 518-828-0135; www.olana.org; Rte 9G, Hudson; grounds ☺ 8am-sunset; 10am-5pm Tue-Sun for tours; adult/child under 12 $3/free) No house tours in 2006 due to renovation.

Springwood (☎ 800-967-2283; Albany Post Rd, Hyde Park; admission $14; ☺ 9am-5pm)

Storm King Art Center (☎ 845-534-3115; www.storm king.org; Old Pleasant Hill Rd, Mountainville; admission $10; ☺ Apr-Nov)

Vassar/Francis Lehman Loeb Center (☎ 845-437-5632; Poughkeepsie; admission free; ☺ 10am-5pm Tue-Sat, 1-5pm Sun)

Val-Kill (☎ 845-229-9115; www.nps.gov/elro; Albany Post Rd, Hyde Park; admission $8; ☺ 9am-5pm May-Oct, Thu-Mon Nov-Apr)

Vanderbilt Mansion (☎ 800-967-2283; www.nps.gov /vama; Rte 9, Hyde Park; admission $8; ☺ 9am-5pm)

Sleeping

Copper Penny Inn (☎ 845-452-3045; www.copperpenny inn.com; 2406 New Hackensack Rd, Poughkeepsie; r $110-199)

Storm King Lodge (☎ 845-534-9421; Mountainville; r $150-190)

THE CATSKILLS

This scenic region of small towns, farms, resorts and forests has become the latest playground for NYC publishing types and various celebrities who have tired of the Hamptons glitz. They've been snapping up historic houses here to serve as second-home getaways, but so far the rural feel of the area has not been compromised. You'll still find quaint small towns and gorgeous countryside – and a surreal swirl of NYC-hipster activity in the area's hottest restaurants once night falls on the weekends.

In the southern Catskills, the town of **Woodstock** symbolizes the tumultuous 1960s, when US youth questioned authority, experimented with freedom and redefined popular culture. Today it's a combination of quaint and hip. The town has been an artists' colony since 1900, and you'll see an eclectic mix of young Phish fans sporting dreadlocks, and old-time, graying hippie throwbacks. The **Woodstock Guild** is a good source for finding out the latest goings-on in the arts and culture scene – such as the annual Woodstock Film Festival, in October, which attracts film fans from all over. The famous 1969 Woodstock music festival actually occurred in **Bethel**, a town over 40 miles southeast, where a simple plaque marks the famous spot. Two not-so-peaceful spin-offs, also named 'Woodstock,' took place in nearby Saugerties (1994) and Rome (1999). **Saugerties,** just a few miles from the town of Woodstock, offers a similar downtown area, with a smaller offering of galleries, cafés and eateries. Area dining is plentiful, and includes the **Blue Mountain Bistro**, which serves four-star French–Mediterranean cuisine and Spanish tapas to a sophisticated crowd; and **New World Home Cooking Co**, focusing on fresh and tasty organic food in a quirky setting.

You'll find plenty of fine inns in the area, but only a couple stand out from the frilly Victorian masses. The **Villa at Saugerties**, run by a young ex-city couple who escaped the rat race, is the sleekest place around. The five amazing rooms are more urban boutique hotel than country B&B. For a true adventure, stay at the remote **Saugerties Lighthouse**, an 1869 lighthouse that sits on a small island in the Esopus Creek. The Saugerties Lighthouse Conservancy operates it as a year-round B&B, boating guests out to one of the three spare and tidy rooms, all with sweeping water views.

South of Saugerties, Rte 28 crosses the Catskills west of Woodstock, then winds past the Ashokan Reservoir and through the 'French Catskills.' Along this way are excellent restaur-

TRANSPORTATION

Distance from New York City 110 miles (Saugerties)

Direction North

Travel Time 2 hours

Car Take the New York State Thruway (via the Henry Hudson Hwy north from Manhattan), or I-87, to Rte 375 for Woodstock, Rte 32 for Saugerties or Rte 28 for other points north.

Bus Adirondack Trailways (☎ 800-858-8555; average round-trip $45) operates daily buses to Kingston, the Catskills' gateway town, as well as to Saugerties, Catskill, Hunter and Woodstock.

ants, camping, inexpensive lodging, antique shops and character galore. In Mt Tremper is the **Catskill Kaleidoscope**, the world's largest. The 60ft tube, an old farm silo, is touristy, but the 10-minute presentation is worthwhile, featuring US history, psychedelic colors and, of course, images of marijuana leaves. It's also where you'll find **Kate's Lazy Meadow Motel**, a hip, kitschy inn owned by Kate Pierson of the B52's. In Arkville, take a scenic ride on the historic **Delaware and Ulster Rail Line**. Nearby Fleischmanns hosts a good, old-fashioned **auction** every Saturday night, where locals pack to the rafters to snap up bargains from cheap old records to furniture.

Go even further north if it's good winter skiing you're looking for. Rtes 23 and 23A lead to **Hunter Mountain Ski Bowl**, a year-round resort with challenging runs and a 1600ft vertical drop, and **Windham Mountain**, with more intermediate runs.

Sights & Information

Delaware and Ulster Rail Line (☎ 845-652-2821; www .durr.org; Hwy 28, Arkville; adult/senior/child $11/8/7; ☺ May-Aug)

Hunter Mountain Ski Bowl (☎ 518-263-4223; www .huntermtn.com; Hunter)

Kaatskill Kaleidoscope (☎ 888-303-3936; Mt Tremper; adult/child under 12 $8/free; ☺ 10am-5pm Sun-Thu, 10am-7pm Fri-Mon)

Windham Mountain (☎ 518-734-4300; www.skiwindham .com; Windham)

Woodstock Guild (☎ 845-679-2079; www.woodstock guild.org; Woodstock; ☺ 9am-5pm Mon-Fri)

Eating

Blue Mountain Bistro (☎ 845-679-8519; Glasco Turnpike, Saugerties; mains $15-25)

New World Home Cooking Co (☎ 845-246-0900; Rte 212, Woodstock; mains $10-20)

Sleeping

Kate's Lazy Meadow Motel (☎ 845-688-7200; 5191 Rte 28, Mt Tremper; r $175-250)

Saugerties Lighthouse (☎ 847-247-0656; www .saugertieslighthouse.com; Saugerties; r $160)

Villa at Saugerties (☎ 845-246-0682; www.thevillaat saugerties.com; 159 Fawn Rd, Saugerties; r $135-235)

NEW JERSEY

New Jersey is often the butt of jokes – for its preponderance of suburbanite-filled malls, its nasal dialect and, most of all, for its polluted manufacturing district off the Jersey Turnpike. But when you take the time to exit the highways and flee the malls, you are privy to a beautiful side of NJ: a surprising 40% of the state is forest, and a quarter is farmland. It has extensive parkland, beautiful Victorian buildings and a full 127 miles of beaches.

SANDY HOOK

Sandy Hook's 1665-acre natural wonderland comprises 7 miles of beach. Like Jones Beach on Long Island, the area blends massive ocean beaches with bay beaches and history. But here, in **Sandy Hook Gateway National Recreation Area**, you'll also find the nation's oldest lighthouse, the Maritime Holly Forest with plentiful opportunities for observing birds (such as the endangered plover), outstanding views of Manhattan's skyline on clear days, a nude beach alongside a gay beach (area G), and a complex system of paved bike paths, which wend their way through the abandoned forts of historic Ft Hancock (what you'll see upon arrival) and white sand-dune peaks. Best of all, you can get here via the **SeaStreak Ferry**, which leaves from Lower Manhattan and gets you here in a cool and salty 45 minutes. Bring your bike along for the ride, and you can pedal to various Jersey Shore areas, including the nearby towns of **Atlantic Highlands** and **Highlands**. The **Atlantic Highlands Chamber of Commerce** can provide you with information on several eating and sleeping options in the area.

If you get hungry on the beach, you'll find plenty of standard concession stands, with a rooftop option, **Seagull's Nest**, serving burgers, fried clams and ice-cold beers. For better grub, ride your bike over the bridge to the mellow, waterfront **Inlet Café** for seafood in the Highlands. The closest place to stay is the gay-owned **Sandy Hook Cottage**, done up with tasteful, beach-house decor. Also nearby is the **Grand Lady By the Sea Bed and Breakfast**, a historic, romantic inn that overlooks the beach.

TRANSPORTATION

Distance from New York City 45 miles
Direction West
Travel Time 1 hour
Car Take the Garden State Parkway to exit 117 and follow Rte 36 east to the beach.
Ferry The SeaStreak Ferry (☎ 732-872-2628; www .seastreak.com; 2 First Ave, Atlantic Highlands; one way $19, round-trip $34, one way bike extra $3) leaves from Pier 11 near Wall St and also from a pier at E 34th St.

Sights & Information

Atlantic Highlands Chamber of Commerce (☎ 732-872-8711; www.atlantichighlands.org; Atlantic Highlands Municipal Harbor; ⏲ 9am-4pm Mon-Fri)

Sandy Hook Gateway National Recreation Area (☎ 732-872-5970)

Eating

Inlet Café (☎ 732-872-9764; 3 Cornwall St, Highlands; mains $8-20)

Seagull's Nest (☎ 732-872-0025; Sandy Hook Area D; mains $5-10)

Sleeping

Grand Lady By the Sea Bed and Breakfast (☎ 732-708-1900; www.grandladybythesea.com; 254 Rte 36, Highlands; r $139-179)

Sandy Hook Cottage (☎ 732-708-1923; www.sandy hookcottage.com; 36 Navesink Ave, Highlands; r $159-289)

Caesar's Atlantic City (opposite)

ATLANTIC CITY

When the railway arrived on Absecon Island in the 1850s, city-dwellers came here for the wide white beach and seaside atmosphere. By 1900 the resort was a hot spot that catered to the affluent; in the 1920s it was a hotbed of vice, with smuggled liquor, speakeasies and illegal gambling. After WWII faster transportation made other destinations more accessible, and Atlantic City went into steep decline. In 1977 the state approved casinos to revitalize the place, and since then, Atlantic City (or 'AC' as it's known locally), has become one of the country's most popular tourist destinations, with 33 million annual visitors spending some $4 billion at its 12 casinos and numerous restaurants. The part of town that sits in the shadows of the oceanfront casinos has been largely left behind – it's rife with empty lots, rough-looking bars and abandoned warehouses. However, AC is still an interesting stopover on your way to Cape May and you may find the anthropology of the surreal scene intriguing. If you're a gambler, you can't beat the selection of nearly 1000 blackjack tables and more than 30,000 slot machines in town.

As in Las Vegas, the hotel–casinos have themes, from the Far East to Ancient Rome, but they're very superficially done here. Inside they're still all basically the same, with clanging

TRANSPORTATION

Distance from New York City 130 miles
Direction South
Travel Time 2¼ hours
Car Leave Manhattan via one of the Hudson River crossings (Holland Tunnel, Lincoln Tunnel, George Washington Bridge). Take the NJ Turnpike to the Garden State Parkway; Atlantic City is exit 38 off the parkway. The Atlantic City Expressway runs directly to Atlantic City from Philadelphia. Casino parking garages cost about $2 per day, but they waive the fee if you have a receipt showing you spent money inside.
Bus Greyhound (☎ 800-231-2222), **Academy** (☎ 800-442-7272) and **New Jersey Transit** (☎ 973-762-5100; www.njtransit.com) buses run from Port Authority; a round-trip costs around $25. **Gray Line** (☎ 212-397-2620) operates from 900 Eighth Ave between W 53rd and 54th Sts in Midtown. A casino will often refund the fare (in chips, coins or coupons) if you get a bus directly to its door. Fares are cheaper Monday to Thursday.
Train New Jersey Transit (☎ 973-762-5100; www.njtransit.com) doesn't go direct to AC, so a train trip requires two connections and about twice the cost of a bus trip. From Penn Station, switch in Trenton to Philadelphia; from Philly, switch to the Atlantic City Line.

slot machines, flashing lights and gluttonous all-you-can-eat food buffets. This is changing, however, as big developers like Donald Trump and Steve Wynn vie for supremacy. The latest addition – the **Borgata Hotel Casino & Spa** – from Boyd Gaming and MGM Mirage, has really upped the ante, offering plush rooms, a full-service spa and five-star restaurants galore. Staying in any of the towering hotels can be cheap or extravagant, depending on the season, with rooms ranging from $50 in winter to $400 in summer.

There are plenty of hotel–casinos. The southernmost casino, **Atlantic City Hilton**, has over 500 hotel rooms. **Caesar's Atlantic City** contains 1000 rooms and Atlantic City's Planet Hollywood theme restaurant, which is just off the gaming area.

Harrah's Marina Hotel Casino is considered the friendliest casino in town. Newbie gamblers might try its floor, which has gracious and instructive dealers. **Tropicana Casino & Entertainment Resort** is one of the biggest places in town, with its own indoor theme park (Tivoli Pier), a 90,000-sq-ft casino and 1020 rooms. Trump's properties include **Trump's Marina Resort**, with an art deco theme; **Trump Plaza Casino Hotel**; and the **Trump Taj Mahal**, where nine two-ton limestone elephants welcome visitors, and 70 bright minarets crown the rooftops. The buffet here is one of the best in town.

Each of the casinos offers a full schedule of entertainment, ranging from ragtime and jazz bands in hotel lobbies to top-name entertainers in the casino auditoriums. Some of this stuff is way over the top, but worth it for the cheese factor alone; think sequins and feathers.

However, there is some life outside of the casinos. Built in 1870, the **Boardwalk** was the first in the world. Enjoy a walk or a hand-pushed **rolling chair ride** (adult $22) and drop in on the informative **Atlantic City Historical Museum**, run by a quirky old-timer. Until recently, the Miss America Pageant was held here at Convention Hall – which is worth a visit if only for its claim of 'world's largest' pipe organ (with 33,000 pipes, it weighs 150 tons). The **Steel Pier** amusement pier, directly in front of the Trump Taj Mahal, belongs to Donald Trump's empire. It used to be the place where the famous diving horse plunged into the Atlantic before crowds of spectators, but today it's a collection of small amusement rides, games of chance, candy stands and 'the biggest Go-Kart track in South Jersey!' The **Visitor Information Center**, under the giant tepee in the middle of the Atlantic City Expressway, can provide you with maps and accommodation deals, as can the various other information booths on or near the Boardwalk.

The **Absecon Lighthouse** dates from 1857 and, at 171ft high, ranks as the tallest in New Jersey and the third-tallest in the country. It's been restored to its original specifications (including the Frensel lens) and you can climb the 228 steps to the top for phenomenal views.

Aside from the Borgata, good food can be found away from the casinos. A few blocks inland from the Boardwalk, **Mexico Lindo** is a favorite among Mexican locals, while **Angelo's Fairmount Tavern** is a beloved family-owned Italian restaurant. The outdoor patio makes a nice spot to take in the sunset and have a pint and a burger. If you've got a car, try **Hannah G's**, an excellent breakfast and lunch spot in nearby Ventnor; or **Maloney's**, a popular seafood-and-steak place. **Ventura's Greenhouse Restaurant**, in next-door Margate City, is an Italian restaurant loved by locals.

Excursions

NEW JERSEY

ATLANTIC CITY

A

SIGHTS & ACTIVITIES
Absecon Lighthouse................1 F4
Atlantic City Historical
  Museum.........................2 F5
Steel Pier..............................3 E5

EATING
Angelo's Fairmount Tavern......4 B5
Mexico Lindo........................5 B5
Restaurants.......................(see 7)

SLEEPING
Atlantic City Hilton................6 A6
Borgata Hotel Casino & Spa.....7 C2
Caesar's Atlantic City.............8 C5
Harrah's Marina Hotel
  Casino..............................9 D1

B

Tropicana Casino & Entertainment
  Resort............................10 B6
Trump Plaza Casino Hotel.........11 C6
Trump Taj Mahal...................12 E5
Trump's Marina Resort............13 D2

TRANSPORT
Bus Station.........................14 C5
Train Station.......................15 C4

INFORMATION
Information Booth..................16 D5
Information Booth..................17 D5
Information Booth..................18 E5
Information Booth..................19 D5
Post Office..........................20 C5
Toilets..............................21 D5

To Center; Garden
State Parkway; Camden;
Philadelphia (PA)

Atlantic City Expressway (toll)
To Visitor
Information;
Garden State Parkway;
Pomona; Camden;
Philadelphia (PA)

Intracoastal Waterway

Farley
State
Marina

Huron Ave

Brigantine Blvd

White Horse Pike

Illinois Ave (Dr Martin Luther King Jr Blvd)

Sewell

Maryland Ave

Virginia Ave

Pennsylvania Ave

North Carolina Ave

Bacharach Blvd

Kirkman Blvd

Baltic Ave

Arctic Ave

Tennessee Ave

South Carolina Ave

Ocean Ave

St James Pl

New York Ave

Kentucky Ave

Atlantic Ave

Indiana Ave

Ohio Ave

Michigan Ave

Pacific Ave

Illinois Ave

Train
Station

Fairmount Ave

Missouri Ave (Christopher Columbus Ave)

Arkansas Ave

Mississippi Ave

Georgia Ave

Florida Ave

California Ave

Iowa Ave

Texas Ave

Brighton Ave

Monroe Ave

Chelsea Ave

Montpelier Ave

Sovereign Ave

Ventnor Ave

Boston Ave

Atlantic Ave

Pacific Ave

Convention
Hall

Boardwalk

Beach

Beach

To Margate;
Cape May

Excursions

ATLANTIC CITY

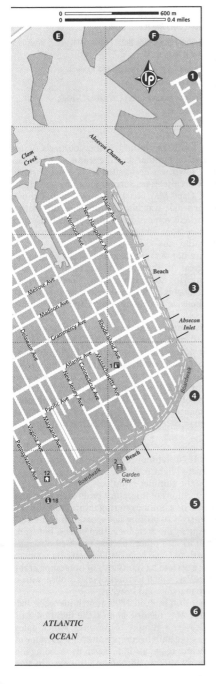

Trump Taj Mahal (p393) trumps the other casinos

Sights & Information

Absecon Lighthouse (☎ 609-449-1360; www.absecon lighthouse.org; cnr Rhode Island & Pacific Aves; 🕙 10am-5pm Jul-Aug; 11am-4pm Mon, Thu-Sun Sep-Jun; adult/child $5/3)

Atlantic City Historical Museum (☎ 609-347-5839; www.acmuseum.org; Garden Pier; admission free; 🕙 10am-4pm)

Visitor Information Center (☎ 609-449-7130; www.atlanticcitynj.com; Garden State Parkway; 🕙 9am-4pm)

Eating

Angelo's Fairmount Tavern (☎ 609-344-2439; Mississippi Ave at Fairmount Ave; mains $13-20)

Hannah G's (☎ 609-823-1466; 7310 Ventnor Ave; mains $5-13)

Maloney's (☎ 609-823-7858; 23 S Washington Ave; mains $14-25)

Mexico Lindo (☎ 609-345-1880; 2435 Atlantic Ave; mains $5-11)

Ventura's Greenhouse Restaurant (☎ 609-822-0140; 106 Benson Ave, Margate City; mains $12-25)

Sleeping

Rates at all of the following places fluctuate hugely, from around $50 to $400 a night, depending on weekend events, time of year, vacancy etc.

Excursions ■ **NEW JERSEY**

Atlantic City Hilton (☎ 609-340-7111; Boston Ave at Boardwalk)

Borgata Hotel Casino & Spa (☎ 866-692-6742; One Borgata Way)

Caesar's Atlantic City (☎ 609-348-4411; Arkansas Ave at Boardwalk)

Harrah's Marina Hotel Casino (☎ 609-441-5000; Brigantine Blvd)

Tropicana Casino & Entertainment Resort (☎ 609-340-4000; Iowa Ave at Boardwalk)

Trump Plaza Casino Hotel (☎ 609-441-6000; Mississippi Ave at Boardwalk)

Trump Taj Mahal (☎ 609-449-1000; 1000 Boardwalk)

Trump's Marina Resort (☎ 609-441-2000; Huron Ave)

CAPE MAY

Founded in 1620, Cape May is on the state's southern tip and is the country's oldest seashore resort. Its sweeping beaches get crowded in summer, but the stunning Victorian architecture is attractive year-round. The entire town was designated a National Historic Landmark in 1976. In addition to its attractive architecture, accommodations (many of them B&Bs in historic homes) and restaurants, Cape May boasts a lovely beach, famous lighthouse, antique shops, and opportunities for whale-watching, fishing and superlative bird-watching. It's the only place in New Jersey where you can watch the sun both rise and set over the water. The quaint area attracts everyone from suburban families to a substantial gay crowd, who are drawn to the many gay-friendly inns.

While summer is high season, when places are hoppin' and beaches can be enjoyed at their full potential, the rest of the year is also great for settling into one of the romantic lodgings, strolling on the deserted beach and enjoying some fine-dining. The **Cape May Jazz Festival** is a biannual affair, and the **Cape May Music Festival** is highlighted by outdoor jazz, classical and chamber music concerts. For comprehensive information on Cape May county attractions, stop at the **Welcome Center**.

The white, sandy beaches are the main attractions in summer months. The narrow **Cape May Beach** requires passes sold at the lifeguard station on the boardwalk at the end of Grant St. **Cape May Point Beach** (admission free) is accessible from the parking lot at Cape May Point State Park near the lighthouse. **Sunset Beach** (admission free) is at the end of Sunset Blvd and is the spot to watch the sunset with a 100% uninterrupted horizon line. This is also the place to begin your hunt for the famed Cape May diamonds – pure quartz crystals that are tumbled smooth by the rolling surf. If you're here between May and September, don't miss the pomp and formalities of the flag-lowering ceremony at Sunset Beach. Offshore, **Cape May Whale Watcher** 'guarantees' sighting a marine mammal on one of its ocean tours.

The 190-acre **Cape May Point State Park**, just off Lighthouse Ave, has 2 miles of trails, plus the famous **Cape May Lighthouse**. Built in 1859, the 157ft lighthouse recently underwent a $2 million restoration, and its completely reconstructed light is visible as far as 25 miles out to sea. You can climb the 199 stairs to the top in the summer months.

The Cape May peninsula is a resting place for millions of migratory birds each year, and the **Cape May Bird Observatory** (☎ 609-898-2473) maintains a hotline offering information on the latest sightings and is considered one of the country's 10 birding hot spots. Fall is the best time to glimpse some of the 400 species that frequent the area, including hawks, but from March through May you can see songbirds, raptors and other species. The bird observatory also offers tours of **Reed's Beach**, 12 miles north of Cape May on Delaware Bay, where migrating shorebirds swoop down to feed on the eggs laid by thousands of horseshoe crabs each May. Also visit the 18-acre **Nature Center of Cape May**, which features open-air observation platforms with wonderful views of the expansive marshes and beaches.

In town, the **Emlen Physick Estate**, an 18-room mansion built in 1879, now houses the **Mid-Atlantic Center for the Arts**, which books tours for Cape May historic homes, the lighthouse or nearby historic Cold Spring Village. You can also get a glimpse of *Atlantus*, which dates from WWI, when 12 experimental concrete ships were built to compensate for a shortage of steel. This surviving example, with its 5-inch concrete aggregate hull, began its seagoing life in 1918, but eight years later it broke free in a storm and ran aground on the western side

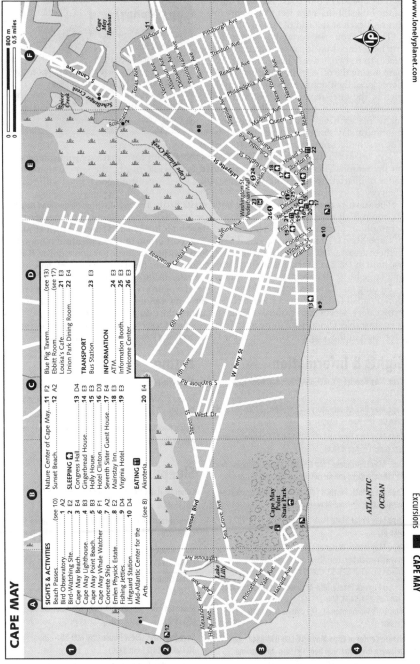

CAPE MAY

SIGHTS & ACTIVITIES
Beach Passes	(see 10)
Bird Observatory	1 A2
Bird-Watching Site	2 F1
Cape May Beach	3 E4
Cape May Lighthouse	4 B3
Cape May Point Beach	5 B3
Cape May Whale Watcher	6 F1
Concrete Ship	7 A2
Emlen Physick Estate	8 E2
Fishing Jetties	9 D4
Lifeguard Station	10 D4
Mid-Atlantic Center for the Arts	(see 8)
Nature Center of Cape May	11 F2
Sunset Beach	12 A2

SLEEPING
Congress Hall	13 D4
Gingerbread House	14 E3
Holly House	15 B3
Hotel Clinton	16 D3
Seventh Sister Guest House	17 E4
Mainstay Inn	18 E3
Virginia Hotel	19 E3

EATING
Akroteria	20 E4
Blue Pig Tavern	(see 13)
Ebbitt Room	(see 17)
Louisa's Cafe	21 E3
Union Park Dining Room	22 E4

TRANSPORT
Bus Station	23 D4

INFORMATION
ATM	24 E3
Information Booth	25 E3
Welcome Center	26 E3

of the Cape May Point coast. A small chunk of the hull still sits a few feet from shore on Sunset Beach at the end of Sunset Blvd.

Though you can certainly make a day trip here, Cape May is packed with excellent places to rest your weary head. If you come here during the off-season many places will have closed their doors, but you'll have your pick of the ones remaining open and at a reasonably cheap price. In high season, many places have a two- to three-night minimum stay during summer weekends. The best budget option remains **Hotel Clinton**.

Classy **Virginia Hotel** has gorgeous old-fashioned rooms with costs that vary wildly depending on the season. The sprawling, just-renovated **Congress Hall**, run by the same owners, has a range of quarters to suit various budgets, plus a long, oceanfront porch lined with rocking chairs.

The town is positively overflowing with small B&Bs; try the darling **Gingerbread House**, a six-room B&B where the rates include a Cape May Beach pass, continental breakfast and scrumptious afternoon tea. **Holly House** is a cottage built in 1890 and run by a former mayor of Cape May. It's one of the so-called Seven Sisters, a group of seven identical homes; five of them are situated along Jackson St. **Seventh Sister Guest House** is just a few doors down. **Mainstay Inn**, built in 1872 as a men's gambling club, features rooms furnished in opulent dark woods and large beds; all have private bathrooms and rates include breakfast.

Finding good food is not a problem at Cape May. For a beach snack, **Akroteria** is a collection of small fast-food shacks. **Louisa's Café**, a tiny, low-ceilinged dining room, is the town's prize eatery, serving up seasonal eclectic specialties; the casual **Blue Pig Tavern** at Congress Hall is comparable. Diners with more upscale tastes should reserve a table at the award-winning **Ebbitt Room** in the Virginia Hotel or at the **Union Park Dining Room**, at Hotel Macomber.

Sights & Information

Cape May Beach (☎ 609-884-9525; day/week pass $4/10)

Cape May Bird Observatory (☎ 609-861-0700; 701 East Lake Dr; ☾ 9am-4:30pm)

Cape May Jazz Festival (☎ 609-884-7277; www.capemay jazz.com; ☾ Apr & Nov)

Cape May Lighthouse (☎ 609-884-2159; Lighthouse Ave; ☾ change daily, call for details; admission $5)

Cape May Music Festival (☎ 609-884-5404; www.cape maymac.org; ☾ mid-May–early Jun)

Cape May Point State Park (☎ 609-884-2159; 707 E Lake Dr)

Cape May Whale Watcher (☎ 609-884-5445; www.cape maywhalewatcher.com; Miss Chris Marina, btwn 2nd Ave & Wilson Dr; adult $23-30, child $12-18)

Emlen Physick Estate/Mid-Atlantic Center for the Arts (☎ 609-884-5404, 800-275-4278; www.capemaymac .org; 1048 Washington St; ☾ change frequently, call for details)

Nature Center of Cape May (☎ 609-898-8848; 1600 Delaware Ave; admission free; ☾ 9am-4pm summer, 10am-1pm winter, 10am-3pm fall & spring)

Welcome Center (405 Lafayette St; ☾ 9am-4pm)

Eating

Akroteria (Beach Ave; mains $2-6)

Louisa's Café (☎ 609-884-5884; 104 Jackson St; mains $12-18)

Union Park Dining Room (☎ 609-884-8811; 727 Beach Ave; mains $18-30)

Sleeping

Congress Hall (☎ 609-884-8422; 251 Beach Ave; r $115-400)

Gingerbread House (☎ 609-884-0211; 28 Gurney St; r $98-260)

Holly House (☎ 609-884-7365; 20 Jackson St; r from $120)

Hotel Clinton (☎ 609-884-3993; 202 Perry St; r $50-60)

Mainstay Inn (☎ 609-884-8690; 635 Columbia Ave; r $115-295)

Seventh Sister Guest House (☎ 609-884-2280; 10 Jackson St; r from $120)

Virginia Hotel (☎ 609-884-8690; 25 Jackson St; r $80-365)

PHILADELPHIA

Only two hours from NYC, Philly provides a great opportunity to get a glimpse of city life beyond New York – especially for history hounds, who will marvel over the abundance of sites that tell the stories of America. It's easy to combine a trip here with one to Atlantic City, Cape May or both.

William Penn made Philadelphia his capital in 1682, basing its plan on a grid with wide streets and public squares – a layout copied by many US cities. For a time the second-largest city in the British Empire (after London), Philadelphia became a center for opposition to British colonial policy. It was the new nation's capital at the start of the Revolutionary War and again after the war until 1790, when Washington DC took over. By the 1800s, New York had superseded Philadelphia as the nation's cultural, commercial and industrial center, and Philly never regained its early preeminent status. But in the 1970s, the nation's bicentennial prompted an urban renewal program that continues to this day.

It's an easy city to get around. Most sights and accommodations are within walking distance of each other, or a short bus ride away. East–west streets are named; north–south streets are numbered, except for Broad and Front Sts. Historic Philadelphia includes Independence National Historic Park and Old City, which extend east to the waterfront.

Perhaps the best way to see all the sites and get an idea of the city's layout, especially if you're only here for the day, is to take advantage of one of the many guided tours. The most complete tour is the 90-minute narrated trolley trip by **Philadelphia Trolley Works**, during which you can hop on and off at designated stops and then reboard when you're ready. For a unique way of getting around, the **76 Carriage Company** will take you around various areas in a horse-drawn carriage. **Phlash** visitor shuttle is a one-hour, do-it-yourself tour that visits about 25 sites. You travel in a bright purple van, which you can hop on and off of whenever you want; there is no tour guide, but you are equipped with a color-coded, easy-to-follow map of the journey. To do it yourself, make your first stop the **Independence Visitors Center**. Run by the knowledgeable folks of the National Park Service, the center distributes the useful *Philadelphia Official Visitors Guide*, maps and brochures. The nearby **Philadelphia Convention & Visitors Bureau** has information about businesses, tours, hotels and package deals.

The L-shaped 45-acre **Independence National Historic Park** (undergoing a major renovation) along with the Old City area, has been dubbed 'America's most historic square mile,' and can feel like a stroll back through time. Concentrating your sightseeing around this area will make the city easier to tackle, and allow you to visit the most renowned sites. **Carpenters' Hall**, owned by the Carpenter Company, is the USA's oldest trade guild and the site of the First Continental Congress in 1774. Housed in the Second Bank of the US and modeled after the Parthenon, is the **National Portrait Gallery**, which includes several portraits of prominent figures by Charles Willson Peale. **Library Hall** is where you'll find a copy of the Declaration of Independence, handwritten in a letter by Thomas Jefferson, plus first editions of Darwin's *On the Origin of Species*, and Lewis and Clark's field notes.

Liberty Bell Center, Philadelphia's premier tourist attraction, was recently moved to a brand new location (just around the corner from its old pavilion, where it had sat since 1976) as part of the extensive Independence Park makeover. Constructed in London and tolled at the first public reading of the Declaration of Independence, the hefty 2080lb bell became famous when abolitionists decided to adopt it as a symbol of freedom. The bell is inscribed, 'Proclaim liberty through all the land, to all the inhabitants thereof. (Leviticus 25:10).' Extensive cracking along the face eventually made the bell unusable way back in 1846.

The **Franklin Court** complex, a row of restored tenements, pays tribute to Benjamin Franklin with an underground museum displaying his inventions. At the **B Free Franklin Post Office**, which has a small US Postal Service Museum, mail receives a special handwritten Franklin postmark. (In addition to being a statesman, author and inventor, the multi-talented Franklin was a postmaster.) **Christ Church**, completed in 1744, is where George Washington and Franklin worshipped.

The **Greek Revival Philadelphia Exchange**, a beautiful Episcopal church designed by William Strickland, is the home of the country's first stock exchange (1834). It's closed to the public, but you can linger at its facade.

Old City – along with Society Hill – comprises the area bounded by Walnut, Vine, Front and 6th Sts. This was early Philadelphia. The 1970s saw its revitalization, when many warehouses were converted into apartments, galleries and small businesses. **Elfreth's Alley** is believed to be the oldest continuously occupied street in the USA; on it, **Mantua Maker's Museum House** has displays of period furniture. **Windsor Chair Maker's House** produced the chairs in Independence Hall. **Fireman's Hall** is where you'll find the nation's oldest fire engine and an exhibit on the rise of organized volunteers, which was led by Ben Franklin. **Betsy Ross House** is where Betsy Griscom Ross (1752–1836), upholsterer and seamstress, is believed to have sewn the first US flag.

National Museum of American Jewish History features exhibits that examine the historical role of Jews in the USA. At the nearby **US Mint**, tours are open to the public. **Arch Street Meeting House** is the USA's largest Quaker meetinghouse, and the **African American Museum in Philadelphia** has excellent collections on black history and culture.

PHILADELPHIA

```
0 _____ 500 m
0 _____ 0.3 miles
```

SIGHTS & ACTIVITIES
African American Museum in
 Philadelphia.............................1 C3
Betsy Ross House............................2 D3
Carpenters' Hall.............................3 D4
Christ Church.................................4 D4
Congress Hall............................(see 8)
Elfreth's Alley................................5 D3
Fireman's Hall................................6 D3
Fireman's Hall................................7 D3
Franklin Court..........................(see 24)
Independence Hall..........................8 C4
Independence National Historic Park..9 D4
Liberty Bell Center........................10 C4

Library Hall...................................11 D4
Mantua Maker's Museum House..(see 6)
National Museum of American Jewish
 History......................................12 D4
National Portrait Gallery...............13 D4
Old City Hall..............................(see 8)
Philosophical Hall.......................(see 8)
US Mint.......................................14 D3
Windsor Chair Maker's House.....(see 6)

EATING 🍴
Buddakan....................................15 D4
Millennium Coffee........................16 B4
Reading Terminal Market.............17 B3

SLEEPING 🛏
Antique Row B&B..........................18 B4
Four Seasons Hotel
 Philadelphia...............................19 A3
Latham Hotel................................20 A4
Penn's View Hotel 21 D4
Shippen Way Inn..........................22 C5

INFORMATION
Arch Street Meeting House........23 D3
B Free Franklin Post Office...........24 D4
Giovanni's Room..........................25 B5
Independence Visitors Center....26 C4
Independence Visitors Center....27 D4

TRANSPORTATION

Distance from New York City 100 miles

Direction Southwest

Travel Time 2 hours

Car Take the Lincoln Tunnel to the NJ Turnpike (I-95) to Rte 73 toward Philadelphia. Merge onto I-295 and then onto US-30, over the Ben Franklin Bridge and onto I-676, which has exits into Philly.

Bus Greyhound (☎ 800-229-9424) and **Capitol Trailways** (☎ 800-444-2877) all go from Port Authority Bus Terminal to Philly. The trip takes two hours and a round-trip ticket costs about $40.

Train Leaving from Penn Station, **Amtrak** (☎ 212-582-6875, 800-872-7245; www.amtrak.com; one way $42) goes to Philly, but a better bargain is **New Jersey Transit** (☎ 973-762-5100; www.njtransit.com; round-trip $40), which runs a commuter service to Philly from Penn Station, requiring a transfer in Trenton.

Gay visitors to Philly will be pleased to know that the Philadelphia Convention and Visitors Bureau launched a major ad campaign in 2004 that was specifically aimed at LGBT travelers. 'Get your history straight and your nightlife gay,' the slogan urged. Though the offerings pale in comparison to what's in NYC, there is a pretty hopping nightlife scene for a small city; plus **Millennium Coffee** is a hip java hang, filled with cute boys, while **Giovanni's Room** is a large, well-stocked gay bookstore on Antique Row, and definitely worth a look.

If you decide to stay the night here, know that you'll mostly find upscale hotel chains and a sprinkling of quaint B&Bs; the city is sorely lacking in classy boutique-style hotels. **Penn's View Hotel** is an old-fashioned inn that overlooks the water. It offers a range of rooms featuring Chippendale-style furniture, many with exposed-brick walls and working fireplaces. A continental breakfast is included. Similarly, the **Latham Hotel** is a classy, European-style hotel with Victorian rooms. **Shippen Way Inn** is a 1750s colonial house containing nine rooms with quilted beds, plus free wine and cheese in the kitchen and a cozy B&B atmosphere. The **Antique Row B&B** has quirky, period-furnished rooms and good breakfasts on hoppin' Antique Row. **Four Seasons Hotel Philadelphia** is the most lavish place in town.

Eating options are plentiful, with some of the cheapest, most interesting edibles found in the city's compact Chinatown and South St areas. Two of Philadelphia's most popular spots for a cheese steak (and you can't leave without trying this regional specialty) are **Geno's** and **Pat's King of Steaks**.

The indoor **Reading Terminal Market** is a wonderful indoor marketplace, offering everything from fresh Amish cheeses and Thai desserts to felafal, cheese steaks, salad bars, sushi, Peking duck and great Mexican. At the high end, an elegant favorite is **Buddakan**, serving Asian-fusion feasts.

For a full rundown of all of Philly's offerings, pick up a copy of LP's *Philadelphia & the Pennsylvania Dutch Country*.

Sights & Information

The phone number for all Independence National Historic Park (INHP) stops is the same (☎ 215-597-8974). Sites are open 9am to 5pm unless otherwise noted.

76 Carriage Company & Philadelphia Trolley Works (☎ 215-923-8516; www.phillytour.com; cnr 6th & Chestnut Sts; adult $20-70, child $4-13)

African American Museum in Philadelphia (☎ 215-574-0380; www.aampmuseum.org; 701 Arch St; admission $8; ⊗ 10am-5pm Thu-Sun, 10:30am-5pm Tue, 10:30am-7pm Wed)

Arch Street Meeting House (320 Arch St; admission by donation; ⊗ closed Sun)

B Free Franklin Post Office (☎ 215-592-1289; 316 Market St)

Betsy Ross House (☎ 215-686-1252; 239 Arch St; admission by donation; ⊗ 9am-5pm)

Carpenters' Hall (INHP, btwn Chestnut & Walnut Sts; ⊗ closed Mon)

Christ Church (☎ 215-922-1695; 2nd St btwn Market & Arch Sts)

Fireman's Hall (☎ 215-923-1438; 147 N 2nd St)

Franklin Court (INHP, Market St btwn S 3rd & S 4th Sts)

Giovanni's Room (☎ 215-923-2960; 345 S 12th St)

Greek Revival Philadelphia Exchange (cnr 3rd & Walnut Sts)

Independence Hall/Congress Hall (INHP, Chestnut St btwn S 5th & S 6th Sts)

Independence National Historic Park (☎ 215-597-8974; www.nps.gov/inde)

Independence Visitor Center (☎ 215-965-7676; www.independencevisitorcenter.com; 6th St btwn Market & Arch Sts; ⏱ 8:30am-5pm)

Liberty Bell Center (INHP, 6th St btwn Market & Sts)

Library Hall (INHP, S 5th btwn Chestnut & Walnut Sts)

Mantua Maker's Museum House (☎ 215-574-0560; admission $2; ⏱ 10am-4pm Sat, noon-4pm Sun)

National Museum of American Jewish History (☎ 215-923-3811; www.nmajh.org; 55 N 5th St; admission free; ⏱ 10am-5pm Mon-Thu, 10am-3pm Fri, noon-5pm Sun)

National Portrait Gallery (INHP, Chestnut St btwn S 4th & S 5th Sts)

Old City Hall/Philosophical Hall (INHP, Chestnut St btwn S 5th & S 6th Sts)

Philadelphia Convention & Visitors Bureau (www.pcvb.org, 215-636-3300) Please note that this is not a place to be visited; it's a marketing office for the city

Phlash (☎ 215-474-5274; all-day pass $4)

US Mint (☎ 215-408-0114; INHP, btwn 4th & 5th Sts; admission free)

Windsor Chair Maker's House (☎ 215-574-0560; 126 Elfreth's Alley; admission $2; ⏱ 10am-4pm Sat, noon-4pm Sun)

Eating

Geno's (☎ 215-389-0659; 1219 S 9th St; mains $3-6)

Buddakan (☎ 215-574-9440; 325 Chestnut St; mains $20-28)

Millennium Coffee (☎ 731-9798; 212 S 12th St; mains $2-6)

Pat's King of Steaks (☎ 215-468-1546; 9th St at Wahrton & Passyunk Aves; mains $3-7; ⏱ 24hr)

Reading Terminal Market (☎ 215-922-2317; www.readingterminalmarket.org; 12th & Arch Sts; mains $2)

Sleeping

Antique Row B&B (☎ 215-592-7802; www.antiquerowbnb.com; 341 S 12th St; r $65-110)

Four Seasons Hotel Philadelphia (☎ 215-963-1500; www.fourseasons.com/philadelphia; One Logan Sq; r $220-300)

Latham Hotel (☎ 215-563-7474; www.lathamhotel.com; 135 S 17th St; r $109-149)

Penn's View Hotel (☎ 215-922-7600; www.pennsview hotel.com; Front & Market Sts; r $165-185)

Shippen Way Inn (☎ 215-627-7266; 416-418 Bainbridge St; r $85-120)

Directory

Directory

ACCOMMODATIONS

With the number of hotel rooms in New York City standing at about 70,000 (and climbing), the question is not *will* you find a room, but where, and for how much? New hotels open regularly in this city, and Dream (p366), Hotel QT (p367) and the Night Hotel (Map p282; 132 W 45th St) are among the newest. And so, although the national trend of converting or partially converting hotels into residential condos has not missed NYC (with the posh Plaza, which lost more than half of its guest rooms, and the Time Warner Center's Mandarin Oriental, p369, as recent examples), so far the impact upon the number of available accommodations has been minimal.

In the Sleeping chapter (p354) of this book you'll find hotels listed alphabetically within their neighborhoods, with price ranges indicated with $ symbols (see p354 for the key). The average room is $300 a night, with some seasonal fluctuations (lowest in January and February, highest in September and October), and plenty of options both below and above (especially above) this rate. Expect rates, in reality, to be even higher when you get your bill, as the hotel will also tack on a 13.625% room tax and $2 to $6 per night occupancy tax. All that said, it's still not so hard to find a budget room (that means less than $200 by New York standards) or even space for $50 in a youth hostel. It's not uncommon to find frequent special rates no matter what time of year it is, but especially in midwinter or midsummer, when weekend rates often get slashed. Other times, you can usually find rates slashed up to 65% on various hotel booking websites, which include the following:

Hotel Conxions (www.hotelconxions.com) A city-specific site with unique results.

Just New York Hotels (www.justnewyorkhotels.com) Four-star options for as low as $171.

Lonely Planet (www.lonelyplanet.com) Go to 'travel services' and then 'hotels' for great deals.

Orbitz (www.orbitz.com) Lets you specify star rating, chain name and other details.

Travelocity (www.travelocity.com) Includes packages with flights, too.

For more tips on finding discounts through Internet reservations, see Bidding for Travel, Pt 1, p373. Know that check-out times vary, but are usually 11am, while check-in time is usually 3pm; if you need to vary either, though, just ask, as most places are flexible – though some could charge up to a half-day's rate for a late checkout.

If you're up for a neighborhood adventure, bedding down in a more unusual area – not Times Sq or Soho, in other words – is a great way to ensure that you'll do some off-the-beaten-path exploring, as well as stay in a place that's more intimate and B&B-like than the majority of NYC hotels. For example, take a look at the offerings in Harlem, like the Harlem Flophouse (p374), or in areas of Brooklyn, including Park Slope's Bed & Breakfast on the Park (p375) or the Carroll Gardens Union Street B&B (p376).

See p356 for information on rental accommodations.

BUSINESS HOURS

Most offices are open 9am to 5pm Monday to Friday, while most shops are on a later clock, typically opening at 10am or 11am or even noon in the Village, and closing between 7pm and 9pm, often later on weekends. Restaurants serve breakfast from about 6am to noon, and then lunch till 3pm or 4pm, with just enough time to start serving dinner by 5pm – although prime dinner hour is more like 8pm (9pm on weekends). Most stores are open on public holidays (except Christmas day) but banks, schools and offices are usually closed. Though most banks are open 9am to 4pm Monday to Friday, a few in Chinatown have limited Saturday hours, and the Commerce Bank chain, with locations all over Manhattan, has daily (including weekend) hours that vary.

CHILDREN

Contrary to popular belief, New York can be a child-friendly city – it just takes a bit of guidance to find all the little creature comforts that you're accustomed to having back home. When seeking accommodations, steer clear of the supertrendy boutique hotels that tend to have tiny rooms and single-person party-monster vibes; there are plenty of other options that welcome kids with open arms. At the **Time Hotel** (Map p282; ☎ 212-246-5252; www.thetimeny .com; 224 W 49th St; d $259-$569), children under 12 stay free and cribs and childcare are both available; same with the Iroquois (p368), Le Parker Meridien (p369) and the Gershwin Hotel (p363). For a longer list of options, visit www.gocitykids.com.

Visiting during warm weather tends to make things easier, as you can always resort to the many parks, playgrounds and zoos to let your kids expel some pent-up energy; the following are just a few of the great parks-with-playscapes options:

Battery Park (p117) Great waterfront location and various activities.

Central Park's Safari Playground (Map p199) Has a fun safari theme.

Central Park's 96th St Playground (Map p199; 96th St at Fifth Ave) Features a safe tree house.

Glass Garden (Map p199; ☎ 212-263-6058; 400 E 34th St at First Ave; ☒ 8am-5:30pm Mon-Fri, 1-5:30pm Sat-Sun) A botanical garden, complete with koi and turtle ponds, plus the educational PlayGarden.

Tompkins Sq Park (p137) Hipster downtown parents and little ones at three playgrounds.

But there are plenty of indoor activities. Museums, especially those geared to kids like the Children's Museum of Manhattan (p158) are great respites, as are children's theaters, movie theaters, book and toy stores, aquariums and kid-friendly restaurants (p94). For more details, pick up Lonely Planet's *Travel With Children*. And when you get to town, get your hands on a copy of the weekly *Time Out Kids* magazine, available at newsstands.

The biggest pitfalls tend to revolve around public transportation, as a startling lack of subway-station elevators will have you lugging strollers up and down flights of stairs (though you'll avoid the turnstile by getting buzzed through an easy-access gate); strollers (unless they're folded up, sans child) are not allowed on public buses. Taxis are easiest.

Babysitting
While major hotels (not boutique-style places) offer babysitting services, or can at least provide you with referrals, you could also turn to a local childcare organization. **Baby Sitters' Guild** (☎ 212-682-0227; www .babysittersguild.com), established back in 1940 specifically to serve travelers staying in hotels with children, has a stable of sitters who speak a range of 16 languages. All are carefully screened, most are CPR-certified and many have nursing backgrounds; they'll come right to your hotel room and even bring games and arts-and-crafts projects. Another good option is **Pinch Sitters** (☎ 212-260-6005). Both will set you back about $20 per hour.

CLIMATE
Spring in New York is absolutely gorgeous – blossoming trees pop into reds and pinks, sunny days glimmer and even rainy days have a lovely, cleansing feel to them. The temperatures can still dip down to a chilly 40°F in early April evenings, but average temperatures hover at around 60°F, creating days that are perfect for strolling in the city.

Summers can be beastly, as temperatures in July and August can climb to the 100°F mark; usually it's between 70°F and 80°F, with occasional thunderstorms that light up the sky and cool everything down until the sun comes out again.

Winters, of course, are cold. It can be gray for days, with sleet and snow showers that quickly turn into a mucky brown film at your feet and temperatures that can easily dip down into the single digits come January. But a good snowstorm is a beautiful thing in these parts, and a cold night inspires cuddling, which can make for a damn romantic visit.

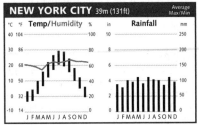

COURSES
New York is brimming with universities, colleges and small, focused schools where students reap the benefits of being in an artistic, culinary and cultural hotspot. Why

not learn a little something while you're here? As a traveler, it's a great way to gain a different perspective on the city.

Cooking

Bouley Test Kitchen's Demonstration Classes (Bouley Bakery, Café & Market, p329) enables you to learn from celeb chef David Bouley, with a single lesson ($175) that includes both food and wine tasting, plus photographs of your creations. Other chefs have jumped on this education bandwagon, including Sue Torres of Sueños (p241), who teaches fine Mexican cooking techniques on Saturday afternoons ($50); and the people at Artisanal (p242), where you will find several open classes that focus on gourmet cheese ($75 to $125). De Gustibus Cooking School at Macy's (p345) offers an impressive lineup of lessons at its in-store facility; subjects range from TV Personalities (Rachael Ray and Daisy Martinez were recent guests) and New and Notable Restaurants (which had local celeb Tom Colicchio preparing a tasting menu recently) to Knife Skills and Clearly Kosher. Single classes average $85 per person.

Writing

Media Bistro (Map p450; ☎ 212-929-2588; www.mediabistro.com; 494 Broadway btwn Spring & Broome Sts; classes $65-125), a networking and educational organization for journalists and other writers, provides regular three-hour seminars that cover topics from Intro to Travel Writing to Pitching Your Novel and How to Write Essays about Sex. It is the perfect opportunity to rub elbows with those in the New York–writer scene.

General

The **Learning Annex** (Map pp452-3; ☎ 212-371-0280; www.learningannex.com; 16 W 53rd St btwn Fifth & Sixth Aves; classes $40-250), an NYC institution, is infamous for its thick catalogues, available for free in street boxes, and its wacky range of classes – feng shui, soap making, in-line skating, real estate, how to fall in love. Classes, often taught by celebs that have included Donald Trump and Suze Orman, are generally held over the course of one day or an evening.

CUSTOMS

US customs allows each person over the age of 21 to bring 1L of liquor (no absinthe!) and 200 cigarettes duty-free into the USA (smokers take note: cigarettes cost around $7 a pack here in the big city, so take advantage of those duty-free shops). US citizens are allowed to import, duty-free, up to $800 worth of gifts from abroad, while non-US citizens are allowed to import $100 worth. If you're carrying more than $10,000 in US and foreign cash, traveler's checks, money orders etc, you need to declare the excess amount. There is no legal restriction on the amount that may be imported, but undeclared sums in excess of $10,000 will probably be subject to investigation. If you're bringing prescription drugs, make sure they're in clearly marked containers; leave the illegal narcotics at home. For updates, check www.customs.gov.

DISABLED TRAVELERS

Federal laws guarantee that all government offices and facilities are accessible to the disabled. For information on specific places, you can contact the mayor's **Office for People with Disabilities** (☎ 212-788-2830; 🕙 9am-5pm Mon-Fri), which will send you a free copy of its *Access New York* guide if you call and request it. Another excellent resource is the **Society for Accessible Travel & Hospitality** (SATH; Map 000; ☎ 212-447-7284; www.sath.org; 347 Fifth Ave at 34th St; 🕙 9am-5pm), which gives advice on how to travel with a wheelchair, kidney disease, sight impairment or deafness.

Though New York is congested and difficult to navigate, things are improving slowly but surely; buses, which all have wheelchair elevation systems and ride space, are definitely the way to go. Subways, on the other hand, are either on elevated tracks or deep below ground and there are very few elevators to access them. For detailed information on subway and bus wheelchair accessibility, call the **Accessible Line** (☎ 718-596-8585). Also visit **NYC & Company** (www.nycvisit.com; click on 'NYC & Company' and then 'Travelers with Disabilities') for more tips.

Movie and Broadway theaters have areas reserved for wheelchairs, and sometimes the newer movie theaters even have these seats near the front, rather than stuck in the back; Broadway theaters also provide live audio description devices for blind theatergoers.

DISCOUNT CARDS

New York City Pass (www.citypass.com), which you can purchase either online or at any major city attraction (museums, historic sites etc), buys you admission into six major attractions for just $53 ($41 for ages six to 17) – a $107.50 value. **New York Pass** (www.newyorkpass.com), meanwhile, sells online for $49 and gives you daylong access to 40 top attractions (Empire State Building, Statue of Liberty, the Guggenheim etc), as well as discounts at 25 stores and restaurants. Two-, three- and seven-day passes are also available, and you can choose to collect them in NYC or have them sent to you before you leave home. The **Entertainment Book** (www.entertainment.com), which you can order for $30 before your arrival, is packed with passes that arm you with dining, shopping and service deals – from 20% off meals at various restaurants to free admission to the South Street Seaport Museum and movie tickets for $6 (as opposed to $10).

ELECTRICITY

The US electric current is 110v to 115v, 60Hz AC. Outlets are made for flat two-prong or three-prong plugs. If your appliance is made for another electrical system, you'll need a US converter, which can be bought from hardware stores and drugstores.

EMBASSIES & CONSULATES

The presence of the United Nations in New York City means that nearly every country in the world maintains diplomatic offices in Manhattan. You can check the listing in the local *Yellow Pages* under 'consulates' for a complete listing. Some foreign consulates, all in Manhattan, include the following:

Australia (Map pp452-3; ☎ 212-351-6500; www.australianyc.org/consulate; 34th fl, 150 E 42nd St; ☯ 8:30am-5pm Mon-Fri)

Brazil (Map pp282-3; ☎ 917-777-7777; www.brazilny.org; 21st fl, 1185 Sixth Ave; ☯ 10am-noon & 2:30-4pm Mon-Fri)

Canada (Map pp282-3; ☎ 212-596-1628; www.canada-ny.org; 1251 Sixth Ave; ☯ 8:45am-5pm Mon-Fri)

France (Map pp454-5; ☎ 212-606-3680; www.consulfrance-newyork.org; 934 Fifth Ave; ☯ 9am-1pm Mon-Fri)

Germany (Map pp452-3; ☎ 212-610-9700; www.german-info.org/newyork/; 871 UN Plaza; ☯ 9am-noon Mon-Fri)

EMERGENCY

Poison control (☎ 800-222-1222)
Police, fire & ambulance (☎ 911)

GAY & LESBIAN TRAVELERS

It's no big deal to be LGBT in New York City, the birthplace of the gay rights movement. The signal moment of the modern gay rights movement occurred in New York on June 27, 1969, when the police launched a raid on the Stonewall Bar (p266), whose patrons were mourning the death of singer Judy Garland, an icon for the gay community. Many angrily resisted the bust, and three nights of riots followed. The Stonewall rebellion and other protests led to the introduction in 1971 of the first bill designed to ban discrimination on the basis of sexual orientation. Several more have been passed since then – though same-sex marriage is still not legal – and the city now has several out-gay political representatives; as of 2006, the position of City Council Speaker, which many officials agree is the second-most powerful local post after mayor, was filled by openly-lesbian City Council Member Christine Quinn.

The Lesbian, Gay, Bisexual & Transgender Pride March (p25) is held each June; for a list of gay bars and clubs, see p266.

A great resource is the **LGBT Community Center** (☎ 212-620-7310; www.gaycenter.org; 208 W 13th St), home base for more than 300 organizations with meeting space, dances and film screenings, drag bingo, and programs on families, health, gay youth, recovery and much more. It's a good place for a gay visitor to make a first stop and get all the info.

Also, for feature stories about and lists of gay and lesbian venues and events, pick up the free publications *HX*, *Next*, *Metrosource* and *Go* (for lesbians) at street boxes and in gay bars and bookstores. Follow news stories about the gay community in the two gay weeklies, the *New York Blade* and *Gay City News*.

HOLIDAYS

Following is a list of major NYC holidays and special events. These holidays may force closure of many businesses or attract crowds, making dining and accommodations reservations difficult. See p23 for a list of more-specific dates.

Directory

Easter Mid-April

Memorial Day Late May

Gay Pride Last Sunday in June

Independence Day July 4

Labor Day Early September

Rosh Hashanah and **Yom Kippur** Mid-September to mid-October

Halloween October 31

Thanksgiving Late November

Christmas Day December 25

Boxing Day December 26

New Year's Eve December 31

INTERNET ACCESS

Internet access is easy in NYC – you can even find it on street corners now (and in the area's airports), with the recent addition of nearly 30 payphones equipped with Internet portals. The TCC Internet Phones, found mostly in Midtown but also sprinkled throughout the East Village, Soho, Chinatown and on the Upper East Side, cost $1 for four minutes, although NYC information websites are free. Best of all, the phones have wireless capabilities (within 300ft), allowing high-speed access to folks who have wireless laptops.

The main branch of the **New York Public Library** (Map pp452-3; ☎ 212-930-0800; E 42nd St at Fifth Ave) offers free half-hour

---

WIFI NYC

Though New York is not totally wired – and is frustratingly behind other cities when it comes to free access spots – there are plenty of places that make for a happy laptop. **NYC Wireless** (www.nycwireless.net) is a local free-WiFi activist team and has an online map of free access points, which require sign-in; the group has advocated to get free hotspots in public parks including Bryant Park (p148), Tompkins Sq Park (p137) and Union Sq Park (p146). You'll find free hotspots on the campus of Columbia University (p166) and at the South Street Seaport (p123), and at businesses including Apple Soho (p325), Chelsea Market (p143), Soy Luck Club (p239) and, oddly enough, the gay bar/club **xl** (p266), where you can surf while sipping a martini. Note that while all the hundreds of Starbucks in the city are wired, you'll be required to sign up for an account, which will run you about $6 an hour – not to mention that $4 latte.

Internet access, though there may be a wait in the afternoons; more than 80 other local branches also have free access and usually with no wait; for locations, visit www.nypl.org/branch/local/. There are many WiFi access hotspots around the city; see the boxed text, left, for a guide.

At Internet cafés, you can surf the Net for an hourly fee, which ranges from $1 to $12, or plug in to free WiFi access. Try the following places, all with their own distinct vibe:

Cyber Café (Map p282; ☎ 212-333-4109; 250 W 49th St btwn Broadway & Eighth Ave; per 30 min $6.40, minimum 30 min; 🕑 8am-11pm Mon-Fri, 11am-11pm Sat-Sun) High-speed computers with color printers, scanners and web cams, plus coffee and wine bar.

Easy Internet Café (Map p282; ☎ 212-398-0724; 234 W 42nd St; per hr $2; 🕑 24hr) This is the cheapest, and possibly the biggest, place in town.

LGBT Community Center (Map p448; ☎ 212-620-7310; 208 W 13th St; suggested donation $3) The cyber-center here has 15 computers, open to all.

Web2Zone (Map p449; ☎ 212-614-7300; 54 Cooper Sq btwn Astor Pl & 4th Ave; per hr $5; 🕑 9am-11pm Mon-Fri, 10am-11pm Sat, noon-10pm Sun) Also has extensive printing and design services, plus computer games.

LEGAL MATTERS

If you're arrested, you have the right to remain silent. There is no legal reason to speak to a police officer if you don't wish to – especially since anything you say 'can and will be used against you' – but never walk away from an officer until given permission. All persons who are arrested have the legal right to make one phone call. If you don't have a lawyer or family member to help you, call your consulate. The police will give you the number upon request.

MAPS

Lonely Planet publishes a pocket-size laminated map of New York City, available at most bookstores. You can also pick up free Downtown Manhattan maps in the lobby of any decent hotel and at tourist information booths run by NYC & Company (p414). If you want to explore the city at large, buy a five-borough street atlas, published by the Long Island City, Queens-based Hagstrom company, which also makes great maps of the individual boroughs.

Most subway stations in Manhattan have 'Passenger Information Centers' next to the token booths; these feature a wonderfully large-scale, detailed map of the surrounding neighborhood, with all points of interest clearly marked. Taking a look before heading aboveground may save you from getting lost. You can get free subway and bus maps from the attendant inside the subway booth (though they're often all out).

You can buy maps at any bookstore (Barnes & Noble, p339, usually has the biggest selection), or directly from Hagstrom Map & Travel Center (p344).

MEDICAL SERVICES

Healthcare is a major problem in this country, as there is no federal law guaranteeing medical care for all citizens, and health insurance is extremely costly. People living below the poverty line are eligible for Medicaid, which covers many costs, and seniors can apply for Medicare, which works in a similar way. As a visitor, know that all hospital emergency rooms are obliged to receive sick or injured patients whether they can pay or not.

Clinics

If you're sick or injured, but not bad enough for an emergency room, try one of the following options:

Michael Callen-Audre Lorde Community Health Center (Map p448; ☎ 212-271-7200; www.callen-lorde.org; 356 W 18th St btwn Eighth & Ninth Aves) This medical center, dedicated to the LGBT community and people living with HIV/AIDS, serves people regardless of their ability to pay.

New York County Medical Society (☎ 212-684-4670; www.nycms.org) Makes doctor referrals by phone based on type of problem and language spoken.

Planned Parenthood (Map pp454-7; ☎ 212-965-7000; www.plannedparenthood.com; 26 Bleecker St) Provides birth control, STD screenings and gynecological care.

Emergency Rooms

New York City emergency rooms are, for the most part, like the ninth circle of hell. Avoid them at all costs. For when you really can't avoid one, consult the local phone directory for a complete listing and prepare for an average four-hour wait (unless you're in dire shape). Following are some major hospitals with emergency rooms:

Beth Israel Medical Center (Map pp446-7; ☎ 212-420-2000; First Ave at E 16th St)

Mount Sinai Hospital (Map pp454-5; ☎ 212-241-6500; 1190 Fifth Ave at 100th St)

New York Presbyterian Columbia University Hospital (Map pp468-9; ☎ 212-305-6204; 622 168th St at Ft Washington Ave)

St Vincent's Medical Center (Map p448; ☎ 212-604-7000; 153 W 11th St at Greenwich Ave)

Pharmacies

New York is practically bursting with 24-hour 'pharmacies,' which are handy all-purpose stores where you can buy over-the-counter medications anytime; the actual pharmaceutical counters have more limited hours. Harder-to-find 24-hour pharmacies include a downtown **Rite Aid** (Map pp446-7; ☎ 212-529-7115; 508 Grand St at Clinton St) and a Midtown **CVS** (Map pp282-3; ☎ 212-245-0636; 400 W 59th St at Columbus Circle).

MONEY

The US dollar (familiarly called a 'buck') is divided into 100 cents (¢). Coins come in denominations of 1¢ (penny), 5¢ (nickel), 10¢ (dime), 25¢ (quarter), the practically extinct 50¢ (half-dollar), and the not-oft-seen golden dollar coin, which was introduced in early 2000, featuring a picture of Sacagawea, the Native American guide who led the explorers Lewis and Clark on their expedition through the western US. Although striking, the new coins are prohibitively heavy and jingle conspicuously, alerting panhandlers to your well-heeled presence. These coins are often dispensed as change from ticket and stamp machines. Notes come in $1, $2, $5, $10, $20, $50 and $100 denominations.

In recent years the US treasury has redesigned the $5, $10, $20, $50 and $100 bills to foil counterfeiters. Yes, they're still green, but the portraits have grown exponentially.

See p35 for information on specific prices of goods and services. To check the exchange rate (though it changes daily), see the Quick Reference guide inside this book's front cover.

ATMs

Automatic teller machines are on practically every corner. You can either use your card at banks – usually a 24-hour-access lobby, filled with up to a dozen monitors at major branches – or you can opt for the lone wolves, which sit in delis, restaurants, bars and grocery stores, charging fierce service fees that go as high as $5 for foreign banks in some places. Most New York banks are linked by the New York Cash Exchange (NYCE) system, and you can use local bank cards interchangeably at ATMs – for an extra fee if you're banking outside your system. Getting money this way saves you a step – no changing money from your own currency – and is a safer way to travel, as you only take out what you need, as you go.

Changing Money

Banks and moneychangers, found all over New York City, will give you US currency based on the current exchange rate. Banks are normally open from 9am to 4pm Monday to Friday. A couple of options:

American Express (Map pp452–3; ☎ 212-421-8240, for locations 800-221-7282; 374 Park Ave at 53rd St; ⏰ 9am-5pm Mon-Fri) American Express has plenty of branches about town.

Travelex (Map p282; ☎ 212-265-6049; 1590 Broadway at 48th St; ⏰ 9am-7pm Mon-Sat, 9am-5pm Sun) Features currency exchange at eight locations in the city, including the Times Sq office.

Credit & Debit Cards

Major credit cards are accepted at most hotels, restaurants and shops throughout New York City. In fact, you'll find it difficult to perform certain transactions, such as purchasing tickets to performances and renting a car, without one.

Stack your deck with either a Visa, MasterCard or American Express, as these are the cards of choice here. Places that accept Visa and MasterCard also accept debit cards, which deduct payments directly from your check or savings account. Be sure to check with your bank to confirm that your debit card will be accepted in other states or countries – debit cards from large commercial banks can often be used worldwide.

If your cards are lost or stolen, contact the company immediately. The following are toll-free numbers for the main credit card companies:

American Express (☎ 800-528-4800)

Diners Club (☎ 800-234-6377)

Discover (☎ 800-347-2683)

MasterCard (☎ 800-826-2181)

Visa (☎ 800-336-8472)

Traveler's Checks

This old-school option offers protection from theft or loss. Checks issued by American Express and Thomas Cook are widely accepted, and both offer efficient replacement policies. Keeping a record of the check numbers and the checks you've used is vital when it comes to replacing lost checks. Keep this record in a separate place from the checks themselves.

Bring most of the checks in large denominations. It's toward the end of a trip that you may want to change a small check to make sure you aren't left with too much local currency. Of course, traveler's checks are losing their popularity due to the explosion of ATMs and you may opt not to carry any at all.

NEWSPAPERS & MAGAZINES

There are scads of periodicals to choose from – but what else would you expect from one of the media capitals of the world? Daily newspapers include the following:

Metro (www.metro.us) Part of a three-city chain that includes Philadelphia and Boston, this weekday-only daily, geared toward subway commuters, delivers the major news in well-written, easy-to-swallow bits.

New York Daily News (www.nydailynews.com) One of two sensationalistic tabloids, this is slightly more staid in tone than the *Post*.

New York Newsday (www.nynewsday.com) Though tabloid in shape, it's broadsheet in tone, and is the city version of *Newsday*, a popular Long Island daily.

New York Observer (www.nyobserver.com) The salmon-colored broadsheet is obsessed with insidery news and gossip of the uptown sort.

New York Post (www.newyorkpost.com) The *Post* is known for screaming headlines, conservative political views and its popular Page Six gossip column.

New York Press (www.nypress.com) The alternative weekly that forced the *Voice* to go free; expect lots of first-person ramblings and a witty edge, plus lots of arts write-ups.

New York Times (www.nytimes.com) 'The gray lady' has gotten hip in recent years, with new sections on technology, arts and dining out.

Village Voice (www.villagevoice.com) Recently purchased by national alternative-newspaper chain New Times, the legendary *Voice* has less bite but still plenty of bark. It's home to everyone's favorite gossip columnist, Michael Musto.

Villager (www.thevillager.com) A local neighborhood weekly, this well-reported paper is a great source of downtown news.

Wall Street Journal (www.wallstreetjournal.com) This intellectual daily has a focus on finance.

Magazines that give a good sense of the local flavor include the following:

BKLYN (www.bklynmagazine.com) This relatively new monthly focuses on 'brownstone Brooklyn,' meaning the gentrified areas including Bococa, Park Slope and Brooklyn Heights.

New York Magazine (www.nymetro.com) The weekly magazine has feature stories and great listings about anything and everything in NYC, with an indispensable website.

Paper (www.papermag.com) This hip monthly favors celebrities, fashion, art and film.

Time Out New York (www.timeout.com) A weekly magazine, its focus is on being complete (as you'll see from its bible-like listings on everything cultural) plus articles and interviews on arts and entertainment.

PHOTOGRAPHY

Just as you can drop your old-school film off at any pharmacy or photo shop for speedy printing, you can now do the same with your digital-camera card, getting photos transferred either onto a disk or printed while you wait – or both. Ubiquitous chains including Rite Aid, CVS and Duane Reade all have photo counters, most equipped with machines that allow you to read your digital card and edit which photos you want printed. For cameras or photo equipment, head to a photo shop such as **B&H Photo and Video** (p344), in Midtown, or **J&R Music and Computer World** (p324) in Lower Manhattan. For prints both film and digital, you'll find several high-quality photo labs, used by professionals, in the blocks of 20th to 24th Sts between Fifth and Sixth Aves; **Duggal** (Map pp446-7; ☎ 212-924-8100; 29 W 23rd St btwn Fifth & Sixth Aves) is a fine example.

POST

Rates for sending mail go up every few years, and with increasing frequency it seems. With the latest increase, rates for first-class mail within the USA are 39¢ for letters up to 1oz and 24¢ for postcards. For package and international letter rates, which vary, check with the post office or with the online **postal-rate calculator** (http://ircalc.usps.gov/). For whatever postal questions you may have, call ☎ 800-275-8777 or visit the **US Post Office** (www.usps.com/welcome.htm) website.

New York City's **General Post Office** (Map pp452-3; ☎ 212-967-8585; James A Foley Bldg, 380 W 33rd St at Eighth St; ☺ 24hr) can help with all your postal requirements, as can the various branch offices, which are listed on the website. Alternatives to post-office mailing include various mail stores, such as the chain **Mailboxes Etc** (www.mbe.com), which has many options around Manhattan. The upside is there's always a much shorter wait, and there are more branches to choose from; the downside is that it's much more expensive.

RADIO

NYC has some mighty excellent radio options beyond the commercial, pop-music dreck. An excellent programming guide can be found in the *New York Times* entertainment section on Sunday. Below are some of the top station picks, all of which can be heard online:

East Village Radio (www.eastvillageradio.com) Community radio with music, talk and political chatter, available online only.

WBAI 99.5FM (www.wbai.org) Hear political talk and news with an activist bent, with highlights featuring shows like *Democracy Now!*, on this local Pacifica Radio affiliate.

WFUV 90.7FM (www.wfuv.org) Fordham University's radio station features excellent indie music – folk, rock and otherwise personable-type sounds – as well as personable DJs.

WLIB 1190AM (www.airamericaradio.com) This is the new Air America station, featuring 24-hour left-leaning talk that's in sharp contrast to the conservative talk shows filling the AM dial.

WNYC 93.9FM and **820AM** (www.wnyc.org) NYC's public radio station is the local NPR affiliate, offering a blend of national and local talk and interview shows, with a switch to classical music in the day on the FM station.

WOR 710AM (www.wor710.com) A talk-show station, it features local maven Joan Hamburg, who doles out pithy advice on where to eat, shop and travel; you'll also hear the national Dr Joy Brown Show, with a call-in therapy format.

SAFETY

Crime rates here remain at their lowest in years. There are few neighborhoods remaining where you can feel scared, no matter what time of night it is. That goes for subway stations, too, though some low-income neighborhoods, especially in the outer boroughs, can be dicey. There's no reason to be paranoid, but it's better to be safe than sorry, so use common sense: don't walk around alone at night in unfamiliar, sparsely populated areas, especially if you're a woman. Don't flash money around on the street. And keep your valuables somewhere safe. Unless you must accessorize with the real thing, leave the good jewelry at home. Carry your daily walking-around money somewhere inside your clothing (in a money belt, bra or sock) rather than in a handbag or an outside pocket, and be aware of pickpockets in particularly mobbed areas, like Times Sq or Penn Station at rush hour.

TAX

Restaurants and retailers never include the tax – 8.625% – in their prices, so beware of ordering the $4.99 lunch special when you only have $5 to your name. Several categories of so-called 'luxury items,' including rental cars and dry-cleaning, carry an additional city surcharge of 5%, so you wind up paying an extra 13.625% in total for these services. Hotel rooms in New York City are subject to a 13.625% tax, plus a flat $2- to $6-per-night occupancy tax. Since the US has no nationwide value-added tax (VAT), there is no opportunity for foreign visitors to make 'tax-free' purchases.

TELEPHONE

Phone numbers within the USA consist of a three-digit area code followed by a seven-digit local number. If you're calling long distance, dial ☎ 1 + the three-digit area code + the seven-digit number.

For local and national directory assistance, dial ☎ 1 + 212 + 555-1212. And, as part of a miraculous citywide system, you can dial ☎ 311 for anything that's city-related – whether you have a noise complaint, have a question about parking regulations or want to find the nearest dog run. Operators are available 24 hours and will quickly connect you to the government office that'll best be able to serve you.

If you're calling New York from abroad, the international country code for the USA is 1. To dial an international number directly, dial ☎ 011, then the country code, followed by the area code and the phone number. (To find the country code, check the phone book or dial ☎ 411 and ask for an international operator.) International rates vary depending on the time of day and the destination.

In New York City, Manhattan phone numbers are in the 212 or 646 area code (although cell phones and some businesses use

a 917 area code) and the four outer boroughs are in the 718 zone. No matter where you're calling within New York City, even if it's just across the street in the same area code, you must *always* dial 1 + the area code first.

All toll-free numbers are prefixed with an 800, 877, 866 or 888 area code. Some toll-free numbers for local businesses or government offices only work within a limited region. But most toll-free phone numbers can be dialed from abroad – just be aware that you'll be connected at regular long-distance rates, which could become a costly option if the line you're dialing regularly parks customers on hold.

Cell Phones

Known in the US as 'cell phones,' these tiny little accessories have taken over the city; plans are even underway to make reception available in the subways. Part communication device and part status symbol, New Yorkers are totally in love with their phones (and their iPods, for that matter; do you sense a pattern?). But as a traveler, you really don't need a cell phone in the city, especially with the preponderance of pay phones. Plus, service is less than stellar, with several silent zones around town.

Pay Phones

Though they seem outmoded, pay phones still exist on NYC streets and are almost always available. Just don't expect to find any phone booths like the kind that Superman changed in, unless you find one of the very few left in existence, such as one on the Upper West Side at West End Ave and 101st St.

To use a pay phone, you can pump in quarters, use a phone credit or debit card or make collect calls. There are thousands of pay telephones on the New York City streets, all with a seemingly different price scheme, though most (especially the Verizon phones, which have yellow handles) are 50¢ for unlimited local calls.

You can also make long-distance calls at global calling stations, which have low by-the-minute rates; you'll find them all over the city, but especially in and around Times Sq.

Phonecards

An excellent long-distance alternative is phone debit cards, which allow you to pay in advance, with access through a toll-free 800 number. In amounts of $5, $10, $20 and $50, these are available from Western Union, machines in airports and train stations, some supermarkets and nearly every corner deli. Certain cards deliver better value depending on where you're calling (eg New York Alliance is better for Brazil, while Payless is better for Ireland) and the purveyors of the cards can usually provide accurate information.

TELEVISION

New Yorkers are pop-culture-obsessed creatures by nature, making them natural TV fans. The most popular shows for locals to chatter on and on about include, not surprisingly, those based here: *Project Runway* (Bravo), a reality show about fashion designers; *Queer Eye For the Straight Guy* (Bravo), another reality show that has a team of gay men giving sorely needed makeovers to hetero men; and *The Apprentice* (NBC), which is – surprise! – another reality show, this one starring Donald Trump.

There are also a few local TV stations worth tuning into (note that the channel number varies depending on the source of programming from the TV that you're watching; options range from Cablevision and Time Warner cable providers to Direct TV satellite TV):

Manhattan Neighborhood Network (www.mnn.org; various channels) The excellent community TV station, MNN, is chock-full of local entertainers, talkers and other assorted narcissists.

Metro TV (Cablevision 60 and Time Warner 70) An affiliate of *New York Magazine*, this station has great programming on local fashion, dating and culture.

MSG Network (www.msgnetwork.com) The local sports station, run by Madison Sq Garden, broadcasts games involving local teams, including the Yankees, Mets, Knicks, Liberty, Jets and Rangers.

New York 1 (www.ny1.com) This 24-hour local news channel, with hourly one-minute updates and 'weather on the 1's' is only on Time Warner Cable channel 1.

NYC TV (Channel 25) The city's official TV station has an excellent line-up of NYC-based programming, including 'Cool in Your Code,' which looks at the cultural perks of a neighborhood based on its zip code, and 'City Classic,' which shows old footage of protests, press conferences and special events.

Time Out On Demand (www.tony.com, Time Warner Digital channel 1112) This new interactive station of Time Out New York magazine has staff editors discussing culture and entertainment picks of the week.

TIME

New York City is in the Eastern Standard Time (EST) zone – five hours behind Greenwich Mean Time, two hours ahead of Mountain Standard Time (including Denver, Colorado) and three hours ahead of Pacific Standard Time (San Francisco and Los Angeles, California). Almost all of the USA observes daylight-saving time: clocks go forward one hour from the first Sunday in April to the last Saturday in October, when the clocks are turned back one hour. (It's easy to remember by the phrase 'spring ahead, fall back.')

TIPPING

Tipping is expected in restaurants, bars and better hotels, taxis, and also by hairdressers and baggage carriers. In restaurants, wait staff are paid less than the minimum wage and they rely upon tips to make a living. Tip at least 15% unless the service is terrible; most New Yorkers either tip a straight 20% or just double the 8.625% sales tax. At bars, bartenders typically expect at least $1 tip for every drink they serve. In fast-food, take-out or deli-counter joints, you'll often find a tip jar on the counter; dropping in a quarter or two is polite.

Taxi drivers and hairdressers expect about 15% if their service is satisfactory. Baggage carriers (skycaps in airports, bellhops in hotels) receive $2 for the first bag and $1 for each additional bag. In hotels, you should tip the cleaning staff about $5 a day. See p227 in the Eating chapter for more details.

TOILETS

New York is downright hostile to the weak of bladder or bowels. The explosion in the homeless population in the 1970s led to the closure of subway facilities, and most places turn away non-patrons from bathrooms. But there are a few public loos left, including those in Grand Central Terminal, Penn Station and Port Authority Bus Terminal, and in parks including Battery Park, Tompkins Sq Park, Washington Sq Park and Columbus Park in Chinatown, plus many scattered around Central Park. The best bet, though, is to pop into a Starbucks (there's one about every three blocks) and head straight to the bathroom in back.

TOURIST INFORMATION

The most reliable tourist information can be found either online or at official city kiosks and offices.

NYC & Company (Map pp282-3; ☎ 212-484-1200; www .visitnyc.com; 810 Seventh Ave btwn 52nd & 53rd Sts) The city's official tourism arm is the extremely helpful NYC & Company, which offers maps and all sorts of pamphlets at its three locations, and endless useful stuff online, from upcoming special events and various discounts to historic tidbits and security updates. Other branches include Lower Manhattan (Map pp444-5; City Hall Park at Broadway), Harlem (Map pp458-9; 163 W 125th St at Adam Clayton Powell Blvd) and Chinatown (Map pp444-5; Canal, Walker and Baxter Sts).

Times Sq Visitors Center (Map pp282-3; ☎ 212-768-1569; www.timessquarenyc.org; Broadway btwn 46th & 47th Sts) This information center, run by the Times Sq Business Improvement District, offers pamphlets, maps and tourism counselors who can advise you in 10 different languages.

Brooklyn Tourism and Visitors Center (Map pp462-3; ☎ 718-802-3846; Brooklyn Borough Hall, 209 Joralemon St btwn Court & Adams Sts; ☟ 10am-6pm Mon-Fri) Get all sorts of info on the other favorite borough.

VISAS

Because of ever-lingering terrorism-fear fallout, foreigners needing visas to travel to the US should plan ahead. However, there is a reciprocal visa-waiver program in which citizens of certain countries may enter the USA for stays of 90 days or less with a passport but without first obtaining a US visa. Currently these countries include Australia, Austria, Denmark, France, Germany, Italy, Japan, the Netherlands, New Zealand, Spain, Sweden, Switzerland and the UK. Under this program you must have a round-trip ticket that is nonrefundable in the USA, and you will not be allowed to extend your stay beyond 90 days.

Other travelers will need to obtain a visa from a US consulate or embassy. In most countries, the process can be done by mail. Visa applicants may be required to 'demonstrate binding obligations' that will ensure their return home. Because of this requirement, those planning to travel through other countries before arriving in the USA are generally better off applying for their US visa while they are still in their home country – rather than after they're already on the road.

The Non-Immigrant Visitors Visa is the most common visa. It is available in two forms, B1 for business purposes and B2 for tourism or visiting friends and relatives. The validity period for US visitor visas depends on which country you're from. The length of time you'll be allowed to stay in the USA is ultimately determined by US immigration authorities at the port of entry. Non-US citizens with HIV should know that they can be excluded from entry to the USA.

Finally, all visa information is very likely to change, as the federal government is actively making changes all the time due to security situations. For updates on visas and other security issues, you can visit the **government's visa page** (www.unitedstatesvisas.gov), the **US Department of State** (www.travel.state.gov) and the **Travel Security Administration** (www.tsa.gov). Check out the Lonely Planet website (www .lonelyplanet.com) for updates as well.

WOMEN TRAVELERS

In general, New York City is a pretty safe place for women travelers, as long as common sense is used. If you are unsure which areas are considered dicey, ask at your hotel or telephone **NYC & Company** (☎ 212-484-1200) for advice; of course, other women are always a great source for the inside scoop. Depending on the neighborhood you're in, you are likely to encounter obnoxious behavior on the street, where men may greet you with whistles and muttered 'compliments.' Any engagement amounts to encouragement – simply walk on. Finally, if you're out late clubbing or at a venue further afield, consider stashing away money for the cab fare home. If you're ever assaulted, call the **police** (☎ 911).

WORK

To work legally in the USA you generally need both a work permit and a working visa. To apply for the correct visa at the US embassy you are generally required to obtain a work permit from the Immigration and Naturalization Service (INS) first. Your prospective employer must file a petition with the INS for permission for you to work, so you will first need to find a company that wants to hire you and is willing to file all the necessary paperwork. You can find more detailed information at the website of the **US Department of State** (www .travel.state.gov).

Directory

Transportation

Transportation

AIR

Three major airports serve New York City. The biggest is John F Kennedy International (JFK), in Queens, about 15 miles from Midtown Manhattan. Northwest of JFK, but also in Queens, is La Guardia Airport (LGA), which is 8 miles from Midtown. Newark International Airport (EWR), in Newark, New Jersey, is about 16 miles from Midtown. There are no baggage-storage facilities at any of these airports.

There are some rules of thumb for buying cheap tickets: start the hunt early – some of the cheapest tickets and best deals must be purchased months in advance, and popular flights tend to sell out early. Be flexible: play with arrival and departure dates, arrival airports and stopovers. Consider a shorter trip, and try search engines in the wee hours, when cheap fares sometimes sneak in.

High season in New York City runs from mid-June to mid-September (summer), and one week before and after Christmas. February and March, and from October to Thanksgiving (the fourth Thursday in November) serve as shoulder seasons, when prices drop slightly. Booking flights is best done online. Among the best websites are the following:

Cheap Tickets (www.cheaptickets.com)

Expedia (www.expedia.com)

Hotwire (www.hotwire.com)

Orbitz (www.orbitz.com)

Priceline (www.priceline.com)

Travelocity (www.travelocity.com)

If your itinerary is complex, travel agents can find great deals. STA Travel (☎ 800-777-0112, reservations 212-627-3111; www.statravel .com) has some very cheap rates, especially for students. It has many offices in Manhattan. The East Coast chain Liberty Travel (☎ 888-271-1584; www.libertytravel.com) has 12 Manhattan offices and 19 in the boroughs.

Airlines

Visiting airline offices is old-fashioned business these days (and most airlines have closed Manhattan locations in recent years). To get the toll-free numbers of airlines in the US, call ☎ 800-555-1212; you could also check the homepage of your airline for further details.

Airports

Three major airports serve the New York metropolitan region.

JFK INTERNATIONAL AIRPORT

This busy airport (Map p442; JFK; ☎ 718-244-4444; www.panynj.gov), out in southeastern Queens, serves 35 million passengers annually and hosts flights coming and going from all corners of the globe. Its nine terminals sprawl and get quite crowded. Major renovations have been in progress for several years; presently Jet Blue is planning to reopen the superb ex-TWA terminal, designed by Finnish architect Eero Saarinen in 1962 (it perfectly evoked the retro vibe in the film *Catch Me If You Can*). The AirTrain offers free service between the terminals.

LA GUARDIA AIRPORT

Generally busier for domestic flights, La Guardia (Map p467; LGA; ☎ 718-533-3400; www.laguardiaairport.com) is slightly more convenient than JFK if you're driving or taking a taxi, as it's smaller and closer to Manhattan. It sees about 25 million passengers per year. It's been open to commercial use since 1939, making it considerably older than its more famous brother JFK. US Airways and Delta have their own terminals.

NEWARK LIBERTY INTERNATIONAL AIRPORT

Those crafty folk in Newark (Map p442; EWR; ☎ 973-961-6000; www.panynj.gov) are starting to undercut flight fares to New York's airports, bringing more and more Manhattan business to this side of the Hudson River. Actually it's just as accessible as the other two airports – and more historical: it became the metropolis' first major airport in 1928. Much of the action is domestic – particularly on Continental Airlines, which treats EWR as a hub – but not all. The passport checks at Newark's

GETTING INTO TOWN

You can get to/from New York's three main airports – JFK, La Guardia or Newark – via several options, none of which are too complicated to figure out once you've arrived. The easiest is following the signs to taxi stands and standing in the organized queue at any of the airports (avoid independent solicitors who sometimes approach new arrivals). Public transportation can take longer.

For a little extra ease, dozens of car services can offer drop-off or pickup service to the airports, including **Tel Aviv** (☎ 212-777-7777, 800-222-9888; www.telavivlimo.com) and **Prime Time** (☎ 718-482-7900, 800-282-3227). Tel Aviv is about $5 to $10 cheaper (from $46 to JFK or Newark, from $31 to La Guardia). Note that taxi or car-service drivers will expect a tip of about $3 to $5.

If you're going to JFK or La Guardia, the **New York Airport Service Express Bus** (☎ 718-875-8200; www.nyair portservice.com; every 20-30min) has routes to/from both, stopping at the Port Authority Bus Terminal, Penn Station and just outside Grand Central Terminal (Map pp452–3) – no reservations needed.

Super Shuttle Manhattan (☎ 800-258-3826) is kind of like a shared-taxi ride that connects all airports. The shuttle requires you to make a reservation and will then pick you up, on schedule, along with several others who are traveling at the same time as you. Reservations from the airport aren't necessary – just stop at the 'ground transportation' desk and call Super Shuttle, or go up to the departures and look for it. A ride to/from JFK or Newark is $19, La Guardia is $15.

To/from JFK

- A yellow **taxi** from Manhattan will use the meter – prices depend on traffic (often about $50) – it can take 45 to 60 minutes.
- A **car service** (see above) has set fares from $46 (plus toll and tip). Note the Williamsburg, Manhattan and Brooklyn Bridge have no toll either way, while the Queens–Midtown Tunnel and Battery Tunnel have tolls going into Manhattan only.
- If you're **driving**, the two main routes are, from the airport, around Brooklyn's south tip via the Belt Parkway to US 278 (the Brooklyn–Queens Expressway, or BQE); or via US 678 (Van Wyck Expressway) to US 495 (Long Island Expressway, or LIE), which head into Manhattan via the Queens–Midtown Tunnel.
- The **New York Airport Service Express Bus** (see above) costs $15/27 one way/round-trip.
- By **subway**, you can take the A line to Howard Beach–JFK Airport Station (bound for the Rockaway Beach), or the E, J or Z line or the Long Island Rail Rd to Sutphin Blvd/Archer Ave (Jamaica Station), where you can catch the AirTrain to JFK. The E express from Midtown has the fewest stops. The AirTrain finishes the trip for $5 one way; you can use a Metrocard to swipe yourself in.

To/from La Guardia

- A **taxi** to/from Manhattan runs about $35 to $40 for the roughly half-hour ride.
- A **car service** (see above) makes trips to La Guardia for $31 (not including tip and toll).
- Most common **driving** route from the airport is along Grand Central Expressway to the BQE (US 278), then to the Queens–Midtown Tunnel via the LIE (US 495); downtown-bound can stay on the BQE and cross (free) via the Williamsburg Bridge.
- The **New York Airport Express Bus** (see above) costs $13/21 one way/round-trip.
- It's less convenient to go to La Guardia by public transportation than the other airports. The best **subway** link is 74 St–Broadway station (7 line, with access to the E, F, G, R, V lines at Jackson Hts–Roosevelt Ave station), where you can pick up the Q33 or Q47 **bus** to the airport; plan on an hour minimum – split evenly on subway and bus.

To/from Newark

- A **car service** (see above) runs about $46 to $60 one way for the 45-minute ride from Midtown – a **taxi** is roughly the same. You only have to pay the toll to go through the Lincoln Tunnel (at 42nd St) or Holland Tunnel (at Canal St) coming *into* Manhattan from Jersey. It's possible to skip the toll roads in Newark; ask your driver to take Hwy 1 or 9 (they should know); otherwise there's an inexpensive toll to pay.
- **Public transportation** to Newark is convenient, but a bit of a rip. The NJ Transit (☎ 800-772-2222; www .njtransit.com) runs an AirTrain between the Newark airport ('EWR') and New York's Penn Station for a shocking $14 each way (hardly worth it if you're traveling with a couple of others). The trip takes 15 minutes and runs every 20 minutes from 4.20am to about 2am. Hold onto your ticket, which you must show exiting the train station. A clumsier alternative to/from Penn Station is with the **PATH train** (www.panynj.com); it's $1.50 between Penn Station in New York and Newark's Penn Station, which is one stop – via NJ Transit – from the airport ($7.50).

immigration hall have the rep for being quicker than JFK's.

BICYCLE

It's not the most bike-friendly city, but New Yorkers are getting better at tolerating cycling, thanks in part to improved road conditions, new bike paths (such as the one that's part of Hudson Park, running the length of Manhattan's west side), and awareness campaigns from environmental groups. **Transportation Alternatives** (Map pp452–3; ☎ 212-629-8080; www.transalt .org; 127 W 26th St, Suite 1002) has cycling maps available for downloading, sponsors Bike Week NYC every May and acts as a clearinghouse for loads of cycling-related resources and tips.

Still, a great many locals are terrified of vying for road space with the oft-oblivious taxis, trucks, cars and buses that fly up and down the avenues. But if you do ride around the city, be smart: always wear a helmet, choose a bike with wide tires to help you handle potholes and other bits of street debris and be alert so you don't get 'doored' by a passenger exiting a taxi. Unless your urban skills are well honed, stick to the pastoral paths in Central and Prospect Parks and along the Hudson River. And don't even think of pedaling on the sidewalks – it's illegal. If you must lock a bike up somewhere in the city, forgo anything that's not the most top-of-the-line U-lock you can find – or, better yet, stick to the $100 coated chains that weigh a ton. Stealthy bike thieves will easily slice through anything else.

You're allowed to bring your bike onto the subway, which is helpful in case you get caught in the rain. But to bring it on a commuter train, which you can only do during nonrush-hour times, you'll need to have first obtained a bike pass at the ticket window. You can get your pass, which is free, during weekday afternoon hours.

See p310 for information on bike clubs and bike rental.

BOAT

It's highly unusual for anyone to yacht their way into town, and those who do will find few ports ready to receive them – just an exclusive boat slip at the World Financial Center and a long-term slip at the 79th St Boathouse on the Upper West Side.

The zippy yellow boats that make up the fleet of **New York Water Taxi** (☎ 212-742-1969; www.nywatertaxi.com; tickets $5 & $10, two-day pass adults $25, children & seniors $15) provide an interesting alternative of getting around (literally) the city (from May through October). Boats stop at 10 landings, starting at West 44th St in the Hudson River, with stops at West 23rd St, Christopher St, World Financial Center, Battery Park, South Street Seaport, Fulton Ferry in Brooklyn's Dumbo, Schaefer Landing on Kent Ave in Williamsburg, East 34th St and Hunter's Point (with a new beach and bar in Long Island City, Queens). A station at Red Hook may open in the near future. A single ride is $5 for one stop, or $10 for any trip longer than a stop.

The water taxis also lead hour-long 'Gateway to America' tours around the New York Harbor sites on the hour from 11am to 4pm weekdays, 11am to 5pm weekends (adult/child/senior $20/12/18); off-season they run on weekends only.

Another bigger, brighter ferry (this one's orange) is the commuter-oriented **Staten Island Ferry** (p116), which makes constant free journeys across the gorgeous New York Harbor to Staten Island.

For information on boat tours, see p110.

BUS

Many New Yorkers don't ever consider the bus as a viable transportation option. But NYC buses aren't too bad and have certainly improved in the past decade or so. They run 24 hours a day and the routes are easily navigable, going crosstown at all the major street byways – 14th, 23rd, 34th, 42nd and 72nd Sts, and all the others that are two-way roads – and all uptown and downtown, depending on which avenue they serve. Stops, many with shelters, are every few blocks and all have maps and clearly marked schedules, which are rough guides as to how often you can expect a bus to pass. The frequency on most routes is remarkably often and, best of all, when you ride a bus instead of a subway, you can look out at the world. That said, buses do get overcrowded at rush hour, as most are smaller than even one subway car, and slow to a crawl in heavy traffic. So when you're in a hurry, stay underground.

The cost of a bus ride is the same as the subway ($2), though express bus routes cost $5 (best for long journeys from the boroughs). You can pay with a Metrocard (p421) or exact change but *not* dollar bills. Transfers from one line to another are free, as are transfers to or from the subway. Transfers are good for two hours and are automatically encoded on the Metrocard when used.

For all suburban and long-distance bus trips, you'll leave and depart from the **Port Authority Bus Terminal** (Map p282; ☎ 212-564-8484; www.panynj.gov; 41st St at Eighth Ave). Though the Port Authority is not quite as rough as its reputation, it's still possible that you may be hassled by panhandlers or shady types offering to carry bags for tips. **Greyhound** (☎ 800-231-2222; www.greyhound .com) connects New York with major cities across the country. **Peter Pan Trailways** (☎ 800-343-9999; www.peterpanbus.com) operates buses to the nearest major cities, including a daily express service to Boston (one way/round-trip $30/55), Washington DC ($37/69) and Philadelphia ($21/40), with a seven-day advance purchase. **Short Line** (☎ 800-631-8405, 212-529-3666; www.shortlinebus.com) operates numerous buses to towns in northern New Jersey and upstate New York, while **New Jersey Transit** (☎ 800-772-2222, 973-762-5100; www.njtransit.com) buses serve all of NJ, with a direct service on bus No 319 to Atlantic City (one way/round-trip $26/28) from Port Authority.

'Chinatown Buses'

Undoubtedly the sweetest bus deals are on the crazy 'Chinatown buses,' which – loosely legal – pack in passengers along 'sidewalk terminals' at various points around Chinatown, bound for Boston, Philadelphia and DC. Typically a ticket doesn't guarantee a seat, so things sometimes get a little push-and-shove at busy times curbing weekends. **Fung Wah** (Map pp444–5; ☎ 212-925-8889; www.fungwahbus.com; 139 Canal St at Bowery) has 10 departures per day between 7am and 10pm for about $15 one way to Boston. You can buy tickets online – and you'll need to pre-buy, especially on weekends. There are many competitors in the area, including **2000 New Century** (Map pp444–5; ☎ 215-627-2666; www.2000coach.com; 88 E Broadway), with $12 service to Philadelphia, $20 to DC.

A Midtown (and saner) version, **Vamoose** (Map pp452–3; ☎ 877-393-2828; www .vamoosebus.com) sends a couple of air-conditioned buses (with movies) most days to Washington DC (one way/round-trip

$25/40); half a dozen make the trip on Friday and Sunday (no service on Saturday). Buses leave from outside Madison Sq Garden, on 31st St between Seventh and Eighth Aves.

CAR & MOTORCYCLE

Driving is not recommended around Manhattan unless it's absolutely necessary. There's always traffic that doesn't want you hogging lanes, gas is pricey, car hire is expensive, the struggles for parking space can age the eternally laid-back and it's a way bigger hassle than it's worth, considering all the excellent mass-transit options.

Driving

If you're in a passenger car in New York that isn't a taxi, and are planning to do much driving outside Manhattan, pick up a Hagstrom five-borough map (p408). A good radio source is WINS 1010-AM, which broadcasts all the gnarly traffic details.

Other than trying to park when/where you want, getting in and out of the city – and dealing with crosstown traffic – are the worst parts. Lanes are loosely adhered to – generally be more aware of what's next to you and before you. Parallel parkers can back up traffic on some streets – so middle lanes go quicker on multilane avenues.

Remember that bridges are your friends. All of the ones linking Manhattan with the other boroughs (but not the George Washington coming in from Jersey) are free both ways. Generally, at peak hours, the tunnels tend to back up more than the bridges too. Besides that, getting around within the city isn't difficult, as most of Manhattan (with the exception of the Village) is laid out in a neat grid, and traffic congestion prevents you from having to move along too swiftly if you're feeling tentative. Just be aware of local laws, such as the fact that you can't make a right on red (as you can in the rest of the state), you can't drive and talk on a cell phone, and also the fact that every other street alternates one-way direction, which can cause inexperienced drivers to drive around in frustrating circles.

LEAVING MANHATTAN?

If going to Queens, you can take the Queens–Midtown Tunnel (off 36th St between First and Second Aves) or the freebie Queensboro Bridge (from 60th St between

First and Second Aves). Brooklyn-bound can consider going over the Williamsburg Bridge on Delancey in the Lower East Side, or tempt fate with busy Canal St to cross the Manhattan Bridge. Most hours you can circle the southern tip of Manhattan via West Side Hwy for an easy hook-up with Brooklyn Bridge (or access from Lafayette St south of Chambers St).

Beyond the metropolis, things are pretty easy (on paper, at least): I-95, which runs from Maine to Florida, cuts east to west through the city as the Cross Bronx Expressway (another nightmare, recognized locally as the worst roadway around). Outside New York City, I-95 continues south as the New Jersey Turnpike; north as the Connecticut Turnpike. Via I-95, Boston is 194 miles to the north, Philadelphia 104 miles to the south and Washington DC 235 miles south.

Highway speed limits in Connecticut and upstate New York are 65mph; in New Jersey, they remain 55mph except on certain interstate roads.

Parking

Finding space in this cramped city to park your car is a challenge, whether you're willing to pay for it or not. Free parking, or parking on the streets, is in short supply – car owners have mastered the knack of moving their vehicles back and forth to alternate sides of the street to make way for the street cleaners. Meters are strictly enforced and on most streets (which run east to west) and avenues (north to south) there are no-parking strips. If you're lucky enough to find a spot, make sure to read every sign posted, as one may appear to make parking legal while another, a few feet away, cancels it out. Fines from violations are big business for the city – infractions will rarely be granted mercy.

Parking in lots and garages is usually what drivers must resort to – prices average $20 to $25 a day but some have daily specials, which require early entrances and departures. Check the New York City Department of Transportation (DOT) site for traffic updates and alternate-side parking schedules at www.nyc.gov/html/dot/home.html.

Because so few city travelers will be driving, restaurant and hotel listings in this book do not list any parking icons – although many city hotels do have deals with local lots and garages, affording minor discounts.

Rental

Hiring a car in the city is mighty expensive and, though agencies advertise bargain rates for weekend or week-long rentals, these deals are almost always blacked out in New York. If you want to rent for a few days, perhaps for a road trip out of town, book through a travel agent or online before leaving home. Without a reservation, a rental car will cost at least $75 per day for a midsize car – and that's before extra charges like the 13.625% tax, various insurance costs etc – and wind up being at least $100 before all is said and done. One trick is to leave the city altogether – at least Manhattan – via mass transit and rent 'over the border,' as rates in the outer boroughs and New Jersey can be much cheaper. The big-name agencies tend to have cheaper rates on multiday deals from Newark airport.

To rent a car, you need a valid driver's license and a major credit card. The law no longer decrees that you need to be over 25 to rent, but companies are still allowed to charge younger folks a higher rate, making it prohibitively expensive for all but trust-fund kids.

Among the many rental agencies in the city are the following:

Avis (☎ 800-331-1212; www.avis.com)

Budget (☎ 800-527-0700; www.budget.com)

Dollar (☎ 800-800-4000; www.dollar.com)

Hertz (☎ 800-654-3131; www.hertz.com)

A friendly family-run rental place, **Autoteam USA** (☎ 866-438-8326, 732-727-7272; www.autoteamusa.com; South Amboy, NJ) has cars with weekly rates (including 100 free miles per day) from $26 per day; insurance is $7 per day extra. They'll pick you up from the South Amboy station on the NJ Transit line.

Another interesting and popular option is the self-service **Zipcar** (☎ 212-691-2884, 866-494-7227; www.zipcar.com) geared mostly to locals who might need a car for errands. Zipcar is an on-demand car-sharing service that's available 24 hours a day, and cars can be hired per hour or per day. The price includes gas, insurance, designated parking and access to one of the cars marked with the cute green Z-logo that are parked all over the city. Rates are generally $8 or $10 per hour, $85 per day (some are just $65). There are 125 free miles per day, then $0.20 per mile. Check the website for availability, location, price and details on getting a Zipcar.

PEDICABS

A fairly new addition to NYC's already-crazed streets is bicycle taxis, similar to rickshaws, which are used mostly for novelty rides by tourists. It's goofy, but at least it's green. General trips cost between about $10 and $30, depending on the distance and number of passengers. For more information, contact **Manhattan Rickshaw** (☎ 212-604-4729; www.manhattanrickshaw.com).

SUBWAY

Iconic, cheap ($2), round-the-clock and a full century old, the New York City subway system is a remarkable example of mass transit that works, in spite of itself. The 656-mile system can be intimidating at first, but dive in and you'll soon be a fan of its many virtues.

An important part of subway travel is knowing how to refer to your train. Every subway is named with a letter or number – and most lines carry a collection of two to four trains on their tracks. For example, the red-colored line in Manhattan is the 1, 2, 3, line; they are separate lines, and though they follow roughly the same path in Manhattan, the 2 and 3 eventually split off on their own in Brooklyn and the Bronx. Plus, the 2 and 3 make express stops in Manhattan, while the 1 is local. Still, if you ask someone which train to take to W 72 St, they may say 'take the one-nine,' even though the 1, 2 or 3 could take you there. The same goes for all the other lines, whether they're lettered or numbered. But don't fret! The maps are surprisingly easy to negotiate, especially because of the different-colored lines.

The New York subway, run by the Metropolitan Transportation Authority (MTA), is the fastest and most reliable way to get around and it's also much safer and cleaner than it used to be. Free maps are available for the taking at every stop and huge route maps are displayed on every platform, as well as on every subway car of every line. You can also ask someone who looks like they know where they're going (although they may not). The mistake most visitors make is boarding an express train only to see it pass by the local stop they wanted. But the subway map delineates between local and express stops by representing local stops as black circles and express stops as white circles. Still, there are no guarantees: tourists and locals alike are constantly baffled by a local train switching

METROCARDS FOR TRAVELERS

Subway tokens are of the ages, now all buses and subways use the yellow-and-blue Metrocard, which you can purchase or add value to at one of several easy-to-use automated machines at any station. You can use cash or an ATM or credit card. Just hit 'get new card' and follow the prompts.

There are two types of Metrocard. The pay-per-ride allows one transfer from subway to bus, or bus to bus, in a two-hour period; it's $2 per ride, though a $20 card gives you two free rides. The other is the excellent-value unlimited-ride card (it's $7 for a one-day 'fun pass' or $24 for a seven-day pass). The unlimited-ride card is a real treat for travelers — particularly if you're planning to brunch in the Village, drop by the Guggenheim, stroll Fifth Ave department stores, get noodles in Chinatown, then a drink in Tribeca. That'll quickly deplete a pay-per-ride card, at $2 a pop.

to an express track without warning and vice versa, but that's usually due to construction (or an emergency), as the system is ancient and constantly under repair.

Another common mistake that visitors make is trying to seem cool, calm and collected by not holding onto anything as the train begins to move. Often, you just get knocked into the lap of a jaded local. So just hold on!

Other than the death of the token, those who haven't been in New York in a while will notice that many of the older trains have been replaced by models with sleek, clean cars that have *cheerful* automated announcements at each stop – much to the chagrin of New Yorkers who were in love with the various gruff, accented inflections of individual announcers (which still do exist on many lines). However, perhaps the most sweeping change has been the recent rerouting of many trains (including the N, R, W, B, D and M lines), restoring full service over the Manhattan Bridge, in and out of Brooklyn, for the first time in many years.

Though there's been a bit of a buzz lately about the construction of a Second Ave subway line (the east side of Manhattan is notoriously underserved), don't expect to notice anything as a visitor. Plans for such a project have been long awaited and, if the MTA stays on schedule, the first phase will be ready for riders in 2011.

For subway updates and information, call ☎ 718-330-1234 or visit www.mta.info.

TAXI

Hailing and riding in a cab are rites of passage in New York – especially when you get a hack (local lingo for 'taxi driver') who drives like a neurotic speed demon, which is often. Still, most taxis in NYC are clean and, compared to those in many international cities, pretty cheap.

The Taxi & Limousine Commission (TLC; ☎ 311), the taxis' governing body, has set fares (which can be paid for with a credit or debit card). It's $2.50 for the initial charge (first one-fifth mile), 40¢ for an extra one-fifth mile as well as per 120 seconds of being stopped in traffic, $1 peak surcharge (weekdays 4pm to 8pm), and a 50¢ night surcharge (8pm to 6am daily). Tips are usually 10% to 15%, but give less if you feel mistreated and be sure to ask for a receipt; use it to note the driver's license number. You can call the TLC with complaints and if anything bothers you about your ride, don't be afraid to speak up, as you're covered by the Passenger's Bill of Rights. This gives you the right to tell the driver which route you want, or ask your driver to stop smoking or turn off an annoying radio station. The driver does not have the right to refuse you a ride based on where you are going; the best thing you can do is not give him or her a chance to, but rather get in, let the meter start, and then give your destination.

To hail a cab, it must have a lit light on its roof. It's particularly difficult to score a taxi in the rain, at rush hour and around 4pm, when many drivers end their shifts.

And note that something called a car service (which is basically a taxi, but the car isn't yellow and you must call or stop into a storefront dispatcher for your ride) is a common taxi-cab alternative in the outer boroughs. Fares differ depending on the neighborhood and length of ride, and must be determined beforehand, as they have no meters. These 'black cars' are quite common in Brooklyn and Queens, but you should never get into one if a driver stops to offer you a ride no matter what borough you're in. It could be a scam, and, to be safe, you should always arrange for these rides through a dispatcher.

TRAIN

Penn Station (Map pp452–3; 33rd St btwn Seventh & Eighth Aves) is the departure point for all Amtrak (☎ 800-872-7245; www.amtrak.com) trains, including the Metroliner

and Acela Express services to Princeton, NJ, and Washington DC. Both will cost twice as much as a normal fare because they are express services with fewer stops. A basic one-way service from New York to Washington DC costs $84. All fares vary, based on the day of the week and the time you want to travel. Call Amtrak for information about special discount passes if you plan on traveling throughout the USA. There is no baggage-storage facility at Penn Station.

Long Island Rail Road (☎ 718-217-5477; www.mta.nyc.ny.us/lirr/) serves several hundred thousand commuters each day, with services from Penn Station to points in Brooklyn, Queens and to the suburbs of Long Island, including the North and South Fork resort areas. Prices are broken down by zones. A peak-hour ride from Penn Station to Jamaica Station (en route to JFK via AirTrain) costs $6.65 if you buy it online (a whopping $12 on board!). New Jersey Transit (☎ 800-772-2222; www.njtransit.com) also operates trains from Penn Station, with services to the suburbs and the Jersey Shore.

Another option for getting into NJ, but strictly northern points such as Hoboken and Newark, is the New Jersey Path (Map pp444–5; ☎ 800-234-7284; www.pathrail.com), which runs trains on a separate-fare system ($1.50) along the length of Sixth Ave, with stops at 34th, 23rd, 14th, 9th and Christopher Sts, as well as at the reopened World Trade Center site.

The only train line that still departs from Grand Central Terminal, Park Ave at 42nd St, is the Metro-North Railroad (☎ 212-532-4900; www.mnr.org/mnr/), which serves the northern city suburbs, Connecticut and the Hudson Valley.

WALKING

Screw the subway and the cabs and buses, the personal 'copter and hot-air balloon you packed in your bag. New York, down deep, can't be seen until you've taken the time to hit the sidewalks. The whole thing, like Nancy Sinatra's boots, is made for the pedestrian transport. Broadway runs 17 miles. Crossing the East River on the pedestrian plank boards of the Brooklyn Bridge is a New York classic. Central Park trails get to pockets where you can't see (and almost can't hear) the city.

For walking-tour operators, see p110, or if you're shy to look where others point, go on your own with one of our walking tours (p206).

Transportation

Behind the Scenes

THE LONELY PLANET STORY

The story begins with a classic travel adventure: Tony and Maureen Wheeler's 1972 journey across Europe and Asia to Australia. There was no useful information about the overland trail then, so Tony and Maureen published the first Lonely Planet guidebook to meet a growing need.

From a kitchen table, Lonely Planet has grown to become the largest independent travel publisher in the world, with offices in Melbourne (Australia), Oakland (USA) and London (UK). Today Lonely Planet guidebooks cover the globe. There is an ever-growing list of books and information in a variety of media. Some things haven't changed. The main aim is still to make it possible for adventurous travelers to get out there – to explore and better understand the world.

At Lonely Planet we believe travelers can make a positive contribution to the countries they visit – if they respect their host communities and spend their money wisely. Every year 5% of company profit is donated to charities around the world.

THIS BOOK

This fifth edition of *New York City* was written by Beth Greenfield, Ginger Adams Otis and Robert Reid. Earlier editions were written by Conner Gorry and David Ellis. The History chapter was based on work by Kathleen Hulser, and the Architecture chapter was based on work by Joyce Mendelsohn.

This guidebook was commissioned in Lonely Planet's Oakland office, and produced by the following:

Commissioning Editors Jay Cooke

Coordinating Editor Melissa Faulkner

Coordinating Cartographer Herman So

Coordinating Layout Designer Jacqui Saunders

Managing Cartographer Alison Lyall

Assisting Editors Carolyn Bain, Michelle Bennett, Monique Choy, Kyla Gillzan, Emma Gilmour, Gina Tsarouhas, Helen Yeates

Assisting Cartographers Amanda Sierp

Assisting Layout Designers Wibowo Rusli

Cover Designers Daniel New, Wendy Wright

Color Designers Daniel New, Wendy Wright

Project Manager Fabrice Rocher

Thanks to Imogen Bannister, Eric Beck, Annie Chambliss, Robert Cooke, Chris Cronis, Sally Darmody, Karina Dea, Heather Dickson, Margaret Doyle, Jennifer Garrett, Mark Germanchis, Brice Gosnell, Robert Hammond, Laura Jane, Jane Hart, Martin Heng, Graham Imeson, Kate McDonald, Kathleen Munnelly, Wayne Murphy, Jane Pennells, Sommai Purintun, Raphael Richards, Frank Ruiz, Fiona Siseman, Andrew Smith, Whit Sotkiewicz, Andrew Tudor, Emily Wolman, Celia Wood

Cover photographs A subway train speeding, underground at the Chambers station, George J Kunze/Photolibrary (front); People contemplating Ground Zero from the World Trade Center Path Station, Corey Wise/Lonely Planet Images (back).

Internal photographs by Dan Herrick/Lonely Planet Images and Angus Oborn/Lonely Planet Images except for the following: p67 (bottom) Adrian Wilson/Photolibrary; p74 Alan Scein/Corbis; p197 Aurora/Getty; p200 Becca Posterino/Lonely Planet Images; p15 (bottom), p16 Carole Martin/Lonely Planet Images; p14 Christopher Groenhout/Lonely Planet Images; p4 (bottom), p6 (top), p7 (right), p12 (top), p15 (top and centre), p72 (left), p73, p191, p199 Corey Wise/Lonely Planet Images; p75 Greg Gawlowski/Lonely Planet Images; p72 (right) James Marshall/Lonely Planet Images; p70 (top) Jeff Greenberg/Lonely Planet Images; p9 (top) Jerry Alexander/Lonely Planet Images; p69 John Neubauer/Lonely Planet Images; p6 (bottom), p70 (bottom), p196 Kim Grant/Lonely Planet Images; p67 (top) Lee Snider/Corbis; p193 (inset) Martin Moos/Lonely Planet Images; p12 (centre) Michael Gebicki/Lonely Planet Images; p192 (bottom) Michael Nichols/Getty; p9 (bottom), p65, p71 (right) Michael Taylor/Lonely Planet Images; p195 (inset) MedioImages/Getty; p190 Neil Setchfield/Lonely Planet Images; p4 (top) Peter Hendriemp/Lonely Planet Images; p195 (main image) Rafael Macia/Lonely Planet Images; p10, p66 Ray Laskowitz/Lonely Planet Images; p189 Rob Blakers/Lonely Planet Images; p76 Timothy Hursley/MoMA; p68 (right) Von Briel Rudi/Photolibrary.

All images are copyright of the photographer unless otherwise indicated. Many of the images in this guide are available for licensing from Lonely Planet Images: www.lonelyplanetimages.com.

THANKS
BETH GREENFIELD

Thanks to Jay Cooke for your support and wonderful editing skills; to Robert Reid and Ginger Adams Otis for great knowledge and teamwork; to Frank Ruiz and Cindy Cohen for getting us attention; to Melissa Faulkner for your cool-under-deadline pressure; to Maya Israel at Top of the Rock for access to the view; to Greg Wessner for your architectural lessons; and to all of my in-the-know friends (you know who you are) for eating, drinking and shopping with me this year. Thank you Mom and Dad for your encouragement and excitement, and thank you Kiki for being there in countless ways.

ROBERT REID

Thanks to Jay Cooke at Lonely Planet's Oakland office for offering the fine book and accompanying me around Manhattan; to Beth Greenfield for being a pal to work with, and Melissa Faulkner at Lonely Planet's Melbourne office for editing the text and putting all the pages together.

GINGER ADAMS OTIS

Thanks to Jay Cooke, first and foremost, for giving me such great assignments; to Melissa Faulkner for corralling the maps, edits and changes that turn out such a great final product, and all those friendly New Yorkers who let me stick a camera at them and ask nosy questions.

OUR READERS

Many thanks to the travelers who used the last edition and wrote to us with helpful hints, useful advice and interesting anecdotes:

A Bas Aldewereld, Emma Allen, Rune Andersen **B** Kirsten Bayly, Jude Bennington, Lisa Borsa, Kevin Bruce, John Burnett **C** Rene Calvo, Colin Campbell, John Carey, Nicolo Carpaneda, Angela Carper, Danny Cha, Alexandra Chimbo, Chungwah Chow, Shane Clark, Barbra Cooper, Andrew Cosgrave, Gavin & Sandra Costigan, Catriona Crawford, Monique Cremers **D** Alessandra D'Agostin, Ake Dahllof, Martin de Lange, Karen de Plater, Anke Dekkers de Wit, David Del Campo Sud, Ellen den Braber, Emma Dougherty, Carolyn Downing, Zac Drumsticks, Windy Dryden, Anne Dukelow **E** Benjamin Elsner, Caroline Evans **F** Roberto Filange, Sarah Florenz, Matteo Franchi, Marty Fullerton **G** Heiko Gabriel, Brett George, Ed Gillard, Ben Godfrey, Helena Golden, Herschel Goldfield, Andac Gursoy **H** William Hackworth, Stephanie Hammonds, Martin Hargous, Julian Hart, Thorbjørn Busk Hededal, Eveliina Hihnala, Jackie Hill, Susan Hodge, Peter Holland, Emma Holmbro, Eric Hormell, Arjen Huiden, Francis Hunger, David M Hunt **J** Darren Jackson, Magnus Jaderbo, Adrian Jones **K** Felicia Kahn,

LONELY PLANET AUTHORS

Why is our travel information the best in the world? It's simple: our authors are independent, dedicated travelers. They don't research using just the Internet or phone, and they don't take freebies in exchange for positive coverage. They travel widely, to all the popular spots and off the beaten track. They personally visit thousands of hotels, restaurants, cafés, bars, galleries, palaces, museums and more – and they take pride in getting all the details right, and telling it how it is. For more, see the authors section on www.lonelyplanet.com.

Farah Karim, Elizabeth Karpinski, Anthony King, Melanie Kite, Wendy Ko **L** Maxime Lachance, Kerstin Lange, Jeremy Lau, Mikelson Leong, Beverly Leu, Brette Luck **M** Nick McDowell, Kerry Mcenaney, Gareth McFeely, Peter McManus, Katie McMurray, Neil McRae, Daniel Mann, Adam Mathews, Michael Matthes, Trevor Mazzucchelli, Robert Mills, Stephanie Monaghan, Heather Monell, Will Moore, Ioan Morris, Elena Mosca, Meaghan Mulvany, Jane Muris, Don Murray **N** Tim Newton, Lilian Noack, Eric Nowitzky **O** Robin O'Donoghue **P** Sam Peacock, Philip Pool, Kenton Price, Eleanor Priestley, Ronald Primas **R** Glen Rajaram, Cathy Ray, John Reeves, M Rehorst, Geoff Rimmer, Ermanno Rizzi, Aaron Romero, Nicky Rowe **S** Jörn Schmidt, Tom Schmidt, Charlotte Seiglow, Mike Shaw, Julia Simeon Foster, Joyce Snipp, Vanessa Sotelo, Donna Spoerl, Rose St John, Christopher Staake, Jane Stewart, Frederick Steyn, Vivi Suharto, Charlie Suisman **T** Janis Takamoto, Daniel Tiede, Maureen Tierney, Scott Toulson, Raymond Tsao, Fredrik Tukk, Colin Turner, Peter Turner, Julie Twitmyer **U** Jorge Urenda Valdés **V** Michiel van Amelsfort, Carlijn van Dehn, Kris van der Meij, Ruud van Leeuwen, Wim Vandenbussche, Marlon Vaughn, Timo-Pekka Viljamaa **W** D M Williams, Scott Williams, Trevor Wilson **Y** Andrew Young **Z** Jay Zasa

ACKNOWLEDGMENTS

Many thanks to the following for use of their content: Museum of Modern Art (MoMA) for their floorplan map © 2006; Metropolitan Transit Authority for New York City subway map © 2006.

SEND US YOUR FEEDBACK

We love to hear from travelers – your comments keep us on our toes and help make our books better. Our well-traveled team reads every word on what you loved or loathed about this book. Although we cannot reply individually to postal submissions, we always guarantee that your feedback goes straight to the appropriate authors, in time for the next edition. Each person who sends us information is thanked in the next edition – and the most useful submissions are rewarded with a free book.

To send us your updates – and find out about Lonely Planet events, newsletters and travel news – visit our award-winning website: www.lonelyplanet.com/feedback.

Note: We may edit, reproduce and incorporate your comments in Lonely Planet products such as guidebooks, websites and digital products, so let us know if you don't want your comments reproduced or your name acknowledged. For a copy of our privacy policy visit www.lonelyplanet.com/privacy.

Notes

Index

See also separate indexes for Drinking (p436), Eating (p436), Entertainment (p437), Shopping (p438) and Sleeping (p438).

Index

000 map pages
000 photographs

Index

435

000 map pages
000 photographs

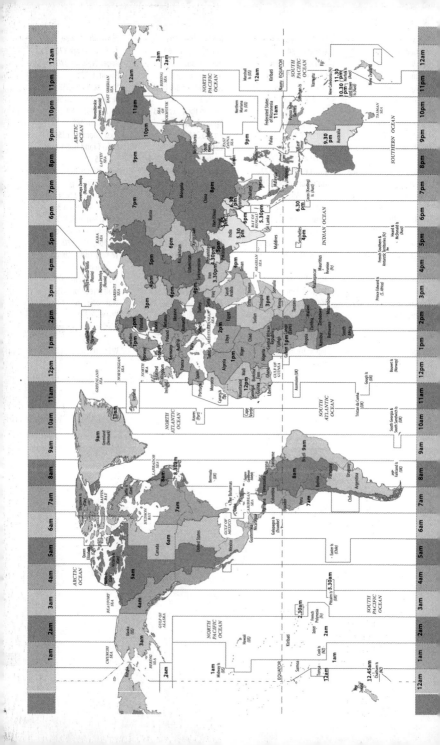

MAP LEGEND

ROUTES

Tollway	One-Way Street
Freeway	Mall/Steps
Primary Road	Tunnel
Secondary Road	Walking Tour
Tertiary Road	Walking Tour Detour
Lane	Walking Trail
Under Construction	Walking Path
Track	Pedestrian Overpass
Unsealed Road	

TRANSPORT

Ferry	Bus Route
Metro	Rail
Monorail	Rail (Underground)

HYDROGRAPHY

River, Creek	Canal
Intermittent River	Water
Swamp	

BOUNDARIES

International	Regional, Suburb
State, Provincial	

AREA FEATURES

Airport	Cemetery, Christian
Area of Interest	Cemetery, Other
Beach, Desert	Forest
Building, Featured	Land
Building, Information	Mall
Building, Other	Park
Building, Transport	Sports

POPULATION

CAPITAL (NATIONAL)	CAPITAL (STATE)
Large City	Medium City
Small City	Town, Village

SYMBOLS

Sights/Activities

- Beach
- Buddhist
- Christian
- Jewish
- Monument
- Museum, Gallery
- Other Site
- Swimming Pool
- Winery, Vineyard
- Zoo, Bird Sanctuary

Eating

- Eating

Drinking

- Drinking
- Café

Entertainment

- Entertainment

Shopping

- Shopping

Sleeping

- Sleeping

Transport

- Airport, Airfield
- Bus Station
- General Transport
- Parking Area
- Petrol Station
- Taxi Rank

Information

- Bank, ATM
- Embassy/Consulate
- Hospital, Medical
- Information
- Internet Facilities
- Police Station
- Post Office, GPO
- Telephone
- Toilets
- Wheelchair Access

Geographic

- Lighthouse
- Lookout
- Mountain, Volcano
- National Park

Maps

NEW YORK CITY

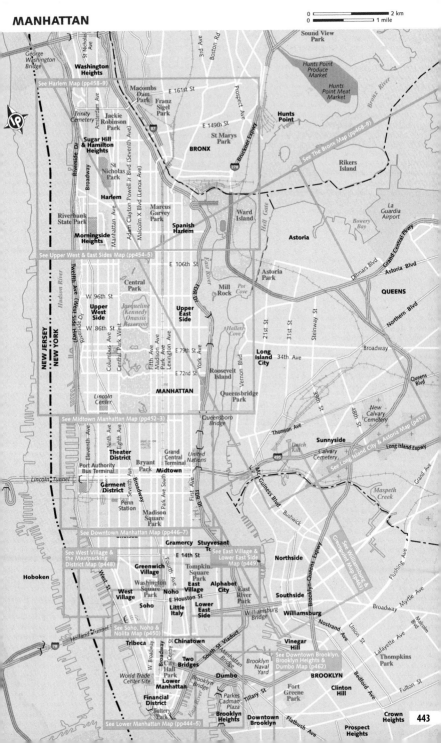

LOWER MANHATTAN

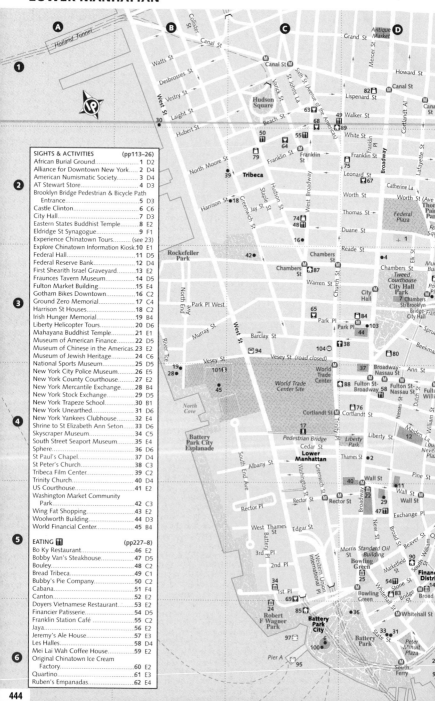

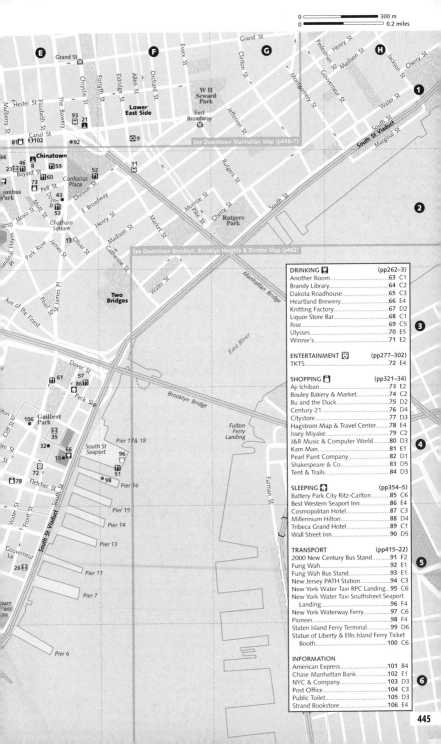

See Downtown Manhattan Map (p446–7)

See Downtown Brooklyn, Brooklyn Heights & Dumbo Map (p462)

DRINKING (pp262–3)
Another Room	63	C1
Brandy Library	64	C2
Dakota Roadhouse	65	C3
Heartland Brewery	66	E4
Knitting Factory	67	D2
Liquor Store Bar	68	C1
Rise	69	C5
Ulysses	70	E5
Winnie's	71	E2

ENTERTAINMENT (pp277–302)
TKTS	72	E4

SHOPPING (pp321–34)
Aji Ichiban	73	E2
Bouley Bakery & Market	74	C2
Bu and the Duck	75	D2
Century 21	76	D4
Citystore	77	D3
Hagstrom Map & Travel Center	78	E4
Issey Miyake	79	C2
J&R Music & Computer World	80	D3
Kam Man	81	E1
Pearl Paint Company	82	D1
Shakespeare & Co	83	D5
Tent & Trails	84	D3

SLEEPING (pp354–5)
Battery Park City Ritz-Carlton	85	C6
Best Western Seaport Inn	86	E4
Cosmopolitan Hotel	87	C3
Millennium Hilton	88	D4
Tribeca Grand Hotel	89	C1
Wall Street Inn	90	D5

TRANSPORT (pp415–22)
2000 New Century Bus Stand	91	F2
Fung Wah	92	E1
Fung Wah Bus Stand	93	E1
New Jersey PATH Station	94	C3
New York Water Taxi BPC Landing	95	C6
New York Water Taxi Southstreet Seaport Landing	96	F4
New York Waterway Ferry	97	C6
Pioneer	98	F4
Staten Island Ferry Terminal	99	D6
Statue of Liberty & Ellis Island Ferry Ticket Booth	100	C6

INFORMATION
American Express	101	B4
Chase Manhattan Bank	102	E1
NYC & Company	103	D3
Post Office	104	C3
Public Toilet	105	D3
Strand Bookstore	106	E4

DOWNTOWN MANHATTAN

West St   **A**

London Terrace Gardens   **B**

W 23rd St

23rd St

23rd St   **D**

23rd St   44   **C**   70

32   28   39

80   3 57 18   16   62   52   **Chelsea**   25

34   **1**   5   7   9   W 22nd St   41   74   58

W 21st St

W 20th St   73   72   68   43

Eleventh Ave

Tenth Ave

Chelsea Piers

51   W 19th St   50 48   24   45   27   13   36

18th St   37   55   23   60

82   W 18th St   59

Ninth Ave   Eighth Ave   Seventh Ave   Sixth Ave (Ave of the Americas)

W 17th St   31   63   64   W 17th St   71

78 42   19   40

West Village & the Meatpacking District (p448)   65

W 16th St

4   W 15th St   20

2

8th Ave-14th St   14th St   6th Ave-14th St

W 14th St

W 13th St   W 13th St

W 12th St

Little W 12th St   W 11th St

Meatpacking District   W 10th St   **Greenwich Village**

Gansevoort St   Horatio St   Abington Square   Waverly Pl   Greenwich Ave   W 9th St

3   Jane St   W 8th St

W 12th St   W 4th St   Gay St   Waverly Pl

Bethune St   Perry St   Charles St

Hudson St   Bank St   Bleecker St   Christopher St-Sheridan Square   **Christopher Park**   Washington Sq West

W 11th St   Washington Pl   Washington Sq

W 10th St   W 4th St

Washington St   Christopher St   Jones St   Cornelia St   W 3rd

Bedford St   Grove St   Minetta

4   Soho, Noho & Nolita (p450)

Greenwich St   Barrow St   Commerce St   Carmine St   Minetta   Bleeck

West Village   Hudson St   Morton St   MacDougal St   Ave of the Americas (Sixth Ave)

St Lukes Pl   Seventh   W Houston

James J Walker Park   W Houston St

Leroy St   King St   Sullivan St

Clarkson St   Charlton St

5   West St   Vandam St   Spring St   Spring St

Hudson River   **NEW YORK**   **NEW JERSEY**

Lower Manhattan (pp444-5)

Dominick St

6   Collister St   Canal St

Broome St   Canal St

Holland Tunnel   Watts St   Vestry St

Desbrosses St   Laight St   Varick St

Hudson Square

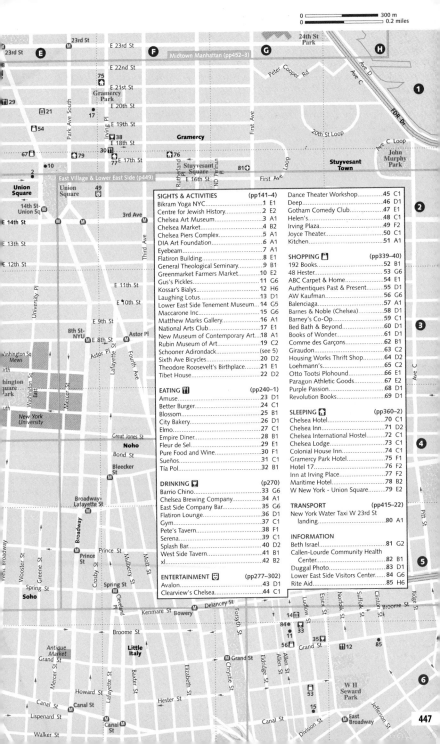

E 22nd St

75
Gramercy Park
E 21st St
E 20th St

29   21   17
54   E 19th St
E 18th St   38   Gramercy
67   79   30   77   E 17th St   76
10   Stuyvesant Square   81   Stuyvesant Town   John Murphy Park
2   E 16th St   First Ave

Union Square   Union Square   49
East Village & Lower East Side (p449)
14th St-Union Sq
E 14th St   3rd Ave

E 13th St

E 12th St

SIGHTS & ACTIVITIES	(pp141–4)
Bikram Yoga NYC	1 E1
Centre for Jewish History	2 E2
Chelsea Art Museum	3 A1
Chelsea Market	4 B2
Chelsea Piers Complex	5 A1
DIA Art Foundation	6 A1
Eyebeam	7 A1
Flatiron Building	8 E1
General Theological Seminary	9 B1
Greenmarket Farmers Market	10 E2
Gus's Pickles	11 G6
Kossar's Bialys	12 H6
Laughing Lotus	13 D1
Lower East Side Tenement Museum	14 G5
Maccarone Inc	15 G6
Matthew Marks Gallery	16 A1
National Arts Club	17 E1
New Museum of Contemporary Art	18 A1
Rubin Museum of Art	19 C2
Schooner Adirondack	(see 5)
Sixth Ave Bicycles	20 D2
Theodore Roosevelt's Birthplace	21 E1
Tibet House	22 D2

EATING	(pp240–1)
Amuse	23 D1
Better Burger	24 C1
Blossom	25 B1
City Bakery	26 D1
Elmo	27 C1
Empire Diner	28 B1
Fleur de Sel	29 E1
Pure Food and Wine	30 F1
Sueños	31 C1
Tía Pol	32 B1

DRINKING	(p270)
Barrio Chino	33 G6
Chelsea Brewing Company	34 A1
East Side Company Bar	35 G6
Flatiron Lounge	36 D1
Gym	37 C1
Pete's Tavern	38 F1
Serena	39 C1
Splash Bar	40 D2
West Side Tavern	41 B1
xl	42 B2

ENTERTAINMENT	(pp277–302)
Avalon	43 D1
Clearview's Chelsea	44 C1

Dance Theater Workshop	45 C1
Deep	46 D1
Gotham Comedy Club	47 E1
Helen's	48 C1
Irving Plaza	49 F2
Joyce Theater	50 C1
Kitchen	51 A1

SHOPPING	(pp339–40)
192 Books	52 B1
48 Hester	53 G6
ABC Carpet & Home	54 E1
Authentiques Past & Present	55 D1
AW Kaufman	56 G6
Balenciaga	57 A1
Barnes & Noble (Chelsea)	58 D1
Barney's Co-Op	59 C1
Bed Bath & Beyond	60 D1
Books of Wonder	61 D1
Comme des Garçons	62 B1
Giraudon	63 C2
Housing Works Thrift Shop	64 D2
Loehmann's	65 C2
Otto Tootsi Plohound	66 E1
Paragon Athletic Goods	67 E2
Purple Passion	68 D1
Revolution Books	69 D1

SLEEPING	(pp360–2)
Chelsea Hotel	70 C1
Chelsea Inn	71 D2
Chelsea International Hostel	72 C1
Chelsea Lodge	73 C1
Colonial House Inn	74 C1
Gramercy Park Hotel	75 F1
Hotel 17	76 F2
Inn at Irving Place	77 F2
Maritime Hotel	78 B2
W New York - Union Square	79 E2

TRANSPORT	(pp415–22)
New York Water Taxi W 23rd St landing	80 A1

INFORMATION	
Beth Israel	81 G2
Callen-Lourde Community Health Center	82 B1
Duggal Photo	83 D1
Lower East Side Visitors Center	84 G6
Rite Aid	85 H6

Washington Sq Mews
Astor Pl   8th St-NYU
Washington Square East   New York University
Great Jones St   Noho   Bond St   Bleecker St
Broadway-Lafayette St
Prince St   Prince St
Spring St   Spring St
Soho
Antique Market Grand St   Little Italy   84   33
56   35   12   85
Broome St   Grand St   Grand St
Howard St   Canal St   Canal St
Hester St   53
Canal St   WH Seward Park   15
Lispenard St   Canal St   East Broadway
Walker St   Division St

0 — 300 m
0 — 0.2 miles

WEST VILLAGE & THE MEATPACKING DISTRICT

0 — 500 m
0 — 0.3 miles

SIGHTS & ACTIVITIES (pp152–7)
6 & B Garden... 1 C2
9th St Garden & La Plaza Cultural. 2 D2
All People's Garden... 3 D3
Astor Place... 4 A2
Blades Downtown... 5 A3
Brisas del Caribe... 6 D3
Essex Street Market... 7 C4
Grace Church... 8 A2
Jivamukti... 9 A3
Merchant's House Museum... 10 A3
Om Yoga Center... 11 A1
Participant Inc... 12 C4
Kiyosgon Arms... 14 C3
Russ & Daughters Appetizing... 15 C2
Russian & Turkish Baths... 16 B2
St Mark's-in-the-Bowery... 17 A1
Tony Pastor's New 14th St Theatre Site. 18 B2
Ukrainian Museum...

EATING (pp233–7)
B&H Dairy... 19 B2
Bao 111... 20 D2
Bereket... 21 C3
Chikalicious... 22 B2
Colors... 23 A3
Cube 63... 25 D4
Il Bagatto... 26 C3
Katz's Deli... 27 C2
Max... 28 B2
Prune... 29 B3
Sammy's Roumanian Steak House 30 B4
Schiller's Liquor Bar... 31 C4
Teany... 32 C4
Two Boots Pizzerias... 33 C3
Veselka... 34 B2
WD50... 35 C4
Yonah Shimmel Bakery... 36 B3
'Inoteca... 37 B2

DRINKING (pp256–8)
11th Street Bar... 38 C2
Angel's Share... 39 B2
Barramundi... 40 C4
Beauty Bar... 41 B1
Chibitini... 42 D4
Clubhouse... 43 D1
DBA... 44 C2
Easternbloc... 45 C2
Gallery Onetwentyeight... 46 C4
Girls Room... 47 D3
Holiday Cocktail Lounge... 48 B2
Joe's Pub... 49 A2
KGB Bar... 50 B3
Kitchen Club... 51 A4
Magician... 52 C4
Mo Pitkin's House of Satisfaction. 53 C2
Odessa Café... 54 C2
Side/Marquee... 55 A3
Suba... 56 C4
Swift... 57 A3
Welcome to the Johnsons... 58 C4

Pyramid... 77 C2
Sapphire... 78 B3
Starlight Bar & Lounge... 79 C4
Tonic... 80 C4

SHOPPING (pp331–7)
360 Toy Group... 81 B4
A Cheng... 82 C3
Alphabets... 83 C3
Babeland... 84 C4
Bluestockings... 85 C4
Breakbeat Science... 86 C4
Dinosaur Hill... 87 B2
Economy Candy... 88 C4
Foley + Corinna... 89 C4
Footlight Records... 90 A1
Forbidden Planet... 91 A1
Fuck Yoga... 92 C4
Jutta Neumann... 93 C4
Kiehl's... 94 A1
Las Venus... 95 B2
Love Saves the Day... 96 B2
Ludlow Guitars... 97 C4
Mary Adams... 98 C4
Mondo Kim's... 99 B2
Other Music... 100 A3
Otto Tootsi Plohound... 101 A4
Physical Graffiti Cover... 102 C2
Screaming Mimi's... 103 A3
Shakespeare & Co... 104 A2
Sounds... 105 B2
Sunrise Mart... 106 A2
Tokyo 7... 107 B2
Tokyo X... 108 B2
Tower Records... 109 A1
Underdog East... 110 C2
Village X... 111 B2
Virgin Megastore... 112 A1
Vlada... 113 C4
Whiskers Holistic Petcare... 114 B2
Yu... 115 C4

ENTERTAINMENT (pp277–302)
Amato Opera Theatre... 59 B3
Anthology Film Archives... 60 B3
Arlene's Grocery... 61 C4
Astor Place Theatre... 62 A2
Bowery Poetry Club... 63 B3
CBGB... 64 B3
Cinema Classics... 65 C1
Danspace Project... (see 16)
Delancey... 66 C4
Gonzalez y Gonzalez... 67 A3
Joseph Papp Public Theater... 68 A3
La Mama ETC... 69 B3
Landmark Sunshine Cinema... 70 B3
Mercury Lounge... 71 C3
Nuyorican Poets Café... 72 D2
Opaline... 73 D3
Orpheum Theater... 74 B2
Pianos... 75 C4

SLEEPING (pp357–8)
East Village B&B... 116 D2
Hotel on Rivington... 117 C4
Howard Johnson Express Inn.118 B3
Jazz on the Town... 119 B1
Second Home on Second Ave.120 B1
St Marks Hotel... 121 B2
Union Square Inn... 122 B1

INFORMATION
alt.office... 123 C2
Post Office... 124 A1
St Mark's Bookshop... 125 A2
Strand Bookstore... 126 A1

Bernard Downing Playground
Hamilton Fish Park
Tompkins Square Park
Sarah D Roosevelt Park
East Village
Lower East Side
Nolita
Noho
Union Square
New York University

SOHO, NOHO & NOLITA

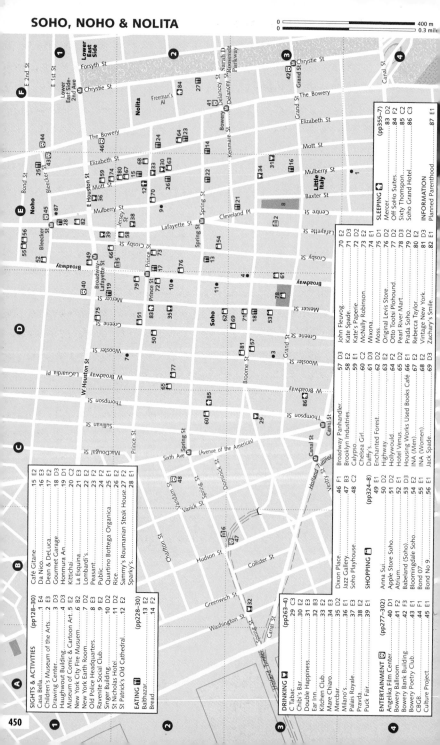

0 ————————— 400 m
0 ————————— 0.3 mile

SIGHTS & ACTIVITIES (pp128–30)
Casa Bella...1 E4
Children's Museum of the Arts...2 E3
Drawing Center...3 D3
Haughwout Building...4 D3
Museum of Comic & Cartoon Art...5 E2
New York City Fire Museum...6 B2
New York Earth Room...7 D2
Old Police Headquarters...8 E3
Ravenite Social Club...9 E2
Singer Building...10 D2
St Nicholas Hotel...11 D2
St Patrick's Old Cathedral...12 E2

EATING (pp228–30)
Balthazar...13 E2
Bread...14 F2
Café Gitane...15 E2
Da Nico...16 E4
Dean & DeLuca...17 E2
Gourmet Garage...18 D3
Hommura An...19 D1
Kittichai...20 C2
La Esquina...21 E2
Lombardi's...22 E2
Mare Chiaro...23 F2
Peasant...24 E3
Public...25 E1
Quartino Bottega Organica...26 E2
Rice...27 F2
Sammy's Roumanian Steak House...28 E1

DRINKING (pp263–4)
C Tabac...29 C3
Chibi's Bar...30 E3
Double Happiness...31 B3
Ear Inn...32 B3
Kitchen Club...33 E3
Mercbar...34 E3
Milano's...35 D2
Palais Royale...36 F1
Pravda...37 E3
Puck Fair...38 E2
Sparky's...39 E1

ENTERTAINMENT (pp277–302)
Angelika Film Center...40 D1
Bowery Ballroom...41 F2
Bowery Bank Building...42 F3
Bowery Poetry Club...43 E1
CBGB...44 F1
Culture Project...45 E1
Dixon Place...46 F1
Jazz Gallery...47 B3
Soho Playhouse...48 C2

SHOPPING (pp324–8)
Anna Sui...49 E1
Apple Store Soho...50 D2
Atrium...51 D2
Babeland (Soho)...52 E3
Bloomingdale Soho...53 D3
Bond 07...54 E1
Bond No 9...55 E1
Broadway Panhandler...56 F1
Brooklyn Industries...57 D3
Calypso...58 E2
Chelsea Girl...59 E1
Daffy's...60 C2
Enchanted Forest...61 D3
Highway...62 D2
Hollywould...63 E2
Hotel Venus...64 D2
Housing Works Used Books Café...65 E1
INA (Men)...66 E1
INA (Women)...67 E2
Jack Spade...68 D3
John Fleuvog...69 D3
Kate Spade...70 E2
Kate's Paperie...71 D3
McNally Robinson...72 D2
Mixona...73 E2
Moss...74 E1
Original Levi's Store...75 D1
Otto Tootsi Plohound...76 D2
Pearl River Mart...77 D3
Prada Soho...78 D2
Rebecca Taylor...79 D2
Vintage New York...80 E2
Zachary's Smile...81 D3

SLEEPING (pp355–7)
Mercer...83 E2
Off SoHo Suites...84 F2
Sixty Thompson...85 C2
Soho Grand Hotel...86 C3

INFORMATION
Planned Parenthood...87 E1

Lower East Side
Lower East Side–2nd Ave
Nolita
Freeman's Al
The Bowery
Noho
Little Italy
Soho
Holland Tunnel

MIDTOWN MANHATTAN

B   W 59th St   7

C

D   Central Park Sout

59th St-
Columbus Circle

Columbus Circle

See Upper West & East Sides Map (pp454-5)

W 58th St

57th St

W 57th St

Carnegie
Hall

●9

W 56th St

W 55th St

55th St

Tenth Ave

Ninth Ave

Eighth Ave

W 54th St

W 54th St

Dewitt
Clinton
Park

W 53rd St

7th Ave

W 52nd St

Seventh Ave

W 51st St

W 51st St

W 50th St

50th St
W 50th St

W 49th St

Worldwide
Plaza

49th St

W 48th St

W 48th St

Hell's
Kitchen

W 47th St

Theater
District

47th St

81

W 46th St

68

W 45th St

16

W 44th St

Times
Square

130

W 43rd St

128

Pier
83

●6

8

42nd St
W 42nd St

Times Sq-
42nd St

W 41st St

W 41st St

Port
Authority
Bus Terminal

W 40th St

Pier
81

W 39th St

Lincoln Tunnel

W 38th St

Broadway

W 37th St

Jacob Javits
Convention
Center
17

Garment
District

W 36th St

See Times Square & Theater District Map (pp282-3)

W 35th St

146

129

48

64

W 34th St

34th St-
Penn Station

59

75

W 33rd St

Twelfth Ave (West Side Hwy)

W 33rd St

147

21

131
Penn
Station

W 32nd S

134

W 31st St

Seventh Ave

●20

Ninth Ave

Tenth Ave

Eleventh Ave

105

104

Eighth Ave

W 30th St

W 29th St

W 28th St

60

61

Chelsea
Park

25

28th St

W 27th St

133

72

62

58

67

73

W 26th St

30

W 25th St

23●

●1

W 24th St

22

London
Terrace
Gardens

53

23rd St

W 23rd St

63

114

110th St • Cathedral Parkway (W 110th St)

W 109th St

W 108th St

W 107th St

Duke Ellington Blvd (W 106th St)

W 105th St

W 104th St

W 103rd St

W 102nd St

W 101st St

W 100th St

W 99th St

W 98th St

W 97th St

W 96th St

W 95th St

W 94th St

W 93rd St

W 92nd St

W 91st St

W 90th St

W 89th St

W 88th St

W 87th St

W 86th St

W 85th St

W 84th St

W 83rd St

W 82nd St

W 81st St

W 80th St

W 79th St

W 78th St

W 77th St

W 76th St

W 75th St

W 74th St

W 73rd St

W 72nd St

W 71st St

W 70th St

W 69th St

W 68th St

W 67th St

W 66th St

W 65th St

W 64th St

W 63rd St

W 62nd St

W 61st St

W 60th St

W 59th St

Cathedral Pkwy (110th St)

Central Park North

Central Park Nc (110th St)

Hudson River

Twelfth Ave (West Side Hwy)

Riverside Dr

Amsterdam Ave

Columbus Ave

Manhattan Ave

Central Park West

Broadway

West End Ave (Eleventh Ave)

West Side Hwy (Twelfth Ave)

Freedom Pl

NEW JERSEY

NEW YORK

Riverbank State Park

Upper West Side

96th St

86th St

72nd St

66th St-Lincoln Center

59th St-Columbus Circle

81st St-Museum of Natural History

Lincoln Center

103rd St

Seneca Village

Central Park

North Meadow Recreation Area

97th St Transverse Rd

86th St Transverse Rd

79th St Transverse Rd

72nd St Transverse

65th St Transverse Rd

Jacqueline Kennedy Onassis Reservoir

Belvedere Lake

The Lake

The Pool

The Loch

Harlem Meer

Seneca Village

Naumburg Bandshell

Literary Walk

The Pond

East Dr

West Dr

Center Dr

East Dr

Columbus Circle

Central Park South

See Midtown Manhattan Map (pp452–3)

0   500 m
0   0.3 miles

110th St 🚇
E 110th St
E 109th St
E 108th St
E 107th St
E 106th St
E 105th St
E 104th St
103rd St 🚇   E 103rd St
E 102nd St
E 101st St
E 100th St
E 99th St
E 98th St
E 97th St
96th St 🚇
E 96th St
Upper East Side
E 95th St
E 94th St
E 93rd St
E 92nd St
E 91st St
E 90th St
E 89th St
E 88th St
E 87th St
86th St 🚇
E 86th St   **Yorkville**
E 85th St
E 84th St
E 83rd St
E 82nd St
E 81st St
E 80th St
E 79th St
E 78th St
77th St 🚇
E 77th St
E 76th St
E 75th St
E 74th St
E 73rd St
E 72nd St
E 71st St
E 70th St
E 69th St
68th St–Hunter College 🚇
E 68th St
E 67th St
E 66th St
E 65th St
E 64th St
E 63rd St
Lexington Ave 🚇
E 62nd St
E 61st St
59th St 🚇
E 60th St
E 59th St

Frawley Cr

Madison Ave
Fifth Ave
Park Ave
Lexington Ave
Third Ave
Second Ave
First Ave
York Ave
East End Ave
Franklin D. Roosevelt Dr

East River

Metropolitan Hospital

Mill Rock Light Park
Mill Rock

Carl Schurz Park

Yorkville

John Jay Park

Roosevelt Island

Rainey Park

Hallets Cove

East River

Main St

Vernon Blvd
Ninth St
Eighth St
First St
Second St
Third St
Fourth St
26th Ave
27th Ave

Pot Cove

Ninth St
Tenth St
Eleventh St
35th Ave

38th Ave
40th Ave
41st Ave

Queensbridge Park

Rockefeller University

Conservatory Pond

Franklin D. Roosevelt Dr

To Long Island City & Astoria Map (p457)

Triborough Bridge

Roosevelt Island Bridge

Queensboro Bridge
59th St Bridge

Eighth Ave
Main St
East Rd

E   F   G   H
1
2
3
4
5
6

25
21
35
38
143
28
16
36
39
47
37
75
133
124
64 56
141
118
23 3
109
27
54
111
53
120
103
33 105
26
136
89 108
137
4
84
24
115
126
45 73
62 59
65
70 106
107
76
74 88
72
93
121
139 104
123
140
138
42

455

0 ———— 600 m
0 ———— 0.4 miles

A B C D

1

W 164th St
W 163rd St
Fort Washington Ave
W 162nd St
163rd St-
Amsterdam Av
W 161st St
21
19
Jumel
Tce
17
W 160th St
13
W 159th St
Edward M
Morgan
W 158th St
157th St
W 157th St
Washington
Heights
Riverside Dr
Amsterdam Ave
St Nicholas Ave
W 156th St
12
Macomb
Dam
Bridge
Macombs
Dam
Park
24

Twelfth Ave (West Side Hwy)

2

W 155th St (Audubon Tce)
Trinity
Cemetery
155th St
W 154th St
W 153rd St
St Nicholas Place
W 152nd St
Jackie
Robinson
Park
W 151st St
W 150th St
41
W 149th St
Harlem-
148th St
W 148th St
Sugar Hill
& Hamilton
Heights
W 147th St
Edgecombe Ave
Macombs Pl
Harlem River Dr

3

22
145th St
145th St
Bradhurst Ave
Frederick Douglass Blvd (Eighth Ave)
W 146th St
W 145th St
145th St
W 144th St
W 143rd St
W 142nd St
Riverbank
State Park
Convent Ave
Hamilton Tce
10
W 141st St
W 140th St
Malcolm X Blvd (Lenox Ave)
W 139th St
W 139th St
29
W 138th St
2
37
Hudson River
Hamilton Pl
W 137th
St
137th St-
City College
St Nicholas Tce
20
136th St
Adam Clayton Powell Jr Blvd (Seventh Ave)
27
W 135th St
135th St

4

NEW YORK
NEW JERSEY
W 135th St
135th St
St Nicholas Park
46
W 134th St
25
W 133rd St
W 132nd St
34
W 131st St
W 130th St
St Nicholas Ave
45
47
W 132nd St
W 131st St
W 130th St
26
W 129th St
W 126th St
Harlem
18
125th St
W 128th St
W 127th St

5

Claremont Ave
Riverside Dr East
Riverside Dr West
LaSalle St
Amsterdam Ave
125th
St
St Nicholas Ave
43
11
3
50
52
51
Martin Luther King Jr Blvd (125th St)
30
40
125th St
W 124th St
23
36
Morningside Park
W 123rd St
48
39
W 122nd St
W 121st St
Morningside Dr
W 120th St
W 119th St
44
W 118th St
Columbia University
42
7
Broadway
33
116th St
W 116th St
Morningside Dr
Morningside Ave
116th St
32
116th St
W 117th St
5
15
16
W 115th St

6

W 115th St
W 114th St
49
W 113th St
W 112th St
W 111th St
Morningside Heights
Manhattan Ave
Cathedral Pkwy (110th St)
Central Park North (110th St)
W 111th
Twelfth Ave (West Side Hwy)
110th St
Cathedral Pkwy (W 110th St)
Mt Morris Park West
Summit Ave
Woodycrest Ave

SIGHTS & ACTIVITIES (pp167–71)

16 Jumel Terrace	1 C1
Abyssinian Baptist Church	2 D3
Apollo Theater	3 D5
Baptist Temple	4 D6
Canaan Baptist Church	5 D6
Cathedral of St John the Divine	6 C6
Columbia University	7 B6
Duke Ellington Statue	8 E6
General US Grant National Memorial	9 B5
Hamilton Grange	10 C3
Harlem USA	11 C5
Hispanic Society of America	12 B1
Jumel Terrace Books	13 C1
La Marqueta	14 E6
Malcolm Shabazz Harlem Market	15 D6
Malcolm Shabazz Mosque	16 D6
Marjorie Eliot	17 C1
Metropolitan Baptist Church	18 D4
Morris-Jumel Mansion	19 C1
Mother African Methodist Episcopal Zion Church	20 D4
Museum of Art and Origins	21 C1
Riverbank State Park Information Center	22 B3
Riverside Church	23 B5
Rucker Park	24 D2
St Paul Baptist Church	25 C4
Salem United Methodist Church	26 D4
Schomburg Center for Research in Black Culture	27 D4
Second Providence Baptist Church	28 D6
Strivers' Row	29 D3
Studio Museum in Harlem	30 D5
Yankee Stadium	31 E1

EATING (pp251–3)

Amy Ruth's Restaurant	32 D6
Caffé Swish	33 B6
Fairway	34 B4
Ginger	35 E6
Màx Soha	36 C5
Miss Maude's Spoonbread Too	37 D3
Patsy's Pizzeria	38 F6
Strictly Roots	39 D5

DRINKING (p274)

Lenox Lounge	40 D5
St Nick's Pub	41 C2

ENTERTAINMENT (pp277–302)

Postcrypt Coffeehouse	42 B6

SHOPPING (pp349–50)

Bobby's Happy House	43 C5
Harlemade	44 D5
Liberation Bookstore	45 D4
Pieces of Harlem	46 D4
Scarf Lady	47 D4

SLEEPING (pp374–5)

Harlem Flophouse	48 D5
Wanderers Inn	49 D6

INFORMATION

Harlem Visitor Information Kiosk	50 D5
NYC & Company	51 D5
NYC & Company	52 D5
Time to Compute	53 E5

See Long Island City & Astoria Map (p457)

See Upper West & East Sides Map (pp454–5)

459

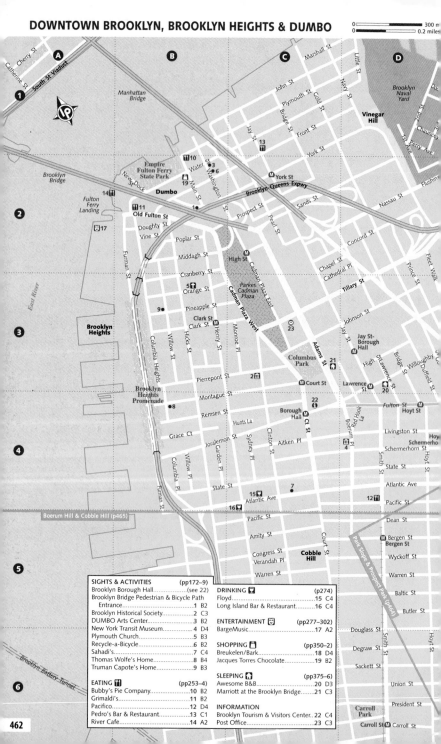

WILLIAMSBURG & GREENPOINT

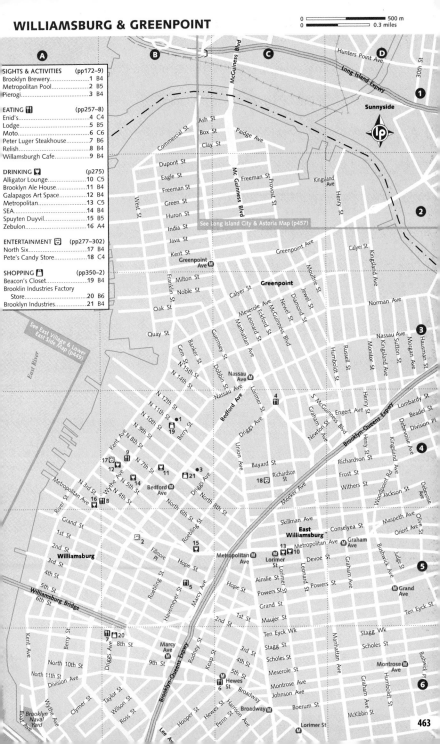

463

PARK SLOPE & PROSPECT PARK

SIGHTS & ACTIVITIES	(pp172–9)
Brooklyn Museum	1 D3
Brooklyn Public Library	2 C3
Carousel	3 D4
Ebbets Field Site	4 D4
Kate Wollman Rink	5 D5
Lefferts Homestead Children's Historic House Museum	6 D4
Prospect Park Tennis Center	7 C6
Soldiers' and Sailors' Memorial Arch	8 C3
Williamsburg Savings Bank	9 B1
Zoo	10 D4

EATING	(pp254–5)
Applewood	11 B4
Blue Ribbon Sushi Brooklyn	12 B3
Tea Lounge	13 B2
Tom's Restaurant	14 D2

DRINKING	(p275)
Cattyshack	15 B2
Excelsior	16 A3
Freddy's	17 C1
Ginger's Bar	18 B3
Great Lakes	(see 12)
O'Connor's	19 B1

ENTERTAINMENT	(pp277–302)
BAM Café	(see 22)
BAM Rose Cinema	(see 22)
Brooklyn Academy of Music	22 B1
Southpaw	23 B2
Up Over Jazz Café	24 C2

SHOPPING	(pp350–2)
Beacon's Closet	25 B2
Brooklyn Industries	26 B2
Flirt	27 B2
Umkarna	28 B2

SLEEPING	(pp375–6)
Bed & Breakfast on the Park	29 B4

INFORMATION	
Audobon Center Boathouse	30 D4

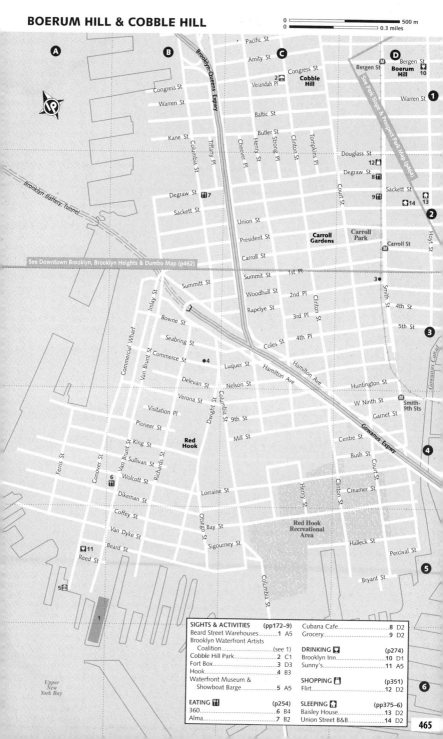

BOERUM HILL & COBBLE HILL

0 ———————— 500 m
0 ———————— 0.3 miles

CONEY ISLAND & BRIGHTON BEACH

| 0 | 1 km |
| 0 | 0.5 miles |

466

SIGHTS & ACTIVITIES (pp179–81)
Astroland..............................1 C3
Clubhouse...........................(see 5)
Coney Island Museum...........(see 5)
Cyclone...............................(see 1)
Deno's Wonder Wheel Amusement Park..2 C3
KeySpan Park.......................3 C3
New York Aquarium..............4 C3
Sideshows by the Seashore.....5 C3

EATING (p256)
Cafe Glechik........................6 D2
M & I International.................7 D2
Nathan's Famous..................8 C3
Restaurant Volna..................9 D3
Tatiana...............................10 D3
Totonno's...........................11 C2

FLUSHING

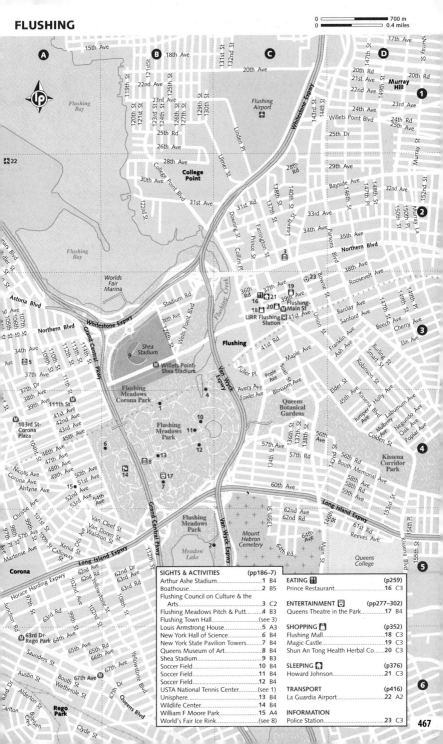

SIGHTS & ACTIVITIES	(pp186–7)
Arthur Ashe Stadium	1 B4
Boathouse	2 B5
Flushing Council on Culture & the Arts	3 C2
Flushing Meadows Pitch & Putt	4 B3
Flushing Town Hall	(see 3)
Louis Armstrong House	5 A3
New York Hall of Science	6 B4
New York State Pavilion Towers	7 B4
Queens Museum of Art	8 B4
Shea Stadium	9 B3
Soccer Field	10 B4
Soccer Field	11 B4
Soccer Field	12 B4
USTA National Tennis Center	(see 1)
Unisphere	13 B4
Wildlife Center	14 B4
William F Moore Park	15 A4
World's Fair Ice Rink	(see 8)

EATING 🍴	(p259)
Prince Restaurant	16 C3

ENTERTAINMENT 🎭	(pp277–302)
Queens Theatre in the Park	17 B4

SHOPPING 🛍	(p352)
Flushing Mall	18 C3
Magic Castle	19 C3
Shun An Tong Health Herbal Co	20 C3

SLEEPING 🛏	(p376)
Howard Johnson	21 C3

TRANSPORT	(p416)
La Guardia Airport	22 A2

INFORMATION	
Police Station	23 C3

467

THE BRONX

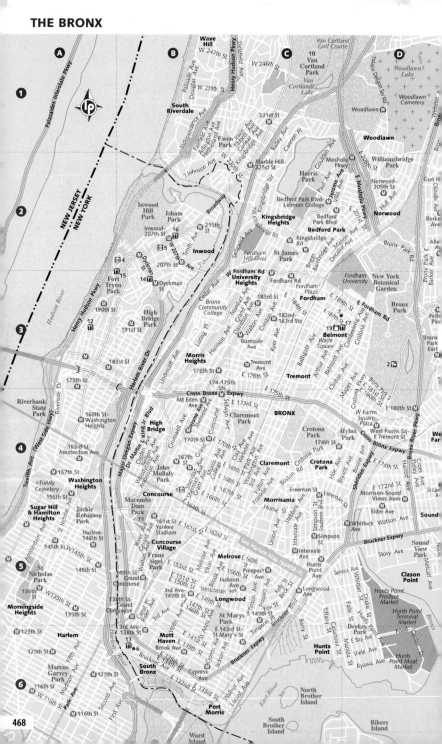

SIGHTS & ACTIVITIES	(pp188–201)
Bronx Museum of the Arts..........1	B4
Bronx Zoo.........................2	D3
Captain Mike's Dive Shop..........3	H3
Cloisters..........................4	B2
Dyckman Farmhouse Museum.....5	B2
Friends of Brook Park..............6	B6
Mario's...........................7	C3
Orchard Beach.....................8	H2
Stickball Blvd.....................9	E5
Van Cortland Park.................10	C1
Yankee Stadium...................11	B5

EATING 🍴	(pp259–60)
Bleu Evolution...................12	A3
Bruckner Bar & Grill.............13	B6
DR-K............................14	B3
New Leaf Café...................15	A2
Park Terrace Bistro...............16	B2
Roberto's........................17	C3
Tony's Pier......................18	H4

SHOPPING 🛍	(p201)
Arthur Avenue Market.............19	C3

MTA Metropolitan Transportation Authority

MTA New York City Subway

with bus, railroad, and ferry connections

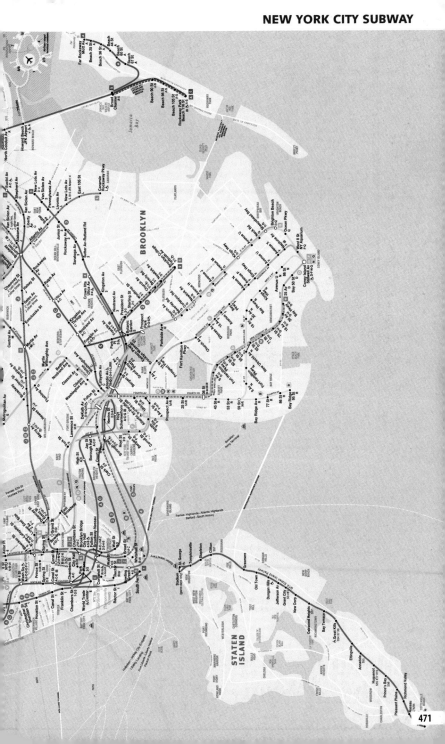

CENTRAL PARK

HUDSON RIVER

EAST RIVER

QUEENS

ROOSEVELT ISLAND

81 St
B·C

79 St   79 ST
1

77 St
6

72 St
1·2·3

72 St
B·C

68 St
6

Lex Av/63 St
F

Roosevelt Island
F

66 St
Lincoln Center
1

CENTRAL PARK WEST

BROADWAY

Free walking transfer with Metrocard

5 Av/59 St
N·R·W

57 St
7 Av

57 St
N·R·W

Lex Av/59 St
N·R·W

59 St
4·5·6

59 St
Columbus Circle
A·B·C·D·1

7 Av
B·D·E

5 Av/53 St
E·V

Lex Av/53 St
E·V

51 St
6

50 St
C·E

50 St
N·R

49 St
N·R

47-50 Sts
Rockefeller Ctr
B·D·F·V

MIDTOWN

METRO NORTH

WEST SIDE

42 St
Port Authority
Bus Terminal
A·C·E

Times Sq
42 St
N·Q·R·S·W
1·2·3
7

42 St
7

5 Av
7
Bryant Pk
B·D·F·V

Grand Central
42 St
S·4·5·6·7

MURRAY HILL

34 St
Penn Station
A·C·E

34 St
Penn Station
B·D·F·N·Q·R·V·W
1·2·3

33 St
6

LIRR/NJ TRANSIT AMTRAK

28 St
1

28 St
6

28 St
N·R·W

23 St
C·E

23 St
1

23 St
F·V

23 St
N·R

23 St
6

MADISON SQ PARK

GRAMERCY PARK

CHELSEA

18 St
1

6 Av
F·V

UNION SQ PARK

14 St-Union Sq
L·N·Q·R·W·4·5·6

3 Av
L

1 Av
L

14 St

14 St
A·C·E

14 St
L

14 St
1·2·3

14 St
F·V

8 St-NYU
N·R·W

Astor Pl
6

GREENWICH VILLAGE

TOMPKINS SQUARE PARK

EAST VILLAGE

Christopher St
Sheridan Sq
1

W 4 St
Wash Sq
A·B·C·D·E·F·V

Broadway
Lafayette St
B·D·F·V

Bleecker St
6

Lower East Side/2 Av
F·V

Houston St
1

Prince St
N·R·W

Spring St
C·E

Spring St
6

Bowery
J·M·Z

Delancey St
F

Essex St
J·M·Z

Canal St
1

Canal St
A·C·E

Grand St
B·D

Canal St
J·M·N·Q·R·W·Z·6

East Broadway
F

SOHO

LITTLE ITALY

CHINATOWN

LOWER EAST SIDE

Franklin St
1

Park Place
2·3

City Hall
R·W

Chambers St
J·M·Z·J·M

Brooklyn Bridge-City Hall
4·5·6·6

TRIBECA

Chambers St
A·C

Chambers St
1·2·3

World Trade Center
E·E

Fulton St-Broadway Nassau
A·C·J·M·Z·2·3·4·5

BATTERY PARK

Cortlandt St 1 (closed)

Cortlandt St
R·W (closed)

Rector St
1

Wall St
4·5

Wall St
2·3

Broad St
J·M·Z·J·Z

Rector St
R·W

Bowling Green
4·5

Whitehall St
South Ferry
R·W

South Ferry
1

WILLIAMSBURG BRIDGE

DELANCEY ST

E B'WAY

SOUTH ST

BROOKLYN

Please check www.mta.info often for latest service advisories.

LEGEND

6   Terminal

Station Name

4·5·6   Part-time line extension

Full-time Part-time Service Service

Local Service only

All trains stop (local and express service)

Free subway transfer

Free out-of-system subway transfer (excluding single-ride ticket)

MTA   New York City Transit

Manhattan Subway Map

March 2006